GERMAN COLONIALISM
IN A GLOBAL AGE

POLITICS, HISTORY, AND CULTURE
A series from the International Institute at the University of Michigan

SERIES EDITORS
George Steinmetz and Julia Adams

SERIES EDITORIAL ADVISORY BOARD

Fernando Coronil	Nancy Rose Hunt	Julie Skurski
Mamadou Diouf	Andreas Kalyvas	Margaret Somers
Michael Dutton	Webb Keane	Ann Laura Stoler
Geoff Eley	David Laitin	Katherine Verdery
Fatma Müge Göcek	Lydia Liu	Elizabeth Wingrove

Sponsored by the International Institute at the University of Michigan and published by Duke University Press, this series centers on cultural and historical studies of power, politics, and the state—a field that cuts across the disciplines of history, sociology, anthropology, political science, and cultural studies. The focus on the relationship between state and culture refers both to a methodological approach—the study of politics and the state using culturalist methods—and a substantive one that treats signifying practices as an essential dimension of politics. The dialectic of politics, culture, and history figures prominently in all the books selected for the series.

GERMAN COLONIALISM IN A GLOBAL AGE

BRADLEY NARANCH AND GEOFF ELEY, EDITORS

Duke University Press · Durham and London · 2014

© 2014 Duke University Press
All rights reserved
Typeset in Arno Pro by Graphic Composition, Inc., Bogart, GA

Library of Congress Cataloging-in-Publication Data
German colonialism in a global age / Bradley Naranch and Geoff Eley, editors.
pages cm—(Politics, history, and culture)
Includes bibliographical references and index.
ISBN 978-0-8223-5711-7 (hardcover : alk. paper)
ISBN 978-0-8223-5723-0 (pbk. : alk. paper)
1. Germany—Colonies. 2. Germany—Colonies–Historiography. 3. Imperialism—Historiography. I. Naranch, Bradley, 1974- II. Eley, Geoff III. Series: Politics, history, and culture.
JV2027.G48 2014
325'.343–dc23
2014024285
ISBN 978-0-8223-7639-2 (e-book)

Duke University Press gratefully acknowledges the support of the University of Michi-gan, OVPR Faculty Grants and Awards Program, which provided funds toward the pub-lication of the book.

Chapter 3 is based on *Networks in Tropical Medicine: Internationalism, Colonialism, and the Rise of a Medical Specialty, 1890–1930*, by Deborah J. Neill. Copyright © 2012 by the Board of Trustees of the Leland Stanford Jr. University. All rights reserved. Used with the permission of Stanford University Press.

Contents

Preface, ix   Acknowledgments, xi

Introduction · German Colonialism Made Simple
BRADLEY NARANCH
1

One · Empire by Land or Sea?
Germany's Imperial Imaginary, 1840–1945
GEOFF ELEY
19

Two · Scientific Autonomy and Empire, 1880–1945
Four German Sociologists
GEORGE STEINMETZ
46

Three · Science and Civilizing Missions
Germans and the Transnational Community of Tropical Medicine
DEBORAH J. NEILL
74

Four · Ruling Africa
Science as Sovereignty in the German Colonial Empire and Its Aftermath
ANDREW ZIMMERMAN
93

Five · Who Is Master in the Colony?
Propriety, Honor, and Manliness in German East Africa
HEIKE I. SCHMIDT
109

Six · A New Imperial Vision?
The Limits of German Colonialism in China
KLAUS MÜHLHAHN
129

Seven · Experts, Migrants, Refugees
Making the German Colony in Iran, 1900–1934
JENNIFER JENKINS
147

Eight · Classroom Colonialism
Race, Pedagogy, and Patriotism in Imperial Germany
JEFF BOWERSOX
170

Nine · Mass-Marketing the Empire
Colonial Fantasies and Advertising Visions
DAVID CIARLO
187

Ten · Colonialism, War, and the German Working Class
Popular Mobilization in the 1907 Reichstag Elections
JOHN PHILLIP SHORT
210

Eleven · Colonialism and the Anti-Semitic Movement in Imperial Germany
CHRISTIAN S. DAVIS
228

Twelve · Internal Colonialism in Germany
Culture Wars, Germanification of the Soil, and the Global Market Imaginary
SEBASTIAN CONRAD
246

Thirteen · Pan-German Conceptions of Colonial Empire
DENNIS SWEENEY
265

Fourteen · Maritime Force and the Limits of Empire
*Warfare, Commerce, and Law in Germany and the
United States before World War I*
DIRK BÖNKER
283

Fifteen · The Rhineland Controversy and Weimar Postcolonialism
BRETT M. VAN HOESEN
302

Sixteen · Colonialism, Imperialism, National Socialism
How Imperial Was the Third Reich?
BIRTHE KUNDRUS
330

Bibliography, 347   List of Contributors, 407   Index, 411

Preface

The past two decades have seen enormous changes in how the history of empire and colonialism has come to be viewed, markedly revising earlier views of Europe's relationship to non-European worlds. German historians have fully participated in this activity. The essays of this volume gather its best results. Our collection presumes a collective conversation occurring in many different venues over the past ten years, including a variety of sessions at the annual meetings of the German Studies and American Historical Associations. It also follows two major international conferences, one at the University of Sheffield (September 2006) and the other at San Francisco State University (September 2007), each of which resulted in key volumes, those edited by Michael Perraudin and Jürgen Zimmerer, *German Colonialism and National Identity* (London: Routledge, 2011), and Volker Langbehn and Mohammad Salama, *German Colonialism: Race, the Holocaust, and Postwar Germany* (New York: Columbia University Press, 2011), respectively. A number of our contributors, including the two editors themselves, were present on those earlier occasions, and our own discussion builds gratefully on this wider activity.

Acknowledgments

We wish to thank all those who made this publication possible, including first and foremost the University of Michigan, whose support was vital in a variety of ways, and Duke University Press, where Valerie Millholland and Miriam Angress guided our progress with no less patience than wisdom. In the closing stages, with painstaking thoroughness and tact, Ken Garner coordinated the manuscript's final preparation, collating the contributions, chasing down references, compiling the bibliography, and generally keeping us to schedule. Otherwise, the countless friends and colleagues who helped shape our thinking are far too numerous to thank each by name; instead, we acknowledge all of the audiences, seminars, and conference groups who responded to the ideas. Some individuals were especially crucial, however. They include Young-Sun Hong, Jennifer Jenkins, Dirk Moses, Roberta Pergher, Hartmut Pogge von Strandmann, George Steinmetz, Dennis Sweeney, Julia Adeney Thomas, Jürgen Zimmerer, and Andrew Zimmerman. Our final and greatest gratitude goes to those closest—namely, Gina Morantz-Sanchez and Camelia Naranch.

INTRODUCTION

German Colonialism Made Simple

BRADLEY NARANCH

Writing the history of German colonialism has never been simple. For decades, scholars consistently underestimated its value by relegating it to a supporting role in their larger accounts of German history, treating it as merely a secondary expression of a larger impulse toward territorial expansion in Europe.[1] An empirically rich story of overseas conquest and cultural change became instead a rather straightforward rendering of government manipulation and political consensus building. This did little to alter the dominant tone or trajectory of historical research; it merely confirmed what was already known from other sources about the dynamic but unstable nature of German society prior to World War I. Despite its limits, this approach held considerable merit. It inspired scholars in West and East Germany to uncover detailed documentary evidence of German colonialism's systemic violence, extreme brutality, and persistent corruption, thereby weakening the residual influence of Weimar and Nazi revisionism, which had misleadingly argued that German colonial administrators, settlers, and missionaries had played progressive roles in African, Asian, and Pacific economic modernization.[2]

Studying the impact of German colonialism on Wilhelmine party politics, interest group formation, and public opinion also yielded meaningful Cold War–era lessons about the past methods used by imperialists to manufacture domestic majorities in support of policies that exploited the lives and resources of foreign others while silencing the voices of domestic critics by portraying them as unpatriotic and racially disloyal. This research model is far from being outdated or irrelevant today, but along with its undoubtedly good intentions came conceptual constraints that limited the story that German colonialism could tell. And it is precisely in pushing past these limits that the compelling complexity of that story is to be revealed.

It was in the mid-1990s that the status quo started to weaken and a new narrative of German colonialism began to take shape.[3] Freed from the strictures of *Sonderweg* methodology that conditioned historians into seeing the exceptional in modern Germany, some discovered new models and inspiration in the discursive theories and textual critical techniques of postcolonial studies.[4] Others looked admiringly to the examples set by their British, American, Dutch, Spanish, and French colleagues who were reviving the study of colonial empire in their own fields of regional expertise. Countering the continental confines of modern German historiography was so clearly a priority that the multicultural transformations taking place in the new Federal Republic would be reflected in its rewritten past, in which the colonial legacy finally was acknowledged as central.[5]

For a number of influential early figures in the field, examining the long history of German colonial and Orientalist discourse played a critical role in reconstructing an extensive genealogy of racism, xenophobia, and right-wing violence that did not take as its endpoint the world wars.[6] The prominence of others interested in the history of women, notably Lora Wildenthal and Birthe Kundrus, in what would become something of a German colonial historiographical renaissance, was reflected in the salience of gender and sexuality in new accounts of German settler society and the domestic colonial movement.[7] Advocates in the field for transnational history were quick to identify German colonialism in its newer, more expansive form as an area rich in possibility.[8] Area specialists in African and East Asian history who had always included the former colonies as part of their research largely encouraged these trends and intervened by raising important concerns about indigenous agency and the importance of on-site archival and oral historical scholarship for understanding the localized dynamics of German overseas rule. Another critical sustaining influence assisting the rise of the "new" German colonial history came from Holocaust scholars and Third Reich historians interested in the colonial connections to the Nazi genocide.[9] The history of colonial warfare and native resistance in German Southwest Africa, in particular, became a touchstone for renewed debate about the Herero and Nama genocides and the future roles played by German settlers, scientists, and soldiers in supporting the racial policies of the Nazi dictatorship as applied to "mixed" populations at home as well as in occupied Poland and the European East.[10] The scholarship of earlier generations of historians on German colonial ideology and its legacy has also been rediscovered and reinterpreted in light of new archival research.[11]

As these discrete communities encountered each other, the trickles became flows and the flows started to converge into a movement with critical mass.[12] Many younger scholars were attracted to the field because it appeared dynamic, interdisciplinary, and driven by a strong desire for change in response to institutional concerns about the viability of German studies as a discipline and the feared decline of academic positions in modern German history at North American, British, and European universities. The result has been a proliferation of conferences, workshops, dissertations, edited volumes, and monographs, as well as greater coverage of German colonialism in major academic journals and annual gatherings.[13] More than a decade has now passed since the first major publications appeared in print seeking to outline an ambitious future agenda. The field continues to grow but in a disparate fashion lacking a fixed center, a leading set of academic players, or a dominant research paradigm. Other than a number of review essays and recent conference-related volumes of essays, there have been few detailed attempts to define the field intellectually or to establish an institutional foundation for furthering its aims.[14] Despite these absences, the field remains both a site of original, creative scholarship and an area for further growth. What sustains its viability and motivates its members? What impact has it had on German historiography and on the study of empire more generally, if at all?

Establishing an explanatory framework to help answer these questions is the purpose of the present volume, not to make German colonialism a discrete area of research or outline a set of principles governing its operation. We are not trying to impose a rigid order on a field of inquiry that seems perfectly content to exist without one and whose attractiveness may in fact be contingent upon this very condition. Past attempts to carve out a subfield dedicated to the study of German colonialism have failed to find for it a lasting and proper place. The geographical and temporal boundaries often used to demarcate Germany's overseas territories have proven too limited for scholars interested in local and regional responses to foreign occupation and the global marketplace whose themes and timelines do not fit neatly within these boundaries. German historians have also found it problematic to focus exclusively on official colonial policy debates and administrative reforms whose outcomes were highly dependent on the overlapping relationship to the larger politics of global expansion and imperial expression.[15] Widely varying relationships between Germany and the colonies were also influenced by differences of class, confession, and political affiliation, making it impractical to speak in terms of a uniform experience.[16]

At the other extreme, approaches to German colonialism that define it primarily as a flexible discourse underwritten by expansive fantasies of conquest, resettlement, and economic domination suffer from an even greater tendency toward analytical imprecision. Much work has pinpointed forms of discursive slippage and ideological overlap in which a comparable language of German colonization is applied equally to parts of Europe and Africa—for example, while showing how once active racial categories could be recycled for future legal or imperial purposes.[17] Yet, however highly productive, such methods cannot substitute for an integrated colonial history fully attuned to the dissonances and disruptions that distinguish one form of German expansion from those that came before, that were coterminous, or that happened much later and in another context.[18]

By choosing between paradigms that result either in minimizing or magnifying the impact of German colonialism, scholars make their stories needlessly difficult to tell. The continual need to correct the distortions disrupts the story line by introducing analytical elements that distract the reader. In the case of minimalist approaches, the comparative methodology is often at fault; the German colonies are judged marginal by juxtaposing them with others of larger spatial expanse or longer duration. The costs and casualties of colonial wars and occupation in German Africa can be made relatively insignificant statistically by invoking the vastly higher numbers from World Wars I and II.[19] Once rendered small by comparison, the overseas colonies are more easily relegated as politically or economically insignificant in principle. That in turn can help to explain their unpopularity with the wider German public and the lack of effective political responses to their loss compared with that of Alsace or East Prussia. Magnifying the colonial lens to embrace a full range of expansionist practices as well as rhetoric and imaginative reconstructions, on the other hand, almost immediately confronts questions of continuity and causality. Simply setting this aside will never satisfy the skeptics who cannot see the implied connections between discrete historical events and experiences often separated by considerable cultural and physical distances.

The approach proposed in this volume moves away from comparisons and causality in the aforementioned forms to focus instead on questions and considerations of scale. Our initial frame of reference becomes the hundred-year history of modern Germany as an expansionism-oriented imperial state. Its early formation dates from the middle decades of the 1800s; it accelerates and expands at the turn of the twentieth century before collapsing in 1918; it is sustained in the 1920s by Weimar colonial revisionists and the new Nazi movement, before being reformulated in radical expansionist ways in the 1930s and during the war years.[20]

Colonialism, in a multiplicity of forms and functions, was a continuous and central concern during the entirety of this period. Its reach was as widely spaced as German transatlantic migration and settlement on the North American frontier and the relocation of ethnic German communities from the Soviet Union into areas of Nazi occupation in eastern Europe.[21] Its topics were extremely divergent: not only Prussian and Austrian efforts at gunboat diplomacy in East Asia but also programs of forced cotton cultivation and mandatory medical testing extending far into the West and East African interiors.[22] Concrete colonial practices in specific overseas locations coexisted with more encompassing conversations about internal developments in Germany's European borderlands and plans for informal economic expansion in the Middle East, southeastern Europe, and central Asia. The impact of colonialism could be as subtle as new sentences embedded within a school geography textbook or as severe as mass murder, internment, and economic enslavement. If not the ultimate expression of German empire, colonialism was certainly one enduring expression.[23] It was ubiquitous without becoming all-encompassing or uniformly powerful. For most of the world most of the time, German colonialism was a relatively easily ignored subject. But it could also be invasive, intrusive, and irritatingly real, as German voters and millions of former colonial subjects would all have to learn during the first decade of the 1900s.[24] Indeed, for any particular moment along the imperial timeline, it is often the fractional scale and restricted reach of German colonialism, separated by sudden spikes of expansionist activity and agitation that emerges as most striking. By examining these shifts in scale as they cycled from one sequence to the next and by tracing the overlapping histories of people, information, commodities, and capital as they flowed across and between imperial networks, historians can create a capacious three-dimensional space where the discrete effects and operations of colonialism may be located across a wider global and locally detailed landscape.

While the resulting picture of German global empire will likely be one of considerable complexity, it is made up of smaller and more manageable moving parts. Colonialism manifested itself at the imperial contact points and serves as a convenient vantage point for observing the changing patterns and pace of German history. The existence for several long and eventful decades of direct overseas rule during a period of elevated German political engagement, economic expansion, and scientific innovation is thus not a situation that can simply be taken for granted.²⁵ It offers German historians a unique opportunity to examine the larger operations and daily transactions of a modern empire whose means of expression were unpredictable and varied, one in which colonialism was present but not central to the lives of most of its citizens.²⁶ The specifically colonial component of the resulting imperial project continued for decades, despite costing millions in tax revenue, consuming the energies of tens of thousands of soldiers, settlers, technical advisors, and administrators, and resulting in a steady stream of stories of political scandal, economic corruption, and violent unrest. To ascribe the situation simply to successful government management of public opinion in order to cater to the needs of interest groups and elite economic stakeholders, while an essential element of the story to tell, stops far short of exhausting the range of reactions that can be charted across the imperial field. Neither does the loss of overseas territory mark an obvious endpoint at which the impact of colonialism on the politics of German empire ceased.²⁷

Once it becomes clear that German colonialism does not have to offer definitive explanations or identify the start of a linear path leading into the future, the reasons for addressing it start to proliferate. While specific topics, particularly those that relate to local responses and regional variations of colonial rule, necessarily require a familiarity with languages, locations, and literature best studied as part of a dedicated specialization in non-European history, the need for German scholars to reconstruct the full dimensions of the imperial state and its effects in central Europe and around the globe remain exceptionally high.²⁸ What will advance our understanding, in other words, is not the cultivation of German colonial specialists but rather the ability to assess colonialism's impact at those points of broader interest where it intersects. Putting colonialism back within the various and overlapping historical contexts from which it first emerged simply means reconnecting a long-separated historiographical branch to where it rightly belongs—with the general ebbs and flows of modern German and global history.²⁹

The transnational turn, combined with the increased visibility of race and empire as necessary categories of cultural and political analysis, makes this task considerably easier than it would once have been. The results will be readily apparent in the chapters that follow and are illuminated in the following brief foray into the world of print culture in the early 1900s, by which time the presence of colonialism in the daily and weekly news cycles of Imperial Germany was all but inevitable.

Regular subscribers to the new Munich-based weekly *Simplicissimus* may have been surprised to learn in April 1904 that Germany had been invaded by an African army intent on liberating factory workers from the bondage of wage slavery. A front-page illustration by Theodore Thomas Heine, "The African Peril," depicts the arrival of an army of dark-skinned soldiers in an unnamed German industrial city. The caricatured spear-waving warriors engage in a violent street battle with uniformed police officers outside a factory building from which white workers are trying to escape.[30] While the police hold back the doors on the bridge, a group of Africans carrying drums, shields, and a red flag leads a second group of emaciated workers to freedom down below. One African soldier mounts a ladder to free two emaciated men chained to a smokestack. Closer scrutiny of the lower image reveals two severed heads of helmeted policemen being carried on spears. "It is high time that the government moved with full force against the Herero," the caption reads, "otherwise the black beasts might eventually come to Germany and abolish the slavery that exists here." The mock invasion was, not the extension into Germany of a race war that radical nationalists had prophesied at the start of the Herero Rebellion in January, but the satirical start of a global class war in which oppressed colonial subjects would liberate urban proletarians from the bondage of wage slavery.

The power of colonialism as a metaphor was intruding around the same time into the ethnic borderlands of the eastern frontier. A 1904 illustration, "The Wild Czechs," invokes the racial imagery of African savagery and Slavic inferiority while redirecting the language of the civilizing mission into east-central Europe. Crudely drawn humans with apelike features and long dark hair hang from trees while others wave clubs and rocks. One stabs a missionary while a second man, dead or unconscious, is robbed of his pocket watch. In the center, an older man dressed in Austrian fashion escorts a young soldier into the fray. "After the suppression of the Herero rebellion," the caption explains, "our colonial policymakers face an even more difficult undertaking: the civilization of Bohemia." This fanciful depiction of a German mission of inner colonization in the East thus blended the events of the colonial periphery with an older trope of Slavic barbarity, evoking in satirical form the more serious efforts on the part of pan-German activists to use the language and iconography of race to conflate the European East with Africa.

The lives of German children were also impacted by the cyclical violence of imperial expansion into new spheres of imperial influence.[31] A front-page illustration from a 1900 issue depicts graphically the consequences of colonial warfare for the next generation of German imperialists. Germany's seizure of the Chinese port city of Qingdao and the punitive expeditions conducted during the Boxer Rebellion generated intense debate at home about the military violence against Chinese civilians that followed.[32] News reports of the alleged atrocities prompted a critical reevaluation of Wilhelm II's speech to departing troops in Bremerhaven harbor in which he exhorted them to act like barbarian Huns in exacting vengeance on the Chinese for threatening the lives of Germans abroad. In the *Simplicissimus* edition, Heine has a group of German schoolboys mimic the violent behavior overseas of their adult male military counterparts. They torture barnyard animals and mount the heads of roosters on nearby fence posts. One boy in the foreground stabs a half-naked baby with a bloody German flag, while another boy attacks a young girl with a sword as if intent on decapitation or rape. The caption provides the necessary connection to the real-world events: "The major's children play China War and spread Prussian culture in the fresh spring breeze."

Domestic concern in Imperial Germany over the violent potential of class conflict, ethnic minority relations, and militarism was not prompted by colonial warfare in Africa and China at the start of the twentieth century. These topics were too large and deeply embedded in the cultural fabric of modern Germany to be traced to colonialism alone. What images such as these from *Simplicissimus* reveal, however, is that neither can they fully be separated from the violent realities of German colonial life on an expanding global frontier. This, too, was an effect of empire, one that was no less harmless because of the imaginative nature of its operation. For Heine and his fellow illustrators, there was no cordon sanitaire shielding German citizens at home from the modalities of colonial governance and military repression, which reached new and unprecedented levels of severity in the early 1900s. The political rights of citizenship would not protect German workers who chose with their votes to cross the racial color line by supporting candidates who were critical of colonial policymakers and expressed concern over the actions of German soldiers overseas. Like the wild Bohemians caricatured in *Simplicissimus*, the Slavic-speaking populations of eastern and central Europe would not be exempted from the territorial ambitions of pan-German activists and their allies, who viewed their lands, labor, and natural resources as the building blocks of a future continental empire less vulnerable to Anglo-American intrusion than scattered overseas possessions. School-age German boys who played at making war in Africa and China would find themselves drafted into later armies of occupation in Belgium, France, and Poland, where scenes similar to those fancifully depicted by Heine could be put into deadly practice.

To hold German colonialism accountable for these future acts of empire is not the primary purpose of this volume. But as the editors of *Simplicissimus* recognized, neither can its effects be ignored or relegated to the margins of collective memory. The task of anchoring Germany's colonial past more firmly into an expanded history of empire is being accomplished without the training of a dedicated army of specialists. The most pressing need is not for the production of new expert knowledge about the colonies, which is actually quite plentiful when compared with a decade ago.[33] Rather, the effects of German colonialism need to be tracked in less obvious ways: through a variety of micropolitical contexts localized in time and space, through the lives and professional career paths of particular groups and individuals, and across and beyond the categorical and chronological boundaries that previous generations had deemed it practical to impose.

As the following chapters reveal, the results of this approach are refreshingly clear. Although they engage deeply and quite differently with the empirical complexities and contradictions of Germany's distinctively discontinuous colonial path, all share two basic assumptions that make their findings accessible and mutually intelligible.

First, when it comes to colonialism, there are no marginal players and no protected places entirely free of its impact. While the influences may initially appear unexpected or unanticipated, our hope is that readers will quickly learn how to spot its effects.

Second, German colonialism in Africa and Asia between 1884 and 1914 was neither the first nor the final expression of a continuing imperial project. That project took multiple forms and functions in the decades that followed but never entirely went away or erased all connecting links to the earlier colonial past. These connections are not always obvious nor are they all-embracing. German territorial ambitions in parts of the European East, for example, easily outlasted the end of colonial experiments in East Africa and East Asia. These respective arenas were never entirely equivalent at any specific moment in time, but they did have connections, and these connections matter. At the same time, the field of connectedness to eastern Europe is not the only reason for writing about colonialism in Africa and Asia.

For the past generation, for reasons entirely intelligible, historians of modern Germany have tended to shape the global dimensions of their work in distinctive ways that culminate on familiar continental ground. All roads of understanding, in one way or another, however foggy or circuitous, eventually end up in the East. Perhaps the simplest lesson of our volume, then, may be the one hardest for many readers to accept. When it comes to German colonialism in a global age, there is no clear necessity to choose. All paths lead somewhere worthwhile, even if the final destinations are not the same, nor are they likely to converge in the near future. It is the journey itself that matters, and this particular one will take readers quite far. For all of its unsettling severity, the subject matter demands our attention.

THE CHAPTERS

In his opening chapter, *Geoff Eley* defines the programmatic agenda of the volume and develops some of its key concepts. He places the formal history of German overseas colonialism within a larger context of German foreign policy initiatives, patterns of global expansion, and informal imperial practices. The repeated recurrences of colonial categories into metropolitan contexts and apparent assimilations in the domestic sphere of colonial prejudices and racial distinctions erase "any firm and fast distinction between forms of colonizing expansionism overseas and forms of landward colonialism inside Europe." Treating German overseas expansion as a peripheral process when compared to subsequent projects of imperialism and genocide externalizes colonialism as an exclusively extra-European project and ignores the complex cultural operations of colonial discourse within German society to internalize the lessons of empire for future projects of expansion. The promiscuous circulation of knowledge and power within and across the diverse spaces of the German empire supported the growth of modern, biopolitical projects of social engineering capable of being deployed overseas in Africa or China, but it also was translated into internal projects of social and political reform in the metropolis and adapted to suit the purposes of economic and territorial expansion into eastern and central Europe.

Next, *George Steinmetz* tracks the rise of German sociology as a modern academic discipline alongside the variable path of German empire from the 1880s to the 1940s. His innovative approach to the relationship between scientific knowledge and imperial rule, along with his detailed discussion of the fate of the German colonial sciences after World War I, plunges the reader deep into the heart of the "new colonial history" and demonstrates its potential for rewriting the history of the modern sciences. Detailed discussions of Max Weber and Richard Thurnwald, in particular, allow Steinmetz to present a nuanced picture of how their respective scientific careers and attitudes toward empire reflected both internal disciplinary struggles for academic freedom and opportunist efforts at rendering scientific knowledge useful to a succession of German imperial projects.

Deborah J. Neill's account of German tropical medicine then adds fascinating new details about the transnational networks of scientific experts who worked across imperial borders to solidify European dominance in equatorial

Africa. Neill examines a wide range of locations, from international sanitary conferences in the heart of metropolitan Europe to isolated experimental research stations in Cameroon and Lake Victoria, to tell a story of how Germans worked closely with French, Belgian, and British counterparts until World War I severed such ties and hampered German efforts at regaining access to their former research sites in the 1920s. Neill's findings underscore the importance of tropical medicine in the establishment of German colonial rule and in the enactment of some of its most discriminatory practices, including compulsory medical experimentation and quarantine systems.[34]

Andrew Zimmerman's investigation of German scientific colonialism shows how aspiring experts in emerging fields of tropical agronomy, botany, zoology, and anthropology seized upon calls to reform the colonial economy by modernizing its means of production and wage labor regimes. In their quest to produce disciplined agricultural wage laborers in both the colonies and the eastern provinces of Prussia, German social scientists looked across the Atlantic for inspiration from the sharecropping system of the American South. Others experimented with monocrop economies like sisal and rubber in their East African research station at Amani. Zimmerman shows how such initiatives garnered international recognition and further legitimized the necessity of European oversight in the "development" of tropical economies. The League of Nations trustees who assumed sovereignty over Germany's lost empire did so on the basis of a discourse of Western scientific authority and economic rationality that German experts had helped to construct.

If scientific experts operating within a complex imperial and international landscape take center stage in the opening chapters, the next section, on forms of colonial state formation within the German empire, explores the complex interplay of administrators, military officials, settlers, servants, indigenous elites, and rebels that accounted for highly variable regimes of power and forms of violence in the colonies. *Heike I. Schmidt* provides an intimate glimpse into the gossip-filled lives of a tiny German community in East Africa. Using a theoretical approach adapted from Ute Frevert's research on dueling and the "crisis of masculinity," Schmidt explores the fragile and fractious nature of white settler life. Internal disputes over honor and accusations of sexual violence, publically played out in court and in front of African servants and witnesses, led colonial administrators to fear that white rule was under threat when class boundaries normally not crossed at home came into conflict on the colonial frontier. Like Klaus Mühlhahn, Schmidt sets her story in the locality of a colonial society forged by interactions *between* white colonists and indigenous residents, but she does so by linking the gender and class politics in Germany with those of East Africa.[35]

Meanwhile, *Klaus Mühlhahn* surveys the history of the German East Asian leasehold of Kiaochow, placing its unique process of state formation within the larger story of Western and Japanese imperialism in late Qing China.[36] He explores how German naval officials created a racially segregated, military-bureaucratic enclave that served as an economic penetration point for German capital. At the same time, he shows the limits of the "model colony" by describing a long pattern of tentative accommodation and outright resistance on the part of Chinese government elites, local merchants, and peasant farmers whose lands and irrigation canals were disrupted by German railway and telegraph networks that emanated from their colonial stronghold on the coast. The relative success of the Qingdao colony relied on heavy government subsidies and on the professional reputation of the Imperial Navy, whose interest in East Asia helped to define the agenda of early twentieth-century *Weltpolitik*.

Jennifer Jenkins looks even farther afield to examine the virtually unknown history of German expatriate communities in twentieth-century Iran. Her account of German efforts at gaining informal influence in central Asia shows how an expansive notion of colonialism can uncover important moments in the redefinition of German identity and citizenship that facilitated the integration of the German diaspora into the national imaginary. Dramatized in a gripping story of ethnic German refugees from Stalinist Russia who attracted the attention of German consular officials in Tehran in 1929, her chapter revises the history of German imperialism to include locations beyond Africa, East Asia, and eastern Europe. In the process, Jenkins shows how discourses of German diaspora once mobilized by colonial activists in the nineteenth century were appropriated and transformed by late Weimar and early Nazi imperialists.[37]

Jeff Bowersox concentrates on an understudied domestic effect of German colonial expansion; namely, its impact upon primary-school education. His chapter delves deep into the history of pedagogical reform and progressive politics to show how nationalist-minded teachers and textbook authors tried to incorporate the history, geography, ethnology, botany, and zoology of the colonies into their lesson plans. In surveying a wide selection of such efforts, Bowersox concludes that the presence of colonial-themed content did increase markedly in the latter half of the empire. At the same time, specific references to the German colonies were partially overshadowed by a larger global story of Western expansion and conquest, one often told with an eye to entertainment and adventure rather than an in-depth account of the specificities of overseas administration, economic development, and settlement.

David Ciarlo also takes a refreshingly provocative view of German colonial politics, especially the organizational efforts of middle- and upper-class colonial lobbyists to win over wider sectors of the population to their movement. He shows how German advertising firms developed an arresting but generic iconography of colonial commodities and caricatured natives that proved more appealing to consumers than the traditional propaganda of the German Colonial Society. These images helped to promote racial attitudes among the German consuming public that competed with the colonial project of Wilhelmine elites. Ciarlo argues that the pervasiveness of such stock images, later adopted by the colonial movement to help broaden its base of support, did less to further any concrete political agenda than to lay the cultural foundation for racist politics and animosity toward people of color more generally.

The next set of chapters focuses on how colonialism functioned in the political discourses and organizational tactics of the radical right. *John Phillip Short*'s chapter, which opens the section on colonial politics and culture, begins in the wake of the Herero genocide with the contentious "Hottentot" federal election campaign of January 1907.[38] He presents what amounts to a microlevel "people's history" of the election by examining the creative electioneering strategies of Social Democratic activists, who were directly targeted as unpatriotic and insufficiently race-conscious by an increasingly vocal conservative press. The distinctly modern political campaign followed years of increasingly hostile confrontations pitting the German left and Catholic Center party against the pro-colonial parliamentary majority. Short reveals the extent of working-class mobilization against German military atrocities and capitalist oppression in the colonies, creating a tradition of anti-imperialist activism that persisted, revisionist trends among party leaders notwithstanding, among more radical sectors of the political left in late Wilhelmine Germany, Weimar, and beyond.

Christian S. Davis rounds out the discussion of Wilhelmine radical nationalism by taking a close look at how anti-Semitic parties responded to the founding of the German colonies and the subsequent controversies over their administration and reform. Davis identifies clear affinities between the domestic agenda of German anti-Semites and the colonial movement. However, he also shows how disagreements over colonial policy—and the prominent roles played by Germans of Jewish background—increased the fractiousness that characterized the anti-Semitic movement. Some members embraced the racial language of segregation, mixed marriage bans, and colonial genocide, while others expressed skepticism about the value of the overseas colonies and questioned the harsh treatment of native workers, especially those who were Protestant converts. Davis's nuanced portrayal of a political movement whose members were often ambivalent about colonialism, while supportive of the national necessity of colonial conquest and racial purity, is an important reminder of how the unpredictable outcomes of colonial rule could disrupt the domestic politics of coalition building as much as it might consolidate them.

Sebastian Conrad examines the structural parallels between projects of internal colonialism in Germany's eastern provinces and the simultaneous settlement of its overseas territories. Conrad contextualizes the struggle on the German-Polish borderlands within larger global concerns over migration, wage labor, and settler colonialism. The increasing tendency of German radical nationalists to describe the Polish population in the Prussian East in colonial terms contributed to a racialization of ethnic difference and helped undermine the political claims of Polish-speaking citizens of Imperial Germany. By placing the Prussian East within the context of global history and by emphasizing the overlapping effects of overseas as well as inner colonization, Conrad gives readers a compelling picture of how a German global imagination formed, an imagination that encompassed overseas and borderlands locations while elevating the issue of race to increasing prominence in debates over national character and culture.

Dennis Sweeney's Foucauldian reading of pan-German colonial propaganda takes up many of Conrad's assertions while providing additional evidence of dramatic transformations in the German imperial imagination during the early twentieth century. While the organizational and ideological linkages between the League and colonial interest groups have long been recognized, Sweeney shows with great precision how leading pan-German theorists were often great innovators in melding the competing strands of German colonial ideology— *Weltpolitik* and *Lebensraum*—into a modern vision of an expanding imperial state. Their image of Greater Germany was not that of a nation-state with defined borders but a "macropolity," a flexible imperial formation with gradations of sovereignty geared toward satisfying the resource and labor needs of a growing capitalist economy as well as the biopolitical imperatives of population management and racial hygiene. Their future vision of a Germanic world empire included the colonies but vastly exceeded them in scale. Sweeney also shows how the events of World War I enabled once radical perspectives to enter the ranks of mainstream conservative and liberal parties. It was the "disturbingly innovative and forward-looking" nature of pan-German visions of world empire, he concludes, that rendered them important in the evolution of a German imperial politics bridging the gap between Wilhelmine nationalists and the Nazis.

The last set of chapters explores some of the complicating factors that limited Germany's ability to maintain an overseas empire and helps account for the distinctive shifts in the German imperial imaginary occurring between 1914 and 1945. Each chapter describes events and ideas that enhance our understanding of how Germany transitioned into something resembling a postcolonial condition, not a postimperial one, after 1914. The limits of empire are seen quite strikingly in Dirk Bönker's transnational account of German and American naval strategy on the eve of World War I. American and German navies played key roles in establishing and policing their new overseas empires, and naval officers were often vocal supporters of the ensuing colonialism. Bönker shows, however, how high-ranking battle-fleet strategists and geopolitical experts minimized the practical necessity of protecting the colonies in favor of a more broadly defined global "command of the seas" that would keep foreign markets open. When plans for a North Atlantic fleet appeared unlikely to deter a British blockade, German naval experts supported international legal guarantees of trade neutrality to keep vital sea lanes open and supply the domestic market with foodstuffs and raw materials. Protecting the colonies, by contrast, received a much lower priority. For Bönker, such decisions amounted not to a rejection of global empire but rather a recalibration of German ambitions in light of geopolitical and commercial calculations.

Brett M. Van Hoesen next moves readers from the waters of the North Atlantic to the occupied territories of the Rhine and Ruhr valleys in the 1920s. Her chapter examines the strange case of Weimar "postcolonialism" through an original analysis of German responses to the stationing of French and Belgian colonial soldiers. She examines how the orchestrated public outcry against these occupying forces overshadowed the revisionist colonial movement that lobbied for the return of Germany's lost overseas territories. Fears of a reverse colonization by North African, Senegalese, and Congolese forces resonated across a broad spectrum of German political life, stoking fears of racial contamination and supporting a revitalized German imperial project.[39] Van Hoesen's visual analysis of the "Black Horror on the Rhine" propaganda adds important new information to a critical chapter in early Weimar history, as does her concluding discussion of Dada montage pioneer Hannah Höch, one of the few left-wing critics who incorporated such imagery into their work.

The relationship between colonialism, German or otherwise, and Nazi territorial conquests during World War II is the subject of Birthe Kundrus's compellingly argued chapter, which concludes the volume. After examining the specific ways in which the German colonial past was appropriated by Nazi thinkers, political elites, and their allies, Kundrus concludes that such impulses, while significant, were only part of what made Nazi imperialism distinctively destructive. The desire to transcend the failures of past German efforts at overseas colonialism, combined with a more general sense of how other world powers functioned, led Nazi elites to imagine forms of conquest that exceeded the scale and scope of previous empires. Germany's colonial past provided lessons to learn, not models to follow. German actions in Poland were a particularly violent form of occupation—"a new system of 'foreign rule' that broke with core elements of imperial hegemony." Colonial history mattered for Nazi Germany, but it offered patterns that Hitler chose not to copy very precisely.

NOTES

1. Wildenthal, "Notes on a History," 144–156; Conrad, "Doppelte Marginalisierung," 145–169.

2. Ames, Wildenthal, and Klotz, eds., *Germany's Colonial Pasts*; Kundrus, ed., *Phantasiereiche*.

3. Kundrus, "Blind Spots," 86–106; Friedrichsmeyer, Lennox, and Zantop, eds., *Imperialist Imagination*.

4. Blackbourn and Eley, "Forum," 229–245; Blackbourn and Eley, *Peculiarities of German History*. On the idea of multiple modernities, see Sweeney, "Reconsidering the Modernity Paradigm," 405–434.

5. Jeffries, *Contesting the German Empire*, 172–178, offers the most up-to-date account of the impact of the new colonial history. For other important initiatives at integrating colonialism within the larger framework of German empire, see Dickinson, "The German Empire," 129–162; Poiger, "Imperialism and Empire," 117–143; Reagin, "Recent Work on German National Identity," 273–289. The foundational test in the debate about colonialism and empire in modern Germany remains Smith, *Ideological Origins*.

6. Zantop, *Colonial Fantasies* and "Colonial Legends, Postcolonial Legacies," 189–205; Berman, *Impossible Missions?*

7. Wildenthal, *German Women for Empire*; "Race, Gender, and Citizenship," 263–283; "'She Is the Victor,'" 371–395; and "'When Men are Weak,'" 53–77; Kundrus, *Moderne Imperialisten*.

8. Conrad, *German Colonialism*; van Laak, *Über alles in der Welt*. A more conventional history of the colonial period, along with a detailed bibliography, is provided by Gründer, *Geschichte der deutschen Kolonien*.

9. The complexities of this debate are expertly explored by Moses, "Colonialism," 68–80, and Kundrus, "Kontinuitäten, Parallelen, Rezeptionen," 45–62. An excellent overview of these debates is provided by Fitzpatrick, "The Pre-History of the Holocaust?," 1–27.

10. Nelson, ed., *Germans, Poland, and Colonial Expansion*.

11. This is particularly so in the case of the origins of the colonial movement in nineteenth-century Germany. See Fitzpatrick, *Liberal Imperialism in Germany*; Müller, "Imperialist Ambitions," 346–368; Fenske, "Imperialistische Tendenzen," 336–383, and "Ungeduldige Zuschauer," 87–123.

12. Noteworthy publications from this period include Grosse, *Kolonialismus, Eugenik*

und bürgerliche Gesellschaft; Zimmerman, *Anthropology and Antihumanism*; and Walther, *Creating Germans Abroad*.

13. Berman, Mühlhahn, and Nganang, eds., *German Colonialism Revisited*; Perraudin and Zimmerer, eds., *German Colonialism and National Identity*. See the works edited by Van der Heyden and Zeller, including *Kolonialismus hierzulande*; *"Macht und Anteil an der Weltherrschaft"*; and *Kolonialmetropole Berlin*. See also Honold and Sherpe, eds., *Mit Deutschland um die Welt*; Bechhaus-Gerst and Leutner, eds., *Frauen in den deutschen Kolonien*; Gründer, ed., *"Da und dort"*; and Möhle, ed., *Branntwein, Bibeln und Bananen*.

14. Langbehn and Salama, eds., *German Colonialism*; and Langbehn, ed., *German Colonialism*.

15. Wielandt and Kascher, "Die Reichstagsdebatten," 183–201; Smith, "Talk of Genocide," 107–123.

16. Sobich, *"Schwarze Bestien, Rote Gefahr"*; and Schröder, *Sozialismus und Imperialismus*.

17. Poley, *Decolonization in Germany*; Maß, *Weisse Helden, Schwarze Krieger*; and Klotz, "Global Visions," 37–68.

18. Eckert and Wirz, "Wir nicht, die Anderen auch," 373–393; Lindner, "Platz an der Sonne?," 487–510; Zimmerer et al., "Forum," 251–271; and Ciarlo, "Globalizing German Colonialism," 285–298.

19. For a full range of the debates and controversies, see Zimmerer and Zeller, eds., *Genocide in Southwest Africa*; and Förster, Henrichsen, and Bollig, eds., *Namibia-Deutschland*. Accounts of the military campaign can be found in Gewald, *Herero Heroes*; Hull, *Absolute Destruction*; and Erichsen, *"The Angel of Death has descended violently among them."* For comparative accounts of colonial warfare that do not single out the events in Namibia, see Klein and Schumacher, eds., *Kolonialkriege*; and von Trotha, "'The Fellows Can Just Starve,'" 415–433.

20. Furber and Lower, "Colonialism and Genocide," 372–400; Majer, "Das Besetzte Osteuropa," 111–34; and Linne, *Deutschland jenseits des Äquators?*

21. Liulevicius, *German Myth of the East*; Thum, ed., *Traumland Osten*.

22. Naranch, "Made in China," 367–381; Zimmerman, "What Do You Really Want?," 419–461; Sunseri, "The Baumwollfrage," 31–51; and Koponen, *Development for Exploitation*.

23. Steinmetz, *The Devil's Handwriting*.

24. Lowry, "African Resistance," 244–269; Short, "Everyman's Colonial Library," 445–475; Grimmer-Solem, "The Professors' Africa," 313–347; and Naranch, "Colonized Body, Oriental Machine," 299–338.

25. Eckert, Wirz, and Brommer, eds., *Alles unter Kontrolle*; von Trotha, *Koloniale Herrschaft*; and Söldenwagner, *Spaces of Negotiation*.

26. Walther, "Racializing Sex," 11–24; and Reagin, "The Imagined Hausfrau," 54–86.

27. Cf. Fehrenbach, *Race after Hitler*; Campt, *Other Germans*; and Höhn, *GIs and Fräuleins*.

28. Deutsch, *Emancipation without Abolition*; Pesek, *Koloniale Herrschaft in Deutsch-Ostafrika*; Zimmerer, *Deutsche Herrschaft über Afrikaner*; Sunseri, *Vilimani*; Eckert,

Grundbesitz, Landkonflikte und kolonialer Wandel; and Krüger, *Kriegsbewältigung und Geschichtsbewusstsein*.

29. Conrad, *Globalisation and the Nation*.

30. Brehl, *Vernichtung der Herero*. On the larger history of African representations in German culture, see Martin, *Schwarze Teufel, edle Mohren*.

31. Holston, "'A Measure of the Nation.'" For Weimar, see Schmidt, *"Was Deutschland mit Blut gewann!"*

32. Kuss, "Deutsche Soldaten während des Boxeraufstands," 165–182; and Dabringshaus, "An Army on Vacation?," 459–476.

33. Orosz, *Religious Conflict*; Aitken, *Exclusion and Inclusion*; Ruppenthal, *Kolonialismus als "Wissenschaft und Technik"*; Gewald and Silvester, eds., *Words Cannot Be Found*; Van der Heyden, ed., *Schwarze Biographien*; Aitken, "From Cameroon to Germany," 597–616; Bechhaus-Gerst and Klein-Arendt, eds., *AfrikanerInnen in Deutschland*; Bechhaus-Gerst, ed., *Die (Koloniale) Begegnung*; and Van Laak, *Imperiale Infrastruktur*.

34. Eckart, *Medizin und Kolonialimperialismus*.

35. Schmidt, "Colonial Intimacy," 25–59.

36. Mühlhahn, *Herrschaft und Widerstand*.

37. O'Donnell, Bridenthal, and Reagin, eds., *The Heimat Abroad*.

38. Sobich, *"Schwarze Bestien"*; Crothers, *German Elections of 1907*; and Fricke, "Der deutsche Imperialismus," 538–576.

39. Wigger, *Die "Schwarze Schmach am Rhein."*

ONE

Empire by Land or Sea?
Germany's Imperial Imaginary, 1840–1945

GEOFF ELEY

FROM *IMPERIALISM* TO *EMPIRE*

After something of a hiatus in the 1980s, interest in imperialism is booming. Yet the language has changed. We prefer the sanitized usage of "empire." "Imperialism" in the 1960s described the coercive domination and exploitative relations imposed by metropolitan countries on the more vulnerable parts of the world. Imperialist expansion was attributed to compulsions from inside the imperialist societies, whether economic, more specifically mercantile, more narrowly strategic, or more grandiosely geopolitical. Usually this was linked to arguments about dominant interests too, variously located among military and naval strategists as well as foreign policymakers, colonial administrators, and civil servants, entrepreneurial and business interests, freebooters and visionaries, or simply "the official mind." Yet these days "empire" often shrinks back to international politics more narrowly understood: foreign policymaking, national security concerns, geopolitical strategy, international monetary policy, trade agreements, international policing, and the deployment of military force. That earlier structural or systemic unity linking power abroad to pressures at home seems far less evident.[1]

For *popular* involvement in imperialism, however, the contrast cuts the other way. Treatments of empire seem *more* capacious rather than less. Social historians' first impulse in the 1960s and 1970s was often to query the extent of working-class identification with colonies, locating imperialist enthusiasm mainly elsewhere, whether among the prosperous educated and propertied bourgeoisie or the self-employed and white-collar lower middle class. From anti-imperialist sentiments or sheer parochialism and indifference to the wider overseas worlds, historians argued, working people remained stubbornly uninvolved. On the evidence of elections and nationalist campaigning groups, workers proved much harder to win for patriotic causes.[2] Yet now, the contrast could hardly be greater. In the wake of cultural history, scholarship shows the penetration of colonial ideas into all possible areas of popular culture and everyday life. Now we emphasize not the *marginality* or *insignificance* of empire for ordinary life but rather its *pervasiveness* and *presence*.

This dichotomy, between stressing the thinness of colonialism's impact inside the home society and seeing its depth, describes most national historiographies. But skepticism has been all the stronger in the German field, given the colonial empire's transitory duration. Because German colonialism lasted only from 1884 to 1919, the argument runs, it makes no sense for German historians to copy the British and French by taking the "imperial turn." By any criteria, German colonialism was a marginal phenomenon, at best a sideshow. For Jürgen Osterhammel, "the social histories above all of Great Britain, Portugal, and the Netherlands, and in some respects of Russia and France, have to remain incomplete or incomprehensible once divorced from their imperial-colonial context," whereas in Germany that is not the case.[3] David Blackbourn agrees: "one could hardly argue that the German colonies possessed the same centrality for domestic political debate as the far larger empires of the British and French"—or for that matter the Belgians and Dutch.[4] Under a "transnational" perspective, moreover, the colonies become recalibrated into just one instance of Germany's growing embeddedness in a larger set of global relations.[5] By relativizing the colonies as such, the transnational perspective as often shrinks their significance as asserts it.

As our volume makes abundantly clear, though, knowledge about the colonies reached far down into German society in manifold ways. From propaganda of the Colonial Society and the Navy League, through the literary and visual landscapes of newspapers, magazines, pulp literature, postcards, schoolbooks, and all the new paraphernalia of advertising and mass marketing, to the public spectacles of museums, *Völkerschauen*, films, slide shows, exhibits, and congresses, the public sphere of the late *Kaiserreich* was saturated with the citations of colonialism overseas. Here the patriotic intensities unleashed in December 1906–January 1907 during the "Hottentot elections" afford a telling illustration. By the first day of polling (January 25, 1907), the Navy League central office, acting as a clearinghouse for the government's electioneering, had dispatched 21 million leaflets highlighting Germany's colonial interests. The most numerous included *Arbeiter, Kolonien und Flotte* (5 million copies),

Für die Kämpfer in Sudwest Afrika (3.5 million), *Die Wahrheit über unsere Kolonien* (2.4 million), *Deutsches Volk, wie sorgt der Reichstag* (2.3 million), and *Warum ist der Reichstag aufgelöst?* (2 million).[6] The use of Gustav Frenssen's 1906 popular novel, *Peter Moors Fahrt nach Südwest—ein Feldzugsbericht*, is especially well documented. Embraced immediately by radical nationalists, Frenssen's account of a young Schleswig-Holstein artisan's experience of the Herero war, which sold 180,000 copies by 1914, brought the violent romance of the colonial frontier vividly home. During the 1907 elections the Navy League purchased a thousand copies for distribution through its regional sections.[7] Frenssen, a best-selling popular novelist from Schleswig-Holstein commonly associated with regionalist *Heimatkunst* but actually far more outward looking, epitomized the colonial world's new allure. Inspired by friendship with Friedrich Naumann, he constructed his fictions around the neo-Nietzschean idealism of his youthful protagonists as they passed from family and farm into the scenes of national grandiosity, which by the 1900s were patently placed on a global-cum-imperial scale.[8]

Frenssen's novel conveyed the German colonies' long afterlife. Never out of print, the Third Reich produced numerous editions for schools and the army. During World War II it surpassed half a million copies; in 1952 it appeared once again.[9] In contrast with the other old-imperial western European countries, (West) Germany faced none of the violence and divisiveness of decolonization, although the large-scale labor migracy from the late 1950s had similar displacement effects. If British and French reactions to immigrants signaled a postcolonial return of the repressed, then so too did West German reactions to *Gastarbeiter*, especially once earlier German imperialisms are brought to mind—from *Mitteleuropa*, Berlin-Baghdad, and the Balkan entanglements of the *Kaiserreich* to the southeastern European and Mediterranean theaters of expansionism under the Nazis. Colonialism not only seared long-lasting legacies into the public cultures of Britain, France, Belgium, the Netherlands, and Portugal; it left their viral traces in German popular memory, too, flaring every so often into life.[10]

In October 1966, at the height of the Fischer Controversy, West German television broadcast a polemical documentary by Ralph Giordano called *Heia Safari*, subtitled *The Legend of the German Colonial Idyll in Africa*. With an audience of some nine million, the reception confirmed German colonialism's ability to continue troubling the political unconscious of the nation. The right-wing press was outraged. Eugen Gerstenmeier and Franz Joseph Strauß telephoned Klaus von Bismarck, head of Westdeutsche Rundfunk (WDR), to demand that the documentary's second part be shelved and a more sympathetic film be produced instead. As a compromise the channel agreed to a studio discussion (aired in February 1967).[11] While German society lacked the permanent reserves of love for the colonies present in Britain, France, and elsewhere, a constructed memory of colonial benevolence continued resurging on occasions like the one above, goading the defenders of Germany's civilizing mission into vociferous voice. In those ways "colonial fantasies" continued to echo.[12]

So we have a paradox, setting long-standing tendencies to *play down* the importance of Germany's formal empire, whether in time or domestic penetration, against current insistence on its *thoroughgoing pervasiveness*, a claim the present volume attests. Hans-Ulrich Wehler offers a revealing example. In Wehler's mature works—whether his multivolume magnum opus, the *Gesellschaftsgeschichte*, or the collections of essays and reviews—colonialism plays virtually no part.[13] This silence seems ironic because Wehler's 1969 classic, *Bismarck und der Imperialismus*, made a compelling case for taking colonies seriously.[14] It also stood plainly alone. There were only Helmut Bley's and Karin Hausen's case studies; a smattering of works by Africanists; and monographs from the DDR. Works that did tackle German colonialism on a broader front were Klaus Bade's study of Friedrich Fabri and Hartmut Pogge's account of the *Kolonialrat*.[15]

Yet once we begin broadening the contexts for colonialism by setting our sights *beyond* direct colonial rule toward German expansion into the wider extra-European world—as soon as we make the conceptual moves of Sebastian Conrad's *Globalisation and Nation*—then older literatures provide far more help.[16] While not formally *about* colonialism, certain works become extremely suggestive once viewed in that light: Mack Walker's study of German emigration; William Hagen's *Germans, Poles, and Jews*; Kenneth Barkin's *Controversy over German Industrialization*; Alfred Vagt's older study of German-US relations in the context of *Weltpolitik*; Fritz Fischer's two great classics; Wolfgang Mommsen's *Max Weber and German Politics*.[17] Each proves very illuminating once colonialism is approached in a more broadly contextualized set of ways.

Where these older works offer little help is with the less direct, less perceptible, and more diffuse consequences of colonialism inside German society at home—all those questions now gathered under the sign of the "cultural turn." Here the decisive departure was certainly the volume edited by Sara Friedrichsmeyer, Sara Lennox, and Susanne Zantop called *The Imperialist Imagination*.[18] If that volume came almost entirely from *literary* studies, moreover, the intervening historical work has now transformed that disciplinary picture, opening German historians in the process to the pertinence of race, gender, and sexuality.[19] In consequence, the salient questions, methodologies, archive types, and grounds of inquiry have come to look profoundly different from those inspiring Bley and Hausen forty years before. The complicated passages between "the social" and "the cultural" experienced by historians during that time are nowhere clearer than in the history of colonialism.[20] As we hope to show, it is exactly the bringing of the cultural and the political together that makes possible the most challenging recent work on the history of German empire making before 1918.

FROM "SOCIAL IMPERIALISM" TO WHAT?

There seems far less interest than during the 1970s in drawing connections from the domestic environment of politics to foreign policy. From the perspective of the "primacy of domestic politics" (*Primat der Innenpolitik*), the new histories seem decoupled from an interest in the societal grounding of German foreign expansionism as more traditionally understood.[21] In the wake of the Fischer Controversy, the continuity thesis originally took its cachet primarily from foreign policy and the similarities linking the war aims of 1914–1918 with the later imperialism of the Nazis. At the outset the continuity argument involved Germany's "grab for world power," after all. In those discussions of the 1960s and 1970s, it was the *compulsion toward empire* that in the first instance defined the postulated continuity.[22]

Conceptually speaking, the sharpest contrast between then and now concerns the idea of "social imperialism," which in the 1970s had been pivotal for new approaches to the *Kaiserreich*. In Wehler's formulation, this denoted a "defensive ideology" against the "disruptive effects of industrialization on the social and economic structure of Germany," one that enabled "the diversion outwards of internal tensions and forces of change in order to preserve the social and political status quo."[23] A more recent iteration puts it thus: "It was only beneath this perspective that Wilhelmine *Weltpolitik* revealed its real meaning, its deeper driving force." By 1914 it was a permanently embedded pattern of politics: "Only this technique of rule seemed to make it possible to continue blocking the reformist modernization of the social and political constitution in the necessary degree."[24] Beginning with Bismarck and continuing from the later 1890s with growing recklessness and escalating results, a fateful pattern was projected into the future: "If there is a continuity in German imperialism," Wehler argued, then it consists in "the primacy of social imperialism from Bismarck to Hitler."[25]

Much of the historiographical excitement then surrounding the *Kaiserreich* came from an insistence that the imperialist drives of the two world wars possessed direct and compelling equivalence. That is, those successive waves of foreign expansionism needed to be understood in relation to the persistence of a domestic political power structure, a definite constellation of dominant class interests and their associated antidemocratic politics. For the Nazi period the analogue to this "Fischerite" approach to the July Crisis was Tim Mason's interpretation of the outbreak of World War II, a more pointed version of the widely shared view that the essential principle of the Third Reich's social system was the drive for war.[26]

Neither of these viewpoints—centrality of "social imperialism" for historiography of the *Kaiserreich* and Mason's thesis about Nazi expansionism—has kept much influence. Yet there are other ways of continuing to connect imperialist expansion to life inside Germany itself: the "racial state" clearly links the drive for foreign expansion to the logics of domestic policymaking, while cultural histories of the salience of the colonial relationship for the life of the German metropole could hardly enjoy greater influence. What *has* been lost is the strong conceptual unity that Wehler's generation constructed, linking the drive for empire, government strategies of rule, dominant class interests, and the structural persistence of authoritarianism. Current work on colonialism is concerned less with the persistence of authoritarian forms of rule than with the broader impact of German interactions with a non-European set of worlds. Rather than show interest mainly in *origins* (in colonial policy as an expression of conflicts and pressures coming from inside German society), recent work focuses on *consequences* and the impact of the colonial encounter. One obvious priority, therefore, would be to find ways of reestablishing concrete linkages from "colonialism" into the mainstream of German politics and policymaking in the early twentieth century.

We get furthest in tackling that question by thinking inside a far more capacious concept of colonialism.[27] Formal colonial rule might be deemed just one instance in a wider repertoire of Germany's expansionist relations with an exploitable world. "German expansionism" might then encompass everything from colonial policy as such to all the other ways in which German interests began seeking global penetration: the arms race and the big Navy; export drives and trading policy; the competitiveness of the German economy in world markets; questions of migration and maintenance of ties with Germans overseas; the "civilizational" impetus behind German culture; German diplomacy and the wider realm of *Weltpolitik*; and finally the July Crisis and Germany's aims in World War I.

Current talk of "empire" in our own time makes it easier to see this wider field of expansionary meanings. In contemporary globalization talk, interestingly, pre-1914 colonialism is now being reclaimed across a wide political spectrum in exactly this way, whether in Britain, France, or the United States.[28] Such arguments bespeak grandiose historical claims about the distinctive global order made by the Soviet Union's collapse and the end of the Cold War; they link to concepts of "failed" or "collapsed" states, they redeploy older liberal-imperialist arguments for new versions of the civilizing mission, and they urge the advanced states—like the United States and prospectively the European Union (EU)—to embrace "their responsibilities in the world" by realizing "a vision of cooperative empire."[29] In such discussion the nineteenth-century Pax Britannica is invariably invoked as a guide. Epitomized by the lionizing of Niall Ferguson, a recharged metanarrative of pre-1914 world history centering on the progressive directionality of "empire" has been circulating through the public sphere with ever greater insistence. The gist of this high Victorian analogy joins a theory of economic modernization to sanitized versions of the "civilizing mission" and the inevitable consequences of European or Western military superiority in order to rationalize a new developmental realism.[30]

For new interest in colonialism and empire before 1914, these contemporary languages of politics have been decisive. Recent historical discussions are simply not thinkable beyond present anxieties about foreignness, cultural belonging, migrancy, and race or beyond post-Saidian critiques of "the West" or beyond the wildly burgeoning discourse of "globalization."[31] For some scholars, the concept of "empire" seems even to acquire analytical or, perhaps, epistemological equivalence with the older category of "society."[32] Since the early 1990s, a set of intensively grounded arguments about the importance of imperialism—meaning both the acquiring of colonies and the informal dynamics of the West's coercive and exploitative impact in the rest of the world—has been slowly transforming the questions British and French historians bring to the study of national history, and the same has become true par excellence for the United States.[33] American studies programs have become entirely suffused with recognitions of empire's importance.[34]

THE NATION'S URGENT NEEDS: AN EXPANDING IMAGINARY

What are the larger contexts that best illuminate German colonialism? The essays assembled between the covers of this volume suggest a wealth of possible answers, but here I consider four.

COMPETITIVE GLOBALIZATION?

How should we read talk of the "great world empires" acquiring ever-greater impetus after the 1880s across German-speaking Europe? That talk suffused the public realms of business, journalism, academic life, and politics, enlisting the imaginations of the Wilhelmine intelligentsia into another version of the "ideological consensus" that Wehler found behind the drive for colonies in the earlier 1880s.[35] In its discursive architecture such talk uncannily resembles the progress of the languages of globalization today. As a deep-lying context of economic projection, hardheaded geopolitical calculation, and visionary thought, it likewise foreshadows one strand of current expectations for European integration.

This "empire talk" explicitly forged connections across the presumptively interlinked priorities of several distinct domains in the life of the nation. The first of these encompassed national efficiency in the economy, including the general projection of continuing economic growth; deployment of tariffs, bilateral trading treaties, and export offensives to ensure the conditions of market viability; and the aggressive securing of Germany's competitiveness in the world economy.[36] Second came the entire domain of social welfare, likewise conceived increasingly under the sign of national efficiency. While social policy was always complexly overdetermined by a plethora of economic, sociopolitical, ethicoreligious, institutional, and short-term political considerations, sometimes strategically conceived but as often undertaken for reasons of expediency, most major initiatives were at some level consciously framed to further the cause of social cohesion and political stability, commonly again under the sign of Germany's national competitiveness.[37] Finally came the sphere of foreign policy and international conflict per se, increasingly defined after the proclamation of *Weltpolitik* in the late 1890s by the arms drive and a diplomacy of aggressive interventions. The urgency of world-political advocacy developed symbiotically across each of these domains.

As a consensus of imposing breadth came together during the *Kaiserreich*, it traveled through perhaps four distinct phases. Each was marked by an intense concentration of public discussion across the press, associations, and the wider domain of publicity, intersecting with the business and government worlds and finding powerful resonance in the parties and the Reichstag. If each was then followed by a relative lull, the political climate had been fatefully ratcheted forward.

- The *first* phase, from the late 1870s to the mid-1880s, was described by Wehler's "ideological consensus" in the third part of his *Bismarck* book. Here, the first surge of colonialism was matched by conventional strategic and diplomatic concerns for stabilizing the new Germany's geopolitical security in central Europe.[38]

- A *second* spurt occurred in the mid-1890s, with the naval expansion, the end of the depression (1895/96), and the huge fanfare of the Kaiser's proclaiming of *Weltpolitik* in January 1896.[39] But concurrent with this new assertiveness about Germany overseas was an equally marked drive for a politically secured and state-guaranteed central European economic trading region, galvanized by the impact of the Caprivi commercial treaties of 1892–1894. The most serious attempt to hold these goals politically together came from the Pan-German League, founded in 1890/91.[40]
- A *third* phase was sparked by the 1902 tariff settlement, the standard of living agitation behind the SPD's 1903 electoral landslide, and the economic recovery after the brief depression of 1900–1902. While enthusiasm for *Weltpolitik* continued apace (dramatized around the first Moroccan Crisis and the radicalizing of naval agitation), the most notable initiative was the founding of the *Mitteleuropäischer Wirtschaftsverein* in 1904, again strongly inflected by Pan-German thinking. It was now that the characteristic oscillation between "world policy" and "continental policy" began to be named.
- The *fourth* phase immediately preceded 1914, introduced by the watershed of the second Moroccan Crisis and the reversion to a military (as opposed to a naval) arms drive in 1911. The intensifying public discussion was classically demonstrated in Fischer's second book, *Krieg der Illusionen*, together with the key supporting works of Dirk Stegmann, Peter-Christian Witt, and Klaus Wernecke.[41]

Running through that discourse from the start was the idea of three existing "world empires"—the British, American, and Russian (plus occasionally the French as a fourth)—against whose global dominance (economically, demographically, geostrategically) Germany would need comparable resources to compete. German unification and French military defeat had already prised open this global constellation of the existing "world nations," but now the urgency of further securing Germany's claims to parity was severe. As Paul Rohrbach succinctly put it: "The fourth nation—that is ourselves."[42] Indeed, a fundamental condition of Great Power standing beneath the pressures of intensifying world economic rivalry, which put into question not just a society's future prosperity but its very survival, would be Germany's ability to assemble an equivalent basis for "world imperial" expansion, usually conceptualized as some version of *Mitteleuropa* but extending (as Fischer said) "from Spitzbergen to the Persian Gulf."[43]

On the outbreak of war Bethmann Hollweg embraced this idea as a customs union between Germany and Austria-Hungary, which Belgium and France would be compelled to join. Crystallizing from earlier discussions with Walter Rathenau and others into the core of his September Program, *Mitteleuropa* hardwired Bethmann's thinking about war aims. During the intensive ministerial discussions of September 1914, Bethmann's main collaborator, Interior Secretary Clemens von Delbrück, projected "a single customs unit stretching from the Pyrenees to Memel, from the Black Sea to the North Sea, from the Mediterranean to the Baltic."[44] This characteristic imagery of the globalized struggle for existence among rival "world nations" or "world empires" had become the default language of international politics in German policymaking circles, organized around the dialectics of prosperity and survival.[45] *This* was how powerful nations—expanding economies, prosperous societies, dynamic cultures, strategically dominant Great Powers—*had* to develop to avoid sinking into stagnation, poverty, decadence, and marginality. The terms of success under the competitive world system *required* such a logic.

Before 1914 such thinking was necessarily more speculative. Sometimes France was part of the projected union, sometimes not; sometimes it was deemed a fourth world empire, sometimes marked as irremediably decadent. In Gustav Roloff's *Kolonialpolitscher Führer*, produced for the 1907 elections, *Mitteleuropa* was a German-centered confederation of states capable of "produc[ing] all modern necessities as successfully as any of the giant empires" of Britain, France, the United States, and Russia: "At the top of a union to which Holland, Belgium, Scandinavia, Austria, and perhaps also Italy and a few extra-European states such as Mexico and Chile could accede, Germany would have nothing to fear from the four others."[46] This continental projection of necessary economic security was always bound integrally to a global imaginary of expanding trade and cultural influence, edged by a history of emigrationist anxieties descending from the early nineteenth century. Here is Gustav Schmoller during the agitation for the 1900 Navy Law, invoking the familiar exclusionary threat from the three "conquering and colonizing empires" of Russia, the United States, and Britain:

> [Germany] no longer wishes to be the nursery and schoolroom of the rest of the world, a land that sends out millions of its sons abroad so that they cease being Germans in the next generation. Its state, its energy, its

scholarship and its technology, its trade and its reputation in the world are so great ... [and] its moral and intellectual qualities, its affective life, its fine arts, its diligence, its institutions, stand so high that it can demand in the interests of the *Kultur* of humanity to assert, on the basis of its own law, own colonies, own stations, its own influence of power, its place in the world economy next to ... the great three world empires.[47]

As Rohrbach said in *Der deutsche Gedanke in der Welt* in 1912: "For us there can be no standing still or stopping, not even a temporary renunciation of the expansion of our sphere of life; our choice is either to decline again ... or to struggle for a place alongside the Anglo-Saxons.... Our growth is a process of elemental natural force."[48] That was partly what Weber had meant in 1895 when he worried caustically that the unification of Germany was starting to seem like a "costly extravagance" and a frivolous "youthful spree," which "would have been better left undone if it was meant to be the end and not the starting point of a German policy of world power."[49] Just as Germany's unification had required war, so too might its future survival. Here is Rohrbach again in 1913:

> *Whether we shall obtain the necessary territorial elbow room to develop as a world power or not* without use of the old recipe of "blood and iron" is anything but certain.... Our situation as a nation today is comparable to that before the wars of 1866 and 1870 which it was necessary to fight to settle the national crisis. At that time it was Germany's political unification which was at stake, today it is Germany's admittance to the circle of World Nations or its exclusion from it.[50]

How are we to judge the effects of this discourse on politics? What was its relationship not only to the making of wartime policy but also over the longer term to the ideas, projects, and ambitions shaping German expansionism under the Third Reich? For that matter, what legitimate lines might be drawn from these earlier projections of *Mitteleuropa* to later images of more peaceful commercial and industrial penetration, including the prospects opened by 1989/90?

GLOBAL GERMANY?

Historians are drawn increasingly to "transnationalism" as a "way of seeing" allowing us to think "beyond the nation" or outside the framework of the nation-state. Without diminishing states, empires, and other forms of bounded sovereignty, this stresses a different field of connections defined more by "networks, processes, beliefs, and institutions that transcend these politically defined spaces."[51] Isabel Hofmeyr amplifies the point: "The key claim of any transnational approach is its central concern with movements, flows, and circulation, not simply as a theme or motif, but as an analytic set of methods which defines the endeavor itself." Citing Arjun Appadurai, she calls this a concern with the "space of the flows," which insists not only on the diverse origins of historical processes (any history will usually be made in more than one place) but also that "they are constructed in the movement between places, sites, and regions."[52]

A transnational perspective has many dimensions. The complicated interconnectedness of nationality and territoriality will not always map easily onto Europe's actual national-state sovereignties of the period, say, between 1859 and 1973. People, goods, and ideas circulate *across* the national frontiers, both actual and imagined, of any particular time. The permeability of geographical borderlands and state-territorial frontier lines allow the porousness and mobility of both cultures and all kinds of personal affiliations. Parochialism can break down in "nonnational" or "prenational" ways. National affiliations might be shaped from margins and across distances markedly separated from the physical heartland of the nation itself, subtly complicating relations of inclusion and exclusion. Any period in a society's history contains a complex repertoire of processes—economic, social, cultural, political—that cut across the main patterns of nation forming, whether in state-territorial or culturalist terms. Such processes work against the grain of either the actually consummated histories or the imagined realizations of the nation form. A transnational history proposes regional contexts for exploring questions a national frame might otherwise obscure.

A transnational optic calls attention to the extra-European and colonial theaters of Germany's metropolitan history. It illumines the earlier nineteenth-century settings in which the *national* itself was yet to be properly formed—before a "national" had arrived that could yet become "trans." Between *Vormärz* and the 1860s, nationhood and national belonging had attained a prefigurative presence even in advance of statehood per se. In a geopolitical environment already occupied by older established national states, where nationalist ideas were palpably circulating through those central European lands soon to be remapped into a new state-bounded entity of Germany and where the urgency of nationalist advocacy saturated the emergent public sphere, the language of the transnational already made sense. As Bradley Naranch has shown, expansionary relations already bound the inhabitants of German-speaking Europe into a set of larger-than-European worlds within an avowedly *national* frame of aspiration yet *in advance* of the national state's actual foundation. Between the 1840s and 1870s, well ahead of the coming unification, Germany's emergent national intelligentsia—writers, journalists, academics, economists, businessmen, political activists—used the visionary landscape of a putative colonial imaginary to do much of the ideological work of describing what the future national government would be expected to do. To secure its popular legitimacy, that government should be capable of defending Germany's interests on the world stage of international competition, as well as sustaining the power of German culture overseas and creating organized ties strong enough to retain the affiliations of those who were leaving German-speaking Europe in such prodigious and disquieting numbers. No mere preamble to the later narrative of the Bismarckian colonial policy of the mid-1880s, this was an integral part of the story itself. It was vital to the process *through which the making of the German nation was accomplished*.[53] By thinking transnationally *in advance* of the national state's creation, we can observe the "boundaries of Germanness" already being fashioned into place.[54]

In this mid-nineteenth-century context a transnational approach unsettles our thinking about where exactly "Germany" was to be found. Before unification itself, the nation coalesced around an imagined topography of European and global locations far larger and more dispersed than the lands to which the political entity fashioned in the period 1864–1871 then became attached. Once Germany had become organized into the "small German" territorial sovereignty that understood itself as a national state—once Germany was unified into the *Kaiserreich* of 1871—the stakes radically changed. The transnational object transmuted from the "not yet national" into the "not yet national enough." For German nationalists, the language of what I am calling "competitive globalization"—the constant invoking of the circle of the "great world empires" to which Germany needed admittance—became a principal means through which that lack was to be bridged.

Andrew Zimmerman's study of the Tuskegee expedition to German Togo in the early 1900s offers a fascinating demonstration. To examine the complex interrelations among ideas of free labor, race, and social science, Zimmerman tracks their journeying back and forth along the Atlantic circuits of influence, ideas, and political economy that joined Germany, Africa, and the United States.[55] By proceeding transnationally, he brings previously separated histories compellingly together. In venturing outside the well-beaten paths of national history, he reconstructs the complex channels that brought a series of paired histories unexpectedly into crosscutting dialogue. The *first* of these couplets sets Booker T. Washington's speech at the Atlanta Cotton States and International Exposition of 1895 alongside Max Weber's Freiburg inaugural address of the same year; the *second* joins the politics of internal colonization in the

Prussian East with the political economy of plantation agriculture in the postslave South; and a *third* juxtaposes the structure of the agricultural labor market in eastern Germany with the range of agrarian labor relations encountered in North America, including the sharecropping system, the various regimes of postemancipation labor coercion, and the "Negro question" in the US New South. In pondering the problem of East Elbian backwardness, seemingly so intractably linked to the codependent inefficiencies of Prussian Junkers and Polish peasants, German economists looked to the labor regimes and models of agricultural economy prevalent in Canada and the United States. The late nineteenth century saw significant traffic of German agronomists to the Canadian prairies, the Great Plains, and the plantation South. Attracted by Washington's Tuskegee experiments, percipient German policymakers saw opportunities for colonial development potentially adaptable for the East Elbian home. Borne by the Tuskegee expedition, these transatlantic links convened in the German colony of Togo, where Washington's ideas inspired an ambitious program for the *Erziehung des Negers zur Arbeit* (the "Education of the Negro for Work"). By situating the Tuskegee expedition in the complex circuitry of influences inside a "German Atlantic," Zimmerman shows how a history located in Germany's "East" disclosed far more complex genealogies, which can be tracked back and forth across some unexpected places in Europe, Africa, and the Americas.[56]

Several particular points arise. First, by following Weber in 1904 to his meetings with Washington in Tuskegee and W. E. B. DuBois in Atlanta, Zimmerman shows how Weber's thinking about ethnicity, labor, and agricultural proletarianization in the Prussian-Polish East became shaped by his understanding of race, land, and agricultural labor across the Atlantic in the United States. German thinking about settlement policies for eastern Europe relied on a reservoir of knowledge about the relative efficiencies of farming on the Canadian prairies, in the US Midwest, and in the plantation economies of the slave and postslave South. German overseas colonialism and German landward expansionism to the east were always in a complex exchange before 1914, involving traceable relays of ideas, influences, and people.[57]

Second, Zimmerman shows how the freshly racialized category of the "Negro" supplanted older anthropological designations of the *Naturvölker* ("natural peoples") or the *Eingeborenen* ("natives") by constructing "an individual capable of improvement, in contrast to the so-called 'natural person,' who was doomed either to extinction or to a travestied approximation of civilization."[58] Under the spell of Tuskegee, German colonial theorists "hoped to make Africans just like US 'Negroes,' only more so—more productive, more docile, more rational and free, and more obedient and constrained."[59] Zimmerman likewise shows how racialized thinking forged in the colonies simultaneously subsisted on social experience back in the metropole, in this case a body of social thought preoccupied with the property relations of eastern Prussian agriculture: "The concept of the 'Negro' buttoned together a number of ideological discourses about race and ethnicity, free labor, and agricultural production in the United States, Africa, and Germany."[60]

Third, this production of ideas about the "Negro" in an apparently unimportant Togolese colonial margin shows racialized categories possessing a *contingency*, a *constructedness*, and a *mobility* that belie our assumptions about national peculiarities, allowing us to track their efficacies into unexpected places. The transnational perspective encourages us not only to follow the genealogies of racialized ideas back and forth across the Atlantic rather than just into the deeper nineteenth-century mists of specifically German time but also to understand the fallout from the "colonial effect" inside the German metropole as far more pervasive than older dismissals of Germany's colonial history could allow. As Zimmerman says, the Tuskegee expedition "stitch[ed] together and thus permanently transform[ed] three powerful networks: German social science, New South race politics, and African cash cropping. At their points of intersection, these three networks produced objects whose apparent stability both conceals and results from a dynamic and transnational history: blackness, peasants, and cotton."[61]

EMPIRE BY SEA OR BY LAND?

Within the commonly agreed "world-imperial" frame of reference, radical nationalists hotly debated the preferred direction for Germany's interests before 1914. Was this to be *Überseepolitik oder Festlandspolitik?* ("Overseas Policy or Continental Policy?"), to invoke a keynote debate at the 1905 Pan-German Congress between the editor of the Essen-based *Rheinisch-Westfälische Zeitung*, Theodor Reismann-Grone, and the former governor of German East Africa and head of the *Reichsverband gegen die Sozialdemokratie* (Imperial League against Social Democracy), Eduard von Liebert.[62] Yet as Sweeney shows, this public exchange only staged a longer-standing Pan-German debate, one explicitly *refusing* any such conflict between landward empire and *Weltpolitik*. Under Ernst Hasse's presiding tutelage, that discussion ambitiously reconceived Germany's imperialist future as a new type of complex macropolity, or "imperial formation," whose spatial reach went far beyond unambiguous colonial government of the direct kind. Instead, it embraced not only "blurred genres of rule and partial sovereignties" but also varying modalities of cultural influence and economic penetration, whether inside Europe or in the wider extra-European world.⁶³ Within a federated European structure linked to variegated global dominion, this empire would combine gradated sovereignties arranged around a dominant German core with integrated economic planning linked to grandiose biopolitical schemes for social engineering and large-scale population transfers. Pan-German visions of a "Greater Germany" specifically held these European and extra-European logics of imperial policymaking together, binding the prospects for colonial expansion overseas to the securing of Germany's dominance inside the continent at home. If the resulting coprosperity zone, a Greater German Federation, would have to include far more heterogeneous populations, it would still be "exclusively ruled" by the ethnic Germans.⁶⁴ For Pan-Germans European empire making also presumed an active social policy at home, one profoundly technocratic and hostile to democracy. As Sweeney argues, it was the racialized logic of this emergent biopolitical program for the management of populations, intensifying on the eve of 1914, that allowed a recognizably fascist conception of the *Volkskörper* (national body) to form.⁶⁵

Pan-German visions were the most radical of the efforts at imagining, consistently and programmatically, how Germany might take its place among the vaunted "world empires." As international tensions escalated toward 1914, others found the simultaneity of overseas and landward expansionism harder to sustain. The government found itself constrained to choose one over the other. The abrupt reversion in 1911/12 to the more orthodox primacy of an army-based armaments policy, after the navy's long dominance ushered in by the call to *Weltpolitik* in 1896, forms the most obvious context for this. The debacle of the second Moroccan Crisis during the summer of 1911, the government's policymaking disarray, and the associated "breakthrough of the national opposition" combined with Germany's deteriorating trading position and the 1913/14 recession to tarnish the appeal of overseas colonialism and bring *Mitteleuropa* strongly back to the fore. With the vital exception of the projected drive through the Balkans, Asia Minor, and the Caucasus along the direction of "Berlin-Baghdad, wartime then necessarily privileged those ideas to the practical exclusion of extra-European goals."⁶⁶

As I have argued, expansionist policies in Europe and colonialism in the rest of the world contained definite logics of equivalence. It was no accident that an infrastructure was being created for internal colonization of eastern Prussia's Polish enclaves just as the Congress of Berlin laid the foundations for Germany's overseas empire. In the event, the Prussian Settlement Commission solidified Polish solidarities as much as it promoted the German presence.⁶⁷ Yet this self-defeating quality of the Germanization measures mattered less than the radical nationalist ambitions they incited or the German-Polish tensions they inflamed. Lack of success diminished neither their place in the colonizing imagination nor their cumulative relation to the more determined policies applied against occupied Poland and the Baltic during the 1914–1918 period. Nor was the scale negligible: the 120,000 German-speakers settled in the eastern provinces before 1914 exceeded by five times the aggregate numbers who settled in colonies overseas.[68]

There remained distinctions. In projecting eastern mastery, German nationalists shied well short of the mass killing and other colonial violence all too prevalent on African land. In that sense the genocidal ruthlessness of Nazi expansion certainly presupposed the brutalizations of 1914 to 1918. But the character of Germany's impact on the extra-European world was actually no less heterogeneous: German migrants to the south of Brazil, German commercial representatives in Chile and Venezuela, or German consular officials in the Ottoman Empire comported themselves very differently from German settlers in Southwest Africa or German administrators in Dar es Salaam. Once we broaden our perspective beyond the colonial empire per se, we see how easily Polish policy fits into the larger repertoire of practice associated with the pre-1914 "colonial ordering of the world." Those practices included settlement policies and property regimes; regional planning and infrastructural investment; the dynamics of labor markets and "education for labor"; schooling and language policies; family relations, sexuality, and miscegenation; and finally, all the discursive machinery associated with the construction and elaboration of colonial hierarchy and difference.[69] It is precisely when anti-Polish policies are viewed in this way that the relevance of the Pan-Germans' racialized biopolitical ambitions emerges more clearly.

What else was at stake in the couplet of "overseas policy" versus "continental policy"? In what precise ways might the overseas colonial contexts of Germanness before 1914 and the eastern European territories into which Germany expanded during the years 1915–1918 be given equivalence? How should we think about this comparison? Whereas German nationalist ideas of the eastern frontier grew from deeply embedded antagonisms going back several centuries, after all, the dynamics of African colonialism involved more novel encounters with foreignness. But the congruence and reciprocities have recently been prompting attention. The possibilities only increase as treatments of the "racial state" and "racialization" under Nazism get pushed back into the *Kaiserreich*. Approaching such questions from each of the respective "peripheries," recent works by Paul Weindling and Pascal Grosse seek to recast the interrelations among race, science, public health, eugenics, social engineering, and the larger complex of modernizing reform before 1914.[70] Similarly, the most recent debates over Nazi "modernity" have unsettling implications for how we approach questions of planning, technology, population, and national efficiency in the earlier period, not only in Germany itself but also with respect to the developmentalist futures projected into the colonial sphere.[71]

How far does it make sense to consider the eastern territories as a *colonial* frontier in these ways? Should we think of the eastern borderlands and the overseas colonies on a plane of equivalence, or do the specificities undermine the usefulness of this comparison? How far should the period between the 1880s and the 1940s be treated as a single entity in this regard? Is there a single chain of equivalence linking, *first*, the ideologies of overseas settlement and colonization feeding from the 1880s into the later radical nationalism of the Wilhelmine Pan-Germans; *second*, the colonization and settlement projects invented for the occupied East during the 1915–1918 period; and *third*, the further radicalization of such thinking about the East under the Third Reich? How do we position the experience of World War I in this overall story? Is there a coherent strand of continuity tying languages of racialization under the Third Reich into the earlier race thinking of the *Kaiserreich*, or are the breaks and disjunctures more decisive?

SOCIAL IMPERIALISM ONCE MORE?

Is there a case for revisiting the explanatory usefulness of Wehler's "social imperialism" thesis of thirty years ago? In that argument the drive for overseas empire was connected to the desire to contain or divert social and political tensions at home.[72] But Wehler focused on the manipulative and directly propagandist aspects of colonialism and other nationalist enthusiasms from a specifically *governmental* point of view. Only recently have historians turned to the wider cultural effects. Via many complicated fields of indebtedness, we now appreciate, forms of social relations, patterns of culture, and increasingly racialized discourses of national superiority fashioned in the colonies became powerfully reinserted into the metropolitan social world. Forms of colonial representation via literature, museums and exhibitions, commercial entertainments, marketing and advertisements, and the widest domain of popular culture all now come into view.[73] The regendering of national identity in this period also acquired colonial dimensions.[74]

We now see more clearly the relays back and forth between the colonial worlds and the German metropole. Diverse categories of German speakers came to define themselves—their Germanness in its social and cultural dimensions, their claims to citizenship, their access to varieties of personhood—via representations of the wider-than-German overseas world as those ideas circulated ever more profusely through the commodified and mass-mediated public spheres of the new German state. It was more *these* discursive materials that assembled the *real* ground of "social imperialism," and *less* the conscious manipulations Wehler ascribed to governing elites. More insidious ideological restructuration was at work, reorienting nationalist assumptions in manifold ways. Yet while many such relays correspond *exactly* to the connectedness addressed by Wehler—the relationship between domestic prosperity and overseas expansion or the political proceeds of artfully mobilized popular nationalism or the propaganda value of foreign adventures and diplomatic coups or the unifying feedback of patriotic rhetorics on popular opinion—any interest in "social imperialism" per se has disappeared.[75]

Yet irrespective of the *term* "social imperialism," we surely need some means of theorizing the long-term domestic consequences of empire—everything generated from the colonial encounter that became assimilated into the metropolitan society's self-understanding with sufficiently potent and pervasive continuity to have helped the later implanting of the "racial state." These discursive consequences of empire included not just formal ideas and easily recognizable prejudices about the colonial world. They worked through insidiously internalized, culturally perduring patterns of belief. Such patterns embraced many transferential conflations from overseas colonial populations to colonized territories inside Europe itself, as well as all the racialized systems of distinction, both sophisticated and crude, defining Germans against their "others." Inside metropolitan social life were produced particular elements of political subjectivity complexly structured around ideas of the colony, forming a metropolitan version of the "colonial effect." By this I mean the sum of the transference and translation of complex and heterogeneous knowledge, idioms of thought, direct and vicarious experiences, spectacular events, arresting and seductive images, compelling arguments about economics, prosperity, and global survival, a visual repertoire of fantasy and desire, manifold forms of everyday consumption, and all the relevant registers of governmentality—in other words, the aggregative, adaptable, and coherent discursive presence we call *colonialism*, whose availability for deployment in the domestic arenas of politics then became capable of producing active forms of political agency and active particular effects.[76]

CONCLUSION

Any firm and fast distinction between colonizing expansionism overseas and landward colonialism inside Europe seems hard to sustain. Colonialism in established usage begins from the seizure and settlement of lands or trading posts and coaling stations overseas, joined to exploitation of resources and people, in a framework of imperial rule and political dispossession. Most working definitions stress destruction of indigenous social relations; imposition of the colonizers' own systems of law, economy, and political rule; denial of rights of all kinds, whether as citizenship, protections under law, and the franchise or as human dignity and access to livelihood; finally of course the exercise of coercion and violence embracing extremes of mass incarceration, mass killing, and genocide. Racialized forms of the overseas colonial encounter come next, with their obsessiveness about skin color and the dangers of race mixing, practices of exoticizing, logics of "othering," and essentializing of human differences. That describes colonial rule during the period of intensified imperialist competition among the industrializing countries before 1914. Yet it likewise offers a compelling inventory of everything the Nazis pursued in the East after 1939. Precisely these planes of equivalence between colonialism overseas and twentieth-century expansionism inside Europe itself are too clear to ignore.

Scholars such as Jürgen Zimmerer, from the pre-1914 vantage point of the overseas, and Wendy Lower, writing from the 1940s, have convincingly thought these histories together.[77] That need not require seeing oversimplified causal or explanatory continuities from one to the other, whether biographically, ideologically, or in some other way. Birthe Kundrus writes instead about specific "chains of influence, transfers, and situational parallels," treating earlier colonial histories as a future reservoir of models and policies, ideas and attitudes, dreams and fantasies, usable practices, modalities of planning, and available blueprints, including those paths *not* to be followed.[78] Nazi expansionism also had its own terrible specificities, never subsumable inside such larger-scale frameworks. But the basic case for placing Nazi empire inside a framework of colonialism, whether in the abstract or for purposes of comparison, seems noncontroversial.

If structures of rule, systems of exploitation, and patterns of expansionism allow colonialism to be historicized across varying contexts of *Kaiserreich* and Third Reich, so too does "civilizationism": the claim to German national superiority based in the empowerment of science and reason, the compulsion to bring progress to the non-European peoples, and the projection outwards of a German national mission.[79] In each case—overseas colonialism and Nazi empire in the East—cultural dominion over the foreign elsewhere converged. Again, theorizing these affinities in an overarching framework of colonialism implies no simplified and linear causal chains.

Finally, each of these concluding propositions—the meaningful equivalence linking colonialism overseas and landward expansionism; the commonalties binding Nazi expansionism and pre-1914 colonialism; the convergence of "civilizationist" ideologies—suggests an argument running throughout this discussion. In recovering the genealogies of Nazism, it is to the connective dynamics of the period between the 1890s and the 1930s that we should look.

NOTES

This essay began at the Midwest German History Workshop in Urbana-Champaign in October 2003 and evolved through various iterations. I am grateful to each of the audiences concerned. I am especially indebted to Sebastian Conrad, Jessica Dubow, Julia Hell, Jennifer Jenkins, Wendy Lower, A. Dirk Moses, Bradley Naranch, Robert L. Nelson, Roberta Pergher, Hartmut Pogge von Strandmann, George Steinmetz, Ronald Grigor Suny, Dennis Sweeney, Lenny Urena-Valerio, Andrew Zimmerman, and Jürgen Zimmerer.

1. For the high tide of earlier interest, see Sutcliffe and Owen, eds., *Studies in the Theory of Imperialism*; and for the tide's receding, Mommsen and Osterhammel, eds., *Imperialism and After*. For current writing: Burton, ed., *After the Imperial Turn*; Maier, *Among Empires*; Miller and Rieber, eds., *Imperial Rule*; Calhoun, Cooper, and Moore, eds., *Lessons of Empire*; and Stoler, McGranahan, and Perdue, eds., *Imperial Formations*. For conceptual guidance: Steinmetz, "Imperialism or Colonialism?" and "Return to Empire." Kramer, "Power and Connection," is a magisterial survey.

2. For my own earliest work: Eley, "Defining Social Imperialism" and "Social Imperialism in Germany." In British history, see Price, *An Imperial War and the British Working Class*.

3. Osterhammel, "Transnationale Gesellschaftsgeschichte: Erweiterung oder Alternative?," 468.

4. Blackbourn, "Das Kaiserreich transnational," 321.

5. See esp. Conrad, *Globalisation and the Nation* and, in Retallack, "Transnational Germany" (esp. 221–223). Significantly, there is no separate chapter or subentry in Retallack's volume for colonies per se. In contrast, Zimmerman, "Race and World Politics," brilliantly integrates treatments of colonies and imperialism.

6. As itemized in August Keim's report to the Reich Chancellery, January 22, 1907, *Zentrales Staatsarchiv Potsdam*, Rkz., 1807, 55–56, cited in Eley, "German Navy League," 420.

7. See Sobich, *"Schwarze Bestien, rote Gefahr,"* 279–281; Benninghoff-Lühl, *Deutsche Kolonialromane*, 111; Wassink, *Auf den Spuren*, 141–144; Eley, *Reshaping the German Right*, 254–267.

8. For Frenssen, see, above all, Pascal, *From Naturalism to Expressionism*, esp. 38–41, 100; Thalmann, *Protestantisme et nationalisme*.

9. Reprinted most recently by BiblioBazaar, Charleston, 2008. The English translation appeared almost immediately: *Peter Moor's Journey to Southwest Africa*.

10. See Eley, "The Trouble with 'Race.'"

11. Michels, "Die WDR-Dokumentation 'Heia Safari.'" I first learned of this in 1969/70

from the consultant to the documentary, Hartmut Pogge von Strandmann, who joined the studio discussion.

12. Zantop, *Colonial Fantasies*.

13. See Wehler, *Deutsche Gesellschaftsgeschichte*, vol. 3, 977–990 and 1137–1141, where colonialism remains confined within two perfunctory subsections with no cross-referencing to economy, culture, or social life. Concepts of imperialism/empire are absent from the successor volume, Wehler, *Deutsche Gesellschaftsgeschichte*, vol. 4, and the collected essays, *Politik in der Geschichte, Umbruch und Kontinuität*, and *Notizen zur deutschen Geschichte*. This isolating of colonialism characterizes Nipperdey's general history too, which briefly notices the topic under foreign policy and *Weltpolitik*. See Nipperdey, *Deutsche Geschichte 1866–1918*, vol. 1, 445–453 and 629–670. The companion volume dealing with social, economic, and cultural history omits any mention. See Nipperdey, *Deutsche Geschichte 1866–1918*, vol. 1.

14. Wehler, *Bismarck und der Imperialismus* and "Industrial Growth." Wehler barely mentions imperialism in his recent interview reflections. See Wehler, *Eine lebhafte Kampfsituation*.

15. Bley, *South-West Africa under German Rule*; Hausen, *Deutsche Kolonialherrschaft in Afrika*; Iliffe, *Tanganyika under German Rule*; Austen, *Northwest Tanzania*; Louis, *Ruanda-Urundi*; Wright, *German Missions in Tanganyika*; Stoecker, *Deutschland und China*; Stoecker, ed., *Kamerun unter deutscher Kolonialherrschaft*; Müller, *Deutschland-Zanzibar-Ostafrika*; Drechsler, *Südwestafrika unter deutscher Kolonialherrschaft*; Bade, *Friedrich Fabri und der Imperialismus*; von Strandmann, *Imperialismus vom Grünen Tisch*. Somewhat later, Smith published his valuable overview, *German Colonial Empire*.

16. Conrad, *Globalisation and Nation*; also Conrad and Osterhammel, eds., *Das Kaiserreich transnational*.

17. Walker, *Germany and the Emigration*, esp. 197–227; Hagen, *Germans, Poles, and Jews*; Barkin, *The Controversy over German Industrialization*; Vagts, *Deutschland und die Vereinigten Staaten*; Fischer, *Germany's Aims* and *War of Illusions*; Mommsen, *Max Weber and German Politics*; also Böhm, *Überseehandel und Flottenbau*.

18. Friedrichsmeyer, Lennox, and Zantop, eds., *Imperialist Imagination*.

19. The plenitude of current research was captured in two major conferences in Sheffield (September 2006) and San Francisco (September 2007), proceedings later published as Perraudin and Zimmerer, with Heady, eds., *German Colonialism and National Identity*, and Langbehn and Salama, eds., *German Colonialism*, respectively. See also Langbehn, ed., *German Colonialism, Visual Culture*; Moses and Stone, eds., *Colonialism and Genocide*; Moses, ed. *Empire, Colony, Genocide*.

20. See Eley, *Crooked Line*.

21. The reference here is to Kehr, *Der Primat der Innenpolitik*, translated as *Economic Interest, Militarism, and Foreign Policy*.

22. See Fischer, *World Power or Decline* and *From Kaiserreich to Third Reich*.

23. Wehler, "Industrial Growth and Early German Imperialism," 87, 88, 89.

24. Wehler, *Deutsche Gesellschaftsgeschicht*, vol. 4, 1139.

25. See, respectively, Wehler, "Bismarcks Imperialismus 1862–1890," 161; and Wehler, "Probleme des Imperialismus," 131.

26. See Mason, "Legacy of 1918 for National Socialism," 218: "National Socialism appears as a radically new variant of the social imperialism of Bismarck and Wilhelm II ... foreign expansion would legitimize not an inherited political and social system but an entirely new one." See also Mason: "Internal Crisis and War of Aggression," and "Domestic Dynamics of Nazi Conquests"; "Domestic Crisis and War, 1939"; "Debate: Germany, 'Domestic Crisis,' and War in 1939," with a reply by Richard J. Overy. For the more diffuse view of the Third Reich as "a regime inherently geared to war," see Noakes and Pridham, eds., *Nazism 1919–1945*, vol. 3 (here 751); Kershaw, *Nazi Dictatorship*, 134–160; Knox, "Conquest, Foreign and Domestic," 1–57, "Expansionist Zeal," 113–133, and *Common Destiny*.

27. Steinmetz properly ties colonial rule to the *colonial state*, defining modern colonialism "as the annexation of a territory by people with ties to a foreign state who perceive the conquered population as culturally distant and inferior." The colonial relationship then presumes both a state apparatus and a regime of cultural inequality that works to fix the subject people's inferiority, by what Chatterjee calls the "rule of colonial difference." Broadening the concept of colonialism risks occluding these specificities, but the heuristic gains outweigh the drawbacks. See Steinmetz, "'Devil's Handwriting,'" 42; Chatterjee, *Nation and Its Fragments*, 14, 20.

28. For the French law of February 2005 affirming French colonialism's positive legacies, see Godoy, "Recasting Colonialism as a Good Thing," www.globalpolicy.org /empire/history/2005/0705empgood.htm; and for Sarkozy's remarkable speech at the University of Dakar on July 28, 2007, see Andriamananjara, "Senegal," at www .globalvoicesonline.org/2007/08/24/senegal-africa-according-to-nicolas-sarkozy/. For the speech itself, see Sarkozy, "Speech at University of Dakar," www.elysee.fr/elysee /elysee.fr/francais/interventions/2007/juillet/allocution_a_1_universite_de_dakar .79184.html.

29. Phrases are taken from Cooper, "New Liberal Imperialism," full text at http:// observer.guardian.co.uk/comment/story/0,,680093,00.html. Robert Cooper, adviser to British Prime Minister Tony Blair, became EU Director-General for External and Politico-Military Affairs in 2002. For his longer essay, see "Post-Modern State," in Foreign Policy Center, ed., *Reordering the World*. See also Cooper, *Post-Modern State* and *Breaking of Nations*; also, "Grand Strategy," 26–32.

30. Ferguson, "America: An Empire in Denial," B7–B10, and *Empire*.

31. See Eley, "Historicizing the Global."

32. See here Hardt and Negri, *Empire*; Balakrishnan, ed., *Debating Empire*; Passavant and Dean, eds., *Empire's New Clothes*; Howe, *Empire*.

33. In general, see Stoler, *Carnal Knowledge*; Burton, ed., *After the Imperial Turn*. For Britain, see Hall, ed., *Cultures of Empire*; Burton, *Empire in Question*. For France, see Wilder, "Unthinking French History" and *French Imperial Nation-State*. For Germany, see Wildenthal, "Notes on a History"; Penny and Bunzl, eds., *Worldly Provincialism*.

34. Foundational was Kaplan and Pease, eds., *Cultures of United States Imperialism*; and for current discussion, Stoler, *Haunted by Empire*; also Kramer, "Power and Connection."

35. See Wehler, *Bismarck*, 112–193; also Bade, *Friedrich Fabri*, 67–79, 80–135; von Strandmann, "Consequences of the Foundation."

36. Wehler, *Bismarck*, 112–142, 423–453, remains the best overall guide, together with Spohn, *Weltmarktkonkurrenz und Industrialisierung Deutschlands*. Also Torp, *Herausforderung der Globalisierung*; and Conrad, *Globalisation and Nation*, 27–76.

37. See here Eley, "Social Imperialism"; Grimmer-Solem, *Rise of Historical Economics*, 89–168, 171–245; Grimmer-Solem, "Imperialist Socialism"; Sheehan, *Career of Lujo Brentano*.

38. See Wehler, *Bismarck*, 112–193; Bade, *Friedrich Fabri*; von Strandmann, "Consequences of the Foundation"; Hayes, *Bismarck and Mitteleuropa*.

39. Vagts, *Deutschland und die Vereinigten Staaten*; Böhm, *Überseehandel und Flottenbau*; Torp, *Herausforderung der Globalisierung*; Conrad, *Globalisation and Nation*.

40. Chickering, *We Men Who Feel Most German*, is silent on this front. But see Stegmann, *Die Erben Bismarcks*, 54–58, and Sweeney's essay in this volume.

41. Fischer, *War of Illusions*; Stegmann, *Erben Bismarcks*; Witt, *Die Finanzpolitik des Deutschen Reiches*; Wernecke, *Der Wille zur Weltgeltung*.

42. Rohrbach, "Das Kriegsziel im Schützengraben," quoted by Fischer, *Germany's Aims*, 160. A Baltic German who came to Germany to escape Russification and complete his PhD in Protestant theology, Paul Rohrbach (1869–1956) was an emblematic figure of the Wilhelmine nationalist intelligentsia. Protégé of Hans Delbrück and Adolf von Harnack, early associate of Friedrich Naumann, regular contributor to *Preußische Jahrbücher*, *Christliche Welt*, and *Die Hilfe*, and sometime secretary of the *Evangelisch-Sozialer Kongreß*, he resists easy categorization. Inveterate Russophobe, his travels across central Asia, Persia, and Turkey from 1897 to 1902 made him an expert advocate of the Baghdad Railway. Serving from 1903 to 1906 as Commissioner for Settlement in South-West Africa, he produced a spate of associated writings, including the two-volume *Deutsche Kolonialwirtschaft*. Teaching from 1912 in the Berlin Handelshochschule, with numerous commissions from the Colonial Office and the Foreign Office, he was linked to Bethmann Hollweg's circle through Delbrück and Ernst Jäckh. Editor of *Das größere Deutschland* (from early 1914) and *Deutsche Politik* (from 1916), he was instrumental in Germany's strategy of destabilizing the Russian Empire, helping in 1918 to form the German-Ukrainian Society. His writings on Germany's arrival as a "world nation" included *Deutschland unter den Weltvölkern*, *Die Bagdadbahn*, *Der deutsche Gedanke in der Welt*, and *Weltpolitisches Wanderbuch, 1897–1915*. See esp. Mogk, *Rohrbach und das "Größere Deutschland"*; Bieber, *Paul Rohrbach*; vom Bruch, *Weltpolitik als Kulturmission*, 73–75; Kouri, *Der deutsche Protestantismus*, 160–161; Smith, *Ideological Origins*, 159–164; Fischer, *War of Illusions*, 42–43; Borowsky, "Paul Rohrbach und die Ukraine"; Meyer, *Mitteleuropa*, 95–99; Bley, *South-West Africa*, 109–110; Wildenthal, *German Women*, 99–104; van Laak, *Imperiale Infrastruktur*, 184–194. See also Rohrbach's autobiography, *Um die Teufels Handschrift*. I am grateful to Jennifer Jenkins for rekindling my interest in Rohrbach.

43. Fischer, *Germany's Aims*, 160.

44. Fischer, *Germany's Aims*, 248. For Under-Secretary Friedrich von Falkenhausen of the Ministry of Agriculture, this was the goal: "To match the great, closed economic

bodies of the United States, the British, and the Russian Empires with an equally solid economic bloc representing all European states, or at least those of Central Europe under German leadership, with a twofold purpose: (1) of assuring the members of this whole, and particularly Germany, the mastery of the European market, and (2) of being able to lead the entire economic strength of allied Europe into the field, as a unified force, in the struggle with those world powers over the conditions of the admission of each to the markets of the others" (250).

45. Delbrück's assistant von Schoenebeck repeated the argument: "Difficulties of procedure should not make us forget the 'great final aim' of creating a great Central European economic unit to enable us to hold our place in the economic struggle for existence of the peoples and to save us from shrinking into economic impotence against the ever-increasing solidarity and power of the economic World Powers, Great Britain with her colonies, the United States, Russia, and Japan with China." Fischer, *Germany's Aims*, 251, 247–256; also von Strandmann, ed., *Walther Rathenau*, 183–191.

46. Roloff extolled the virtues of this centered cultural heterogeneity: " . . . this coalition of territory would have the enormous cultural advantage over the giant empires in that not one nation, not one language dominates, but instead that almost all nations that have created modern *Kultur* would be represented and protected from decline." See Kolonialpolitisches Aktionskomité, ed., *Kolonialpolitischer Führer*, cited by Grimmer-Solem, "The Professor's Africa," 333.

47. G. Schmoller, "Wirtschaftliche Zukunft Deutschlands," in L. Schmoller, ed., *Zwanzig Jahre*, 20, cited by Grimmer-Solem, "The Professors' Africa," 320.

48. Fischer, *War of Illusions*, 264.

49. Mommsen, *Max Weber and German Politics*, 69. See Weber's Freiburg inaugural address (May 1895), "The National State and Economic Policy," and Tribe's "Introduction to Weber."

50. Fischer, *War of Illusions*, 264.

51. Beckert in Bayley, Beckert, Connelly, Hofmeyr, Kozol, and Seed, "AHR Conversation," 1459, 1446.

52. Hofmeyr, "AHR Conversation," 1444. See Appadurai, *Modernity at Large*; also H-German Forum on "Transnationalism," January 2006, with Ronald J. Granieri, Nina Berman, Young-Sun Hong, Konrad H. Jarausch, and Jennifer Jenkins: www.h-net.org/~german/discuss/Trans/forum_trans_index.htm.

53. Naranch, *Beyond the Fatherland*.

54. See O'Donnell, Bridenthal, and Reagin, eds., *Heimat Abroad*.

55. Zimmerman, "German Alabama" and *Alabama in Africa*.

56. See here Nelson, ed., *Germans, Poland, and Colonial Expansion* and, esp., "Archive for Inner Colonization"; Zimmerman, "Booker T. Washington," 12–15; Beckert, "From Tuskegee to Togo"; more broadly, Conrad, *Globalisation and Nation*, 77–143.

57. See Mommsen, *Max Weber*, 68–90; Grant, *Migration and Inequality*, 181–252; Tribe, "Prussian Agriculture—German Politics"; Perkins, "Agricultural Revolution in Germany."

58. Zimmerman, "German Alabama," 1377–1378.

59. This was further linked to a Christian ideal of household structure and family

life and to an economic postulate of the free peasant farmer. On the ground, as Zimmerman compellingly shows, these ideas could only be practiced via the most brutal forms of coercion. His account acutely captures this basis of German colonial practice in ideals of family relations and household production linked to a cotton-based economy and *Volkskultur* rooted in "a patriarchal, monogamous domesticity." Such a model presumed violently reordering Togolese social relations. The Germans "imagined that this [reordering] would result in cultural transformations that would bring the normal bourgeois Christian family to Togo. Indeed, their actions may have revealed an uncomfortable truth about the normal bourgeois Christian family. Germans could call this attempt to radically restructure the Togolese economy *Volkskultur* only because they identified Africans with the imaginary 'Negroes' concocted by New South ideologues—inherently pathological agents requiring outside force to become what they purportedly had always, essentially, been." See Zimmerman, "German Alabama," 1388.

60. Zimmerman, "German Alabama," 1378.

61. Zimmerman, "German Alabama," 1362–1363.

62. See Reismann-Grone and von Liebert, *Überseepolitik oder Festlandspolitik?* A charter signatory of the Pan-Germans' founding manifesto in 1891, Reismann-Grone (1863–1949) eventually broke with the leadership around Heinrich Claß during World War I. After serving several years as general secretary of the Ruhr Mine Owners' Association, he devoted himself full-time to his newspaper, making it a leading organ of pro-industrial and overtly radical nationalist opinion. Backing Hitler from the 1920s, he ended his career after 1933 as the first Nazi mayor of Essen. A career officer of bourgeois provenance, von Liebert (1850–1934) served in the Russian section of the general staff, became interested in colonies, and was appointed in 1897 governor of German East Africa before being ennobled and retired in 1900/1. In 1904 he headed the Imperial League in the aftermath of the SPD's success in the 1903 elections and in 1907 entered the Reichstag as a Free Conservative. An early Pan-German, he joined its national leadership toward 1914. He entered the Reichstag as a Nazi in 1928. See Eley, *Reshaping*, 54–57, 108–11, 229–35; Frech, *Wegbereiter Hitlers?*; von Liebert, *Aus einem bewegten Leben*.

63. Stoler, "On Degrees of Imperial Sovereignty," 125–146.

64. Hasse, *Großdeutschland und Mitteleuropa*, 47, cited by Sweeney, "Pan-German Conceptions," chapter 13 in this volume.

65. See Sweeney, "Pan-German Conceptions."

66. Berghahn sees this as a "Retreat to the European Continent." See *Germany and the Approach of War*, 136–155, plus the preceding discussion, 97–135; also Fischer, *War of Illusions*, 71–159, 291–329, 355–369, 439–458.

67. See Eddie, "The Prussian Settlement Commission"; Hagen, *Germans, Poles, and Jews*, 159–287; Blanke, *Prussian Poland*.

68. A point made by Conrad, *Deutsche Kolonialgeschichte*, 98.

69. Conrad, *Deutsche Kolonialgeschichte*, 100. In the radicalizing of German nationalism against the Poles from the early 1900s, we can see a cumulative realization in Steinmetz's definition, where colonialism required ruthless abrogating of Polish rights: "The core of colonial policy is an image of the native's essential distance from, or

proximity to, the culture of the colonizer. Colonial policy organizes its stabilizing projects around this image of the sociocultural essence of the colonized. Native policy can thus be defined as an attempt to lock the colonized into a single, stable position somewhere along a spectrum ranging from absolute difference to absolute identity, but not encompassing either of those extremes. Complete identity, or genuine assimilation, was incompatible with the rule of colonial difference." By 1914, as far as the Polish East was concerned, Pan-Germans had crossed the Rubicon of the colonial wish. By 1915, as the annexationist logic of the war aims unfolded, government had joined them. See Steinmetz, "'The Devil's Handwriting,'" 47.

70. Weindling, *Epidemics and Genocide*; Grosse, *Kolonialismus*. See also Urena, "The Stakes of Empire"; Nelson, ed., *German, Poland, and Colonial Expansion*; Kopp, "Constructing Racial Difference."

71. See esp. Naranch, "'Colonized Body,' 'Oriental Machine'"; Koponen, *Development for Exploitation*; Sunseri, *Vilimani*; van Laak, *Imperiale Infrastruktur*; Zimmerman, "Counterinsurgency and the Science Effect" and "A German Alabama."

72. See Wehler, "Bismarck's Imperialism"; Wehler, "Industrial Growth"; Eley, "Defining Social Imperialism" and "Social Imperialism."

73. See essays in this volume by David Ciarlo, Jeff Bowersox, and Brett van Hoesen; also Ciarlo, *Advertising Empire*; Short, *Magic Lantern Empire*; Langbehn, ed., *German Colonialism*.

74. See Wildenthal, "'She Is the Victor,'" and her important book, *German Women*; also Stoler, "Sexual Affronts and Racial Frontiers" and *Carnal Knowledge and Imperial Power*.

75. As a concept "social imperialism" appears nowhere in the new works on German imperialism.

76. See also Eley, "Imperial Imaginary, Colonial Effect."

77. See Zimmerer, "The Birth of the *Ostland*" and "Colonialism and the Holocaust"; Lower, *Nazi Empire-Building*; also Furber, "Near as Far in the Colonies"; Grosse, "What Does German Colonialism Have to Do with National Socialism?"

78. Kundrus, "Kontinuitäten, Parallelen, Rezeptionen." In *Deutsche Kolonialgeschichte*, 96–106, Conrad makes a similar argument.

79. Klotz, "Global Visions" and "The Weimar Republic."

TWO

Scientific Autonomy and Empire, 1880–1945
Four German Sociologists
GEORGE STEINMETZ

Studies of the relations between science and colonialism have looked mainly at anthropology, geography, and the natural sciences. But sociologists have also been preoccupied with questions of empire since the beginnings of the sociological field and continuing into the recent past. Although this chapter focuses on German and German-language sociologists, it is important to keep in mind that sociologists in most other national contexts also wrote about overseas colonies and empires, modern and ancient.[1]

This chapter explores the ways in which sociologists have related to the interests and demands of the empires they study, paying special attention to questions of academic autonomy and heteronomy.[2] German sociology was concerned from the start with questions of the independence of social science from values or politics, just as the leading theorists of the role of the German university insisted that *Wissenschaft* should provide its own ends rather than be a means to external ends.[3] Due to the powerful influence of Max Weber, questions of scientific objectivity and *Wertfreiheit* dominated the first meeting of the *Deutsche Gesellschaft für Soziologie* in 1910 and roiled the meeting of the *Verein für Sozialpolitik* in 1913.[4] The question of autonomy gains a special urgency in the German context due to the severe assault on academic freedom by the Nazi state and because of German academics' widely varying approaches to questions of collaboration and self-*Gleichschaltung*. But even in more democratic regimes such as the *Kaiserreich* and the Weimar Republic or in our own contemporary contexts, questions of scientific autonomy arise repeatedly and force intellectuals to make difficult choices.

FOUR IMPERIAL SOCIOLOGISTS

Richard Thurnwald (1869–1954) was one of the most prominent German colonial ethnographers during the first half of the twentieth century. He was seen as a founder of economic anthropology and research on gift exchange. His work was praised by Marcel Mauss and Karl Polanyi. Thurnwald carried out extensive ethnographic research in German New Guinea before World War I and British East Africa during the first half of the 1930s. During World War I, Thurnwald argued that "the war must bring us an expansion of our *Lebensraum*, it has to bring us an adequate holding of colonies" and that retaining the colonies would be the best guarantee of long-term peace.[5] After 1936 Thurnwald began drawing up guidelines for the administration of the planned German colonial empire in Africa along specifically National Socialist lines.[6] In 1938 he presented a paper on colonial policy to the *Akademie für Deutsches Recht*, whose president was Hans Frank, the *Reichsjustizkommissar* since 1933 and the future *Generalgouverneur* of the occupied Polish territories.[7] In 1939 Thurnwald associated himself with the Nazi *Kolonialpolitisches Amt* and in 1940 joined the NSDAP. He published in propagandistic journals, including *Koloniale Rundschau, Der Kolonialfreund*, and the Nazi weekly *Das Reich*. After Hitler dissolved the *Kolonialpolitisches Amt* in early 1943, Thurnwald turned his attention to questions of land empire, although he was less involved in this "continental turn" than his student Wilhelm Mühlmann. After World War II he was one of the founders of the Free University of Berlin.

It is revealing to compare Thurnwald's imperial analyses and his strategic stance toward questions of scientific autonomy with those of three other German sociologists who studied empires: Max and Alfred Weber and Wilhelm Mühlmann. Max Weber (1864–1920) returned to the topic of traditional and contemporary land empires throughout his lifetime. Weber's *Habilitation* thesis dealt with the reasons for the Roman empire's decline.[8] He completed a book-length comparative study of ancient empires in 1909[9] and devoted part of his three-volume sociology of religion to analyzing the Chinese empire.[10] In *Economy and Society*, Weber brought traditional land-based empires and modern imperialism into the same analytic framework, claiming to detect "features that have since recurred in basic outline again and again and which still recur today," such as the reciprocal impact of economic and political impulses and the centrality of "honor" or "the prestige of power."[11]

With respect to scientific autonomy, Weber's position is more ambiguous than his defense of value freedom might initially suggest. Weber was obsessed with increasing Germany's geopolitical power. He focused at several points in his life on intensifying German hegemony over eastern Europe and fortifying its eastern border against Polish immigration and cultural influence.[12] His inaugural address at Freiburg University in 1895 defended a muscular German *Weltpolitik*.[13] In the decade before World War I, however, Weber began to denounce any mixing of politics and scholarship. He managed to keep his academic studies of empires largely free of explicit political polemics, even in his public lecture in 1896 on the reasons for Rome's decline.[14] Max Weber departed in other ways from the model of the typical nineteenth-century conservative German mandarin professor. He supported the modernization of higher education, defended socialist scholars, like Robert Michels, and Jewish scholars, like Georg Simmel and Arthur Salz, and contributed to the Weimar constitution.[15] Nonetheless, Weber's analysis of China, like his view of the Poles, seems to echo the worst racial and cultural stereotypes of his era.[16] We return to these contradictions below.

Alfred Weber (1868–1958) was a central figure in Weimar sociology, presiding over the most important center of social science research during the 1920s, the *Institut für Sozial- und Staatswissenschaften* at Heidelberg University, where he supervised many of the rising stars of Weimar sociology, including Erich Fromm, Karl Mannheim, and Norbert Elias.[17] Like his older brother, Alfred Weber was interested in empires and colonialism throughout his career. In an article published before World War I, he argued that German capitalists could profit handily by doing business in other countries' empires and did not even need their own German colonies.[18] During the latter years of World War I, both Max and Alfred Weber became involved in projects aimed at strengthening German hegemony over *Mitteleuropa*. Alfred hoped at that time that the smaller nations to Germany's east would become dependent on the larger "leading nation"; Poland, he hoped, would become a "kingdom with military and economic dependence on Germany."[19] After 1918, however, Alfred became extremely critical of European imperialism and began defending the self-determination of the colonized peoples.[20] His treatise on world history, published in the Netherlands during his period of "inner exile," summarized modernity under the conceptual heading of Western expansion (*"das expansive Abendland seit 1500"*) and a "global Occident" (*Welt-Abendland*) with its colonial empires. Already in 1935 Alfred Weber was forecasting an "uprising of the masses" in the colonies.[21]

Alfred Weber also promoted his own distinctive version of the value-free science doctrine before 1933. Weber's concept of a "socially unattached intelligentsia" (*sozial freischwebende Intelligenz*) was popularized by his student Karl Mannheim.[22] After 1945, however, Alfred began to distance himself sharply from the idea of value-free science, seeing it as partially responsible for Nazism.[23]

Wilhelm Mühlmann (1904–1988) was considerably younger than the other three sociologists considered here, all of whom were born in the 1860s. Mühlmann completed his doctoral dissertation, which dealt with the secret Arioi society in precolonial Tahiti, in 1932, and most of his publications appeared after 1933.[24] Mühlmann worked as an editorial assistant for his mentor Richard Thurnwald, taking responsibility for much of the editorial correspondence for Thurnwald's journal *Sociologus* while Thurnwald was in the United States.[25] Mühlmann's writing clarified Thurnwald's vaguely formulated "functionalism," his epistemological realism, and his thesis of social "sifting" (*Siebung*). Mühlmann also followed Thurnwald in describing his own work as a mix of ethnology and sociology, a combination that was much more common in British and French social science at the time than in Germany.[26] Mühlmann's earliest publications seemed distant from any political concerns.[27] As the Nazis ascended to power, however, Mühlmann aligned his thinking even more assiduously with the new order than Thurnwald did.[28] The culmination of Mühlmann's transformation into a Nazi social scientist involved a change in his main object of research from Polynesians to eastern Europeans. Already in 1932 Mühlmann had published an article comparing "cornerstones and horns" in Tahitian and Jewish culture.[29] Having previously adopted Thurnwald's nonracialist theory of social selection or "sifting," he moved now in a more explicitly racial and biological direction, discussing for example the "hypothesis of the Aryan origins of the Polynesians."[30] By 1935 Mühlmann began turning his ethnic expertise to the study of ethnic assimilation or, in the phrase used during the Nazi era, trans-folking (*Umvolkung*)—a neologism for the Germanization of certain ethnic groups in the occupied zones or the absorption of smaller ethnic groups into larger, more powerful ones. He focused increasingly on the occupied regions that were subject to "historical German eastern colonization," which was "the greatest process in German history," since the "German first reaches true self-consciousness in contrast to the inferior" populations of the East. For Mühlmann, "German history" was "in a very important sense colonial history."[31] The corollary of trans-folking in actual policy was, of course, the extermination of the Jews and other inhabitants of the occupied zones who were seen as enemies or as noncandidates for assimilation. Mühlmann explained this process in one of his "scientific" essays:

> trans-folking as a process obeys geopolitical-strategic laws. Just as the aim of war is the annihilation of the enemy, so the goal of trans-folking is ethnic extermination. Subjective ethnic conversion under the superior weight of the foreign ethnic gradient corresponds to surrendering to the enemy in war. . . . The suffering ethnos constitutes small and tiny ethnic

islands that become ever more tightly surrounded and finally give way before the flood of the stronger ethnic group.[32]

Mühlmann described these noncandidates as a "rootless or uprooted" *Scheinvolk* ("sham people"), "sifting itself again and again out of all ethnic communities of vagabonds, vagrants, bums, and so on, whose sociological connections with Jews and Gypsies have been amply demonstrated."[33] He published a book-length study of trans-folking and also wrote on the ethnic composition of eastern and southeast Europe.[34] He defended the Nazi ban on marriage between Christians and Jews.[35] He wrote a memo arguing that ethnologists who did not adhere to modern (Nazi) sociobiological views should be fired from positions at ethnographic museums—at a time when he was trying to obtain just such a position.[36] He attacked the rival *Kulturkreis* ethnological school as a "degeneration of science" pursued by "Catholic Jews" like Wilhelm Schmidt, the founder of the Vienna school that denied the importance of race in explaining culture.[37]

Mühlmann's intellectual autonomy from the Nazi regime was thus almost nonexistent. He appeared frequently as a speaker at the Berlin Institute for Border and Foreign Studies, which conducted applied research on ethnic issues in the occupied zones. Mühlmann was closely connected to the Berlin *Auslandswissenschaftliche Fakultät*, which was directed by the sociologist and SS-Gruppenführer Prof. Dr. Franz Six and, after 1942, by Karl-Heinz Pfeffer, a sociologist specializing in British imperialism and settler colonies who led a "European Studies Seminar" with the goal of elaborating "suggestions to secure the . . . subjugation of the occupied states and regions" and "the unity of Europe under German leadership."[38] Mühlmann's career benefited from close connections to key figures inside the notorious Rosenberg Office. Alfred Rosenberg directly funded Mühlmann's research, and Mühlmann wrote reports for Rosenberg's office on the "sociological views of Durkheim and the Lévy-Bruhl school."[39]

Taken together, these four sociologists present a spectrum of possible approaches to scientific autonomy. The two Webers represent different versions of extreme autonomy, while Thurnwald and Mühlmann describe two forms of heteronomization. Seen historically, the overall trajectory from Max Weber to Wilhelm Mühlmann illustrates the growing dependence of German social scientists on the field of the state.[40]

MAX WEBER: SCIENTIFIC AUTONOMY AND IMPERIAL HISTORY

How can we understand the seeming contradiction between Max Weber's openly expressed support for German imperialism and his adamant defense of scientific value neutrality? I leave aside his articles in obviously political venues like *Die Hilfe*, since these would have been characterized by Weber himself as nonscientific. I also ignore his writings on Poland, which mainly appeared before Weber developed his doctrine of value neutrality.[41] I will also overlook Weber's 1909 comparative study of ancient empires, which had only the most oblique connections to contemporary politics. Instead I focus on the *Religion of China*. Of all Weber's late scientific writings this is the one that touches most directly on current imperial politics. Several of the other cultures Weber discussed in his three-volume *Sociology of Religion*, especially India, had also been subjected to European imperialist attacks and colonial conquests during his lifetime. But China was closest to Weber's interests in German *Weltpolitik*. Prussia had concluded a separate treaty with China after the Second Opium War, opening China to Prussian traders and missionaries and allowing Prussia to open a legation in Beijing. In 1897 Germany seized Qingdao, triggering a chain reaction of European annexations of Chinese coastal colonies. Qingdao was the only German colony run by the Navy rather than the Colonial Department, and the Navy was at the heart of German *Weltpolitik*. In 1901 Germany was at the head of the international imperialist campaign against the Boxer Rebellion. In the decade before World War I forces inside the German government started backing away from the policy of continuing to occupy a formal colony inside China, advocating instead peaceful cultural penetration of the country and cultivation of China as a potential military ally. Weber supported this prioritization of *Weltpolitik* over *Kolonialpolitik*, imperialism over colonialism.[42]

The *Religion of China* is therefore the text in which Weber's scientific neutrality seems most at risk of breaking down. Weber completed his analysis of China while Germany still possessed its colony in Qingdao. His central question was why China had failed to develop a modern form of rational capitalism, and his answer was that the economic ethics of Confucianism had hindered capitalism's development. Confucianism was oriented toward "adjustment to the world" rather than the "rational transformation of the world."[43] Confucianism also prevented the rationalization of the state, law, education, poetry, and even the basic Chinese personality structure.[44] Weber avoided discussing the possible effects of imperialism on China's development.

Although Weber's arguments about China were wrong, it is more interesting to focus on the process by which he assembled the analytic models and raw materials for his text. Weber made systematic and patterned selections from the literature available to him in the Berlin libraries where he was working at the time. Some of the authorities cited by Weber had spent time in Qingdao; others were in the employ of British or Dutch colonizers.

Weber's decision to begin his three-volume sociology of religion with China—after first presenting the case for Protestantism—was not at all arbitrary. This framework emphasized Weber's debt to Hegel, who had also started his philosophy of history in China. Weber echoed Hegel's uncompromising Sinophobia, which had itself been a philosophical translation of the discourse of the European merchants in East Asia in Hegel's own era.[45] The overall design of Weber's comparative religion project, organized around a discourse of lack, echoed the well-established thesis of Chinese stasis and lack, which in Hegel took the form of the arrested development of Oriental freedom ("The Oriental World knows only that One is Free").

An opposing view that painted a more nuanced picture of Confucianism and Chinese history was present, however, among well-known German sinologists and in German universities. Weber dismissed these alternative, more "Sinophilic" approaches. He ignored scholarship from the Berlin Seminar for Oriental Languages, for example, as well as the more political texts by Ku Hung-Ming, a neo-Confucian intellectual and anti-imperialist who had studied and published in Germany. Weber downplayed the work of Richard Wilhelm, the founder of the Confucius Society in colonial Qingdao which tried to strengthen the Confucian tradition. Contrary to Weber, Wilhelm traced China's problems to "alienation and despiritualization" resulting from Western interventions and called for strengthening Confucianism. Weber relied instead on the literature of the European merchants in China and their organic intellectuals, first and foremost the Berlin University professors Ferdinand von Richthofen and J. J. De Groot. Richthofen, a geographer, and de Groot, a sinologist, had forged their Sinophobic views while working and travelling in China and East Asia.

One possible explanation for Weber's choice of authorities and selection of evidence is simple "cherry picking": he wanted to prove at all costs that ascetic Protestantism alone was capable of generating capitalism. Although this seems entirely plausible, it is difficult to reconcile with Weber's "ascetic" scientific program and the care he took with evidence in other writings. Another possibility would be that Weber was, as he himself said, a "class conscious bourgeois." His work could then be read as a more or less direct transcription of merchant capitalist consciousness.[46] But there are also problems with this account. First, the typical merchant class discourse on China was drenched in straightforward biological racism. Weber's texts, while exemplifying a form of cultural racism, never strayed into sociobiological explanations of Chinese backwardness. Even more importantly, Weber is best characterized neither as bourgeois nor as a *Bildungsbürger* but rather as located simultaneously in both classes and as having a divided or cleft scientific habitus.[47] Weber's social background and class properties were not expressed directly in the academic field but were translated into positions and practices appropriate to that field.[48] The overarching field of the social and human sciences in Germany was divided at the time between two poles: on the one hand, the various historicisms codified as *Geisteswissenschaften*; on the other hand, the array of positivisms and naturalisms that denied any difference between the natural and human sciences. The first grouping was associated with Ringer's German "mandarins."[49] Weber himself compared the old-style German professoriat, with their "humanist, exclusive and bookish literary education" that stamped them as "belonging socially to the cultured status group," to the Chinese mandarins.[50]

The second group consisted of "modernists," in Ringer's terms, who challenged the long-lasting hegemony of the mandarins and their classical, philological humanism. Despite Weber's frequent jibes, he was not as unambiguously allied with the academic modernists as Ringer suggests.[51] There is a rather consistent pattern in Weber's work of seeking a *middle ground* position between the two poles. He wrote his *Habilitation* thesis in a classic German mandarin field, Roman history, and he addressed a classic problem: Rome's decline. But he constantly compared Roman land policy to contemporary Prussian policy, a nonhistoricist move. His *Habilitation* thesis on ancient Rome was seen by the *Verein für Sozialpolitik* as qualifying Weber for the study of Polish laborers in the present. In his epistemological writings Weber sought to overcome the split between historicism and positivism, interpretive description and causal explanation. His argument in favor of *specialized* sciences, as against the traditional *generalism* of the German mandarins, was coupled with a vehement campaign to exclude specialized practical policy research from sociology. Weber's pursuit of this median strategy inside the academic field did not directly reflect his social class background but was an attempt to occupy a position that was homologous to or isomorphic with his position in the wider field of power. The midpoint between bourgeois and *Bildungsbürger* in the field of power was homologous to the midpoint between mandarin and modernist in the social scientific field.

Weber's sociology of religion project has this same intermediary quality. He concerned himself in the midst of the Great War with the seemingly esoteric topics of Confucianism, Daoism, Buddhism, and Hinduism. He studied British censuses of India in the Prussian State Library rather than fight on the battlefield. However, he also refused to accept the traditional mandarin sinologists as his guides to Chinese history. Weber's central question was also "modernist": rather than ask why China had declined—a question linked to ancient visions of history as a cycle of empires—Weber asked why China had supposedly *always* been stagnant. In making these arguments Weber aligned himself with more modern economic and social theories of modernization. Above all, Weber adopted the views of De Groot and von Richthofen. Both of these China specialists occupied the most prestigious category of academic position in Germany: *Professor Ordinarius* at Berlin University.[52] This points to the other key principle of Weber's scientific strategy. In addition to seeking a middle ground between German mandarin and modernist positions within a given scientific field, his strategy when dealing with new fields of inquiry was to identify and ally himself with members of that field who occupied positions structurally analogous to his own.

Von Richthofen and de Groot seemed to fit this bill. Both were academic modernists. Richthofen was located in a modern discipline, geography, and had a highly practical background, having traveled in China in the pay of a European chamber of commerce and having worked as geographer in the California gold mines. De Groot's social trajectory also differed from the German mandarin sinologists'. His background was in the Dutch East Indies, where he had worked for years as a missionary and colonizer. Both men held views of China that were closer to those of typical colonial merchants than of classic German sinologists. On the other hand, being a modernist expert was not enough for Weber; he sought out experts who occupied dominant positions in their respective fields. Weber thus paid less attention to the interpretations of the sinologists Richard Wilhelm and Otto Franke, Sinophiles with practical backgrounds (as a missionary and a diplomatic interpreter, respectively). When Weber was working on his study of China, both of these men were associated with less prestigious institutions—the Hamburg Colonial Institute in Franke's case, the Protestant Weimar mission society in Wilhelm's.[53] They were also associated with a growing, cosmopolitan, and anti-imperialist group of intellectuals that started to emerge in Europe and the colonies before 1914, gaining strength during the interwar period. Sinologists who took a position favorable to China and opposed to Western imperialism were even more untouchable for Weber than traditional German mandarins. The anti-imperialist position might have appeared to Weber as a threat to academic freedom. Faculty at the SOL were divided from the regular faculty at Berlin University by a powerful social barrier rooted in the more practical orientation of the former group and in the fact that the SOL had "native" language teachers. Some of the latter published in the seminar's journal. One of the seminar's Chinese language instructors, Wang Ching Dao, published what amounted to a refutation of Weber's thesis in the journal at the moment when Weber was beginning work on the China text.⁵⁴ An example of a leftist who adopted the "native" voice with regard to China was Alfons Paquet, whose essays praising Ku Hung-Ming and Chinese resistance to the West were completely ignored by Weber.⁵⁵

A similar pattern of alignment with the most prestigious scholars in the relevant field characterizes Weber's analysis of India. Here Weber relied heavily on the work of "outstanding German Indologists" (*"hervorragenden deutschen Indologen"*) like Albrecht Weber (Berlin University *Ordinarius*, 1867–1901) and Richard Pischel (also a Berlin *Ordinarius*, 1902–1908).⁵⁶ Pischel criticized earlier Indologists for the "vehemence" with which they "insisted on the superiority of European science" over "indigenous Vedic criticism."⁵⁷ If Weber's analysis of India was less permeated by imperialist racism than his discussion of China, this was partly because Pischel and other scholars who dominated the German Indological field after 1900 did not typically depict India as stagnant, despotic, or racially inferior.

In sum, Weber sought out authorities in the sinology field whose positions were structurally similar to his own—those of a modernist university mandarin. Weber's strategizing led him to select the very Sinophobic tropes that his thesis on the uniqueness of the Protestant ethic required and for which he should have had a natural predilection according to reductionist sociologies of knowledge. My hypothesis, however, is that Weber would have been more favorable to less Sinophobic experts like Wilhelm and Franke if the latter had already occupied the high-profile university posts that they would later attain.⁵⁸

THURNWALD'S MOBILE HETERONOMY

The contrast between the Webers, on the one hand, and Thurnwald and Mühlmann, on the other, with respect to the question of scientific autonomy seems dramatic at first glance. Thurnwald, the son of an Austrian *Fabrikleiter*, had studied law, sociology, *Staatswissenschaften*, and Orientalism.⁵⁹ He published two of his earliest articles on the typically *bildungsbürgerliche* topics of ancient Egypt and Babylonia. At the outset, then, Thurnwald seemed to combine *Besitz* and *Bildung*, as did the Webers and many other nineteenth-century German professors. Thurnwald's shift from ancient history to the ethnology of Melanesians and Africans corresponded to his increasing personal economic difficulties. Born in the 1860s like Max and Alfred Weber, Thurnwald was *sociologically* younger than them, an eternal "newcomer" in the German social scientific field, closer in this sense to the academics who came of age during the Weimar Republic. He spent fourteen years outside Germany, beginning with research trips to New Guinea (1906–1909 and 1912–1914), began his academic career as a private docent at Halle (1919–1923), and became an "extraordinary" professor (i.e., without full health and pension benefits) at Berlin University in 1923 at the age of 56. According to his biographer, Thurnwald lost money in the post–World War I inflation and struggled financially due to a messy divorce. He eagerly accepted offers as visiting professor at Yale and broadcast his willingness to take almost any permanent job at an American college or university, but he was unsuccessful and had to return to Germany in 1936.[60] He was now promoted to the rank of honorary professor.[61] Only at the age of 77 did he finally obtain a position as professor at Berlin University (now Humboldt University). Thurnwald gave up that position in 1949 and moved to the newly founded Free University in Berlin, with the reduced rank of honorary professor.[62]

Thurnwald frequently received outside funding and other forms of support for his research. Before his first trip to New Guinea, he was employed by the Berlin Ethnological Museum as a scientific assistant under the ethnologist Felix von Luschan. Thurnwald's first three-year trip to German New Guinea was financed by the Berlin Ethnological Museum and the private Baessler Foundation. While in New Guinea, he received extensive assistance from the colony's governor, Albert Hahl, who took the ethnographer on trips around the islands on a government steamer and contributed to one of Thurnwald's early articles on the use of native labor.[63] Thurnwald's second trip to New Guinea (1912) was financed by the German Colonial Office and the German Colonial Society. During these early research trips, Thurnwald became known to his sponsors as being particularly *"bedürfnislos"* (frugal).[64] In letters from that period he described his situation as arduous but liberating, and he seemed to relish his independence and isolation. The first European to make contact with certain populations in New Guinea, he was often the only "white man" around, given the thinness of the German colonial administration.

Thurnwald's career and research program seemed to be on an uphill trajectory during the Weimar Republic. His new work on Africa was sponsored by the London-based International Institute of African Languages and Cultures, and he also received funding from the Australian National Research Council.[65] The scholarly journal he founded (see below) was subsidized by the *Notgemeinschaft der deutschen Wissenschaft* (Emergency Association of German Science), a government-financed organization created in 1920.[66] Thurnwald does not seem to have received any additional grants from the *Notgemeinschaft* after his return to Germany in 1936. He later claimed to have created an "institute for sociological research" at Berlin University during the Nazi era using private funds.[67]

Thurnwald's economic situation was often precarious. His letters to the Berlin University administration in the late 1930s and early 1940s contain constant complaints of poverty and frequent requests for emergency funds. In the report on his personal and racial background from 1935, Thurnwald explained that his poverty had made it impossible for him and his second wife to have children. He defended his acceptance of invitations to work in the United States "because this seemed advisable given my low salary and the beginners' status that I was granted as long as I was in Berlin."[68]

In light of his employment before 1914 at the Berlin Ethnological Museum, the history of his research funding, and the nature of his early publications, it is clear that Thurnwald saw himself as located primarily in the academic field of ethnology before World War I. His evolving efforts to enter the academic field of sociology after 1918 present a more complicated picture, however, and one that is relevant for assessing the question of Thurnwald's scientific autonomy. When Thurnwald was recruited in 1919 to Halle University, he asked that his professorship title include three disciplines: ethnology, sociology, and social psychology (*Völkerpsychologie*).[69] This request was supported by the Science Minister of the state of Saxony, but the university's *Dekan* refused to include sociology in Thurnwald's title, arguing that he had made his reputation as "a serious and very experienced researcher" only in the other two fields.[70] Starting in 1923, Thurnwald began systematically publishing in core sociological venues, including the *Kölner Vierteljahrshefte für Soziologie* and the famous 1923 Festschrift (*Erinnerungsgabe*) for Max Weber.[71] In 1924 he published an article in *Archiv für Sozialwissenschaft und Sozialpolitik*, the celebrated journal that had been cofounded by Max Weber. It was in this article that Thurnwald distanced himself from the sociobiological framework with which he had been closely associated in the preceding years. By doing that, Thurnwald simultaneously aligned himself with the legacy of Max Weber, still the central figure in German sociology after his death in 1920. When Thurnwald then received a "call" to join Berlin University in 1923 he once again requested that his professorship include the word sociology. His title at Berlin was "Extraordinary Professor of Ethnology, Social Psychology, and Sociology."

There were greater divisions between the academic fields of sociology and ethnology in Germany than in France or Britain between the wars, and this made Thurnwald's efforts more difficult. Thurnwald's "functionalism" remained an isolated theoretical position in German sociology. His insistence on a "realistic," presentist, empirically oriented sociology was orthogonal to the two dominant approaches in Weimar sociology, formalism and historicism.[72] Thurnwald was not invited to participate in the meetings of the German Sociological Society until 1928, and he was not invited back to the sociologists' meetings in 1930 or 1934.[73]

Thurnwald's rather marginal status in the German sociological field is also suggested by the journal he created in 1925, the *Zeitschrift für Völkerpsychologie und Soziologie* (*Journal for Ethnic Psychology and Sociology*). Although his collaborating editors included two of the leading American sociologists, W. F. Ogburn and P. A. Sorokin, none of his German collaborators were central members of their own sociology field.[74] Nonetheless, most of the American authors Thurnwald recruited to publish in his journal were sociologists, not anthropologists. This underscores the seriousness of his effort to move into sociology and his sense that he might have greater luck via a lateral move into the American rather than the German field.[75]

Indeed, when Thurnwald moved to the United States in 1931, he changed the journal's title to *Sociologus*, signaling its disciplinary priorities even more clearly. He began publishing in English. Although Thurnwald was active in both the American sociology and anthropology fields during his time at Yale, most of his efforts to find employment in the United States were directed toward sociology. In 1932 he was invited to become an affiliate of the American Sociological Society and to speak at a dinner event at its annual meetings. Harvard and the University of Buffalo asked him to teach summer courses in sociology.[76] He published in the leading US sociology journals, including *American Journal of Sociology* and *Social Forces*. He was invited to join a group of sociologists who met regularly in the New York City area.[77] That said, Thurnwald remained active in anthropology and actively disputed the need for disciplinary divisions between "sociology, anthropology and ethnology."[78]

The conditions seemed propitious for Thurnwald's entry into the sociology field once he returned to Germany. Sociology had by no means disappeared in 1933 but was transformed into an applied discipline with a heavy emphasis on ethnic and foreign studies, Thurnwald's specialties. Most of the field's older leaders, who do not seem to have thought too highly of Thurnwald, had emigrated or withdrawn into private life. Thurnwald's extensive research in colonial settings and his orientation toward applied native policies pointed to a closer fit with the priorities of the Nazi regime. His arguments against sharp disciplinary boundaries, especially between sociology and ethnology, corresponded with the Nazis' own "interdisciplinarity," their emphasis on transcending narrow scientific specializations. Thurnwald seemed poised to join the ranks of those academics whose careers took off after Hitler's rise to power.

Thurnwald's writing on colonialism and native policy falls into four main periods, and each of these corresponds to a specific structure of relations between his resources, his position in academic fields, and the changing constraints, pressures, and opportunities emanating from outside the university field, especially from colonial and other government offices. Before 1914 Thurnwald's views on colonialism are often framed as if he were participating in the colonial state field rather than the metropolitian academic field. In his first article on colonialism (1905), he argued that the control of native labor was the "actual problem of native policy" in colonies, since Europeans and North Americans were unsuited for physical labor in the tropics and since the raison d'être of colonialism was economic exploitation.[79] The African's passivity, Thurnwald reasoned, "predestines him to be a *Knecht* of the *Herrenvölker*, the prototype of the slave." According to Thurnwald the key question for the colonizers was "which qualities he finds already present in the Negro, qualities that can be used to contribute to the cultural development that is being directed by the whites." Thurnwald was thus occupying an ideological posture more closely associated with owners of colonial mines, plantations, and other businesses than with *Bildungsbürger* like himself. This is surprising because, as I have shown elsewhere, university-educated German officials active in colonial state fields tended to base their claims to field-specific authority on displays of hermeneutic insight, linguistic ability, and ethnographic finesse, rather than crude assessments of natives' racially-grounded readiness to work. Although Thurnwald never showed any interest in becoming a colonial official, his publications between 1905 and 1923 were actively oriented toward colonial practitioners and the colonial state field even when they were published in metropolitan social science journals.

Thurnwald's seeming inability to recognize the identity of the field in which he was actually participating is also revealed in his views of the scientific status of "race." Starting in 1904 Thurnwald aligned himself with race theory and began contributing to the *Archiv für Rassen- und Gesellschafts-Biologie* (Journal of Racial and Social Biology). At the beginning of the 1920s he was still viewed as the ideal candidate for writing the entries on "race," "racial hygiene," and "racial struggle" for a *Dictionary of Politics*.[80] Although Thurnwald's "racialist" position had not been unusual among nineteenth-century German proto-sociologists and ethnologists, many of the leading figures in both disciplines had moved away from race science around the turn of the century. Felix von Luschan (1854–1924), Thurnwald's supervisor at the Berlin Ethnological Museum, had initially been a proponent of biological theories of race and anthropometric measurements of skulls, skin color, and the like. But in the decade before World War I von Luschan began arguing that "the concept of 'race' as a whole [was] imprecise," that all races were equal, and that "the only savages in

Africa are whites."[81] Max Weber expressed deep skepticism about race theories at the first meeting of the German Sociological Society in 1910. Thurnwald's views of race before 1914 thus seemed to "lag behind" the leading figures in the academic disciplines who were most relevant for him. His views were closer to those of the more conservative colonial officials. There was a persistent gap between Thurnwald's (scientific) habitus and the scientific field in which he was active, reminiscent of the mismatch between habitus of Algerian workers and their modernizing colonial *Umwelt* identified by Bourdieu in his research at the turn of the 1950s.[82]

After returning to Germany from his first expedition to New Guinea Thurnwald finally began to make arguments that seemed more appropriate to the position he would have occupied had he actually been a participant in the colonial state field. The ethnographer was now said to have talents that distinguished him from the average colonizer. "If the white man wants to use his superior intellect to influence and guide the laborer," he wrote, "he needs to know how the native feels and thinks, what he views as right and wrong."[83] Having lived for three years in an overseas colony, Thurnwald seemed to have internalized the rules of the colonial state field. As an intellectual schooled in foreign languages and several disciplines, he had gravitated toward the pole of the colonial state field that made his own social properties appear to be essential to the colony's success. In an essay called "Applied Ethnology in Colonial Policy" (1912), he argued that "native policy . . . circles around [the] problem" of controlling native workers "through our cultural power resources" ("*durch geistige Machtmittel*").[84] Thurnwald also now embraced a mild relativism, also typical of colonial *Bildungsbürger* at the time, arguing that "there is no absolute measure of the worth of a given culture." He endorsed a policy of regulated preservation of indigenous culture—the approach associated with Wilhelm Solf and other university-educated middle-class German colonial governors and officials. In a book about his first expedition to New Guinea, Thurnwald argued for seeking "an appropriate symbiosis" between European and local culture.[85] This was also a "liberal" position insofar as colonial racists were opposed to any such synthesis and supported laws banning racial intermarriage in the colonies.

Between 1905 and 1910, in other words, Thurnwald's views had become sociologically appropriate for a university-educated colonizer operating inside a colonial state field. But his arguments were still anomalous in that Thurnwald was never actually a member of that field; that is, he was never an employee of a colonial government. Thurnwald seemed to be engaging in battles over native policy even though he was not active on that battlefield. This shadow boxing suggests that Thurnwald failed to understand his own social reality. At the same time this pattern pulled Thurnwald to the margins of the academic fields in which he was engaged and reproduced his own marginality. Thurnwald's comments about the joy he felt in New Guinea, far from any European, also suggest a certain attraction to "social weightlessness" along the lines discussed by Bourdieu in *The Rules of Art*, that is, a fantasy of escaping from all social determinations.[86] Such a desire for social weightlessness is often associated with social marginality or with periods of rapid change in which individuals or groups experience a widening gap between their internalized dispositions and inherited resources and the social positions available to them.

In his 1912 lecture "Applied Ethnology in Colonial Policy," Thurnwald initiated a polemic against the dominant cultural-historical and *Kulturkreis* schools in German ethnology. Ethnology was the academic field to which Thurnwald most securely belonged. In addition to his "protest" against the "poor understanding" of native subjectivity by colonial officials, Thurnwald insisted against the cultural-historical school that "ethnography is not exhausted by illuminating historical influences." Thurnwald's employer at the Berlin Ethnological Museum, von Luschan, had recently aligned himself with the rising *Kulturkreis* school.[87] As an alternative, Thurnwald suggested opening ethnology up to disciplines like sociology, law, psychology, and biology. In a period in which history and historicism were still dominant within the overall field of the German *Geisteswissenschaften*, organizing their work like an "invisible hand" (Karl Mannheim),[88] Thurnwald made a move against history and in a more scientistic direction. And in an era in which social scientific disciplinary boundaries were beginning to emerge, Thurnwald made a strong argument for interdisciplinarity. When he finally reentered the academic field and severed his investments in the overseas colonial field, he did so by embracing a kind of interdisciplinarity that was not coupled with a strong hierarchy of disciplines, in contrast to thinkers like Durkheim, Mauss, and Braudel.[89]

The second phase of Thurnwald's colonial research began during the last two years of World War I after his return to Germany and ended with his move from Halle to Berlin in 1923. At the end of the war Thurnwald wrote a series of articles echoing the colonial movement's insistence that Germany be allowed to keep its colonies. As debates swirled around German war aims, Thurnwald wrote early in 1918 that "the war must bring us an expansion of our *Lebensraum*," including "adequate colonial possessions."[90] While his pleas before 1918 for a humane native policy had been directed at other Germans, his insistence now that "native policy in German colonies before [the] war was much more humane than in English ones" resonated with efforts to rebut British claims that Germany had been an "immature" and brutal colonizer.[91] Thurnwald took up his new professorship at Halle and joined the university's Colonial Academy just as Germany was losing its colonies. He participated in discussions about transforming the Halle Colonial Academy into a school of foreign studies, along the lines followed by other German colonial training schools during the same period.[92] In 1922 he lectured at Halle on the possibility of a peaceful (*unkriegerische*) form of colonialism.[93] This was Thurnwald's last intervention on colonial questions until the end of the decade.

Rather than become an embittered German colonial revanchist, as many of the former colonial governors and officials did, Thurnwald shifted his scientific-libidinal investments into noncolonial pursuits. Although he had participated in all three German colonial congresses before the war, he did not participate in the fourth colonial congress in 1924.[94] The colonial movement no longer seemed to offer any attractive opportunities or publication venues, even if a journal like *Deutsche Kolonialzeitung* continued to appear. During the 1920s Thurnwald worked on his massive 5-volume *Die menschliche Gesellschaft*.[95] In the introduction to the first volume he briefly addressed the "crisis" in native life that had been precipitated by sustained contact with western culture and technology. But this theme was not taken up again in the remaining 1,618 pages, which dealt exclusively with non-European "traditional" societies without thematizing the impact of European imperialism or processes of colonial transculturation.[96] The 1920s therefore did not really mark a separate phase in Thurnwald's work on colonialism but demonstrated once again his pattern of flexibly shifting focus in response to changing external events—in this case, shifting his attention entirely away from colonialism. In this respect Thurnwald's work was aligned with that of most other European ethnologists during the 1920s. Nearly all of them tended to depict colonized cultures as pure, traditional, and untouched by outside influences.

In the third period, starting at the end of the 1920s, Thurnwald again reversed course, focusing on the impact of western rule on the colonized. Thurnwald claimed that his new attention to problems of "acculturation" was a direct response to the shock of visiting Tanganyika and seeing a "Negro at the typewriter" (the title of one of his articles) in 1932, as well as his return visit to New Guinea in 1934, where he witnessed the "transition of a savage society from almost complete integrity to a growing disintegration of the old order."[97] European colonialism may have brought peace and economic development to these societies, he wrote, but authority relations and traditions had been smashed and the "spice had been taken out of native life."[98] Thurnwald's discussions of cultural mixing were accompanied by his first expressions of skepticism about European cultural superiority. Cultural hybridity and "primitive thinking," he argued, were found among Europeans as well as the colonized.[99] Thurnwald pointed to embryonic anticolonialism in an "awakening Africa."[100] In 1936 Thurnwald participated in discussions of the "crisis of imperialism" with "colored Americans" and representatives from Africa, China, and India at a conference at Howard University's Sociology Department. Thurnwald argued here that "inherent in imperialism is the 'hybris,' the overbearing insolence of the dominant stratum," which "inescapably leads to its nemesis."[101]

Thurnwald's writing in the third phase underscores the fact that he was now highly responsive not just to political and temporal forces but also to shifts in his immediate academic environment. The themes of anticolonialism and cultural hybridity filtered into his work through discussions with academics in the United States and the United Kingdom. After all, the colonized world had been undergoing cultural change and "crisis" since the onset of colonial conquest without those topics necessarily registering in the work of European ethnographers.[102] By the 1930s however Malinowski, Herskovits, Gluckman, Mauss, Monica Wilson, and others had started to reorient anthropology away from its obsession with the supposedly pure native, untouched by outside influences. The shift in Thurnwald's thinking seems to have been a direct response to this intellectual shift and to the work of some of his Jewish American colleagues in the United States, including Boas, Lowie, Herskovits, Sapir, and Wirth.

The fourth and final phase in Thurnwald's work on colonialism corresponds to his return to Germany in 1936 and his alignment with the regime's anti-Semitism and its imperial aims. In 1933 Thurnwald had attacked Nazism in letters to Boas, writing

> we learn with disgust and consternation of the occurrences provoked by the new government in Germany. We *Auslandsdeutsche* should also all dissociate ourselves from this government.... I should be prepared to manifest this standing publicly.[103]

At the same time, however, Thurnwald speculated darkly in a letter to Mühlmann that the German Jews would only be quiet "for a short period of time, in order to gather power and organize. They will try to destroy Nazism from the inside.... And then one day the same thing may occur, only from the opposing side. But that would be a bloody revolution ... it would be carried out by red hordes, raging and pillaging."[104] Thurnwald's dislike for Horkheimer and the Frankfurt Institute for Social Research also intensified during this period.[105]

When Thurnwald began requesting permission to return to Berlin University from the United States in autumn 1936, his reappointment was opposed by the leader of the Nazi professors' organization there, who argued that Thurnwald was "already too old and . . . in addition could not be called a National Socialist in political terms."[106] But the university's new *Dekan*, the eugenicist and physical anthropologist Eugen Fischer, was sympathetic to Thurnwald, partially due to his older work on sociobiology, and supported his return. After he returned to Germany in 1936, Thurnwald defended his decision to go to the United States by arguing that American sociology was "not Jewish dominated" and by attacking the "completely Marxist, Talmudic-contaminated sociology that is represented in Germany above all by a group of Frankfurt Jews."[107]

Thurnwald's ability to adopt the voices of anticolonial pan-Africanism and right-wing anti-Semitism at the same time suggests an extreme opportunism and possibly even a failure to form a systematic habitus. In *Pascalian Meditations* Bourdieu referred to individual differences in the ability to form an integrated habitus and speculated that while an overaccommodating personality may form a "rigid, self-enclosed, overintegrated habitus," an adaptive personality type might allow the habitus to dissolve "into a kind of *mens momentanea*, incapable of . . . having an integrated sense of self."[108] Thurnwald seems to fit this picture of *mens momentanea*, a man without stable qualities.

The final phase in Thurnwald's work on colonialism also encompassed a realignment of his work with the imperial agencies and academic institutions of the Nazi state. Thurnwald's 1937 article "The Colonial Question" represented an abrupt return to his line of argumentation between 1905 and the early 1920s. Whereas his 1936 "Crisis of Imperialism" paper had condemned colonial hubris, the 1937 piece argued once again against the "colonial lie"—that is, the disqualification of Germany as a competent colonial power. Thurnwald also returned to his earlier argument that Germany required *Lebensraum* and tropical raw materials.[109] He compared Germany's pre-1918 colonial practices favorably with British and French policies.[110] The fact that Thurnwald must have been aware of the political compromises he was making is revealed by a marginal comment his ethnographer wife Hilde Thurnwald wrote on the proofs of his 1937 article: *"Blut und Boden!"*[111] Nonetheless, Thurnwald began to sign his letters "Heil Hitler!"

In the following years Thurnwald developed a detailed model for a future Nazi colonial occupation and administration of Africa. Nazi terminology and concepts like race, space (*Raum*), and *Lebensraum* structured his analysis. German colonialism was to be organized around the *"Führer* principle." The expropriation of African land was defended as making it more productive and allowing the native to increase his *"Lebensraum."*[112] Thurnwald attributed the threat of anticolonial resistance to "Bolshevist" propaganda coming from African Americans, whereas several years earlier he had traced it to the "hubris" of imperialism itself.[113] Thurnwald polemicized against "the numerous South African Jews" who had joined the British in opposing the Boers' segregation policies, which were exemplary.[114] Nazi colonies in Africa, he argued, should be divided into three zones: one restricted to whites, a mixed zone, and native reservations. Natives would need a "work card" to work in the white zone. The colonized would govern themselves within their reservations under the oversight of a German resident, described as a *"Betreuer der Eingeborenen."* Rather than lump all natives under a single rubric, Thurnwald insisted that there be one "black space" for each tribe. It was important to him that Africans "mainly pursue their traditional agrarian activities" and "be allowed to put on their old festivals and dances." One goal of German colonialism was to *prevent* "the rise of a black proletariat," which would have "nasty consequences."[115] Thurnwald still tried to maintain some distance from Nazi ideology: he did not introduce a racial explanatory framework. His proposed reservations looked no different from native locations in Southern Africa or British doctrines of "indirect rule" as codified by Lord Lugard.[116] Thurnwald's abhorrence for urbanized and proletarianized Africans was shared by most British colonial governors.[117]

The next stage of Thurnwald's self-*Gleichschaltung* was his proposal for an institute for ethnological research that would encompass "ethnographic research at home" (*Volksforschung in der Heimat*) alongside research on overseas and colonized societies.[118] Of course, he had long insisted that sociology should not respect the distinction between primitive and modern, European and non-European societies. Similar moves to bridge metropolitan and colonial ethnography were already being made in the US by Lloyd Warner and in Britain by the creators of Mass Observation. But by calling on Berlin University to bridge this particular gap at this particular moment, Thurnwald was essentially giving his approval to projects of putting European ethnosociology to work in the service of Nazi colonization, ethnic cleansing, and genocide in Germany and Eastern Europe. German research on Eastern Europe was focusing at this moment on sorting out the populations that could be successfully Germanized. Mühlmann, with whom Thurnwald remained in close contact, was deeply involved in this work. By linking metropolitan and overseas social research, Thurnwald was forging bridges to the Institute of Foreign Studies, discussed above. Given his earlier comments on the attacks on Jews in Germany while he was still in the United States, it seems impossible that he could not have imagined what would happen to the populations and individuals who were not deemed useful for slave labor or ethnic assimilation.

The final stage of this self-*Gleichschaltung* and the erasure of all scientific autonomy occurred in 1942 when Thurnwald's earlier expertise on questions of colonial labor was put to use within Nazi Germany. On October 31 Thurnwald asked Berlin University's *Dekan* for a reduction in his teaching load because he was working on "a series of reports on the labor deployment of foreign workers" for the Ministry for Armaments and Munition (see figure 2.1).[119] By the mid-1940s, the distance between Thurnwald's scientific work and Nazi imperial policy had narrowed to the vanishing point.

CONCLUSION: FIELD, HABITUS, AND SCIENTIFIC AUTONOMY

Scientific autonomy requires more than liberties and regulations, more than material resources and money. Individual scientific strategies are also driven by holdings of economic and symbolic capital and by basic structures of the scientific habitus and personality. The four sociologists examined here illustrate four different constellations of material resources and opportunities, habitus and personality.

Alfred Weber's habitus was perhaps the most strongly characterized by a fundamental desire for autonomy: both scientific autonomy and ego autonomy—that is, independence from the more famous older brother and from his domineering family. If Max Weber contributed to the creation of a new discipline, sociology, Alfred Weber was centrally involved in the creation of two new subfields, cultural sociology and historical sociology, and he coined the terms *Geschichts-Soziologie* and *Kultursoziologie*.[120] And Alfred took the more dramatic step of directly opposing German imperialism, both before and after World War I. Not everyone with Alfred Weber's symbolic and economic capital took the extreme step of withdrawing almost entirely from public life when the Nazis took power.

Wilhelm Mühlmann sought to walk a fine line between heteronomous, applied work and work that retained some degree of independence from immediate policy concerns. Nonetheless, he was drawn inexorably into the practical, applied domains of Nazi policymaking in the field of *Ostpolitik*. In direct contrast to Alfred Weber, Mühlmann seems to have had almost no resources for resisting this cooptation by the regime.

Max Weber's habitus was, as I have argued, fundamentally divided, but he was nonetheless able to generate a fairly stable set of scientific choices. Weber constantly sought out academic fields that were located between the modernist and mandarin poles and seems to have felt most comfortable in economics and law. When moving in traditional mandarin fields like sinology and Roman

```
Libellenstr.17
Bln-Nikolassee                    31. 10. 1942


Herrn Dekan der philosophischen Fakultät
Berlin  C  2

Sehr geehrter Herr Dekan,
                    Jetzt erst kam eine Vereinbarung zu Stande,
wonach ich für das Ministerium für Bewaffnung und Munition eine
Reihe von Schriften über den Arbeitseinsatz ausländischer Arbeiter
teils herausgeben, teils selbst verfassen soll. Dadurch wird ein
erheblicher Teil meiner Zeit in Anspruch genommen werden. Daher
werde ich nicht, wie beabsichtigt, die Vorlesungen wöchentlich
halten können, sondern jede Vorlesung mit den dazu gehörigen Übun-
gen nur vierzehntätigig, so dass jede Woche abwechselnd die eine,
dann die ander Vorlesung und Übung stattfindet.

        Ich erbitte dazu Ihre Genehmigung, da im Vorlseungsverzeich-
nis und auf dem schwarzen Brett die Ankündigung für die Woche lau-
tet. Ich weiss nicht, ob vom Dekanat aus die entsprechende Ände-
rung der Ankündigung vorgenommen werden kann, oder ob ich auf neu-
en Blättern sie vornehmen soll.

                            Heil Hitler

Es würde sich darum handeln, die
Vorlesungen am 4. und 11. Dezember
beginnen zu lassen.
```

FIGURE 2.1 · Letter from Thurnwald requesting reduction in his teaching for work on "a series of reports on the labor deployment of foreign workers." Courtesy of Humboldt University archives, Berlin.

history, he allied himself with modernist experts who nonetheless occupied the most prestigious, dominant positions within the field.

Richard Thurnwald's scientific habitus was not just divided but seemingly unstable. He seems to have repositioned himself constantly in the German and American sociological fields. Often he seems to have failed to understand what field he was in. This highly unstable scientific habitus may not even have the consistency to be called a habitus. In any case, its result for Thurnwald's intellectual production was a tendency to try to please a shifting array of external audiences and patrons.

Why does all of this matter? It is one thing to say that science and society are "co-produced" or that colonial social science is co-produced by colonial states and imperial offices.[121] We can state with some certainty that colonial native policies have been profoundly shaped by the ideas of expert and non-expert knowledge producers.[122] There is less evidence, however, about the ways expert and non-expert knowledge have been shaped by imperial policies and practices. Critics of colonial knowledge have often fallen back into simplistic models that have long been rejected within science studies and the sociology of knowledge. This chapter has shown that colonial, imperial, and Nazi politics influenced sociological production in a variety of ways. In order to understand how scientists respond to extra-scientific pressures, resources, and opportunities, we need to pay attention to the structures of cultural fields and individual habitus, holdings of capital, and psychic structures. Colonial history and colonial cultural criticism need to avoid falling into reductionist epistemologies and explanatory short-circuits.

NOTES

1. Steinmetz, "Imperial Entanglements," 1–56; Connell, "Why Is Classical Theory Classical?," 1511–1557; and Steinmetz, ed., *Sociology and Empire*. By the mid-1950s nearly half of the professional sociological field in the UK and France and their respective empires were working in colonial contexts or on imperial questions; see Steinmetz, "A Child of the Empire."

2. Sociology in Germany before 1933 was a nascent academic *field* in Bourdieu's sense, defined by a recognized set of founders and foundational texts and ideas and by field-specific symbolic capital, stakes, and hierarchies of distinction. By 1933, some forty German professorships included the word "sociology" in their title, and ten were exclusively dedicated to sociology; see Kaesler, *Die frühe deutsche Soziologie*, 626–628.

3. Platt, "'Im ertödtenden Blicke des todten Beschauers,'" 63.

4. Nau, *Der Werturteilsstreit*.

5. Thurnwald, "Der Wert von Neu-Guinea als Deutsche Kolonie," 43; also Thurnwald, "Die Kolonien als Friedensbürgschaft," 170–185.

6. Thurnwald, "Die Kolonialfrage," 66–86; "Kolonialwirtschaftliche Betriebe," 48–62; and *Koloniale Gestaltung*.

7. Thurnwald, "Bericht zu der Sitzung," 617–627.

8. M. Weber, *Die römische Agrargeschichte*.

9. M. Weber, *The Agrarian Sociology of Ancient Civilizations* and *The Religion of China*.

10. M. Weber, *Die Wirtschaftsethik der Weltreligionen*; translation: *The Religion of China*.

11. M. Weber, *Economy and Society*, vol. 2, 910–921.

12. Mommsen, *Max Weber and German Politics*; and Konno, *Max Weber*.

13. M. Weber, "The National State and Economic Policy," 188–209.

14. M. Weber, "Social Causes," 75–88.

15. There is no evidence that Weber took any specific interest in the notorious article 48 of the Weimar Constitution, although he supported the constitution's plebiscitary aspects; see Mommsen, *Max Weber and German Politics*, 378.

16. M. Weber, *Die Lage der Landarbeiter* and *The Religion of China*; Zimmerman, "Decolonizing Weber," 53–80.

17. Demm, "Alfred Weber als Wissenschaftsorganisator," 97–116. Frankfurt began to outshine Heidelberg as a center for social research only in 1930, when Horkheimer took over the directorship of the Institute for Social Research and Karl Mannheim moved to Frankfurt as a sociology professor and was followed by Norbert Elias and Hans Gerth. See N. Gerth, "'Between Two Worlds,'" 37–38.

18. A. Weber, "Deutschland und der wirtschaftlicher Imperialismus," 298–324.

19. Demm, *Ein Liberaler in Kaiserreich und Republik*, 209, 207; Weber to Arthur Zimmermann, September 22, 1916, in Demm and Soell, *Alfred-Weber-Gesamtausgabe*, 232.

20. A. Weber, "Selbstbestimmungsrecht," 60–71, and "Deutschland und die europäische Kulturkrise," 308–321.

21. A. Weber, *Kulturgeschichte als Kultursoziologie*, 405, 408.

22. Demm, *Geist und Politik im 20. Jahrhundert*, 264.

23. A. Weber, "Gibt es wertfreie Soziologie?," 37–43; Weber to Otto von Zwiedineck-Südenhorst, September 1948, *Alfred-Weber-Gesamtausgabe*, 147.

24. Mühlmann, "Die geheime Gesellschaft der Arioi."

25. Thurnwald papers, Yale University Library (YUL Thurnwald).

26. Evans-Pritchard argued that anthropology and sociology were "inseparable" and should be combined, while Marcel Mauss maintained that ethnography was a descriptive subfield within sociology. Evans-Pritchard, "Social Anthropology," 172–173; Clifford, *The Predicament of Culture*, 63.

27. Mühlmann, "Die Begriffe 'Ati und Mataeinaa," 739–756.

28. *Pace* Fischer, *Völkerkunde im Nationalsozialismus*, 42.

29. Mühlmann to Thurnwald, October 18, 1932. YUL Thurnwald, box 2, folder 28; Mühlmann, "Eckstein und Horn," 173–180.

30. Mühlmann, "Frage der arischen Herkunft," 3–16. This article stands in a long lineage of European thought. See Thomas, "Melanesians and Polynesians," 133–155, and Steinmetz, *The Devil's Handwriting*, ch. 4.

31. Mühlmann, "Echtes und unechtes Slawentum," 69, 75.

32. Mühlmann, "Umvolkung und Volkwerdung," 296.

33. Mühlmann, "Umvolkung und Volkwerdung," 294.

34. Mühlmann, *Assimilation, Umvolkung, Volkwerdung*; Loesch and Mühlman, *Die Völker und Rassen Südosteuropas*.

35. Mühlmann, *Rassen- und Völkerkunde*, 536–537.

36. Michel, "Neue ethnologisches Forschungsansätze im Nationalsozialismus?," 150.

37. Mühlmann, "Umvolkung und Volkwerdung," 292; Michel, "Neue ethnologisches Forschungsansätze im Nationalsozialismus?," 151; Mühlmann, "Politisch-katholische Rassenforschung?," 35–38.

38. Karl-Marx-Universität Leipzig, *Eine Dokumentation*, 15–16; Botsch, *Politische Wissenschaft im Zweiten Weltkrieg*. Mühlmann and the other defenders of "trans-folking" ultimately lost out to the more brutal "race faction" inside the *Auslandswissenschaftliche Fakultät*; see Klingemann, "Angewandte Soziologie im Nationalsozialismus," 21.

39. Michel, "Wilhelm Emil Mühlmann," 91, 93; Thurnwald to *Dekan*, Berlin University, October 12, 1942 in Thurnwald's personnel file, Humboldt University Archive, Berlin (TP HUAB), vol. 6, 202.

40. On the state as field see Bourdieu (1999, 2014); Steinmetz (2008, 2014).

41. Thus Weber's "rural laborer study" analyzed the alleged threat to the eastern German border zones posed by Polish immigration and combined "sociological analysis with '*volkstumspolitischer Agitation.*'" Klingemann, "Ostforschung und Soziologie," 177.

42. As Mommsen ([1959] 1984) point out, Weber evinced no interest in the German African colonies.

43. Weber, *The Religion of China*, 235–242, 249.

44. Confucianism had undergone a certain rationalization, according to Weber, but in a form that was antithetical to the socioeconomic rationalization.

45. Steinmetz, *The Devil's Handwriting*, 402. This point is made by Schmidt-Glintzer, "Einleitung, Editorischer Bericht," 6.

46. This seems to be the argument of Allen, *Max Weber*.

47. See Bourdieu, *Pascalian Meditations* and *Sketch for a Self-Analysis*.

48. On homologies and isomorphisms among fields see Bourdieu, *The Rules of Art*.

49. Ringer, *The Decline of the German Mandarins*.

50. Weber, *The Religion of China*, 121.

51. Ringer, *Max Weber*.

52. Von Richthofen was *Dekan* of Berlin University in 1900; de Groot took up an appointment at Berlin as Professor Ordinarius in 1912.

53. Wilhelm worked as a missionary and teacher in Kiaochow from 1899 to 1919, received an honorary doctorate from Frankfurt University in 1922, and was given a *Honorarprofessur* in 1924; see Steinmetz, *The Devil's Handwriting*. Franke was appointed to the first German chair in sinology at the Hamburg Colonial Institute in 1909 and later held de Groot's chair at Berlin University (1923–1931). In both of these careers, the rise to academic respectability came too late to influence Weber's source selection in his China study.

54. Wang, "Die Staatsidee des Konfuzius," 1–49.

55. Paquet, "Vorwort," in Ku Hung-Ming, *Chinas Verteidigung gegen europäische Ideen*, i–xiv; Paquet, *Li, oder Im neuen Osten*; Paquet, "Der Kaisergedanke," 45–62.

56. M. Weber, "Hinduismus und Buddhismus," 2, n. 1.

57. Pischel and Geldner, *Vedische Studien*, iv; Sengupta, *From Salon to Discipline*, 114.

58. On the German sinological field before 1918, see Steinmetz, *The Devil's Handwriting*, ch. 6; Leutner, "Sinologie in Berlin," 31–56.

59. Melk-Koch, *Auf der Suche*, 31.

60. L. L. Bernard explained to Thurnwald the reasons for the latter's failure to find employment in an American sociology department in a letter from June 26, 1936, YUL Thurnwald.

61. "Fragebogen an sämtiche Mitglieder des Lehrkörpers der Universität Berlin," November 25, 1936, TP HUAB, vol. 2, 25; *Chronik der königlichen Friedrich-Wilhelms-Universität*, 20.

62. Melk-Koch, *Auf der Suche*, 281–282. Thurnwald participated in planning meetings for the new Free University.

63. Thurnwald, "Die eingeborenen Arbeitskräfte im Südseeschutzgebeit," 607–632; Melk-Koch, *Auf der Suche*, 135.

64. Melk-Koch, *Auf der Suche*, 162.

65. Stoecker, "The Advancement of African Studies," 75.

66. Thurnwald to Thomas, May 3, 1932, YUL Thurnwald.

67. Thurnwald to *Dekan*, April 30, 1946, vol. 6, TP HUAB, 240.

68. Report on Thurnwald's background (*Abstammung*), vol. 1, TP HUAB, 7.

69. Problems of "ethnic psychology" had been central to Thurnwald's arguments about understanding colonial subjects in order to motivate them to work.

70. Vorländer, acting dean of the Philosophical Faculty, University of Halle–Wittenberg, to the university's curators, May 7, 1919, vol. 4, TP HUAB, 7.

71. Palyi, ed., *Hauptprobleme der Soziologie*.

72. Aron, *La sociologie allemande contemporaine*.

73. Deutsche Gesellschaft für Soziologie, *Verhandlungen des Deutschen Soziologentages*, 248–288.

74. On the central and peripheral members of the German sociological field, see Kaesler, *Die frühe deutsche Soziologie*.

75. On scholars' differing strategies in moving internationally between nationally-specific academic fields and their varying success see Steinmetz (2010).

76. P. A. Sorokin, chairman, Department of Sociology, Harvard University, to Thurnwald, January 2, 1932; Louis Wirth, secretary of the ASS, to Thurnwald, July 28, 1932; L. L. Bernard to Thurnwald, December 8, 1932 (all in YUL Thurnwald).

77. Frederic M. Thrasher to Thurnwald, November 4, 1932. Thurnwald was included in a list of "New York sociologists 1932–33" (State of New York). YUL Thurnwald.

78. Thurnwald to W. Mühlmann, February 3, 1933, in YUL Thurnwald.

79. Thurnwald, "Koloniale Eingeborenenpolitik," 632.

80. Herre, ed., *Politisches Handwörterbuch*.

81. Laukötter, "The Time after Adolf Bastian," 159; von Luschan, *Anthropological View of Race*, 11.

82. On Bourdieu's concept of habitus as an attempt to make sense of this gap between subjectivity and the social *Umwelt* see Mead (2013).

83. Thurnwald, "Das Rechtsleben der Eingeborenen," 192.

84. Thurnwald, "Angewandte Ethnologie in der Kolonialpolitik," 59–69.

85. Thurnwald, *Forschungen auf den Salomo-Inseln*, 19.

86. Bourdieu, *The Rules of Art*, 12.

87. von Luschan, "Rassen und Völker," 48.

88. Mannheim, "Historicism," 84.

89. On the asymmetries of power among disciplines in different forms of interdisciplinarity see Steinmetz, "Transdisciplinarity as a Nonimperial Encounter," 48–65; and Steinmetz, "Historicizing and Spatializing Field Theory."

90. Thurnwald, "Der Wert von Neu-Guinea," 43.

91. Thurnwald, "Der Wert von Neu-Guinea," 53–54.

92. See "Gründung einer Kolonialakademie," in Bundesarchiv Berlin, R 8023 (Deutsche Kolonialgesellschaft). Thurnwald to Geheimrat, February 23, 1921; and "Eine neue Aktionsprogramm der Kolonialakademie," Halle, February 25, 1921, YUL Thurnwald.

93. "Wie weit ist unkriegersiche Kolonisation möglich?," notes for a lecture at the Halle Colonial Academy, July 17, 1922, YUL Thurnwald.

94. *Verhandlungen des deutschen Kolonialkongresses.*

95. Melk-Koch, "Richard Thurnwald," 481. On the Emergency Association of German Science see Flachowsky (2008).

96. Thurnwald, *Die menschliche Gesellschaft,* 21–22.

97. Thurnwald, "Die Neger an der Schreibmaschine"; Thurnwald, "The Price of the White Man's Peace," 347.

98. Thurnwald, "The Price of the White Man's Peace," 353.

99. Thurnwald, *Black and White,* 211, 288.

100. Thurnwald, *Black and White,* 80.

101. Thurnwald, "The Crisis of Imperialism," 84.

102. As I showed in *The Devil's Handwriting* (2007), 19th century European descriptions of the cultures soon to be subjected to colonial rule focused on mimicry and instability. Europeans understood indigenous cultural slippage as a threat to their rule and sought to rein it in through native policy. Ethnographic descriptions before conquest and during the early decades of colonial consolidation differed in this respect from most official ethnography carried out between the wars, which was directed toward (re)discovering stable cultural traditions and patterns and using this information to guide policies of indirect rule. This approach was most explicit in places like British Tanganyika, where Governor Cameron instructed district officials to gather information on ancient tribal customs which could then be resurrected through careful policy (Austen, 1968).

103. Thurnwald to Boas, March 26, 1933, YUL Thurnwald.

104. Thurnwald to Mühlmann, April 2, 1933, YUL Thurnwald.

105. Amidon, "'Diesmal fehlt die Biologie!"

106. Die Dozentenschaft der Friedrich-Wilhelms-Universität Berlin to Rektor, September 7, 1935, TP HUAB, vol. 5, 3.

107. Thurnwald to Berlin University *Dekan,* April 22, 1936, TP HUAB, vol. 5, 8.

108. Bourdieu, *Pascalian Meditations,* 161.

109. Thurnwald, "Die Kolonialfrage."

110. Thurnwald, "Die fremden Eingriffe."

111. Melk-Koch, *Auf der Suche,* 278.

112. Thurnwald, "Methoden in der Völkerkunde," 433.

113. Thurnwald, *Koloniale Gestaltung*, 378.
114. Thurnwald, "Bericht zu der Sitzung der Arbeitsgemeinschaft," 625.
115. Thurnwald, "Bericht zu der Sitzung der Arbeitsgemeinschaft," 625.
116. Lugard, *The Dual Mandate*; Faught, *Into Africa*.
117. Steinmetz, "Colonialism and British Sociology."
118. Timm, "Richard Thurnwald," 622.
119. Thurnwald to *Dekan*, October 31, 1942, vol. 6, TP HUAB, 200; Thurnwald to Westermann, February–May 1946, vol. 6, TP HUAB, 238.
120. A. Weber, *Schriften zur Kultur- und Geschichtssoziologie*.
121. See Jasanoff, "The Idiom of Co-production."
122. For evidence see Steinmetz, *The Devil's Handwriting*.

THREE

Science and Civilizing Missions
Germans and the Transnational Community of Tropical Medicine
DEBORAH J. NEILL

In a draft history of Hamburg's *Institut für Schiffs- und Tropenkrankheiten* (now the Bernhard Nocht Institute for Tropical Medicine), written after much of the institution had been destroyed in World War II, the author reflected on a happier moment in time, the opening of a new building in May of 1914. Leading up to that year, "international scientific connections in the field of tropical medicine had grown significantly. The scholars of all countries seemed to want to work in a friendly competition on the solutions to questions of hygiene, the settlement in tropical countries of the white race as well as the opening up of the colonial countries connected with that." The attendance of experts from all over Europe at the inauguration, the author noted, "gave eloquent expression to these future dreams." And then came the war. It "brought the cultural-intellectual work—carefully nourished in a community for many decades—to a halt, if not even to a collapse."[1] The war, which damaged many of the transnational connections that had been forged among tropical medicine specialists all across Europe in the previous two decades, altered the profession and was particularly difficult for Germans whose research depended on access to African and other tropical colonies.

Although the author undoubtedly exaggerates the extent of the goodwill between European scientists in an era characterized by national and imperial rivalries, the prewar "friendly competition" he describes encouraged innovation, and there was a significant amount of cooperation between German scientists and their foreign counterparts that led to exchanges, new training opportunities, and collaborative research. International connections were vital to furthering the projects of ambitious scientists, as well as cementing the reputations and authority of major research institutions. Many tropical medicine specialists also believed that beyond their personal career goals and their desire to assist in national projects of expansion, their task was to more broadly bring the benefits of Western civilization, modern science, and technological expertise to the world.[2] The author's lament about the loss of this collective spirit after 1918 was a lament for Germany's lost place at the forefront of a vibrant transnational scientific community united by a common global mission.

Recent historical scholarship reveals not only the ways in which colonial expansion in the late nineteenth and early twentieth centuries furthered Germany's own territorial and political ambitions, but also how Germans involved in transnational networks helped to facilitate greater Western control over an increasingly interconnected world.[3] In the new field of tropical medicine, national efforts to build the specialty were fundamental, as several major studies have effectively demonstrated.[4] But the field's development before 1914, in Germany and elsewhere, was also deeply indebted to a well-connected community of scientific experts whose cross-border, collaborative work helped to establish the standards of medical research and clinical practice in many different colonial empires. Their culture of "friendly competition" was sorely challenged by World War I, which significantly altered relationships between leading German researchers and their counterparts in Belgium, Britain, and France. In this chapter I explore some of the ways in which German doctors contributed to the prewar transnational specialty and then examine the impact of the war, both in terms of how it led to reinterpretations of Germany's record as a colonial power and "civilizing" force in Africa, and how it had practical implications for the continuation of German tropical medicine research in the 1920s and 1930s.

TROPICAL MEDICINE IN GERMANY

The modern specialty of tropical medicine developed in the late nineteenth century and grew out of the microbiological revolution spearheaded by Germany's Robert Koch and France's Louis Pasteur. Other major contributors to the new field were the scientists Alphonse Laveran and Patrick Manson, who introduced the study of parasitology and scored a major victory in 1898 when Britain's Ronald Ross proved their theory that malaria was caused by a mosquito.[5] The scientific breakthroughs were extraordinary and were facilitated by Western Europe's colonization of Africa and Asia which gave scientists unprecedented opportunities to conduct research, collect data, and identify new microbes. In Germany, scientific opportunities arose in significant part because of the establishment of German protectorates in Cameroon, Togo, East Africa, and Southwest Africa. The government sought to train colonial doctors to protect the health of officials, traders, and settlers, and support also came from members of the business community with tropical interests.[6] The *Institut für Schiffs- und Tropenkrankheiten*, founded in 1900 in Hamburg, provided dedicated space for laboratory research as well as an infrastructure to train Germany's doctors before they were sent to colonial posts.[7] The Hamburg Institute was modeled in significant part on similar centers in London and Liverpool, and gave Germany a base from which scientists could build networks, conduct research, and organize scientific expeditions. Their work became even more pressing after the 1901 outbreak of a major sleeping sickness epidemic in eastern Africa; this epidemic was particularly worrisome because the disease attacked young, able-bodied workers—workers whose labor was vital to the success of major economic initiatives in railway, mining, and agriculture.

Even before the opening of the Hamburg institute, the German scientific community, with its well-organized universities and medical departments, was in a strong position to take a leading role in the new field. Foreign scientists recognized their indebtedness to German work; in one letter to his mother, the young Liverpool researcher John Todd noted that he had hired a clerk to help him brush up on his German, since "I find that a working knowledge of the tongue is absolutely essential to me in doing any research work, for over half the references are to work done by Germans and therefore printed in Deutsch."[8] Todd's reading list included some new studies by Robert Koch and his students. Todd both envied and admired Koch, expressing his respect for the quality of research coming out of Koch's well-funded and well-staffed laboratory but complaining about Koch's tendency to claim credit for the work of his junior colleagues.[9] Todd felt competitive, but he also took great pride in belonging to what he considered to be a cutting-edge field with high-profile practitioners from across Europe. Members of the small tropical medicine community cultivated ties with cross-border colleagues; even as scientists raced to be the first to publish meaningful results, they relied on their foreign counterparts to assure the veracity of their findings and bolster their claims to truth. Because research and travel were almost always funded within national systems, having the support of foreign colleagues could benefit scientists looking to boost their profiles, bolster the reputation of their institutions, and compete for government funding and other forms of financial aid.[10]

Tropical medicine research was concentrated in several European centers;

researchers exchanged samples, offprints, experimental medications, students and speaking invitations. German scientists were highly active in these exchanges and used their contacts extensively to further their work. Claus Schilling, for example, who headed the tropical section at Koch's Berlin laboratory, cultivated ties to scientists in Liverpool, London, Paris, and Brussels through letters, attendance at international conferences, and personal visits. He was able to use his connections to gain permission for field research in the Belgian Congo and in French Central and West Africa.[11] Schilling was not unique; at the Hamburg institute, researcher Friedrich Fülleborn was a guest at the British Medical Association meeting of 1904, and established friendly ties to London's Patrick Manson, as well as Ronald Ross and other members of the Liverpool school.[12] Hamburg's institute welcomed foreign scientists, such as London's F. M. Sandwith, and alumni recounted the importance of the many foreign scientists who presented lectures and mingled with faculty and students at the Hamburg school.[13] The school also trained foreign students from many countries, including Hungary, the Netherlands, Russia, Brazil, England, Belgium, and Australia.[14] Publicizing and formalizing cross-border ties was a declared goal of the Hamburg group; researchers there not only established a national Tropical Medicine Society in 1907 but also spearheaded a push for an international society at the same time. Thanks to their efforts, as well as those of their colleagues in Britain and France, a permanent subsection for tropical medicine was established in time for the 1912 meeting of the International Medical Congress in London.[15]

German field doctors also forged connections to foreign colleagues. Examples include Cameroon's Hans Ziemann, who befriended Ross and France's trypanosomiasis research pioneer Emile Brumpt.[16] Ziemann pursued publishing opportunities in Britain's *Journal of Tropical Medicine*, was well known on the international conference circuit, and conducted research not just in German colonies but also in British Nigeria.[17] Similarly, Ludwig Külz visited and reported on French and British tropical medicine institutions for the government and, while serving in western Africa, enjoyed trips to neighboring French colonies that gave him material for publications.[18] Another example is Friedrich Karl Kleine; he served on Koch's Ugandan expedition and from late 1907 was the head of the sleeping sickness program in German East Africa. This post brought him into contact with British scientists and officials who supported his work.[19] Kleine was also well respected by the French; he became a Corresponding Member of the prestigious French Society for Exotic Pathology, along with Fülleborn and Schilling. The French society was proud of its German members: Ziemann and the Hamburg school director, Bernhard Nocht, were also members, and Robert Koch and his fellow Nobel Prize winner Paul Ehrlich were named in the prestigious category of Honorary Members.[20]

Aside from the obvious practical benefits to knowing colleagues in foreign countries, many specialists shared a bond because a similar worldview united them. This included a belief in the universal value of Western medicine, the idea that Europeans had a duty to elevate "inferior" races, and a sense that scientists were united by their common professional, gender, and racial identities. German specialists enthusiastically embraced this idea of a shared medical "civilizing mission." In an after-dinner speech to his colleagues at an international meeting in London, Koch argued that scientists and doctors were in many ways above politics, because although they came from different countries, they "had but one aim, viz., the effective prosecution of their humanitarian work."[21] The idea of scientists as objective truth seekers with a humanitarian agenda was coupled with a belief that colonialism was the best way to universalize the benefits of European medicine. Claus Schilling called the European doctor "the most important carrier of modern culture in the colonies" and stated that "to a race of lower standing, the physician is representative of the most noble and sublime [ideals] produced by our European culture, for he represents science in the service of humanity."[22] Schilling also cast the work of physicians and scientists in a moral light:

> These *Naturvölker* are completely and helplessly exposed to the dangers resulting from climate and illness. Is it not revealing that the Indians, who every year are decimated by plague and cholera, have not found the means to heal or prevent these epidemics, and have not even uncovered the way in which these diseases are transmitted from person to person? Only European science has provided clarity on this issue and thus has provided the possibility of fighting these epidemics. And it is like this with all tropical diseases: the protection afforded by smallpox vaccinations, for example, was transplanted by the Europeans to the tropics.[23]

The goal of rescuing "backward" races from disease dovetailed with the individual ambitions of many scientists to find paths to advancement and fame, and they shared their ideas, publications, and research with each other across borders to further both their professional and personal aims. Nowhere was this combination of "moral" and strategic motivation more apparent than in the response to sleeping sickness in Africa; the epidemic deepened the existing connections between field doctors and metropolitan scientists in all of the colonizing countries.

SLEEPING SICKNESS (HUMAN TRYPANOSOMIASIS) AND CROSS-BORDER CONNECTIONS

Sleeping sickness, caused by trypanosomes and transmitted by the tsetse fly, is fatal without treatment; by 1907 it had already claimed, according to one estimate, 200,000 to 300,000 lives in Uganda alone.[24] British researchers had successfully identified the carrier by 1903, but aside from atoxyl, a dangerous arsenic-based compound, there were few options for treating the disease.[25] A collective response was necessary because sleeping sickness had the potential to spread rapidly across colonial borders, and it developed not only in Uganda but in German East Africa, the Congo Free State, Portuguese territories, and, further afield, French Equatorial Africa and British, German, and French West Africa.[26] The race to find both prevention and cure dominated tropical medicine research in the early twentieth century.

Scientists in pursuit of patients and flies crisscrossed the continent on high-profile research missions, and Koch's drug therapy research work in British Uganda and German East Africa in 1906–1907 confirmed the standard for medications and dosages in many affected colonies.[27] Transnational partnerships involving individuals, research institutes, and German drug companies were also established. For example, the pharmaceutical company Bayer engaged the assistance of Pasteur Institute scientists Maurice Nicolle and Félix Mesnil to test dyes they hoped would be effective in attacking trypanosomes in a patient's blood.[28] Paul Ehrlich also carried out drug therapy research via a network of field physicians in German, British, French, and Belgian colonies.[29] Ehrlich's network also gave him an influential role in international agenda setting; he served as the president of the Medical Sub-Commission at the 1907 sleeping sickness meeting in London and, together with Laveran, kept the quest for an effective drug therapy at the center of the campaign against the disease. The meeting also led to a bilateral agreement between the Germans and the British that saw the introduction of common measures in East Africa, including the creation of a joint commission and a commitment to building segregation camps on each side of the shared border.[30] These formal arrangements cemented preexisting connections between German and British doctors in East Africa. The contact between Germany's Oskar Feldmann and Britain's Cuthbert Christy, for example, had helped the German government keep abreast of developments in Uganda in the initial stages of the epidemic.[31] The British also provided the German medical officer Dr. Lott with access to facilities in infected zones in Uganda to conduct sleeping sickness investigations.[32]

Because of the proximity of Cameroon and French Equatorial Africa, German and French doctors also shared information and ideas about combating the disease. The Molundu station doctor, Geisler, for example, visited his

French counterpart in Wesso in 1909 to confer, while his colleague Dr. Haberer traveled in French territory and even provided temporary medical assistance at a French station.[33] Despite the challenges of long-distance travel in the region, Germans visited the Pasteur Institute in Brazzaville multiple times. Examples include Schilling's trip in 1907 and the 1913 expedition of Philalethes Kuhn, the head of the sleeping sickness program in Cameroon. Kuhn's visit included strategy sessions with French colleagues about mutual measures to enforce sleeping sickness regulations; he also opened negotiations about forging a Franco-German bilateral border agreement.[34] In remote locations, European scientists, regardless of nationality, came together to trade ideas and knowledge.

These meetings were crucial because physicians and researchers relied on sharing information in order to make stronger recommendations to their home governments.[35] Koch's experiences in Uganda, for example, introduced him to the idea of the controversial British "concentration camps." These camps housed African patients or suspected carriers of the disease in a single center for clinical and research purposes. Koch suggested a similar system for German East Africa—a system adopted by the German government in 1907.[36] Policies of brush burning and clearing to destroy the habitat of the fly, border controls, and the surveillance of local populations also developed in German East Africa and Cameroon in part due to discussions among German advisers and their foreign counterparts. The idea of giving atoxyl prophylactically and on a mass scale in German Cameroon was greeted with approval when German doctors discussed the matter with French colleagues in Brazzaville in 1913. The Germans even hoped that they would be given administrative control of entire regions of the colony, and French doctors agreed that only greater regional medical authority would allow them to truly conquer the disease.[37] The increasing conformity of ideas and policies in the region contributed more broadly to the growing hegemony of Western medicine in Africa, with its emphasis on laboratories, "campaigns" against specific diseases, and isolation and control.[38] Government officials were more likely to listen to Europeans who backed each other's opinions and spoke their own technical language and less likely to consider the views of the local people who were most affected by the European measures. Africans had little voice in decision making and were the primary targets of intrusive and aggressive policies, including drug therapy experimentation, intensive surveillance, forcible confinement and quarantine.[39]

Partnerships reinforced the sense of common purpose and contributed to the confidence that many Europeans had in their global mission. In a speech to the German Colonial Society, for example, a former special commissioner of Uganda, Harry Johnston, praised British-German cooperation, declaring that "[w]e have both learned to walk hand in hand in our great battles with rebellious nature, in tasks such as combating tropical diseases and other problems."[40] French observers also commented favorably about Germany's sleeping sickness program, with one 1909 article stating that in the German colonies, "hygiene and the campaign against infectious diseases are objects of serious preoccupations." The French author approvingly described Germany's many colonial medical facilities, including large hospitals and well-appointed sanatoriums, and also praised the abundance of doctors. He seemed to be implying that his own government should follow the German lead and invest more in colonial health care.[41]

All of this "friendly competition" and the transnational connections between German tropical medicine specialists and their foreign peers would change as a result of World War I. The length of the conflict and the demands it made on doctors' time and energy halted most scientific research in the African colonies. When the war finally ended, Germany lost all of its colonial holdings in the peace agreement. This loss meant that German scientists no longer had easy access to the raw materials, laboratories, and other necessities that made research possible. They also saw their prewar record reinterpreted by their wartime enemies in light of new political priorities.

POSTWAR STRUGGLES: WAR OF WORDS

If various forms of cross-border connections had tempered the rivalries in tropical medicine before the war, the reverse was true in the postwar period, where many of the ties had been severed and the bitterness of the war augmented the atmosphere of competition. Without colonies, Germans were now in a position of serious weakness, and their foreign colleagues were far from willing to provide them with the opportunities that would keep them in their former position of dominance in the field. Cross-border cooperation continued among the allied powers, but although there was some softening in German-English relations over time, German scientists were largely excluded from their former networks, and some of them responded with vitriolic attacks that made their situation worse.

Allied references to German colonial barbarism began during the war and accelerated in its aftermath. In 1915, Harry Johnston, so emphatic in his praise of German colonization before the war, now argued that Germany should be excluded from the colonies altogether.[42] In 1918, Britain's Sir Hugh Clifford announced, "Germany has besmirched the escutcheon of Europe in Africa," and continued, "we may thank God that throughout the Dark Continent 'white men' and 'Germans' are regarded and spoken of by the natives as two utterly distinct species of mankind."[43] In 1920, the British government published an aggressively critical pamphlet entitled *Treatment of Natives in the German Colonies*.[44] British attempts to disassociate Germans from both the civilizing mission and the racial category of "white men" were motivated in large part by the desire to assume control of Germany's African colonies. The French made similar interventions with the same goal in mind, and political and popular writings also focused on Germany's alleged abusive rule. Even travel guides, such as one by Maurice Rondet-Saint, noted that

> Germany considers that in its capacity as a grand civilized nation, a share of Africa should be returned to it in order to allow Germans to bring the civilizing mission to the backwards people of tropical Africa. But once we knew the way in which German nationals proceeded before the war under this mandate, and the role that the cudgel played in the civilizing mission, we are permitted to find this argument specious, if not even audacious.[45]

Comments like this one challenged the idea that Germans, including German scientists and physicians, shared the same values, worldview, and "civilizing mission" as their colleagues from other colonizing countries. Predictably, German tropical medicine specialists reacted with rage to the accusations. "With astonishment," Hamburg's Bernhard Nocht wrote, on behalf of the German Tropical Medicine Society in 1919, "the tropical doctor sees his vocation—which easily withstands comparisons with those of doctors in foreign colonies—pilfered, in order to find arguments for this hostile smear campaign. This is obviously only because demagoguery is necessary to obtain the support of the masses at home and among neutral observers."[46] The bitterness of Hamburg Institute supporters was also obvious in an open letter in 1921, where they protested that "before the war, German science was almost universally *the leader*." Now, "German researchers and all German surgeons have been excluded by our enemies from international society, and have been brought into disrepute, because we protested in the time of the greatest need, when almost the entire world stood against us, against the shameless slandering of our army and our people."[47] Along with feeling marginalized by former colleagues, researchers also worried that they would have great difficulty conducting field work. They also feared that the German government, in light of the loss of the African territories, might withdraw crucial support for Hamburg-based work.

Scientists with international profiles and strong prewar connections to foreign colleagues were the most likely to receive permission to continue research work in Africa, but these rights were hard won. The case of Friedrich Kleine demonstrates this. Kleine had the opportunity to travel to British-held Northern Rhodesia and the Belgian Congo between 1921 and 1923, but this was largely because the drug company Bayer had introduced a promising new sleeping sickness drug, Bayer 205 (commonly called Germanin), and did not initially wish to provide it to foreign scientists until Kleine had proven its efficacy and thus demonstrated the value of German research.[48] This desire to refuse test samples to foreign scientists was in marked contrast to the easy, informal collaboration that Paul Ehrlich and his foreign colleagues had developed before the war. In this new context, wartime enemies were highly suspicious of each other, and Kleine's presence made officials very uneasy. Even Ehrlich's former collaborator in the Belgian Congo, drug therapy researcher Alphonse Broden, expressed his fears about being at the mercy of Bayer. In fact the tensions surrounding Bayer 205 led to attempts by Belgian officials to obtain the drug by demanding it as part of German reparation payments.[49] It is no surprise, therefore, that Kleine's nationality continued to be a problem for him and that he struggled to be included in international meetings, research, and forums.[50] But Kleine did benefit from a slight thaw in British attitudes toward German tropical medicine in the late 1920s and the 1930s, particularly as the sleeping sickness epidemic in French Cameroon and Equatorial Africa grew worse and British commentators weighed in on French efforts. One article in *The African World* argued that "[u]nder the tragic circumstances existing in the mandated Cameroons to-day, the French authorities would be well advised to avail themselves of the Locarno spirit and apply to the German experts who so successfully fought the scourge up to the time of the war for their prompt assistance in this matter, which could not be otherwise than to their own best interests."[51] Despite British respect for German science, Kleine did face difficulties in 1929 when his proposed trip to Tanzania, hosted by the White Fathers Missionary Society, caught the attention of nationalists at the British Joint East African Board and subsequently the British House of Commons. There was concern that the presence of a German doctor in the British colony would create "confusion in the native mind," given that Kleine was not going as a member of the International Sleeping Sickness Bureau. He was eventually allowed to go, but one British newspaper assured its readers that Kleine was traveling as a private individual and being hosted by missionaries. The article also confirmed that the British government had decided that any research on the disease would continue to be carried out in Entebbe, Uganda, "on a purely British basis."[52]

Although Kleine had to work hard to regain access to the colonies, his experiences prove that it was not impossible. This was in part because the British and Belgians were willing to concede that German scientists still had something to offer the African colonies. The French were less likely to make such concessions; they were adamant that they were better off without German involvement, and they made repeated accusations against the Germans in their scientific and popular publications. In 1924, Doctors Louis Tanon and Eugène Jamot published an article in a prestigious French journal where they claimed that during the war the Germans had "liberated the sick who had been detained in the segregation camps, which facilitated the dissemination of the disease." They also accused the Germans of using the camps to house prisoners of war.[53] In 1929, another article noted that in the prewar period, Germany's "very modest and insufficiently equipped laboratories did not respond to the gravity and the extent of the epidemic."[54] A 1930 article in *Le Temps* made the same assertion, arguing that in Cameroon, Germany had, despite recognizing the problem by 1900, "still waited thirteen years before equipping, on paper, a mission of disease prevention. . . ."[55] Given the praise meted out to the German medical establishment before the war, this revised view of pre-1914 German actions in Africa is particularly striking. Still, not every French doctor was unrelentingly harsh. Gustave Martin, who before the war had been the director of the Brazzaville Pasteur Institute, did criticize Germany's prewar record; he noted, for example, that German doctors had relied on military escorts, implying that the Germans had required the threat of force to carry out sleeping sickness investigations and medical treatment.[56] But Martin was dismissive of some of the other criticisms that his administration and some missionaries leveled at the Germans, noting that many people were "badly informed or ignorant of technical or scientific questions." Although he stated that before the war, "in [German] Cameroon, not all was best in the best of all worlds," he maintained that the Germans had not been much worse than their colleagues in neighboring colonies in responding to what were, in fact, very difficult health care challenges. Martin then revealed his own sensitivities when he noted that "our German colleagues would do well to remember that before they blame the organization of the medical services on neighboring colonies."[57]

Martin's sensitivities about German critiques are revealing: if some German scientists found it difficult to conduct research in their former colonies after the war, their attacks on French colonial governance and their own ambitious plans did not help their cause. Many Germans expressed outrage at French plans to control German Africa, but one senior doctor, writing in early 1918, had already envisioned a "greater German colonial empire in the African tropics" and submitted plans to reorganize health services in territories acquired at Allied expense.[58] The attempts to use Bayer 205 for political gain also enraged the allies. The British newspaper *The Times* reported in 1922 that at a tropical medicine meeting in Hamburg, one speaker had argued that sharing the drug "must be made conditional upon the restoration to Germany of her colonial empire." The article also noted a claim by a former East African official, Dr. Zache, that the discovery of the drug "will be the key of Africa in German hands."[59] British annoyance at German rhetoric is evident in a 1924 article in the *British Medical Journal* where the author commented dryly that "little of the altruism of pure science is discernible in the sentiments expressed at the Hamburg meeting."[60] In any event, German strategies for using Bayer 205 as leverage failed: a French chemist managed to re-create the drug in 1924 and brought out a French version known as Fourneau 309.[61] German drugs were not completely excluded from Africa, but Fourneau 309 became a standard medication, and Bayer lost its leading role in drug therapy research in Africa.

A number of German specialists also added fuel to the fire by making aggressive, relentless, and very public attacks on French strategies for fighting sleeping sickness in Cameroon in the 1920s and 1930s. The steadiest stream of scornful articles came from the pen of the high-ranking Emil Steudel.[62] In one seventeen-page report, Steudel maintained that Allied forces, including infected Africans from the Belgian Congo, had traveled through German colonies and brought the disease to new areas.[63] It still might have been contained, he lamented, but "the German doctors, who were relatively numerous and very zealous in the combating of epidemics, have been removed." Steudel noted that other colonial powers were "not everywhere in the position entirely to fulfill the hygienic responsibilities accruing from them." In Steudel's view, this particular inadequacy applied less to Britain (whose scientists were presented as well intentioned but slightly overextended) than to Belgium, which simply could not cope with "a colony 84 times larger than itself," and especially to France, where officials "were very tardy in adopting practical measures to combat sleeping sickness." He argued that "the French watched the penetration of the epidemic into their colony before the Great War, without raising a finger against it. They devoted little interest, especially in matters of public health, to this colony."[64] Steudel's report also noted:

> The saving of the natives is not only a demand based upon economic reasons, but also a task imposed upon us by civilization, the performance

of which must be considered as a duty of honor of the white races to the primitive natives, and especially as sleeping-sickness first attained its present proportions owing to the increased communication and trade developed by the white race in Africa.[65]

Steudel's words reveal the persistence of the belief that European doctors were engaged in a noble undertaking to save indigenous peoples, and he makes a case for Germany's moral right to continue participating in the project. His report also fits more broadly into the dispute between wartime enemies about Germany's prewar record and its rights within the new political realities of the 1920s and 1930s. Both sides engaged in reinterpretations of the historical record: the allies, motivated by a desire to keep the Germans out, recast Germany as a "barbarous" power, unworthy of participating in the "civilizing" of the tropics. German specialists, whose careers depended on access to colonial centers and participation in the international tropical medicine community, depicted themselves as victims whose exclusion would greatly inhibit campaigns to fight sleeping sickness and other infectious diseases in the colonies. Both sides minimized the transnational realities of the pre-1914 world of colonialism and tropical medicine and obscured what were in fact important similarities between the colonial powers' approaches to health care in Africa before the war.

CONCLUSION

The prewar world of tropical medicine was a competitive one; researchers shared results but guarded secrets, rushed to print their findings before their colleagues could do the same, and cooperated primarily when they were not competing for the same specific opportunities or where the urgency of the problem demanded some forms of collective action. But what had genuinely transcended national rivalries was the idea of a pan-European professional identity and the shared goal of a medical "civilizing mission." After the war, the allies largely excluded Germany from participation in this mission in Africa, and their insistence that Germans were not worthy "civilizers" led to bewilderment and rage among German scientists, who had lost their access to field work. Given the dual blow—the practical loss of fields of research and the accusations of barbarity by the allies—it is worth noting how German tropical medicine and its practitioners were affected in other ways by the "war of words" that continued after 1918.

Most practically, Germany's exclusion from Africa quickened attempts by

German researchers to find new places to forge partnerships. Many looked east. Hamburg scientist Hans Zeiss, for example, won the right to experiment with Bayer 205 on camels in the Soviet Union in the early 1920s.[66] The pioneering work of men like Zeiss opened up new possibilities for partnerships with the Russians.[67] German researchers also worked effectively to strengthen ties with partners in the Dutch colonies, as well as in Turkey and Latin America. Their already established ties to Brazilian specialists also helped them in the postwar years.[68] These friendships helped the Hamburg Institute to survive, but it did limit German sleeping sickness research in particular and did nothing to alleviate the bitterness of some specialists who longed to recover their leading position as researchers and colonizers in Africa.

The difficulties created by the war and the postwar political climate gave right-wing groups, including the Nazis, a strategic opportunity to appeal to German specialists who lamented the loss of the empire and of their personal opportunities. In his postwar appointment at the Military Medical Academy, Hans Ziemann demonstrated his attraction to the idea of restoring Germany's overseas empire. In 1939 he submitted a major report to the government on tropical medicine and colonialism; in his introduction he noted that "all of Germany desires, with a burning interest, the return to us of the colonies that we were robbed of in the peace at Versailles." He then outlined how the medical administration would be organized once the Germans had their African colonies restored to them.[69] Other tropical medicine specialists sought to further their careers by cooperating with the Nazis. Ernst Rodenwaldt, a physician who had served in German Togo before 1914, won posts at Heidelberg and in the military after 1933, gave courses on "racial hygiene," and was appointed surgeon-general during the war. Most notoriously, Claus Schilling carried out malaria experiments on prisoners in the Dachau concentration camp. He was executed after a military trial conducted by the Americans in 1946 found him guilty of war crimes.[70]

German specialists did not respond favorably to Nazism en masse, but it is not surprising that some physicians were attracted to a movement that promised to restore their profession's reputation and their fields for research.[71] More curious is how the Nazis were able to utilize the perceived plight of German tropical medicine experts to further their own agenda among the German population more broadly. This is demonstrated by the film *Germanin*, made by Goebbels's brother-in-law, filmmaker Max Wilhelm Kimmich, in 1942.[72] A gross distortion of Kleine's research and the story of Bayer 205, the film begins with a brilliant German doctor named Achenbach watching helplessly as British troops burn down his African laboratory during World War I. Achenbach returns to Germany, where he discovers a cure for sleeping sickness, but although he is eventually granted permission to test the drug in the British colonies, he faces obtuse resistance from local British officials who obstruct his attempts to bring it to the people. Ultimately both the villainous British commander and Achenbach contract the disease, but there is only one vial of the serum left, so the good German doctor gives it to the unworthy Englishman. The film, which was given an award for "national political value," presents German doctors as civilizers, humanitarians, and noble colonizers, while the British are depicted as insensitive, racist and inhumane. The film is cartoonish in its stereotypes and falsely claims that Germanin was the definitive cure for the disease. Without any nuance, it ignores the complexities of interwar colonial politics and the Germans' own role in creating tensions in the 1920s. More than two decades after the end of World War I, the Nazis were able to capitalize on the German grievance that their participation in a moral global civilizing mission had come to an unfair end due to Allied perfidy. But the Nazis added a new twist: in their version, Germany is presented as the *only* power worthy of bringing civilization through medicine to tropical peoples.

NOTES

This chapter is based on material taken from my book *Networks in Tropical Medicine*; I am grateful to Stanford University Press for permission to use this material.

1. From an anonymous draft of a history of the Bernhard Nocht Institute, "Neubau," n.d. (probably written between 1945 and 1950), Bernhard Nocht Institute Archives, Hamburg (hereafter BNI), 2–115B, Geschichte und Struktur, 1907–1945.

2. On European views about their technological superiority, see Adas, *Machines as the Measure of Men*.

3. See Zimmerman, *Alabama in Africa*; Conrad, *Globalisierung und Nation*; Winseck and Pike, *Communication and Empire*; Lindner, "Imperialism and Globalization" and "Colonialism as a European Project?"

4. See Eckart, *Medizin und Kolonialimperialismus* and, for the British case, Farley, *Bilharzia*.

5. On the origins of tropical medicine, see Worboys, "Germs."

6. German firms with tropical interests included the shipping company Woermann. See Hücking and Launer, *Aus Menschen Neger machen*.

7. On the institute's founding, see Eckart, "Die Anfänge der deutschen Tropenmedizin."

8. John Todd to Rosanna Todd, letter of December 3, 1901, in Todd, *Letters*, 106.

9. John Todd to Rosanna Todd, letters of June 11 and December 12, 1906, in Todd, *Letters*, 255, 260. For more on Koch's life and work, see Christoph Gradmann, *Krankheit im Labor*.

10. British scientists in Uganda, for example, cooperated with Germany's Paul Ehr-

lich in part to further their own ambitions; see Neill, "Paul Ehrlich's Colonial Connections." And the Liverpool school advertised Koch's friendship with his former student, pathologist Henry Edward Annett, to demonstrate the school's international credibility. See Power, *Tropical Medicine in the Twentieth Century*, 22.

11. Schilling, "Die Schulen für Tropenmedizin in England." For his report on his African research, see "Bericht über eine Studienreise nach West-Afrika."

12. Fülleborn, "Reisebericht" and "Bericht über eine Reise," August 1, 1904, Geheimes Staatsarchiv Preußischer Kulturbesitz [GStA PK] I. HA Rep. 76 VIIIB, Kultusministerium. Nr. 4117, Bl. 298–300.

13. Sandwith, "Visit to the Tropical School," and Werner, *Ein Tropenarzt sah Afrika*.

14. Sandwith, "Visit to the Tropical School," 64.

15. Laveran, "Section de médecine tropicale."

16. See letters from Ziemann to Ross, ranging from 1900 to 1905, London School of Hygiene and Tropical Medicine Archives [LSHTM] GB0809 Ross. In an inscription to an offprint he sent to Brumpt, Ziemann wrote, "Übersandt im Auftrage meines in Kamerun weilenden Bruders." Archives de l'Institut Pasteur [FR IP] Fonds Emile Brumpt.

17. Ziemann caused a stir with a British journal article, translated from an earlier German article, entitled "Is Sleeping Sickness of the Negroes an Intoxication or an Infection?" His lectures included "Second Report on Malaria and Mosquitos on the West Coast of Africa" at an international meeting in Paris, referenced in the *Journal of Tropical Medicine* 5 (1902), 309. On Nigeria, Ziemann mentions a research trip to Lagos in a letter to Ross. See letter from Ziemann to Ross, March 5, 1903, LSHTM GB0809 Ross/146/05/24/112.

18. Külz, "Bericht über die Organisation, den Unterricht und die praktische Betätigung der belgischen und französischen Kolonialhygiene," BArch Bundesarchiv Berlin R1001 5994, Bl. 138–182, and "Guinée française und Kamerun."

19. Berichte, Friedrich Karl Kleine, Muansa, June 10, 1909, GStA PK I. HA. Rep. 76 VIIIB Kultusministerium, Nr. 4121, Bl. 2.

20. Letter of thanks from Friedrich Karl Kleine to Alphonse Laveran, Udjidji, March 15, 1910, FR IP SPE.02. See also the Société de pathologie exotique membership lists, including the one in the *Bulletin de la Société de pathologie exotique* 3 (1910) ii–iii, v, viii–ix.

21. Report on Koch's speech in "Dinner to the Delegates of the International Conference on Sleeping Sickness," *Journal of Tropical Medicine and Hygiene* 11 (1908) 127–128.

22. Schilling, "Über den ärztlichen Dienst," 32.

23. Schilling, "Welche Bedeutung," 163.

24. Address of Lord Fitzmaurice, International Conference on Sleeping Sickness, Protocol No. 1, Sitting of Monday, June 17, 1907, London, 6.

25. Both trypanosomes and tsetse flies were identified by Royal Society researchers David Bruce and Aldo Castellani, but there was some controversy as to who would receive the credit. See Boyd, "Sleeping Sickness." Atoxyl was dangerous because it caused blindness in some patients; it was also largely ineffective in treating the disease.

26. The history of sleeping sickness between 1901–1914 in specific territories has

been told in Isobe, *Medizin und Kolonialgesellschaft*; Lyons, *The Colonial Disease*; Hoppe, *Lords of the Fly*; Headrick, *Colonialism, Health and Illness*. For a recent innovative regional study on Eastern Africa, see Webel, "Borderlands of Research."

27. For the impact of Koch's drug therapy trials on African patients, see Eckart, "The Colony as Laboratory" and Gradmann, *Krankheit im Labor*.

28. Although animal experiments carried out by the French researchers showed that the test medications held some promise, this line of research did not end in finding a drug that could be effectively used on human patients. See Steverding, "Development of Drugs," 3.

29. Neill, "Paul Ehrlich's Colonial Connections."

30. For Ehrlich's involvement in the international meeting, see *International Conference on Sleeping Sickness*. London: His Majesty's Stationary Office, 1907. On the British-German agreement, see Treaty Series No. 28, "Agreement and Protocol," signed at London, October 27, 1908.

31. Feldmann, "Betr. Arbeiten," Bukoba, November 26, 1902, GStA PK I. HA Rep. 76 VIIIB Kultusministerium, Nr. 4117, Bl. 55–56.

32. British official (signature not distinguishable) to David Bruce, Entebbe, May 13, 1903, Wellcome Institute Archives [WL] WTI/RST/G 26/19.

33. Stabsarzt Geisler, "Bericht," Molundu, August 24, 1909, BArch R1001 5913, Bl. 155; *Medizinal Berichte*, 1909/1910: 305–307.

34. Kuhn, "Reise des Chefarztes," 1913, BArch R1001 5914, Bl., 324–325.

35. Various expert committees provided advice to the government. Examples include the German Reichs-Gesundheitsrats (Ausschuß für Schiffs- und Tropenhygiene und Unterausschuß für Cholera), later the Reichs-Gesundheitsrats (Unterausschuß für Schlafkrankheit), the British Royal Society, and the French Société de pathologie exotique.

36. For the discussion see Aufzeichnung über die Sitzung des Reichs-Gesundheitsrats (Ausschuß für Schiffs- und Tropenhygiene und Unterausschuß für Cholera) vom 18, November 1907, BArch R1001 5876. The camps were controversial and deeply unpopular with many Africans. For an overview of the British camps, see Hoppe, *Lords of the Fly*.

37. Kuhn, "Reise des Chefarztes," Bl. 327–328. The German prophylactic program and bid for total administrative control was not achieved before 1914, but the French did implement some of these ideas in the postwar period. For more on the French case, see Lachenal, "Le médecin qui voulut être roi."

38. For more on medicine as a "campaign," see Vaughan, *Curing their Ills*.

39. For more on the impact of sleeping sickness measures on patients, see Neill, *Networks in Tropical Medicine*, chs. 4–6; Lyons, *The Colonial Disease*; Bauche, "Medizin und Kolonialismus."

40. Quoted in Lindner, "Imperialism and Globalization," 11.

41. Martin, "Publications diverses sur les colonies allemandes," 56.

42. E. D. Morel discusses Johnston's position in the *African Mail*, October 15, 1915; clipping found in Archives nationales d'outre-mer (hereafter ANOM) FM SG AEF/ii/7.

43. Clifford, *German Colonies*, 113.

44. Great Britain, Foreign Office, *Treatment of Natives in the German Colonies.*

45. Rondet-Saint, *Sur les Routes du Cameroun*, 32–33.

46. Nocht, "Zur Abwehr!" *Sonder-Abdruck*, 101.

47. Emphasis in original. Signed by Professor Dr. Arning, Geheimrat Cuno, F. C. H. Heye, Professor Dr. Nocht, Alfred O'Swald, L. Sanne, Dr. Julius Schlinck, M. Thiel, Max Warburg, and F. H. Witthoefft, "Für das Hamburger Institut," Vertrauliche Denkschrift, Hamburg, August 1921, Nocht Korrespondenz (1902–1932), BNI, 2–1.

48. Mertens, "Chemical Compounds in the Congo," 18–19. I am grateful to Myriam for providing me with a copy of this paper. Bayer 205 was the most effective medication to date, but it did not offer a complete cure. To date, there is no definitive cure for late-stage sleeping sickness, although there are some medications that work on early stage cases. See Hotez, *Forgotten People, Forgotten Diseases.*

49. Mertens, "Chemical Compounds," 18–20; Mertens and Lachenal, "History of Belgian Tropical Medicine."

50. See "Sleeping Sickness Inquiry," *The Times*, May 15, 1925, in BArch R1001 5894; Kleine an das Auswärtiges Amt, Berlin, June 1, 1925, BArch R1001 5894, Bl. 4.

51. Anon, "Sleeping Sickness in the Cameroons," *African World*, May 24, 1930, in BArch R1001 5917 Bl. 215.

52. "Return of Dr. Kleine to East Africa," *The Standard*, January 1929, in BArch R1001 5894, Bl. 115.

53. Tanon and Jamot, "La maladie du sommeil au Cameroun," 1428.

54. Legrand, "La maladie du sommeil au Cameroun," *La Dépêche coloniale*, June 15, 1929, in BArch R1001 5917, Bl. 201–204.

55. "Critiques intéressées," reprinted from *Le Temps*, in BArch R1001 5917, Bl. 216.

56. Martin, *L'existence au Cameroun*, 200–202.

57. Martin, *L'existence au Cameroun*, 205.

58. Zupitza, "Aussichten für die Schlafkrankheitsbekämpfung," January 2, 1918, in BArch R1001 5881, Bl. 32–39.

59. Both speakers are quoted in "Cure of Sleeping Sickness," *The Times*, Friday, August 25, 1922, 7.

60. Pope, "Synthetic Therapeutic Agents," *British Medical Journal*, March 8, 1924, 413.

61. Mertens, "Chemical Compounds," 20.

62. Examples include Steudel, "Die Ärztenot in Afrika"; "Der Mangel an französischen Kolonialärzten."

63. Steudel, "Die afrikanische Schlafkrankheit." There was also an English translation, "The African Sleeping Sickness." Both in BArch R1001 5881.

64. Steudel, "Die afrikanische Schlafkrankheit," Bl. 222–224.

65. Steudel, "Die afrikanische Schlafkrankheit," Bl. 234.

66. Hachten, "How to Win Friends and Influence People."

67. Solomon, "Introduction: Germany, Russia, and Medical Cooperation."

68. In 1922, delegates from these countries attended a Hamburg Tropical Medicine meeting. See "Cure of Sleeping Sickness," *The Times*, Friday, August 25, 1922. For more on the connections between Hamburg and Latin American researchers, see Brahm, "Die Lateinamerikabeziehungen."

69. Ziemann, "Einige Hauptrichtlinien," October 1939, BArch R1001 5641, Bl. 30–31.

70. On Rodenwaldt, see Eckart, "Generalarzt Ernst Rodenwaldt," 210–222. For Schilling, see Eckart and Vondra, "Malaria and World War II."

71. More on tropical medicine and Nazism can be found in Eckart, *Medizin und Kolonialimperialismus*.

72. The film can be viewed at the Internet Archive, http://archive.org/details/1942-Germanin (accessed March 28, 2014). For an interesting analysis of the film and of Nazi visions of Africa, see Hake, "Mapping the Native Body." For more on Kimmich, see Eoin Bourke, "Two Foxes of Glenarvon."

FOUR

Ruling Africa

Science as Sovereignty in the German Colonial Empire and Its Aftermath

ANDREW ZIMMERMAN

The European partition of Africa, given formal sanction at the Berlin West Africa Conference of 1884–1885, is often treated as an expression of exuberant nationalism in which each nation, vying for what Germans would come to call a "place in the sun," sought to outdo the others in sticking their flags in far-flung territories. In fact, it was an expression of exuberant humanitarianism, guaranteed by such state power as the signatories of the General Act of the Berlin Conference were willing to provide. The General Act guaranteed a free flow of commerce along the African coast and in the Congo and Niger Rivers and their tributaries. The signatories also vowed to fight slavery in Africa; "watch over the preservation of the native tribes, and to care for the improvement of the conditions of their moral and material well-being"; guarantee "freedom of conscience and religious toleration" for foreigners and Africans alike; and protect "Christian missionaries, scientists and explorers." The signatories of the act "recognize[d] the obligation to ensure the establishment of authority in the regions occupied by them on the coasts of the African Continent sufficient to protect existing rights, and, as the case may be, freedom of trade and of transit under the conditions agreed upon."[1] "Effective occupation" replaced conquest as a form of land appropriation. Like the signatories of the Covenant of the League of Nations almost thirty-five years later, these powers bound themselves to serve humanity, a service they would carry out through institutions of their particular national states.

"[W]hoever invokes humanity wants to cheat." This was the judgment of Carl Schmitt, the German political theorist who, in his revolt against the terms of the Treaty of Versailles, produced perhaps the most insightful criticisms of imperial sovereignty yet written. "The concept of humanity," he explained, "is an especially useful ideological instrument of imperialist expansion."[2] By 1950, Schmitt would recognize the 1885 Berlin Act as the decisive turning point from the old world order, or *nomos*, of the law of sovereign nation-states, to a new *Nomos of the Earth*, as he called it, in which the "vested rights" of individual states gave way to "the safeguarding of free trade," which for liberals meant "a guarantee of progress, civilization, and freedom."[3] At Versailles the victors of the Great War expelled Germany from the international community defined in the Berlin West Africa Conference, accusing Wilhelm II, the former kaiser, and by implication the whole German state, of "a supreme offence against international morality and the sanctity of treaties." "[I]nternational morality and the sanctity of treaties," in fact, formed the entire content of European sovereignty in Africa, which was, after all, not conquest but rather "effective occupation" to protect humanity, including free trade and other liberal idols, with European military and police power. When taking German territories in Africa, Britain, France, and South Africa acted not from their own sovereignty but rather as administrators of "a sacred trust of civilization."[4]

That Germany had organized the 1884/85 conference from which sprang the international and humanitarian form of sovereignty that would eventually strip it of its colonies and even much of its European territory is only one of the ironies of the Treaty of Versailles. Prior to the outbreak of hostilities in August 1914, the methods by which Germany administered its protectorates in Africa had long served other European powers as models for their own colonial administrations. Already by the 1890s, the foreign admirers of German overseas administration applauded the methods of colonial rule carried out by German states. Generally, these admirers pointed to the relatively generous support given to social and natural scientific researchers in the protectorates as well as to the application of this new knowledge in day-to-day colonial administration. German East Africa, a territory comprising present-day mainland Tanzania as well as Rwanda and Burundi, long served as the best example of this method of colonial administration. British administrators, when they took over Tanganyika territory as part of their share in the "sacred trust of civilization," struggled to maintain the scientific institutions they were allegedly rescuing from German misrule.

Scientific colonization was, in fact, not merely one particular way of administering international, humanitarian sovereignty among others; rather, it was inseparable from this very form of sovereignty. Science has also long been recognized as, in itself, a form of sovereignty.[5] Jeremy Bentham, for example, criticizing the French Declaration of the Rights of Man and Citizen, contrasted the "execrable trash" of French legislation with the "systematic views" of French chemistry that "Europe has beheld with admiration, and adopted with unanimity and gratitude."[6] Writing a century and a half after Bentham, the sociologist of science Joseph Needham wrote "Democracy"—he meant liberalism—"might... almost in a sense be termed that practice of which science is the theory."[7] Scientific law is universal, indifferent to political boundaries, and allowing of no dissent, not because it is tyrannical, but because it is true. Science, in short, corresponded precisely to the new sovereignty proclaimed over Africa in 1885 and exercised in much of the world today. Just as international sovereignty became valid in Africa only, as all recognized, when administered by individual European states with "effective control" over specific territories, so too did science in Africa come to depend on and also support European domination. The Berlin Conference had grasped Africa primarily as freely navigable water, both coastal and riverine, and primarily in its venerable economic role as trading partner with Europe. With the terrestrial expansion of European states, the fluidity of water and commerce gave way to the violence of bounded terrestrial states and European capital. This violence produced what I have called elsewhere state, capital, and science effects.[8] Science was an integral part of colonial sovereignty, a cause and an effect of the permanent violence that constitutes the peace of the state. Germany was a model colonizer in precisely this sense.

Germany initiated its scientific approach to colonialism in East Africa where, with the exception of Zanzibar, there were no long-standing trade relations between Europeans and Africans, such as had existed for centuries in West Africa. East Africa had a thriving economy based on trade networks and plantations managed by Swahili-speaking coastal elites.[9] In West Africa, where European and African merchants had engaged in a brisk coastal trade for centuries, first primarily in gold, then in slaves, and finally, with the gradual abolition of the Atlantic slave trade, in palm oil. By the second half of the nineteenth century, Hamburg merchants played an enormous role, handling nearly a third of all trade between Europe and West Africa by 1880.[10] In East Africa, by contrast, as the great British colonial administrator and writer Frederick Lugard explained in 1893, "there is no staple of commerce—such as the palm-kernel on the West Coast, the clove in Zanzibar, or coffee in Nyasaland," but "there are many articles which may become staples." Lugard found in the paucity of the East African mainland certain advantages. "Our West Coast possessions," he explained, "depend for their returns on the illegal traffic in arms and spirits.... That neither arms, spirits, nor gold are the sources to which we look for revenue is, in my view, one of the greatest advantages of East Africa." Lugard encouraged British administrators of East Africa to follow "our German neighbours," who "have set us an example in the thorough and practical way in which they set about to develop their territories." He praised the expeditions of "experts and scientists, to report on the geology, climate, soil, and vegetation," and the research that led to the establishment of plantations to produce in East Africa the staples that Europeans, rather than Africans, chose.[11]

The Germans understood the difference between the emptiness that Europeans saw in the East African economies they wished to destroy and the plentitude of the plantation crops they would introduce in the region as one between nature and culture. For Germans, culture was not a universal human property but rather the exclusive possession of Europeans and other "historical peoples" or "cultured peoples" (*Kulturvölker*). Africa, as well as most of the rest of the world, was a static realm of nature, including so-called natural peoples. Natural peoples were natural both because they did not change historically and also because they could not transform nature.[12] Colonial states would transform East Africa by cultivating nature, including Africans themselves, with the help of modern science. An expert for the government of German East Africa, writing in 1912, explained the peculiar role that nature played in colonial economies:

> In the more established national economies . . . the factor of production "nature" is of course not excluded, but it does appear to be susceptible to far-reaching influence by capital and labor. This is not the case for this primitive region that is now to be opened up. The entire economic development of a newly acquired country . . . depends upon natural conditions.[13]

While capital and labor ruled nature in "established national economies," in Africa, for this author, nature remained dominant. Thus economic control would mean the control of nature, including "natural peoples," by science, as much as the control of workers by managers.

Germans brought colonial experimentations to East Africa on a scale previously known only in British India and the Dutch East Indies. Cultivating the African landscape meant using agricultural science to introduce sisal and other new crops. Cultivating Africans meant transforming them into sources of commodified labor power for use as a factor of production on capitalist plantations. In the fields of Africa, like the factories of Europe, extracting labor power from living labor meant the discipline of workers.[14] Ernst Vohsen made this point clearly in an 1891 memorandum he prepared for the *Kolonialrat*, an advisory board to the German government on colonial matters, of which he was a leading member. "The current cultural conditions of the mass of Negroes," Vohsen explained, "is not congenial to regular labor such as is required for plantation work. Their needs are small and are satisfied with a small amount of work. Collecting the products with which nature has so richly endowed their land gives them . . . all that they need for survival." Vohsen recommended "education of natives to long-term plantation work," primarily through three-year labor contracts backed by government coercion.[15] Franz Stuhlmann, one of the central figures in official colonial science in East Africa, applauded "the education of the Negro on European plantations," noting that plantation workers arrive "savage" and, in less than a year, "wear white clothes and eat well," eventually leaving the plantation with "new needs and thus with the necessity of working."[16]

German colonial science, like its European counterparts, privileged agriculture both as an object of scientific inquiry, a point of penetration for the political and economic regulation of Africans, and as a model for colonial rule generally. (Medicine was also of great importance, and after World War I, brush-clearing operations to clear tsetse fly infestations also allowed for great political and economic interventions by British authorities in African life.) At the most basic level, the economic innovations that Europeans hoped to introduce in tropical Africa generally involved introducing commercial crops, like sisal, or transforming the cultivation of already existing commercial crops, like cotton and rubber. Agricultural programs also, however, intervened directly in African households, seeking to transform not just what crops grew in African soil but also the gendered division of labor and African relations with European merchant and industrial capital.

German colonial agriculture, like much other colonial and postcolonial agriculture to this day, focused on introducing the plow into African agriculture, which more typically relied on hoe cultivation. Plows, unlike hoes, employed animal power and thus, it was hoped, would increase the area Africans could cultivate. Plows also required Africans to switch from intercropping to fields with neat rows of single crops. Most African agriculturalists mixed many crops in a single field, a system of intercropping that historian Paul Richards has described as "one of the great glories of African science. It is to African agriculture as polyrhythmic drumming is to African music and carving to African art."[17] Because draft animals could not survive the sleeping sickness endemic to much of the continent, African farmers cultivated with hand tools, which did not require neat rows of single crops in fields plowed, planted, and harvested all at once. Interplanting meant that fields constantly produced various crops and were never left to lie fallow and become overgrown with weeds. African fields, though mere overgrown chaos to most European eyes, were in fact intensively farmed and constantly productive.

Europeans hoped that the plow would not merely increase agricultural output and thus the profitability of cash crops but would also introduce patriarchal domesticity into African families. Much agriculture in Africa was carried out by women, which offended the domestic and economic sensibilities of many Europeans. It was widely believed that plow agriculture could only be done by men, thus confining women to the domestic sphere and men to the fields, preventing both from taking part in a range of activities that Europeans found threatening. These included not working at all, wandering long distances as merchants or migrant laborers, competing with European merchants, and generally avoiding state oversight.

From the beginning, agricultural science in German East Africa was bound up with labor discipline and state formation. Founded in 1896, Culture Station Kwai, as it was known, was the first European settlement in the West Usambara Mountains in northern Tanzania. Even just setting the station up extended the effective range of German sovereignty. Kwai not only experimented with crops for European planters in the region but also used what the station manager described as "gentle pressure"—a fuller account, he feared, would be regarded as "a fairy tale or an exaggeration"—to force local Africans to work for local planters.[18] When the government began encouraging Nyamwezi, who commonly worked as migrant laborers throughout East Africa, to settle in the Usambaras and work for planters, Kwai tested the speed at which these workers could perform various tasks, such as clearing land or planting seeds, and determined the cost in wages per hectare.[19] Developing a plantation economy required such experiments in the commodification of labor at least as much as more strictly botanical experiments with agricultural commodities.

The German government in Dar es Salaam reported its efforts to improve indigenous agricultural production and to induce Africans to work on German plantations as "cultural efforts" (*Kulturbestrebungen*).[20] Both civilian administrators and the officers of military outposts were actively involved in improving the "culture" of their areas of operation.[21] German colonial authorities did not understand these cultural efforts as facilitating the autonomous development of Africans but rather as subordinating Africans to state authority so that they might be improved by European science and technology. As Franz Stuhlmann, who held a number of positions in East Africa, including director of the Amani Institute, explained, "the Negro ... although he certainly belongs like us to the human race, does not have in himself the same possibilities for development as do other peoples."[22] Development would thus come exclusively from European direction.

The Amani Institute in the East Usambaras was set up in 1902 to replace Kwai. The original purpose of the institute was to conduct agricultural research and test various tropical plants in experimental fields. The station at Amani employed a German botanist, a chemist, and an entomologist, as well as several hundred African workers to tend experimental fields. Despite intentions that Amani be purely biological, the scientists there found that they could not separate considerations of agricultural research from concerns about indigenous workers. Amani ultimately faced labor shortages similar to those of every East African plantation. To encourage wage labor among the local populations, the Amani Institute set up a savings bank, encouraged the development of a weekly market, and even briefly brought in plantation overseers from Ceylon and Java. Even the apparently "pure" agricultural science of Amani ultimately had to participate in the larger discourse of "elevation" of Africans prevalent in the rest of the colony. Amani soon became a center for a broad range of natural and social scientific research in East Africa.[23]

Amani became one of the premiere institutes of colonial science in the world, rivaling Buitenzorg in Dutch Java and Pusa and Behar in India.[24] Indeed, the scientific director of Amani, Albrecht Zimmermann, had been hired away from the Dutch institute at Buitenzorg. Zimmermann rejected early proposals to have Amani simply assist local plantations and insisted that it pursue questions of a more general scientific nature, though always related to the political-economic concerns of the colony. Robert Koch, who conducted some of his sleeping sickness research at Amani in 1906, was only the most famous of the institute's numerous visitors who pursued science beyond the confines of plantation agriculture.[25] Like Kwai, Amani functioned as a scientific research station, an outpost of governmental authority, and an organ of labor discipline. The government located the Amani Institute in an area with African settlements, which it kept as a "native reserve" and a source of laborers, supplemented with Nyamwezi and other migrant workers.[26] Disciplining African workers was an important function of Amani station, and one potential station officer was rejected when it was learned that he had once been beaten by his own African employees.[27] Amani also advised local planters on labor as well as on botanical questions.[28] Amani and Kwai were hybrid institutions of state, capital, and science. It was from Amani and Kwai that the liberal humanitarianism of the Berlin conference took concrete form in labor discipline and plantation agriculture.

German sovereignty in West Africa utilized the social sciences that emerged in the United States and in Germany to manage the transition from bound to free agricultural labor in each of those countries.[29] Unlike East Africa, West

Africa had enjoyed commercial relations with Europe since the sixteenth century. As palm oil prices declined and European textile industries expanded, every colonial power turned to West Africa as a source of cotton as an industrial raw material. While West Africans had long grown cotton for local textile production, the cotton they cultivated was unsuitable for the mechanized mills of Europe, and the fact that Africans spun and wove kept local cotton from European industry. Germans were the first to export significant quantities of cotton from West Africa to Europe, an achievement they attained by combining forms of coerced—but formally free—agricultural smallholding from both sides of the Atlantic. Employing African American instructors from Tuskegee Institute, the Germans imposed a form of household cotton farming that combined elements of American sharecropping, German cottage tenancy, and the supervised settlement of Prussian "internal colonization." Those involved in the project imagined that they were Americanizing (and improving) the African cotton industry. In fact, their efforts helped deindustrialize West Africa and, where they were successful, brought Africans down to the subordinate status of a range of only nominally free agricultural laborers around the world, including African American sharecroppers. This peasantization program also attacked the extended, polygamous households of Togo, seeking to create the patriarchal monogamous families advocated by colonial states and succeeding, at least, in undercutting the political and economic autonomy afforded by African households.

Colonial policymakers in Togo, like those in Prussia, relied on and contributed to the historical economics developed by Gustav Schmoller and his colleagues in the *Verein für Sozialpolitik*, who had long looked to the United States as a model of controlled free labor that might be applied in Germany to check what Max Weber called "the dark urge for personal freedom."[30] German Togo appeared to many observers an example of free peasant agriculture, although in fact it involved at least as much coercion as the plantations and big colonial science of German East Africa. It was this apparent peasantization that won both German colonialism and Tuskegee Institute the admiration of Congo Reform Association head E. D. Morel, who contrasted peasantized, cotton-producing Togo with the coercion he saw in the Belgian Congo.

The methods of colonization developed around the turn of the century in Togo and in German East Africa became the basis for the national policy proclaimed by Colonial Secretary Bernhard Dernburg during his rise to power in the so-called Hottentot elections of 1906–1907.[31] Supported by an organization of scholars founded and led by Gustav Schmoller, Dernburg offered "scientific colonization" as a response to the Center Party's accusations of brutality. At the most famous speech of the campaign, Dernburg, after a brief introduction by Gustav Schmoller, reminded his audience that Germany, as the "nation of thinkers and poets," had long led other nations in the humanities and social sciences and had more recently taken the lead in applied science and technology. These areas were, the colonial director explained, "the modern means of developing foreign parts of the world, raising up lower cultures, and improving the conditions of life for blacks and whites."[32] He contrasted the new colonization, based on science and technology, with an older model in which merchants sold destructive goods, including liquor and firearms, to indigenous populations without a thought for the long-term welfare of the colony.

This was precisely the contrast that Lugard had drawn between West Coast and East Coast colonialism almost fifteen years earlier, although Dernburg now had equal praise for German efforts on both sides of Africa. The new colonization, Dernburg explained, meant "making useful the earth, its resources, the flora, the fauna, and above all the people for the benefit of the economy of the colonizing nation, which is then obliged to give in return its higher culture, its ethical concepts, its better methods." The old colonialism itself had in fact paved the way for the new scientific colonization, for by continually expanding its exploitation of existing resources such as rubber and ivory, it had directly or indirectly caused the extinction of native animals and plants and forced colonizers to replace them with new, superior varieties.[33] Germans in Africa had improved both humans and agriculture as part of a comprehensive cultivation of nature. Africans would be transformed by attending schools, adopting the language of the colonizer, and taking up "new beliefs, new moral concepts." He declared it "doubtless," though regrettable, that "many native tribes, like many animals, will become extinct in civilization, if they are not to degenerate and become wards of the state." Dernburg, however, hoped to make most of the indigenous populations, like the rest of nature, contribute to the expansion of colonial capital. Such transformations would be fostered by the work of the "missionary, the physician, the railroad, the machine, that is, the advanced theoretical and applied sciences in all areas."[34] Thanks in large part to Dernburg and his scientific and scholarly supporters, the Bülow government reestablished the old coalition of liberals and conservatives against the old *Reichsfeinde*, the Catholics and Social Democrats. Once again, liberals rallied to a *Kulturkampf*, a struggle for *Kultur*, this time not only against Catholics in Germany but also against untamed nature in Africa.

The leading theorist of the Social Democratic Party, Karl Kautsky, objected to colonialism as a form of domination masking itself as development. Writing in 1907, Kautsky explained that capitalism itself, whether in Germany or in

Africa, is "a relationship of control and tutelage." Capitalism, Kautsky explained, turns "the economic freedom of the individual" into "subjection by the fact that one side possesses nothing whilst the other monopolizes the means of production." This monopoly included a monopoly over "cultural resources" so that the class rule of the bourgeoisie gains "the appearance of the rule of culture over barbarism, of select intelligence over . . . 'the great unwashed,' as the English say." The working class could not endorse colonial rule in the name of cultural progress for Africans "without sanctioning its own exploitation and disavowing its own fight for emancipation." Cultural progress, Kautsky warned, "has always occurred against and not through the upper classes."[35] Kautsky's explanation of the position of the Social Democrats gives the lie to assertions that colonial domination, the hypocrisy of the Berlin West Africa Conference and of "scientific colonization," was a European phenomenon. It was a liberal political enterprise and a structural component of turn-of-the-century capitalism.

Dernburg institutionalized his understanding of "scientific colonization" in the Hamburg Colonial Institute, which opened in 1908. The Colonial Institute conceived of itself as an institution of science, unlike either the Colonial School at Witzenhausen or the Seminar for Oriental Languages in Berlin.[36] The Witzenhausen school, modeled, according to its founder, on American agricultural colleges, had been founded in 1899 to train Germans planning to settle abroad as farmers, not necessarily in the German protectorates.[37] These settlers would be, as the school newsletter had it, "German cultural pioneers."[38] At the Seminar for Oriental Languages, which opened in Berlin in 1887, government officials, soldiers, and merchants bound for the colonies could learn the languages of their areas of activity, as well as basic skills necessary to colonial service. Both the Prussian Minister of Culture and the seminar's director, Eduard Sachau, stressed that the teaching of languages in the seminar was not "scientific" but rather "for practical use as tools for goals which lie outside the realm of philology."[39] German texts on African languages tended to present themselves as practical rather than scientific. The practical nature of colonial language instruction at this time meant two things: 1) there was no attempt to connect these language studies to the comparative, historical linguistics pursued in universities; 2) most seminar publications were language primers explicitly addressed to the practical exigencies of colonial rule. Perhaps the most jarring example is the primer that teaches its readers to say "clean my boots!" in the Bo language of Cameroon.[40] Few primers were quite so obvious in their practical orientation, although the exercises assigned in each generally make clear their colonial focus.

In contrast to the Colonial School at Witzenhausen and the Seminar for

Oriental Languages, as well as several smaller institutions of colonial education, the Hamburg Institute was to focus on all aspects of colonization, not just language instruction or agriculture, and would undertake research that its advocates regarded as scientific rather than merely practical.[41] This "colonial science" has, as Erik Grimmer-Solem has shown, emerged as a branch of the social science of the *Verein für Sozialpolitik*, especially in the work of the Gustav Schmoller student and Colonial Institute economist Karl Rathgen.[42] Georg Thilenius, a leading faculty member at the institute, understood it as a realization of the "scientific colonization" that Dernburg had described in his 1907 campaign speech, dealing with "natural science . . . because our immediate task in the colonies is making useful soil, flora, fauna, and humans, that is, natural scientific objects."[43] Understanding the colonies as nature allowed the Hamburg Colonial Institute to unify a practically limitless range of disciplines around a common project of cultivation. Agriculture thus continued as a founding image for the colonial sciences, bringing together disciplines including history, jurisprudence, political science, colonial economics, ethnography, natural sciences, and tropical medicine. Each would form part of a totalizing discourse of the colonies, which would improve, cultivate, and discipline the colonial space, understood as nature.

The scholarly study of Islam was unique among the disciplines identified as colonial sciences at the Hamburg Institute. Rather than contribute to the project of development itself, Islamic studies sought to combat what was regarded as an obstacle to the development that other disciplines offered. Especially in German East Africa, although also in other African colonies, Germans had to compete with Islam as a form of cultural development and empire building. The Hamburg Institute Orientalist Carl Becker founded the journal *Der Islam* in order, in his words, to "free Islam from Oriental philology" so that he might focus on it as a cultural and political obstacle to development in the colonies.[44] Martin Hartmann, a specialist in the study of Islam at the Seminar for Oriental Languages, wrote in Becker's journal: "In Africa, Germany and Islam compete for influence over the natives."[45] Hartmann advocated studying Islam not as a religion but rather as a regionally varying cultural and political system. In doing so he hoped to "strengthen the national thought, since a real, lasting elevation of cultural conditions is only possible on a national basis."[46] To this end, *Der Islam* published articles emphasizing the range of regional diversity in Islamic religion, customs, and laws. The editors sought to treat Islam as a local phenomenon without the universal validity needed to challenge European rule. On one occasion, for example, Becker provided expert testimony for a German court in East Africa, denying the applicability of sharia law to the property of the sultan of Zanzibar, since sharia was "a purely ideal recommendation" and not actual law like Roman or German law.⁴⁷ The study of Islam, rather than seek to develop colonial nature, sought to clear the way for German scientific authority.

During World War I, Germany was cast from its position as model colonizer and transformed into a countermodel justifying the international sovereignty reaffirmed at Versailles. The genocidal war against the Herero and Nama of Southwest Africa (1904–1907), which, according to William Roger Lewis, played only a minor role in public discussions of German colonialism prior to the war, came to replace the Amani Institute of German East Africa and the Tuskegee-run cotton programs of German Togo as the emblem of a peculiarly German colonialism. Colonial liberals like E. D. Morel and John H. Harris, who had advocated transferring the Belgian Congo to Germany before the war, either changed their positions or were silenced.⁴⁸ Belgium, meanwhile, found itself transformed in the discourse of humanitarian internationalism from the brutal ruler of the Congo to the innocent victim of German brutality. Modern imperialism, from the Scramble for Africa to today's neoliberal globalization, has so far justified itself in part as a correction of some earlier, abusive form of European intervention, whether the slave trade, the Belgian Congo, German colonialism, or even the brutality of direct colonial rule. Because of an ideological racism and a structural commitment to political and economic domination by core capitalist countries, colonial powers respond to each atrocity with an ostensibly better racism, better colonialism, rather than an outright rejection of racism or colonialism, thus continuing an often genocidal cycle.⁴⁹ Scientific sovereignty, worked out in exemplary fashion in German Africa, continues to serve as one of the most powerful forms of imperial humanitarianism. The fundamentally racist nature of this humanitarianism finds no better example than in the power chosen to rescue the inhabitants of Southwest Africa from German misrule: South Africa, which imposed its segregationist and, later, apartheid regime on Namibia until Africans themselves expelled these trustees of civilization in 1988.

The Amani Institute occupied a fraught position in the colonial sovereignty that emerged under the League of Nations after World War I. On the one hand, Britain controlled German East Africa—now Tanganyika Territory—as part of the "sacred trust of civilization" created by the League of Nations to rule the territories taken from Germany and the Ottoman Empire, both of which were declared unfit to exercise this trust. On the other hand, Amani had been widely recognized, in the period before the war, as perhaps the greatest institution in Africa exercising precisely the kind of international sovereignty established at the Berlin Conference in 1885 and reaffirmed and expanded by the League of Nations. Thus, the British rejected an early proposal to turn the German scientific station, located in the temperate and scenic Usambara Mountains, into a health resort for colonial officers.[50] British neglect of scientific research at Amani in the years immediately following the war led to official concern that this would give the impression that British administration was less able than the Germans to help Africa, in the words of the director of Kew Gardens, "work out her own agricultural salvation."[51]

The British in fact expanded the reach of the scientific colonization carried out at Amani, reopening the institute in 1927 as a center for scientific experimentation for the entire British region made up by Kenya, Uganda, Zanzibar, Nyasaland, and Zanzibar, as well as Tanganyika Territory.[52] British scientists working for colonial governments in East Africa welcomed the prospect of a less applied colonial science being carried on at Amani, far from the interruptions of practical day-to-day agricultural and other local crises.[53] From the beginning, the unification of these British East African territories scientifically at Amani was part of a drive to bring the East African territories into "closer union," a demand ultimately rejected by the League of Nations as a violation of the terms of the mandate status of Tanganyika Territory.[54] At the close of World War II, some in East Africa again turned to the science carried out at Amani as a rationale of colonial sovereignty under what they expected to be the even more stringent internationalism after the war. The director of Kenya's Central Veterinary Research Institute worried in 1943 that the United States would become more involved in "international trusteeship" than it had been in the interwar period and that Americans would demand "large scale scientific planning of colonial development" of a sort even greater than that carried out at Amani.[55] By World War II, most considered Amani itself to be located unfavorably for such centralized scientific research, but the connection forged at Amani between science and sovereignty continued to play out in British rule in East Africa until independence.[56]

The idea of ruling through science played an important ideological role in imagining and justifying colonial state formation as the exercise of international law rather than territorial annexation. What laws, after all, are more international than the universal laws of science? What laws depend less for their legitimacy upon the consent of the people or things they govern than the objective laws of science? Yet far more important than their ideological function were the practical political and economic routines of colonial governance developed as ruling with science. These included treating—not just imagining—subjugated territory as a natural space to be cultivated, simultaneously introducing new crops, new farming techniques, new family structures, and new forms of labor control. Each of these is as political as it is economic. Indeed, the colonial science carried out at Kwai and Amani in German East Africa or in the cotton program in Togo depended as much on state and capital formation as state and capital formation depended on the newly emerging colonial-scientific disciplines. These disciplines evolved as a component part of the international and asymmetric sovereignty that continues to subject most people around the world to a small political and economic elite, concentrated mostly in the Northern Hemisphere.

NOTES

1. General Act of the Berlin Conference, signed February 26, 1885.
2. Schmitt, *The Concept of the Political*, 54.
3. Schmitt, *Nomos of the Earth*, 219.
4. Treaty of Versailles, signed June 28, 1919, articles 227, 22.
5. Shapin and Schaffer, *Leviathan and the Air-Pump*.
6. Bentham, "Anarchical Fallacies," 489–534, 521.
7. Needham, "On Science and Social Change," 145.
8. Zimmerman, "'What Do You Really Want?'"
9. Glassman, *Feasts and Riot*.
10. Hopkins, *An Economic History of West Africa*, 130; Harding, "Hamburg's West Africa Trade," 363–391.
11. Lugard, *The Rise of Our East African Empire*, vol. 1, 389, 402–403.
12. I discuss the concept of "natural peoples" in Zimmerman, *Anthropology and Antihumanism in Imperial Germany*.
13. Vageler, "Ugogo," 1.
14. There is a well-developed literature on the relation of discipline and the sale of labor power, beginning with Marx, *Capital*, vol. 1, and including Thompson, "Time, Work-Discipline, and Industrial Capitalism," 56–97, and Postone, *Time, Labor, and Social Domination*.
15. Vohsen, "Bericht über die Baumwollenkultur," 7–12.
16. Stuhlmann, *Beiträge zur Kulturgeschichte von Ostafrika*, 874.
17. Richards, "Ecological Change and the Politics of African Land Use," 27.
18. Kulturstation Kwai to the Imperial Government of German East Africa [GEA], "Einiges über die Entwickelung," January 9, 1901, Tanzania National Archives, Dar es Salaam [TNA], G8/37, Bd. 4, Bl. 21–24.
19. "Versuchs-Arbeitern der Kulturstation Kwai," [n.d., but position in file suggests around 1901], TNA, German Records, G8/37, Bl. 25. On Nyamwezi workers in precolonial and colonial Tanzania, see Rockel, "'A Nation of Porters,'" 173–195.
20. See Stuhlmann, "Übersicht über Land- und Forstwirtschaft," 1–23, and "Auszüge aus den Berichten," 205–323. See also the programmatic statements by the editors of

the *Tropenpflanzer* and *Koloniale Rundschau*, such as Wohltmann, "Die wirtschaftliche Entwicklung unserer Kolonien," 53–66; Warburg, "Zum neuen Jahr," 1–22; and Vohsen and Westermann, "Unser Programm," 1–7.

21. See, for example, "Auszüge aus den Jahresberichten," 26–27, 28; "Auszüge aus den Berichten," 216–223.

22. Stuhlmann, *Handwerk und Industrie in Ostafrika*, 84.

23. On Amani Institute, see the reports in *Berichte über Land- und Forstwirtschaft*, 325–329; Zimmermann, "Erster Jahresbericht." For secondary accounts, see Bald and Bald, *Das Forschungsinstitut Amani*; Conte, "Imperial Science, Tropical Ecology," 246–261; and Koponen, *Development for Exploitation*, 252.

24. When the British took over the institute after World War I, the director of Kew Gardens praised it as the most important scientific institute in Africa. D. Prain, Royal Botanic Gardens, Kew [to Milner], June 28, 1920, sent by Milner to Governor H. A. Byatt, August 12, 1920, TNA, Early Secretariat Files, AB 607.

25. Bald and Bald, *Das Forschungsinstitut Amani*, 88.

26. See Amani Institute, note, July 18, 1902, TNA, G8/42, Bl. 94–95; Zimmermann to GEA Government, August 14, 1902, TNA, G8/42, Amani (1902), Bl. 147–148; St. Paul-Illaire et al., *Taschenbuch für Deutsch-Ostafrika*, 331.

27. District officer in Tanga to governor, Dar es Salaam, January 11, 1902, TNA, G8/42, Amani (1902), Bl. 25.

28. See, for example, Zimmermann, "Bericht über die Pflanzungen" (n.d.), copy sent by Zimmermann to GEA Government, January 29, 1913, TNA, G8/163, Bl. 8–12.

29. See Zimmerman, *Alabama in Africa*.

30. Weber, "Entwicklungstendenz," 492–493.

31. Marcia Wright was the first to make this point about East Africa, in "Local Roots of Policy," 621–630.

32. Schmoller, Dernburg, Delbrück, et al., *Reichstagsauflösung und Kolonialpolitik*, 5.

33. Dernburg, *Zielpunkte des Kolonialwesens Deutschen*, 5–9.

34. Dernburg, *Zielpunkte des Kolonialwesens Deutschen*, 9.

35. Kautsky, *Sozialismus und Kolonialpolitik*, 18–20.

36. Pugach, *Africa in Translation*; on the Colonial Institute, see Ruppenthal, *Kolonialismus als Wissenschaft und Technik*.

37. Fabarius, "Ausbildung für den Kolonialdienst," 135–148.

38. *Der deutsche Kulturpionier*.

39. Sachau, *Bericht über die Eröffnung*. See also Sachau, *Bericht über die Wirksamkeit*, in GStA PK, Rep. 89, Nr. 21531, Bl. 50–55 (M); Sachau, *Vorlesungsverzeichnis*; Sachau, *Denkschrift über das Seminar*.

40. Spellenberg, *Die Sprache der Bo*. Although not published until 1922, the text was written in 1912.

41. While the Hamburg Institute did teach languages, the head of language instruction, Carl Meinhof, emphasized that they would be a part of academic linguistics. See Meinhof, "Das Studium der Kolonialsprachen," 1–4.

42. Erik Grimmer-Solem, "The Professors' Africa," 313–347.

43. Thilenius, "Bericht über die Konferenz," May 14, 1907, HStA, 364–6, A I 1, 24–28.

44. Becker, "Der Islam als Problem," 1–21.

45. Hartmann, "Deutschland und der Islam," 72.

46. Hartmann, "Deutschland und der Islam," 84.

47. Becker, "Islamisches und modernes Recht," 169–172.

48. See Louis, "Great Britain and German Expansion," 35. See also Catherine Ann Cline, "Introduction" to Morel, *Truth and the War*. John H. Harris similarly proposed that the Belgian Congo be transferred to Germany to improve colonial government of the region; see Harris, *Dawn in Darkest Africa*, 87–90, 294–303. Lord Cromer endorsed Harris's plan in his preface to *Dawn in Darkest Africa*, viii–xi.

49. Dominick J. Schaller has suggested, in a comparative analysis of the genocide in Southwest Africa and the even more deadly suppression of the Maji Maji uprising in German East Africa, that all colonialism is genocidal. See Schaller, "From Conquest to Genocide," 296–324.

50. Allystre Leechmann, Director, Survey of the Amani Institute, January 23, 1920, TNA, Early Secretariat Files, AB 607.

51. D. Prain, Royal Botanic Gardens, Kew [to Milner], June 28, 1920, sent by Milner to Governor H. A. Byatt, August 12, 1920, TNA, Early Secretariat Files, AB 607. See the similar concerns in White, *Mandates*, and Lugard, *Preface*. Zimmermann, who had headed Amani under the Germans, welcomed British plans to continue work at Amani as a contrast to the general view of Germany as an unfit colonizer; A. Zimmermann, "Erster Jahresbericht."

52. Colonial Office to Treasury, April 15, 1924 (copy), TNA, Early Secretariat Files, AB 607; Colonial Office to Governor Donald Cameron, January 19, 1928, TNA, Secretariat Files, 12209, Provision of Funds for East African Agricultural Research Station at Amani, vol. 2, 1–7.

53. Director of Agriculture (Morogoro), Memorandum on Various Technical Research Activities of Agricultural Departments, March 19, 1935, TNA, Secretariat Files, 21810, vol. 1, "Coordination of Research (Scientific Services) Agricultural Conference," 156–159.

54. Acting Chief Secretary, September 27, 1927, to Comptroller of Customs, Director of Public Works, General Manager of Railways, Director of Medical and Sanitary Services, Secretary for Native Affairs, Director of Agriculture, Director of Veterinary Services, Director of Amani Institute, Officer Commanding Troops, TNA, Secretariat Files, 11283.

55. Director, Central Veterinary Research Institute, Kabete, "The Organisation of Scientific Research in East Africa," July 24, 1943, TNA, Secretariat Files, 28675, 8a.

56. On Amani as unsuitable for centralized East African research, see the memorandum by the Director of Agriculture, Uganda, to the Conference of Governors of British East African Territories, April 3, 1940, TNA, Secretariat Files, 28675, 1. On the politics of closer union, see Mitchell, *African Afterthoughts*, 106–123, and Dumbuya, *Tanganyika under International Mandate*.

FIVE

Who Is Master in the Colony?
Propriety, Honor, and Manliness in German East Africa

HEIKE I. SCHMIDT

At the end of August 1915, the magistrate court in Dar es Salaam declined to investigate the charge against a German settler woman accused of having slandered a colonial government employee.[1] This outcome is certainly not surprising considering that the case was filed at a time when the administration was preoccupied with more important concerns. German East Africa, today Tanzania, had turned into a theater of war and was engaged in land and sea battles with the British army on its borders which, together with its allies, began to take over the territory from March of 1916.[2] What might be seen as remarkable, though, is that the district office indicted the woman in the first place. This particular case was one of at least eight defamation charges filed among the European population resident in Songea, the capital of the district of the same name located in southwestern Tanzania, inhabited by only eight Europeans on the eve of World War I. What this chapter will demonstrate is that tensions and conflict between Germans about questions of honor and propriety in the colony were common and were usually addressed through judicial channels, while paradoxically the colony served also as an experimental playground for alternative lifestyles that were not easily tolerated in the metropole, as has been argued elsewhere.[3] Also important in German East Africa were rumor and gossip, inextricably linked to notions of propriety and honor.[4] The focus here, for reasons of conciseness, is on the latter two normative concepts.[5]

This study argues that the crisis of masculinity in the German metropole manifested itself in a colonial guise, where German men in the colony both were to be undisputed masters carrying themselves with manly honor at all times while at the same time frequently challenging each other's manliness in court. In short, the colonialists, in particular colonial officers, saw propriety and honor as central elements in upholding white civilization, with German manliness at its very core.[6] In the thinking of the time, it was the white man who, from the governor and administrative officers to every male settler, upheld colonial power. Colonialists tended to perceive any suggestion of flaws in Teutonic masculinity as a direct threat to the colonial project. Consequently, disputes about manliness highlight the very frailty of colonial power.

This study hopes to contribute to the new historiography on colonialism and gender by illuminating the complexity of German colonial experiences and practices beyond a simplifying power paradigm or a colonizer-colonized dichotomy that frames the colonial subject as merely victimized by or responding to imperial initiative.[7] This challenge, which has led to a call to investigate mutual flows of knowledge between colony and metropole, so far has produced few studies that show new perspectives on the metropole gained from the colony rather than vice versa.[8] One approach taken here is to examine the everyday life in the colonial household, where the lifeworlds of the colonizer and colonized most intimately intersected. The omnipresent African servants gained detailed knowledge of colonial society while they in turn shaped German practices of honor and propriety. A second and related approach taken here stems from Frederick Cooper's recent observation that empires only became nation-states through the process of decolonization.[9] German identity practices in the colony, deeply rooted in notions of manliness, honor, and propriety, were informed by what Cooper calls "thinking like an empire."[10] Hence in the colony the German man had to be master, and he was prone to use judicial procedure to uphold his manliness to what can only be seen as an absurd extent.

This chapter examines in detail criminal cases heard in German East Africa by the colonial courts. These sources may not be representative, but they certainly dispute the notion that the colonizers involved are merely quarrelsome personalities. More importantly, conflict and dispute, especially in the arenas of court hearings and petitions, can serve as crucial pathways for historians to gain insight into everyday negotiations of identity, power, and status.[11] It should be added that during World War I the governor gave the order to destroy all administrative files. Dozens of dockets survived from the magistrate and appeal courts, which heard cases involving European citizens and Indians as either plaintiffs or defendants, but many files were lost, including all cases heard by the *Eingeborenengerichte* (native courts). At the same time, unlike the judicial procedures of other colonial powers, there is here a wealth of witness material. The quality of the testimony is unique and allows insight into the everyday life in a German colony of a sort granted by no other corpus of sources.[12]

EMPIRE AND MANLINESS

Germany presents an unusually bountiful case study in colonialism, power, and identity, with the country emerging almost simultaneously as an internationally recognized nation-state and as an empire in practice and political stance.[13] This constitutes one reason why the everyday imprint of its colonies in the metropolitan discourse does not compare to that of Britain's or France's of the same time. It has been shown elsewhere that at the turn from the nineteenth to the twentieth century, the latter two countries experienced interplay of continuity and change rooted in their imperial pasts.[14] In contrast, Germany industrialized late and rapidly and traversed a path of restoration, revolution, wars, and territorial competition, which only in 1871 culminated in the unified German nation-state. During the Wilhelmine era, in particular at the turn of the century, the country was characterized by tremendous economic and social change. The mobilization of the labor force, urbanization, the emergence of an ever-strengthening bourgeoisie—numerically, politically, and not least, economically—all contributed to what became known as the social question and the crisis of German masculinity, both seen as part of the crisis of modernity.[15] The paternalism and patronage as well as self-assured autocracy of the aristocratic order was—if not in practice then ideologically—replaced or at least rivaled by capital. Meanwhile, social networks fragmented as industrial labor conditions and hurried urbanization were taking their toll and male identity stumbled into crisis.[16]

German men began to feel that they were losing their bearings at a time of social transformations when formerly clearly delineated lifeworlds of master-and-servant or patron-and-client now merged in the university classroom or officers' mess. In her work on dueling, Ute Frevert has shown that one possible response in the metropole was to provide the "proof of manliness," which resulted in the astounding number of eight thousand duels among university students in the 1890s alone.[17] Having the right to demand satisfaction, an honorable status in society, was still held only by a few. Maybe better than any historian, Theodor Fontane's novels, such as *Irrungen Wirrungen* (1888), *Stine* (1890), *Frau Jenny Treibel* (1892), and the novella *L'Adultera* (1882), are vivid *Sittengemälde* (genre pictures) of Berlin's changing social landscape, an environment many colonial officers were familiar with because they trained at the Seminar for Oriental Languages, which since 1887 had served as a colonial academy at the Friedrich-Wilhelms University (today Humboldt University). A look at the colonies, German East Africa in particular, reveals their similarities with and differences from the metropole.[18] The social diversity of colonial society, together with the inevitably merged social spheres between the classes, led to a situation where conflicts relating to notions of honor and propriety occurred frequently. Such quarrels could, however, not be addressed through duels. Few colonialists had the right of satisfaction; hence, class differences negated reconciliation through a duel, which required shared ideas of reciprocity, civility, and civilization.[19]

In the early years of formal colonization, when the administration successively established military stations in the interior, military officers were commonly aristocrats. Between the German-French wars and World War I, colonial conquest followed by punitive expeditions was a rare opportunity for the second or third son—or even the firstborn of a not-so-well-to-do family—as well as for any young man who wanted to prove himself in battle, encounter combat, and have an honorable career. That, together with the perceived dangers of the "dark continent," proved to be strong pull factors for these aristocrats. However, it appears that they were very well aware of their societal status, and when exploration and combat shifted into military administration, the young officers did not hesitate to demand that the government account for their elevated rank in society.

The question of outfitting the military district stations in the interior of German East Africa provides an example for this sense of entitlement. In 1895 the central government responded to colonial officers' orders for drinking glasses instead of tumblers, as well as champagne glasses, as standard issue.[20] The complete list of requested supplies illustrates a combination of conspicuous consumption and the expectation of a certain comfort level in the living quarters—clearly an expression of the administration's class profile at the time. When the requests came to Governor Wissmann's attention, he responded by pointing out that "pacification" had not sufficiently advanced to elevate the stations in the interior to a level of comfort comparable to the coast's. He continued to emphasize that the officers might consider themselves satisfied with serving the empire and that, after all, though they might face the hardship of being stationed in the interior, they also enjoyed the privilege of participating in hunting expeditions.[21]

It was in the years leading up to the Maji Maji war (1905–1907), a largely anticolonial uprising, that the colonial state almost entirely transitioned to civil administration in German East Africa. Not least because of the demands arising from the increase in personnel, more and more men of bourgeois background who qualified through a law degree or through having attended the colonial academy in Berlin were posted to the colony, at times in high-ranking positions. Though intended as a settler colony, its numbers always remained low, ranging between 1,390 Europeans in 1904 and 4,998 in 1913.[22] The result was a settlement pattern of small European, mostly German, enclaves, presenting a tremendous mix of social backgrounds. Wilhelm Methner, who served as colonial officer in German East Africa from 1902 until Germany lost control of the colony in World War I, was much concerned with the influx of Germans he considered to be of low moral standing. He thought that their behavior sabotaged the colonial effort. Serving as judge at the time, Methner tried a case of a German planter who had been indicted for gross brutality toward his workers. On appeal, the man was sentenced to prison and exiled from the colony. Later, however, he apparently continued his abusive behavior; when laborers on an East Prussian farm complained, he was dismissed and shot himself to death.[23] The building of railway lines spurred the lower classes' influx. The Philip-Holzman Construction Company appears to have been a willing employer of shifty or even previously convicted men. However, the evidence is not sufficient for a substantial statement on the issue.[24]

In 1902 Governor Graf von Götzen issued a circular to all the officers in charge of military stations and posts regarding the state of the colony. He emphasized that it was crucial for colonial officers to seek a pleasant coexistence with the common man—"*mit dem einfachen Mann,*" except for "notorious lowlifes."[25] The governor explained: "Some socializing even with those persons one would not seek at home is necessary. In this regard public interest may require the individual to make personal sacrifices, but that is a necessary burden for those who dedicate themselves to the colonial service, and sacrifices one may make without compromising oneself if one understands one's own standing properly."[26] Governor Götzen continued to emphasize that colonial history showed that those who moved to the colony in order to earn a living were not the most pleasant "elements of society. . . . The common man, who cannot be considered for socializing with officers will, however, always be receptive of a friendly complaisance."[27]

Dar es Salaam, the capital city, was a rare exception to the suffocating smallness and constraints of colonial society; the German presence there made for social life that was in some aspects comparable to the metropole. For European entertainment, there was the German officers' club, a homosocial and class-defined place of leisure; the dinners and parties at the governor's palace, which, depending on the officeholders' countenance, at times included numbers of honorable citizens such as merchants; and the local inn, the Kaiserhof, a place where Europeans of all backgrounds socialized, enjoyed their beer, and also found European sex workers. The focus of this chapter, however, is the more common experience, that of the small enclave and, in particular, the district capital Songea. Slander and libel were apparently common in Dar es Salaam, too, but the small communities were where the full extent of rivalry and class tensions was most manifest.

PROPRIETY: THE MORALE OF APPEARANCES

The narrow-minded insistence on appearances in German small town life is well established. As Berlin and other cities evolved into metropoles of political power, cultural and social experimentation, and economic opportunity for some, it appears that in smaller communities, but also in urban neighborhoods, a sense of insisting on propriety gained exigency. Eric Hobsbawm and others observed that in times of rapid economic, social, political, and technological transformation, nations emerge and traditions are invented.[28] This certainly applies to Germany during the period under investigation. Following Cambridge historian John Lonsdale, a nation can be understood as a moral ethnicity, a community of people who negotiate membership through a continuous, contested debate over civic virtue, over the question of what makes somebody a valuable member of the ethnicity and thus a contributor to social well-being and cohesion. Following this definition, it does not come as a surprise that it was during the rise of nations in early modern Europe when respectability became a societal concept that reflected the changing times.[29] A central "virtue" characterizing the moral ethnicity of Germans in the colony was propriety.

The colonial project was inherently fragile because it featured a small minority facing a large majority of colonized subjects; permanently relying on sheer force and menace was a practical and ideological impossibility. This fracture line became most apparent in the colonial household, whose concern was demonstrating superior civilization, class status, and heteronormativity and which was characterized by daily encounters between colonizer and colonized in the most intimate colonial space.[30] Without disregarding the violence that was part of daily life for colonial subjects, these encounters can be characterized as "colonial intimacy." As I observed elsewhere, their consequences were twofold: first, from the colonizers' perspective it was crucial to keep up appearances at all times, to demonstrate the superiority of their race over all people of color, including the appearance of racial unity and solidarity. Second, it was particularly important to do so in the colonial household, because it was there that the colonized other gained deepest insight into the colonizer's lifeworld.[31]

A case that illustrates the moral corset of propriety that appeared to suffocate German colonial society at times occurred in Morogoro, a district capital, close to Dar es Salaam and located on the first railway line, built between Dar es Salaam and Tanga. The court case reveals that a German woman who felt sexually violated nevertheless upheld propriety over her humiliation. In 1909 Berta Sahm had intercourse with a man she knew, Friedrich Kuhnle, after they got drunk together in her home at the train station. Sahm, married to the railway station master in Morogoro, accused Kuhnle, a train driver, of having intoxicated her in order to commit adultery and of having assaulted her.[32] All protagonists were in their early thirties at the time. Plaintiff and defendant agreed in their testimonies on part of the occurrences. At half past five in the afternoon, Kuhnle had paid Sahm a social visit since she was upset that her husband was away in Dar es Salaam facing a court trial. They chatted and spent the hours until three in the morning drinking together; eventually she invited Kuhnle to spend the night, sleeping on a bench.[33] Their accounts of the following morning differ.

Kuhnle claimed that he awoke and left quietly.[34] Berta Sahm, on the other hand, said that her servant, knocking on the door to be let in, woke her from her drunken stupor. Sahm stated that to her shock she found Kuhnle in bed with her, sucking her breast. After she handed the key for the chicken coop to the servant, she returned to get fully dressed and had to pass Kuhnle who was still lying on the bed. She claimed that on that occasion, Kuhnle grabbed her, put his hand under her slip and had intercourse with her. She emphasized that she did not resist his advances or shout for help because she was weak from alcohol consumption and exhaustion. She merely repeatedly said to him: "Herr Kuhnle, what are you doing?"[35] This is when Sahm's account takes a bizarre turn, considering she claimed he had raped her. "After a short while Kuhnle got up and sat on the bench. We talked about what had happened and I offered him a cup of cocoa which he drank. He said he was sorry and that I should not tell my husband about it. I said he would learn of it anyway because the other train drivers knew perfectly well that he had spent the entire night and they would tell my husband. . . ."[36] Sahm then asked Kuhnle to stay long enough for the next train to pass through because the station would be busy and he had a chance to slip out undetected.[37]

Confronted with Sahm's account, Kuhnle changed his testimony. He insisted that Sahm had encouraged him to keep drinking and stay the night. He agreed that they had slept half-dressed but that in the morning when they woke up, both hung over, it was Sahm who pulled him to bed, saying, "Stay, now it does not matter anymore." At this point, Kuhnle confessed that they had had intercourse, but he insisted that he had assumed that it was consensual and that she did not resist his advances. In response, Sahm admitted that she had been too drunk to remember whether she had encouraged him to spend the night in the first place. The judge then dismissed the charges for lack of evidence, declaring that her testimony could not be trusted.[38]

This is a case where it is impossible to conclusively establish whether the plaintiff was sexually assaulted or not. Both Sahm and Kuhnle agree that she was severely hung over in the morning and that the defendant initially lied. This, together with the tone and content of Sahm's testimony, make it most likely that she was raped by the standards of our time. But it is possible that the distress of her spouse's trial and absence did push her to initiate contact with Kuhnle. Either way, her morning-after vulnerability is striking. She clearly felt violated and humiliated. Nevertheless, she did send her servant away, prepared a cup of hot cocoa, and asked her attacker or illicit lover, depending on what happened, to stay until the morning train arrived to keep up appearances.

The legal understanding of a woman's sexual honor at the time gave European women very limited access to protection from sexual violence. According to §177 of the German penal code, the definition of rape required proof either that a woman put up serious physical resistance or that her attacker had rendered her helpless. Legal experts assumed that women of propriety who were in full control of their mental and physical capacity could almost always fend off unwanted advances.[39] This is also the reason why, despite overwhelming evidence, charges of sexual assault did not lead to an indictment in another case. In the District Kilosa, a German hotel owner accused his own hotel manager, Captain Bender, of having violated a *Missionsbraut* (celibate woman who dedicates her life to the mission). Apparently Bender had boasted the morning after that he had lured the young woman outside town and then coerced her to have intercourse, threatening to reveal to her mission superiors that she had had a male visitor, another hotel guest, in her room the previous night. Bender reenacted for his employer how the young woman fell to her knees, begging him to leave her alone, but said he nevertheless dragged her into the bushes and assaulted her.[40] The judge found that this did not constitute a criminal offense.[41]

The Kilosa case adds to an understanding of German notions of propriety that emphasize that honor was thoroughly gendered both in legal understanding and in societal practice. Here a young woman, who either had met a lover the previous night or might have been assaulted already in the hotel by a guest, was raped and forced to remain silent about the incident because her honor was already compromised. In this case, it was a German male witness who felt that justice had to be pursued. During the proceedings it turned out that Bender had also recounted his exploits to a German planter, but the latter testified, "I would have already filed charges had I not felt sorry for Bender."[42] In other words, the consideration that such a case might harm the reputation of a German man was more important to the planter than knowing of the rape of a young Christian woman who had dedicated her life to the church. In such cases the law was of little assistance to women. The Morogoro and Kilosa cases are merely two examples, but they illustrate the strong sense of propriety at any cost that permeated German colonial society. Not only government officials such as the governor and judges but a cross section of German colonial society was concerned that the other Europeans and—even more important, as the Sahm case illustrates—the servants were not to see any fracture lines in the mask of high morale. This posturing demonstrates the fragility of colonial society with a particularly weak link: German manliness.

DISPUTED MANLINESS

Songea District, located in southwestern Tanzania, had just transitioned to civil administration when the Maji Maji war began in September 1905. The area saw that conflict's most rigorous counterinsurgency campaign, which led to the death or displacement of about 40 percent of the African district population. Typical for German colonialism in East Africa, actual colonial rule began only in 1896 with a punitive expedition that established the town of Songea as the administrative headquarters. The administration's presence coincided with the arrival of German and Swiss Benedictine missionaries, who in 1898 founded the Peramiho mission station, located about sixteen miles from town. The only settler in the district appears to have been John Booth, a farmer and rancher. Other outsiders whose presence contributes to an understanding of the dynamics in the area are coastal traders who identified themselves as Arab. Songea was an ideal location for their interests because the politically dominant local ethnicity in that part of the district, the Wangoni, were a slave-raiding, slave-trading, and slave-owning society.[43] Songea town itself had a very small European population. The three colonial administrators normally present, the district commissioner (DC), the district secretary, and the assistant district secretary, were at times accompanied by wives, although that was a rare exception for this interior station. The administrators were complemented by a coastal Muslim man, a former slave hired by the government to preside over the "native court" and to hear minor matters of dispute among the African population.⁴⁴ Some Indian merchants lived in town, too. The only German businessman was Emil Blohm, a merchant who also ran the town inn. A retired professor from Berlin's prestigious teaching hospital, the Charité, Geheimer Medizinalrat Professor Doctor Beck and his wife decided to abandon the metropole for this location that was rather remote even by German East African standards. At times military officers, too, were temporarily stationed in Songea with units of the colonial army.

The *boma*, the actual administrative headquarters, was a building atop a hill in town. The European houses were located on the slope in front of the *boma*, leading down toward the European cemetery and not far from what became in 1905 the local Maji Maji mass burial place for the executed Wangoni war leaders. The houses were located so close to each other that, after the war, aware of security concerns, Emil Blohm was told that his house was too close to the *boma* and had to be demolished because it blocked the line of fire.⁴⁵ The degree of intimacy in this suffocatingly small colonial world cannot be overemphasized. Nobody could leave the house, sit on the colonial veranda, or frequent the local inn without being seen. This culture of mutual surveillance included African servants, whose omnipresence meant that rumors of goings-on quickly spread through town and that gossip was not contained within colonial society. It was against this background that the German residents filed defamation charges against each other, cases that showed a high degree of both pettiness and helplessness.

On March 5, 1915, Professor Beck accused DC Keudel of slander. The magistrate court judge in Dar es Salaam declined to indict. Beck had accused Keudel of slandering his wife when, sharing a sundowner, Keudel remarked casually that "Your wife certainly has a weakness for Lieutenant Schröder." Beck argued that Keudel must have made the remark on purpose in order to defame his wife in his eyes.⁴⁶ Only a few weeks later, on March 30, Beck filed another case against the DC for slandering his wife. According to the professor, for nine months his wife had been responsible for distributing milk among the European households. Keudel then accused Mrs. Beck of having taken advantage of her position by allotting herself a larger share; he therefore delegated the task to Secretary Peters. Professor Beck considered that a "serious accusation," which had to be followed up with charges.⁴⁷ In contrast in the metropole frequenting a socially diverse bar on the west side of Friedrichstrasse in Berlin was possible, while formal socializing such as evening drinks would usually have taken place only among Germans who viewed each other as social equals. The composition of the administrative staff and the smallness of colonial society, however, led to unusual social encounters, which in turn could cause awkwardness. Here, Beck could not respond to Keudel's perceived affront by asking him for satisfaction; hence he had little choice but to prove his manliness by filing charges, petty as this might appear from today's (and quite possibly even the contemporary) vantage point. At the same time, had he felt more self-assured, Beck could have also let the remarks pass. There is too little in the case files for one to decide whether it was the Becks' character, anything that might have previously happened, or the lack of self-assurance in this new social realm that led to the escalation of a minor incident into a major conflict.

In December 1914, Mrs. Beck publicly stated, "My boys never lie, but the officers here lie . . . they even defraud."[48] She was apparently referring to District Secretary Johannes Peters, who promptly filed charges against her for slander, specifically asking the court not to consider atonement. The district judge, however, gave instructions to attempt reconciliation, and in February 1915, when the case was heard in Songea, Mrs. Beck said that she had spoken wrongly and would never insult Peters. In response, the plaintiff withdrew his charges.[49]

The Becks in turn were also charged with slander. In August 1915 Mrs. Beck got into trouble, again with District Secretary Peters. She was not pleased to find an *askari*, an African policeman, in the process of extinguishing the fire she had ordered to be set to burn the grass around her house right next to the *boma*. Controlled fire was—and is—commonly used to control vermin and keep the fire hazard down and security up. She instructed the *askari* to stop, putting the African man into a difficult situation. He had the choice of angering and being insolent toward a white woman or of defying Peters's orders to put out the fire. He tried to negotiate but abandoned the task when Mrs. Beck became assertive, insisting that she was ordering him to stop and that she would take care of it as she was responsible for the fire. She stated sternly that Peters's order did not matter because, after all, he was not, as the *askari* reported, *bwana mkubwa* (master); he was merely *bwana fedha* (tax collector). She also added that if the *askari* did not leave right away, she would slap him in the face. When the policeman reported the incident to his commander and then to Peters, he was ordered to return but was again chased away by Mrs. Beck. Apparently Peters's wife overheard the exchange.[50]

The issue was taken seriously in Songea. Beck's insult carried a double sneer: any male person of sufficient standing was referred to as *bwana mkubwa*—in Kiswahili, "big man." Specifically, the term at the time could also apply to a slave owner or political ruler. Using the term *bwana fedha*, tax collector, implied that Peters was not a master, merely a servant—in this case a civil servant—and thus derogatory in nature. Questioning a colonial administrator's standing, even if he held a low-ranking position, undermined colonial power. DC Keudel decided to follow juridical procedure rather than take a conciliatory approach. This escalation probably resulted from the fact that the insult happened with several African witnesses to it, and it cannot have helped that during this time no love was lost between the Germans. The Becks might appear to be a particularly litigious couple, but they had compatriots in Songea and throughout the colony who were as prone to engage the judicial system to settle personal conflicts regarding honor and propriety. In sum, these examples illustrate that propriety was on Germans' minds in the colony and that legal proceedings were the chosen means of securing justice even for the smallest infractions.

MASTER AND NATIVE

In his 1902 circular to the military stations and posts, Governor Graf von Götzen emphasized that all Europeans clearly had to be masters in the eyes of the colonial subjects at all times. He explained that while "natives" naturally feared only those who have power, it was dangerous to the colony that they paid *heshima* (respect) to administrative officers and soldiers but not as much to private citizens. Götzen emphasized that the private individual "also belonged to the ruling class." The governor was concerned with sensibilities, and the insistence on honor and propriety was most pronounced when colonial subjects witnessed moral shortcomings or were directly involved in conflicts between colonizers. Götzen emphasized that respectability in the eyes of Africans was important also regarding missionaries, who in addition served a greater good and who with their superior linguistic and ethnographic knowledge could be most useful to the administration.[51] The feared infraction became the center of the so-called Gare War of 1908, between a Catholic priest, Father Joseph Stiegler, and a Protestant pastor, Franz Gliess.[52] This conflict illustrates not only the commonly occurring squabbles between missionaries of different confessions but more importantly the significance given to German men asserting themselves as masters. Reading through the case rhetoric, the connections of manliness, master, and corporal punishment become apparent.

Stiegler and Gliess served on neighboring mission stations in the District Wilhelmsthal, a circumstance that had apparently already caused conflict. Things came to a head on August 24, 1908, when Father Stiegler found that the Protestant station was breaking an agreement that stipulated that music practice had to be restricted to certain hours, because otherwise preaching, teaching, and other activities at the Catholic station Neu-Köln would be affected. Father Stiegler went to investigate and noticed the culprit, a student practicing the trumpet, in African teacher Eliezer's house. Stiegler called the student, Kipingu, outside but he initially refused to comply. Eventually Stiegler went inside and kicked the boy "because he disobeyed a European."[53] Kipingu ran away; when a Catholic teacher, Josef, who had accompanied Stiegler, returned the boy to the priest, he slapped Kipingu in the face "because he kept trying to escape."[54] Kipingu then filed charges against Stiegler for assault.[55]

The preliminary hearings began in September 1908 in Wilhelmsthal with thirty-one-year-old Joseph Stiegler's testimony. He admitted to having kicked and slapped Kipingu. He reasoned that the boy deserved the treatment because he had refused to talk to him. The priest argued that "black insolence towards a European, I think, is something one cannot allow to go on without punishment." Stiegler concluded his testimony, in turn, by filing charges against Kipingu because of his "disrespectful (*unerzogen*) behavior towards a European, and for disturbing school teaching."[56] The Protestants argued their position along the lines of private property and "the right to blow a trumpet" and that Kipingu had not blown it into the direction of the Catholic station.[57] The underlying issue was clearly the long-simmering competition between the confessions. The judge indicted Stiegler for grievous bodily harm because he had no right to enact authority on the Protestant station.

In this context Gliess's reflections on power in the colony are significant. He argued that the squabbles between the missionaries sadly resulted in Africans no longer paying respect to Europeans and added that surely one could understand that Kipingu had run away after being kicked and refused to return when called to do so. The pastor emphasized that "his people considered Father Stiegler ... not a European as other Europeans, but a representative of an assault force (*angreifende Macht*)."[58]

With the indictment, conflicting legal grounds appeared to be laid out, but things took a turn for the worse. The incident escalated into what became known as the Gare War, a self-righteous dispute. Five days after the indictment, on November 16, 1908, Kipingu withdrew his complaint.[59] Still, Stiegler's confession induced the magistrate court at Tanga to hear the case. The judge found the priest guilty and sentenced him to pay fifty marks or spend five days in prison and pay the costs for the court proceedings.[60] Stiegler petitioned for an appeal, and the case was heard by the appeals court in Dar es Salaam in April 1909. In the end, Judge Vortisch passed a lighter sentence of twenty marks or two days' imprisonment.[61] Vortisch found Stiegler guilty of assault because he had no right to inflict corporal punishment on a student of another mission society. The judge listed as aggravating circumstances that Stiegler had the boy returned to him to inflict further punishment and had no immediate reason to forbid the trumpet playing and that such actions endangered the confessional peace. He noted that the trumpet playing served merely instructional purposes, albeit with "shrill dissonances," and that the event had brought about an agreement between the mission stations. The judge continued to also identify mitigating circumstances:

> [Stiegler] is very nervous and irritable, and the blowing of the trumpet caused him to become aggravated so that the punishments were not unreasonable; also kicking appears excusable to the court, because the accused might have interpreted Kipingu's passive behavior as insolence towards him.[62]

Judge Vortisch's opinion is significant in allowing insight into the balancing act of running an effective colonial state. The colonial enterprise was based on an ideology of absolute racial and cultural superiority and juxtaposed all Europeans against all Africans, as clearly shown in his support of Stiegler's right to use violence, even toward a Christian boy. The colonial state struggled to establish and maintain a monopoly of violence through both the *pax colonia* and regulating settlers' use of violence. Therefore, with the colonial judicial system discriminating as to whether a German could consider himself master of all Africans or only of a specific African in a given situation, conflict over corporal punishment between settlers and the colonial state was not uncommon. The main issue of disagreement between the two interest groups was over the means of controlling labor, though those court cases usually involved major incidents of brutality.[63]

Despite this ongoing contestation, part and parcel of German colonial manliness was being master. In his opinion, Vortisch mentioned Stiegler's psychological makeup, his nervousness, which resonates with a major tenet in colonial culture. As I have argued elsewhere, irritability and what was perceived to be abnormal behavior were often explained by the impact of the tropics on the white civilized mind. Instead, it was the constant tension created by the necessity to affirm one's superiority at all times that took its toll.[64] The Europeans in Songea District serve as an example for this common affliction.

By late 1915, the Germans in Songea, vulnerable due to their proximity to the border with Portuguese East Africa and Lake Nyassa, expected the arrival of the Allied forces.[65] Even then disputes continued. In November of that year, District Assistant Secretary Erich Nodoph was sentenced to pay five rupees or spend one day in prison for *"Gebrauch einer Schusswaffe in geschlossener*

Ortschaft," breaking the gun law, because he had shot a stray dog in town.[66] Nodoph appealed and in the end was forced to settle his fine through foreclosure in February 1916.[67] Meanwhile Professor Beck filed his own charges. Nodoph's case must have been the talk of the town; Beck believed that Secretary Peters had reported his own colleague, Nodoph, and that he would be next. Beck decided to do something unprecedented, even in the quarrelsome Songea community: he preemptively charged Peters for *"Missbrauch der Amtsgewalt"* (abuse of his official powers). He reported that he had witnessed Peters himself shoot his gun within the confines of Songea town, as Europeans did, and explained he took action against him in anticipation of Peters's accusing him, Beck, of a gun infraction. Beck insisted *"Gleiches Recht für Alle"* (equal justice for all).[68]

CONCLUSION

This chapter examines a phenomenon apparent in court cases in German East Africa: the widespread defamation accusations between Germans in the colony and concern with propriety and honor, often addressed through judicial channels. The causes for these social tensions and practices of conflict resolution can be found both in the metropole and the inherent friction between power and violence in the colony. The crisis of modernity in Germany manifested itself in part as a crisis of masculinity in the late nineteenth century leading up to World War I. Subsequently, honor and propriety became ever more important in German society, with its rapidly changing social and economic configurations. Small-town life especially was notorious for its narrow-mindedness, with neighbors observing and commenting on each other. This sense of social control also permeated colonial society in German East Africa. The European presence in the colony consisted of tiny white enclaves of German identity. While one might expect a sense of solidarity in a difficult and—especially until after the Maji Maji war (1905–1907)—hostile environment, it appears that often the opposite was the case. In Germany, the middle and upper classes frequently chose the duel for conflict resolution; the outcome could be deadly, but the practice at the same time reinforced shared notions of honor and manliness. In German East Africa, however, settlers and colonial officials articulated class tensions in a discourse of propriety that led to numerous slander cases and often resulted in an exacerbation of conflict. In short, German men in the colony proved their manliness in the courtroom.

In sum, the argument is threefold: First, in the colony, the crisis in German modernity articulated itself in concern over upholding honor and propriety in the name of white civilization, with manliness at its very core. Second, German colonial society was fraught with conflict. Empire exported the German crisis of masculinity into the colony, albeit exacerbated by even closer intermixing of the classes in the workplace and in social situations, but without the outlet available to some in the metropole: dueling. In the colony much of that conflict found an arena in the judicial system through slander and libel cases; rumor and gossip were also widespread. Third, the dispute among Germans of who deserved to be seen as master in the colonial context was mirrored by the fear of African witnesses to lapses of morale among Europeans; hence appearances were important to colonial society. Imperative in this discourse and practice of propriety was the claim of a clear-cut dichotomy between "master" and "native," colonialist and colonial subject, under all circumstances. No fracture line in the facade of colonial authority could be allowed, the difficulty of which was enhanced by the omnipresence of African men and women as labor and servants but also as neighbors and companions. A question that remains is whether the litigious practices served as a safety valve allowing pressure to be released or as an aggravation of intrasocietal stress. Either way, the judicial system leant itself to Beck's passionate claim; justice was to be blind to class and power differences within colonial society: *Gleiches Recht für Alle*.

NOTES

1. Indictment of Mrs. Professor Beck for slander, Ssongea, August 2, 1915; handwritten remark, August 26, 1915, 1, Magistrate Court Dar es Salaam, G21/646, Tanzania National Archives [TNA]. Note that modern spelling is used throughout this article with the exception of citations. During the German colonial period Songea, for example, was spelled Ssongea. All translations from German and Kiswahili into English are mine.

2. For a concise and authoritative treatment of German East Africa as a theater of World War I, see Iliffe, *A Modern History of Tanganyika*, ch. 8.

3. See Stoler, *Carnal Knowledge and Imperial Power*; Aldrich, *Colonialism and Homosexuality*; and Hyam, *Empire and Sexuality*.

4. For a call to connect studies of respectability and the bourgeoisie with German colonial studies as well as a thorough examination of these connections with masculinity, see W. D. Smith, "Colonialism and the Culture of Respectability" and *Consumption and the Makings of Respectability*. See also Stoler, "Making Empire Respectable." The only comprehensive study so far on honor in Africa south of the Sahara, albeit exclusively examining African societies, is Iliffe, *Honour in African History*.

5. For a detailed discussion of rumor, gossip, and defamation in German East Africa, see Schmidt, "Colonial Intimacy."

6. This stands somewhat in contrast to the notion of the housewife as the up-

holder of civilization, fostered in most colonies, in particular through missionaries. See Hunt, "Colonial Fairy Tales." For the role of the German woman in the colony, in particular as an advocate of Germanness, see the detailed study by Wildenthal, *German Women for Empire*, ch. 4, and Bechhaus-Gerst and Leutner, eds., *Frauen in den deutschen Kolonien*.

7. For a useful brief review of the paradigm shifts in the historiography of German colonialism, see Kundrus, "Blind Spots." Kundrus, however, overlooks the fact that studies claiming to examine colonial identities are usually still written in an antiquated mode, at least as far as gender is concerned. Examples are Pesek, *Koloniale Herrschaft in Deutsch-Ostafrika*; and Perras, *Carl Peters and German Imperialism*. For a more vigorous critical stance toward the new colonial history, see Smith, "Colonialism and the Culture of Respectability," 3.

8. See Ballantyne and Burton, eds., *Bodies in Contact*; Hall and Rose, eds., *At Home with the Empire*; Phillips, *Sex, Politics and Empire*; and Thompson, *The Empire Strikes Back?*

9. Cooper discusses a broad range of examples but not the German empire. See Cooper, *Colonialism in Question*, ch. 6.

10. Cooper, *Colonialism in Question*, 188.

11. Peterson, "Morality Plays"; Roberts, *Litigants and Households*; Schmidt, *Peasants, Traders, and Wives*; Chanock, *Law, Custom, and Social Order*.

12. The sudden end of empire with World War I and the impact of defeat led to the immediate rise of colonial nostalgia that colored memoirs and other treatments of colonial experiences written after 1916. See Friedrichsmeyer et al., eds., *The Imperialist Imagination*.

13. Historians debate whether Germany was reluctant to become a colonial power. Gründer, *Geschichte der deutschen Kolonien*; von Strandmann, "Consequences of the Foundation"; and Bade, "Imperial Germany and West Africa."

14. On comparative studies, for Britain: Porter, *The Absent-Minded Imperialists*; Hall, ed., *Cultures of Empire*; for France: Aldrich, *Greater France*; for Germany: with a literary and cultural studies approach, Zantop, *Colonial Fantasies*; Friedrichsmeyer et al., eds., *The Imperialist Imagination*. See also Wildenthal, "Notes on a History."

15. For the social question as a debate over "the intricate links between social and sexual order," see Canning, *Gender History in Practice*, ch. 5.

16. Studies on the crisis of masculinity in Germany tend to be either broadly conceptual or very specific. Bublitz, "Zur Konstruktion von 'Kultur'"; Bublitz, ed., *Das Geschlecht der Moderne*; Hastings, "Fears of a Feminized Church." See also Mosse, *The Image of Man*.

17. Frevert, "The Taming of the Noble Ruffian," 48, 50, 55 and *Men of Honor*. For a new model of middle-class manliness, developed in the gymnastics movement leading up to 1871, see Dencker, "Class and the Construction of the 19th Century German Male Body."

18. For the discussion of German society in other colonies, see Walther, *Creating Germans Abroad*; Zurstrassen, *Ein Stück deutscher Erde schaffen*, esp. ch. 4.

19. Frevert, "Noble Ruffian," 37–39.

20. Wissmann, "Governements-Befehl," No. 41, Dar es Salaam, October 15, 1895, 64, Militärstationen, R1001/1026, German Federal Archives [BArch].

21. Wissmann, "Governements-Befehl," 64.

22. Iliffe, *A Modern History of Tanganyika*, 141.

23. Methner, *Unter drei Gouverneuren*, 25–26.

24. Indictment of the Greek entrepreneur Marras Salvatore for attempted sexual assault and abuse, kilometer 412 of the Central Line, October 1, 1910, G21/686, and indictment of the Assistant District Secretary Heinrich Klemp for sexual assault, Morogoro, August 17, 1900, 45, G21/210, Magistrate Court Dar es Salaam, TNA.

25. Governor von Götzen, "Confidential Circular," Dar es Salaam, July 7, 1902, 100, R1001/1026, BArch.

26. von Götzen, "Confidential Circular."

27. von Götzen, "Confidential Circular."

28. Hobsbawm, "Introduction: Inventing Traditions."

29. Lonsdale, "The Moral Economy of Mau Mau" and "Moral Ethnicity and Political Tribalism." See also Smith, *Consumption and the Makings of Respectability*.

30. Bhabha, "Of Mimicry and Man"; Stoler and Cooper, "Between Metropole and Colony"; Arendt, *On Violence*, 56. Ferdinand Oyono portrays brilliantly that servants knew best the goings-on in the colonial household in his novel *Une vie de boy*, translated as *The Houseboy*, 71.

31. Schmidt, "Colonial Intimacy." Stoler has done pathbreaking work on the colonial household with *Carnal Knowledge and Imperial Power* and *Haunted by Empire*. See also Clancy-Smith and Gouda, eds., *Domesticating the Empire*.

32. Indictment of Friedrich Kuhnle for sexual assault, arrest warrant, Dar es Salaam, August 19, 1909, 2, Magistrate Court Dar es Salaam, G21/256, TNA.

33. Indictment of Friedrich Kuhnle, testimony by Friedrich Kuhnle, August 19, 1909, 4f, and testimony by Bertha Sahm, August 20, 1909, 6f.

34. Indictment of Friedrich Kuhnle, testimony by Friedrich Kuhnle, August 19, 1909, 5.

35. Indictment of Friedrich Kuhnle, testimony by Bertha Sahm, August 20, 1909, 7.

36. Indictment of Friedrich Kuhnle, 7.

37. Indictment of Friedrich Kuhnle, 7.

38. Indictment of Friedrich Kuhnle, testimony by Friedrich Kuhnle, August 20, 1909, 8f, and testimony by Bertha Sahm, August 20, 1909, 9. Otto Sahm's case against Friedrich Kuhnle for adultery was also dismissed; G21/258.

39. Hommen, *Sittlichkeitsverbrechen*, 28, 35.

40. Indictment against Bender for sexual assault, Kilossa, December 16, 1911, 1, Magistrate Court Dar es Salaam, G21/398, TNA.

41. Indictment against Bender for sexual assault, judge's annotation, Dar es Salaam, December 21, 1911, 1.

42. Indictment against Bender for sexual assault.

43. For details on the dynamics between the population groups in the area in the early twentieth century, see Schmidt, "The Maji Maji War."

44. DC Albinus, "Dienstreise im Bezirk Ssongea," Ssongea, November 15, 1904, 10, R1001/234, BArch.

45. Governor to Emil Blohm, Dar es Salaam, August 28, 1912, District Office, Ssongea, G49/13, TNA.

46. Charges by Professor Beck against DC Keudel for slander, March 5, 1915, Magistrate Court Dar es Salaam, G21/613, TNA.

47. Charges by Professor Beck against DC Keudel for slander, March 30, 1915, Magistrate Court Dar es Salaam, G21/613a, TNA.

48. Charges by Johannes Peters against the wife of Professor Beck for slander, December 13, 1914, Magistrate Court Dar es Salaam, G21/901, TNA.

49. Charges by Johannes Peters against the wife of Professor Beck for slander, December 13, 1914, Magistrate Court Dar es Salaam, G21/901, TNA.

50. Preliminary hearing, Ssongea, August 2, 1915, 1–3, G21/646, TNA.

51. Governor von Götzen, confidential circular, 101–102.

52. DC Wilhelmsthal to Magistrate Court Tanga, November 16, 1908, 12, indictment against Father Josef Stiegler for grievous bodily harm, G23/58, TNA.

53. DC Wilhelmsthal to Magistrate Court Tanga, November 16, 1908, 12, indictment against Father Josef Stiegler for grievous bodily harm, testimony Josef Stiegler, Neu-Köln, September 13, 1908, 2f.

54. DC Wilhelmsthal to Magistrate Court Tanga, November 16, 1908, 12, indictment against Father Josef Stiegler for grievous bodily harm, testimony Josef Stiegler, Neu-Köln, September 13, 1908, 2f.

55. DC Wilhelmsthal to Magistrate Court Tanga, November 16, 1908, 12, indictment against Father Josef Stiegler for grievous bodily harm, testimony Josef Stiegler, Neu-Köln, September 13, 1908, 1.

56. DC Wilhelmsthal to Magistrate Court Tanga, November 16, 1908, 12, indictment against Father Josef Stiegler for grievous bodily harm, testimony Josef Stiegler, Neu-Köln, September 13, 1908, 3.

57. DC Wilhelmsthal to Magistrate Court Tanga, November 16, 1908, 12, indictment against Father Josef Stiegler for grievous bodily harm, testimony Franz Gliess, Bungu, September 26, 1908, 4.

58. DC Wilhelmsthal to Magistrate Court Tanga, November 16, 1908, 12, indictment against Father Josef Stiegler for grievous bodily harm, testimony Franz Gliess, Bungu, September 26, 1908, 5.

59. DC Wilhelmsthal to Magistrate Court Tanga, November 16, 1908, 10.

60. DC Wilhelmsthal to Magistrate Court Tanga, November 16, 1908, Judge Fehlen, verdict, Tanga, November 17, 1908, 18f.

61. DC Wilhelmsthal to Magistrate Court Tanga, November 16, 1908, appeals court, Dar es Salaam, verdict, April 28, 1909, 32f.

62. DC Wilhelmsthal to Magistrate Court Tanga, November 16, 1908, appeals court, Dar es Salaam, verdict, April 28, 1909, 33.

63. Schröder, *Prügelstrafe und Züchtigungsrecht*; Achilles, *Prügelstrafe und Züchtigungsrecht*.

64. Schmidt, "Colonial Intimacy."

65. The Allied forces captured Songea District in September 1916. Doerr, ed., *Peramiho 1898–1998*, vol. 1, 83.

66. Indictment against Assistant District Secretary Erich Nodoph, Ssongea, October 14, 1915, 9, Magistrate Court Dar es Salaam, G21/46, TNA.

67. Indictment against Assistant District Secretary Erich Nodoph, testimony Nodoph, February 10, 1916, 2.

68. Charges by Professor Beck against District Secretary Peters for slander, November 3, 1915, Magistrate Court Dar es Salaam, G21/669, TNA.

SIX

A New Imperial Vision?
The Limits of German Colonialism in China

KLAUS MÜHLHAHN

In a 1908 Reichstag speech, Center Party spokesman Mathias Erzberger sharply criticized the expenditure of 110 million Reichsmark for the German leasehold Kiaochow since its founding in 1897. "If the 110 million had been spent in Germany," he remarked, "one could make the finest garden in the world even out of the Mark of Brandenburg."[1] At that time he could not know that the final bill for Kiaochow would run much higher—almost double, in fact, the amount discussed in 1908. Six years later, in 1914, when Kiaochow surrendered to the Japanese Imperial Army, the German Reich had spent at minimum 200 million Reichsmark in Kiaochow, more than in any other German colony. Independently run by the German navy, Kiaochow was distinct in other respects, too. It was, for instance, the only German colony that had a colonial college.

Kiaochow exemplifies the variety of colonial forms in the European overseas empires more generally.[2] Particular forms and unique formations were the rule rather than the exception. Ann Stoler and Carole MacGranahan have argued that "imperial formations neither imagined uniform sorts of rule nor subscribed to uniform vocabularies."[3] Differentiation, particular forms and blurred categories resulted from efforts of active realignment and attempts of continuous reformation and adaptation. The case of Kiaochow is well suited to demonstrate that modern empires were diverse and variable state formations. This flexible adaptation was based on ongoing transfers of ideas, practices and technologies between the metropolitan regions and their far-flung colonies across fixed boundaries and political forms. Colonies were terrains where projects of power and concepts of superiority were not only imposed, but also engaged and contested in the colonies and at home.[4] Circuits of ideas and rhetoric that upheld or subverted colonialism connected metropolitan society to colonial dominions. Alan Lester pointed to the existence of a metropolitan-colonial network of linked sites across which "colonial discourses were made and remade."[5] The effects of imperial rule were thus felt in the European societies as well as in the colonies themselves, albeit to varying degrees and in divergent ways.[6]

This chapter examines the relationship between German colonial authorities and the Chinese population in the colonial society in Kiaochow and in the larger German sphere of influence in the province of Shandong, 1897–1914. In particular, I consider how various actors maneuvered within this particular colonial space, how the dislocation of colonial rule was experienced and modified, and what imprint the colonial state left on local society in Qingdao and Shandong. The German colonial authorities in Qingdao used a variety of new techniques and visions in order to maintain authority and control among the Chinese population. To achieve these goals, colonial authorities had to deal or interact with the Chinese people, making them stakeholders in the imperial order and allowing them to shape the social order in which both they and the German colonists resided.[7]

SEMICOLONIAL FORMATIONS ON THE CHINESE COAST

Since the 1860s, German overseas activists had sought to obtain a naval base on the Chinese coast. The base was to serve as a coaling station for German warships and as an entry point for German businesses to expand into inland China. In East Asia, harbor colonies or colonial bases were perhaps the most prevalent form of colonial rule. Here European adventurers, merchants, or officers encountered sophisticated forms of indigenous governance, highly developed economies, and complex societies that were difficult to penetrate and control. Any territorial settlement by Europeans and long-term direct rule over large territories were quickly deemed unattainable and also undesirable. European powers also confronted determined efforts of defending East Asian empires to retain a core of sovereignty; they managed to hold the foreign powers at bay, despite some signs of weakness and internal crisis.

But small colonial possessions were still useful to European powers as logistical bases for the operation of mercantile fleets and military warships. European powers mainly aimed at obtaining harbor colonies or colonial bases along the seacoast and the major rivers.[8] In China, most colonial bases were leased from the Qing empire for a contractually limited term.[9] European powers sought to establish so-called urban settlements or urban colonies in major Chinese cities and treaty ports. There were roughly twenty settlements in China, the best known being the international settlement in Shanghai.[10]

Settlements, leaseholds, and colonial bases were means rather than ends: to extend influence into the hinterland of a colonial base. In these spheres of foreign influence, the Chinese government typically retained full sovereignty over its subjects but otherwise obliged itself to lend preferential treatment to a foreign government and its nationals. In various treaties, European powers forced the Chinese government to guarantee that their own businesses would be preferred by providing provincial governments with capital, receiving concessions for the construction of railway links or for setting up educational projects. By the turn of the century, a unique imperial formation had emerged on the Chinese coast. Colonial ports under foreign control served as bases for the economic, cultural, and military penetration of a large hinterland region that remained outside direct colonial control.

Western historians of colonialism have rarely discussed the historical specifics of colonial bases or harbor colonies in China and beyond.[11] But Chinese historians have long held that the existence of particular colonial forms was indicative of a special manifestation of colonial rule, which they called semicolonialism, a term describing a transitional state wherein various forms of foreign hegemony coexisted with remnants of formal political sovereignty of the dominated country. Global colonialist and capitalist practices colliding with indigenous local practices created a transitory social formation that was caught between conflicting forces in the global, national, and local realms. The outcome of these transactions was open; it could lead either to independence or full colonization.[12] Rather than a mere step to formal empire, semicolonization in China opened up spaces of resistance against a more expansive form of outside imperial rule.

THE GERMAN COLONIAL SYSTEM IN QINGDAO

The murder of two German missionaries in the prefecture of Caozhou, West Shandong, in November 1897 gave Germany the long-awaited opportunity for the military occupation of the Jiao'ao Bay, in the eastern part of Shandong province. In March 1898, a treaty with China was signed that gave Germany a ninety-nine-year lease of a territory in Jiao'ao Bay. German interests in China were by no means limited to this small territory directly ruled by German colonial authorities. With this treaty Germany also secured rights to build railways, start mining operations in a corridor along the railway lines, and deploy troops in Shandong.[13] Shandong became Germany's primary entry point to the Chinese market. The influential secretary of state of the Naval Ministry, Alfred von Tirpitz, made sure, however, that no other government agency would get authority over Kiaochow. Based on his personal intervention in mid-January 1898, Emperor Wilhelm II placed Kiaochow under the jurisdiction of the Naval Ministry.[14] This was an unusual step, because the ministry was thought to be a purely political office representing the navy's interests and financial claims in the Reichstag. During the whole existence of the German colony, Tirpitz maintained a leading role in all major policy decisions concerning Kiaochow.

In a note dated January 1898, Tirpitz emphasized Kiaochow's importance for the navy. He wrote: "If the navy is on the top of the colonial movement, the colonial successes as well as the results will benefit the navy."[15] Tirpitz's political calculations were right. In March 1898 a German newspaper commented: "The events in Kiaochow and the new hopes for commerce and the missions increased the willingness to make sacrifices for the navy."[16] One month later, in April, the Reichstag finally approved the so-called Tirpitz Plan, which envisioned the building of a large, technologically advanced German naval force. If Tirpitz's overall naval plans loomed very large in his policy toward China and its German colony, he also pursued more general geopolitical goals. In 1896, when he spent a year in China as commander of the German Squadron in East Asia, Tirpitz became convinced that Germany had to move quickly if it wanted to be an actor on the global stage. In private correspondence with his family, he wrote: "The accumulation of giant nations like Panamerica, Greater Britain, the Slavic race or the Mongolian race under the leadership of Japan will destroy or almost extinguish Germany [. . .] in the course of the next century, if Germany does not become a great power outside the borders of the European continent. The imperative basis for that [. . .] is a fleet."[17] Like many contemporaries, especially in the military, Tirpitz had a Darwinistic understanding of modern international relations, seeing it as a fight for survival between nations. He was convinced that colonial bases in combination with a worldwide operating fleet formed the backbone of any global aspirations. This alone could guarantee the survival of the German "race" in the long run. Not economic or diplomatic but, above all, strategic considerations were at the very center of Tirpitz's colonial ambitions for China.

The German colony in China was of highest priority to Tirpitz. From his year there he understood very well the unique structural conditions for colonial possessions in China, conditions that, as we have seen, can be well described as semicolonial. He viewed semicolonial formations not as limitations but as innovative openings for a new, reformed, and advanced type of imperial expansion, one that allowed colonial authorities to avoid the unnecessary costs associated with the maintenance of large territorial dependencies, including territorial defense, maintenance of security over a large indigenous population, dealing with potential rebellions and upheavals, and expenses for large administrations and infrastructures. By limiting itself to a small territory, colonial rule could be intensified, could become more concentrated and more efficient. The hinterland remained outside direct colonial control but was accessible to colonial agents for their economic, political, and cultural projects of domination.

The colonial system that emerged in Kiaochow consistently emphasized the role of the colonial state in supervising and steering the development of the colony. With these considerations in mind, Tirpitz was eager to forestall any possible disruption by local colonizers or domestic political groups. Tirpitz's overpowering role massively limited the powers of the governors of Kiaochow.[18] The governor, who had to come from the ranks of the navy, had to report monthly about important developments within the colony. Every ordinance issued by the governor had to be countersigned by Tirpitz.[19] When governors failed to carry out the policy expected by Tirpitz, they were dismissed.[20] By declaring Kiaochow an imperial "protectorate" (*Kaiserliches Schutzgebiet*) in April 1898, the constitutional organs of the German Reich, such as the Reichstag and Bundestag, were barred from legislating for Kiaochow. Unlike the British crown colony Hong Kong, Kiaochow was under tight supervision by the authorities of the motherland, with little room left for self-government or self-administration.[21]

In building up the colonial economy, Tirpitz and the various governors favored a corporate system. Kiaochow was set up as a free port, duties were charged only for goods that passed through Kiaochow and entered Chinese territory or were exported abroad. Private firms and enterprises were welcome to open local branches or initiate local manufacturing, but they had to apply for various concessions before they were allowed to go into business. There were several guidelines and regulations for businesses. The government also sought to persuade large German enterprises such as Siemens and Krupp to become investors in Kiaochow. But as both were unwilling to make large investments, the colonial authorities ended up running the naval shipyard, harbor operations, the power generator, and most other key industries.[22] They often operated at the expense of small businesses, whose owners, local German entrepreneurs, eventually went out of business.

The role of the state was particularly marked in setting up two key industries that have been described as the central economic reason for the occupation of Kiaochow. The government in Berlin and colonial authorities in Kiaochow formed two major syndicates, for the railway and for mining operations, that were composed of large banks, heavy industries, shipping companies, and trading houses. These syndicates raised capital for two companies established in 1899. The Shandong Railway Company built the railway form Qingdao to Jinan, the provincial capital of Shangdong. The Shandong Mining Company exploited mineral resources along the railway. The companies were obliged to use supplies from Germany, to apply German technologies and standards, to coordinate the price policy with colonial authorities, and finally to yield a part of their profits to the German government.[23]

MANAGING DIFFERENCE IN QINGDAO

Constructing and upholding differences between the colonizers and the colonized has long been identified as an important tenet of colonial rule. Colonialism, contingent on discourses that create otherness and turn differences into hierarchies, implies inequitable treatment, hierarchical relations, and unequal rule. Efforts by authorities in Qingdao to produce and sustain differences between Europeans and Chinese populations were multifold and complex, entailing scientific epistemologies, spatial segregation, and development of a dual legal system.

From the very beginning the colonial administration in Qingdao pursued a policy of creating a segregated colonial space in Qingdao. One of the most important goals was to avoid uncontrolled mingling and mixing of different races or social groups (like soldiers and civilians). The urban plan and several administrative decisions created spatially separated zones for different populations. The European district was home to the colonial administration, European businesses, and the residences of German and European settlers. It was made up of European-style buildings and villas along the southern bays.[24] The streets were wide and bordered by trees and other plants. Many of the buildings were luxurious and lavishly appointed. In 1913, 2,069 Europeans, among them 1,855 Germans, lived there.[25] In the area where Chinese businessmen and the well-to-do lived, called Dabaodao, streets were smaller and the houses less luxurious. Over time some Germans also settled here. Workers and less educated Chinese resided in the new towns of Taidongzhen and Taixizhen that were exclusively for Chinese residents. Building regulations for Dabaodao, Taixizhen, and Taidongzhen allowed for higher building density. The building plans followed checkerboard patterns, with all buildings having the same height and width. In 1913, 53,312 Chinese lived in these districts. There was also the harbor district, which consisted of functional and industrial buildings and dormitories for workers and apprentices.

The civilian administration of Kiaochow consisted of three departments:[26] The governor's office was responsible for the colony's general administration; excluded, however, were all affairs involving the Chinese population. Their affairs were administered by the district office of Qingdao. The district office in Licun was in charge of the Chinese population living in the rural areas outside Qingdao. Both district offices were headed by a commissioner appointed by the governor. While in rural areas the district commissioner tried to avoid any changes in jurisdiction and administration and therefore cooperated with village heads and other traditional community leaders who remained in power, the Qingdao administration issued new regulations for the Chinese population in the urban areas. The relationship between the colonial government and the Chinese subjects in Qingdao was governed by the "Ordinance for Chinese living in the urban area"[27] of June 14, 1900. Its Part B, "Maintenance of Public Order and Security," ruled that Chinese living in Qingdao had to register with the commissioner for Chinese affairs.[28] Chinese were also not allowed to have public gatherings or post notices in public. The most important instruction, however, forbade any Chinese to settle in the European city of Qingdao, supposedly for sanitary reasons.

The segregation of Chinese and Europeans was mainly justified as a "sanitary measure." In medical publications, the Chinese were frequently described as "unclean" and "infectious" because of their "promiscuous" and "unhealthy" way of living.[29]

The legal system was also based fundamentally on the distinction between Chinese and Europeans.[30] The "Governor's Order on the Legal Affairs of the Chinese" (April 15, 1899) created distinct civil and penal laws for the Chinese and for Europeans.[31] In the civil law part, §17 ruled that the local common law should be applied to the "natives" in the rural district. The district commissioners were required to explore and codify local common law for use by the German courts. Lesser litigation cases were to be settled in the traditional way by the village heads. Only if traditional Chinese mediation failed to produce a settlement could the case be brought to the district commissioner, who was then authorized to make a final decision.

In the part on penal law, it was decided (§5) that Chinese law had to be applied to the Chinese population. For that reason, the law code of the Qing dynasty was translated by the district commissioners.[32] Most of the cases involving the Chinese were dealt with by the district commissioners, who were sinologists but had no judicial training. The law was vague and ambiguous. For example, in §5 it was stated that all actions "which constitute an offense" are punishable. There was neither a definition nor an enumeration of what would be considered an offense. This paragraph is an obvious violation of an essential principle of European law: *"nulla poena sine lege"* (no punishment without law). One has to note that there is also no explanation of what kind of offense would trigger what form of punishment. In practice, this meant an offender could be sentenced to severe penalties even for a minor crime.

Lashing was allowed as the most frequent form of punishment for the Chinese but not for Europeans. For minor offenses like spitting or urinating on the street, a policemen could impose a punishment of ten strokes on the spot without any trial. Moreover, the district commissioner was not required to record minutes of the proceedings or to explain his legal reasoning. He merely recorded the sentences in a verdict book.[33] Georg Crusen, the high judge of Kiaochow from 1903 to 1914,[34] wrote several essays on the legal system in Kiaochow. One of the important issues was who, in a legal sense, should be considered a native in Kiaochow. Since the colonial legal system was based on the distinction between natives and Europeans, this matter was very significant. Crusen explained that the natives in Kiaochow "are Chinese in an ethnological-cultural sense."[35] He further explained that "it had to be avoided that German law was applied to people who lack the basis for such an application." He noted that law was related to the cultural standards and values of a people and thus reflected their beliefs and ethics. Only after the modernization of Chinese culture would the "natives" qualify for equal legal treatment with Europeans.

Crusen went on to compare Chinese law with medieval European law. By stressing culture, Crusen did not exclude the possibility of development for China. The colonial power had the mission to help China slowly modernize its culture and law. Parallel to the development of the colony and the improvement of the education of the Chinese population, modern law should be incrementally introduced to the Chinese legal system.[36] This demonstrates that Qingdao's colonial society was fundamentally dependent on postponements and deferrals. The granting of rights and equality was delayed and promised for the future. The emerging legal and social order managed and produced scales of differentiation and gradations of rights.

The colonial society in Qingdao was distinctive. Unlike other German colonies in Africa, Kiaochow was never considered a colony for settlement. Whoever from Germany wanted to settle in the colony had first to apply to the governor of Kiaochow.[37] Only Germans with special skills and experiences in trade, engineering, or construction were allowed to move to Qingdao. The

German society within the colony consisted mainly of soldiers, merchants, professionals, and specialists who had been assigned to fulfill certain tasks. There were few German families or women. The male population sought amusement in sports like tennis and polo. There were also frequent military parades and festivities on the birthday of the royal family. The Chinese population was distinctive, too, as it was mostly formed by sojourners. Merchants and workers lived in Qingdao only seasonally. In the urban areas, too, there were only a few women and families. As a result, prostitution was rampant throughout the whole period of German rule.[38] Within a short time a large Chinese pleasure quarter came into being. Different cultures and social worlds coexisted in Qingdao but were separated by legal and social barriers. Within the colony Chinese and Germans lived in segregated social worlds. There were contacts and interactions between Chinese workers and German businessmen, students and teachers, officials on both sides, but all these interactions unfolded within a framework of difference and asymmetry.

WAR IN SHANDONG

During the first years, from 1898 to 1901, a series of violent conflicts between Germany and China led to a tense situation in and around Kiaochow. Both sides saw themselves caught not only in a military and economic conflict but also in a clash of civilizations. The site of these conflicts was the "sphere of influence" in the hinterland of the colony. This region, with large coal seams in Boshan and Weixian along the proposed railway line from Qingdao to Jinan, represented the focus of German economic interests. The construction of the railway and the mining operations were not only expected to become profitable enterprises; their quick completion was also seen as a precondition for Kiaochow's overall development. Every delay would cause losses for the companies and delay the economic development of the colony.

From the start, however, the German companies encountered numerous problems. Peasants were unwilling to sell their land because they were not satisfied with German offers. Despite protests, the companies decided to continue construction, even if some plots of the land had not been bought. This policy antagonized the rural population. It took only a minor incident, like a small dispute between a local peasant and German railway worker at a market in Dalü, to ignite an outbreak of violence. Angry peasants gathered and decided to stop the railway workers from continuing their work.[39] As news of a popular unrest spread to Qingdao, the governor of Kiaochow, Jaeschke, decided "to teach the peasants a lesson." He swiftly ordered about a hundred soldiers to move to Dalü and nearby Tidong to quell the unrest. The troops stormed three villages, killing twenty-five people.[40]

Following these events, German soldiers occupied the city of Gaomi for two weeks. Here an incident occurred that drew the attention of officials all over China. Gaomi was the seat of the local magistrate. A relatively wealthy city, it was well known for its high number of successful literati and degree holders.[41] Many houses displayed signs of academic honors or official appointments. The German troops took up quarter in the academy (*shu yuan*) of Gaomi, which housed a famous library. On leaving Gaomi, German soldiers destroyed the academy and burned the books of the library.[42] The auto-da-fé of Confucian classics symbolized the widespread belief among Germans in Qingdao that more was at stake in the conflict than the mere construction of a railway line. Colonial authorities saw themselves in the midst of a war against not only rebellious peasants but Chinese civilization in general. As they saw it, the enlightened, progressive civilization of the West faced the challenge of overcoming the backward Confucian civilization, if necessary with arms. In 1900 Jaeschke wrote to Berlin: "In China there is at the moment a fierce struggle between two different ideologies: the national Chinese Weltanschauung, which rests on centuries-old traditions, and the cosmopolitan occidental Weltanschauung."[43]

Chinese resistance continued. Peasants repeatedly removed surveyors' rods. In the spring of 1900 a new conflict arose. In the lowlands of the Haoli district north of Gaomi, the population feared that the railway would block the delicate drainage systems of the lowlands and cause floods. But the railway company portrayed these fears as a mere pretext to prevent the construction of the railway at all.[44] Again, the company urged the governor to resort to military measures to protect the construction. In the meantime, the people of Haoli invited leaders of the spreading Boxer movement to teach them their fighting techniques and magic. The Boxers, too, saw the war in Shandong in terms of a clash between civilizations. For them, the presence of foreigners and especially the construction of the railway angered the ancestors and gods. The Boxers believed that this was the real reason behind the drought and other natural calamities that had hit Shandong in recent years.[45] Facing the rapid spread of the Boxers over northern China, the growing attacks on foreigners, and the declaration of war by the Qing dynasty,[46] the colonial authorities decided to retreat for the time being. Jaeschke ordered all German personnel back to Qingdao. The railway construction was stopped. The peasants of Haoli celebrated their victory.

The situation changed with the arrival of an international relief force. In September 1900, under the command of Count von Waldersee, sizable German reinforcements disembarked at Tianjin. On October 6 and 7, Waldersee and Jaeschke met in Tianjin to discuss further German military actions in China. They agreed on the need to quickly suppress the Chinese resistance in the hinterland of Kiaochow to avoid further delays in the railway construction. They authorized German troops to carry out so-called punitive actions, not only against the Boxers themselves but also against the Chinese civilian population, which supposedly provided support to the insurgency. On October 23 and November 1, three villages were taken under artillery fire and destroyed. More than 450 people were killed, among them many women and children.[47]

Through these aggressive campaigns and punitive actions, German colonial authorities succeeded in quelling resistance to the colonial power in and around Qingdao. They also demonstrated their determination to extend German sovereignty beyond the colony's borders. Permanent barracks were built in Jiaozhou and Gaomi so that both were located within the German sphere of interest. German troops stayed there until 1905. The colonial project thus extended beyond the borders of the colony. It made use of a number of innovative arrangements: partial sovereignty, temporary occupations, limited incursions, and punitive strikes against selected targets. All this points to the production and proliferation of geopolitical ambiguities as new and innovative forms of maintaining control without direct territorial occupation.

QINGDAO AS A COLONIAL CONTACT ZONE

Colonies were not simply constructs of power projected unilaterally on a local population; they also became "zones of contact" between colonizers and the colonized. Although colonies were sites of asymmetrical relations, they hosted widely divergent local arrangements whereby different strategies were promoted by different social groups. Tensions and conflicts emerged not only between colonizers and colonized but also between different German and Chinese groups.[48]

For Chinese authorities, the violent conflicts between the population and the foreigners represented a crucial factor for the spread of social instability during the Boxer movement. After 1900, Chinese officials pursued a strategy of de-escalation. Governor Yuan Shikai and his most important successors, Zhou Fu and Yang Shixiang, developed a "new policy," which tried to establish communications in order to negotiate with the German colonial administration. Starting in 1902 there were regular visits by the governor of Shandong to Kiaochow. Lower civil and military Chinese officials also started to visit Qingdao frequently. Zhou Fu, who was the first Chinese governor to visit Kiaochow, described the construction projects and the enormous amount of money the German administration was investing in a memorial.[49] Many other Chinese visitors expressed a similar admiration for the German efforts. Another equally important intention was to protect the Chinese population in Qingdao. In 1902, Zhou Fu reported that he had sent agents to Kiaochow for restoring the *baojia* system (an organization of households in a local community for welfare provision and social control).[50] In this way the interests of the Chinese population could be defended against the colonial authorities, but at the same time this insured that spontaneous resistance was also discouraged. Chinese and German officials were both concerned about possible unplanned and uncontrolled actions by Kiaochow's Chinese population.

When German authorities noticed the Chinese efforts to reestablish informal structures of control over the Chinese population, Governor Oskar von Truppel was alarmed. When he met with the Chinese governor Zhou Fu, Truppel stated the German position that the Chinese population was subject to the German colonial authorities. Zhou Fu disagreed. He explained that the "Chinese people in Qingdao still belonged to their families and clans, they therefore were still under Chinese law, and should and must seek help from there."[51] He demanded the establishment of Chinese representatives who would represent Chinese interests and deal with the Germans. Zhou Fu also said: "Although the territory of Qingdao is leased to Germany, it is still Shandong earth." The question of who asserted control over the population in Qingdao continued to be the source of conflicts between German and Chinese authorities. Despite German objections, Chinese officials felt responsible for the population in Qingdao. Excellent relations existed between the merchants in Qingdao and the officials in Jinan. In particular, after the completion of the railway in 1904, educated, well-off Chinese traders and business people interested in taking advantage of the facilities built by the colonial government came to Qingdao. Many of them possessed official ranks.[52] The Chinese merchants in Qingdao soon wanted to participate in the colonial administration. After lengthy negotiations, Truppel approved the demand by Chinese guilds to form a committee in 1902.[53] The so-called Chinese Committee was allowed to comment on specific economic questions. Members of the committee were elected by the merchants through votes in the guilds. While the German administration wanted the Chinese merchants to bear responsibility for certain decisions, the committee became powerful and self-confident over time. In 1908 the committee felt strong enough to organize a boycott and protest against the colonial administration. The cause was a rise in depot tariffs in the harbor. The Chinese Committee succeeded in mobilizing almost the entire Chinese population to stop buying German goods and visiting German stores. Only after the tariff hike was rescinded did the committee agree to end the boycott. Recalling the conflict of 1908, the German governor stated with disappointment: "The population still feels and thinks Chinese."[54] Because of these events, the Chinese Committee was dissolved in 1910 and replaced by Chinese counselors who were appointed by the governor.

While antagonism between Germans and Chinese remained in place, their relations in Qingdao also became more cooperative and constructive. A jointly operated German-Chinese college was founded in Qingdao in 1909. It had a German director and a Chinese inspector. Students were selected by the Chinese government. Western education by German teachers in the morning was supplemented by teachings in the Confucian classics by Chinese instructors in the afternoon. The changing political climate in China was a factor in the establishment of the school. After the fall of the Qing dynasty in 1911, many former Qing officials fled to the German leasehold and purchased homes there.[55] They sent their children to German schools.

Like its predecessor, the new republican government was interested in maintaining peaceful relations with the German colony. In September 1912, much to the surprise of the German authorities, Sun Yat-sen, the former president, indicated that he would like to visit Kiaochow. Since Germany had not even officially recognized the Chinese Republic, the colonial authorities in Qingdao had very mixed feelings about this proposition. They decided to treat Sun's visit as a private endeavor and refrain from any official reception. When the approximately four hundred Chinese students in Qingdao heard of the upcoming visit, they immediately agreed to give Sun a public reception at the Chinese theater in Dabaodao. Upon learning about this, the German government tried to keep students from attending. The German director of the college maintained that the reception was a political event in which, according to the school regulations, students were not allowed to participate. The students responded by sending back their student IDs. Thus tensions were running high when Sun Yat-sen finally arrived in Qingdao on October 2. Urging the students to end their protest and go back to school, he explained that students had to serve their country and could not fully enjoy all the freedoms granted by the new republic. On his second day he paid a visit to the college. In a speech to the students, he called Kiaochow a "model settlement for China."[56] He continued: "In three thousand years, China has not achieved what Germany did in Kiaochow within fifteen years." He was so impressed that he later read the book of Commissioner Schrameier about the land system in Kiaochow. In 1924, he invited Schrameier to Canton (now Guangzhou) to work out a land policy for Guangdong province. In interviews he gave after his visit, no mention was made of any discrimination or mistreatment of the Chinese in Kiaochow, nor did he speak of the loss of rights or sovereignty.

In the beginning, the occupation of Kiaochow was met with fierce Chinese resistance. Boycotts and protests, as well as violent upheavals in the surrounding areas, document the resentment against the foreign occupation in the first years of German rule. In later years, relations with the Chinese population improved somewhat, as the colonial authorities were more willing to give Chinese representatives a say in the colony's economic affairs. After the completion of major infrastructure construction in the colony and the hinterland (railway, mines, harbor) around 1907, an economic upswing began; it started to transform the colony into a busy marketplace connecting the hinterland to national and international markets reaching from East Asia to Europe. By 1914, Kiaochow had indeed become an evolving imperial outpost where segregation and discrimination were practiced but where at the same time contacts, cooperation, and exchanges began to undermine the legal and political barriers erected by German colonial authorities.

CONCLUSION

The German colony Kiaochow was an example of a new form of imperial rule, one that operated outside the framework of the classical colonial model built on territorial control and bounded space.[57] "Nation building" and developmentalism went hand in hand with extensive territorial rule in the classical imperial vision that flourished in the nineteenth century. But instead of control over and development of a large dependent territory, colonial authorities in Qingdao limited their efforts to building a colonial base there from which a larger informal colonial presence in the hinterland was erected and maintained. This form of colonialism was less expansionist and territorial than intensive and concentrated. In his work on Japanese-controlled Manchukuo, Prasenjit Duara describes this phenomenon as "new imperialism."[58] Imperialism has thus moved in a different direction, weakening the link between empire and nation building. While this shift has been most starkly evident since the Cold War, it originated earlier. To be sure, great powers continued to abridge the sovereignty of others, often by force or threat of force. Twentieth-century empires still invoked a rationale of benevolent transformation, but the nature of the rationale had changed. As a result, the imperial vision of the new imperialism was quite different from earlier imperial visions. The new imperial vision was much more global yet made fewer commitments involving any particular place.

Qingdao also reveals the transformative possibilities of an evolving colonial space. In Qingdao, the colonial society continued to emerge and change; through migration, exile, and trade it became a complex, highly diffuse zone of contact. The semicolonial situation produced a broad range of liminal identities and collaborations that thrived in its ambivalent circumstances. "Zone of contact" as a term connotes an area where "foci of cultural contact in a zone of dispute" can stimulate "cultural dissonance,"[59] as well as more open forms of conflict and cooperation. Within these contact zones, colonial agency was produced, attracted, contended with, and negotiated among various Chinese social groups and networks. Qingdao was a colonial base for the projection of German power in East Asia, but it also became a fluid zone of contact between cultures and a place where experiments in commerce and communication emerged. These developments challenged the colonial power to move beyond the formal colonialism of the previous century as the German Reich competed to control global resources.

Frederic Cooper advocates thinking about multiple colonialisms so as "not to diminish the importance of the specific forms of colonization" and to enable precise analysis of colonial processes.[60] The semicolonial condition in China challenged German authorities to rethink and reform imperial policies. A more flexible form of empire emerged that was more efficient, more dynamic, and less violent. Despite the fact that this colony was small and short lived, it marks a significant conceptual change in the history of empire. Kiaochow signaled a far-reaching transition in imperial forms, from direct control over territory to a flexible deterritorialized form of domination that cultivates imperial connections to noncitizen subjects in ambivalent and opaque circumstances.

NOTES

1. Quoted in Schrecker, *Imperialism and Chinese Nationalism*, 220.
2. Steinmetz, *The Devil's Handwriting*, 5ff. 19ff.
3. Stoler and MacGranahan, "Refiguring Imperial Terrains," 23.
4. See Cooper, *Colonialism in Question*, 3–32.
5. Lester, *Imperial Networks*, 5–7.
6. See Prakash, *Another Reason*.
7. Berman, Mühlhahn, and Nganang, *German Colonialism Revisited*, 1–28.
8. Osterhammel, "Lemmata."
9. Five leaseholds were established by European powers: Guangzhouwan (1898, Guangdong Province) by France; Weihaiwei (1898, Shandong Province) by Great Britain; Jiaozhou (1898, Shandong Province) by the German Reich; Kowloon/Jiulong (1898, next to Hong Kong in Guangdong Province) by Great Britain; Dalian (1896) and Port Arthur/Lüshun (1898, Manchuria) by the Russian czarist empire.

10. There were only two instances where this occurred: Hong Kong was ceded to Great Britain in the Treaty of Nanjing (1842) and Taiwan went to Japan in 1895.

11. Osterhammel, *Kolonialismus*, 15ff; and Osterhammel, "Semicolonialism and Informal Empire."

12. Karl, "On Comparability and Continuity."

13. Schrecker, *Imperialism and Chinese Nationalism*; Seeleman, *Social and Economic Development*; Shouzhong, *Deguo qinlüe Shandongshi*; Stichler, *Das Gouvernement Jiaozhou*; Leutner and Mühlhahn, *Musterkolonie Kiautschou*; Biener, *Das deutsche Pachtgebiet Tsingtau*; Steinmetz, *The Devil's Handwriting*, 433–508. Shorter overviews are Zhang, *Qingdao de shili juan*; Henderson, *The German Colonial Empire*.

14. See Documents 42 and 43 in Leutner and Mühlhahn, *Musterkolonie Kiautschou*, 181–184.

15. Note Tirpitz, January 1898, BArch/MA, RM3/6699, Bl. 1–11.

16. Centrumskorrespondenz, March 2, 1898, quoted in Canis, *Von Bismarck zur Weltpolitik*, 273.

17. Quoted in Deist, *Flottenpolitik und Flottenpropaganda*, 111.

18. Kiaochow had four governors: Oskar Truppel (1897–1899; 1901–1911), Carl Rosendahl (1898–1899), Paul Jaeschke (1899–1901), Alfred Meyer-Waldeck (1911–1914).

19. Mühlhahn, *Herrschaft und Widerstand*, 204–205.

20. This happened to Governor Rosendahl in 1898 because Tirpitz felt that he had neglected the economic development, see Tirpitz to Wilhelm II, October 7, 1898, in BArch/MA, RM2/1837, Bl. 126–128, in Leutner and Mühlhahn, *Musterkolonie Kiautschou*, 352–353. It happened to Governor Truppel in 1910, too, when he failed to support the German-Chinese College. See Pyenson, *Cultural Imperialism and Exact Sciences*, 258.

21. Hövermann, *Kiautschou*, 29; Biener, *Das deutsche Pachtgebiet Tsingtau*, 209, 213–214.

22. Mühlhahn, *Herrschaft und Widerstand*, 143–146.

23. Schmidt, *Die deutsche Eisenbahnpolitik in Shantung*, 65–66.

24. See Warner, "Aufbau der Kolonialstadt Tsingtau," 89.

25. Throughout the period 1897–1914, the German population of Qingdao remained relatively small. German military personnel amounted to only 2,400; see Mohr, *Handbuch für das Schutzgebiet Kiautschou*, 442, and Leutner and Mühlhahn, *Musterkolonie Kiautschou*, 238–239.

26. Norem, *Kiaochow Leased Territory*, 107ff., and Schrecker, *Imperialism and Chinese Nationalism*, 70f., were among the few who paid attention to this feature of Kiaochow.

27. See Leutner and Mühlhahn, *Musterkolonie Kiautschou*, 213–218, and Mohr, *Handbuch für das Schutzgebiet Kiautschou*, 22–29.

28. There was in fact only one "commissioner for Chinese affairs." The translator and sinologist Wilhelm Schrameier was commissioner from December 1897 to January 1909. After his departure, the tasks were given to the civil commissioner (Zivilkommissar); see Biener, *Das deutsche Pachtgebiet Tsingtau*, 216.

29. Uthemann and Fürth, *Tsingtau*, 35–36; Kronecker, *15 Jahre Kiautschou*.

30. Seeleman, *Social and Economic Development*, 76–96.

31. Ordinance concerning the legal position of the Chinese population, April 15, 1899; see Mohr, *Handbuch für das Schutzgebiet Kiautschou*, 72–77.

32. For an overview, see Krebs, "Chinesisches Strafrecht."

33. On the legal system, see Steinmetz, *The Devil's Handwriting*, 452ff., and Mühlhahn, "Staatsgewalt und Disziplin."

34. For biographical details on Crusen, see Degener, *Wer ist's?*, 268–269.

35. Crusen, "Die rechtliche Stellung der Chinesen," 5.

36. See Crusen, "Moderne Gedanken im Chinesenstrafrecht," 142.

37. In a letter to the chief of the naval cabinet, Senden-Bibran, the secretary of state of the Naval Ministry, Alfred von Tirpitz, stressed that everybody has to make an application before settling in Qingdao; Tirpitz to Senden-Bibran, June 2, 1898, BArch/MA, RM 2/1836, fol. 237.

38. See Eckart, *Deutsche Ärzte in China*, 31–33.

39. Ge Zhitan to Yu Xian, June 20, 1899, FHA 5012/0–2, Nr. 292.

40. See Leutner and Mühlhahn, *Musterkolonie Kiautschou*, 248.

41. Sixty percent of the degree holders of Shandong came from Gaomi or Jiaozhou; see Esherick, *The Origins of the Boxer Uprising*, 30, and Zhengjian, *Qingdao*, 1.

42. Ge Zhitan to Yu Xian, July 3, 1899, FHA 501/0–2, Nr. 292.

43. Memorial of Governor Jaeschke, October 9, 1900, BArch/MA, RM3/6782, Bl. 276–308.

44. The fears of the Chinese population proved right. In 1902 the whole region was flooded, destroying the year's harvest and washing away whole villages. The German governor sent a specialist in the Haoli district to investigate the causes. See report of engineer Born to Governor Truppel, September 4, 1902, in Leutner and Mühlhahn, *Musterkolonie Kiautschou*, 300–302.

45. See Cohen, *History in Three Keys*, 84–85.

46. Cohen, *History in Three Keys*, 14–56.

47. See Leutner and Mühlhahn, *Musterkolonie Kiautschou*, 250.

48. For reasons of space I cannot elaborate on the role of gender and sex. Gender and sexuality are important and contested issues in the colonial contact zone. It provides a glimpse into the impact colonialism had on the everyday lives of local women and men. Cf. Bechhaus-Gerst and Leutner, *Frauen in den deutschen Kolonien*.

49. Memorial of Zhou Fu to the Grand Council, December 31, 1902, AS/JYS 02–11–13 (1).

50. Memorial of Zhou Fu to the Grand Council, December 31, 1902, AS/JYS 02–11–13 (1).

51. Letter of Truppel to Tirpitz, December 30, 1903, in: BArch/MA, RM3/6718, Bl. 71–74.

52. The Chinese merchants in Kiaochow had formed several guilds to represent their interests. On the guilds, see Zhang Yufa, *Qingdao de shili juan*, 835–836.

53. See Leutner and Mühlhahn, *Musterkolonie Kiautschou*, 179–180.

54. Truppel to Naval Ministry, November 4, 1908, BA/MA, RM 3/6721, fol. 220–223.

55. In 1912 there were twelve Qing governors and general-governors living in Qingdao; see Mayer-Waldeck to Naval Ministry, February 24, 1912, BArch/MA, RM3/6723, fol. 84–85.

56. Mayer-Waldeck to Naval Ministry, October 14, 1912, BArch/MA, RM3/6723, fol. 316–322.

57. Stoler and MacGranahan, "Refiguring Imperial Terrains," 5.

58. Duara, "Imperialism of 'Free Nations,'" 212.

59. Wolf, "Cultural Dissonance in the Italian Alps," 1.

60. Cooper, *Colonialism in Question*, 52–53.

SEVEN

Experts, Migrants, Refugees

Making the German Colony in Iran, 1900–1934

JENNIFER JENKINS

In the summer of 1928, in the border areas of the new Soviet empire, a mass movement was in the making. Starting with a few caravans, loaded with household goods and trailing draft animals, groups began to trek toward the southern borders. In those warm summer months, a caravan of sixty-nine people crossed the Soviet-Iranian border into the northeastern corner of Iran. Members of interconnected families with the names Flegel, Kuntz, and Krebs, they had left the village of Marienbrunn in the Terek area of the Caucasus in June, headed toward Turkmenistan, and passed into Iran one month later. Inside Iran they found work in rural areas close to the border, where they escaped detection by the Persian authorities. After a year of working as agricultural laborers and doing odd jobs, such as carrying loads and driving trucks, in June 1929 they landed in the vicinity of Mashad, an Iranian city of sacred shrines and the capital of the country's northeastern province of Khorassan. Desperately poor and with members who were ill, the families mixed with a much larger assemblage of Soviet refugees, who were coming into Iran in increasing numbers. In Mashad the families did not go unnoticed. Their arrival caught the attention of Adolf Franke, a German employee with the Hamburg firm Wönckhaus and Company. Franke saw the presence of these families in Iran as cause for alarm. Their poverty and what he saw as their Germanness were issues of concern. Taking up his pen, Franke wrote to the German Consulate in Tehran and to its head, Minister Count Friedrich Werner von der Schulenburg. Describing the families as Germans and as fellow nationals in need, Franke asked what he should do.[1]

Schulenburg in Tehran quickly assessed the situation, placing information about the events in Mashad together with news coming in about refugee movements in other parts of the country. At the same time as the Mashad families, a number of German-speaking Mennonites had entered Iran at its opposite corner. Also fleeing from villages in the Caucasus, they had crossed into the Iranian province of Azerbaijan on the country's northwestern side. Several had arrived in Tabriz, the province's largest city and a commercial center, while others trekked to Mashad or sat in prisons on the border, suspected by Iranian officials of spying for the Soviet Union. Rather than a set of interconnected families, as in Mashad, these refugees were individual men who had left their wives and children behind.[2] Young and with skills ranging from vintner to blacksmith, they had fled either individually or in small groups. Schulenburg put the two sets of refugees together and defined them in the same terms. They were victims of Bolshevik actions, he claimed, innocent peoples under threat who had been driven over the border by Soviet policies.[3] He then went further. Although the new arrivals were possessors of ethnic identities of some complexity, one factor was seized upon by Schulenburg and by Franke: the people sitting in Mashad and Tabriz were not Soviet citizens, nor were they "stateless peoples" in need of Nansen papers. They were "Germans," and they were "colonists." In fact, they were colonists two times over. In the eyes of the Prussian diplomat and the Hamburg businessman, the refugees were "returning" colonists who were engaged in the process of emigrating "back" into Germany (*Rückwanderer*), retracing the paths of their grandparents and great-grandparents, who had left the German-speaking regions of central Europe for the wide spaces of the Russian Empire starting in the late eighteenth century.[4]

Issues of ethnicity and citizenship—how to define the first and how to grant the second—were central to how both the German and Iranian governments sought to manage the refugees coming into Iran in increasing numbers following the onset of Soviet collectivization after 1929. In the 1930s several hundred *Russlanddeutsche* entered Iran from the Soviet Union.[5] They came from villages in the Caucasus, from the Don and Volga regions and as far north as Volhynia, in the borderland between Poland and Ukraine. They came from areas that had witnessed severe disturbances as the targets of Russian state deportation policies during World War I.[6] In many cases the refugees' stop in Iran was the latest in a long chain of forced relocations. These families had been on the move before.[7] In Iran they joined a small and very different group of Germans living in the country, and their arrival sparked a great deal of discussion and activity.

This chapter explores the making of the German colony in Iran, focusing in particular on its shifts in self-perception. As is argued here, the programs set up to aid the refugees changed how the German professionals resident in Tehran—businessmen, diplomats, engineers, bankers, doctors, and teachers—spoke about their ethnicity. Drawing inspiration from Judith Walkowitz's work on prostitution and its social anxieties, one could conceptualize the arrival of the refugees as opening a wound—what Walkowitz calls both a "plague spot" and a sore—around which anxieties about belonging were articulated and state policies were forged.[8]

GERMANS IN IRAN

Virtually nothing is known about the Germans in Iran—the few hundred people living in the country in the early 1930s and the refugees who joined them, whether those from the Soviet Union or the German Jewish refugees from Nazism, who began arriving after 1933.[9] In 1933 an estimated 590 Germans lived in Iran, half of them in the capital, Tehran, half spread over the rest of the country.[10] The group grew by several hundred over the following years. Their stories fit uncomfortably in the literature on German colonialism, for Iran was never the site of a formal colony. A brief flirtation with the idea of Near Eastern settlement was put to rest in 1905.[11] Rather, Iran, like the Ottoman Empire, was envisioned as a site of economic penetration. Since the 1880s German diplomats, politicians, journalists, and businessmen had discussed Iran as a zone of economic investment and activity, a site where Germany would engage in specific strategies of economic competition with its imperial rivals. Germans who went to Iran were driven primarily by economic motives, whether the more extravagant ones involving oil or the more modestly sized ambition to start and own a business. Most went for professional reasons. This was in keeping with the official relationship between Germany and Iran, which rested first and foremost on commercial interests. A Prussian treaty of "commerce and friendship" in 1857 inaugurated their modern diplomatic contact. A Prussian commercial mission followed in 1860, and a treaty of "friendship, navigation and commerce" was signed between Germany and Iran in 1873. In an effort to promote economic expansion, in 1885 Germany opened consulates in the capital city of Tehran and in the Persian Gulf port of Bushehr.[12] From the Iranian side, the shahs of the ruling Qajar dynasty took a keen interest in German involvement. Looking to preserve their power and autonomy, they requested German military protection and financial support in an effort to stave off the predatory interests of Great Britain and Russia. As the largest imperial players in the region, Britain and Russia were bent on hollowing out the sovereignty of the Persian state. In this project they were largely successful, dividing Iran between them in 1907. Bismarck largely decided against German action in Iran, privileging stable Russian relations over imperial ambition, but a row of colonial publicists and representatives from German industry, banking, and business trumpeted the possibilities of expansion. Economic expansion into the Near East was expressed as vital to the growth and future survival of Germany as an imperial power. In 1885 the journalist Paul Dehn wrote in the *Deutsche Kolonialzeitung* that Near Eastern involvement was something that "the German state of the future ... must consider [as] one of its permanent objectives. ... Germany and central Europe (*Mitteleuropa*) must establish themselves in the Near, Middle and Far East ... before other countries, Russia from the north, England from the south ... take the East for themselves."[13]

The diplomatic establishment followed suit. Marshall von Bieberstein, foreign secretary from 1890 to 1896, ambassador to the Porte (1896–1912), and the "chief architect" of Germany's Near Eastern policy, spent his tenure in Constantinople advancing the idea that "countries whose economic structure offered opportunities to German industry should be bound closely to Germany."[14] By 1914 German economic involvement in Iran had begun in earnest. In 1907, a German school was established in Tehran, and the Hamburg-America shipping line extended service to Persian Gulf ports.[15] The German School—conceptualized as a *Realschule* and employing eight German and eight Persian teachers for the teaching of three hundred Persian students—with its scientific laboratories and sporting facilities, symbolized in Iran what it meant to be "German" and "modern." Between 1906 and 1910 diplomats and businessmen sought to establish a national bank in Iran under German auspices, and the trade representative Kurt Jung wrote a voluminous report in 1909–1910 on the possibilities Iran offered to German industry and commerce.[16] While Germany's largest firms engaged in Persian Gulf shipping, transporting the material and machinery needed for the building of the Baghdad railway, smaller firms engaged in trade between Iran and Europe via Black Sea steamer routes. Trading in dried fruits, nuts, silk, cotton, and agricultural machinery, they operated out of Tabriz in northwestern Iran. The Deutsche Levante Linie did a good business in Black Sea shipping, with goods brought overland from the Ottoman port of Trabzon to Tabriz.[17] German involvement was multifaceted. In Tabriz and Isfahan German firms experimented with supplying agricultural machinery to local landowners and with mechanizing the production of Persian carpets for European and North American markets.[18] German and European missions and orphanages dotted the countryside around Tabriz, reaching up to Khoi and Julfa on the Russian-Armenian border and down to Lake Urmia, close to the Armenian communities in Van, on the other side of the Ottoman border.

A strong sense of ethnic identity was generally not in evidence amongst the small numbers of Germans living in Iran before 1914, and it varied by region and city. The diplomat Friedrich Rosen, who had served in the Tehran Consulate in the late nineteenth century, spoke of the friendly relations between German diplomats and those of the other missions. "At the time of my visit to Tehran, in the spring of 1887, there was no idea of an Anglo-German misunderstanding," he wrote. "The relations between the two countries and the two reigning families appeared to be normal, if not friendly."[19] While the German diplomats in Tehran often thought of themselves internationally as well as nationally, in Tabriz a more assertive sense of Germanness emerged in the years before the war. The Foreign Office appointed a consular agent for the area in 1908 in response to requests from businessmen. This was followed by the establishment of an official consulate in 1914. As the new consul, the East Prussian Wilhelm Litten, arrived in Tabriz, the local German *Honoratioren* greeted him in front of their proudest accomplishment, the new textile factory on the outskirts of the city. Litten was given a grand reception at Tabriz's German club, and the outgoing consular agent, the businessman Max Schünemann, gave a stirring speech on the arrival of the German state in this northwestern corner of Iranian Azerbaijan. Linking the fortunes of the local Germans in Tabriz to the expansionist aims of *Weltpolitik* and its forward march through the world, Schünemann roused his audience with evocations of the bright future ahead for "Germandom in Azerbaijan." Litten, with his career connections to the Foreign Office and his familiarity with the more cosmopolitan and international atmosphere of Germany's consulate in Tehran, watched all of this with carefully hidden amusement. The strident evocations of provincial *Deutschtum* struck him as quaint, but he was careful to uphold a serious mien. The celebration at the German club was taken very seriously by Tabriz's notables, with the establishment of a consulate clearly seen as a vital accomplishment.[20]

Declared with great optimism, Schünemann's bright future for Near Eastern Germandom was not meant to be. World War I started early and brutally in this area, which would also later witness the spreading bloodshed of genocide.[21] While the cohesiveness of the German community in Tabriz owed a great deal to both local and international trade and to Schünemann's charismatic personality, it was also forged by a sense of external threat. Russian troops were stationed in the city and countryside after 1909 and brutally suppressed the local Persian population, which had recently risen in revolt against the Qajar shah and his Russian backers.[22] In the opening months of World War I—before hostilities in the area had officially started—the German colony in Tabriz was attacked and scattered, its members sent wandering on the road to Tehran. Fleeing Russian hostility, Litten and his wife sought shelter in the American Consulate.[23] The war and the seizure of Iran by the British in 1919 ended the life of Iran's first German community. Destroyed by war, it was diplomatically forbidden to rebuild. Inscribed on a "Black List" put out by the British government were the names of seventy-three Germans: diplomats, businessmen, Orientalist professors, and members of the military, many of whom had played important roles in Iran, the Ottoman Empire, and the Caucasus before 1918 and who were now forbidden to set foot in the country.[24]

With the reestablishment of diplomatic ties in 1923, the German government called for the abolition of the black list and restarted plans for capital expansion into Iran. In a sign of the importance it accorded to the region, the Foreign Office assigned one of its best-known diplomats to Tehran. The appointment of Count Friedrich Werner von der Schulenburg as German Minister in 1923 signaled Germany's continuing economic and political interest in the region. An expert on Russia and the Caucasus, and the consul in Tiflis after 1913, Schulenburg was an able and energetic representative of Germany's global ambitions. He had mobilized nationalist groups throughout the former Russian Empire during the war (the Georgians in particular) and had traveled throughout the Ottoman Empire after 1916, serving as vice-consul in Anatolian Erzerum following the Armenian genocide of 1915–1916.[25] With his connections to the military, to business interests, and to the foreign policy establishment, Schulenburg was a well-placed *Weltpolitiker* of the Wilhelminian school. His years of service in Tiflis and Constantinople provided him with intimate knowledge of the Near East, and he strongly supported Germany's continued presence in the region. Tracking delicately between Soviet and British interests, Schulenburg opened a space for Germany to become a vital economic actor in Iran, and his presence, diplomatic skill, and connections played a significant role in bringing the next group of Germans into the country.

Schulenburg's ambitions matched the plans of Iran's new ruler, Reza Shah Pahlavi. Coming to power through a British-supported coup in 1921, this former Cossack officer served as war minister before his coronation as shah in 1925. Starting in the mid-1920s, his government energetically pursued a plan to modernize the country with the aid of European capital and expertise. As Atatürk had done in neighboring Turkey, Reza Shah, following a turn away from the possibility of greater involvement with the Soviet Union, began to invite companies and "experts" from various European countries—namely, France, Germany, and the United States—to build Iranian industry and infrastructure. Germany held a particular place in his strategy: the Iranian state began to invite German experts to serve as official consultants to its government.[26] The engineer Georg Hartmann was the first such expert to arrive in Tehran under these auspices, and he held one of the most important state positions. Hired at the Persian Arsenal in 1924, Hartmann was responsible for arms and munitions and was given the specific task of drawing up plans for a modern weapons factory.[27]

The years 1927–1928 marked an important conjuncture for the Iranian economy, which provided significant economic opportunities to Germany. After 1928 German firms became deeply involved in the industrial modernization of the country, as Reza Shah broke the grip of the extralegal forms of sovereignty (capitulations) that had characterized British and Russian imperial power in the region and aggressively opened the national economy to international competition. German diplomats wrote deliriously about the possibility of Germany achieving a new "monopoly position" in the region, and the number of invited experts steadily increased.[28] "Persia is rich in oil and minerals," wrote a Foreign Ministry official in Berlin. "It generates large amounts of agricultural goods—grains, rice, cotton, dried fruits, opium, silk, wool, hides.... Large contracts will be handed out in the near future: the building of the national railroad, the creation of an iron industry, the construction of electrical plants, exploitation of the Caspian Sea fisheries, and the like."[29] Projects came thick and fast, with top positions placed in the hands of German companies: a national bank was founded in 1927 under German directorship; the weapons firm Fritz Wehner established connections in the country; the Junkers aircraft company provided the country's air transportation network and established regularly scheduled flights between Iran and Europe; German firms constructed sugar refineries, electricity stations, and textile factories. In 1928 the Iranian government signed a contract with a German-American consortium for civil engineering projects, including the construction of a national railroad network. These projects brought German experts and employees—highly educated, mobile professionals—to Iran. The firms Philipp Holzmann AG, Julius Berger Tiefbau AG, and Siemens Bauunion sent engineers, with the first group of fifty arriving in the summer of 1928.[30] The foot soldiers of the German corporations, they moved into the area as Reza Shah drew on international competition to forge Iran's industrial economy.

State employment also brought Germans to Iran. Many experts—on the whole an older and more established group than the engineers and white-collar employees—arrived to work as consultants for Iran's government ministries. As Consular Secretary Meyer wrote in 1928, "a German geologist and a surveyor came to ascertain the country's mineral wealth. An expert in steel production, a chemist . . . and an expert to serve as director of the newly founded Persian National Bank [arrived] . . . a German expert has been proposed to direct the archaeological exploration of the country, as well as a German financial advisor and a [national] financial inspector." As he summed up, "the participation of German forces in the building and modernization of the country is happily increasing."[31]

The Iranian enthusiasm for German expertise passed from industry to art. In 1937 Reza Shah invited a little known painter, a two-bit Saxon talent named Albert Hunnemann who held a professorship at Tehran's Art Academy, to paint murals of the Trans-Iranian railroad for the palace in Tehran. Hunnemann's bombastic depictions of shining rails winding through perilously steep mountain ranges and across gorgeously colored landscapes said little about the state of modern German painting but a great deal about Iranian nationalist enthusiasm for things technological and things German.[32]

Yet as Schulenburg wrote in 1927, these Germans in Iran—numerous, energetic and well-connected as they were—did not form a colony or see themselves as such. In response to an inquiry from Berlin, Schulenburg provided information on the German community to the Foreign Office. He estimated the overall number to be "around 250, including women and children." Less than half this number lived in Teheran (100); the rest were spread throughout the country. Asked about the community's level of national and/or ethnic identification, he warned against high expectations. Although several hundred Germans lived in this country, he wrote, one could not speak of a colony. A feeling of cohesiveness was distinctly absent. There was no larger sense of ethnic belonging in this group, as evidenced by the absence of German clubs (*Vereine*) and political parties. He chalked up this development to a marked diversity in class and educational backgrounds. "The level of education of the Germans living here is very diverse. For this reason the formation of German associations and groups has not occurred. For the formation of one German club, the composition of the German colony is too unequal; for the creation of a set of clubs we lack sufficient numbers. In my opinion," he concluded, "the time has not yet come for a closer coming together of Germans living here." Asked whether Germans in Persia would be interested in joining the *Bund der Auslandsdeutschen*, he replied that they were "more or less indifferent" to this idea.[33] This would change in the 1930s.

PERSERFLÜCHTLINGE AND SCHUTZSCHEINE

The arrival of the *Russlanddeutsche* in Iran was part of the much larger movement of peoples of all nationalities out of the Soviet Union in the late 1920s. The onset of collectivization in 1929, coupled with the ongoing persecution of religious and national minorities, set thousands of people into motion inside the Soviet Union and over its borders. As was clear from the papers they carried, the Russian Germans were possessors of hybrid identities of some complexity. It was their Germanness, however, that the Tehran Consulate chose to highlight and to act upon. What Schulenburg, Franke, and others defined as an ethnic German identity—audible to them in the language spoken by the refugees and visible in their attitudes toward work and hygiene—was central to how the refugees were seen and to the rationale for why they were to be helped. There were many factors bringing ethnicity to the fore in the policies and practices of the Tehran Consulate in the 1930s; the importance of defining and tending to the mobile poverty of the *Russlanddeutsche* was a major concern. For their part, the Iranian police viewed the refugees through a state administrative lens—focusing on recording and controlling their movements through the country. German officials, in contrast, approached the issue via a language suffused with national affect. As suffering Germans and nationals in need, the *Russlanddeutsche* were to be taken under the protection of the German state. They were to be legally protected from the encroachment of other state policies (the Iranian and the Soviet), socially protected from economic want, and physically protected from harm. Practically speaking, this meant protection from the three dangers of deportation, destitution, and disease. Franke, in particular, worried about the dangers of physical and moral degeneration facing the families in Iran; Schulenburg wrote to the Foreign Office of the refugees' inevitable descent into indebtedness. As foreigners were barred from owning land, these German farmers, he claimed, would sink to the level of the Persian farmer or lower, becoming effectively enserfed to Persian landowners.[34] Franke wrote with concern that the Russian Germans would degenerate into a rural proletariat, standing economically lower than "Orientals." German poverty would be on display on eastern land, a possibility he viewed with horror. Others concurred. The Russian Germans, they agreed, could not remain in Iran. As Germans and "returning colonists," they must be transported to Germany as soon as possible.

As Schulenburg wrote to fellow diplomat Werner Otto von Hentig in 1930, the situation was straightforward. Persecution and poverty in the Soviet Union were uprooting "German farmers" (*Deutsche Bauern*) and propelling them over the border into Iran. "The unbearable conditions in Soviet Russia, the religious persecutions and the abolition of private property, are forcing these people over the border of the Soviet paradise in all directions," he wrote. Fleeing persecution in the USSR, "a whole number of such families have come to Persia and more will follow."[35] Tagged by the Foreign Office with the label *Perserflüchtlinge* (Persian refugees), these "returning colonists" (*Rückwanderer*) belonged, as Schulenburg stated, to "the same category of Russian Germans who appeared last year in the tens of thousands in Moscow" and had been granted permission to emigrate to Germany. Once in the country they were encouraged to emigrate further. Schulenburg described to Hentig an ethnic German refugee stream flowing out of the Soviet Union, settling temporarily in Germany, and then "sent with German support, at least in part, to Canada and Brazil." He saw the refugees in Iran in similar terms and set out his policies in a similar way. "The only possibility of improving the lot of the German Russian farmers and of rescuing them from ruin is, as I see it, in transporting them out of Persia," he wrote. Like the group from Moscow, these Russian Germans should also be sent to Germany. Once in Germany, they should be encouraged to emigrate further, if possible to North and South America.[36]

It was decided that the refugees were to be economically secured, healed of disease, and provided with various forms of welfare while waiting for transport. Writing letters and meeting with Iranian landowners and officials, Franke found work for the Mashad families on agricultural estates outside the city. The families lived in sod houses, worked assigned pieces of land, and were lent money, seed, machinery, and draft animals in exchange for their labor.[37] In the fall they raised wheat, rye, and poppies. In the spring they planted cotton and melons.[38] Transport proceeded as planned in the fall of 1930. Following the harvest, Schulenburg sent a group of ninety-eight Russian Germans from Tehran to Germany, covering the costs through a combination of public and private funds. His resourcefulness brought together monies from associations as varied as the Reich Aid for Russian Peasants, the Association of Caucasus Germans, and the Canadian Mennonite Board of Colonization. Moreover, he connected the transport of these families to the larger *Hilfsaktion* for Russian Germans spearheaded by the Foreign Office. The *Perserflüchtlinge* became part of the total of 6,700 Russian Germans who arrived in Germany after 1929, paid for through a "discretionary fund" from Reich President von Hindenburg, with monies from "labor, business, religious and Red Cross organizations" and from Russian German exile groups in Germany. Most of the larger group went on to North or South America, but not all made the further trip.[39] Landing in the Mölln refugee camp outside Lübeck in the winter of 1930–31, the Russian

Germans from Iran were first interned. Several families were later resettled as farmers in Mecklenburg.[40]

Following the successful transport of the first group, Schulenburg aimed to process subsequent sets of *Russlanddeutsche* in a similar manner. The route, while treacherous and long, was passable; the funds were in place, and the entry point in Germany was secure. But the worsening economic and political situation in Germany blocked his plans. By late 1931 the Mölln camp had been closed, and restrictions on immigration had been tightened.[41] Without an explicit pledge of financial support—either relatives in Germany or an outside supporting agency that would pay for their passage—it became impossible to secure transport out of Iran for the *Russlanddeutsche*. The Foreign Office in Berlin had begun to look on such refugees with increasing distaste, seeing them as an economic burden that the state could ill afford. It became clear to German consular officials in Tehran and Tabriz that the Russian Germans, with more arriving every day, would have to stay in Iran. This entailed a new set of practices, all of which circulated around the ethnicity of the refugees, highlighting the Consulate's need to define and categorize what was, in reality, a tangle of cultures and identities. Through the work of the Consulate and in discussion with Persian officials, defining the Germanness of the refugees became the preferred mechanism for providing legal and economic security to them. This factor was continually emphasized in the charged context in the 1930s by the Consulate, by members of the German community, by the Persian authorities, and by the refugees themselves.

Schulenburg and Franke liked to emphasize that the Russian Germans were "model colonists."[42] Model colonists they may have been but not for the situation in which they found themselves. Looming over them were the strong possibilities of deportation and destitution. The Iranian government viewed the refugees through an administrative lens, seeing the Russian Germans as largely indistinguishable from the larger group of Soviet refugees breaching the country's borders.[43] Their administrative approach to population movement had developed in the late nineteenth century in response to mass epidemics. Passports had first appeared in Iran in the context of the public health crisis brought on by cholera. Documents registering the internal movements of the population came with the late nineteenth-century cholera epidemics, as the state struggled to record the presence and spread of disease.[44] This disease model was applied to the Soviet refugees, as Iranian authorities spoke of Bolshevism as a contagion that could not be allowed to spread. Although Franke liked to claim that the Russian Germans arrived with nothing, this was a half-truth. Many had arrived with Soviet papers. For the Iranian police these papers and passports proved that the refugees were not stateless peoples but Soviet citizens.⁴⁵ They had entered the country over the Soviet border, bringing their contagion with them, and according to treaties in force between Iran and the Soviet Union, they were to be sent back. Franke wrote with alarm on the deportation from Mashad of Russian German refugees, and reports from Tabriz spoke of shooting at the border. Deporting the *Russlanddeutsche*, stated the German consular official in Tabriz, meant death at the hands of Soviet authorities. "Deportation is execution," he wrote.⁴⁶

In this context Schulenburg began in 1929 to document the *Russlanddeutsche*. In order to stay in Iran, they needed official papers defining them as German, and Schulenburg issued forms that distinguished them from the general mass of Soviet refugees by highlighting their ethnic identity. Listing names, birthplaces, birthdates, and occupations, the forms (*Personalausweise*) covered whole families. Termed a "passport substitute" with a length of one year, the document defined its holder or the holder's family as German. Following correspondence between the Consulate and the Iranian Interior Ministry, these papers were honored by the Iranian police.⁴⁷ Schulenburg made the *Personalausweise* easy to obtain. Refugees were to provide what papers they had, but in the absence of documents—the situation confronting many—Schulenburg had them sign an oath stating that, to the best of their knowledge, they were German. The refugees signed the oaths and received the papers. Families received one *Personalausweis* each, with family photographs taken as documentation. The refugees called them their "protection papers" (*Schutzscheine*).⁴⁸

Rather than an action directed by Berlin and implemented in Iran, Schulenburg's entrepreneurial granting of German status ran in the opposite direction. The Foreign Office strongly objected to the practice, telling Schulenburg it had "fundamental reservations" about giving Reich citizenship to refugees who might be of German descent but where the fact of descent was unproven.⁴⁹ The Reich Ministry of the Interior agreed. Both officials asked Schulenburg "to seek ways to avoid issuing this sort of documentation," stating that the security of such refugees was the responsibility of the Persian government.⁵⁰ Schulenburg ignored the warnings, pressed on with issuing the documents and insisted on their necessity. "If we wish to help these people," he wrote, "the issuing of personal papers is unavoidable.... The Persian government sees people who come over the Russian border without papers as fundamentally illegitimate." They faced immediate deportation, and, he wrote, "you can imagine that in the Soviet Union they will not be treated particularly kindly. We can only protect these people from that fate *when we take ours in* right from the beginning." The vehicle for "tak[ing] ours in" was the *Personalausweis*.⁵¹ By May 1931, Schulenburg had issued documents to 220 families and kept issuing more.[52] The filling out of the forms he viewed pragmatically, focusing mainly on the response of the Iranian authorities. As he wrote to the Tabriz Consulate, "I would request that when issuing such personal documents for the ethnic German refugees that 'German' always be given as their citizenship (*Staatsangehörigkeit*). The columns for 'previous citizenship' and the date should be left bare or crossed out in order to sidestep problems with the Persian ministries when obtaining the necessary stamps."[53]

Together with Schulenburg, the consular staff in Tehran actively reached out to the refugees. Through their efforts and actions a broad definition of German ethnicity became the avenue for the refugees to secure legal status as well as the rationale for aid. But how was Germanness defined? As Renate Bridenthal and Doris Bergen have emphasized, most Germans in the Russian Empire had assimilated into their local societies over generations, particularly through intermarriage.[54] This made the ethnic identity of the families anything but straightforward. German consular officials in Tehran worked with a cultural definition of ethnic identity, focusing on the possession of language and custom, manners and values (the "German" values of thrift, industriousness, cleanliness), and downplaying both passports and international law. The language spoken by the refugees and their habits and mannerisms, as well as their religion (if that were either Lutheran or Mennonite), were taken as the most potent indicators of their ethnic identity.[55] Officials acted as if this were a straightforward calculation, and their pragmatism often made it so. As Franke described the first set of families to Schulenburg: "All of them are Lutherans. They speak good, almost error-free German, and the adults can read and write. All of the children, and a portion of the women, speak only German and know no Russian. All of them leave an orderly and hardworking impression, and the Persians, with whom they have worked, will give them the best of recommendations."[56] Later Franke speedily determined the ethnicity of a group of twenty-four *Russlanddeutsche*, who arrived in Mashad in June 1933, exclusively in terms of their language. "If these people are Soviet state citizens," he wrote, "there can be no doubt of their German background. They all speak good, error-free German, as a German farmer would speak."[57] Plucking the Russian Germans out of the overall refugee stream found favor with some Persian authorities. As the Persian governor of Khorassan, Mirza Mahmoud Khan, mentioned approvingly to Franke, the Russian Germans were different from the other refugees. With the *Russlanddeutsche*, he said, "it is a matter of pure-German farmers and not in any case of those infected by Bolshevism."[58]

German policies regarding the refugees in the period up to 1934 concentrated mainly on responding to Persian measures, as the Iranian government passed new laws regulating the movement of the Soviet refugees. These had a direct impact on the lives of the Russian Germans, determining how they could live and work. As Schulenburg's successor, Consul Wipert von Blücher, wrote in September 1934 with regard to the new Iranian policy of "cleansing" the cities of the Soviet refugees: "Russian refugees, including the ethnic German ones, are no longer welcome in Tehran, Tabriz, Mazanderan, Mashad, or any of the areas bordering Russia; rather they will be resettled in the interior of the country."[59] This new law, passed in March 1934, forced the refugees into the center of the country, moving them specifically toward the construction sites of the Trans-Iranian railroad. Work permits and travel documents were now required for employment, residence, or movement through the country. The Persian police conducted document checks. Through this law the *Personalausweis* issued by the German Consulate was transformed into an *Identitätsbescheinigung* (identity papers). Required for work, it was granted for one year. Armed with what had essentially become guest worker status, which they could and did renew over the years, many *Russlanddeutsche* moved their families to Broujerd and Saliabad and became part of the wildly international force of forty thousand laborers building the Iranian national railroad.

A language of shared ethnicity circulated between the refugees and German officials in Tehran; it also moved between the refugee families and began to circulate within the German community as a whole. As the first set of families arrived in 1929, the Consulate appealed directly to the sentiments of German professionals and business owners in Tehran to provide money and work for the newcomers. Philanthropic activities followed. Frau Dora Scheer, wife of the head of the German Railroad Syndicate, Eduard Scheer, took up a collection for the Mashad families. Advertising in newspapers and on local radio, she asked the Germans in Tehran to donate money, clothing, household items, and schoolbooks for the Russian German children. In December 1929 she held a fund-raising dinner and dance; the proceeds paid down the families' debts to Persian landowners. In Mashad the Wönckhaus firm, in tandem with the American Presbyterian Mission, raised further funds. The Hamburg School Board sent schoolbooks, and the city's Inner Mission sent religious texts. Refugees were treated free of charge at the American Mission hospital. No gift was overlooked. A Mrs. Miller in Mashad, for example, gave two cows, one specifically to provide milk for the children.[60]

The circulation of goods and services — and discussions about who would receive them and who was deserving of help — further heightened the language of ethnic belonging. Consular employees had previously carried out only standard tasks for members of the German community: they notarized documents, arranged for mail to be delivered, issued passports, renewed documents, and contacted relatives. With the arrival of the refugees, the Consulate's work changed, as its employees began to actively provide new forms of social welfare. New arrivals found temporary documents awaiting them. They received initial monetary support. As they could stay legally only a few days in either Mashad or Tabriz, travel to Tehran was organized for them. Once at the Consulate, they were provided with additional funds and received their *Schutzscheine*. Between consular employees and the leads provided by German businesses in Tehran, employment was sought. Doctors were found for those who were ill, with German doctors often charging little to nothing.[61] All such social welfare services were offered in the name of preserving and protecting members of the German community in Iran, with the proffered services described in familial terms. Consular employees wrote often to German professionals living in Isfahan, Tabriz, and Shiraz to inquire after refugees who had recently arrived and to request help in getting them settled. The Consulate set up accounts with the refugee families for monies loaned and carried on an active correspondence with them. These letters between the Consulate and the refugee families reveal not only how the families kept track of the small amounts that had been expended on their welfare but also document the language of Germanness that connected them to the consular officials. The letters document a language of shared values and mores. The refugees continually expressed their willingness to work, their thrift, and their honesty. The emphasis on work was so pronounced that Johannes Rossmann, a refugee working on the railroad in Broujerd, wrote an angry letter to the Consulate when he thought they had spread a rumor claiming that he was "work shy."

The largest service provided to the refugees by the Consulate was in applying for German citizenship. The majority of the *Russlanddeutsche* applied for citizenship but not out of nationalist fervor. Their letters show their pragmatism, their wish for stable status and state protection. The Consulate intervened for the refugees in the search for the all-important papers—the birth certificates, baptismal records, and marriage documents—that served as the currency of ethnic identity. With the coming to power of the National Socialists in 1933 and as the German Consulate in Tehran became an arm of the National Socialist state, Schulenburg's informal means of assigning Germanness was changed. Signed statements were no longer accepted as sufficient documentation. Refugees were now required to extensively document their ethnic backgrounds and provide the racial composition of their family tree. They had to undergo medical examinations by the Consulate's doctor—a Russian

German refugee himself from the Caucasus and a central figure in the Tehran branch of the NSDAP—and provide physical and racial information on their forms, such as the shape of their heads and faces. Photographs were no longer solely to show the existence of the families but were used to assess racial fitness. As the informal signed form gave way to the official "Aryan" family tree, the family photograph became the "scientific" individual head shot, taken from the front and the side. Furthermore, the Consulate no longer handled citizenship cases on its own but frequently passed files to the local NSDAP for assessment. By 1934, a new system of documenting, categorizing, and defining "Aryanness" was being put into place, and members of the NSDAP were called upon to assess the "fitness" of the refugees for citizenship. This was done through documentation and medical examination but also through rumor and secret communications inquiring after the character of the applicants. The majority of the *Russlanddeutsche* did not join the NSDAP branch in Tehran, but the party began nevertheless to play a coercive role in their lives, with increasing power over their labor, mobility, and ability to stay in the country.

The branch of the NSDAP in Tehran stayed small, but its influence was augmented by its position in the diplomatic apparatus that Germany had built up in the country. Hitler's Germany increased its economic and political involvement in Iran after 1935, and by the late 1930s large firms specializing in pharmaceuticals, electricity, construction, and chemicals had an established presence in the country. These existed, however, together with the older layers of capital investment, just as the Nazi party members in Tehran shared space with German refugees of every political direction. Many different forms of Germanness were on display in Iran in the 1930s, but the importance of Germanness as a whole had been heightened. The "colony" began to call itself such and to address itself in these terms to the new arrivals in its midst.

EXPERTS, MIGRANTS, REFUGEES

By 1939 the German community in Iran numbered around a thousand people. The refugees had joined a very different group of German nationals—largely educated, middle class, and of professional backgrounds—who had come to the country in the 1920s to work. The difference between the two groups was striking. One was urban, educated, and in the country by invitation; the other was poor, rural, without papers, and largely unwanted. The offices in which Reich German professionals worked in Tehran, Tabriz, Mashad, and Bushehr were in stark contrast to the jail cells in which many *Russlanddeutsche* spent time before being released into the country. Yet when looking at the longer chronology of German involvement in the area, this jagged encounter between different sets of Germans in Iran in the 1930s was nothing new. Commercial interests and economic forces had repeatedly brought such mixed groups together. The German community in Iran was not and had never been a "colony" in an official or traditional sense. It was not composed of settlers, nor did it have a continuous history. It was only sporadically conceived as a firm outpost of the fatherland, a colony in a true sense, and this sentiment was voiced only by its most nationalistic members. Rather than present a real or imagined homogeneity, its pronounced heterogeneity was its most striking feature. It had been composed of distinct occupational groups who came into the country at different times and under different auspices. Germans who went to Iran and those who landed there accidentally did so for very different reasons. Nationalism was one strong and compelling force, opportunism a second, need a definite third. Over its lifetime the colony had been peopled by diplomats, businessmen, and missionaries, by educated experts and trained, salaried professionals, but also by refugees, impoverished migrants, and persecuted minorities.

One can argue that global commerce and the force of global events, as they translated into the changing economic and political relations between states, exerted a far more potent influence than did nationalist ideology in the making and breaking of the German colony in Iran.[62] For when seen against the backdrop of conventional conceptions of colonies and settlers, the German colony in Iran was a strange sort of animal. For most of its existence it had no real center, and its numbers changed dramatically over the decades, driven by the impact of twentieth-century events. It was not a planned or organized settlement or any kind of organically growing group. It was not even, in any sense, a stable entity. Rather, it was a collective that was made and remade as the relations between states changed and as the global economic and political context shifted through the impact of international conflict, war, and revolution. In other words, one can see the presence and growth of a German "colony" in Iran more as the product of global forces than the outcome of national efforts. It was not exported outward from Germany; it was not a self-conscious national project.

This sort of planned and nationalistically motivated German settlement in the Ottoman Empire and Persia had never borne fruit. Efforts to create communities of settlers and farmers in central Asia had repeatedly failed. Although Persia and the Ottoman Empire had not been seen as an area for German settlement, what Germans called the Orient, centered in the Ottoman Empire and radiating outwards, was the locus of a powerful imperial imaginary. It was the site of empires, both ancient (Sumerian, Assyrian, Babylonian, Persian, Mongol) and modern (British, Russian/Soviet). German diplomats and businessmen, from the late nineteenth century onward, conceptualized it as a zone for a future German empire, which would be established through the expansion of German business. Germany's Oriental empire was to be a space for German capital and a market for German goods.[63] The larger project, of which this chapter is a part, analyzes Iran as at the cutting edge of this idea of German globality, focusing on the strategies for expansion that filled Foreign Office files through the entire period from 1898 to 1941. These sharply defined and described how Germany imagined itself as an imperial competitor, as an inheritor to this territory of ancient empire, and as a modern economic power on a future world stage.[64]

We can see Iran as a site in which Germany imagined itself inhabiting a "dynamic field of global Germanness."[65] This story has been all but forgotten, buried first in the rubble of World War II and then through the Islamic Revolution of 1979, after which Iran's leaders sought to erase the memory of the country's complicated European pasts. It is worth unearthing and analyzing through a detailed and microhistorical look at the zones of encounter between states, businesses, and official interests, both German and Iranian, and between Germans and Iranians themselves. This perspective uncovers the webs of connections and the traffic in people, ideas, labor, and goods that give the topic its depth and meaning. Moreover, an awareness of these networks, in all of their detail, gives human form and agency to the ideas of circulation and translation so important to transnational histories.

NOTES

1. Politisches Archiv des Auswärtigen Amtes Berlin [PA AA Berlin]: Deutsche Gesandtschaft Teheran, Box 18, File 1: Adolf Franke to Count Friedrich Werner von der Schulenburg, August 9, 1929; Franke to Schulenburg, August 20, 1929. A list of names was attached to the second letter.

2. PA AA Berlin, Deutsche Gesandtschaft Teheran [DGT], Box 18, File 2: List from Deutsches Konsulat Täbris, August 19, 1930.

3. PA AA Berlin, DGT, Box 18, File 2: DGT to Werner von Hentig in San Francisco, Nr. 3071, November 14, 1930.

4. On German emigration to the Russian Empire, see Fleischhauer, *Die Deutschen im Zarenreich*.

5. Theirs is an invisible history, covered neither by European nor by Persian historical works and found in virtually no existing book or article. Missing from scholarly accounts, their life stories appear in the records kept by the German Consulate in Teh-

ran. The consulate tracked the presence of Russian Germans in the country, following their lives from the point of arrival, through the years of labor and deprivation, to the final chapters of deportation and internment between 1938 and 1941. This chapter draws on this archival material, found at PA AA Berlin, DGT, boxes 17–20 ("Deutsche Kolonisten").

6. Gatrell, *A Whole Empire Walking*.

7. David Flegel's family, for example, had moved to Marienbrunn from Kulm in Bessarabia. The farmer Reinhold Litz brought his family to Mashad in June 1933. He and his wife were born in the Kuban area; their two children were born in Stavropol. They were sent out of Teheran in 1934, with the law "clearing" the cities, and made their way to Saliabad, where Reinhold Litz worked for a time on construction for the Trans-Iranian railroad. PA AA Berlin, DGT, Box 19, File 4: Franke to DGT, June 7, 1933; Franke to DGT, June 28, 1933; Box 19, File 5: handwritten list, ca. April 1934.

8. Walkowitz, *Prostitution and Victorian Society*. For studies focusing on the transnational parameters for thinking about Germanness, see O'Donnell, Bridenthal, and Reagin, eds., *The Heimat Abroad*.

9. The existing literature on Germany and Iran focuses on official German policies, not on the experiences of Germans living in the country. It is a history of international relations between states rather than an economic and cultural history of imperial contact. There is a small literature on Germany's diplomatic, military and economic policies: Martin, *German Persian Diplomatic Relations 1873–1912*; Gehrke, *Persien in der deutschen Orientpolitik*; and Hirschfeld, *Deutschland und Iran*, are three of the best. This literature operates exclusively at the level of state politics and international relations. One knows little on how these relations were lived. The histories of the Germans in Iran and the ways in which the relations between the two countries were inhabited—and the hybrid German-Persian lifeworlds that this created—have not yet been explored or analyzed. This chapter and the larger study of which it is a part cross this terrain.

10. PA AA Berlin, DGT, Box 23, File 4: Consul Wipert von Blücher to Auswärtiges Amt / Berlin [AA/Berlin], July 22, 1933.

11. A revival of settlement plans in the 1920s also ended in disaster. PA AA Berlin, R 67206: "Deutsche Einwanderer in Persien," *Bank Börsen-Zeitung*, June 24, 1924; Schulenburg report to AA/Berlin, Nr. 127, May 16, 1924; Klötzel, "Erlebnisse deutscher Auswanderer in Persien," *Berliner Tageblatt*, September 23, 1924. See Hirschfeld, *Deutschland und Iran*, 43–46, for a summary of the rise and fall of the Gesellschaft GEROPERS (Gesellschaft zur Rohstofferschliessung Persiens).

12. See Martin, *German Persian Diplomatic Relations*, 20–31. On Iran as a site of commercial possibility, see Stolze and Andreas, *Die Handelsverhältnisse Persiens*.

13. As quoted in Martin, *German Persian Diplomatic Relations*, 38. As Martin states, Dehn wrote his article on the occasion of the establishment of the German Consulate in Tehran. Dehn wrote extensively on Germany's imperial competition with Britain and set his writings on a world stage. His *Weltpolitische Neubildungen* (1905) covers naval competition and trade with China and East Asia; his *Von deutscher Kolonial- und Weltpolitik* (1907) covers strategies of imperial expansion in the non-European world

from the cotton trade to the building of railroads. As did many imperial publicists at the time, Dehn linked disparate imperial projects into a world system, signaled by him with the term *Weltpolitik*.

14. Martin, *German-Persian Diplomatic Relations*, 57.

15. Martin, *German-Persian Diplomatic Relations*, 204–205.

16. PA AA Berlin, R 14593 A 10745: Richthofen to Reich Chancellor von Bülow, June 4, 1906, on the possibility of establishing a German bank in Persia.

17. Issawi, "The Tabriz-Trabzon Trade, 1830–1900."

18. PA AA Berlin, R 19091: "Übersetzung des Leitartikels der Handels- und Gewerbezeitung Aserbeidschanski Listek," in Täbris, No. 5, March 16–29, 1914; Letter from PETAG (Persische Teppichgesellschaft AG) to AA/Berlin, May 9, 1914.

19. Rosen, *Oriental Memories of a German Diplomatist*, 73.

20. Bundesarchiv [BA] Berlin-Lichterfelde, R 9333 Deutsches Konsulat Täbris, File 18: Deutsches Konsulat Täbris to Prinz Heinrich XXXI, Reuss Tehran, March 4, 1914.

21. Shahbaz, *The Rage of Islam*.

22. Browne, *The Reign of Terror in Tabriz*, and Katouzian, *State and Society in Iran*, 25–54.

23. PA AA Berlin, R 19092, Telegram A 21440: Wangenheim to AA Berlin, September 11, 1914; and A 29904: Report of von Oppenheim, November 7, 1914. See also the report from Wilhelm Litten in his memoir *Persische Flitterwochen*, 14–42.

24. PA AA Berlin, R 19096, A 30049: "Liste der Deutschen denen die Rückkehr nach Persien für zehn Jahre untersagt ist" (1919), with seventy-four names, one being that of the Hamburg firm Wönckhaus and Company.

25. Nadolny, *Mein Beitrag*, 54–55, 86, 92–93; PA AA Berlin, Personalakte 13948, Graf v. d. Schulenburg, especially copy I c 3438, letter from Richard von Kuehlmann to the Legationskasse in Berlin, July 24, 1918.

26. Germany's role in this story is not well known, as most Iranian historians do not read German sources. Other than Hirschfeld's *Deutschland und Iran*, which covers German economic and state actors, there is a striking absence in the literature. For a recent account of Iran's modernization that leaves Germany out of the story, see Marashi, *Nationalizing Iran*.

27. Hirschfeld, *Deutschland und Iran*, 42.

28. For details on the sort of economic plans envisioned by Germany, see PA AA Berlin, R 78105: "Gesprächstoff für den Herrn Reichsaussenminister bei dem morgigen Frühstück in der Persischen Gesandtschaft" (talking points for a meeting between Gustav Stresemann and the Iranian Consulate), April 16, 1928; and Hirschfeld, *Deutschland und Iran*, 64–75.

29. Report from the Foreign Ministry in Berlin, 1927, quoted in Hirschfeld, *Deutschland und Iran*, 64.

30. PA AA Berlin, DGT, Box 25, File 1: Letter and list to the German Consulate from the Konsortium für Bauausführungen in Persien (Julius Berger-Konsortium, Berlin; Siemens-Bauunion GmbH, Berlin; Philipp Holzmann AG, Frankfurt am Main), November 20, 1928.

31. PA AA Berlin DGT, Box 23, File 3: Report from Consulate Secretary Meyer, 1928.

32. Hunnemann became professor of drawing and painting at the Tehran Art Academy in 1937. He painted "Industriebilder" for the Iranian Economic Ministry and received the invitation to paint the murals for the Shah's palace in 1937. PA AA Berlin, DGT, Box 27, File III. 10, Nr. 2143/41: Ettel/DGT to AA/Berlin, May 12, 1941.

33. PA AA Berlin, DGT, Box 23, File 3: Schulenburg to AA/Berlin, December 10, 1927.

34. PA AA Berlin, DGT, Box 18, File 1: Schulenburg to AA/Berlin, December 13, 1929. Stoler's *Carnal Knowledge and Imperial Power* analyzes the damage that European/white pauperization in the colonies would do to the "image of a healthy and vigorous race" that the colonial powers sought to present (35). As she writes, "the potential and actual presence of poor, 'unfit' whites was central to reformist social policies in colonies across the globe. British, Dutch, and French colonial businessmen and policymakers designed pay scales, housing, medical facilities, marriage restrictions, and labor contracts to ensure that colonial ventures appeared a middle-class phenomenon" (35). The German Consulate in Tehran wished to attempt something similar in their support of the *Russlanddeutsche*. However, they were ultimately too weak to be able to carry out such an extensive set of policies. The poverty of the Russian Germans was on full display as they labored on the Trans-Iranian Railroad.

35. PA AA Berlin, DGT, Box 18, File 2: Nr. 3071, DGT/Schulenburg to Hentig in San Francisco, November 14, 1930. Schulenburg's reference was to the thousands of Russian Germans who fled to Moscow in 1929 from the "terrors of collectivization," which included the "grain collection campaign, new taxes and compulsory entry into collective farms." The Soviet government, under German pressure, "finally agreed to permit a number of them to emigrate." Williams, *Culture in Exile*, 355.

36. Schulenburg wrote that a portion of the families had relatives in East Prussia and another group had relatives in Canada. PA AA Berlin, DGT, Box 18, File 1: "Unterstützung der deutsch-russischen Bauern in Persien," Telegram Nr. 472 from Schulenburg to AA/Berlin, December 13, 1929.

37. PA AA Berlin, DGT, Box 19, File 4: Franke to DGT, June 7, 1933. This was to provide adequate support prior to transport. This plan did not work well, as the families became indebted.

38. PA AA Berlin, DGT, Box 18, File 1: Franke to Dr. Staudacher/DGT, December 17, 1929.

39. Williams, *Culture in Exile*, 355–356. The Persian refugees are not mentioned specifically in this work, and they remain largely invisible in the literature.

40. Williams, *Culture in Exile*, 355.

41. PA AA Berlin, DGT, Box 18, File 3: Freytag/AA Berlin to DGT, April 9, 1931.

42. See the telegram from Egger, Deutsches Konsulat Täbris to DGT, January 1, 1930, and Schulenburg's response, January 21, 1930, in PA AA Berlin, DGT, Box 18, File 2.

43. The refugee stream was fairly constant, and overall numbers were considerable. In a single six-month period (January–June 1933), seven hundred Russians and several hundred families from Soviet Turkmenistan had arrived in Mashad alone. PA AA Berlin, DGT, Box 19, File 4: Franke to DGT, June 12, 1933.

44. Kashani-Sabet, *Frontier Fictions*, 53–55.

45. For German officials, the moment of crossing the border made a Russian Ger-

man into a stateless person. See the letter from the Tabriz Consulate to DGT, December 28, 1934, in PA AA Berlin, DGT, Box 19, File 5.

46. PA AA Berlin, DGT, Box 18, File 2: Telegram from Egger / Deutsches Konsulat Täbris to DGT, January 16, 1930.

47. Discussion between the consulate and the Iranian police on this matter began in 1929. See PA AA Berlin, DGT, Box 18, File 1: Letter from Dr. Staudacher to the Iranian Ministry of Police, September 20, 1929. Staudacher's letter listed the names of the Russian Germans who had arrived in the country, stated that they had no passports, said that the question of their German citizenship was being explored, and requested that the police give them "politzeilichen Schutz."

48. See, for example, PA AA Berlin, DGT, Box 19, File 5: Letter from the Russian German farmer Friedrich Euteneier to Repnow/DGT, November 27, 1934, thanking Repnow for sending the "Schutzschein."

49. PA AA Berlin, DGT, Box 18, File 1: Telegram from Freytag /AA Berlin to DGT, January 27, 1930.

50. PA AA Berlin, DGT, Box 18, File 2: AA/Berlin to Schulenburg, September 11, 1930.

51. PA AA Berlin, DGT, Box 18, File 2: Letter Nr. 2513 from DGT to Geheimrat Martius/AA Berlin, Abt. V, November 4, 1930. Emphasis added. The Foreign Ministry in Berlin consented to Schulenburg's measures only in April 1931, claiming that they were convinced by the reports of the refugees who had arrived in Mölln the preceding fall. PA AA Berlin, DGT, Box 18, File 3: Freytag /AA Berlin to DGT, April 9, 1931.

52. PA AA Berlin, DGT, Box 18, File 3: Franke to Meyer, May 5, 1931.

53. PA AA Berlin, DGT, Box 18, File 1: Schulenburg to Deutsches Konsulat Täbris, February 14, 1930.

54. Bridenthal, "Germans from Russia," and Bergen, "Tenuousness and Tenacity."

55. On the cultural determinants of "race" in a colonial context, see Stoler, *Carnal Knowledge and Imperial Power*, 79–111.

56. PA AA Berlin, DGT, Box 18, File 1: Franke to DGT, August 9, 1929.

57. PA AA Berlin, DGT, Box 19, File 4: Franke to DGT, June 7, 1933.

58. PA AA Berlin, DGT, Box 19, File 4: Franke to DGT, June 12, 1933.

59. PA AA Berlin, DGT, Box 17, File 3: Telegram to AA/Berlin from Blücher/DGT, September 26, 1934.

60. PA AA Berlin, DGT, Box 18, File 1: DGT Tagebuch Nr. 2300–29, November 5, 1929; Franke to Staudacher/DGT, December 6, 1929.

61. PA AA Berlin, DGT, Box 25: Letter from Georg Bausch to DGT, dated February 2, 1929, is a good example of the correspondence that circulated between the refugees and the consulate.

62. In this sense the historical factors in play were more akin to the economic and political factors that created ethnic diasporas in Europe and North America than to the type of organized colonial settlements characteristic of the high phase of imperialism. The topic of German diasporas in the Russian and Habsburg empires and in North and South America has been recently analyzed in O'Donnell, Bridenthal, and Reagin, eds., *The Heimat Abroad*.

63. See, for example, BA Berlin, R 901, Auswärtiges Amt, Nrs. 4916–4920: Handels- und Schiffahrtsverhältnisse mit Persien, Reisebericht Jung, 5 vols. (1910).

64. For a fascinating analysis of what it means to write histories of "globality," see Geyer and Bright, "World History in a Global Age."

65. This is derived from Geoff Eley's description of Bill Schwarz's work and its outlining of "dynamic fields of global Britishness." See Eley, "What Was/Is the Imperial Imaginary?," 2.

EIGHT

Classroom Colonialism
Race, Pedagogy, and Patriotism in Imperial Germany
JEFF BOWERSOX

As Germans struggled to define themselves as citizens of a recently unified nation-state after 1871, they did so with an eye toward a wider world being made ever smaller. The unprecedented expansion of global transportation, commercial, and communications networks, as well as the various scientific, military, and economic interventions they facilitated, were bringing the peoples of the world into ever closer contact. At the same time, the development of mass commercial culture, mass education, and mass politics provided new ways of mediating these encounters to ever-expanding publics at home. Of course, this global interaction around the turn of the twentieth century unfolded under the sign of empire. Accordingly, as distant and exotic lands progressively fell under the influence of Europeans and their descendants abroad, so did Germans, across lines of class, gender, region, and religion, come to see the world in colonial terms. Theirs was a world that could be ordered according to hierarchies of civilization defined by the orderliness of spaces and the progressiveness of races. Theirs was also a world in which collective progress and prosperity depended on the beneficent intervention of those higher on the scale in the affairs of those below.[1] Indeed, the ability to exercise such influence was the clearest manifestation of national vitality in an era defined by a Darwinian spirit of struggle. Seen in this context, empire, far from a matter of marginal interest, was rather a defining feature of how Germans understood themselves as a modern, civilized nation within a globalizing world.

Articulated in various confused, contradictory, and even conflicting forms throughout popular and official culture, a language of empire became a familiar part of everyday life over the course of the *Kaiserreich*. This was not primarily the product of cynical efforts to indoctrinate the public in a particular political message but rather part of a broader cultural conversation about the workings of a rapidly changing world and Germans' place within it.[2] This chapter examines one critical site for working out the parameters of this relationship, namely, the classroom. Beginning in earnest in the 1880s, German elementary and secondary school students began to wrestle with the non-European world in a variety of disciplines. In German lessons, Ferdinand Freiligrath's poem "Lion Ride" ("Löwenritt") encouraged students to follow the "gruesome trail" (*grausenvolle Fährte*) of the "King of the Desert" as he rode on the back of a giraffe, teeth planted firmly in its neck.[3] Natural history lessons familiarized students with markers of the colonial world ranging from elephants to ostriches and from coffee to coconuts, while history lessons by the late 1890s were beginning to include Germany's recent colonial acquisitions and, later, the wars in China and Southwest Africa. By the first decade of the twentieth century students were even grappling with the economic productivity of Germany's colonies and their country's overseas trade in their math assignments.[4]

However, for German students at all levels and in all types of preuniversity schools, the chief point of contact with the non-European world was within the discipline of geography. In geography lessons teachers brought students face to face with such "characteristic" subjects as the deserts of North Africa, the jungles of South America, and the typhoons of the South China Sea, not to mention the various racial "types" that populated the planet. Young Germans did not only learn about their own recently acquired colonial possessions and new "countrymen" (*Landsleute*) abroad, although these became more prominent as wars in China and Africa focused public attention on them. Students also studied those other areas of the world "colonized" by the German public imagination and by German economic interests, as well as those regions under the sway of other European and North American powers. Their lessons presented them with a progressively exoticized "colonial" world portrayed in terms of its potential for exploitation by able colonizers. If successful, this education would convince students not only that the world could be understood in terms of empire but also that they, too, belonged among the colonizers and, as adults, could promote the cause of progress at home and abroad.

Perhaps surprisingly, this colonial education did not become institutionalized in German curricula as a result of efforts by colonialist activists or organizations.[5] A body of reform-minded school geographers (*Schulgeographen*)[6] were the driving force behind this development. Although some of them were indeed colonial enthusiasts, their motivations were primarily professional and pedagogical. They aimed first and foremost to shape their undervalued discipline in such a way that it appealed to education authorities and teachers updating curricula and instructional practices for the modern age. The opportunities and challenges that attended the introduction of mass education added urgency to these efforts. The new school geography conveyed useful information about the workings of the world as well as patriotic virtues; at the same time, lessons were used to encourage students' interest in the subject through the obvious appeal of the unfamiliar and adventurous. Empire came to occupy and maintain a central place within German curricula by the turn of the century because school geographers employed it in ways that satisfied, on the one hand, teachers' demands for engaging and illustrative material and, on the other, authorities' demands for practical lessons for raising citizens who could promote Germany's well-being around the globe and at home. Understanding the acceptance of colonial education in these terms, rather than as part of the pursuit of a relatively narrow political agenda, helps us better appreciate the wider resonance of empire among the German public during the Imperial period.

Before the founding of Germany's overseas colonial empire in 1884, there were obviously no German colonies in classroom instruction. But there was also relatively little instruction on the rest of the non-European world up to this time. Because relatively few resources were devoted to training geography teachers and because most curricular guidelines designated geography as a subset of history, the subject was largely taught by historians or philologists who had little training in the discipline. When these teachers used the dedicated class time for geography instruction, they taught primarily the geography of the Mediterranean and northern European worlds, along with their lessons on classical languages and Greek, Roman, and German histories.[7] This geography instruction was, as a rule, a dry affair all across Germany. Teachers generally gave their lessons in the form of lectures, and students at both the elementary and secondary levels were expected to memorize and regurgitate extensive lists of names, facts, and figures. Given this emphasis, it is not surprising that most critics and commentators considered geography an "unuseful, intellectually killing, statistical memory cram" and thus the "most sterile" of school subjects.[8]

School geographers and other commentators frequently lamented the state of geography instruction and from the 1860s began to discuss in a more organized fashion how to make their discipline more effective.[9] In correspondence, lectures, and articles they petitioned officials across Germany to dedicate more classroom time to geography instruction independent of that of history and other humanities and to devote more resources to training geography teachers. Most of the German states, particularly in the south, were not overly receptive to their suggestions, but geographers' appeals did not fall on deaf ears in Prussia.[10] The Prussian Ministry of Culture, as the largest and most reform-minded of the German education ministries, became the particular focus of school geographers' attentions as they reformed their discipline. Prussian officials were in the process of reforming the nature and goals of education to suit the practical needs of the state.[11] These administrators saw a particular need to produce a citizenry with a better awareness of the world around them, given the rapid expansion of German economic and military interests around the globe. In exchange for extra resources devoted to training geography teachers and some minor curriculum changes, Prussian officials called on geographers to create, as Minister of Culture Gustav von Gossler proclaimed to the Deutscher Geographentag (Conference of German Geographers) in 1889, a geography "suited to the needs of today."[12] Teachers needed lessons that provided practical information relevant to an expansive Germany, and they also required a more effective manner of instruction appropriate to an age of mass culture and spectacular entertainments.

How best to reshape the practice of classroom instruction to suit the modern age had become a topic of considerable interest, especially for an influential, international circle of educators collected under the umbrella of "reform pedagogy" (*Reformpädagogik*). In all their diversity these pedagogues were united in their critique of modern industrial society and its mechanistic teaching methods, which did not deal with students as individuals with unique interests and abilities and sought to suppress or overcome childish tendencies as quickly as possible. Reaching back to Rousseau and Pestalozzi, reformers called instead for a pedagogy "that begins with the child" (*vom Kinde aus*): teaching strategies must be tailored to each student, and they must embrace the unique qualities of childhood. These educators started from the premise that imagination was the most effective teaching tool and developing self-reliance its most important goal. While school geographers did not endorse the most progressive, even utopian goals of leading reform pedagogues, many were captivated by the practical teaching strategies they encouraged. Through "illustrative" (*anschaulich*) teaching methods and practical applications, teachers could help students come to an understanding of the material at hand through their own efforts.[13] Young Germans would learn more effectively, and, with their creative faculties engaged with enriching lessons, they would be less susceptible to the much-disparaged mass commercial culture coming into its own during this same period.[14]

The undeniable appeal of mass entertainments—more to the point, the degeneracy many presumed they inspired—lent special urgency to the quest for an engaging pedagogy, but it also inspired effective teaching tools that school geographers later turned to their advantage. As the Strasbourg geographer Rudolf Langenbeck noted during a discussion about the value of local studies (*Heimatkunde*) for introducing geographical concepts in the first years of elementary schooling, the young student was especially "thirsty for the new, his interest is directed far more at foreign lands and peoples than the narrow homeland." To fellow school geographer Heinrich Matzat's concern that this interest derived from sensationalized Indian stories and adventure tales, Langenbeck argued that teachers should use this interest to make their teaching more effective:

> It is certainly true to an extent, but who is keeping teachers of VI [approximately age 8] from livening up their stories by weaving in tales of individual exploits, from telling students—in appropriate places—about lion and elephant hunts, about battles between Europeans and natives, about travelers' trials and tribulations while crossing Africa or on a polar journey? It is certainly also true that kids are more interested in getting to know the site of their heroes' great deeds than to be chained for a whole year in the narrow confines of their own neighborhood.... [Focusing only on the local] means fundamentally spoiling the joy of geography from the outset.[15]

Indeed, school geographers predicated their claim to be the very "science of illustration," to use the eminent atlas maker Hermann Kropatschek's description of his own discipline, on their ability to take students on imaginary journeys around the globe.[16] Tapping into the appeal of the exoticized and unfamiliar without degenerating into the voyeurism of trashy entertainments, geography teachers could keep their students interested in illustrative lessons about how the contemporary world worked.

As school geographers reshaped their discipline to meet "the needs of today," they devoted considerable energy to positioning geography as the subject best suited to prepare students to succeed in the contemporary world. After intensive discussions amongst themselves and in consultation with Prussian officials, they rallied around the so-called land-and-people (*Land-und-Leute*) approach, which encouraged reflection on the reciprocal influence between an environment and its inhabitants. More than simply pointing out geographic formations on a map, reformist school geographers argued for a methodology that started with understanding the features of a landscape before moving on to the ways that humans had developed that landscape and then addressing the political structures that humans developed to manage the resulting societies. In an intellectual climate in which the relative value of the humanities vis-à-vis the sciences was an explosive issue among education officials and competing interest groups, geographers claimed they could bridge the gap between the two by approaching human civilization as a form of adaptation to given natural conditions.[17]

Attention to geographical relationships not only promoted the illustrative lessons the most modern pedagogy demanded; it also allowed teachers to address what one teacher in training described as the "ethical side of instruction." Teaching students that "the features of the earth's surface exist in particular dependent relationships" necessarily required directing them "to the fact that under the same natural conditions the same is not always achieved." Thinking in terms of the hierarchies of race and civilization that were one of the first topics covered in the geography curriculum, he continued: "Because man is not unconditionally subject to the rule of nature it is left to his free will to decide whether to take advantage of the benefits of a territory or not."[18] By the 1890s, the object of geography instruction had become not only how the environment conditioned human development but also the extent to which humans successfully exploited available natural resources. School geographers intended this instruction to frame the very narrative of world history, illustrating the conditions under which nations rise and fall. Those nations that chose to successfully utilize their resources succeeded, and those that did not were destined to decline or fall under the influence of more innovative and efficient peoples.

The practical uses of such knowledge were clear. As early as 1879 one commentator on the controversial question of secondary school reform included among the "characteristics of every educated man" a familiarity with "the newest discoveries in the field, so important nowadays, of non-European geography." In an age when industry and commerce constituted the world's "main arteries" (*Hauptpulsadern*), the writer continued, educated Germans could not do without a "pretty comprehensive familiarity with the geographic and ethnographic relations of our earth, some familiarity with the production strength of countries, and the trading relationships of nations."[19] Indeed, as school geographers made the case for their discipline's practical value, they increasingly made economic production, the exploitation of available natural resources, and commercial relations—as the primary measures of a nation's strength—the focus of their teaching recommendations. In an environment of increasing competition over lucrative markets and limited but necessary resources beyond the boundaries of the civilized world, school geographers increasingly presented the non-European world in terms of its potential for economic exploitation and thus for strengthening Germany's trade relations vis-à-vis the rest of the world. This colonial world, including but not limited to Germany's young colonial empire, had become "so important nowadays" because it was the site where national strength would be tested.

With the land-and-people approach school geographers explicitly put their discipline in the service of German expansion. School geography became a matter of surveying, explaining, and thereby facilitating the expansion of colonial influence around the globe. Richard Lehmann, speaking at the eleventh Deutscher Geographentag in Bremen in 1895, insisted that the importance of geography was "greater than ever before." At the end of the nineteenth century European civilization was spreading over the entire earth "and indeed in ever growing expansion and strength." Germans, Lehmann continued, did not live in some isolated corner where it was possible to hide from the world around them. On the contrary, "our country is the central country of the most powerfully civilized continent," and Germany's expanding world trade, which was of such importance for their way of life, could only grow more in the next century. Lehmann pointed specifically to the recent entry of Germany into the family of colonizing peoples, noting that even if "the development [*Nutzbarmachung*] of the [colonies] is still small at first and everything there is still in the process of becoming, much can develop out of them in the course of time." The coming twentieth century would require students to look beyond Europe and familiarize themselves with the United States, the "colossus" China, and an already modernizing Japan. Given all of this, Lehmann asked rhetorically, should an awareness of the wider world and its inhabitants not be something that "must belong in the required kit of every educated person?"[20]

It was as the object of both exotic entertainment and potential economic exploitation that the non-European world found its way into German secondary and elementary school curricula beginning in the 1880s and 1890s. As more material became available on Germany's colonies specifically, the *Schutzgebiete* took on ever more importance as the exotic sites where Germans' competence was most directly tested and proven. This process was by no means uniform or consistent across Germany. School geographers praised certain states (Prussia, Saxony, Bremen) rather than others (Baden, Württemberg, Bavaria) for their willingness to promote the teaching of geography.[21] While elementary schools did not vary significantly in their teaching emphases, at the secondary level the humanist *Gymnasien* and girls' schools took up school geographers' suggestions far less readily than did the more practically oriented *Realschulen*, *Oberre-*

alschulen, and continuation schools (*Fortbildungsschulen*).[22] It also took time to marshal the resources needed to properly train teachers. Nevertheless, by the turn of the century state and school officials and teachers generally accepted that Germany's relationship with the wider world was worthy of attention, even if they disagreed on precisely how much in relation to other subjects.[23] While important for establishing the outlines of geography instruction, general curricular suggestions did not represent school geographers' greatest impact on the teaching of their discipline. Rather, they hoped to intervene directly in the classroom through the teaching materials they produced. Because teachers all across Germany and in all types of schools tended to rely on the same basic materials, it is worth taking a closer look at teaching resources to illustrate how school geographers employed empire to shape instructional practice.

Despite differences in form, style, and content, the materials produced by the 1890s maintained a striking uniformity in the narrative they presented to teachers and students, and editors developed increasingly more sophisticated textual and visual techniques to effectively "illustrate" their lessons in the sense encouraged by reform pedagogy. There were three basic types of geography resources in use by the turn of the century. Textual materials, readers chief among them, provided intensive and engaging discussions on a variety of subjects, while increasingly sophisticated collections of images (drawings and later photographs) or products provided visual and tactile resources for students to interpret in the classroom. Textbooks, although meant chiefly as references to be used by teachers to construct lessons and by students to review at home, served as the crucial backbone of instruction. Their factual details and narrative surveys provided the interpretive context within which world relations could be understood. A survey of the three most widely used textbook series in Prussia by the turn of the century—those originally founded by H. A. Daniel, Ernst von Seydlitz, and Alfred Kirchhoff—illustrates the common narrative, drawn from Ritter's land-and-people approach with its emphasis on the interaction between environment and humans.[24] All human development was bound together in a history of ever-expanding contact among the world's peoples driven by advances in commerce and transportation. Interaction offered opportunities for nations that successfully exploited their own wealth to prove their strength by exploiting and assisting those unable to do so on their own. All people were part of a grand quest to settle and develop the entire world, a quest whose end goal was "the economic satisfaction of humanity."[25]

Students learned most explicitly about Europe's position of leadership among the world's races, in this process of "mutual" development, through lessons on the racial divisions of humanity.[26] Although the specific information contained in these sections changed to suit new research and although the textbooks sometimes disagreed about such things as the number of races on the planet and the most important defining characteristics, they all nonetheless agreed on how ethnology contributed to an understanding of the interaction of humanity and nature. The standard overviews of skin color, skull shapes, and facial features of the races usually led readers to discussions of the diverse ways of life associated with them and, necessarily, their ranking according to contemporary standards of civilization. As the 1891 edition of Daniel's *Leitfaden für den Unterricht in der Geographie* explained, physiological characteristics were intimately intertwined with sociocultural habits determined in part by environment. After asking readers to name the races that live in Africa, the review questions at the end of the introduction asked about those races' ways of life: "Why do herding and hunting peoples not carry out agriculture? And what disadvantages do they derive from this?" The answer to these leading questions can be found on the previous page:

> Only the necessity of life forced these [peoples] to their nomad lifestyle or to their hunting and fishing life and holds them firmly to it. Their life represents a step backwards from agriculture. By contrast, agriculture offers a peaceful, quiet life, without the exhausting concerns about acquiring sustenance, rich in sociability and leisure. Crafts, arts, trades, commerce easily develop out of this: in this way it [agriculture] leads man to higher development [*Bildung*], to civilization [*Civilisation*].[27]

All agreed that the "caucasian," or "white," race was the most "important" of the world's races, and this was reflected both in the sophistication of its sedentary civilization and its "beautiful physical build [*Gliederbau*] and noble facial features."[28] As the twentieth edition of Seydlitz's *Kleine Schul-Geographie* explained to readers, "The Europeans—best enabled by the climate to lasting exertions of strength, developed by the diverse topography of their continent in the most varied ways, further blessed by the location of [the continent] in the middle of the three largest continents—has known, since the beginning of historical time, how to win and maintain first place among the populations of the earth."[29] Thus not only through geographic advantage but, in Kirchhoff's words, "through diligent work in the intellectual and economic realms Europe became the most powerful and wealthy of the continents."[30] The potential for civilization was determined only in part by given natural conditions; the rest was a matter of choice and dedicated effort.

Their leading position in the world had driven Europeans to spread beyond the boundaries of their continent. Not only did they become the "most capable emigrants, who now have begun to make Europe's culture into that of the world, Christianity to the religion of the world"; European explorers were the agents who brought the world's distant regions into ever closer contact.[31] Textbooks related the deeds of explorers like Marco Polo, Christopher Columbus, Ferdinand Magellan, and James Cook, who had done so much to expand European knowledge of the distant world in centuries past. In a transparent effort to grab students' interest, they included more recent celebrities—such internationally renowned names as Henry Morton Stanley, David Livingstone, and Sven Hedin—but also devoted themselves to introducing students and teachers to the Germans who belonged in the pantheon of great explorers. Men such as Heinrich Barths, Gerhard Rohlfs, and Gustav Nachtigal had also played an important role, at great personal risk, in the "entirely new epoch in the illumination of inner Africa."[32]

By the 1890s, with the growing official interest in a practical education centered on world commerce, textbook series inserted these explorers into an appropriate narrative. From the ancient Phoenicians who first spread their culture across the Mediterranean, to the Italian and German city-states who dominated trade in the Middle Ages, to the great European sea powers who established colonies around the world, economic competition and advances in transportation promoted world trade and brought civilization to those areas that lacked it.[33] Atlases and wall maps, such as in figure 8.1, made visible the growing interconnectedness via world commerce.[34] Where they had previously provided only political boundaries and topographical features, over the course of the 1890s they began to include important transportation and communications networks. The presentation of railroads, steamer routes, and telegraph lines enclosed the world in a net whose strings were tightened in Europe.

These networks bound Europe to a colonial world in need of assistance, a world defined, in all its diversity, as fundamentally chaotic, backwards, and, as a result, underdeveloped. Locals' inability—in the case of the *Naturvölker* of the "dark continent"—or stubborn unwillingness—in the case of the ancient but declining *Kulturvölker* of India and China—to develop the wealth of their lands not only bred disorder and stagnation in their own lands but also limited the economic progress of all peoples around the globe. For the mutual benefit of all concerned, then, capable colonizers had to overcome this backwardness; empire, as the antidote for the ills of the colonial world, was not only a reflection of the vitality of a nation but also the expression of a humanitarian imperative.

To buttress this perspective and to keep students' attention, textbooks and other teaching materials pursued a twin strategy in their portrayals of the

FIGURE 8.1 · Global transportation and communication networks represented in Diercke and Gaebler's *Schul-Atlas* (1900). Image courtesy of the Georg Eckert Institute for International Textbook Research.

colonial world, emphasizing chaos and underdevelopment and the potential for future exploitation. Students learned in particular about the raw materials necessary to produce the industrial and consumer goods recognizable from advertising or their household pantries.[35] Where they had previously focused on matters of historical or religious interest, textbooks increasingly focused their summary overviews on listing mineral resources and "usable plants" (*Nutzpflanzen*). Representational drawings, photographs, and product collections allowed students to see or handle such mundane items as rice, cotton, rubber, tea, and coffee in their raw form, while readers provided longer readings on their cultivation and processing. Such materials gave students a "grasp," both literal and figurative, of the available wealth outside Europe and of their own intimate connections with distant lands.[36] At the same time, they established a distance between the colonial world that provided raw materials and the civilized world that processed and consumed them.

Material surveying the colonial world's landscapes and fauna fulfilled the purpose of livening up instruction by constructing a titillatingly uncivilized colonial world. In image collections, quaintly idyllic pastoral scenes or bustling urban scenes defined images of Europe's "characteristic" landscapes, while common markers of underdevelopment, such as the untamed jungles, deserts, and animals that made adventure novels so exciting, became more prevalent and more pronounced in images of the colonial world.[37] Textbooks always listed game animals along with the various other natural resources, and readers, especially those used in elementary schools, emphasized danger and excitement in the colonial world by describing how lions, elephants, and other wild creatures interacted with humans in the still untamed areas they inhabited. Such descriptions did not shy away from providing gruesome accounts of the perils and thrills that such encounters could provide. To wit, an instructional essay on lions in an 1890 edition of Ferdinand Hirt's *Lesebuch für Volksschulen* described in detail the discomfort a traveling party experienced when a lion with a taste for human flesh slipped into camp one night, dragged a traveler away by the throat, and proceeded to crunch his bones within clear hearing distance of the camp. The article assuaged sensitive readers' fears by assuring them that a single pistol shot will drive away such a beast and by advising that the best time to hunt such creatures is when they sleep around midday.[38]

However much school geographers hoped to draw lessons from the world of popular culture, they always tempered their portrayals of the colonial world with an interest in taming the wilderness and ordering the chaos through development and integration into global trading networks. We can see in figure 8.2, which portrays "Papuas" from the German colony of Kaiser-Wilhelms-Land (on New Guinea), how school geographers situated all the necessary ethnographic and economic details within the colonial narrative of the new school geography.[39] Here we see "natives" (*Eingeborene*) taking proper advantage of their tropical paradise. The accompanying text by Alfred Kirchhoff takes time to outline for teachers the exotic physiognomic and cultural features of the Papua "race" that students should note, from their facial features and skin color to their skimpy skirts and colorful jewelry. Their appearance, superstitions, and characteristic wooden pole houses—"as were also common on the inland shores of prehistoric Europe"—mark them as a *Naturvolk* on a lower stage of development than readers (but "not at all so low"), but the Papuas are nevertheless "clever little people."

They obviously live off the abundant fruits of their local environment, and they have also become linked into the global economy. Women and men hand the result of a successful day's fishing to the pilots of outriggers, and others prepare yams, coconuts, and a spitted Papua pig. While one woman brings a pot of tuna, another man directs a girl to gather a bunch of bananas. In the background towers that ubiquitous marker of tropical bounty, the palm tree. The man at the very center of the image explains all the activity by pointing to the German steamer that has appeared on the horizon, their link to the world economy.[40] Overcoming their initial fears when they first encountered white men, the Papuas have distinguished themselves as a people willing to take ad-

FIGURE 8.2 · "Papuas," from Leutemann's *Bilder aus dem Völkerleben* (1888). Image courtesy of Amherst College Archives and Special Collections.

vantage of the connection their German colonial rulers have provided to a wider world of which they formerly knew little. In Kirchhoff's estimation, this interaction represents a "promising beginning to establishing peace and order among these tribes, to putting our trade and our industry to use, to blessing the cultural development of the natives."[41]

In their various teaching materials, school geographers hoped to fix in students' minds the relationship between the local and global in a world defined by empire. This project entailed making students aware of connections and opportunities all around the globe, but Germany's overseas empire became a focal point of lessons on the colonial world soon after the founding of the first colonies in the mid-1880s. Even before the newly acquired territories became a required subject of instruction, textbooks provided what limited and inconsistent details they could gather.[42] Their formal inclusion in the Prussian secondary school curricular revisions of 1892 spurred the introduction of more detailed surveys in textbooks, as well as the production of various supplementary aids focused exclusively on the colonies.[43] As more information and materials became available over the course of the 1890s and thereafter, the *Schutzgebiete* took an ever more central role within instruction on the colonial world. By the turn of the century, only India and China received equal attention in textbooks, and thereafter students increasingly found their lessons focused around such readings as "An Ostrich Hunt in Southwest Africa," "Our Togo Negroes as Farmers," and "A Coffee Plantation in East Africa."[44] For school geographers, lessons on Germany's efforts to civilize their own colonies most directly illustrated Germany's positive contributions to world development, but they also reflected the rising strength of a nation divided until 1871.[45] Indeed, given school geographers' basic assumptions about the rise and fall of nations in the modern era, these were intimately intertwined.

As they tried to familiarize German students with the workings of the world around them, school geographers pursued a project at once pedagogical, political, and practical. They claimed for their discipline a unique ability both to effectively engage students drawn to the charms of spectacular mass culture and to effectively prepare them to promote their nation's interests in a world being drawn ever closer together. They responded to the demands of education authorities, pedagogical reformers, and their own professional self-interest with their vision of a world defined by empire, a world in which vigorous peoples expanded their influence while decline awaited those that did not. Given contemporary concerns over the possible degeneracy that attended industrial modernity, this vision, in turn, lent urgency to school geographers' claims. Although they never achieved quite the expansion of their subject they desired, they did succeed in convincing officials and teachers across Germany that their instruction was a valuable tool for preparing young Germans to succeed as adults. By the turn of the century, lessons on the colonial world, especially Germany's overseas empire, had become institutionalized, and suitable teaching materials were both readily available and widely used. Increasingly over the course of the Imperial period, when teachers told their students stories about the wider world, they did so in the language of empire.

As historians Hans-Dietrich Schultz and Heinz Peter Brogatio point out with regard to the professionalization of geography at the university level, we make an important mistake if we reduce this development to "an organized form of colonial agitation."[46] On the one hand, this is a matter of chronology. Colonialist activists and organizations in general did play an important role in producing, promoting, and facilitating access to a wide range of teaching materials in high demand among officials and teachers, but they only began to do so from the turn of the century. They expanded and refined what school geographers had already achieved. On the other hand, this is a matter of context. The vision of the world that school geographers created and disseminated was only one contributor to a much broader societal engagement with empire that extended far beyond the sphere of education, although it did play an important role in setting the context and providing the terms for encounters in other spheres. By recognizing this fact—that school geographers actively responded to and engaged with other, more popular forms of colonial knowledge—we make it possible to distinguish the many competing, confused, and conflicting manifestations of empire that ran throughout German culture during the Imperial era and beyond.

NOTES

This author wishes to acknowledge Oxford University Press for publishing the original essay upon which this chapter is based.

1. In the context of European hegemony, the position of colonial cultivator was a generally understood metaphor for progress and power; contemporary Germans found it useful for framing relationships that extended beyond those traditionally understood as "colonial"—for example, between Germans and Poles in the East or between social reformers and the marginalized subjects of their zeal. See, for example, Ketelsen, "Der koloniale Diskurs"; Kopp, *Germany's Wild East*; Kopp and Müller-Richter, eds., *Die "Großstadt" und das "Primitive."*

2. For further discussion of the uses of colonialism in media aimed at youth during the imperial period, see my *Raising Germans in the Age of Empire*.

3. See Freiligrath, "Löwenritt."

4. *Schwelmer's Rechenbuch* asked students to compare the size and population of the colonies with those of the metropole and assess the increasing profitability of the colonies. See Barth, *Unsere Kolonien im Schulunterricht*, 17–18.

5. For a comprehensive survey of educational efforts by the organized colonial movement that nevertheless overemphasizes their role and identifies colonial enthusiasm too narrowly with *Kolonialpolitik*, see Holston, "'A Measure of the Nation.'"

6. The term refers specifically to those geographers whose focus was on the teaching of the subject at the pre-university level, to differentiate them from university faculty or various other researchers.

7. Sperling, "Zur Darstellung der deutschen Kolonien," 388.

8. "Der geographische Unterricht auf der höheren Schulen," *Die Post*, Nr. 230 (August 21, 1888); Kühne to Falk (February 8, 1874), Geheimes Staatsarchiv Preußischer Kulturbesitz [GStA PK] I. HA Rep. 76 Kultusministerium VI Sekt. I z Nr. 32 Bd. IV Bl. 247.

9. Schultz, *Die Geographie als Bildungsfach*, 64–72.

10. Kropatschek, *Zur geschichtlichen Entwicklung*, 18; Naumann, "Geographische Tagesfragen"; Kirchhoff, "Über die Vorbereitung der Geographielehrer," 127.

11. Nipperdey, *Arbeitswelt und Bürgergeist*, 537–540, 549–554.

12. "Deutscher Geographentag," *Volkszeitung* (April 25, 1889).

13. Herrmann, "Pädagogisches Denken und Anfänge der Reformpädagogik," 161–171.

14. For a good introduction to the development of mass culture in Germany and its attendant anxieties, see Maase and Kaschuba, eds., *Schund und Schönheit*.

15. Langenbeck, "Der Erdkundliche Unterricht nach den neuen Lehrpläne," 196–207.
16. Kropatschek, *Zur geschichtlichen Entwicklung*, 161–172.
17. For a more detailed survey of the complicated debates and competing positions among school geographers during this period of transition, see Schultz, *Die Geographie als Bildungsfach*, esp. 111–124, 267–298.
18. Maurer, "Seminararbeit" (January 7, 1887), 1, Hessisches Staatsarchiv Darmstadt Best. G 53 Gießen-LLG Nr. 375.
19. E. S., *Zur Reorganisation der höheren Schulanstalten*, GStA PK I. HA Rep. 76, Kultusministerium VI Sekt. I z Nr. 20 Bd. V Bl. 18.
20. Lehmann, "Der Bildungswert der Erdkunde," 192, 195–198.
21. "Bericht über den Verlauf," x–xi; Rößger, "Die Pflege der Erdkunde"; Schultz, *Die Geographie als Bildungsfach*, 160–169.
22. This was a frequent complaint that had more to do with the politics of school reform than any negative value ascribed to instruction on the colonial world. See the discussion in "Bericht über die Hauptversammlung," Bundesarchiv [BArch] R 8023/952 Bl. 113.
23. See the results of surveys carried out by the Deutsche Kolonialgesellschaft in 1900 and 1911. BArch R 8023/941 Bl. 129; BArch R 8023/952 Bl. 194.
24. After Seydlitz's death in 1849 and Daniel's in 1871, their august series were continued by different editors. After editing Daniel's series for a number of years, Kirchhoff decided to create his own textbook. His was an explicit and successful attempt to create a new series appropriate to the new ideas in school geography, ideas he did more than anyone to promote.
25. Oehlmann, ed., *E. v. Seydlitz'sche Geographie*, 315.
26. These sections simplified the most contemporary research for students. See Zimmerman, *Anthropology and Antihumanism in Imperial Germany*; Penny, *Objects of Culture*.
27. Volz, *Leitfaden für den Unterricht*, 176th ed., 29–30.
28. Kirchhoff, ed., *Leitfaden für den Unterricht*, 21; *Kleine Schul-Geographie*, 31.
29. Simon and Oehlmann, eds., *E. v. Seydlitz'sche Geographie*, 78–79.
30. Kirchhoff, *Erdkunde für Schulen*, 10.
31. Kirchhoff, *Erdkunde für Schulen*, 9–10. For a concise, schematic model of this narrative and its fundamental axioms that nonetheless relies on an overly simplistic model of top-down manipulation by a vaguely defined "European elite" to explain its construction, see Blaut, *The Colonizer's Model of the World*, 1–30.
32. Kirchhoff, ed., *Lehrbuch der Geographie*, 98–99.
33. See, for example, Volz, ed., *Leitfaden für den Unterricht*, 210th ed., 212–220; Oehlmann, ed., *E. v. Seydlitz'sche Geographie*, 314–326; Kirchhoff, *Erdkunde für Schulen*, 224–236.
34. Diercke and Gaebler, *Schul-Atlas für höhere Lehranstalten*.
35. Ciarlo, *Advertising Empire*.
36. Badenberg, "Zwischen Kairo und Alt-Berlin," 355.
37. This was the case even in the earliest collections of images found in textbooks. See Simon, ed., *E. v. Seydlitz'sche Geographie*, 169–183.

38. Anon. "Der Löwe," in *Ferdinand Hirts Lesebuch für Volksschulen*, 301–302.

39. Photographs were not widely used as a teaching resource until after the turn of the century. Before this, narrative or pictorial overviews of a region, called *Charakterbilder*, provided teachers the best tool for illustrating their geography lessons. Each *Charakterbild* was meant to provide a single coherent "picture" that illustrated the interactions between land and people and, thus, the essential "character" of the region. Besides the best-known works, those edited by Hölzel, Leutemann, and Lehmann, there were also less expensive collections, like Hirt's, that, while not as acclaimed, served the same basic purpose. For a discussion of different *Charakterbilder* series available around the turn of the century, see Nowack et al., eds., *Der Unterricht in den Realien*, 43–44.

40. Although the illustration identifies it only as a "European" steamship, the text is more specific about its provenance.

41. "Papuas," in Leutemann, ed., *Bilder aus dem Völkerleben*.

42. Volz, ed., *Lehrbuch der Geographie*, 64th ed., 113; Simon and Oehlmann, eds., *E. v. Seydlitz'sche Geographie*, 171.

43. See, for example, Kirchhoff, *Die Schutzgebiete des deutschen Reiches*, and Partsch, *Die Schutzgebiete des Deutschen Reiches*. Partsch's booklet was the textual accompaniment to his friend Richard Kiepert's *Deutscher Kolonialatlas*.

44. Jenetzky and Hellmuth, eds., *R. u. W. Dietleins Deutsches Lesebuch*.

45. Volz, ed., *Leitfaden für den Unterricht*, 210th ed., 212–220; Oehlmann, ed., *E. v. Seydlitz'sche Geographie*, 314–326; Kirchhoff, *Erdkunde für Schulen*, 224–236.

46. Schultz and Brogatio, "'Gesellschaft für Erdkunde zu Berlin,'" 87.

NINE

Mass-Marketing the Empire
Colonial Fantasies and Advertising Visions
DAVID CIARLO

In 1908, an advertisement for Bergmann and Company's "Hobbyhorse Lily Soap" appeared in the pages of the magazine *Colony and Home*; it depicted a neatly wrapped bar of soap as an object of awe to childlike African natives (see figure 9.1). This tableau epitomizes the aesthetics of what might be termed the colonial cargo cult: primitive natives transfixed by the wondrously modern European commodity. The scene incorporates two powerful strands of imperialist ideology: the civilizing mission and racial difference. With the first, the commodity here stands as "civilizer": the brand-name soap represents not just a cleaning product but the superiority of industrial production, the global reach of commerce, and the very value of cleanliness.[1] The figures' facial expressions and postures and the way that other figures come running from afar demonstrate *ad oculos* that such Western goods (and values) have a culturally transcendent and inherently inescapable appeal. At the same time, the natives are racially differentiated: their culture is manifestly savage, as seen in their state of undress, and their intellectual inferiority is shown by the immaturity of their facial features. Since this advertisement appears in a publication devoted to promoting German colonialism to the German public, it might seem to reflect a politicization of commerce—namely, an example of one way in which colonialist ideology was deliberately disseminated to the broader German public.

The story, however, is not so simple. The relationship between this particular advertisement and the ideology of German colonialism is fraught with countervailing forces. At first glance, the congruence of this visual commercial

FIGURE 9.1 · "Hobbyhorse Lily-Milk Soap. For tender white skin." Bergmann & Co, Radebeul. Source: Kolonie und Heimat (1908).

motif with those ideological constructions of the civilizing mission or of ineluctable racial difference found in colonialist writings appears to offer a compelling argument that colonialism—and those who advocated it—had begun to penetrate the world of business. The history of visuality follows a trajectory different from the history of ideology's, and they cannot be so casually coupled together. In fact, a deeper look into the intersections of colonialist advocacy and the broader world of advertising suggests a different relationship: not an established political ideology ultimately penetrating the commercial world but rather the new practices of commerce reconfiguring a traditional sphere of political ideology. First, the style of Bergmann's ad—the way it is designed to convey information—could not be further from the traditional formats of German colonialist ideology. Moreover, the vehicle for this new communicative style and the scope of its circulation reflect a radical transformation already under way in German society. Bergmann's ad represents not the victory of colonial ideology in the German public sphere but rather its defeat.

The Bergmann Company embodied a new mode of business. A multinational company, Bergmann mass-produced a product that became a brand-name commodity (*Markenartikel*) by means of the new methods and technologies of modern advertising.² Just before the fin de siècle, Bergmann began to circulate an array of images in advertising inserts and on posters and packaging labels to define and characterize its *Steckenpferde* (hobbyhorse) brand soap. These included romanticized tableaus: an attractive young maiden (in the style of art nouveau) gazing into a sunset (emblazoned with the brand name); a cute little girl in a sun hat, carrying flowers; a cherubic child stepping into a washtub.³ Such images of idealized womanhood and romanticized childhood infused the product with larger meanings (in this case, gendered and maternal). Soap manufacturers were at the cutting edge of modern German advertising. Indeed, it is likely that one of Bergmann's brands, Dada hair conditioner, even provided the eponym for the infamous avant-garde movement.⁴ None of Bergmann's soap ingredients came from the German colonies, however. It therefore might seem odd that its 1908 ad seemingly promotes a German colonialist agenda.

What is the relationship between commercial incarnations of colonial fantasy and the escalating tempo of colonial politics in Germany? While scholars have studied the operations of colonialist *ideology* in the political sphere, the role of *fantasy* in that sphere has proven more difficult to tackle.⁵ One reason for this is that the disseminators of colonialist ideology were quite distinct from the more diffuse generators of commercial colonial fantasy. They came from different social strata, they had different aims and strategies, and they had different influences upon the larger course of German history. A great deal of scholarship has revealed the contours of the "colonial archive"—the governmental, quasi-official scientific and educational establishments that have left extensive written records. Exploring the visual archive puts the very notion of ideology in a different light, exposing the shifting social and cultural contours of colonialist culture itself.

CLASSIFYING COLONIALISTS

From the broadest perspective, the German colonial project began as an armchair fantasy for educated readers. As Suzanne Zantop has shown, it emerged first in the imaginative world of print, stretching back to works of drama and fiction in the eighteenth century.⁶ Even the origin of organized colonialist politics is usually traced back to a publication: Friedrich Fabri's 1879 pamphlet *Does Germany Need Colonies?*⁷ In the wake of Fabri's publishing success, colonialist politics in Germany soon came to be monopolized by a single institution, the German Colonial Union, which emerged out of the array of different colonial clubs and commercial geography societies and quickly subsumed them.

In 1887, two years after Germany acquired colonies, the union merged with its only remaining rival to become the German Colonial Society. Its goal was "agitation" for the colonial idea.[8]

Despite its organizational growth, the Colonial Society's membership remained fairly insular throughout its history, self-selecting by social class, professional inclination and political stance. Society members came overwhelmingly from the conservative echelons of German society, and at the level of the national leadership, the society had close ties with the German state.[9] Its professional secretariat, meanwhile, became the primary clearinghouse for all issues relating to the colonies, often working closely with the Colonial Section of the Foreign Office.

What is less often discussed is the degree to which the German Colonial Society as an organization was able to steer, manage, and ultimately monopolize a great deal of the print culture of German colonialism. Before 1900, most German publications that dealt with the colonies emerged from a small web of conservative publishing houses that had personal connections to both the German state and members of the upper ranks of the Colonial Society. For instance, Ernst Vohsen, who owned the press of Dietrich Reimer, was a key member of the executive board of the Colonial Society, and his publishing house received lucrative contracts for a vast number of printing projects, including the *German Colonial Atlas*.[10] A great deal of colonialist literature came from publishing houses with connections to the state, such as E. S. Mittler and Sons.[11] Even more importantly, the professional secretariat of the Colonial Society and its chief editor, Gustav Meinecke, salted countless essays and articles in mainstream media, from daily newspapers across Germany to the *Illustrierte Zeitung, Daheim*, and *Gartenlaube*.[12] Thus, much of the print circulating about the colonies, whether books or articles in seemingly apolitical magazines, remained tightly enmeshed in the institutional structures of colonial enthusiasm, which calls into question the relationship of this colonialist discourse to the mentality of the German public more broadly.

An alternative way to chart the relationship between colonial enthusiasm and the broader public is through commercial relationships, for these were not so obviously staged with "agitation" (i.e., propaganda) in mind. Indeed, it is possible to map the "consumer identity" of colonial enthusiasm; that is, its character as delineated in the classified advertising that underwrote its publications. The practice of appending classifieds to the end of a periodical or book to help defray printing costs was a century old. The *German Colonial News*, the organ of the German Colonial Society, appended classified pages, and so too did other colonial enthusiast periodicals, from the *Tropenpflanzer* to the state-sponsored *German Colonial Bulletin*. Serialized books, such as the annual *German Colonial Calendar*, were particularly laden with long appendices of classifieds. One interesting aspect to the classifieds in colonialist publications is their continuity: the range of businesses running classifieds in the *German Colonial News* is quite small in any given year of the late 1880s, with the same twenty- or thirty-odd businesses appearing over and over again.

Given the Colonial Society's mission, one might naturally assume that such classified advertising would be geared toward future or would-be colonists.[13] Indeed, there were some classified ads for goods useful for colonization, whether seeds, tools, and farm implements or jam packaged for export. Machinery, too, along with materials for railroad and mine cart construction, also makes the occasional appearance and even (in one exceptional instance) iron steamboats "for the cheapest price of 1000 Mk."[14] If illustrated at all, these classifieds might feature a simple drawing of the tool or material. Overall, however, such classifieds for the tools of colonization were a minority. Given that, in the 1880s, only a tiny number of Germans were emigrating or visiting the new German colonies, it is improbable that sales to would-be colonists generated by these classifieds would have covered these ads' cost.

The preeminent product advertised in 1880s–1890s colonialist literature was other colonialist literature. The classifieds of the 1889 *Colonial News* promoted books that ran the gamut from the pragmatic to the scientific; how-to books on emigrating to Argentina or on successful tobacco planting were promoted alongside treatises on German colonial law and overviews of the land and people of Samoa.[15] Interestingly enough, classified ads for how-to colonization literature declines after 1890; they were increasingly overshadowed by geographical overviews or boosterish evaluations of the colonial economy— literature directed more at metropolitan readers. Literature speaking to *Bildungsbürger* or to nationalists more broadly also appeared, though less and less over the course of the 1890s.[16]

The single largest product category after colonialist literature was alcohol. Classifieds for champagne, wine, beer, and all sorts of liquor were ubiquitous. Other consumables were nonalcoholic; the most common was cigars, a staple of *Bildungsbürgerlich* leisure.[17] There were also classifieds for cocoa; Dresden's Hartwig and Vogel, for instance, ran ornate classifieds in the *Colonial News* through the 1890s. Lübeck tea importers and even a Weimar cigarette company likewise advertised in the *Colonial News*. Since tobacco, tea, and cocoa were the most common consumables to appear in colonial literature classifieds, it is tempting to see these classifieds as an early attempt by companies to link such goods to the *German* colonies (and thereby inspire purchase) through taxonomic fiat. Few colonial enthusiasts would have been fooled. In fact, many colonial enthusiasts, belaboring Germany's need for "real" colonial wares, eschewed the word *Kolonialwaren* altogether and insisted on the cumbersome phrase "Produkten aus die deutschen Kolonien."

Colonialist classifieds did offer some types of consumables that were truly colonial in their origins. A Karlsruhe Apotheke advertised its Kolabiscuits and Kolabread in 1889, for instance. Another relatively new product with a strong whiff of tropical colonies was coconut butter. The Müller firm of Mannheim advertised its coconut butter in the *Colonial News* around 1890, but Germany's fledgling colonies played no role, as the requisite tropical oils came from established trade networks in West Africa. Taken collectively, the classifieds of colonial enthusiast literature in the 1880s and 1890s speak to a very distinct consumer; namely, one who was male, middle-class, well-read, and nationalist. The Colonial Society leadership may have endlessly discussed efforts to bring the colonial message to "wider circles," but the ads in colonialist publications make such talk ring hollow. What defined the colonial enthusiast first and foremost was the consumption of literature, literature that was made interesting by its exotic locale but remained serious through the authority of its scientific legitimacy. The cocoa or tea he saw in the classified pages was "colonial" only by linguistic tradition, although some novelties, like the cola nut, certainly conveyed a flash of tropical exoticism. In all of these classifieds, the appeal to the reader was first and foremost on the standard assurance of the product's quality. If the classified included any larger message, it spoke to the product's connection to social class or to Germany.

A decade later, a far broader range of goods were being advertised in the *Colonial News*. By 1900, more and more of the goods in these classifieds might appeal simultaneously to the colonial adventurer, the recreational traveler, and perhaps most importantly, the stay-at-home, nationally minded consumer. Colonial Brew brand beer (for export), steamer trunks (for travelers more generally), and Cito bicycle tires (for domestic use) were intermingled on a typical ad page (see figure 9.2). Mauser handguns, Friedrich Haag pocket knives, and Maggi soup powder were also offered in colonialist literature classifieds as uniquely "suitable for the colonies."[18] It seems unlikely that the limited sales of ads by Mauser and Maggi to the handful of Germans actually traveling to the colonies circa 1900 could have recouped the ads' costs; but handguns and soup powder most likely found their way into the desk drawers or kitchens of colonial enthusiasts whose feet remained firmly planted in Germany. The attestation of a product's suitability "in the colonies" spoke to its durability and worth rather than its actual use. Full-page ads by Heinrich Jordan, for exam-

FIGURE 9.2 · Excerpt of a classified ad page from the *German Colonial News*. Source: *Deutsche Kolonialzeitung* (1899).

ple, appearing regularly in the *Colonial News* and the annual *German Colonial Calendar* of the 1890s, offered full tropical outfits, from white cotton suits to pith helmets, boots, and riding crops. Yet Heinrich Jordan also sold entirely mundane clothing, from pajamas to socks, as advertisements from 1898 show (see figure 9.3). The appellation "suitable for the colonies" could spice up a mundane purchase of soup bouillon or socks with a flash of imaginative travel. Even today, outdoor gear such as North Face alpine jackets and Land Rover off-road vehicles rarely find use outside urban or suburban areas, but their suitability for more rugged conditions is a precondition of their purchase.

Yet the importance of imaginative travel to advertisers in the *Colonial News* should not be overstated. Even in 1900, most classifieds in the *Colonial News* held no explicit colonial or colonialist reference whatsoever. Classifieds for cigars, the quintessential conservative male middle-class luxury good, most often featured nationalistic brand names such as "Kaiser" and "Germania."[19] Ads by larger firms from the mainstream of the German business world, such as Hartwig and Vogel (cocoa), Hildebrand and Sons (chocolate), Liebig (beef bouillon), and Panther (bicycle tires), appear more frequently in the years just

Mass-Marketing the Empire · 193

Heinrich Jordan
Berlin SW.12, Markgrafenstr. 105-107.

Gegründet 1839. — Deutschlands grösstes Kaufhaus — **Gegründet 1839.**

für

Fertige Wäsche jeder Art.

Die Firma empfiehlt in hervorragend guter Ausführung:

Tropen-Anzüge

aus weissem, extra starkem Cutil
für die Herren Offiziere in vorschriftsmässiger, wie auch in jeder anderen gewünschten Form.

Preis für den Anzug, je nach Grösse Mk. **9.75** und **10.00**.

Besonders beachtenswert für die Offiziers-Chargen der Kaiserl. Marine.

Schlaf-Anzüge — Padjamas —
für den Tropen-Aufenthalt unerlässlich.

aus Hemdentuch. Anzug M. **5.25**	Verschiedene Formen und Ausführungen.	aus gestr. Baumwoll. Flanell **5.50**
aus Engl. Zephyr, gestr. M. **8.25**	aus gestr. Halbwoll. Flanell **11.00**	aus gestr. Reinwoll. Flanell **15.50**
aus gestr. Halbseid. Flanell **18.75**	Preise für normale Grössen.	aus schwerer Chines. Seide **25.50**

Tropen-Anzug. — Schlaf-Anzug.

Flanell-Hemden für Tropen-Aufenthalt, Reise, Jagd und Sport
in den Preislagen: das Stück Mk. **2.50, 3.50, 6.00—12.00**.

Porös. — **Unterkleid der Zukunft.** — **Wolle — Baumwolle — Leinen**
in einem Gewebe — nicht Trikot gewirkt — vereinigt.
Nicht einlaufend. — Für die Tropen besonders geeignet. — Stets porös bleibend.
Artikel aus dem neuen Gewebe — Unterkleid der Zukunft:
Unterhemden — Unterbeinkleider — Sporthemden — Taghemden — Reisehemden — Schlafhemden. — **Unterkleid der Zukunft.** **Porös.**

Trikot-Hemden aus: | ### Trikot-Beinkleider aus:

Ungebleichter Baumwolle — feines leichtes Gewebe — vorn zum Knöpfen mit Hals- und Handprisen versehen . das Stück Mk. **2.40**
Grauer Reform-Baumwolle — feines, weiches Gewebe — sehr haltbar, doppelte Brust-, Hals- u. Handprisen u. Schulterschluss, das Stück M. **2.50**
Vigogne (aus Wolle und Baumwolle bestehend) — modemeliert — feine, bewährte Qualität, in der Wäsche nicht einlaufend, doppelte Brust, Schulterschluss, Hals- und Handprisen . . . . das Stück Mk. **3.75**
Reinwollenem Kammgarn — modemeliert — feine, leichte Qual., mit dopp. Brust, Schulterschluss, Hals- und Handprisen, das Stück M. **4.25**

Ungebleichter Baumwolle — ganz leichte Qualität, das Paar Mk. **1.75**
Ungebleichter Egyptischer Baumwolle (Maco) — feine erprobte Qualität (sehr haltbar) . das Paar Mk. **3.50**
Vigogne (aus Wolle und Baumwolle bestehend) — modemeliert — feine sehr haltbare Qualität, nicht einlaufend in der Wäsche . . . . das Paar Mk. **3.00**
Reinwollenem Kammgarn — modemeliert, feine, leichte Qual., d. Paar Mk. **4.00**
Leibbinden aus Trikotstoff das Stück Mk. **1.70** gestrickt das Stück Mk. **1.40**

Socken aus: Baumwolle **0.15-2.00** | Vigogne **0.75-3.00** | Reiner Wolle **1.00-4.00**
das Paar Mk.

Reise-Mützen, Stück Mk. **0.75-6.00** | **Original-Spessart-Mützen** Stück Mk. **6.00** | **Reise Schuhe** das Paar Mk. **1.75-4.50**

Die Firma versendet franko Proben und Preislisten, sowie jeden Auftrag im Betrage von 20 Mark an.

FIGURE 9.3 · Heinrich Jordan, "Germany's Largest Department Store. Ready-Made Clothing of Every Sort. Tropical wear; sleepwear/pajamas." Source: *Deutsche Kolonialzeitung* 15, Nr. 12 (1899): 95.

before 1900. These ads are illustrated. Not only did such larger firms possess the capital to invest in more expensive illustrated ads; they also were familiar with professional advertising's latest methods, which stressed the effectiveness of visual appeal. Absent was any allegiance to the colonial "cause." In the pages of the *Colonial News*, therefore, one could see the growth of a visual dissonance between traditional small businessmen, who promoted wares with textual classified ads laden with political overtones, and larger firms, which deployed the latest visual techniques without any reference to politics at all.[20]

Nonetheless, the larger firms needed to remain within the restrictions of colonial enthusiasts' class- and political predilections For instance, a Cito bicycle ad (cf. figure 9.2), featuring a woman astride that modern gadget, stands out from the other ads in the *Colonial News*. The ad, following the lead of such industry giants as Reithoffer, Durkopp, and Excelsior, conveys its message primarily through imagery. Unlike bicycle ads in the mainstream press, however, Cito's female cyclist is depicted in very conservative garb: a long dress and elaborate hat convey an unmistakably conservative decorum. Yet this ad, one of the most visually sophisticated to appear in a colonial enthusiast publication before 1900, looks a bit archaic next to more freewheeling ones in the mainstream press.[21] Also around 1900, mainstream bicycle ads, particularly those of Reithoffer and Excelsior, began deploying images of blacks, usually in racialized depictions as minstrel figures.[22] In the classified pages of the *Colonial News*, no such minstrel motifs are to be found.

THE COLONIZATION OF ADVERTISING

Colonial enthusiasts might have their insiders' club and proclaim their expertise in all things colonial, but they could not maintain proprietary control over colonialism's image. Beginning around 1900, the nascent field of German visual advertising used more and more images that deliberately sought to draw upon the colonial aura broadly construed. Mainstream advertising illustrations increasingly showed scenes of a white colonizer directing native labor, for instance; even more commonly, Africans might be depicted so as to show them laboring for the viewer.[23] An advertisement for Odol mouthwash that appeared in the tabloid *Die Woche*, for instance, depicts a line of African women carrying bundles of Odol out of the dark jungle (see figure 9.4).[24] Yet nothing in its ingredients or manufacture had to do with Germany's African colonies. Trademarked in 1893, Odol, an oral antiseptic made from willow bark, was among the first branded commodities to become a household name in Germany; its manufacturer, the firm of Karl August, was a pioneer in modern advertising

FIGURE 9.4 · Odol mouthwash, "Absolute best mouthwash in the world! Distributed over the entire globe!" Source: *Die Woche* III, Nr. 6 (1901).

methods. Around the turn of the century, Odol ads appeared in *Die Jugend* and other cutting-edge magazines; only much later in the decade did Odol advertisements begin to turn up in colonial enthusiast publications.[25]

Companies like Karl August increasingly turned to African figures for strategic reasons, not because their products had a real connection to colonies. The use of Africans allowed advertisers to stage a visual performance of labor, one showing the modern product carried, as it were, directly to the viewer. Indeed, a close look at the Odol illustration reveals sophisticated visual techniques at work. The line of figures emerge from the darkness of the background and into the lighted foreground—a march from darkness toward civilization. It is the name-brand commodity—the "absolute best mouthwash in the world! Spread over the entire earth!"—that is the driving force behind this developmental progress. For when the African porters carry the bundled commodity on their heads, moreover, they are *literally* elevating it above themselves. Setting the scene in the colonial realm offered avenues of representation useful to the advertiser, even when the product had nothing to do with the colonies. In this way, Africa became "fashionable," in the words of one advertising writer.[26]

True, the control of African labor formed one of the linchpins of German colonialist ideology.[27] Yet with this one notable exception, colonial enthusiast enterprises were curiously little enamored with deploying the ideology of colonized labor *visually*, at least in commercial illustrations.[28] One of the most visually elaborate ads in the *Colonial News* of 1899, for instance, was for Emde

FIGURE 9.5 · Emde Düsseldorf Cigar Factory advertisement, featuring "Prime New Guinea" and "Prime Bibundi" sorts. Source: classified advertisement from the *Deutsche Kolonialzeitung* (1899).

cigars, the product of a Düsseldorf cigar maker (see figure 9.5). The focal point of the illustration is an unremarkable drawing of the product. At the ad's sides are two mustached archetypes of the conservative upper class, a naval officer and a businessman with a monocle, top hat, tie, and jacket, smoking the cigars. Only the names of the tobacco blends—Bibundi, New Guinea—refer to these cigars' origins in the German colonies. The visual emphasis is on the class of German that purchases these cigars. This then is an ad for insiders, not one legible to a wide audience. Compared to Odol's transparent distillation of colonial power—an ad for a *noncolonial* product geared to wide audience— the contrast could not be more striking.

Whether as a niche market or a paying readership, middle-class colonialists were not entirely inconsequential commercially; the *Colonial News* could claim a circulation of 18,500 copies in 1889.[29] Yet by comparison, the paragon of middle-class-leisure print culture, *Die Gartenlaube*, had attained a circulation of 385,000 in 1875 (it declined thereafter).[30] The first true mass-circulation papers, like the *Berliner Lokal-Anzeiger*, attained daily circulations of 123,500 by the late 1880s and continued to grow dramatically. By 1914, some tabloids had a circulation exceeding a million copies; such massive numbers relied utterly on advertising to keep paper costs low enough to make the cover price widely affordable.[31] In the face of such developments, the few thousand subscribers of the *Colonial News* were a paltry sum.

By 1900, the Colonial Society and its offshoots were pursuing a number of enterprises that strayed from the political mission of colonial agitation into the business of print media and even consumer goods.[32] Unfortunately for colonial enthusiasts, Germany's colonies never grew into the fabled German India. Even fifteen years after the declaration of German sovereignty over regions of Africa, there were precious few goods from the German colonies to sell. Cigars from New Guinea, cocoa from Cameroon, and coffee from East Africa—and that was all. The German colonial economy relied upon its loyal colonial-enthusiast consumers to purchase what was often an inferior product, at best an equivalent one, at a higher price.[33] The only real success story was cocoa exported from Kamerun; it reached 260,000 kilograms annually by 1900. But cocoa consumption in Germany that year was 19.2 million kilograms. So German colonial production could fill only a fraction of domestic needs, and the German cocoa manufacturing giant Stollwerck acquired the vast majority of its cocoa from independent producers.[34]

Cocoa consumption in Germany would only keep growing. In 1890, it was 0.10 kilograms per capita; by 1912, it had risen more than eightfold, to 0.81. This consumption surge stemmed in a large part from new advertising practices, as even contemporaries realized.[35] From the 1890s onwards, chromolithographed posters and tins and illustrated inserts for such brands as Ruger, Tell, and Van Houten made strong, seemingly irresistible visual arguments for cocoa's benefits. On the package one could see cherubic children made visibly healthy and happy by the product within. On posters and ad inserts everywhere, svelte modern women displayed maternal competence by serving the healthy product to their children.[36] Two decades later, with hot cocoa firmly established as a necessity of the domestic sphere, Sarotti and other popular brands turned to more exotic themes, from anonymous African laborers carrying the valuable product to Orientalized minions serving it on trays.[37]

A second hurdle that colonialists faced lay in the visual realm. German colonial enterprises by and large did not use vivid illustrations of colonial power,

FIGURE 9.6 · Hönig and Bauhardt's "Kamerun Cocoa." The packaging is black, white, and red—the colors of the imperial German flag. Source: *Warenzeichenblatt des Kaiserliches Patentamts* (1901), 500, reg. no. 49000.

exotic terrain, erotically posed natives, or laboring colonial subordinates to sell their wares. Indeed, German companies selling Kamerun cocoa often deployed expressly conservative packaging forms when marketing it as "German colonial." The 1901 packaging for Hönig and Bauhardt's Kamerun Cocoa, for example, carries a design with primarily textual impact (see figure 9.6). Its visual components—a picture of a cocoa bean, a handful of gold medallions—belong to the packaging style of the 1880s and so had grown a bit quaint.[38] The packaging was striped in black, white, and red—a reference to the German flag meant to inspire patriotic purchase. Yet there is no attempt to illustrate the exotic or colonial origins of the product or to meaningfully connect them in the visual realm to the German consumer.[39] Six years later, a trademark registration by Georg Schepeler for Usambara Blend coffee includes a greater visual component but one that still does not reflect anything expressly "colonial." It shows two men wearing sombreros loading cocoa onto donkeys—a tropical scene so generic that the illustration must have simply been borrowed from another label.[40] Right up to the eve of the World War, German colonial companies and marketers continued to deploy very traditional motifs to sell German colonial products.[41]

In 1911, the Deutsche Tabakbau-Gesellschaft Kamerun mbH trademarked a logo of classical motifs that seemed straight out of the late 1880s. Centering on a classically inspired Mercury in front of a shield of Germany's national colors (black, white, and red), it includes a sailing ship (three-quarters of a

Mass-Marketing the Empire · 199

FIGURE 9.7 · Deutsche Tabakbau-GMBH Kamerun. Note the black, white, and red blazon behind the figure of Mercury (god of trade). Source: *Warenzeichenblatt des Kaiserliches Patentamts* (1911), 2260, reg. no. 149584.

century into the age of steam!) and an antique train chuffing under some palm trees (see figure 9.7). This type of classical collage—a diverse array of antique symbols of industry grouped together—could be found on the masthead of publications like *Die Gartenlaube* and *Über Land und Meer* in the 1860s. By 1911, such collages were a half-century out of date. In that year, for instance, Tengelmann, a mass-market coffee and cocoa grocery chain with more than five hundred retail locations, trademarked an eye-catching advertisement (see figure 9.8). In it, African laborers, wearing exotic coolie hats, unfurl a banner listing the brand-name goods. While the Africans' massively distorted facial features highlight their inferiority, their artfully depicted musculature hints at the labor going into the commodity. Also, the figures are posed to draw attention by meeting the gaze of the viewer and directing it to the brand name.[42] Tengelmann's mix of Orientalizing, exotic, and preposterously racialized elements was aimed at the general public, not the expert colonialist. In this broader marketplace, the drab packaging (cf. Figure 9.6) or classical allegories (cf. figure 9.7) of German colonial companies selling "genuine products from the German colonies" could not possibly compete.

The conservatism of German colonial product advertising might derive from the audience for these niche products. Even mass-market firms that normally invested a great deal of creative energy in packaging played down dynamic and imaginative elements when marketing colonial products to

FIGURE 9.8 · Hamburger Kaffee-Import Geschäft Emil Tengelmann. This advertisement was directed at the general public and did not appear in colonialist publications. Source: *Warenzeichenblatt des Kaiserliches Patentamts* (1911), 104, reg. no. 138038.

colonial-enthusiast consumers. The Riquet Company, for instance, trademarked several labels for cocoa from the German colonies in 1910. Their packaging for "Kamerun Cocoa" shows a grainy map of the colony—nothing more than a cartographic ink blot, buttressed by a poorly crafted German imperial eagle. Even the brand name is lettered in old German script, and the packaging includes a lengthy exposition that begins "Kamerun cocoa, because it is of suitable quality for household use, is in fact an *achievement* of the German colonial effort, for it cost such great effort [*Mühe*] to come so far"—not exactly inspirational in this new age of the superlative. Riquet also trademarked packaging for Samoan chocolate with a similarly bland cartographic theme; Samoa is illustrated as six unimpressive ink splotches with the numerical population of each printed underneath.[43] Even the cocoa manufacturer Stollwerck, with its world-renowned logo of a mighty eagle straddling two globes, used its drabbest and most amateurish packaging ever to market its German-colonial brand Unser Kakao.[44] Was Stollwerck's use of an outmoded style a deliberate appeal to colonialists' traditionalism or simple inattention to a fringe market? Either way, the optical obsolescence of the advertisements for German colonial products insured that the scarce products themselves would remain at the margins of both the physical economy and the commercial imaginary. It was a curious fact of fin de siècle German commercial culture that mass marketers, who knew little of the colonial project and still less of the politics of colonial enthusiasm, turned to images of colonial rule (cf. figure 9.4) to lend their wares exotic flair and eye-catching scenes of power, whereas the promoters of genuinely colonial products deployed old-fashioned, lackluster imagery largely lacking in exotic flair or enthralling panache.

IMAGERY'S EMPIRE

Given the dearth of actual material products, literature remained the primary "consumer good" of colonial enthusiasts over the course of Germany's tenure as a colonial power. The dynamics of this literary consumption changed dramatically, however. In the 1890s, colonialist publications had been characterized by the authority of scientific expertise backed up by the institutional weight of the Colonial Society (with its ties to conservative publishing houses). By 1910, a new array of periodicals and books emerged, increasingly aimed at a wider audience in a newly competitive publishing field. A change in the tenor of the rhetoric of the Colonial Society after 1907 has been noticed by historians, who have ascribed it to the work of a new "populist" wing of the colonial enthusiast movement, energized by the so-called Hottentot elections.[45] In fact, between the Herero War of 1904 and the ensuing victory of pro-colonialists in the 1907 elections, membership in the Colonial Society grew by 7,000 members, to 38,000. (The society could still hardly compare with the Navy League, however, which claimed almost ten times the membership at its height in 1914.)[46]

Yet the post-1907 electoral enthusiasm (and upswing in Colonial Society membership) followed on the heels of an outpouring of *commercial* enthusiasm after the 1904 Herero uprising. Images of the uprising in the colonies, which flooded the mass illustrated dailies during the course of the war, paralleled the racialization of blacks in advertising across the mass media.[47] The war in Southwest Africa showed advertisers that colonialism, if simply and powerfully packaged, could be salable to a broad German public. Typical of this trend was the new, inexpensive illustrated magazine, *Colony and Home in Words and Pictures*, which began publication in 1907. Its editorial staff was intentionally drawn from a variety of social backgrounds.[48] Most importantly, drawing a lesson from the tabloids, the entire publication was built around images, whether illustrations or photographs; promotions for *Colony and Home* boasted that "every issue contains over 30 good pictures!"[49]

The character of this visuality, however, is what differentiates it so dramatically from the photographs and illustrations in the previous decades' colonialist literature. Rather than those grainy landscapes, photos of colonial outbuildings, or sketches of tropical plants that had dotted the *Colonial News* between 1890 and 1900, *Colony and Home* published vivid "ethnographic" photographs that are striking for their blatant eroticism. The very first issue, in fact, featured a young "Wageia-Girl" on the cover. Had her bare breasts been those of a European woman, they would have violated public decorum, not to mention the strict Wilhelmine censorship laws.[50] Yet the veil of ethnography legitimized the nudity, and so no discernible protest arose.[51]

Colony and Home was also steeped in sensationalist imagery of race. An illustrated layout of the "Peoples of Togo" for instance, presented dozens of hand-drawn profiles of African natives, from "Bassarimann" to "Ewefrau," arranged in neat rows for phrenological evaluation; the drawings emphasized and exaggerated physiognomic features (see figure 9.9). With its photographs, such manipulation of facial features was more difficult. Yet sensationalistic racism could be brought into photography by staging scenes of power: a particularly notorious example is the cover photo of a 1910 issue of *Colony and Home* that featured an African being electrocuted, his face and body contorted in a spasm of agony. The caption simply read: "The effects of electric current on a Negro."[52] Such an image would have been literally unthinkable in the public sphere two decades before; now it led as the cover illustration.

Other publishing houses joined the swell of *volkstümlich* (populist) illustrated colonialist literature. One such, the Berlin firm of Wilhelm Süsserott, came on the scene after 1901. By 1909 it specialized in serialized colonialist literature (it even tried muscling in on the contract for the official *German Colonial Bulletin*).[53] Süsserott's flagship publication was the *Illustrated Colonial Calendar*; heavily illustrated and with a large circulation, this annual usually featured a bust of an attractive native woman on the front cover, and images of seminude native women appeared in its pages.[54] After 1912, it also included a humor section, which featured extremely racialized and often racist caricatures of a type never found in the *Colonial News* (see figure 9.10). Other rivals leapt into the market. Wilhelm Köhler, also a newcomer to colonial enthusiast publishing, printed its competing annual calendar starting the same year

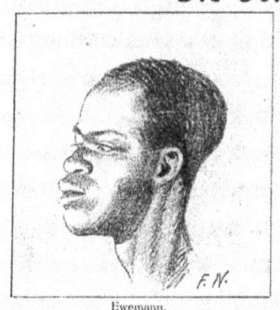 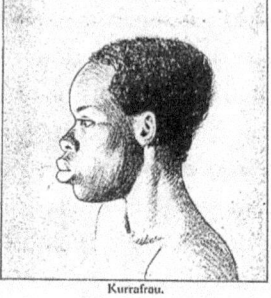

FIGURE 9.9 · "The Peoples of Togo." Ethnographic sketches in *Colony and Home*. Note the deliberate exaggeration of skull shape and other supposedly-racial features. Source: *Kolonie und Heimat* (1912), 222.

FIGURE 9.10 · Cartoon, "In the Rain": "Slowly, slowly, no need to trot; because our color won't wash off!" Note the exaggerated lips and distorted bodily features seen in popular caricature. Source: *Süsserott's Illustrierter Kolonial-Kalender* (1912), 222.

(1909). The prospectus for Köhler's *Illustrated German Colonial Calendar* of 1910 boasted to potential advertisers that it would have a minimum circulation of 130,000 copies—a very high number that would allow Köhler to charge much higher fees to advertisers.[55] The competition grew fierce. The firm of Wilhelm Süsserott aggressively demanded subsidies from the Colonial Office, claiming its rival had received one. When an official reply maintained that no such subsidy had been given, Süsserott retorted that its rival was claiming to enjoy the *"Mitwirkung"* of the Colonial Office. It turns out that Köhler had indeed trumpeted this spurious claim in promotional material circulated to prospective advertisers.[56]

New illustrated weeklies, like *Colony and Home*, and popular serialized calendars, like those printed by Süsserott and Köhler, had finally turned to the modern business model, one where extensive advertising could defray the bulk of publication costs, keep the cover price low, and thereby increase circulation. Süsserott's 240-page calendar came with an astounding 150 pages of advertising, many for mass-market brands. Ads for name-brand products like Odol and Palmin and for a department store like Berlin's *Kaufhaus des Westens* appeared in *Colony and Home*. While most of the ads in Süsserott's 1909 *Illustrated Colonial Calendar* were for colonialist literature, by 1912 there were many mass-market products as well, including Immalin shoe polish, Salem Aleikum cigarettes, and Bergmann's Hobbyhorse Soap (see figure 9.1), The mass-market businesses did not orient themselves to the conservative, traditionalist sensibility seen in the colonial enthusiast classifieds of the 1890s; they simply imported their textual and visual ads from other media and other publications. The advertisements in *Colony and Home*, therefore, increasingly reflected larger trends in German mass-produced commercial culture—including trends toward racially inflected depictions of colonial rule.

This, then, is the larger historical arc behind the ad for Bergmann's Hobbyhorse Lily Soap in *Colony and Home* of 1908, an ad that also appeared in *Süsserott's Illustrated Colonial Calendar* in 1910 and represents less the politicization of commerce than the commercialization of politics. Bergmann's soap ad, featuring overawed, childlike African natives, was crafted for an audience far broader than *Colony and Home*'s readers—indeed, it had appeared prominently in the *Leipziger Illustrierte Zeitung* and similar magazines years earlier[57]—and was part of a series of scenes of Hobbyhorse "around the world," most of them giving little hint of colonialist ideology. In the advertisement, the distant homes at the edge of the jungle appear to be teepees. While such an out-of-place detail would certainly arouse the ire of a colonialist-cum-amateur ethnologist, it was a perfectly legible icon of exotic primitivism to an audience raised on Karl May rather than Karl Dove.[58] Similarly, while the odd immaturity of the facial features seems out of place, we now know Bergmann's image was crafted not for colonialists but for Germans who didn't know a "Bassarimann" from a "Massai" and didn't care; the advertisement's figures are drawn with features of children to emphasize their inferiority, not for phrenological study. The point was to sell soap, not colonies.

CONCLUSION

The appearance of exaggerated racialization in the pages of colonialist publications suggests, with no small degree of irony, that the old self-contained circle of colonial enthusiasts was beginning to be pulled apart by new forces in Germany: from one direction, mass-market businesses sought to distill colonialism and racism to sell products; from the other, new rival publishers sought to compete by bringing new business practices into the clubhouse of the colonialist movement. Major chocolate manufacturers, margarine producers, and grocery chains set the agenda for advertising throughout Germany, and images of blacks in advertising were crafted not by colonial enthusiasts but by companies pursuing a logic of mass appeal. When some colonialist publishers began to not only print these advertisements but also deploy this style of imagery within their pages to attract the attention of a wider German audience, it represented the logic of mass culture taking away possession of the German colonial project from the experts who had long been the backbone of the German colonial movement. This process began to erode the politics of colonialism, leaving behind only a simplified racial fantasy. If the former helped to lead Germany into the First World War, the latter helped to lead Germany into the Second.

NOTES

1. McClintock, *Imperial Leather*, 207–231; Ramamurthy, *Imperial Persuaders*, 24–62; Ciarlo, *Advertising Empire*, 108–113, 135–138, 240–245, 259–265.

2. On *Markenartikel*, see Schwartz, "Commodity Signs"; Reinhardt, *Von der Reklame zum Marketing*; Lamberty, *Reklame in Deutschland 1890–1914*; and esp. Borscheid and Wischermann, eds., *Bilderwelt des Alltags*.

3. Some Bergmann posters are in Anna, ed., *Historische Plakate 1890–1914*, 105, and Hollmann et al., eds., *Das frühe Plakat*.

4. Bergmann and Company issued its Dada brand hair conditioner (colloquial French for "hobbyhorse") after 1906, and the word was taken up in 1916 by a soon-to-be-infamous Zurich cabaret act. Bolliger, Magnaguagno, and Meyer, *Dada in Zürich*, 85.

5. For colonialist ideology in politics, see Grimmer-Solem, "The Professors' Africa,"

and Schubert, *Der schwarze Fremde*. For colonial fantasy in politics, see Mass, *Weisse Helden schwarze Krieger*.

6. Zantop, *Colonial Fantasies*.

7. Breuning and Chamberlain, eds., *Bedarf Deutschland der Kolonien*, 28.

8. Präger, *Die Deutsche Kolonialgesellschaft 1882–1907*, 25.

9. The elitist inclination of the society is emphasized by Eley, *Reshaping the German Right*, 46, 120–123, 156–157. In cities like Solingen and Essen there was higher participation of industrialists and bankers (and fewer officers), while academics dominated the Bonn chapter; Soenius, *Koloniale Begeisterung im Rheinland*, 39–40.

10. Bundesarchiv [BArch] R8023/911, "Ausschussberichte von 1896," no. 2 (January 7) and no. 7 (February 27); *Deutsche Kolonialzeitung* [DKZ] 13 (1896), 125. For a list of this firm's publications, see Verlag, *Verlags-Katalog*; also useful is von Wolzogen, *Zur Geschichte des Dietrich Reimer Verlages*.

11. See Mittler and Sohn, *Königliche Hofbuchhandlung*, 284–301. An overview of colonialist publishers can be glimpsed in Brose, *Des Deutschen Reiches Kolonial-litteratur*, and Brose, ed., *Repertorium der deutsch-Kolonialen Litteratur*. Brose was the librarian of the Colonial Society.

12. Newspapers and magazines in Germany often incorporated essays or articles handed to them by various organizations or institutions. See *Illustrierte Zeitung* Nr. 2387 (1889), 304, or "Emin Pascha Expedition," *Über Land und Meer* (1890), 448.

13. See Held, "Kolonialismus und Werbung."

14. DKZ (1889); seeds were offered by J. C. Schmidt of Erfurt, tools by the Gebr. Brüninghaus of Werdohl.

15. DKZ (1889).

16. A classified for the *Tägliche Rundschau* boasted that it was "Für die Gebildeten aller Stände!" with only a typesetter's drop-in certifying that the *Tägliche Rundschau* committed itself to German *Kolonialpolitik*. DKZ Nr. 4 (1889).

17. For cigar culture, see Kölling, "Das Öl im Kompass."

18. DKZ (1899), appended classifieds.

19. DKZ (1898). For cigar and cigarette advertising in Germany, see Moeller, *Plakate für den blauen Dunst*, and Weisser, *Cigaretten-Reclame*.

20. See esp. Schwarz, *Bildannoncen aus der Jahrhundertwende*, and Borscheid and Wischermann, eds., *Bilderwelt des Alltags*, esp. 44–77. See also Aynsley, *Graphic Design*.

21. For bicycle and tire ads, see Meißner, ed., *Strategien der Werbekunst*.

22. See Ciarlo, *Advertising Empire*, 196–199, 221–222, and the Reithoffer ads in Scholz-Hänsel, ed., *Das exotische Plakat*.

23. Ciarlo, *Advertising Empire*, 148–212.

24. *Die Woche*, III Jg. Nr. 6 (1901).

25. See Väth-Hinz, *Odol Reklame-Kunst um 1900*, and Ciarlo, *Advertising Empire*, 89–90.

26. "Wie man in Deutschland annoncirt [sic]," in *Die Reklame* 5, 19 (1895), 334.

27. On the ideological significance of African labor, see van Laak, *Imperiale Infrastruktur*, and Naranch, "Colonized Body, Oriental Machine."

28. The exception is the advertising for Bruno Antelmann's Kolonialhaus.

29. DKZ (February 2, 1889).

30. See Belgum, *Popularizing the Nation*, 12; for the role of advertising in *Die Gartenlaube*'s success, see Homburg, "Werbung."

31. See esp. Reuveni, "Lesen und Konsum"; Fritzsche, *Reading Berlin 1900*, 73; Stöber, *Deutsche Pressegeschichte*, 231–237.

32. First among these was the German Colonial Exhibition in Berlin in 1896; another was the German Kolonialhaus–Bruno Antelmann.

33. When the Colonial Economic Committee sent samples of Togo cocoa to a number of prominent cocoa manufacturers, Stollwerck declared it "only suitable for blending small quantities in with better cocoa sorts." Meanwhile, a colonial-enthusiast business, Antelmann's Kolonialhaus, unhesitatingly "certified" the Togo cocoa as high quality; *Tropenpflanzer* (1902), 249–250.

34. Germany imported 2,211,312 kg of cocoa from Ecuador alone in 1900. See Stollwerck, *Der Kakao und die Schokoladenindustrie*, 11, 30, 61. Stollwerck gets his statistics on German colonial production from the *Tropenpflanzer* and the *Deutsche Kolonialblatt*; they should be regarded with suspicion, as both periodicals were unrelenting boosters of German colonial enterprise in order to attract German investors.

35. As one advertising expert attested in 1914; see Seÿffert, *Die Reklame des Kaufmanns*, 186.

36. For examples, see Scholz-Hänsel, *Das exotische Plakat*; Feuerhorst and Steinle, *Die Bunte Verführung*; Schmidt-Linsenhoff, Wettengl, and Junker, eds., *Plakate 1880–1914*.

37. For the former, see *Monographien Deutscher Reklamekunstler 6* (1912), 40.

38. See Leitherer and Wichmann, eds., *Reiz und Hülle*.

39. Another trademark by this same firm included even less illustration; see *Warenzeichenblatt des Kaiserliches Patentamts* [WZB] (1901), 595, no. 49523.

40. Georg Schepeler, Frankfurt am Main, WZB (1907), 2384, no. 102741. Usambara, in German East Africa, was the only successful coffee-producing region in the German empire.

41. There are exceptions, such as the packaging for Carl Grunow's Deutscher Ost-Afrikanischer Cacao; see Deutsches Historisches Museum item AK 94/516.2113, reproduced in Ciarlo, *Advertising Empire*, plate 11.

42. See Ciarlo, *Advertising Empire*, 259–304, esp. 286–287.

43. Riquet, chocolate packaging, WZB (1910), 1810, no. 133826.

44. "UNSER KAKAO: Hergestellt ausschliesslich aus Roh-Kakao unserer DEUTSCHEN KOLONIEN." Stollwerck AG, Cöln, WZB (1909), 1515, no. 120010. On Stollwerck advertising, see Epple, "Das Auge Schmeckt Stollwerck."

45. See van der Heyden, "Der 'Hottentottenwahlen' von 1907"; Soenius, *Koloniale Begeisterung im Rheinland*, 47–48; and Smith, *The German Colonial Empire*, 183–191.

46. The Colonial Society claimed 43,000 members in 1914, the Navy League 330,000; Eley, *Reshaping the German Right*, 36.

47. See Ciarlo, "Picturing Genocide."

48. Wildenthal, *German Women for Empire*, 146. For the start-up negotiations, see BArch R1001/4581. Early issues dwelt on the aftermath of the recent war; see *Kolonie*

und Heimat 1, 1 (1907), 2. The magazine sought to appeal to "wide, varied circles" and the "very plain elements, mostly also women"; Wildenthal, 147.

49. Cf. Sembritzki, *Der Kolonialfreund*, 207.

50. *Kolonie und Heimat* 1, 1 (1907).

51. One organization against public immorality did in fact protest erotic images in the *Colonial News*—in its classified section. A complaint from the *Verband der Männerverein zur Bekämpfung der öffentlichen Unsittlichkeit* to the Colonial Office vehemently protested the ad for Richard Ungewitter's illustrated "art" book *Nackt* (Stuttgart, 1909). The Colonial Office's response was to evade responsibility, insisting it had no connection with the *Colonial News*. BArch R4691, doc. 52; the classified appeared in DKZ 26, 24 (1909), 396.

52. *Kolonie und Heimat* 4, 3 (1910).

53. The *Deutsche Kolonialblatt* was published by E. S. Mittler under contract to the Colonial Office. Süserotts offered its "Kolonial Bibliothek"—popular books on a wide range of topics—serialized as a "library" to boost sales.

54. See the photo plate "Samoan Beauties," in *Süsserott's Illustrierter Kolonial-Kalender* (1914), xiii.

55. BArch R1001/4536, doc. 80 (ad flyer: Illustrierter deutscher Kolonial-Kalender für 1910).

56. BArch R1001/4536, docs. 67, 68, 76–86, 94 (1909).

57. *Leipziger Illustrierte Zeitung* (1909), 636.

58. See Bowersox, *Raising Germans in the Age of Empire*.

TEN

Colonialism, War, and the German Working Class
Popular Mobilization in the 1907 Reichstag Elections

JOHN PHILLIP SHORT

We imagine the scene: a cold, damp December night in Hamburg, ten or twelve people in a small pub in the Nagelsweg, the dim room thick with tobacco smoke and the smell of beer. A man named Hinz, a spy for the Hamburg police, arrives about twenty minutes before ten o'clock to listen. It is mid-December 1904, several months after the Herero revolt in German Southwest Africa, and a conversation among four of the patrons—they appear to be workers—turns to the unfolding German war there. One worker, pessimistic about German prospects, predicts that the "uprising in Southwest Africa will not be put down for a long time yet and that probably at least as many soldiers as are already there now must be sent over." His companion, bitterly resentful, condemns as "a scandal" that "so many people have been sacrificed" for "a worthless desert that will yield nothing in the foreseeable future." It's regrettable, he thinks, that so many people are drawn into such "nonsense," to which another retorts, "If people are so stupid and care so little for their own lives, then it's their fault; one has to just let them go." More important, he wants to know, "who is supposed to pay the huge costs" of the war? Still another is thinking about how to educate and mobilize Germans, complaining that there had been insufficient protest, that the "protest rallies must be repeated at brief intervals and extended all across Germany."[1]

When, with our police spy Hinz, we overhear such rancorous working-class talk of worthless sacrifice, of blood and money squandered in the desert, and of hatching plans to mobilize the indifferent or misguided masses, we hear a kind of collective ventriloquism: the embodied rhetoric of countless Social

Democratic headlines and slogans, articles and leaflets, lectures and speeches. Ordinarily, of course, beer and brutishness—pubs and empire—are thought to go hand in hand. As J. A. Hobson put it in *Imperialism* just two years before, "'*Panem et circenses*' interpreted into English means cheap booze."[2] Cheap booze and, moreover, cheap talk. "The saloon, the club, the train, and other common avenues of conversation helped in the work of propaganda," he argued, feeding a political discourse of "short stories and bar tittle-tattle."[3] But in Germany, with its strong Social Democratic Party, circumstances were quite different. The machinery of imperial propaganda and of commercial mass amusement was powerful, but as we shall see, the force and momentum of the SPD critique and mobilization nevertheless enabled a stubborn working-class resistance. Such barroom chatter, right in the bustling imperial entrepôt of Hamburg, is but one vivid reflection of a discourse widely diffused among workers and local organizers of the SPD.

By February 1907, two years on, such working-class anticolonialism would be severely tested—although events in Southwest Africa had vindicated the pessimism and anger voiced in the Hamburg pub. By all accounts, even among many Social Democrats, that winter marked the apotheosis of colonial enthusiasm in Germany: the dramatic dissolution of parliament and fierce elections following it—national elections fought for the first time over the "colonial question." These were the so-called Hottentot elections, occasioned by the protracted, brutal, very costly war in German Southwest Africa, first against the Herero and then against the Nama, the eponymous Hottentots. Nationalist fervor and the passions stirred by war combined, crystallizing in a new mass imperialism that, for the first time, transcended the class divisions that had bedeviled German colonialism from its origins.

The German Colonial Society, the center of an institutional network that had, since the 1870s, developed into an influential colonial movement, was powerfully defined by these divisions: a membership carefully limited to the propertied and the educated, a pessimistic, sharply attenuated apprehension of "the masses," and a fundamental antagonism toward the vigorously anticolonial SPD. After some twenty years of perplexed, halting efforts to make the overseas empire popular, colonialists in 1907 believed they had finally achieved some success among the "broad masses" of factory workers, peasants, shopkeepers, and artisans. It was the heyday of a robust and vicious propagandism against the "enemies" of the Reich: the bloodthirsty savages of Southwest Africa and their sympathizers, Social Democracy and the Catholic Center Party. As one colonialist put it, with characteristic derision, there was "gradual clarification, too, of the colonial policy of the barroom [*Stammtisch*]. One no longer looks for Southwest Africa in the South Seas, and even knows better now than to mistake Togo for Tokyo."[4] The ordinary German seemed, at last, within reach.

Even Lenin, driven by no less antipathy toward German Social Democracy than were the bourgeois colonialists themselves, argued in *Imperialism* (1916) that "the signs of the times are a ... passionate defense of imperialism, and every possible embellishment of its real nature. The imperialist ideology also penetrates the working class. There is no Chinese Wall between it and other classes."[5] This came in response to the enthusiasm for war in 1914, but likewise to the quickening revisionism among German Social Democrats, the growing acceptance of a "reformed," "humane" idea of imperialism that had taken root already before 1907, part loss of political nerve, part surrender to the economic axioms of imperial ideology. The electoral defeat of 1907 energized this tendency. Such leading Social Democrats as Eduard Bernstein, Gustav Noske, and Richard Calwer produced controversial analyses portending a socialist embrace of some version of empire.

But what of the workers themselves? What do we find if we look beyond the world of party intellectuals and leaders into the proletarian public sphere, into political life at the grass roots? If ever there were a moment in the Kaiserreich when the machinery of imperial manipulation might implant among the German working class its particular racist and economic worldview, it had come. Certainly this is how Hobson understood the British–South African War, which had, he wrote, opened up a "panorama of vulgar pride and crude sensationalism to a great inert mass."[6] But there was no real jingoist mob, no working-class *Hurrahkanaille* in Germany, nor even anything to match, for example, the more extreme passions of the middle-class Pan-German League. The popular reception of empire was often less vivid and altogether more elusive. The revisionist drift in the national SPD at precisely this moment belies the local reality of a persistent, unmistakable anticolonialism among workers. There is a history of powerful anticolonial conviction in the Kaiserreich; it flourished among politicized working people even as the leaders who had given it direction and momentum began themselves to succumb to the blandishments of empire. The "colonial policy of the barroom" turns out to be hard-edged socialist critique.

In the effort to say something about the mass politics of imperialism, historians tend to scrutinize the response to empire by the leadership of the Social Democratic Party, ostensibly the party of the German working class.[7] Conclusions about working-class attitudes scarcely gesture toward the everyday action and opinion of rank-and-file Social Democrats, much less the ill-defined proletarian world beyond the party.[8] Yet if in 1907 Social Democracy seemed to waver before the powerful strategy of the right and indeed to grow ever more receptive to imperialism, the experience of workers themselves tells a different story. With the elections, German colonial policy became an important political issue for workers. Colonialism made headlines, filled newspaper columns and public meetings, and pulled thousands of new working-class voters into the electoral process. But it was really only the scale of the working-class response that was new. The SPD had worked since before the turn of the century to shape a discourse among working people that would enable a broadly based critique of empire. Working-class responses to the war in Southwest Africa evolved out of this older, broader discourse on imperialist violence and exploitation, provoked especially at the turn of the century by the Boer War and the Boxer Rebellion.[9] In the multiple forms of working-class engagement in early 1907—through local party institutions and in the language of local party organs—we observe the fruition of this strong countervailing force. If "revisionism" had begun to erode the powerful, united front of SPD anticolonialism at the top among the leadership, the very success of anticolonial policy, its rhetoric and activism, suggest that any neutralization or retreat among the more radical rank and file was anything but a foregone conclusion in the immediate aftermath of 1907 or in 1914.

The elections followed immediately upon Chancellor von Bülow's dramatic dissolution of the Reichstag on December 13, 1906, prompted by the Center Party's rejection of a request for 29 million marks in supplementary funding for the expedition in Southwest Africa.[10] The previous two years had been a trying time for supporters of German *Weltpolitik*—and an extended field day for their critics. In 1905, the Maji Maji rebellion had broken out in East Africa, and the kaiser's trip to Tangier had precipitated the first Morocco Crisis.[11] Colonial scandals continued to generate sensational press reports of greed, corruption, brutality, and sex. Most troubling of all, however, was the army's inability to crush the uprising in Southwest Africa. Despite spending nearly 600 million marks and General Lothar von Trotha's notorious extermination policy, the Herero and, later, the Nama were able to tie down some 14,000 troops in the colony. Disease and the implacable, waterless terrain prolonged the bitter campaign.[12]

With the rejection of the colonial spending measure, however, the nationalist right had its own scandal to conjure with: the betrayal by Center and SPD politicians of German youths struggling against cruel savages under a pitiless sun. The elections would not be about suffrage, tariff, tax reform, or any of the myriad matters of conflicting material interest that commonly defined politics. They were to be about national honor and loyalty to the nation on the field of empire. Bülow's government, together with the Colonial Office, the parties of the nationalist right, and the powerful *nationale Verbände*, orchestrated the elections as an appeal to patriotic sentiment, colonial race hatred, and fear of socialism.[13]

Working-class voters were important targets for the barrage of colonialist and nationalist propaganda. "Up to now," complained Colonial Secretary Bernhard Dernburg in an election speech, "only the industrial workers have had true benefits from the colonies—they who now want to condemn wholesale the entire colonial policy."[14] The president of the Colonial Society urged its members to take advantage of the "exceptional and auspicious opportunity" to "strengthen the colonial conscience of the voting masses."[15] The society collaborated with the Pan-Germans, the Navy League, nationalist publishers, and others to distribute flyers, brochures, postcards, and newspaper articles, often through factory owners.[16] They distributed some 150,000 copies of "Soldiers' Letters from German Southwest" and over a million of "Germany, Hold on to Your Colonies."[17] A propaganda leaflet headlined "That Is the Truth!" depicted the horrors of war in Southwest Africa, the terrifying black enemy, German heroism, and the criminal responsibility of the SPD and Center. The dramatic picture on the cover shows a family of German settlers under attack by demonic blacks, the sky aflame in the lurid red and yellow of their burning farm.[18] The Colonial Society also coordinated the performance of short dramatic pieces and patriotic tableaux vivants in "theaters, circuses, and similar institutions," where patriots acted out scenes from military life in uniforms furnished by the army.[19] The Social Democrat Carl Severing later remembered how, since the main elections had been scheduled for the kaiser's birthday, by electing "deputies loyal to the government the voters were supposed to offer the monarch a kind of birthday present."[20] Propagandists railed against the "*Hottentottenblock*" of SPD and Center, the "black-red League for the Defense of Kaffirdom against Germans."[21] They tried to lure workers away from the SPD both by appealing to feelings of national identity and solidarity and by reiterating the material benefits of colonialism to workers.[22]

Still, it does not automatically follow that local contests revolved around colonial policy in the way suggested by the national political discourse. Leading SPD members later disagreed about whether the elections had really been about colonialism in the first place. There were many other social, political, and economic matters of particular municipal or regional significance for working-class voters.[23] In Leipzig, for example, the unequal franchise for both the city government and the Saxon Landtag excited strong feelings and had already alienated many working-class voters from the parties of the Bülow bloc.

In Düsseldorf, the particular local configuration of politics, together with SPD ambivalence toward the whole issue of empire, likewise marked the contest.[24] Whatever the appeal of jingoism to local workers, nationalists had to contend with long-standing class antagonisms over food prices, housing, labor issues, and glaring inequalities in the political and judicial systems. The nationalist parties exerted every effort to transform the elections into a rush of patriotic feeling, a mass rite of devotion to the fatherland. If their victory suggests that they were successful, neither their intentions nor the overall results are by themselves sufficient evidence that, for workers, the elections turned mainly on the matter of empire or fatherland among many long-standing issues.[25]

Very often, though, they did. Whatever fissures divided party leadership, local branches of the SPD frequently took up the challenge of the nationalist parties and fought the elections squarely on the national-colonial ground chosen by the Bülow government and its allies.[26] As Eduard Bernstein observed following the elections, if "the parties, and not least Social Democracy, also raised an abundance of other questions in election speeches and literature," it was "still the colonial question that set the tone of the campaign."[27] Colonialist discourse that had already penetrated the experience of working-class voters or readers or spectators at the panoramas or cinematographs now became prominent in the arena of SPD electoral politics. Colonialism by no means eclipsed other contentious issues. It did, however, supply the main topic of SPD headlines, meetings, posters, speeches, and pamphlets as organizers and journalists wove anti-imperialism into their propaganda:

DOWN WITH ALL BRUTAL MEN WHO BY THEIR CRUELTY HAVE SHAMED GERMANY'S REPUTATION! DOWN WITH REACTION AND THE PRISON BILL! DOWN WITH THE THREE-CLASS VOTING LAW IN SAXONY![28]

The drama of the election, the vivid rhetoric of both socialists and nationalists, and the catastrophic results for the SPD transformed colonialism for the first time into a general theme of working-class politics. Even if many working-class voters remained politically indifferent to German colonialism, after the winter of 1907 they could no longer ignore it.

Eduard Bernstein, reflecting retrospectively on working-class mobilization that year, observed that the rank and file collectively amounted to a "proletarian army," many of them "vigorous enthusiasts in the prime of life, and ready to take upon themselves any work necessary for the distribution of the electoral literature of the party and the working up of the electors." And not only in cities: "Clubs of Socialist Cyclists exist in large numbers and train their members for efforts in rural districts."²⁹ Across Germany, the forms of local engagement had been prepared over the previous eight or ten years. In Leipzig, SPD newspapers and public meetings had long before introduced many workers to a clamorous anti-imperialism.³⁰ As early as 1900, an urgent address "To Our Readers!" in the *Leipziger Volkszeitung* had begun to interpret the seizure of Kiaochow, the Boxer Rebellion, and the Boer War as related parts of a single capitalist-imperialist system that threatened to bring about world war. In October 1906, a series of articles on "colonial policy" criticized and condemned both the economic and the emigrationist strands of German colonialism. The paper explained imperialism in the conventional economic terms of capitalist overproduction, the acquisition of markets, and the export of capital. It went on to ridicule the German colonies as a costly failure by comparison with other European colonial empires: "The difference consists only in that, in other countries, where a continual stream of gold flows in from the colonies, these riches are realized from the plundered natives, while in Germany, where the colonial policy is only a failed caricature—not producing gold but consuming it—gold for Tippelskirch and Woermann must be raised from German taxpayers, and 'colonial policy' is only a pretext to exploit their own people for the benefit of a few capitalists."³¹ The failed colonial policy was not even successful in the brutal exploitation of native peoples, scoffed the *Volkszeitung*, as it relied instead on the exploitation of overtaxed German workers to provide "colonial profits" for a few firms and individuals.

In parts of Bavaria, local SPD branches successfully mobilized workers to protest colonial violence in Africa and Asia. In 1900, for example, workers rallied in Lechhausen, Augsburg, and across southern Bavaria against *Weltpolitik* and the China expedition.³² The socialist *Augsburger Volkszeitung* continually attacked colonial policy, even comparing the condition of German workers to colonized Africans. "The very ruling classes who brutalize and enslave the workers here in Germany carry on the same fine business with the blacks there [in the colonies]."³³ The workers were the "worst affected" by the "monstrous, heavy consequences" of the China expedition, which "cut so deeply into the life of the German people."³⁴ The 1905 Berlin Colonial Congress was painted as a "colorful society of dukes and counts, generals and Christian servants of God, of privy councilors, professors, and bankers, ever ready to grant, in uncounted millions, the money of the German worker" for a colonial policy (*"Wüstensandpolitik"*) that served only the lust for adventure of the few.³⁵ After the turn of the century, readers encountered ever more sensational headlines: "COLONIAL SWAMP," "HORRIBLE REVELATIONS FROM SOUTHWEST AFRICA," "COLONIAL FIASCO," "THE ADVENTURE IN

SOUTHWEST AFRICA," "COLONIZATION WITH THE WHIP," "COLONIAL ABOMINATION," and "A BLOODY DEFEAT IN SOUTHWEST AFRICA."

When in 1900 a Hamburg worker accused the European powers of "snipping off" Chinese lands and introducing "European culture with force" or in 1905 a Saxon factory worker sarcastically mocked the "stroll to China" by "defenders of the fatherland," they reproduced the language and tone then being popularized by the SPD.[36] The same rhetoric colored the *Leipziger Volkszeitung* during the elections, when it attacked the "colonial swindle" perpetrated by the National Liberals and the Conservatives—the "*Schutztruppe* of corruption"—who concealed a "barbaric war of extermination" caused by the dispossession and mistreatment of the Herero by German settlers. "Robbed of their property, often ill treated, almost without rights, abandoned to ... foreign intruders," the Herero "finally grasped at the most extreme means, rebellion against the oppressor."[37] Reasoning of this sort represented bold dissent from the jingoism and racist demonization of the Herero common in the German press. Indeed, the Leipzig police observed a stubborn radicalism in the *Volkszeitung*, even as other elements in the SPD were beginning to articulate a more moderate position on imperialism. Police reports warned that in 1907, as in the previous year, the paper "represented the radical faction in the Social Democratic Party" by continuing to condemn men like Eduard Bernstein, Richard Calwer, Max Schippel, and other "opportunists and revisionists on the military question and colonial policy."

The scandalmongering and hyperbole in the *Leipziger Volkszeitung*, then edited by Franz Mehring, were but one aspect of a local politics that became, as police observers put it, "extraordinarily lively" in January 1907. Immediately following the dissolution of the Reichstag, the national parties united into a local cartel against the SPD. According to Leipzig police reports, they were "extremely active," holding "numerous large election meetings, at which Social Democrats were usually present in large numbers, so that some of these meetings took on a truly tumultuous character."[38] The full panoply of nationalist associations worked to excite patriotic fervor. The Colonial Society itself sponsored three meetings in Leipzig.[39] Also very active were the "many national 'Patriotic Associations' [*Vaterländische Vereine*], the *Vereine reichstreuer Männer*, etc., district associations and groups, which through their painstaking work contributed substantially to the election of the national candidates. They held numerous district meetings, nearly always well attended, distributed appealing leaflets, and in particular helped the nationalist press win voters."[40] Even the local Evangelical Workers Associations entered the fray, going so far as to recommend outright that their members vote for the bloc candidates.[41]

The SPD Leipzig responded with energy and venom. The *Volkszeitung* attacked Colonial Director Dernburg's campaign as a "rivulet of the shallowest phrases [that] burbles, burbles, burbles along. The imagination of an Arabian storyteller"—Dernburg himself—"unfolds enchanting pictures for the listeners." The task of disenchantment fell to the propagandists of the SPD, for whom Dernburg was like "a drunken petit bourgeois making barroom propaganda for a veterans association; the more pitying smiles he gets, the wilder and more enthusiastic he acts."[42] The SPD agitation committee coordinated the campaign in Leipzig, flooding the city with propaganda, leaflets, and posters publicizing colonial corruption and brutality, the Carl Peters affair, and the worthlessness of Southwest Africa.[43] SPD campaign workers plastered the four central and outer districts with nearly twelve thousand posters and distributed over a hundred thousand handbills. A half million leaflets blanketed outlying districts and as many more the center of the city, although "snow, cold, and bad road conditions hindered the agitation profoundly."[44]

The intense excitement of the contest was keenest in the many political meetings held throughout December and January. There were great election rallies at which, for example, Bebel or Heinrich Lange, the SPD candidate for central Leipzig, addressed crowds of Social Democrats on the theme of colonialism. There were also numerous smaller meetings in different working-class neighborhoods across the city. Many of these occurred under the surveillance of the municipal authorities, whose handwritten reports describe something of their atmosphere. On January 12, for example, the SPD sponsored a meeting at the Gasthof zu den drei Linden in Liebertwolkwitz, in the mostly working-class Thirteenth District. Some 250 to 300 people came to hear the speaker, Ludwig Bartels, who, according to the official report, at first "spoke very slowly, agreeably, [then] maliciously and sneeringly and then became in his lecture extraordinarily abusive. He began with the 'murderer Peters' and repeated, 'He is a murderer! . . . [T]he government is pursuing a criminal, a bestial and murderous colonial policy.' . . . At the end of his performance, Bartels's speech received lively applause."[45] Bartels addressed another crowd the following day on the Peters and Puttkamer scandals, the extermination order of General von Trotha in Southwest Africa, and the "bestial atrocities" committed there.[46]

The Social Democrats held nearly three hundred such meetings in Leipzig and particularly in the new industrial suburbs.[47] Speakers did not always emphasize colonialism as the principal theme; tariffs, food costs, and the Saxon franchise were among other topics addressed. German colonial policy was, however, either the most important matter or among the most important discussed at virtually every one of the meetings subject to surveillance. Around 400 men and 5 women attended a meeting on colonialism in Möckern. Some 150 to 180 people attended a meeting in Eythra, where the SPD representative spoke on the "dissolution of the Reichstag, on domestic, foreign, and colonial policy, navalism and militarism, on indirect taxes . . . and on the current condition of the German worker." The meeting was broken up by the police.[48] At a small meeting of about 50 in Schönau, the speaker attacked Trotha's extermination order, Dernburg as a "failed banker," and colonialism as the "cheap finery" and "plaything of the ruling classes." A few days later in Markkleeberg, an SPD speaker addressed about 120 people on the Peters case and the economic injustice of colonialism, a policy "in the interest of a small group of capitalists like Krupp and Tippelskirch."[49] SPD members also displayed their fiery rhetoric in meetings held by opposition parties. Using tactics long employed to disrupt meetings like those of the Evangelical Workers Associations, hecklers attended thirteen meetings in Leipzig and seventy-one more in outlying areas.[50]

In Augsburg during the elections, the party mobilized trade unions, the Women's Educational Association, and singing, gymnastics, and other clubs to distribute handbills in town and surrounding areas. A corps of *Rote Radler*—members of the Workers Cycling Association—carried leaflets to outlying villages.[51] On Sundays, organized leafleting in the mornings preceded large afternoon *Volksversammlungen* in local beer halls, not only in Augsburg but beyond, in comparative hamlets like Inningen, Bobingen, Schwabmünchen, Pfersee, and Steppach. In Kriegshaben, a woman speaker railed against the "colonial swindle." The meeting in Stadtbergen drew both workers and peasant smallholders, and in Langweid "a magnificent attendance from all circles of the population."[52] The *Schwäbische Volkszeitung* provided substantial coverage of the war—under headlines like "MOLOCH AFRICA" and "THE WHIP AS INSTRUMENT OF GERMAN CULTURE"—as it had of the stormy 1906 Reichstag debates on Germany's *Wüstenpolitik*. Under the headline "THE BLEEDING DESERT," the paper attacked Gustav Frenssen's novel *Peter Moors Fahrt nach Südwest* and its warm reception by critics who, they charged, "must either have not read it or have become so hardened that the most terrible accusations of human barbarism and blind madness no longer arouse in them any feeling." As a representation of colonial violence, it argued, the novel was "more reliable than any government report or colonialist travelogue, a ringing accusation against the decay of German culture apparent in our colonial policy."

When the hard-fought elections were over, the intellectuals and ideologues of the SPD disagreed about the implications of colonialism for the party. Revisionists argued in favor of empire on both political and economic grounds.[53]

Radicals insisted that, however potent the spell of colonialism over elements of the bourgeoisie, the working class remained largely unaffected. For Karl Kautsky, the SPD had "underestimated the power of the colonial idea in bourgeois circles."⁵⁴ Rosa Luxemburg argued in a Berlin speech that among the mass of new voters whose participation proved decisive, the greater share "belongs to the Mittelstand, [though] a smaller part may belong to the working class." She interpreted the elections as a battle between Social Democracy and the *Kleinbürgertum*, "a struggle of a dying class against a rising one, a class struggle *par excellence*."⁵⁵ Indeed, in Protestant Germany as a whole, the parties of the bloc did benefit from the increased participation of farmers and the urban middle classes, whose votes went largely to the liberals. Many middle-class voters who had chosen the SPD in 1903 voted for the "national cartel." Altogether, the SPD received some quarter of a million more votes in 1907 than in 1903, but since it was unable likewise to increase its percentage of the total vote and overall participation was substantially greater (rising from 76% to 84% of those eligible), the parties of the Bülow bloc were able to claim victory.⁵⁶

But even in the most unassailable concentrations of working-class Social Democracy, there is evidence of imperialist gains among workers. In the longtime SPD stronghold of Nuremberg, the share of the vote fell from 60 to 56 percent.⁵⁷ In Leipzig, in the "Red Kingdom of Saxony," although the results were mixed, the SPD experienced them as a serious defeat at the hands of the local cartel. After having "exerted all of their energies to keep the Leipzig-Stadt electoral district," which they had won from the Pan-German leader Ernst Hasse in 1903, they lost it to the National Liberal candidate.⁵⁸ In the Twelfth District in 1907, there were 42,938 eligible voters, of whom 38,637 (90%) voted. Of votes cast, 24,044 (62%) were for the cartel and only 14,366 (37%) for City Councillor Lange, the SPD candidate.⁵⁹ The SPD received 1,774 (10.9%) fewer votes than in 1903.⁶⁰ The local agitation committee advanced a sociological analysis of voting patterns in central Leipzig to explain the loss. In areas with heavier concentrations of workers, they reported, voter participation was the least, as low as 82 percent, while in bourgeois areas participation rose as high as 95 percent. They attributed the lower numbers partially to the wintertime absence of seasonal workers in the building trades and to areas where "many unskilled and barely organized workers" did not bother to vote at all. Their report also suggests that working-class voters were not immune to the appeal of nationalism and colonialism: "The loss of seasonal workers' votes does not, in and of itself, account for the Social Democratic loss. Rather, the conclusion that a substantial part of the working-class electorate must have voted for the bourgeois candidate is justified and well founded. The 'affectionate coaching' on the part of the opposition must have been effective here, according to the results from wards inhabited almost exclusively by workers."[61]

The 1903 SPD victory in Leipzig-Stadt turned out to be exceptional in a district that was otherwise solidly National Liberal from 1871 through the elections of 1912.[62] The results for the surrounding industrial and working-class suburbs of Leipzig-Land, on the other hand, held much greater significance for the party. Even though the Social Democratic candidate won, the results for the much larger district, "populated for the most part by the industrial working class," were nevertheless "fully unsatisfactory" to the SPD.[63] There were 112,537 eligible voters in the Thirteenth District in 1907, of whom 97,592 (87%) cast votes. Of these, 39,689 (41%) were for the cartel, as against 56,712 (58%) for the incumbent, Social Democrat Friedrich Geyer.[64] This represented a clear SPD victory and a slight gain of 1,893 votes (3.4%) over 1903.[65] The SPD nevertheless interpreted the outcome as a disappointment and a warning for the future. In this heavily industrialized, heavily working-class, and heavily Social Democratic part of the "Red Kingdom," the cartel won some 16,000 votes more than it had in 1903.[66] The feeling that the Thirteenth District was "an impregnable socialist stronghold" had turned out to be a dangerous illusion. Party analysts argued that the nonparticipation of nearly 15,000 eligible voters reflected insufficient propaganda and agitation among workers. At 87 percent, voter participation was higher than in 1903 (82%) and surpassed the national average (84%).[67] However, the influx of new voters failed to help the SPD. Its share of eligible voters declined from 57 percent in 1903 to about 50 percent.[68] The appeal of nationalism and colonialism was clearly a factor even among working-class voters in a bastion of SPD strength.

Immediately following the elections, the Leipzig SPD dropped colonialism and once more took up the matter of the unequal Saxon suffrage. Yet the colonial question did not really go away. The local police noted that it, along with the rancorous division between stalwart anticolonialists and revisionists, was much discussed at the congress of the Socialist International held that August in Stuttgart and then again three weeks later at the Essen party congress.[69] Leipzig itself remained the stronghold of the SPD left-center during the last years before the war, and left-wing radicals gathered around their banner paper, the *Leipziger Volkszeitung*.[70] According to the police, the SPD had been badly burned by anticolonialism in 1907, and the party was hesitant to muster its usual outrage in the face of the Second Morocco Crisis in July 1911. Such "considerations were not, however, shared by the most extreme elements of Social

Democracy and its press, the *Leipziger Volkszeitung* in particular. These factors worked incessantly and with success to induce the party leadership to action against war and especially against Germany's efforts [abroad]." The month after the Agadir Crisis, the SPD agitation committee organized a mass demonstration at a brewery in Stötteritz; it was attended by some 10,000 protesters (and of course agents for the police).[71] In the 1912 elections, which the SPD again lost in Leipzig-Stadt (with 46% of the vote) but won in Leipzig-Land (with nearly 70%), colonialism persisted as an issue of the second rank, overshadowed by food prices and tax policy but still marked by the local authorities.[72] Only the war would finally end the local battle over colonialism. As the ever-perceptive police put it, "The year 1914 stood in its first half still entirely under the sign of class struggle, while it was dominated in the second half by the World War and the political truce between parties."[73]

All parties, Kautsky argued in 1907, need a "program for the future" to "unite the broader sections of society under their flags." Accordingly, many workers dreamed of a future Social Democratic state, just as the nationalist middle classes looked to the colonial empire as the solution to economic problems and the intractable social question. "The more unsatisfactory and confused the conditions at home, the more longingly the bourgeois elements in all large capitalist states gaze toward the colonies." Socialism and colonialism, Kautsky pointed out, were linked. Fear of an expanding SPD fed enthusiasm for the colonial future. "The fascination exerted by the colonial state of the future on the entire bourgeois world ... is closely related to growing fear of the Social Democratic future state."[74] But Kautsky's pairing of rival "future states" likewise, if inadvertently, suggests the outlines of an unrecognized utopian sodality encompassing socialists and colonialists. Perhaps colonialism appealed to some workers—readers of colonial adventure, visitors to the colonial wax museum or panorama—in the same way the socialist *Zukunftsstaat* transfixed others: as an escape, a dream, a promise of hope for the future—or a worldview adequate to the times.

Nevertheless, the prevailing interpretation of German Social Democracy as "revisionist," as increasingly "colonialist," implies a distortion of perspective. At the *local* level, in terms of everyday political discourse and practice, the SPD was forcefully anticolonialist—in 1907, as over the preceding ten years, and beyond. The successful mobilization of rank-and-file workers and the wide penetration of anticolonial rhetoric indicates a substantial political anticolonialism belied by accounts of an acquiescent SPD leadership. This is one of the outstanding facts of the German colonial period, distinguishing it from its

European counterparts. Key here is the *productive* nature of the conflict itself: a bitter antagonism between bourgeois colonialism and its SPD opponents that was political, intellectual and moral. Colonialism both reproduced and eroded class division in Germany, and it was out of this tension that, ultimately, a more supple, sinuous colonial discourse developed, one reflected in revisionism and the eventual eclipse of grassroots anticolonialism.

The politics of SPD anticolonialism and its mutations does not, finally, tell a complete story, because it omits the more indirect mediation of colonialism, its assimilation into a specifically working-class culture, often in the form of "colonial knowledge," even as a robustly, surprisingly critical attitude flourished among ordinary working men and women. To understand the cultural significance of colonialism in Germany and its role in the dissemination of racism, it is necessary to proceed by way of social history, to disaggregate by social class and consider how class difference shaped the reception and formation of discourse. But the transmission of colonial knowledge among socialists and workers occurred not just in electoral contests or the political arena more broadly but also in the diffuse sphere of culture—the world, much maligned by contemporaries, of dime novels, the cinematograph, the *Panoptikum*, and also, paradoxically, in SPD libraries and adult education, of popular science.[75] Whether as mass culture or mass politics, colonial discourse acted gradually, as a form of working-class or mass initiation into capitalist market modernity: into international exchange relations, via the discourses of commodity consumption, mass production, and global competition. It was also, inseparably, a form of initiation into the nation-state. Here, perhaps, the diffusion of racist cultural codes and iconographies framed the formation, much contested, of national subjectivity among German workers. The SPD was quite obviously susceptible of assimilation to this most modern image of the global and Germany's place within it—not only in its revisionist impulse but in an orthodox critique of empire that itself took colonial political economy increasingly seriously.[76] Still, the vigorous, popular engagement in anticolonial critique and protest, the strong countervailing currents that long thwarted colonialist aims, above all in a time of war from 1904 to 1907, suggests that this was hardly inevitable.

NOTES

1. Evans, *Kneipengespräche im Kaiserreich*, 353–354.
2. Hobson, *Imperialism*, 101.
3. Hobson, *The Psychology of Jingoism*, 117.

4. *Deutsche Kolonialzeitung* [DKZ], April 27, 1907.

5. Lenin, *Imperialism*, 109.

6. Hobson, *Imperialism*, 101.

7. Among the considerable literature treating German Social Democracy and imperialism, see Ascher, "Imperialists within German Social Democracy"; Fletcher, *Revisionism and Empire*; Schorske, *German Social Democracy*; Schröder, *Gustav Noske*; Schröder, *Sozialismus und Imperialismus*; and Stoecker and Sebald, "Enemies of the Colonial Idea."

8. For example, Stoecker and Sebald conclude that the "German working class could indeed not be won over to colonial aims," but virtually all their evidence concerns the anticolonialism of SPD leaders, intellectuals, and the press. See Stoecker and Sebald, "Enemies of the Colonial Idea," 66. Conversely, Fletcher's speculation on working-class receptivity to imperialism reflects his interest in SPD revisionism: "Although the workers did not succumb to the populist nationalism of the Navy League and similar non-socialist agitational groups, the aggregate impact of traditional values, uprooting, material and status deprivation, structural change, the work experience and social controls undoubtedly made many workers more susceptible to the kind of nationalist fare offered by avowedly socialist organs like the *Sozialistische Monatshefte* than historians have hitherto cared to contemplate. This was not a case of workers being betrayed or misled by opportunistic leaders so much as a matter of autonomous working-class radicalism seeking, and to some extent finding, an outlet for its grievances in an avenue that was compatible with social reality as it appeared to the ordinary shop-floor worker." Fletcher, *Revisionism and Empire*, 34.

9. See the police reports on conversations overheard in working-class pubs in Hamburg, transcribed and compiled in Evans, *Kneipengespräche im Kaiserreich* and "Proletarian Mentalities."

10. On the elections of 1907, see Sobich, *"Schwarze Bestien, rote Gefahr"*; Becker, "Kulturkampf als Vorwand"; Crothers, *The German Elections of 1907*; Fricke, "Der deutsche Imperialismus"; Reinhard, "'Sozialimperialismus?'"

11. On the Maji Maji rebellion, see Iliffe, "Effects of the Maji Maji Rebellion"; Iliffe, "The Organization of the Maji Maji Rebellion"; Seeberg, *Der Maji-Maji-Krieg*; Wright, "Maji Maji."

12. On the German-Herero war, see Bridgman, *The Revolt of the Hereros*; Drechsler, *"Let Us Die Fighting"*; Hull, *Absolute Destruction*; Krüger, *Kriegsbewältigung und Geschichtsbewußtsein*; Zimmerer, *Deutsche Herrschaft über Afrikaner*.

13. Sobich, *"Schwarze Bestien, rote Gefahr."* Among many German Protestants, anti-Catholicism also played an important role in the elections. See Crothers, *The German Elections of 1907*, 177–178, and Sperber, *The Kaiser's Voters*, 245, 254.

14. Dernburg, *Zielpunkte des Deutschen Kolonialwesens*.

15. Bundesarchiv Berlin-Lichterfelde [BA], R8023/509, Deutsche Kolonialgesellschaft [DKG], Bl. 12, president of DKG to local chairmen, December 21, 1906.

16. Soénius, *Koloniale Begeisterung im Rheinland*, 62, 108–109.

17. DKZ, January 24, 1907. The DKG distributed some four million pieces of literature altogether. See Pierard, "The German Colonial Society," 31.

18. BA, R8023/509, DKG, Bl. 316–317.
19. BA, R8023/510, DKG.
20. Severing, *Mein Lebensweg*, 155.
21. BA, R8023/510, DKG, Bl. 412–413, "Die Koloniale Lügenfabrik."
22. Severing, *Mein Lebensweg*, 155; Dernburg, *Zielpunkte des Deutschen Kolonialwesens*, 20; Sobich, "*Schwarze Bestien, rote Gefahr*," 258, 284–285.
23. Crothers, *The German Elections of 1907*, 153, 176–178; Nolan, *Social Democracy and Society*, 177–180.
24. Nolan, *Social Democracy and Society*.
25. In his examination of the so-called Khaki Election in Britain in 1900, Richard Price emphasizes the election as a chiefly *local* phenomenon in which there was "very little correlation between imperial appeal and electoral success." Price, *An Imperial War*.
26. The SPD did not, of course, allow the imperialism debate to obscure longstanding issues like tariffs or social insurance. See, for example, *Leipziger Volkszeitung* [LVZ], December 15, 1906.
27. Bernstein, "Was folgt aus dem Ergebnis?," 110.
28. Sächsisches Staatsarchiv Leipzig [StAL], Amtshauptmannschaft [AH] Oschatz 17, Reichstagswahl 1907.
29. Bernstein, "The German Elections and the Social Democrats," 489.
30. Fletcher, in his work on imperialism and revisionism in the SPD, observes before 1911 a "general indifference [to imperialism], punctuated by largely formal, hyperbolical and desultory forays against imperialist excesses. . . . Such interest as was expressed in foreign policy problems was usually vague and woolly-minded, reflecting a clear ambivalence in Social Democratic thinking." The idea that the SPD had no consistent response to imperialism and remained indifferent to diplomatic and international matters makes less sense in the *local* context when one considers the SPD press. Beginning in at least 1900, readers of local SPD papers encountered strong, consistent criticism of colonialism over a period of many years. Fletcher, *Revisionism and Empire*, 34. See also Ascher, "Imperialists within German Social Democracy," 402–403; Nolan, *Social Democracy and Society*, 176; Schorske, *German Social Democracy*, 66–68.
31. LVZ, June 26, 1900, October 8–10, 1906. The sneering accusation about "Gold für die Tippelskirche und die Wörmänner" refers to a colonial financial scandal in the Tippelskirch firm and to the influential Hamburg shipping and trading firm C. Woermann. See Epstein, "Erzberger and the German Colonial Scandals," 644–645.
32. *Augsburger Volkszeitung* [AVZ], October 12 and 16, 1900.
33. AVZ, October 18, 1904.
34. AVZ, October 12, 1900.
35. *Schwäbische Volkszeitung* [SVZ], October 10, 1905. The AVZ became the SVZ on April 1, 1905.
36. Evans, *Kneipengespräche im Kaiserreich*, 357; Bromme, *Lebensgeschichte eines modernen Fabrikarbeiters*, 320.
37. LVZ, December 14 and 15, 1906. The paper gave a detailed account of the costs of empire, estimating that in 1905 Germany's colonial trade amounted to just 0.5 percent of its entire world trade, LVZ, December 15, 1906.

38. Stadtarchiv Leipzig [SAL], Polizeiberichte [PB] 1907, 113, 1, 5.
39. DKZ, January 24, 1907. The DKG held thirteen meetings altogether in Saxony.
40. SAL, PB 1907, 5.
41. SAL, PB 1907, 101.
42. LVZ, January 22, 1907.
43. StAL, AH Oschatz 17, Reichstagswahl 1907.
44. *Bericht über die Tätigkeit*, 5–6, 7.
45. StAL, AH 2675, Öffentliche Versammlungen 1907, Bl. 29–31.
46. StAL, AH 2675, Öffentliche Versammlungen 1907, Bl. 33–5. Trotha had issued the proclamation early in the war, on October 2, 1904.
47. *Bericht über die Tätigkeit*, 6.
48. StAL, AH 2675, Öffentliche Versammlungen 1907, Bl. 167–169. LVZ, January 24, 1907.
49. StAL, AH 2675, Öffentliche Versammlungen 1907, Bl. 76–78, 110–111.
50. *Bericht über die Tätigkeit*, 6.
51. SVZ, December 20, 1906.
52. SVZ, January 21, 1907.
53. Bernstein, "Was folgt aus dem Ergebnis?" and "Die Kolonialfrage und der Klassenkampf," 988–996; Calwer, "Der 25. Januar," 101–107. Of course, it was to the revisionists' advantage to portray colonialism as a decisive issue in the elections.
54. Kautsky, "Der 25. Januar," 589.
55. Luxemburg, "Die Lehren der letzten Reichstagswahl," 192, 194.
56. Sperber, *Kaiser's Voters*, 249–251. The SPD lost nearly half of its deputies, falling from 81 to 43 seats. Sobich, *"Schwarze Bestien, rote Gefahr,"* 319–322, 346.
57. Bauernfeind, *Bürgermeister Georg Ritter von Schuh*, 457.
58. SAL, PB 1907, 3.
59. SAL, PB 1907, 5. Of 42,197 eligible voters in Leipzig-Stadt in 1903, 36,153 (86%) cast votes.
60. *Bericht über die Tätigkeit*, 6.
61. *Bericht über die Tätigkeit*, 8.
62. Rudolph, *Die sächsische Sozialdemokratie*, 66, n. 9.
63. *Bericht über die Tätigkeit*, 9.
64. SAL, PB 1907, 5. Of 96,927 eligible voters in Leipzig-Land in 1903, 79,389 (82%) cast votes. PB 1907, 6.
65. *Bericht über die Tätigkeit*, 6.
66. *Bericht über die Tätigkeit*, 9.
67. Sperber, *Kaiser's Voters*, 249.
68. The SPD won 48 percent of the Saxon vote, down from 58 percent in 1903. Crothers, *German Elections*, 178.
69. SAL, PB 1907, 14, 26–27.
70. Rudolph, "Das 'rote Königreich,'" 77–78.
71. SAL, PB 1911, 33.
72. SAL, PB 1912, 2–3. Nationally, the SPD drew 42 percent of eligible working-class

voters in 1912, representing 49 percent of all working-class votes cast. Sperber, *Kaiser's Voters*, 264.

73. SAL, PB 1914, 1.
74. Kautsky, "Der 25. Januar," 589.
75. Short, "Everyman's Colonial Library," 445–475.
76. In, for example, Hilferding, *Das Finanzkapital*.

ELEVEN

Colonialism and the Anti-Semitic
Movement in Imperial Germany

CHRISTIAN S. DAVIS

On April 24, 1884, the German consul at Cape Town received a telegram from Bismarck declaring coastal regions of Southwest Africa purchased from local notables by the Bremen tobacco merchant, Adolf Lüerditz, to be under the official protection of the German emperor.[1] Several months later, the chancellor extended further protection to German interests in Togo and Cameroon. He offered similar guarantees early the next year to the German East Africa Company, which claimed large areas off the coast of Zanzibar. Anti-Semites enthusiastically joined the pro-colonial forces marshaling support behind Bismarck. The anti-Semitic *Staatsbürger-Zeitung* stated in May that "We would be extraordinarily happy if the German flag suddenly fluttered on the coast of Africa and are convinced that England and France would reckon silently with this fait accompli, albeit with envious eyes."[2] Months later, the paper insisted that "every German patriot" would greet "with open joy" the acquisition of colonies.[3]

As this reaction in the press suggests, some anti-Semites strongly favored the idea of colonial empire. In addition, the major anti-Semitic political parties of the *Kaiserreich* era all endorsed colonialism explicitly. Ernst Henrici's short-lived anti-Semitic Social Reich party, created in 1880, was the first political party in Germany to advocate overseas empire.[4] The longer-lasting and more successful Christian Social, German Reform, and German Social parties supported colonialism as well, either in their party platforms and party papers or through their representatives in the Reichstag. Many of their leading men belonged to the Pan-German League — one of the major extraparliamentary pressure groups that agitated for a strong pro-colonial policy—and the political parties benefited politically from their support of the colonial cause: in the election of 1907, the anti-Semitic parties rode the wave of nationalist fervor sparked by the parliamentary defeat of the colonial budget to emerge with increased representation in the Reichstag long after the heyday of political anti-Semitism had come and gone.[5]

The relationship between colonialism and the anti-Semitic movement, however, was more complex than these facts imply. Despite the overwhelming support for colonialism within the anti-Semitic political parties, influential voices in the more radical wing of the anti-Semitic press questioned the wisdom of maintaining overseas colonies. Additionally, pro-colonial anti-Semites were often at odds with the government over colonial policy. Significant differences of opinion also existed among the former on a variety of matters, from the type of colonialism to be pursued to the treatment of the colonized. Instead of unifying anti-Semites, colonialism introduced new divisions into an already fragmented movement. What is more, colonialism did not automatically advance the domestic agenda of racial anti-Semites, despite the weight colonies gave to theories of racial difference. This is because German colonialism provided opportunities for men of Jewish descent to craft colonial policy and, in a few instances, to even become popular heroes due to their pro-colonial efforts. Their participation refuted the anti-Semitic principle that Jewish citizens were unpatriotic.

This chapter complicates prior historical understandings of the relationship between colonialism and anti-Semites in Imperial Germany.[6] It examines the anti-Semites' engagement with colonialism, detailing the perspectives of the pro-colonial majority before discussing some of their disagreements with the government over colonial policy. It considers the divisions within the anti-Semitic movement over colonial empire, including prominent voices of opposition within Theodor Fritsch's *Hammer* magazine. A final section analyzes the discord among anti-Semites over two Germans of Jewish descent who became celebrated figures in connection with their colonizing activities: Karl Oscar Theodor Schnitzer, widely known as Emin Pasha, and Bernhard Dernburg, the director of the Colonial Division of the Foreign Office in 1906, who later became state secretary of the newly independent Colonial Office.

The idea that Germany needed a colonial empire in order to maintain its great power status and compete economically with rival states coexisted in the *Weltanschauung* of most pro-colonial political anti-Semites with a powerful conviction that colonies could promote the racial health and cultural unity of the German people. Most pro-colonial anti-Semites therefore subscribed to a mixture of what Woodruff D. Smith identified as the two competing imperialist ideologies of the Wilhelminian era: economic imperialism, sometimes called *Weltpolitik*, and migrationist colonialism, which Smith denotes with the anachronism *Lebensraum*.

According to Smith, the first envisioned a worldwide foreign policy aimed at protecting and promoting Germany's industrial economy. Its proponents assigned government an important role in planning the nation's economic development, and they valued colonies as markets for German goods or sources of raw materials for German industry. Advocates of *Lebensraum* were less concerned with the material benefits that colonialism might bring. For them, the colonies were important first and foremost as settlement areas where German immigrants would maintain their cultural and linguistic ties to the homeland, as opposed to the United States, where such ties quickly dissipated. They saw the spread of the German *Volk* across the globe, undiluted by foreign influences, as necessary if Germans were to successfully compete on the world stage with other ethnic communities.[7] Anti-Semites of different stripes subscribed to the two imperialist ideologies to different degrees, but many, if not most, borrowed from both to make the strongest possible argument for the creation and retention of colonies.

The German Reform Party adopted this strategy. The inaugural issue of its party organ, the *Deutsche Wacht*, pledged the party's support in 1887 for "German colonial policy," and its representatives in parliament identified the colonies as potential exporters of raw materials and importers of German goods as well as targets for immigration.[8] In his capacity as a parliamentary deputy, party member Ludwig Werner advocated the development of small farm settlements in German Africa in order to relieve Germany's "surplus population,"[9] but he also insisted that the success of the large cotton plantations was something "to which all must subscribe who intend to take the blossoming of the colonies seriously and wish to make Germany independent from foreign countries."[10] The party's leader, Oswald Zimmermann, held out the additional hope that colonialism could blunt the threat posed by social democracy. As a deputy in the mid-1890s, Zimmermann envisioned sending Germany's unemployed to the African colonies, and he claimed that such a program, if applied to the *Mittelstand*, would help prevent its proletarianization.[11]

The leadership of the German Social Party embraced the *Weltpolitik* and *Lebensraum* ideologies as well, advocating within their party program of 1890 "an active and purposeful colonial policy aimed at the acquisition of trade and farmer colonies."[12] Accordingly, the party's organ, the *Deutsch-Soziale Blätter*, explicitly linked economic imperialism with settler colonialism when making the case for overseas colonies. Without settlements abroad, the argument ran, Germany's "excess population" would continue to flow into foreign states, thereby strengthening its "economic enemies." The *Blätter* reasoned that settlement colonies would prevent this from happening by creating Reich territories for German immigrants while allowing Germany to create its own exclusive foreign markets.[13]

The German Social point man on colonial matters in the legislature, deputy Wilhelm Lattmann, also borrowed from both imperialist ideologies, emphasizing the potential economic advantages of colonial possessions while arguing for the necessity of large German settlements within the colonies. Lattmann claimed that both the working-class and *Mittelstand* would benefit immensely from a sensible colonial policy, which he defined as "the creation of export markets and the expansion over there of production, in order to secure for us an importation of goods that we either don't produce, or don't produce in sufficient quantity."[14] He also insisted that "the farmer, the settler, and the German peasantry abroad must form the backbone of our colonies."[15] In this, he departed from staunch *Weltpolitikers* who opposed colonial settlements and favored instead the large company-owned plantation as the way to develop the colonies.

Of the three major anti-Semitic parties, only the more conservative Christian Socials departed from the strategy of drawing heavily upon the arguments of both the *Weltpolitikers* and the *Lebensraum* advocates. Unlike the German Reformers and German Socials, the religiously oriented Christian Socials identified spreading Christianity as the most important reason for possessing colonies. The proselytizing impulse played a significant role in the party founder's own support for the colonial project; when the court chaplain Adolf Stoecker interceded in Reichstag debates on colonial matters, he frequently did so to promote missionary activity or to champion the causes connected with the missions, like abolishing the liquor trade and combating the spread of Islam. Even so, Stoecker still expressed an appreciation for some of the goals of *Weltpolitik*. Like Ludwig Werner, he argued that tropical colonies might liberate German industry from its reliance on foreign imports of raw materials, a policy that would strengthen Germany's hand internationally.[16]

Significant backing for colonialism also existed among the more radical anti-Semites who shunned conventional politicking. The most important such voice in the last two decades of empire belonged to the ideologue Friedrich Lange, founder of the Deutschbund, an exclusive anti-Semitic organization whose members embraced *völkisch* nationalism and practiced a near-religious worship of German ethnicity and culture. Although he advocated the acquirement of overseas *Lebensraum*, Lange also expressed the sentiments of the *Weltpolitikers*, since he viewed colonial possessions as necessary to strengthen Germany's national economy. His support for colonialism was an outgrowth of his militant Social Darwinism as well, and he valued colonies as "coaling stations" in distant lands.[17] Lange advanced the colonial cause in his daily paper, the *Deutsche Zeitung*, which he controlled from Berlin between the years 1896 and 1912. Along with its weekly addition, the *Deutsche Welt*, the DZ became the anti-Semitic movement's most consistent and enthusiastic advocate of the colonies.

With the exception of perhaps the Christian Socials, the pro-colonial anti-Semites were also motivated, no doubt, by colonialism's apparent confirmation of their racist *Weltanschauung*. Friedrich Lange, the German Socials, and the German Reformers all championed the new racial anti-Semitism and, by extension, the idea of racial hierarchies. The creation of colonial racial states bolstered theories about the reality and importance of racial divides, and some anti-Semites used the colonial example to argue for the significance of racial differences at home. The *völkisch* ideologue and literary historian Adolf Bartels did this in the *Deutsche Welt* during the Herero uprising in Southwest Africa in 1904. Bartels lamented the conservatism of German scholars, arguing that it prevented them from embracing racial science, and he concluded that a consideration of the Hereros might "open the eyes wide." Speaking of the Hereros and Jews together, Bartels wrote, "Indeed, they are also men, but that a Jew will become a true German poet and one of the Hereros a professor of Ethnology in the not-too-distant future is, in the end . . . surely to be rejected."[18] Similar arguments appeared elsewhere in the anti-Semitic press, especially toward the end of empire.[19]

Support for colonialism among these anti-Semites did not, however, entail an unquestioning acceptance of the government's colonial policies. The parliamentary deputies of the anti-Semitic political parties were, in fact, sharply critical of the government throughout much of the colonial era. When the government renounced its aspirations to parts of mainland eastern Africa in 1890 and agreed to the establishment of a British protectorate over the islands of Zanzibar and Pemba in exchange for the small North Sea island of Helgoland, the anti-Semites denounced this action loudly.[20] The parliamentary representatives also criticized the slow pace of colonial development. Despite their support for some of the goals of *Weltpolitik*, pro-colonial anti-Semites both inside and outside the Reichstag vehemently rejected government policies that favored big business at the expense of colonial settlers or provided what the anti-Semites considered excessive remunerations to colonial land, mining, and railroad companies.

Anti-Semites were especially vexed by these latter policies. Beginning in the 1890s, the government attempted to foster colonial development through private capital, in large part because the Reichstag would not approve the necessary public funds. The government gave away extensive land, mining, and other rights to a handful of private corporations, in exchange for which these "concession companies" were obligated to construct roads and explore their territories. Contrary to expectations, this arrangement actually hindered colonial development. Some companies neglected to build the necessary infrastructure within their regions, and their monopolistic rights prevented local colonial governments from taking action.[21] Others interpreted the government's concessions as giving them greater control over the exploitation of natural resources than the government intended, a reading that led some companies to exclude rival trading houses from their zones of influence despite government promises of free trade. The slow pace of colonial development hampered the materialization of the economic and industrial benefits that the anti-Semites insisted colonialism would bring. The enrichment of a few private corporations at the expense of national blood and treasure undermined their claim that the German people would benefit as a whole from the colonies. The fact that some of the largest concession companies were partly foreign owned exacerbated the anti-Semites' anger, as did the government's extensive extra aid to the companies.

The anticapitalist ethos of the anti-Semitic movement drove its members to vehemently condemn these policies, and the Herero War galvanized their opposition, as it necessitated a massive infusion of money into a colony that had failed to live up to its promise. It was the German Social Party's spokesman on colonial matters, Wilhelm Lattmann, who led the charge, sounding the alarm against "the brutal predominance of monopolistic capitalism," "the growing influence of foreign capital," "land speculation," and the "failures of concessionary policy" in almost a dozen deliveries on colonial matters in the Reichstag, as well as numerous published articles.[22] Several months after the outbreak of violence in 1904, Lattmann proclaimed that the German Social delegates were ready to approve a resolution for Southwest Africa to compensate for economic losses from the uprisings but requested that the resolution exclude the land companies.[23] Six years later, Lattmann sparked considerable debate when he proposed a one-time 1 percent levy on landed wealth of 300,000 marks or higher, intended to make wealthy investors shoulder a greater part of the financial burden of maintaining the colony.[24]

Anger over specific government actions and policies did not, however, prevent the parliamentary anti-Semites from rallying behind the government in defense of colonialism when the colonial empire appeared in danger. Following a brief period of national unity in 1904, when even the anticolonial Social Democrats did not oppose sending reinforcement troops to the colony, criticisms of the government mounted as critics accused it of generating the conditions for rebellion through flawed colonial policies. The parliamentary representatives of the anti-Semitic political parties joined other nationalists in censuring the critics, demanding a patriotic front "as long as the bloody battle over there has not ended."[25]

Another crisis arose in 1906, when a number of scandals concerning German Africa erupted in rapid succession. Renewed efforts by critics on the left and center to publicize allegations of the horrific abuse of African indigenes coincided with dramatic new revelations about some of the monopolistic privileges granted by the government to large companies doing business in the colonies. These disclosures motivated the Catholic Center Party to unite with the Social Democrats at the year's end to vote down the government's request for a supplementary appropriation of funds to continue the war in Southwest Africa, providing Chancellor Bülow an excuse to dissolve the Reichstag. Although the anti-Semitic parliamentary deputies joined the chorus criticizing the business monopolies, they attacked the allegations of atrocities as sensationalistic and out of bounds.[26] The parliamentary representatives of the German Social, Christian Social, and German Reform parties sided with the government in voting for the requested funds, proving that their general commitment to colonialism surmounted their disappointment over the way that colonialism had turned out.[27]

The widespread support for colonialism within the anti-Semitic political parties and segments of the anti-Semitic press belied the existence of significant differences over colonialism among them. The most important early difference arose before the creation of colonial empire; it concerned the very nature and purpose of colonies. On one side stood the more orthodox procolonial advocates, like Friedrich Lange, who embraced aspects of both the *Lebensraum* and *Weltpolitik* philosophies. These individuals preached the immaterial racial and cultural benefits they believed colonies would bring but also expressed the hope that colonial possessions would strengthen the German economy and augment the power of the German nation-state vis-à-vis other colonizing powers. On the other side stood anti-Semites who concentrated solely on the imagined spiritual, cultural, and racial benefits of colonies. The former believed that colonies should retain their political ties with the homeland, but the latter deemed this unimportant or even counterproductive to the very purpose of having colonies.

Bernhard Förster and his wife, Elisabeth Förster-Nietzsche, the sister of Friedrich Nietzsche, emerged in the 1880s as the most forceful and active advocates of the second colonial philosophy. A Berlin schoolteacher who helped organize the Anti-Semites' Petition of 1880, Förster became convinced after its failure of the futility of using conventional politics to solve Germany's problems, which he defined as the corruption of German culture through Jewish capitalism. He identified colonialism as crucial to the future of the German people but argued that colonies should remain separate and independent from a Germany that had degenerated into a "step-fatherland" as a result of Jewish influences.[28] For Förster, colonies were not meant to strengthen the economic or military capabilities or international prestige of Germany but to enable the "preservation of human culture" and the "purification and rebirth of the human race" through the isolated breeding of pure Aryans.[29] After several years of raising funds, the Försters set sail with fourteen German families in the winter of 1886 for Nueva Germania, an isolated spot in central Paraguay, which they identified as a potential new fatherland, one free of Jewish influence. The venture quickly fell apart, but the colonial philosophy that underlay it—the idea that colonies were strictly a means to racial and spiritual rebirth—lived on among a minority of anti-Semites.[30]

A more significant divide emerged over the idea of a "civilizing mission," with pro-colonial anti-Semites in sharp disagreement as to whether the well-being of the colonized—their material, spiritual, and cultural uplift—should be a goal of German colonial policy. A strict utilitarianism combined with an unshakable belief in German racial superiority informed the outlook on the treatment of the colonized among the most enthusiastic and outspoken advocates of colonialism from the German Social and German Reform parties. For Wilhelm Lattmann, Ludwig Werner, and men like them, excessive cruelties were to be avoided and the indigenous populations preserved, but for practical reasons like the need for a pliable and sizable labor force, not out of a sense of duty to or shared humanity with the colonized. From this perspective, forced labor, corporal punishment, and other harsh measures were permissible provided that they enabled the success of the colonial project for the long-term benefit of the German *Volk* back home, not the short-term interests of a small number of planters or settlers. This philosophy led Lattmann and Werner to reject the more radical demands of colonial settlers, but it also led them to view the colonized strictly as objects of exploitation.

The utilitarian outlook aroused fierce opposition within a vocal segment of the pro-colonial anti-Semitic community led by Adolf Stöcker, who had employed paternalistic rhetoric when speaking of the colonized as far back as the 1880s, when he argued for the abolition of the liquor trade in German Africa to protect colonial populations from "the dangers of a false civilization."[31] But it was the Herero and Nama wars in Southwest Africa that brought the differences between his perspective and that of the more hard-edged racists most clearly to light. In the months and years after the outbreak of violence, voices in the *Deutsch-Soziale Blätter* and *Deutsche Zeitung* called for forced labor and for strict restrictions on the freedom of blacks. Stöcker, however, rejected such notions, insisting before the Reichstag in late 1904 that the idea of transforming "natives" into "bondsmen without further ado in order to gain laborers" was "not in accord with the promises made and the dignity of the Reich." Stöcker argued that Germans were "only protectors in Southwest Africa," not "masters of the land and the people." He also blamed the revolt on the behavior of whites; specifically, on "the clumsy handling of the land question and the boundless arrogance of the traders."[32] This was a dramatic departure from German Social Party founder Liebermann von Sonnenburg, who attributed the uprising to the Hereros' desire to return to their precolonial customs of "theft, robbery, and murder."[33]

The discord among pro-colonial anti-Semites over the proper attitude toward and treatment of the colonized also played out in the anti-Semitic press. In September of 1904, the *Deutsch-Soziale Blätter* printed a letter from a reader arguing for the application of Christian principles toward the rebelling Hereros. The DSB editors rejected this position, labeling the application of Christian love toward non-Germans as a type a "religious fanaticism" and faulting the government for an "all-too-great compliance" toward blacks.[34] Later in the war, the *Staatsbürger-Zeitung* echoed Stöcker's paternalism in a series of front-page articles that argued for a more humane treatment of the colonized. One piece advocated policies of "education" instead of "extermination" in German Africa and insisted that Germans had a duty to bring "Christianity and the guarantee of law" as well as "economic improvement" to the colonized.[35] Another criticized the tendency within "many colonial circles" to treat blacks as nothing more than "work animals."[36] A third demanded an end to "the slavery-like handling of the coloreds."[37] Such pronouncements contrasted sharply with warnings in the *Deutsch-Soziale Blätter* against "weak sentimentality" in the treatment of "Negroes."[38] They also contrasted with support in the *Deutsche Welt* and *Deutsche Zeitung* for a forced labor system and calls for the creation of a strict master and servant relationship between whites and blacks.[39]

Opponents on these issues shared, at the very least, an appreciation for the colonial project. But a minority of anti-Semites—typically found in the movement's "nonpolitical" wing—questioned the very wisdom of holding colonies.

These individuals saw the government's colonizing endeavors as failing to address the erosion of traditional German culture, the degeneration of the German racial stock, and the alienation of the German people from their inborn sensibilities, all paramount concerns for movement radicals. Highly critical of the modern capitalist, industrialized economy, these colonial critics sharply attacked any concessions in colonial matters to the interests of big business and industry. Concerned to the point of paranoia about racial intermixing, they also pointed out the potential dangers that colonialism posed to German racial purity.

The ambivalence toward and occasional outright opposition to colonialism among these anti-Semites could be seen most clearly in the pages of Theodor Fritsch's *Hammer* magazine. A founding member of the German Social Party and the onetime publisher of the *Deutsch-Soziale Blätter*, Fritsch turned his back on party politics to found his own "unpolitical" anti-Semitic periodical and organizations. From 1902 until his death in 1933, he devoted much of his energy to publishing the Leipzig-based *Hammer*, a magazine that espoused a combination of scientific racial anti-Semitism and *völkisch* nationalism that presaged the National Socialists' beliefs.[40] In marked contrast to the frequent discussion of colonialism in the *Staatsbürger-Zeitung* and other periodicals, colonial matters did not feature prominently in the *Hammer*, a fact suggestive of the low regard Fritsch had for the colonies. The handful of articles and occasional letters and short, often anonymous annotations concerning colonialism that did appear were overwhelmingly critical of colonial conditions or government policies. This negativity was almost never moderated by the sort of impassioned defense of the idea of colonialism that mitigated similar criticisms in pro-colonial anti-Semitic papers.

For example, the *Deutsch-Soziale Blätter* was quite critical of government policy in German Southwest Africa during the Herero uprising. In 1904, it printed several long articles attacking Governor Leutwein's supposed leniency toward the Africans and the government's privileging of the interests of large, often foreign-owned land and mining companies.[41] Nevertheless, the *Blätter* defended the idea of colonialism. Approximately a month after printing its stinging indictment of Leutwein, it published two front-page articles discussing Southwest Africa's merits as a colony and outlining the rationale for colonial possessions overall.[42] The *Deutsche Zeitung* followed suit. In 1904, several weeks after its weekly edition, the *Deutsche Welt*, harshly critiqued government policy in Southwest Africa, the DZ ran a piece emphasizing the dire need for colonies. It claimed that degeneration through excessive urbanization threatened the German race if it failed to plant its excess people in outer territories.[43]

By contrast, the *Hammer* editors let stand unchallenged the anticolonial comments of a contributor who wrote in 1904 that "if today a good friend entered my room and said he wanted to settle in our colonies, I would immediately send for a doctor and have him examined for sunstroke."[44] No rejoinder was made to another contributor in 1908 who, shaken by encounters with Africans in German cities, suggested that the colonies had come at too great a price; namely, Germany's "negroization."[45] This remained the last word on the colonies in the *Hammer* for almost two years, as it was that long before the magazine again discussed colonial matters.

On occasion, participants in this debate identified the opposing view as "Jewish." In 1906, the *Hammer* magazine printed a letter from "J.H.," who denigrated the German African colonies as "crumbs that have fallen from the table" of the other great powers. He wrote of the illnesses, malaria and blackwater fever, that endangered "thousands of soldiers, officials, and colonists." He speculated that "to dispose of the most devoted and brave offspring of German blood" in this way accorded, perhaps, with the plans of "our large Jewish papers," especially if "Romanians and Slavs" took their places back in Germany. The author recommended "inner … colonization" instead, citing the "thousands of square kilometers at home" as well as "the rich arable land of the Danube" that awaited "clearing."[46]

Another reader, H.R., answered J.H. the following year in one of the only unambiguously pro-colonial pieces to appear in the *Hammer*.[47] He contested assertions about the health dangers of the colonies and argued that they offered more "fecund land" for "our *Volk*" than existed in "Polish and Danube" regions.[48] Concerning the latter's claims about "Jewish papers," H.R. countered that it was precisely the "Jewish left-liberal" and "Jewish democratic" press that had "vigorously fought against our colonial policy" and "had tried to make the colonies loathsome to us Germans." H.R. remarked upon the "voluntary enthusiasm of the sons of our people for the colonies" that existed "despite the steadily preached antipathy for and propaganda against our colonies by the Jewish and related press." He insisted upon harnessing this enthusiasm for the advantage of "our German nationality" abroad.[49]

For outside observers, the divisions among anti-Semites discussed so far would not have been obvious because the arguments were largely confined to the pages of the anti-Semitic press, which had a limited readership and catered to movement members. More importantly, none of these positions could be easily read as contradicting anti-Semitism's core beliefs. As seen in the exchange between J.H. and H.R., movement members could marshal anti-Semitic arguments either for or against the overseas colonies. So there was little reason for opponents of the movement to pay attention to the differences among anti-Semites over the purpose and wisdom of colonies or the treatment of their native inhabitants. This was not the case, however, when it came to the discord among anti-Semites over the involvement of Germans of Jewish descent in the colonial project.

Significantly, Germans of Jewish descent numbered among the most prominent personalities of the colonial movement; the newness of colonial empire meant the absence of an entrenched elite in the colonial bureaucracy that, had it existed, would have prevented individuals identified as Jewish by their peers from participating at the highest levels. Surprisingly, Germans of Jewish descent also produced some of the best-loved colonial actors, individuals who became incredibly popular with the wider pro-colonial German public. The most colorful such figure was the explorer Emin Pasha, who converted from Judaism to Christianity as a child. Emin gained national acclaim and worldwide fame during the Mahdist uprising of the 1880s as the besieged European governor of the Egyptian province of Equatoria. He later entered German service, busying himself establishing a presence in the northeastern regions of German East Africa. Emin's popularity within Germany was arguably surpassed in the final decade of empire by that of the outspoken colonial director and then state secretary of the new Colonial Office, Bernhard Dernburg, a man with a once Jewish father.[50] Both men achieved hero status among colonialism's supporters despite public knowledge of their Jewish ancestry; opponents of the anti-Semitic movement noted the discord this caused among pro-colonial anti-Semites.[51]

The anti-Semitic press, for example, was sharply divided over Emin Pasha. The German Reform Party's *Deutsche Wacht* denounced him as a Jew, outlining his family history in an 1888 article. The paper condemned the effort by the German explorer Carl Peters to rescue him from Equatoria, insisting that Emin was "a genuine international Jew," not a German subject, and that Germany had no duty toward him.[52] Other papers denounced him as "a Jewish-African idler" or derided him as "the ivory-Jew Schnitzer" and accused the "Jewish press" of falsely creating excitement about him."[53] But these sentiments were not unanimous. The *Staatsbürger-Zeitung* did not join these attacks and instead published detailed accounts of Emin's exploits. The anti-Semitic Protestant paper *Der Reichsbote* even defended the explorer from anti-Semitic critics, insisting in an article after his death that he had done more "than all Ahlwardts, Pikenbachs, Schwennbagens, and Böckels combined."[54] This split in anti-Semitic ranks caught the attention of the Union of Defense against Anti-Semitism—an organization that monitored the anti-Semitic movement—which reported it in its periodical.[55]

Similar divisions emerged over Bernhard Dernburg. Some anti-Semites rallied to him and overlooked his Jewish heritage, while others opposed him and fixated on it. Those who supported Dernburg were impressed by the energy and determination with which he pursued a policy of reform in colonial matters. During his first months in office, Dernburg announced the cancellation of two much-criticized government contracts with companies that, as had been recently revealed, vastly overcharged for their services. At the same time, Dernburg went on the offense against the detractors of empire, passionately defending the majority of colonial officials against "unjustified and malicious attacks."[56] In his very first address before the Reichstag, he also set forth a positive new vision of colonial development, declaring his intention to create "administratively independent, economically healthy colonies" run by an "efficient and reliable civil service" composed of "the best men and characters."[57] All this won him the admiration of colonial enthusiasts across the Reich.

The *Deutsche Zeitung* emerged as Dernburg's strongest and most consistent supporter in the anti-Semitic press, despite reporting on his Jewish heritage early on. Following his debut in parliament, the paper published an extremely positive review of Dernburg's early speeches, noting with approval his emphasis on railroad construction as well as his exclusion of military costs from his memoranda on the colonies. The DZ remarked with satisfaction that "we, ourselves, advanced a similar . . . perspective twenty-four hours before Dernburg's speech."[58] Later, a DZ contributor actually chastised the anti-Semitic *Deutsche Tageszeitung* for poking fun at Dernburg for his electioneering activities on behalf of the pro-colonial position during the so-called Hottentot election, when Dernburg traveled the country speaking on the importance and viability of the colonies. "What does one want from this man?," A.Pz. asked bluntly in 1907. "Why doesn't one let him alone? Why doesn't one help him with pleasure? . . . Shouldn't we gladly, loudly cry out: Thank God that finally a man of the government with fresh energy steps before the nation and shows it that the government finally wants something and what it wants?"[59]

The DZ maintained its general support for Dernburg over the years, despite disagreeing with him on certain matters. In particular, the paper opposed his privileging of indigenous cultivation over white plantation agriculture and his eventual push for a more humane treatment of colonized Africans, but this never drove it to repudiate him. The *Staatsbürger-Zeitung* also emerged as friendly to Dernburg, albeit after a brief period of initial suspicion. Unlike the DZ, it favored Dernburg in part because of, rather than despite, his stance on the so-called native question, which reflected the paper's own. In addition,

Deputies Wilhelm Lattmann and Ludwig Werner backed Dernburg in parliament. They recognized him as an ally in colonial reform and appreciated his activism on behalf of the colonial project.

This contrasted sharply with the anti-Dernburg stance of the leadership of the *Hammer*, which complained of the "gradual surrender of imperial power to the Jews" upon Dernburg's appointment and referred to him as a "Jewish Colonial Director."[60] The leadership maintained this negative outlook even in the face of pro-Dernburg sentiments among its readers, as expressed in the periodical's letters section. The enthusiasm of the DZ and the SBZ also contrasted with the outlook of the *Deutsch-Soziale Blätter*. The organ of the German Social Party maintained an essentially neutral position for much of Dernburg's tenure, but this changed in 1909 when the paper started to sharply criticize his so-called native policies. Early 1910 witnessed a further shift in the paper's attitude. It began emphasizing Dernburg's Jewish roots, expressing a hostility that approximated that of the *Hammer* leadership.

Opponents of the anti-Semitic movement noticed the support that Dernburg received within it. August Bebel of the Social Democratic Party pointed out the hypocrisy of parliamentary deputies who backed Dernburg in spite of their anti-Semitism. Speaking in the Reichstag in late 1906, Bebel announced his happiness that "the savior of the German colonial calamity has again had to come, like so many other saviors, from Israel," adding that "this time, even the Herr Anti-Semites expect good from there, completely against their usual habits and beliefs."[61] Other opponents noted the discord that Dernburg caused; the Union for Defense against Anti-Semitism reported on the different opinions about him in anti-Semitic newspapers.[62]

Recent scholarship posits a fairly straightforward relationship between colonialism and anti-Semitism, arguing, for example, that colonialism provided ideas about racial domination that anti-Semites applied to Jews—"a set of concepts that were easily translated to continental concerns."[63] This chapter demonstrates that the reality of the relationship between colonialism and anti-Semitism was much more complicated.

On the one hand, it confirms that the anti-Semitic movement successfully drew upon colonialism in a number of ways during the *Kaiserreich* era. First and foremost, the political anti-Semites used colonialism to make common cause with the more mainstream parties after the popularity of political anti-Semitism had declined. This paid dividends during the Hottentot election of 1907, when they sided with the pro-colonial majority against the colonial critics in the Social Democratic and Catholic Center parties. Colonialism also gave the political parties opportunities to publicly expound on key elements of their anti-Semitic *Weltanschauung*—like the evils of big capitalism—without having to address the so-called Jewish question. This was undoubtedly useful after the public had wearied of anti-Semitic politics.[64] Finally, colonialism provided anti-Semites with new ways to intimate the reality and importance of racial differences at home by holding up the colonized as proof of the significance and universality of racial divides.

On the other hand, this chapter demonstrates that colonialism presented the anti-Semites with serious problems. Rather than strengthen the anti-Semitic movement by unifying it unequivocally around the nationalist project of empire building, colonialism generated additional internal strife. Despite the popularity that the idea of colonies enjoyed with a majority of anti-Semites, they did not present a united front on colonial matters. They disagreed over the treatment of the colonized and the nature, purpose, and even wisdom of overseas empire. The existence of influential Germans of Jewish descent involved with the colonies divided the anti-Semites even further, between those who could and those who could not overlook the Jewish heritage of such men in light of their colonial accomplishments. Moreover, the public acclaim won by Emin Pasha and Bernhard Dernburg could only damage the cause of the racial anti-Semites; when colonial enthusiasts lauded both men as German patriots despite their Jewish heritage, it was in direct contradiction to the anti-Semites' claim that a patriotic Jew was an oxymoron. This suggests that the lessons of colonialism in racial matters were not immediately transferable to the Jewish question in the public mind.

By engaging in colonial politics, German anti-Semites helped shape the colonial movement and influence its overseas and domestic policies. The ideological discord that plagued the anti-Semitic movement, however, prevented its members from playing a decisive role. Colonial debates exposed the ideological confusion that characterized the anti-Semitic movement in Imperial Germany. It revealed the persistence of universalist visions of humanity among some movement members, like Adolf Stoecker, which clashed with their public anti-Semitic personae. It encouraged the rise of a hardened racism among the more unequivocal advocates of colonialism, anti-Semites who saw Jews in racialized terms but sometimes made exceptions for individuals who were colonial supporters. The relationship between colonialism and anti-Semitism was thus marked by persistent contradictions that the support for colonialism among a majority of anti-Semites did little, if anything, to resolve.

NOTES

1. For a more detailed examination of the arguments developed in this chapter, see Davis, *Colonialism, Antisemitism*.
2. "Weltlage," *Staatsbürger-Zeitung*, May 25, 1884.
3. "Angra Pequena," *Staatsbürger-Zeitung*, June 12, 1884.
4. Levy, *Downfall of the Anti-Semitic Political Parties*, 23.
5. Wertheimer, *The Pan-German League*, 133. According to Wertheimer, 15 percent of the league's members were from anti-Semitic political parties.
6. Von Joeden-Forgey, "Race Power, Freedom," 21–39.
7. Smith, *The Ideological Origins of Nazi Imperialism*, 52–111.
8. "Was wir wollen," *Deutsche Wacht*, April 5, 1887.
9. *Stenographische Berichte über die Verhandlungen des Reichstags* [Sten. Ber.] XII/I/125, 18 March 1908, 4086.
10. Sten. Ber. XII/I/216, March 1, 1909, 7228.
11. Sten. Ber. IX/IV/6, December 12, 1895, 85.
12. Bernstein, "Anti-Semitism in Imperial Germany," 376.
13. "Südwestafrika und die Sozialdemocratie—Rothäute und Schwarzhäute," *Deutsch-Soziale Blätter*, November 12, 1904.
14. Sten. Ber. XII/I/125, March 18, 1908, 4084.
15. Sten. Ber. XII/II/76, April 30, 1910, 2790.
16. Sten. Ber. XI/I/108, December 9, 1904, 3453.
17. Lange, *Reines Deutschtum*, 286.
18. Bartels, "Zur Rassenforschung."
19. Wardein, "Deutsche Kolonialgesellschaft."
20. Lahme, *Deutsche Außenpolitik*, 116–179.
21. Bley, *Namibia under German Rule*, 131–132.
22. Lattmann, "Küstenklatsch und Kolonialpolitik." Sten. Ber. XI/II/130, November 30, 1906, 4019; Sten. Ber. XI/II/24, January 19, 1906, 677.
23. Sten. Ber. XI/I/87, May 9, 1904, 2808.
24. Sten. Ber. XII/II/76, April 30, 1910. Lattmann's proposal did not pass, despite support from outside the anti-Semitic parties.
25. Sten. Ber. XI/I/107, December 7, 1904, 3424. The speaker is representative Oswald Zimmermann of the German Reform Party.
26. See Lattmann, "Küstenklatsch und Kolonialpolitik." Sten. Ber. XI/II/130, November 30, 1906, 4017; and Werner, Sten. Ber. XI/II/133, December 4, 1906, 4125.
27. The Reichstag rejected the government's request for a supplemental appropriation of 29.2 million marks by 177 to 168, but deputies from the Center Party appeared ready to approve a smaller sum. See Epstein, "Erzberger and the German Colonial Scandals," 659–661.
28. Macintyre, *Forgotten Fatherland*, 111.
29. Förster, *Deutsche Colonien*, 221.
30. In 1909, racial anti-Semites and *völkisch* nationalists formed an organization called the *Siedlungs-Gesellschaft Heimland* and purchased 117 hectares of land north-

west of Berlin for settlement purposes. See Puschner, *Die völkische Bewegung*, 195–201, 188–95.

31. Sten. Ber. 67, May 14, 1889, 1738.

32. Sten. Ber. XI/I/108, December 9, 1904, 3454.

33. Sten. Ber. XI/I/14, January 19, 1904, 370.

34. "Ein Wort über unsere Kolonialpolitik," *Deutsch-Soziale Blätter* [DSB], September 14, 1904.

35. M., "Deutschland in Afrika," *Staatsburger-Zeitung*, November 28, 1906, morning edition.

36. Monheim, "Kolonialkrisis—zur Gesundung," *Staatsbürger-Zeitung*, November 29, 1906, morning edition.

37. von Hassell, "Die Bilanz der Kolonialpolitik für 1906."

38. Stein, "Die Bastardgefahr."

39. Henkel, "Der Hereroaufstand"; K. L., "Thomas Carlyle und die Negerfrage"; "Um Deutsch-Ostafrika," *Deutsche Zeitung*, January 10, 1908; "Der Beginn der Kolonialdebatte," *Deutsche Zeitung*, March 18, 1908.

40. Upon Fritsch's death in 1933, prominent Nazis sent telegrams and letters of condolence to the *Hammer*. See Volland, "Theodor Fritsch," 16.

41. "Zur Verschlimmerung in Südwest-Afrika," DSB, October 19, 1904; "Unsere Kolonien," DSB, December 31, 1904.

42. "Südwestafrika und die Sozialdemokratie—Rothäute und Schwarzhäute," DSB, November 12, 1904; "Südwestafrika und die Sozialdemokratie—Rothäute und Schwarzhäute," DSB, November 15, 1904.

43. Henkel, "Der Hereroaufstand"; Eichler, "Im Kampf um die Weltmachtungstellung."

44. von Schwießel, "Kolonial-Dummheiten," 400.

45. Grimpen, "Die Negerfrage in Deutschland," 147.

46. J.H., "Innere oder äußere Kolonisation?," 723.

47. H.R., "Zur Kolonial-Frage," 186.

48. H.R., "Zur Kolonial-Frage," 187.

49. H.R., "Zur Kolonial-Frage," 188.

50. Dernburg's father had been born a Jew but was baptized as a child when his own father converted to Christianity. See Davis, "Colonialism and Antisemitism," 31–56.

51. "Zum Wechsel in der Kolonialabteilung," *Neue Preußische (Kreuz-) Zeitung*, September 4, 1906, evening edition; *Der Wahre Jacob*, October 16, 1906.

52. "Zur Judenfrage," *Deutsche Wachte*, October 7, 1888.

53. "Vermischtes," *Mittheilungen* 3 (1893), 333; "Der conservativ-antisemitische 'Reichsbote,'" *Mittheilungen* 3 (1893), 236; "Die Wahrheit über Emin Pasha," *Antisemitisches Volksblatt*, June 30, 1894.

54. "Der conservativ-antisemitische 'Reichsbote,'" *Mittheilungen* 3 (1893), 236.

55. "Der conservativ-antisemitische 'Reichsbote,'" *Mittheilungen* 3 (1893), 236.

56. Sten. Ber. XI/II/128, November 28, 1906, 3962.

57. Sten. Ber. XI/II/128, November 28, 1906, 3961–62.

58. O.E., "Dernburgs Programm-Rede."

59. A.Pz., "Dernburg," *Deutsche Zeitung*, January 25, 1907.
60. "Der neue Kolonial-Direktor," *Hammer: Blätter fur deutschen Sinn* 5 (September 1906), 555.
61. Sten. Ber. XI/11/131, December 1, 1906, 4057.
62. "Vermischtes," *Mittheilungen* 16 (1906), 286–287.
63. Von Joeden-Forgey, "Race Power, Freedom," 33.
64. Levy, *Downfall of the Anti-Semitic Political Parties*, 231.

TWELVE

Internal Colonialism in Germany

Culture Wars, Germanification of the Soil, and the Global Market Imaginary

SEBASTIAN CONRAD

On a wintry and snowy February evening in 1885, the Berlin conference—organized by Bismarck and attended by delegates of fourteen treaty powers—closed with the ceremonial signing of the General Act. The conference, officially conducted in French, had been called mainly to solve the Congo question. Beyond this particular issue, however, the treaty has generally been referred to as a watershed in the history of colonialism in that it formalized and regulated the "scramble for Africa" and rang in the period of high imperialism. At the same time, it sealed Germany's acquisitions in Africa and marked her ascendancy as a colonial power in her own right.[1] In that same year, as it happened, the conservative president of Bromberg, Christoph von Tiedemann, published a memorandum in which he called for the colonization of the German East. A few months later, the project of "internal colonialism" in the eastern provinces of Prussia reached new heights as the settlement laws initiated a politics of "Germanification of the soil." It signaled a move toward segregation that led a critic like the leader of the Catholic Zentrum (Center) Party, Ludwig Windthorst, to speak of the "proclamation of a total state of exception" for the Polish population.[2]

Were these parallels and synchronicities mere coincidence? Or was there a connection between overseas and continental expansion, between colonization, settlement, and segregation in Posen (Poznan) and in Tanzania? Traditionally, these two spheres of imperial projection have been treated in virtual isolation from each other. The literature situates German colonies in Africa and in the South Pacific, and it presupposes racial difference, cultural incompatibility, and an ocean safely separating colony and metropole. For a long time, historical analysis has eschewed the question of colonialism in Europe. This perspective was supported by definitions of colonialism that hinge on the assumption of "structures of dependency" vis-à-vis "a geographically remote 'mother country.'"[3] Possible colonial relations within Europe were thus rendered invisible by conceptual barriers.

In recent years, attempts have been made to correct this view and to bring the notion of colonialism to bear on European history and on the *Kaiserreich*. "The true German counterpart to India or Algeria," David Blackbourn, among others, has suggested, "was not Cameroon: it was *Mitteleuropa*."[4] In what follows, I build on this literature and argue that German encounters with the European East can indeed be read as a form of colonialism—but colonialism, literally, with a difference. On the one hand, the notion of "difference," central to the colonial endeavor, was also present in eastern Prussia but with a specific tinge that cannot be simply equated with conceptual hierarchies elsewhere. On the other hand, the "colonial" dimension of Polish Prussia was not only the result of notions of superiority and of the similarity of discursive tropes. Rather, it must be seen as part and parcel of processes of global integration and the forms of difference it produced between various locations.

CIVILIZING MISSIONS AND CULTURE WARS

In the late nineteenth century, German notions of the Polish-speaking territories in eastern Prussia and of their population were multiple and complex. They were the product of a long and often conflict-ridden history that had led, in contemporary parlance, to a dichotomy of "inland Poles" and "foreign Poles." Larger Polish-speaking minorities had been incorporated into the Prussian state since the conquest of Silesia, in the course of the three partitions at the end of the eighteenth century and as a result of the reordering of Europe in 1815. In the wake of the Congress of Vienna, Prussia's policies continued to be guided by a notion of enlightened absolutism that was sensible to linguistic, religious, and national difference. In 1830 the uprising in Congress Poland against Russia found the enthusiastic support of the German national movement, which adopted the Polish cause as a proxy of its own national ambitions. The government, instead, increasingly came to view the Polish population as a political problem and periodically subjected it to a politics of Germanization, as was the case in the 1830s, when Eduard Flottwell, in the Prussian province of Poznan, aimed for a "total unification of both nationalities."[5] Flottwell's "new course," however, was not yet guided by nationalist concerns but rather by state and dynastic interests and aimed not at assimilation but at political loyalty.⁶

After 1848, German and Polish nationalisms were increasingly pitted against each other. This relationship was exacerbated by German unification (1871). In particular among the Polish-speaking population, the foundation of the nation-state was seen as a threat, but in German nationalist discourse, too, the attitude toward minority groups was transformed. Among them, the 2.4 million Poles were clearly the largest group, representing about 10 percent of the population in Prussia. In comparison with Danish or French minorities, the situation of German Poles was complicated by the fact that no Polish nation-state existed on which to call for political support. At the same time, national sovereignty remained on the agenda of Polish elites, and as a consequence, a generalized suspicion that the Polish-speaking population was engaging in separatist activities prevailed.⁷

This was particularly obvious in the case of the "foreign Poles," who many observers depicted as a national threat. Since the 1880s, fears of a "Polonization of regions that had already been won over to German customs, culture, and language" were increasingly voiced in public.⁸ These concerns were not only caused by political agitation of the nationalist nobility and the cleric, but were elicited at the same time by large-scale immigration of Polish labor, both to the industrial centers and to the Prussian countryside. The rhetoric of an imminent "flooding" and of "foreign infiltration" abounded in the nationalist press.⁹

The situation of the "internal Poles" was different: As inhabitants of Prussia, they indirectly held German citizenship, even if the equality of their legal status was limited in social and sometimes juridical practice. As Prussian citizens, they were subject to politics of assimilation and "Germanification," in particular the more than 500,000 "Ruhr Poles" who since the 1880s had migrated to the industrial centers in the West.¹⁰ The situation was more complex in the eastern provinces; for example, in Posen, where the majority of the population spoke Polish and where government policies tended to elicit more resistance. However, intervention remained, on the whole, geared toward linguistic and cultural homogenization. Only occasionally were legal provisions designed to reinforce national difference.¹¹

In general, therefore, Prussian politics vis-à-vis the Polish population was aimed at "improvement" and cultural "betterment." Recruiting Polish labor for the industrial centers, for example, was motivated not only by economics but also in cultural terms: "It is a good deed performed," a memorandum of Konrad von Studt, *Oberpräsident* of the province of Westphalia, declared in 1898, "on the Poles themselves."¹² The prevailing language of *Hebung* rested on a general assumption of superiority, one expressed increasingly in terms of a civilizing mission. "It is to the Prussian rulers that the Polish peasant owes his humane form of existence," as the German-language journal *Lehrer-Zeitung* typically phrased it in 1900, making reference to German work, culture, and education as the appropriate means to propel the Polish population into modernity. The hegemony of the discourse of improvement was further corroborated by its appropriation by reform-minded Polish elites, who frequently subscribed to a notion of modernization in which German culture was a central model.[13]

It is striking to what extent the rhetorical arsenal leveled against the Polish groups was reminiscent of the synchronous attempts to legitimize control in the overseas colonies. When Studt propagated the Germanification of the Polish population in order to improve the "inferior elements, prone as they are to excesses, and featuring questionable characteristics, in particular among the women," his choice of vocabulary did not differ substantially from the rhetoric of missionaries and governmental "native policy" in Germany's African colonies: the aim was to have the subject population "benefit from the economic and moral superiority of Germanness."[14]

The colonial rhetoric was not entirely a new phenomenon.[15] Beginning in the 1830s and especially after 1848, the German notion of Poland was gradually transformed and, increasingly, reconfigured within national and, soon also, colonial parameters. The colonial overtones of the Polish question and explicit references to colonization were prominent features of the discourse of the times. They played a central role in attempts to connect the civilizing project of the nineteenth century to long-standing traditions of German settlement in the European East. Accounts of Poznan and Silesia regularly alluded to the "drive towards the East" and the expansion of the Teutonic Order. The civilizing-mission rhetoric typically appropriated the medieval notion of German "bringers of culture" (*Kulturträgertum*).[16]

Clearly, settler "colonization" since the Middle Ages needs to be differentiated from modern colonialism, as it was not tied to an expansionist nation-state, not premised on the centrality of national discourse, and not predicated on notions of race that became crucial for modern forms of colonialism.[17] Even if, in contemporary parlance, there was a strong sense of continuity, it is important to recognize the extent to which the German-Polish encounter had been transformed. Geographic and cultural difference—not necessarily pejorative but also encompassing tropes such as the "noble Polish folk"—had been replaced since the 1830s by linear concepts of development and hierarchies of progress. In the accounts of German travelers to the Polish provinces, for example, the Poles were no longer primarily strange and different but increasingly characterized in terms of lack and backwardness.[18] Visits to distant lands interpreted as travels into the past—this resembles what Johannes Fabian describes as the emergence of a colonizing gaze and, in his terms, the "denial of co-evalness." Again, therefore, it is instructive to note the synchronicity of this transformation on the Prussian eastern borders with a general shift toward thinking in developmental stages and concepts of temporality in Europe's relation to the colonial world.[19]

Gustav Freytag's immensely popular novel *Debit and Credit*, originally published in 1854 and soaring to over a hundred editions before World War I, is surely the best known example of the emergence of a colonizing consciousness in Germany. Freytag describes the Polish population as culturally and also racially inferior. For him, the civilizational improvement and the establishment of order in Poland is essentially a German task.[20] The central trope lending coherence to a wide array of anti-Polish stereotypes was the notion of *polnische Wirtschaft* ("Polish business"). It denoted a broad spectrum of undesirable characteristics, ranging from chaos, frivolousness, and laziness to outright ignorance and uncleanliness. Clearly a long-standing concept, it acquired new meanings in the context of colonial expansion and the global integration of markets. *Polnische Wirtschaft* was synonymous with backwardness, and it helped legitimize the German presence in the region.[21]

One of the privileged sites where developmentalist tropes were linked to the notion of colonial expansion was the *Ostmarkenroman* (novel of the eastern marches). Kristin Kopp has persuasively argued that this literature, originating in the early 1890s, fused tropes from the colonial movement with the *Heimat* idea. It depicted German Poland as a wasteland, as a landscape of colonial conquest, as a "Wild East" with many parallels to the "Wild West" in North America. The novels were characterized by rural settings, imbued with traditional social values, and based on a civilizing-mission rhetoric that also allowed maintaining discursively the border between Germans and Poles.[22] The texts bespeak a fear of nonidentifiability and a lack of clearly marked boundaries that are typical, as Ann Stoler has argued, of colonial frontiers.[23]

While the discursive appropriation of the European East thus owed much to colonial rhetoric, it is worth remembering that it was employed in a particular situation, as one of its background elements was the culture wars of the 1870s and 1880s. The concept of culture, in this context, indicated a double reference: On the one hand, it was directed against ultramontanist Catholicism as the principal target of governmental policies to separate church from state. At the same time, it included a nationalist dimension and fed into the anti-Polish measures of internal nation building. This overlap of interests was one of the reasons that the culture wars did not end, as is usually assumed, in 1887, at least not in the Polish-speaking regions of Prussia, where, unlike the rest of the country, many of the provisions were not rescinded. Through World War I, German *Polenpolitik* retained elements of the culture war in which anti-Catholicism and anti-Polish sentiments reinforced each other.[24]

This double thrust of the culture wars, however, was complicated by the fact that here, too, a colonial dynamic was at work. As is well known, the term "culture wars" (*Kulturkampf*) was coined by the medical doctor, anthropologist, and liberal politician Rudolf Virchow. What is less recognized is that his terminological invention referred not just to the deep cultural gap between liberal modernism and Catholic traditionalism. In addition, it was related to a shift in the meaning of "culture" that owed much to the colonial context. In a departure from the historicist perception, which, seeing culture mainly as a result of humanist education, was essentially relativist, Virchow employed what he perceived as a decidedly modern understanding of culture in the fledgling discipline of anthropology. Crucial here was a dichotomy of *Kulturvölker* (civilized peoples) and *Naturvölker* (primitive peoples) wherein only the former were capable of progress and development, while the latter appeared as true "peoples without history" and the appropriate objects of anthropological science.[25]

This notion of culture, then, with its developmental overtones and temporal hierarchies of colonial discourse, turned the culture wars into a conflict between premodern backwardness and cultural progress. When Constantin Rössler, one of the foremost protagonists of anti-Catholic polemics, foresaw at the end of the conflict a role for the German nation as "model for the spiritual life of the civilized peoples (*Kulturvölker*)," then both paradigms of the culture wars—Catholicism as different but also as an earlier stage of development—were present.[26] Virchow, too, saw Catholicism as "absolutely incompatible with the culture as whose bearers we see ourselves." This was so not only due to a perceived cultural difference, as the historicist concept suggested, but also because Catholicism seemed to have been unaffected by historical progress. The "antagonism of papism to the modern world" was then no longer understood in relativist terms but rather as expressive of the diachronic stages of obsolete and modern.[27]

SETTLEMENT AND "GERMANIFICATION OF THE SOIL"

The appropriation of the Polish-speaking territories as a form of colonial wasteland was not, however, a matter of discourse alone. Similarities can be observed on a more profound and more material level. In striking synchronicity, an overseas colony such as Southwest Africa and the Polish-speaking provinces in eastern Prussia were subjected to policies of settlement. The redirection of outbound migration to Africa had been one of the raisons d'être of the colonial project; the agitation of the colonial movement aimed at establishing large diaspora communities in "New Germany." At virtually the same time, the "internal colonization" of Polish Prussia became a central concern in nationalist circles, social science debates, and government policies.

In the literature, the settlement policies in the German East are typically seen as part of a long history of Prussian attempts to come to terms with its Polish population. What was called the Germanification of the soil then appeared as the culmination or escalation of a politics of homogenization that assumed a new urgency after unification. Assimilation of linguistic minorities, a central tenet of government policies, can be interpreted as an element both of internal nation building and of the attempt to repress the Polish nationalist movement. Particular attention was paid to the gradual limitation of the use of the Polish language in schools, churches, and political associations. For several decades anti-Polish measures (the so-called *Polenpolitik*) were framed in cultural terms, with a focus on language and religion.

From the mid-1880s, however, the character of intervention changed. The politics of Germanification came to center on migration and settlement and included cases of forced expulsion, border control, and expropriation of territory. Bismarck spoke of a "struggle for existence" raging between the Germans and the Poles.[28] Many protagonists, with most historians in their wake, have interpreted these measures as a radicalization of earlier strategies, as they departed from the hallowed principles of legal equality and benevolent improvement.[29] It is important, however, to acknowledge the broader context of this radicalization, which cannot be understood solely as the continuation of earlier trajectories. Observable in these years was a fundamental transformation of the logic of intervention, whose thrust shifted from culture to demography and biopolitics.

In 1886, the Royal Prussian Colonization Commission (*Königlich Preußische Ansiedlungskommission*) was established to buy up large Polish estates. It subsequently sold them in smaller plots to German farmers, who were lured to the East by state subsidies. The commission was supported by the Eastern Marches Society (*Ostmarkenverein*), founded in 1894 to supply both a political lobby and publicity for the project. Largely composed of bureaucrats and members of the lower-educational strata, such as schoolteachers, the society was the most important pressure group for a redefinition of Germanness along ethnic lines. Increasingly, its members argued for technologies of population that included the forced movement and relocation of large groups. Typically, these proposals are read as part of a prehistory of the genocidal measures of National Socialism.[30] It is more instructive, however, to see the correspondences with similar population policies in the overseas colonies, such as Governor Lindequist's call to move "the whole tribe of Witboois to Samoa" in order to stabilize colonial rule in German West Africa. Racial segregation and ethnic separation, as well as deportation of large populations after the turn of the century, was common practice in the colonial arena.[31]

On the nationalist fringe, consequently, calls for a politics of segregation and legal separation were frequently voiced. Alfred Hugenberg, cofounder of the Pan-German League, called in 1902 for "subject[ing] the German colonists to separate jurisdiction," reserving the schools for the German population, and restricting political rights to ethnic Germans.[32] Only three years earlier, he had openly envisioned the eventual "annihilation" of the Polish population.[33] These propositions, as well as governmental settlement politics, met fierce criticism, in particular from Social Democrats and the Center Party.[34] But over the course of time, in particular during World War I, ever-larger parts of the population tapped into the colonialist rhetoric. The idea of a colonial tabula rasa culminated in discussions about war aims in which the "resettlement of large groups of people" was accepted as a precondition to fulfill Germany's "colonial mission" in the East.[35] When Heinrich Class, president of the Pan-German League, called for a colonial territory "free of people," he could count on the support of many intellectuals and government representatives.[36] In order not to increase the number of "foreign people" (*fremdstämmig*) in Germany, annexed territories were "to be affiliated to the Empire under provisions of international law, but not integrated in terms of constitutional law." This was nothing less than the legal definition of a colony.[37]

The politics of settlement in Polish Prussia, then, were framed in colonial terms. This should be seen, however, not as the simple result of rhetorical interference and articulation but rather as the effect of a shared problematic. On one level, politics of settlement were presented as a solution to the problem of mobility and the centrifugal projection of Germans into the world. This was true for overseas expansion motivated by the alleged need to prevent the "loss of national energies" to the United States and to redirect migration flows to New Germany in Africa. At precisely the same time, the German Eastern Marches Society urged peasants "not even to think about migrating to the United States" but instead to "find a new *Heimat* in the East of the German fatherland."[38] On a second level, the debate on migration and demography found its ideological structure in the concept of Lebensraum. Here, too, territorial acquisitions overseas and in eastern Europe operated within a shared paradigm.[39]

The population politics in eastern Germany were, in the end, not successful; they eventually strengthened rather than weakened Polish nationalism in the region. In comparison with the colonial settlements, however, the figures are staggering: more than 120,000 Germans were settled in the Prussian East, more than five times as many as ever lived in the entire colonial empire.[40]

RACIALIZATION OF DIFFERENCE

When discussing the validity of the colonial paradigm to analyze the German-Polish relations in Prussia and beyond, one of the main concerns is related to the issue of race. Already in the earliest statements on the problem by Hannah Arendt, race was a central ingredient of the argument. In *The Origins of Totalitarianism*, she posed the question of mutual influences between what she called "continental" and "overseas" imperialism. For her, both forms of territorial expansion were predicated upon a biological notion of difference expressed in terms of race and *Volk*, respectively.[41] In particular, she was interested in the "colonial" character of Nazi rule in eastern Europe, an issue only recently arrived on the scholarly agenda.[42]

Heuristically useful as it may be, combining the reading of overseas and colonial forms of imperialism should not, however, lead us to slight the differences between the colonial empire and eastern Prussia. This is clear already from an administrative point of view: Poznan and Silesia were not treated as colonial territories. More importantly, assimilation was always a political and cultural option. For a long time, acculturation of the Polish-speaking population was the stated aim of governmental interventions—and not only in the Ruhr region. Social actors were frequently in a position to articulate different notions of subjecthood, nationality, and modernity and to appropriate them to their own purposes. Moreover, large groups of the Polish-speaking population possessed German citizenship (unlike migrants and seasonal workers from Galicia and Russia). This was crucially different from the overseas empire. The colonies belonged to Germany according to international law, but this status did not imply German citizenship for the indigenous populations. In fact, there were virtually no cases of colonial subjects' naturalization.[43]

The practices of separation and segregation, in other words, suggest a different quality of life under colonial conditions vis-à-vis more conventional forms of prejudice and repression in Prussia's eastern provinces. Indeed, the situations were specific in each case. The argument here, therefore, is not one of sameness but of difference. This is corroborated by the fact that even in the overseas empire, the colonial encounter was by no means uniform. German rule in the African colonies differed markedly from that in Kiaochow (Jiaozhou), in China, where higher education and a university were part of the colonial modernization project. But even in Africa, social realities were highly heterogeneous: "There was no singular German approach to colonial governance."[44] If colonialism was predicated on the "rule of difference," as Partha Chatterjee has forcefully argued, this difference was not defined by race alone; rather, it depended on a set of criteria that included regional particularities, affiliation with a "tribe" or linguistic community, and the import of gender and social status.[45]

Moreover, the impact of racial categories on colonial domination was varied and complex. Colonial policy in the French and Japanese empires, in their different ways and with different limitations, aimed at cultural convergence and assimilation. The colonial experience, in other words, was not monolithic; it differed markedly. The politics of race, too, could range from forceful integration and assimilation to regimes of apartheid. This was not just a reflection of the peculiarities of competing governmental strategies; rather, it was the expression of a fundamental tension in the colonial project in general. Technologies of difference and assimilation, in an ambivalent dialectic, were mutually reinforcing and undermining. The fundamental separation of colonizers and colonized, frequently framed in racial categories, was continually in tension with the ideology of cultural "improvement" that was at the heart of the colonial dynamic.[46]

The notion of race, at the turn of the century, was thus not a universal concept. As Rebecca Karl, drawing on the Chinese case, has argued, racial analogies and attributions could vary and owed much of their dynamic not only to biological criteria but to differing geopolitical contexts.[47] While "race" was clearly an obstacle to empowerment, let alone equality, in many colonies, its status was very different in the eastern provinces of Prussia. This is not to say that the notion of "race" played no role in the European context. Referring to the Polish population as the "Slavic race" was common practice in the *Kaiserreich*. Anton Wohlfahrt, for example, the hero in Gustav Freytag's *Credit and Debit*, defined himself as "one of the conquerors who, for the sake of free labor and human culture, have taken away rule of this territory from a weaker race."[48] The propaganda of the Eastern Marches Society was also replete with a racial vocabulary. Its frequent use was not least an attempt to banish the specter of mixing, hybridity, and the evanescence of boundaries.

As in the overseas colonies, the racializing rhetoric was frequently directed against women. The Hakatists (another term for the *Ostmarkenverein*) called the Polish women "our most efficient and dangerous enemies in the East," referring both to their fertility and the danger of marrying German men and thus degenerating virtuous German families.⁴⁹ The parallels to the fear of hybridization and *Verkafferung* in the African colonies, a form of reverse colonization, are obvious. But just as obvious again were the differences: While warnings of miscegenation in the Prussian East were limited to rhetoric, they were translated into administrative practice in the colonial empire. After 1905, marriage of German citizens with indigenous partners was legally banned in Southwest Africa (from 1912 in Samoa). A similar regulation never existed in the Polish-speaking territories of Prussia—not, that is, before the blatantly racist politics of the National Socialists during World War II.⁵⁰

The use and implementation of racial categories, then, diverged from colonial practice and was specific to the particular situation in Poznan and Silesia. It is equally clear, however, that notions of race increasingly tinted the discourse and practices of belonging. A striking offshoot of this gradual racialization was the tendency to treat Jews and Poles as part of the same group; for example, in cases of immigration and naturalization. In the eyes of the bureaucracy, this seemed legitimate, as both groups frequently overlapped. What it also shows, however, is the complex process in which the radicalization of anti-Semitism and the racialization of anti-Polish sentiments informed each other.⁵¹

This was particularly evident in debates about the so-called eastern Jews (*Ostjuden*), which preoccupied the public in Wilhelmine Germany. The immigration and subsequent settlement of almost 80,000 Jews from Russia unleashed an arsenal of xenophobic, apocalyptic scenarios of an imminent "flood from the East," exacerbated by the alleged backwardness if not outright "barbarity" of the Jews.⁵² These fears, not infrequently supported by German Jews, were nourished not only by social resentment but also by their connection to the much larger flow of over five million transitory migrants (*Durchwanderer*), mostly Poles and Jews, who passed through Germany on their way across the Atlantic. The association of *Ostjuden* with political radicalism, with poverty, with the trafficking of women in the "white slave trade," with a lack of hygiene, and with the spread of diseases—as in the case of the cholera epidemic in the early 1890s—further contributed to a mechanism in which anti-Semitic stereotypes were connected to the fear of the East and "Asian" influences, just as the threat of Polonization was associated with anti-Semitic notions. "Together with the Poles, the Polish Jews will complete the work of the destruction of Germanicness (*Germanenthum*)," as Albert von Randow predicted.⁵³ This mechanism was not confined to the rhetorical level, as the case of forced expulsion of forty thousand Poles and Jews without Prussian citizenship in 1885 demonstrated.[54] The 1890s, as Massimo Ferrari Zumbini has concluded, were characterized by a fusion of anti-Slavism and anti-Semitism in Imperial Germany.[55]

It is this gradual racialization of Polishness that rendered conceivable an otherwise entirely unlikely proposal made by a certain Adolf Hentze in 1907 to Bernhard Dernburg, secretary of state of the Colonial Office. Hentze suggested employing sixteen thousand Herero and Nama, who had lived as prisoners of war in Southwest African camps since the Herero war in 1904, as agricultural workers in the Prussian East. There they were supposed to learn the necessary "civilized customs, the language and the cultivation of the land," and over the course of time be "educated to work." From the perspective of the government in Windhoek this project may have appeared as part of the civilizing mission and the overall "improvement" of colonial subjects while at the same time contributing to the security of the colony. But Hentze's initiative had broader implications, in particular since moving the Herero to Prussia was meant to replace Polish seasonal workers. This plan was thinkable only in the context of a radicalization of difference along the Polish border. Only now could Africans stand in for, indeed serve as substitutes for, Polish workers.[56]

It is important in this context to recognize, finally, that "race" could be linked not only to biology but also to culture. Étienne Balibar, for instance, has forcefully argued that "culture can also function like a nature, and it can in particular function as a way of locking individuals and groups a priori into a genealogy, into a determination that is immutable and intangible in origin." In the late nineteenth century, alongside the biological definition of race there emerged a second powerful strand of racialized thinking, one premised on a system of cultural differences, that functions as effectively as a means of accounting for social and economic inequality.[57] One of the mechanisms to link these two paradigms was the reference to Lamarckian notions of the inheritability of acquired characteristics, notions whose influence persisted into the early decades of the twentieth century. The concept of adaptation to the social and cultural environment could thus assume a pivotal position in racial thinking. "This Lamarckian feature of eugenic thinking," as Ann Laura Stoler has argued, "was central to colonial discourses that linked racial degeneracy to the sexual transmission of cultural contagions."[58]

In this context, Polonization could be perceived as a powerful threat, one as dangerous as the implications of racial mixing in the colonies. To be sure, it was not the same threat. Polish women, for example, were credited with forms of agency that African women—objects of legal provisions against miscegenation—were not associated with in colonial discourse. Moreover, Polonization was frequently couched in a language of nationalism that at the time was not yet at the disposal of most social actors in the African colonies. But it would be reductionist to assume a global order in which nationalism and colonialism functioned as mutually exclusive forms of discourse and practice. Instead, it is important to recognize that in an age of high imperialism differences of nation, culture, and class in the Prussian East were increasingly underwritten by and articulated with notions of colonial difference.

ECONOMIC INTEGRATION, MARKET IMAGINARIES, AND GLOBAL CONSCIOUSNESS

While imperialism from the 1880s on was increasingly shaping the structures of political exchange, it cannot be detached from forms of capitalist integration that were pivotal for the globalization process in the latter half of the nineteenth century. Economic historians, in recent years, have done much to document the gradual price convergence, the emergence of new forms of migration, and the integration of labor markets before World War I.[59] What was of particular relevance in this context was the mobility of workers under conditions marked, on the one hand, by the end of slavery, new forms of servitude and indenture, and the ideology of "free labor" and, on the other hand by the asymmetries of the colonial world order.[60]

It is important not to discuss issues of political discourse—of race, culture, and the nation—outside a framework that is cognizant of the structures of economic integration. Instead, the constitution of difference must be seen as part of this transformation under the auspices of capitalist reordering. One important feature of this process was the emergence of dependent agricultural spheres of production catering to the needs of expanding global markets. These agricultural peripheries were linked directly by trade with the large industrialized port cities and via a steady stream of migrant labor made accessible by new forms of communication and transportation. At the same time, they were connected via a social imagination that made it possible to establish links between places that the capitalist/colonial order had formatted in compatible ways.

One example of this form of global consciousness was the debate among social scientists on the applicability of racialized labor relations to the Polish territories in the Prussian East. *Verein für Sozialpolitik* members such as Georg Friedrich Knapp and Max Weber were interested in the role of race and ethnicity in agricultural labor; for this reason they undertook study tours to the United States. As Andrew Zimmerman has cogently argued, these debates were tied to a set of social interventions in the African colonies modeled on the example of the post-Reconstruction "New South." The technologies developed in Booker T. Washington's Tuskegee Institute, in particular, were exported to the German colony of Togo on the shared assumption that Africans and African Americans, because they were of the same "race," could be subjected to similar social reforms and labor relations. The "education for work" in Togo, which included thorough interventions into local social relations, was then interpreted as a possible blueprint for the reorganization of conditions of production in the Prussian countryside. The inclusion by contemporaries of Alabama, Togo, and Poznan in a comprehensive field of analysis illustrates the transformative power of economic integration, of the volatility of labor markets, and of the belief in the translatability of "race" on a global scale.[61]

A similar chain of equivalences was at work in the attempts to look for substitutes for immigrant Poles from Russia and Galicia. With increasing frequency since the early 1890s, these debates included proposals for the "import of Chinese, a sober and diligent people with very modest needs."[62] Plans to recruit temporary workers from China were an integral part of the displacement of large numbers of Chinese workers in the late nineteenth century. Of particular relevance here was the so-called coolie trade that propelled close to a million Chinese workers to South Africa, Cuba, Hawaii, and Southeast Asia. Formally based on contracts signed with European employers, the coolie trade had many commonalities with the earlier slave trade: brutal patterns of recruitment, frequent kidnappings, inhuman conditions of transport, and a high mortality rate during plantation labor. The demand for Asian workers from China, Java, and India rose sharply as a result both of the end of slavery and of the expansion of the plantation complex, with its concomitant demand for mobile and flexible labor, in the context of high imperialism.[63]

Under the pressure of massive protests in the press, the German government finally decided to abolish the plans. The public outcry, influenced by the transnational discourse of the "yellow peril," depicted the coolies as a threat to the German nation.[64] As a result, Chinese agricultural workers never made it to Germany—even if several thousand coolies were recruited for the German colonies in the Pacific. But quantities are less the issue here than is a focus on the way the restructuring of the global economy allowed for a superimposition—not equation—of Poles and Chinese within a shared set of cultural and geopolitical hierarchies.[65]

In the light of the mutual interference of anti-Polish and anti-Jewish practices mentioned above, it is interesting to note that arguments against the influx of Chinese, too, were frequently couched in the terminology of anti-Semitism, and vice versa. The frequent comparison of Chinese and Jews rested on the alleged economic proficiencies of the Chinese, which turned them into a "by far more dangerous people than the Jews." The possibility that these two marginalized groups might coalesce and unite the entrepreneurial capabilities of the Jews with the hardworking attitudes of the Chinese created further apprehension: "Between these two tribes the Germans would run the risk of being crushed completely."[66]

What are at stake here are not cultural similarities and overlapping stereotypes. Rather, it is about patterns of signification under the auspices of a global consciousness that emerged as a response to increasing global integration. The discourse of the "yellow peril" allowed German nationalists to link anti-Semitism with larger global trends and thus imbue seemingly local issues with forms of transnational legitimacy. The anti-Semitic journal *Neue Deutsche Volkszeitung*, for example, saw "welcome parallels" between the "exclusion laws against the Chinese in North America and the need for a law banning the immigration of Jews" in Germany.[67] California and New South Wales in Australia thus emerged as central points of reference when the demographics of border control were discussed. In the context of an influx of Jews from Russia and Galicia after 1890, in particular, the anti-Semitic press readily drew on anti-Chinese rhetoric and directed it against the Jews.[68]

And against the Poles. Here, too, interferences were the result of close international monitoring and observation. The Prussian countryside, the Polish population, Chinese coolies, and a colonialist rhetoric were linked by a global imaginary of imperialist/capitalist integration that rendered the populations of the globe legible.[69] Apprehending Polish Prussia in tropes such as the danger of cultural degradation and the fear of racial mixing, then, was not only the result of discursive repercussions from the colonies; rather, it was the effect of a specific reading of the globalization process. Max Weber, typically, looked to Australia, where "the immigration of Chinese is banned," only to warn that "the Poles are even more dangerous due to the possibility of mixing and of bringing down German culture."[70]

When analyzing the dynamics of German-Polish relations in the eastern provinces of Prussia, it is productive to work within a framework of colonialism broadly defined. For many social actors in the *Kaiserreich*, the interaction with the Polish-speaking populations in Prussia and beyond bore traces of colonial structures. The civilizing-mission rhetoric, the racial overtones, and the logic of settlement policies all bespoke affinities with colonial settings. To be sure, it was colonialism with a difference. The structures of rule, the systems of exploitation, and the patterns of social and gender hierarchies were not at all equivalent to those in Togo and Cameroon. Rather, they corresponded to the specific context; one shaped, among other things, by the longer history of German-Polish relations, by the culture wars and the role of religion, and by the nationality conflict in the region.

The colonial dimensions of Germany's appropriation of the "East" are typically discussed by reconstructing similarities and explaining them in terms of "repercussions" of the colonial experience. This mode of causation presupposes direct interactions between overseas and continental colonies, linked through flows of people, institutions, and discourse. The argument, then, is one of translation from the colonial world to other locations that are then influenced by colonial tropes. The discussion that ensues focuses on weighing the colonial dimension of social practices against others: nationalism, class difference, gender. This paradigm, however, and the pros and cons that go along with it, rests on a simplified view of the world, one assuming neatly confined spheres of social experience that can then influence each other. It rests, ultimately, on a *Schutzgebiete* view of German colonialism. What I have suggested instead is that the "colonial" character of Polish Prussia can be grasped only by seeing it as part of the global interactions in a world deeply structured—albeit unevenly—by capitalism and imperialism. This larger context is what enables colonial dimensions to structure social experience in highly diverse places— without, to be sure, erasing the particularities of the situation in question. Rather than looking at colonial empires as a specific form of territoriality, then, I suggest understanding Polish Prussia in the framework of global modernity that was marked by colonialism globally.[71]

NOTES

This article was originally written, for this volume, in 2008. Literature published after that date has been incorporated only in a few cases. Parts of the argument presented here have in the meantime appeared in my article "Rethinking German Colonialism in a Global Age," *Journal of Imperial and Commonwealth History* 41 (2013), 543–566.

1. Förster, ed., *Bismarck, Europe, and Africa*.
2. Quoted in Wehler, *Sozialdemokratie und Nationalstaat*.
3. Osterhammel, *Colonialism*, 10.
4. Blackbourn, "Das Kaiserreich transnational." For similar arguments, see Kopp, *Germany's Wild East*, and Ther, "Deutsche Geschichte als imperiale Geschichte."
5. Quoted in Frauendienst, "Preußisches Staatsbewußtsein und polnischer Nationalismus."
6. On the history of German-Polish relations, see Blanke, *Prussian Poland*; Broszat,

Zweihundert Jahre deutsche Polenpolitik; Eley, "German Politics and Polish Nationality"; Hagen, *Germans, Poles, and Jews*; and Wehler, "Polenpolitik im Deutschen Kaiserreich."

7. Conze, "Nationsbildung durch Trennung."

8. Quoted in Bade, "'Kulturkampf' auf dem Arbeitsmarkt."

9. See Herbert, *Geschichte der Ausländerpolitik in Deutschland*; and Nichtweiß, *Die ausländischen Saisonarbeiter*.

10. See Kleßmann, *Polnische Bergarbeiter im Ruhrgebiet*.

11. See Gosewinkel, *Einbürgern und Ausschließen*, 211–218.

12. Quoted in Kleßmann, *Polnische Bergarbeiter*, 63.

13. See Serrier, *Provinz Posen*, 114.

14. Quoted from Kleßmann, *Polnische Bergarbeiter*.

15. See Nelson, ed., *Germans, Poland*.

16. Kaczmarczyk, "German Colonisation in Medieval Poland"; Meyer, *"Drang nach Osten."*

17. On medieval German "colonization," see Schlesinger, ed., *Die deutsche Ostsiedlung des Mittelalters*; Wippermann, *Der "Deutsche Drang nach Osten"*; and Liulevicius, *The German Myth of the East*.

18. See Struck, *Nicht West—nicht Ost*.

19. Fabian, *Time and the Other*.

20. Freytag, *Soll und Haben*. See Feindt, ed., *Studien zur Kulturgeschichte*.

21. See Orlowski, *"Polnische Wirtschaft."*

22. Kopp, "Constructing Racial Difference in Colonial Poland."

23. Stoler, "Rethinking Colonial Categories."

24. See H. W. Smith, *German Nationalism and Religious Conflict*, and Trzeciakowski, *The Kulturkampf in Prussian Poland*.

25. Zimmerman, *Anthropology and Antihumanism in Imperial Germany*.

26. Rössler, *Das deutsche Reich und die kirchliche Frage*, 439.

27. Virchow, *Stenographische Berichte*, 1798, 1800.

28. Cited in Kohl, ed., *Die politischen Reden des Fürsten Bismarck*, 300.

29. See Gosewinkel, *Einbürgern und Ausschließen*, 211–218, 63–77; Walkenhorst, *Nation-Volk-Rasse*; Wehler, *Sozialdemokratie*.

30. Wehler, "Polenpolitik." On the Ostmarkenverein, see Galos, Gentzen, and Jakóbczyk, *Die Hakatisten*, and Grabowski, *Deutscher und polnischer Nationalismus*. For a critical reading of such continuity theses, see Chu, Kauffman and Meng, "A Sonderweg through Eastern Europe?"

31. See Mühlhahn, *Herrschaft und Widerstand*, 185–284; and Zimmerer, *Deutsche Herrschaft über Afrikaner*.

32. Hugenberg, *Streiflichter aus der Vergangenheit und Gegenwart*, 280.

33. *Alldeutsche Blätter* 9 (1899), 86.

34. Wehler, *Sozialdemokratie und Nationalstaat*, 165–182.

35. Cited in Geiss, *Der polnische Grenzstreifen*, 78.

36. Basler, *Deutschlands Annexionspolitik*, and Broszat, *Zweihundert Jahre*, 184.

37. "Denkschrift über die künftige staatsrechtliche und national-politische Gestal-

tung der von Rußland abzutrennenden östlichen Nachbargebiete des Deutschen Reiches," cited in Oldenburg, *Der deutsche Ostmarkenverein*, 231.

38. Cited in Oldenburg, *Der deutsche Ostmarkenverein*, 147.

39. W. D. Smith, *The Ideological Origins of Nazi Imperialism*, 83–111.

40. See Balzer, *Die preußische Polenpolitik*, and Broszat, *Zweihundert Jahre*, 142–72.

41. Arendt, *The Origins of Totalitarianism*. See Grosse, "From Colonialism to National Socialism to Postcolonialism," 35–52.

42. Furber, "Near as Far in the Colonies"; Lower, *Nazi Empire-Building and the Holocaust in Ukraine*; and Zimmerer, "The Birth of the Ostland out of the Spirit of Colonialism."

43. See Nagl, *Grenzfälle*, 249–72; and Wagner, *Die deutschen Schutzgebiete*.

44. Steinmetz, *The Devil's Handwriting*, 19.

45. Chatterjee, *The Nation and Its Fragments*. For an attempt to go beyond Chatterjee's notion of race, see Kolsky, "Codification and the Rule of Colonial Difference."

46. For an overview of this problematic in the German Empire, see Conrad, *German Colonialism*, 134–165.

47. Karl, "Race, Colonialism and History."

48. Freytag, *Soll und Haben*, 163. See also Kopp, *Germany's Wild East*.

49. Quoted in Drummond, "'Durch Liebe stark, deutsch bis ins Mark,'" 152.

50. On "mixed marriage" in the German colonies, see Grosse, *Kolonialismus, Eugenik*, 145–192; Kundrus, *Moderne Imperialisten*; and Wildenthal, *German Women for Empire*, 79–130.

51. See Gosewinkel, *Einbürgern und Ausschließen*, 263–277.

52. Aschheim, *Brothers and Strangers*; Maurer, *Ostjuden in Deutschland*; Wertheimer, *Unwelcome Strangers*.

53. Von Randow, "Die Landesverweisungen aus Preußen."

54. Neubach, *Die Ausweisung von Polen*.

55. Zumbini, *"Die Wurzeln des Bösen,"* 556.

56. Adolf Hentze to Colonial Office, March 1, 1907, Federal Archives Berlin Lichterfelde (henceforth FABL), R1001/2090, 109a–f. See also Zimmerer, *Deutsche Herrschaft*, 52–55.

57. Balibar, "Is There a 'Neo-Racism'?," 22.

58. Stoler, *Carnal Knowledge and Imperial Power*, 72.

59. O'Rourke and Williamson, *Globalization and History*, and Torp, *Die Herausforderung der Globalisierung*.

60. McKeown, "Global Migration," and Northrup, *Indentured Labor in the Age of Imperialism*.

61. Zimmerman, *Alabama in Africa*.

62. FABL, R8034 II, Nr. 5801, 52.

63. Conrad and Mühlhahn, "Global Mobility and Nationalism"; Gungwu, *China and the Chinese Overseas*.

64. For national variations, see Gollwitzer, *Die gelbe Gefahr*.

65. See Karl, *Staging the World*.

66. "Drohende Chinesen-Einwanderung" (June 14, 1889), in Secret Central Archives Berlin, I. HA Rep 77, Tit 922, No. 2.
67. Quoted in Wawrzinek, *Entstehung der deutschen Antisemitenparteien*, 44.
68. See Gollwitzer, *Die gelbe Gefahr*, 174.
69. See Lake and Reynolds, eds., *Drawing the Global Colour Line*.
70. M. Weber, "Die nationalen Grundlagen der Volkswirtschaft," 724–725.
71. See Dirlik, *Global Modernity*.

THIRTEEN

Pan-German Conceptions of Colonial Empire

DENNIS SWEENEY

In a 1905 essay "The Settlement of German Territory," Chairman Ernst Hasse of the Pan-German League, the leading nationalist pressure group in imperial Germany, asserted that the "German Reich is a colonial empire." After providing a brief history of the expansion of the "Germanic" peoples throughout Europe, especially eastern and southern Europe, since the fourth century, Hasse declared that "Germanization of the non-German border regions must not be stopped until it has succeeded in bringing German lands into alignment with the boundaries of the German Reich, Germanized all of the remaining lands of the Reich still settled by foreign peoples, and made new land available to the expansion-needy German people according to its capacity and desires for expansion." This colonial mission, he insisted, should command all of the legal, economic, and political resources of the state and promote an economic-social model based on a healthy mixture of "large, medium-sized and small enterprises" in agriculture. The "foreign and domestic policies of the German Reich," Hasse concluded, "must be subordinated to these central ideas."[1]

At first glance, Hasse's essay appears to confirm prevailing scholarly interpretations of pan-German imperialism as a primitive geopolitical vision shaped by the antimaterialism and self-contained ethnic absolutism predominant within the educated middle classes during the Wilhelmine era. According to this perspective, the pan-Germans articulated a radical-right ideology of settler or "migrationist colonialism" centered on the acquisition of *Lebensraum* for the growing population of Germans and a social vision of "romantic agrarianism," which celebrated the "self-reliant" small farmer as the bedrock of the

German nation. In contrast to a "modern" version of *Weltpolitik*, informed by industrial-capitalist understandings of "economic colonialism" in pursuit of "markets and raw materials, thus jobs and profits" in the global economy, the pan-Germans are thought to have envisioned an expanded Germany forged out of overseas colonies of German immigrant settlement and a territorially contiguous German Reich in central Europe. The latter, according to this line of interpretation, formed a clearly bounded polity that would enclose Germans in an ethnically or racially sealed territory and escape the spatial volatility and systemic imperatives of global capitalism.[2]

This perspective on radical-right imperialism is important owing to the influence of the Pan-German League on the German right and German politics more generally during the first half of the twentieth century. With 18,000 members in 1914, mostly from the ranks of academia, the free professions, commerce, and industry, the Pan-German League was home to the most influential exponents of radical or *völkisch* nationalism: a new ideological formation on the German right, emphasizing the ethnoracial unity of "Germandom," the centrality of "the people" to all policymaking, and aggressive imperial expansion, which defined the "national opposition" to the German government and its foreign policy after 1903.[3] Pan-Germans mobilized this opposition through an extensive network of newspapers, cross-memberships in other nationalist pressure groups, and agitation within the main right-wing political parties in Germany, the National Liberal, Free Conservative, and Conservative parties. They even began to appeal to a number of left-liberals.[4] In these ways, pan-German perspectives on imperial expansion became increasingly influential before but especially during World War I, when league leaders spearheaded the annexationist movement and entered into close collaboration with the German government and military high command.[5]

The pan-Germans largely defined the ideological universe of the "new right" out of which the Nazis emerged during the 1920s. Pan-German ideas about imperial expansion were especially formative in this regard, and historians have noted the similarities between, on the one hand, pan-German demands for German continental hegemony and *Lebensraum* in the east and, on the other, Nazi plans for German economic autarky on the European continent and the racial-demographic transformation of Europe by means of ethnic cleansing and genocide in the east during the Second World War. On this reading, racialized pan-German and Nazi versions of expansionism emerged directly from their shared nationalism and differed from other versions of imperialism by virtue of their territorial conceptions of space, opposition to "modern" industrial-capitalist imperatives, rejection of colonial rule over "others," and exclusive focus on colonial projects of pure German settlement.⁶

This chapter offers an alternative reading of Hasse's views on colonialism at the borders of Germany by situating them within the wider corpus of the league's imperialist literature and colonialist advocacy from 1894 to 1918. My central aim is to demonstrate that Hasse was attempting to articulate a colonial policy only for the core region, or national state, of a more broadly conceived German "world empire," or Greater Germany, in his text from 1905 and that pan-German colonialism must be situated within this wider imperialist framework in order to make sense of its racializing impulses after 1900. First, I argue that pan-German conceptions of a Greater Germany figured not a spatially fixed and racially enclosed nation-state but rather a complex "imperial formation": an uneven and "mobile macropolity" centered on a nation-state core but radiating outward in a complex "architecture" of multiple, ambiguous, and gradated zones of territorial and nonterritorial sovereignty and anchored in discourses about diverse human populations and shifting "categories of subject and citizen" within Europe and overseas.⁷ Second, I suggest that these versions of a German nation-state empire rested on new definitions of nonterritorial or relational space and mechanisms of imperial control at a distance, including communications infrastructure and economic activities, which departed from the geopolitical languages that sustained previous European projects of land-based colonial expansion. Third, I try to show how these definitions of space, economic means of control, and discourses about human populations intersected after 1900 to produce new pan-German strategies for remaking the colonial social order in German Southwest Africa. This remaking relied on the "rule of colonial difference," which defined the "alienness of the ruling group" of German colonizers in relation to the colonized African other, and on new forms of "native policy" for the definition and management of various colonized peoples in Southwest Africa.⁸

Finally, I argue that this focus on defining and managing populations in German Southwest Africa proved to be the generative context for the articulation of a new variant of radical-right racism: a biopolitical racism that constituted entire human populations as discrete biological entities and established links between efforts to manage, relocate, or destroy "racially foreign" populations and the imperative to cultivate the health and reproduction of Germans as a "racial body" (*Volkskörper*).⁹ This orientation informed schemes for population "exchanges," "transfers," and "evacuations" directed at other Europeans by 1912 and intensified during World War I, when the pan-Germans called openly for "racial cleansing" on the borders of Germany in their public agitation for the creation of a world empire. Accordingly, I identify the conditions of emergence of newly racialized versions of pan-German ideology in the conjunction of new conceptions of nonterritorial space, capitalist rationalities, and biopolitical strategies for managing colonized peoples that constituted wider visions of Greater Germany after 1900.

GREATER GERMANY AS IMPERIAL FORMATION

Historians who regard the Pan-German League primarily as an ethnic nationalist organization often overlook the fact that the pan-Germans always defined their national mission in much broader imperial terms. The General German League, as it was initially called, was created in 1891 in response to the perceived failures of the Helgoland-Zanzibar Treaty and the desire not only to retain the loyalties of Germans emigrating abroad but also to lead "the German colonial movement to practical results," to "cultivate" or develop German colonial territories, and to expand "overseas" in order to develop German national and "economic interests" as a "world power."[10] After refounding their organization in 1894, league leaders incorporated these aims into the core definition of the pan-German movement and focused their agitation on creating a greater German empire via two interrelated means: an aggressive colonial policy overseas and the formation of a German-dominated sphere of influence in central and eastern Europe.

Pan-German colonial policy initially focused on the demand for new territories abroad in order both to accommodate the increasing population of Germany and to satisfy the economic needs of an expanding German economy. They stressed the importance of colonies for German settlement overseas as the primary means to prevent Germans from migrating to foreign countries. In the case of the economy, early pan-Germans' colonial aims were manifold. They sought to facilitate agricultural production in overseas territories by proposing plans for land acquisition and clearance, the provision of credit and other assistance to colonists, and the systematic development of colonial infrastructure that would allow the "opening up" of German colonies to full-scale "economic development."[11] These plans were based largely on Alfred Hugenberg's capitalist model for "internal colonization" or economic regeneration of uncultivated and unproductive marshlands and peat bogs and their transformation into settlement "colonies" of competitive agricultural production in northwestern and eastern Germany.[12] Accordingly, they privileged the small or medium-sized farmer at the expense of corporate interests, which were criticized as monopolies that squeezed out competition, favored speculative schemes leading to bankruptcy, or benefited foreign investors at the expense of German banks and stockholders. In addition, the pan-Germans emphasized the importance of colonies as sources of raw materials and "articles of mass consumption," especially "colonial commodities" from Africa, for German consumers.[13] Finally, they also pointed to the value of colonies as markets for German goods and nodal points of global trade.[14]

The second key component of this early version of Greater Germany was a constitutional structure involving a central European federation and customs union, which would ostensibly unite ethnic Germans within a single continental space and provide new conditions for trade in a "closed economic region."[15] In 1895, Hasse provided an outline of this scheme, which included a "Greater German Federation," a polity comprising Germany, Luxembourg, the Netherlands, Belgium, Switzerland, and Austria-Hungary, and a Greater German customs union, an economic zone encompassing the new federation of states along with the Baltic lands, Poland, Ruthenia, Romania, and Serbia. This required efforts at German "colonization" within Europe that would bring Germans together into a single "national state," "Germanize" the "lesser peoples" of southeastern Europe, expropriate the property of non-German peoples, and even require a "population exchange" between a future German-Austrian province of Bessarabia and Russia.[16]

To realize these plans, however, pan-Germans also called for the creation of a Greater German federation and a customs union as different but overlapping political and economic structures. They envisaged the federation as a polity anchored in multiple forms of sovereignty and gradations of rights for its own members.[17] In this regard, it is important to note that Hasse made clear that "The Greater German Federation is a German People's State, which includes the large majority of Germans living in Europe but is not composed solely of Germans; rather, it is to be exclusively ruled by Germans." The latter would tolerate the presence in the federation of some non-Germans, who would not have the same rights to serve in the military or to own property but would "carry out lower forms of manual labor."[18]

Pan-German visions of a hierarchically structured customs union were not bound by simplistic notions of isolated, noncapitalist economic production. The union instead would regulate the terms and conditions of trade and production in ways that would conduce to competitive production in all sectors of economic life. With this goal in mind, the pan-Germans were preoccupied with mapping out the communications infrastructure on the continent—the road, rail, canal, and river networks—that would facilitate trade and productivity across the trading zone.[19] In conjunction with overseas colonies, this would allow the German-dominated continental economy to compete in "global markets" against the rival empires of Britain, Russia, and the United States.[20] According to Hasse, "Only when we are strong overseas will the other global powers, ill intentioned toward us, allow us to found a central European economic union and to bring the disparate segments of Germandom together. And only when we have established ourselves on a broad central European basis can we secure and maintain our position as a global power in foreign lands—a position that we, the most economically productive people of Europe, need in order to secure future generations of Germans."[21] Germans would assume their position in this empire as a "ruling people," with control "over the lower peoples in Europe and over the primitive peoples in the colonial territories" overseas.[22]

EMPIRES, *WELTPOLITIK*, AND SPACE

After the turn of the century, dominant pan-German conceptions of a German colonial empire, based in *Mitteleuropa* but extending to colonies overseas, were transformed by new geographical understandings of space. They changed as pan-Germans entered into a broader public debate over imperial policy, inaugurated by Kaiser Wilhelm II's speech announcing the birth of Germany as a world power (January 1896). In this context, they promoted the creation of Greater Germany as a "world empire" that could compete with other world empires of the day—Britain, Russia, France, and the newly emergent United States—in a global system of imperial rivalry. The pan-Germans imagined this world empire in relation to the modern conditions of "time-space compression": the extraordinary "speed-up in the pace of life" and the collapse of "spatial barriers" occasioned by new technologies of transportation and communication and global economic integration.[23] These changes brought once isolated places into a network of interconnected global spaces and unsettled long-standing conceptions of space that informed European expansion abroad: that is, conceptions of "absolute space," defined as a homogeneous and universal frame or "field of action" in which imperial and colonial activities and events took place. From this perspective, European colonizers identified territorial expansion with the conquest of empty or "unused" space and thus equated territory with space. By contrast, pan-German visions of empire reveal newly emergent understandings of "relational space": a heterogeneous and historically contingent space that is not the frame for but rather the product of imperial and colonial activities.[24] These understandings ruptured the link between territory and space and allowed the pan-Germans to theorize anew about the "political ordering of space" and the varied, nonterritorial mechanisms of imperial rule:[25] the multiple sovereign forms deployed beyond territorial borders, circuits of long-distance communication, and economic influence activated through an array of trade treaties, markets transactions, and extractive commercial endeavors.

This rethinking is evident in the terms of pan-German debates over empire around the turn of the century. In 1901, Paul Dehn, recognizing the obliteration of place and the copresence of disparate global spaces driven by capitalist development, insisted that "modern communications technologies" for the first time brought "all parts of the earth" and "all countries" into a common "global economy," with "world markets" and "world prices" that left no region or state untouched.[26] This recognition prompted an enduring debate about the preferred direction of German imperial policy, a debate pitting supporters of a more determined "continental policy" focused on developing plans for a German-dominated continental Europe (e.g., Essen-based editor Theodor Reismann-Grone) against advocates of more concerted efforts at overseas colonial expansion, including Eduard von Liebert, former colonial governor of German East Africa. Aired openly during the league's annual meeting in Worms in June 1905, this debate was never definitively settled, not least because most pan-German leaders did not want to neglect any domain of imperial expansion entirely. Its importance lay not in the direction chosen for German imperial expansion but rather in the way it opened up discussion of the nature of empire itself—involving systematic comparisons with rival Western empires, as well as ancient and contemporary non-Western powers, like Japan, in efforts to specify the diverse modalities of imperial rule.

These comparisons were worked out most systematically in the writings of the league's chairman, Hasse. In his 1908 treatise *World Policy, Imperialism, and Colonial Policy*, which focused on the history and morphology of the British, US, and Russian empires, Hasse explicitly recognized the importance of the distinctive spatial practices that characterized modern forms of imperial rule. The "possibilities of expansion for states" in the contemporary context, he suggested, "were spatial in nature":

> They exist in the creation of connections with foreign states, in the order of such connections and in their transformation into relationships of dependence, in the peaceful or military acquisition of territories outside current borders, whether in Europe or overseas. For us Germans, it is a matter of expanding the borders of the Reich and the acquisition of European spheres of influence (customs union), of the acquisition of

indirect dependencies in Europe, of the acquisition of overseas trusteeships and spheres of influence or of the acquisition of colonies and protectorates in the form of plantation colonies or overseas settlement territories (colonies in the narrow sense of the word).[27]

Hasse distinguished colonialism, which involved the direct acquisition of or control over territories or the creation of settlement colonies, from imperialism, the wider ensemble of expansionist efforts that propel a state beyond its own borders in search of new "governing relationships" over not only "its own people" but also "foreign" peoples. As a "system of foreign policy," he continued, imperialism encompasses both colonialism and *Weltpolitik*—the various policies designed to secure economic advantage in global markets—and seeks to create through military and economic means "a higher order" or "empire," a polity that "stands above a single nation or state."[28]

Understanding imperialism in this way, according to Hasse, revealed the distinctiveness of the current moment of global imperial competition, in which all borders and human affairs were "in flux" and the previous era of colonization, involving the acquisition of territory not currently controlled by a dominant power, "appeared to be over." In this context, Hasse called for more robust forms of German imperialism:

> A different partitioning of the globe is now beginning. We don't want to be too late this time around or to arrive unnecessarily late to this process. To the next generation, we can hand the task of creating specific organizations to manage the evolving greater-German area of domination, which will extend beyond the German nation-state to the furthest borders by means of gradated imperial connections of all kinds. But we ourselves must first acquire this area, an empire that will secure for us and our descendants what we need: expansion, freedom to develop, and dependencies.[29]

From this perspective, Hasse developed a vision of a German world empire that began with the nation-state core, which would remain free of "foreign peoples" and extend outward via "buffer states" (glacis) constituted by a "German economic region," whence it could secure influence and territories across Eurasia and overseas. More specifically, the "German economic region" would consist of Germany, Austria-Hungary, Belgium, and the Netherlands and extend German influence "from the North Sea and the Baltic Sea over the Netherlands and Luxembourg, and including Switzerland, over the entire Danube region, the Balkan Peninsula, and Asia Minor up to the Persian Gulf."

It would also be the base from which Germany could sustain and develop its overseas colonies. This larger empire would assume the shape of an uneven federated structure, characterized by the "most varied gradations and forms" of imperial dependency and control, rather than come in the form of a "rigid centralized state."[30]

COLONIAL DIFFERENCE AND BIOPOLITICAL RACISM

It was in relation to understandings of a spatially variegated and economically dynamic imperial macropolity of global reach that pan-Germans embraced biopolitical definitions of race. After 1900, these more complex imperial ambitions transformed earlier colonial strategies, based strictly on resource extraction, trading relations, and German settlement, into schemes of direct social organization and the remaking of colonial space in Germany's African colonies, especially Southwest Africa. The transition to schemes of direct social organization in Southwest Africa generated new bioracial discourses, cast in the register of science, about "native" peoples in order to define, subordinate, manage, or eradicate them. After emerging from this violent matrix of colonial domination, this biopolitical framework became the basis of subsequent pan-German understandings of European populations and the German *Volkskörper* as racial collectivities.

In Southwest Africa, pan-German colonialism rested on two main initiatives, which became infused with new bioracial understandings of human populations. First, it sought to promote forms of settler capitalism by attracting colonists from Germany and other parts of Africa, especially the racially "related" South Africa Boers, to the region and providing the material and social support necessary for their resettlement.[31] Second, it lobbied for a clearly defined native policy that would classify, manage, "transfer," or in certain cases "exterminate" indigenous populations.[32] These two aspects of a pan-German *Kolonialpolitik* came together in the work of Max Robert Gerstenhauer, the first to combine them in a coherent bioracial framework defined by and seeking to assert the rule of colonial difference. In 1902, Gerstenhauer pointed to what he deemed the existential "danger" of social and sexual interactions between Germans and indigenous peoples and the importance of maintaining the "purity of the blood" of the "higher valued race" of Germans to colonial rule in Southwest Africa. He decried "mixed marriages" and the presence of "half-breed" children, born to "black women" in nonmarital and marital relationships with German men, and their access to the social and political world of their German colonial rulers. Drawing on the example of the Boers, who had allegedly maintained their "race consciousness" and "racial purity" for a century, Gerstenhauer called for forms of legal and social segregation to effect a "separation" of the "ruling race" from the "native population," expel the "half-breeds" from "white" society, prevent them from acting as "political and social intermediaries between the white and colored races," and outlaw marriage and sexual relations between Germans and colonized peoples in Southwest Africa.[33]

The war against the Herero and Nama prompted a deeper engagement with the racial order in colonial Southwest Africa. In response to the armed anticolonial resistance of the Herero beginning in January 1904, the pan-German leadership called on the government to introduce a series of new economic initiatives, ranging from reduction of customs fees and construction of new railways and roads to expropriation of the land companies in order to facilitate the "natural economic development of the protectorate" by removing the obstacles to the "economic activity of the individual."[34] They also lobbied for financial and social support for Germans, especially women, and South African Boers, who might be attracted to settle in Southwest Africa. Finally, they demanded the military suppression and even mass killing of the rebellious Herero, the full "dispossession" of the remaining Herero, and more developed forms of native policy to control the surviving Herero and to manage (or eradicate) other "native" populations, including the Basters, Damara, Hottentots (Nama), and Bushmen (San). These included the transfer of the Herero to large "reservations" and their systematic exploitation as forced labor; the introduction of an internal passport system for all "natives"; and a ban on marriages and sexual relations between "whites and coloreds" in order to prevent the "racial degeneration" of the German and Boer populations.[35]

These preoccupations with the rule of colonial difference and biopolitical management of populations as races in Southwest Africa paved the way for new bioracial definitions of eastern, southern, and northern European peoples after 1904. At the Pan-German League's June 1905 meeting, Ludwig Kuhlenbeck delivered the first pan-German speech on the "race question" and the political significance of "racial value" in a world defined by "increasing global interaction." Kuhlenbeck described what he called the "three main races" of human beings, the "white," "yellow," and "black" races, as well as the three main divisions within "the white race," the Germanic, Roman, and Slavic "peoples," in terms of their collective biological endowment and shared physical characteristics; ranked them in descending order of "value"; and warned of the dangers of "blood mixing" and "degeneration." He singled out what he considered the threat posed by Polish-speaking migrants in Westphalia—"Slavs" who constituted a racial-biological, rather than a cultural and political, danger to this "heretofore most racially pure" region of Germany.[36] In this way, Kuhlenbeck jettisoned a cultural and political definition of Polish nationality in favor of a new bioracial definition of the Polish "people," which the league had explicitly rejected three years earlier.[37] He went on to address the problem of the demand for cheap "Slavic" labor and the concomitant threat of race "mixing" with reference to Gerstenhauer's proposed measures to keep the "races" apart in German Southwest Africa.[38]

As pan-Germans began to focus on domestic politics in relation to empire, these deliberations were followed by new categorizations of Germans as a collective biological entity. In December 1905, Armin Tille published an essay advocating a scientifically based "pan-German social policy," necessitated by the global "struggle among peoples and races," which would introduce forms of medical, welfare, and economic assistance to promote the "physical and mental health" of the German "social body as a whole," at the expense of misplaced "sympathy for the needs of the individual," and privilege the strong, the "healthy," and the "most capable" over the "sick" and the "weak."[39] Two years later, as part of a new "racial politics," Hasse outlined a similar scheme for *Sozialpolitik*, understood as "health care in the widest sense of the word," concerned with public health, the economy, and reproduction, including a proposal for "planned racial breeding" proscribing "marriages between Germans and Hereros or Hottentots" and between healthy and "mentally or physically sick or degenerate" Germans.[40] In 1912, Heinrich Class, who had become the league's chairman four years earlier, also engaged these themes in his blueprint for domestic "reform" entitled *If I Were the Kaiser*, which called for medical intervention in support of the "bodily health of the German race" and a program of "internal colonization" involving schemes for agricultural settlement and housing construction to relieve overcrowding in the cities and thereby sustain the "valuable elements of the population."[41] Class pointed to the presence of Poles, Russians, Italians, Croats, and especially Jews living in Germany itself, who were now defined in biological terms. Class demanded the "clearance" of "foreigners" from German soil and the creation of "empty" space by means of the "evacuation" of foreign populations on the other side of Germany's western and eastern borders in order to make room for and to cultivate the health of an expanding German population.[42]

As a biopolitical concept, the term *Volkskörper* first appeared in league discussions in a talk entitled "The National Significance of the Race Question," which Arnim Tille delivered to the general assembly of the Dresden branch of the Pan-German League in March 1911. By contrast with the racial "mixing" that took place between Germans and "Slavic" peoples and French Huguenots during an earlier "colonial period," Tille argued, the present era of "global interaction" posed two distinctive threats: the permanent "blood mixing" between Germans and "representatives" of other "peoples and races" ("negroes" and "Mongolians" in German colonies in Africa and Asia) and the continued presence of "racially poor elements" ("criminals," "cripples," the deaf, and the blind) "inside our own *Volkskörper*." Tille focused his remarks on reproductive matters, including measures designed to promote marriages among the "higher" classes and laws that would require medical certificates attesting to the physical and mental health of couples entering into marriage.[43] But by the spring of 1914, this discussion expanded to include biomedical, economic, and social programs for internal colonization as the means of bringing about the "recuperation of our *Volkskörper*"—a biopolitical aim that formed the basis of later claims for territorial, state-constitutional, and demographic changes in Europe.[44]

PAN-GERMAN EMPIRE AND RACE WAR

The connections between new spatializations of empire, economic modalities of imperial control, and bioracial discourse matured during World War I, when pan-German leaders entered into the debate over German war aims in relation to what they defined as a "race war" and radically escalated their demands for imperial expansion. The opening salvo in this debate was the pan-German war aims memorandum, written by Class and published in September 1914, which called for the creation of a German empire on the continent founded upon territorial and nonterritorial forms of political control, blurred sovereignties, and gradated forms of "citizenship" based on ethnoracial categories. Class demanded a large strip of French territory running from the English Channel to Switzerland as a "military border," settled by German soldiers and their families and governed "dictatorially," as well as the political incorporation of Belgium, which Germans would also rule by "dictatorial" means. But in Belgium, German rule would differentiate between Walloons, a "degenerated people," who would be disenfranchised but allowed to maintain their own schools and languages, and the Flemish, who, "related by blood" to Germans, would be allowed to keep their language and schools, required to learn German, serve in the German army and navy, and possibly be granted "codetermination" and "full citizenship rights" after a long "period of education."[45] Class envisioned the incorporation of Scandinavia into a "Greater

German Reich" under a "League of Germanic States" and the creation of a common "Germanic citizenship" to encompass Germans, Danes, Swedes, and Norwegians.[46] He called for the annexation of Lithuania, Latvia, and Estonia and allowed for the possibility of granting some kind of civic status, short of full citizenship, to the "foreign-blood" inhabitants brought into the expanded Reich.[47] Finally, Class demanded the acquisition of French Morocco, Senegal, and Congo, the Belgian Congo, and British Egypt, though he insisted that the German metropole be "kept clean" of all "blacks" and people with "brown" or "yellow" skin color, unless confined to certain districts in German seaports where their labor would be desirable.[48]

Pan-German plans for new forms of imperial incorporation during the war were entwined with schemes for German economic dispossession of and hegemony over other Europeans and European states—schemes that acquired a much broader appeal. Over the course of 1915 and 1916, the pan-Germans established closer contacts with the leaders of heavy industry and began to lead the annexationist movement. Pan-German economic proposals found their way into the war aims petition of the six main economic pressure groups submitted to the chancellor in March 1915. Written over the course of a series of meetings organized by Hugenberg and Class, the petition called for expansion of the German "colonial empire" and acquisition of agricultural land in the Baltic region, but it focused on economic exactions in the West, including the economic subordination of Belgium and parts of northern France to Germany: the "transfer" of Belgian coal and ore fields and iron and steel factories "into German hands," the incorporation of the Belgian currency, banking system, postal system, railroads, and canals into German financial and communications networks, and the acquisition of the French iron ore region of Brey and the coal regions of the Nord and Pas de Calais.[49] Similar demands were inserted into the pan-German-sponsored "Intellectuals Declaration," a petition signed by 1,347 prominent figures in German academic, business, and public life and submitted to the government in July 1915. It called for far-reaching economic "reparations" in relation to France and Belgium but focused on the acquisition of vast areas of Russian territory as agricultural land, including a German "border belt" next to Posen, Silesia, and East Prussia and the entire Baltic region; the creation of a "comprehensive continental economic region," extending German capital into southeastern Europe, Turkey, the Near East, and the Persian Gulf; and measures to facilitate German access to global markets. The last included securing control over Belgian and French ports and dismantling British naval bases; eliminating the British monopoly on currency transactions, arbitrage, shipping insurance, overseas transport, and international cable and wire services; and creating a "colonial empire" in central Africa and extending it to other regions by means of "our contacts with the Islamic world."[50]

Long-standing pan-German designs for a continental European customs union informed official efforts to create a customs union between Germany and Austria-Hungary during the war. Chancellor Theobald von Bethmann Hollweg included a demand for a German-dominated customs union in the government's official war aims memorandum of September 1914, and a public campaign on behalf of the creation of a *Mitteleuropa* during the war reached its peak when the liberal Friedrich Naumann published his book advocating a left-liberal version of a central European customs confederation in 1915. But the most active proponents were leaders of the Central European Economic Associations and the pan-Germans, especially Class and Hugenberg, who orchestrated the conferences held for the purpose of negotiating a customs union between German and Austria-Hungarian businessmen over the course of 1915–1916. Chaired by the former Navy League president Prince Otto zu Salm-Horstmar, these conferences brought government officials from both axis powers and leading representatives of German and Austrian industry and agriculture together to discuss the general and specific terms of a future customs union in central Europe.[51] They included detailed discussions of the possibilities for tariff reform, the introduction of most-favored-nation status, trading conditions between the two countries by economic sector, and extra-European trade. The presentations at these meetings, many of which were delivered by pan-Germans, focused on the possibilities of economic expansion for the future of "Germandom."

The focus on Germandom also led to efforts to systematize plans for the creation of vacant space via the expulsion of non-German populations from newly acquired territories and for the cultivation of the German *Volkskörper*.[52] In order to satisfy what they called Germany's "hunger for land" and to protect its "racial constitution," the pan-Germans demanded territory "free of human beings."[53] In addition to a population "exchange" with Denmark in the north, they called for population "clearances" in northern France and ethnic or "racial cleansing" (*völkische Flurbereinigung*)—a term the Pan-Germans coined— from the vast eastern territories seized from Russia. Pan-German war aims also mooted plans for the removal of eastern European Jews living in Germany's *Ost-Neuland*, including the "transfer" of all Jews eastwards into a truncated Russia, to a new nation-state in the east created out of territory detached from Russia, or to Palestine.[54] The vacated territories would then be resettled by the ethnic Germans from various regions of Russia, whose "return" to the homeland would be negotiated via population "exchanges," as well as by German soldiers, who would become farmers in the border regions. At the same time, the pan-Germans crafted specific proposals for a "domestic" policy designed to promote racial "selection" and to cultivate the health and growth of the "living" German *Volkskörper*. Its cultivation required not only individual measures related to the declining birthrate (e.g., a ban on contraception; tax rebates or premiums for "child-rich" families) and reproductive "mixing" with other races, especially with "black or yellow blood," but also a broad range of social policies. Assembled into a "total plan," these included new lands for German settlement, solutions to the urban "housing question," provisions for indebtedness, and economic initiatives aimed at the German youth.[55]

This concern for the German *Volkskörper* figured in a wide range of wartime strategies for securing imperial control over different countries, but the most expansive set of proposals came from colonial expert Felix Hänsch, who envisioned a "greater" Germany that would span the entire globe—an empire anchored in the manifold political dimensions of "space," including "productive space," "commercial space," "colonial space," and "open space," and their relation to imperial order. In his ambitious plan from 1917, Hänsch combined pan-German designs for racial cleansing and "Germanization" in areas of eastern Europe with a host of proposals for new economic mechanisms, ranging from trade treaties and commercial privileges favorable to German capital to German ownership of key industrial and communications infrastructure, over various subordinated states within *Mitteleuropa* and discussions of the legal mechanisms of imperial incorporation of previously non-German territories and residents, including definitions of graduated property rights, varied "citizenship" rights, and schemes of limited sovereignty. In addition, Hänsch called for the unification of German colonies in western, southwestern, and eastern Africa into a "Central Africa" governed by Germans relying on Islamic subalterns as intermediaries and "black troops under German leadership." The German empire would thus extend across the globe by means of a German-controlled "communications chain" comprising telegraph posts, military bases, naval ports, trading centers, and colonies across the North Sea, the Mediterranean Sea, and the Atlantic and Pacific oceans.[56]

CONCLUSION

In light of these detailed cartographies of empire, current interpretations of radical-right colonialism in the early twentieth century call for significant revision. The tendency to see in pan-German visions of empire static, territorially bounded imperial polities anchored only in forms of direct domination, racially "pure" colonial (re)settlement, and "romantic agrarianism" or even noncapitalist economic isolationism overlooks the complexity of debate within the league, even within individual pan-German texts, over the shape and tasks of a Greater Germany. It ignores the economically dynamic and varied conceptions of sovereignty and domination put forward by the pan-Germans and scants analysis of the economic and spatial conditions of emergence of what was unique to the radical right during the late Wilhelmine era: namely, its embrace of new bioracial definitions of human populations, political organization, and imperial rivalry. This new form of racism secured a place in pan-German discourse in the wake of efforts to formulate new imperatives of colonial rule over racial "others" in German Southwest Africa. Its novelty lay in the way it introduced a violent colonial logic that required either the domination or the expulsion of the bioracial other as a means of fostering the health and future prospects of a putative German *Volkskörper* overseas and on the European continent.

These pan-German visions of a dynamic colonial empire and their distinctive bioracial dimensions should also prompt us to rethink interpretations of radical-right ideology as a self-contained form of ethnic nationalism insulated from the effects of globalization or as a "reactionary modernist" refusal of Enlightenment reason cast in irrational longings for a racist utopia.[57] The pan-German right emerged out of schemas and practices of an expanding world empire and its colonizing initiatives. It defined populations as living and evolving entities in scientific terms and turned the cultivation of the German *Volkskörper* into the existential imperative for no less "rational" demands for unending imperial expansion.

Finally, compelling interpretations of radical-right ideology as an attempt to construct a "deep mythology of place" in response to the collapse of spatial barriers associated with modernity risk downplaying the novel understandings of spatial relations that characterized pan-German visions of world empires after 1900.[58] For the pan-Germans were well attuned to the sociospatial and economic transformations of their era and even sought to harness and remake them in support of an expanded German empire. Pan-German imperialism thus appears disturbingly innovative and in many respects forward looking, distinctive for its ruthless determination to overturn the existing global order so that a bioracially founded Greater Germany could become a reality—not just in Africa and Asia but also on the European continent.[59] It was in these ways that pan-German demands for world empire informed the subsequent imperial projects of German fascism.

NOTES

1. Hasse, *Die Besiedelung des deutschen Volksbodens*, 125, 136.
2. Smith, *The Ideological Origins of Nazi Imperialism*, 92. See also Walkenhorst, *Nation-Volk-Rasse*, 172ff., 209–210, 225.
3. Eley, *Reshaping the German Right*, 48–58; Frech, *Wegbereiter Hitlers?*; Walkenhorst, *Nation-Volk-Rasse*; Hering, *Konstruierte Nation*; Chickering, *We Men Who Feel Most German*.
4. Fischer, *Krieg der Illusionen*; Kurlander, *The Price of Exclusion*.
5. Fischer, *Germany's Aims in the First World War*.
6. Jürgen Zimmerer, "Birth of the Ostland"; Mazower, *Hitler's Empire*; Arendt, *The Origins of Totalitarianism*, 222–225.
7. Stoler, "On Degrees of Imperial Sovereignty," 125–146.
8. Chatterjee, *The Nation and Its Fragment*, 10, 18; Steinmetz, *The Devil's Handwriting*.
9. Foucault, *"Society Must Be Defended,"* 245–256.
10. "Aufruf zum ersten allgemeinen deutschen Kongreß zur Förderung überseeischen Interessen," in Bundesarchiv Berlin (hereafter BArch), R8048/1, 5–10; and "Satzungen des Allgemeinen Deutschen Verbandes," in BArch, R8048/1, 44.
11. "Die Bewirtschaftung unserer Kolonien," *Alldeutsche Blätter* [AB], September 2, 1894, No. 36, 4 Jg., 145–146.
12. Hugenberg, *Innere Colonisation im Nordwesten Deutschlands*, esp. 408–409, 417, 420.
13. "Der Handelsverkehr der deutschen Kolonien," AB, August 29, 1897, Nr. 35, 7 Jg., 174.
14. "Die Bedeutung der Erwerbung der Kiau-Tschou-Bucht," AB, December 19, 1897, Nr. 51, 7 Jg., 266–7.
15. "Deutschlands Weltstellung und der Weiterbau am deutschen Nationalstaat," AB, January 7, 1894, No. 2, 4 Jg., 5–7.
16. Hasse, *Großdeutschland*.
17. Hasse, *Großdeutschland*, 11–14, 45–46.
18. Hasse, *Großdeutschland*, 47, 48.
19. "Mittelländische Verkehrspläne," AB, November 24, 1895, No. 47, 5 Jg., 213–214.
20. "Deutschlands Weltstellung und der Weiterbau am deutschen Nationalstaat," 5.
21. Hasse, "Europäische oder Weltpolitik?" AB, June 11, 1899, Nr. 24, 9 Jg., 194.
22. Hasse, *Großdeutschland*, 8.
23. Harvey, *The Condition of Postmodernity*, 240, 250, 254–259.
24. Smith, *American Empire*, 12–15, and the classic Lefebvre, *The Social Production of Space*.
25. Steinmetz, "Return to Empire," 350.
26. Dehn, "Die weltwirtschaftliche Entwickelung," AB, January 6, 1901, Nr. 1, 11 Jg., 4–6.
27. Hasse, *Weltpolitik*, 2.
28. Hasse, *Weltpolitik*, 11, 12, 13.
29. Hasse, *Weltpolitik*, 71.
30. Hasse, *Weltpolitik*, 51–52, 63, 65.

31. Gerstenhauer, "Deutschsüdwestafrika alldeutsch!" *AB*, July 9, 1899, No. 28, 226–227.

32. "Die Erzeihung der Neger zur Arbeit," *AB*, September 7, 1901, No. 36, 412.

33. Gerstenhauer's article from the *Deutsche Kolonialzeitung* is reprinted in "Der Rassenverderb in Deutsch-Südwestafrika," in *AB*, December 20, 1902, No. 51, 457.

34. *AB*, June 4, 1904, No. 23, 194.

35. *AB*, June 4, 1904, No. 23, 193–194.

36. Kuhlenbeck, "Die politischen Ergebnisse der Rassenforschung," *AB*, June 25, 1905, No. 25, 215–216.

37. Sitzung des Gesamtausschusses, May 23/24, 1902, in BArch, R8048/34, 4–8.

38. Kuhlenbeck, "Die politischen Ergebnisse der Rassenforschung," 216.

39. Tille, "Alldeutsche Sozialpolitik," *AB*, December 16, 1905, No. 50, 428–429.

40. Hasse, *Die Zukunft des deutschen Volkstums*, 55, 72, 83.

41. Fryman, *Wenn ich der Kaiser wär'*, 93, 105–106, 142.

42. Fryman, *Wenn ich der Kaiser wär'*, 93, 141, 152, 170.

43. *AB*, May 5, 1911, No. 18, 157–158.

44. "Die Aufgabe des Alldeutschen Verbandes in der Frage der inneren Kolonisation," *AB*, May 9, 1914, No. 19, 173–74.

45. Class, *Denkschrift*, in BArch, R8048/638, 28–33, 23–27.

46. Class, *Denkschrift*, in BArch, R8048/638, 63–64.

47. Class, *Denkschrift*, in BArch, R8048/638, 39–41.

48. Class, *Denkschrift*, in BArch, R8048/638, 54–57, 65–66.

49. See the petition in BArch, R8048/647, 5–10.

50. See the petition and list of signatures in BArch, R8048/638, 65–68, 93–98.

51. "Bericht über die deutsch-österreichischen Besprechung in Berlin vom 8. Oktober 1916," in BArch, R8048/453, 269.

52. Class, *Denkschrift*, 45.

53. Sitzung des Gesamtausschusses, August 28, 1914, in BArch, R8048/96, 8, 17–18, 26–27.

54. Class, *Denkschrift*, in BArch, R8048/633, 30–32, 43–45, 65, 49–50.

55. Leopold von Vietinghoff-Scheel, "Grundlinien künftiger innerer Arbeit," 1198–1221.

56. Hänsch, *An der Schwelle des grösseren Reichs*, 3, 10, 61, 160, 184.

57. Walkenhorst, *Nation-Volk-Rasse*, 14, 101, 166; Chickering, *We Men Who Feel Most German*, 96; Herf, *Reactionary Modernism*.

58. Harvey, *The Condition of Postmodernity*, 277.

59. Césaire, *Discourse on Colonialism*.

FOURTEEN

Maritime Force and the Limits of Empire

Warfare, Commerce, and Law in Germany and the United States before World War I

DIRK BÖNKER

After the mid-nineteenth century, Germany and the United States emerged as prime movers in the militarization of the globe. During the nationalizing wars of the 1860s, the two countries charted new forms of the wartime mobilization of people, ideologies, and industries within the framework of an integral nation-state. Some thirty years later, the same powers became key actors in the naval arms race for global power and built the world's second and third most formidable navies. These pursuits of force, in turn, were part of strikingly similar and parallel trajectories along which the two countries moved in the developing new global age. These paths, which ultimately collided in the two world wars, involved the territorializing projects of two nation-states, one newly made and one reforged, that aimed at self-development and industrial transformation within a protected national space and then at the outward projection of productive power and military force. National mobilization and global competition coalesced as networks of capital, markets, knowledge, dominion, and force turned the world into the "globe" and ushered in a new competitive global geopolitics of war and empire by the end of the nineteenth century.[1]

In both countries, the military took a front seat in national pursuits of maritime force. Stressing the paramount importance of sea power in a new global age, naval officers were the prime movers of navalism, the militarist formation that emerged as a distinct regime of power and knowledge on both sides of the Atlantic. Rallying support from broad political coalitions and large cross sections of national publics, navalism was a militarism of experts that fused the causes of nation, global power, elite rule, and navy while stressing the professional mastery of maritime warfare and sharing an investment in the model of professionalism and science of war associated with the Prussian-German army.[2]

This chapter focuses on naval elites as a key group that lent meaning to and acted on the global and imperial entanglements of the two most rapidly developing nation-states of the modern North Atlantic world.[3] Focusing on the professional-military thought of the German and US navies in tandem, I delineate the ways in which the two militaries conceptualized the wartime use of maritime force and its boundaries at the beginning of the twentieth century. In an age of "competitive globalization,"[4] the navies' strategists presented themselves as guardians of empire who harnessed force to pursue a muscular politics of maritime threat and deterrence and to prepare for big-power wars of nation and industry.

This examination of German and US approaches to maritime warfare revisits narratives of a peculiar German militarism that continue to capture the imagination of historians of modern Germany. Recent work by John Horne and Alan Kramer and by Isabel Hull on the Imperial German way of war has breathed new life into this narrative, if not the *Sonderweg* question in general, by focusing on the military itself (army and navy) and its "extremist" approach toward the use of force.[5] The notion of the German armed forces' predilection for excessive violence and disregard for regimes of military and legal limitation, which allegedly spanned Imperial and Nazi Germanies and helped to mold their violent engagements with the world, have come to play a central role in current thinking about trajectories of German histories before 1945. Thus Helmuth Walser Smith and Michael Geyer have invoked the Imperial German military and its penchant for absolute violence to make arguments about the peculiarities and deep continuities of German history, culminating in the Nazi pursuit of war, mass murder, and racial empire.[6]

To consider this notion of German military "extremism" in a transatlantic perspective is to confront the fact that historians of the US military have long been making similar arguments about a distinct American commitment to a military strategy of absolute destruction. In a much celebrated work, first published in 1973, Russell Weigley famously argues that a strategy of annihilation directed at the "complete overthrow of the enemy, the destruction of his military power" had come to dominate the thinking of most American strategists, army and navy, and characterize the "American Way of War" since the US Civil War. Driven by the country's ever-increasing wealth and its "adoption of unlimited war aims," the US pursuit of the "total submission of the enemy" was directed first and foremost at destruction of the "enemy's armed force," yet it also targeted the enemy's resources and will in general, including the safety of its people. Early on, the commitment to the destruction of the enemy nation's military power had also contributed to the pursuit of genocidal goals in the wars against Native Americans.[7]

In contrast, in what follows, I make a case for both German-American commonality and shared investment in a "way of war" that imposed clear boundaries on the wartime use of force. The German and US navies moved along similar paths when they conceived of maritime warfare in the developing global age before World War I. The common outlook of these two armed services, which understood themselves as the vanguard of modern navalism, was marked by a firm investment in the battle-oriented contest of fighting fleets, cast in the image of "regular" terrestrial warfare. Yet far from indulging a predilection for unlimited military violence and the relentless instrumentalization of civilian life and property in pursuit of victory, the two navies' strategists adhered to a regime of limitation in conceptualizing naval warfare in terms of economic pressure and the application of military force against the opponent's civilian trade.

SEA POWER SHOWDOWNS

The German and US navies carved out a common approach to matters of naval warfare and fleet operations before World War I. The idea of battle-driven combat between battle fleets grounded the military thought the German and US naval elites developed by the beginning of the twentieth century. The expectation of a decisive naval encounter became the regulative idea of maritime strategy that imagined victory through climactic battle in temporally confined wars. This approach coalesced in the United States and Germany in the 1890s; by 1900, it had become firmly embedded in operational doctrine, war plans, naval programs, and the curricula of naval war schools.[8]

Naval strategists moved to center stage the battle-fleet contest, the *Flottenkampf*. It served a clearly defined purpose: to gain "command of the sea" by defeating the enemy's naval forces and driving them off the sea. Operational planning provided the ultimate field of enactment for the commitment to battle-fleet warfare and climactic combat. Casting the war at sea as a discrete undertaking, planners strove to assure wartime military success in decisive battle in their scenarios, which assumed symmetrical commitments to this kind of warfare on both sides. The cult of the decisive battle and visions of large-scale fleet operations became the hallmark of the war plans both navies devised for such hypothetical big-power scenarios as American-Japanese, German-American, and Anglo-German armed confrontations.[9]

The concept of battle-fleet warfare represented a self-conscious effort to apply allegedly axiomatic principles of land warfare and the notion of an all-decisive battle of annihilation to war at sea. The major US and German theorists of naval warfare, Alfred Thayer Mahan and Alfred von Tirpitz, explicitly took key ideas of the new doctrine of offensive sea warfare from the works of the most prominent theorists of land warfare in their respective countries. Mahan and the Americans borrowed their main operational principles from the eminent Swiss strategist Antoine-Henri Jomini, a highly revered authority in the United States, and Tirpitz and the Germans, with the same results, turned to Karl von Clausewitz's *On War* (and also incorporated Mahan's work).[10]

Moving along common paths and engaging in acts of mimicry in relation to terrestrial professional warfare, Mahan, Tirpitz, and their fellow theorists of naval warfare explicitly set up the paradigm of battle-fleet warfare against another approach to waging maritime war. This approach placed cruisers and their use as commerce raiders at the center of naval warfare (and of building policy, too, for that matter). Casting cruisers' operations against opponents' seaborne trade as the war-winning proposition, it paid little attention to the direct contest between fighting fleets as a primary venue of military action. Cruiser warfare had been the primary operational mission of the US Navy throughout the nineteenth century.[11] Notions of cruiser warfare against the enemy's commerce had also gained considerable ground within the German navy. Drawing on the experiences of the US Civil War and the Franco-Prussian war, many officers championed cruisers as an important means of waging war because they could deny essential supplies to the enemy's armed forces.[12] But the considerable popularity of the idea of cruiser warfare also drew directly on another source, the teachings of the *Jeune École*, a French school of naval thought that had emerged by the 1880s.[13]

Mahan and Tirpitz offered straightforward critiques of cruiser warfare geared toward commerce raiding as a military doctrine prescribing the primary conduct of war.[14] Yet they also undercut this type of warfare on other grounds: precisely by transforming the understanding of the navy's peacetime commercialist service. A key appeal of cruiser warfare as an operational doctrine had been that it also fit perfectly with the use of cruisers as an instrument of a gunboat diplomacy directed against "local" rulers and peoples across the globe, not other imperial powers.[15] But the advocates of battle-fleet strategy maintained that in the new age of global empire, the pursuit of imperial opportunity had become a matter of great power rivalry; it depended on threat and deterrence that targeted rival global empires. Proponents of battle-fleet warfare prioritized big-power wars over gunboat diplomacy as the focal point of strategies of maritime control.[16] In so doing, they promoted the principle of military concentration in distinct regional settings such as the North Sea, the North Atlantic, the Caribbean, and the Pacific. While German and US strategists envisioned large-scale transoceanic battle-fleet warfare and deployed naval vessels in far-flung places to promote economic interests and guard colonial empires by a show of force on the spot, they cast their capital-ship navies nonetheless as regional forces. Following this approach, the German navy simply wrote off the wartime maritime protection of Germany's entire overseas colonial empire in case of a big-power war.[17]

Regional bids for maritime force shaped US and German operational planning, peacetime deployment, naval programs, and specific technological choices; it also set German and US approaches apart from the truly global strategy of maritime projection that the British Empire had originally pioneered at midcentury, a strategy based on a relay of global networks of force, supply, communications, and repair, and to which that empire's policymakers remained committed throughout (and beyond) the entire prewar period.[18]

GLOBAL COMMERCE AND COMMAND OF THE SEA

The two navies' common vision of naval warfare always transcended the notion of the contest between battle fleets even as newly emerging military technologies, such as submarines and battle cruisers, were fitted into it. Naval war was still defined as a war of commerce and economic pressure that targeted the enemy nation beyond its armed forces. This remained a peculiar feature of maritime warfare, reflected in turn in the special meanings of "command of the sea," which lacked a direct equivalent in the realm of army combat. Such command was never conceptualized as an end in itself; rather, it appeared as a means to a larger end in a war that involved more than the destruction of the enemy's fighting fleets.

The "struggle" for "command of the sea" would be the "first task," *Service Memorandum IX*, the foundational text for German naval thinking, written in 1894, explained, "because only once the command of the sea is gained, the real means become available that force the enemy to sue for peace." The list of these means included commercial blockades, operations against enemy transoceanic trade and colonies, bombardments of enemy shorelines and coastal cities, and the landing of troops and creation of bases for the army.[19] In 1899, a lecture on naval preparations for war by Captain Stockton, the president of the US

Naval War College, summarized his navy's thinking on this issue by dividing maritime warfare into three "general forms of action." The "war of fleets and squadrons" would secure "command of sea" and, thus, be the "greater movement" that would in turn "give freedom for and allow or accompany the minor movements of commerce-destroying and territorial attack." These so-called minor movements would "of course" be the "element[s] making for successful termination of war."[20]

In his writings on naval strategy, Mahan himself was most adamant about the overall significance of the war of economic pressure. "For what purposes, primarily, do navies exist?" he once asked. "If navies, as all agree, exist for the protection of commerce, it inevitably follows that in war they must aim at depriving their enemy of that great resource." "Blows against commerce" would be the "most deadly that can be struck"; they would be "blows at the communications of the states; they intercept its nourishment, they starve its life; they cut the roots of its powers, the sinews of its war."[21] Mahan had little doubt that the commercial blockade, based on "command of the sea," was the superior form of a war of economic pressure, as opposed to cruiser warfare on the open sea. According to Mahan, a blockade of the enemy coast would be "the most systematic, regularized and extensive form of commerce destruction known to war."[22] Sharing the same thoughts, Tirpitz expressly characterized the blockade as the "natural course of action" for the superior maritime power that also "commands a strong position."[23] Both writers identified the same advantages of a blockade; namely, its relentless concentration of force and its comprehensiveness in cutting off the enemy seaborne trade at its very source, the enemy ports.

Maritime commercial warfare had a firm place in the two navies' operational planning. To be sure, strategists marginalized direct operations against the opponent's commerce in their plans for war, focusing on the struggle over "command of the sea" and seldom looking beyond the battle of annihilation. But overall, the war of commerce and trade cast a long shadow on the two navies' war strategy. While not mapped out in detail, it was assigned war-ending significance whenever one side was in a position to exercise command of the sea. The specter of British economic warfare, based on the Royal Navy's control of the North Sea, for example, haunted German planners. According to US planners, the "commercial isolation" of Japan would end a Japanese-American war.[24] Their German counterparts envisioned raids against American trade and commerce, the blockade of ports on its eastern coast, and amphibious attacks against major industrial and commercial centers as the means to bring a war against the United States to a successful conclusion.[25]

Official German war plans included designs for limited cruiser-based commercial maritime warfare to parallel the operations of the battle fleet. The handful of regular cruisers and other naval vessels deployed abroad in peacetime were to engage in "ruthless warfare" against trade and enemy possessions, as one planner put it in 1901.[26] The major naval force abroad, the cruiser squadron, based in Kiaochow, was, in case of war with England or the United States, to proceed against the enemy's lines of communication, its shipping routes, and its colonial possessions and inflict maximum damage.

Tirpitz and other German naval strategists generally agreed that the principal value of cruiser warfare was against trade lines if an Anglo-German war broke out while the German battle fleet was still too weak to effectively challenge the English battle fleet. Tirpitz stressed this warfare's many values in 1907. After a lost battle, a campaign against England's trade routes would be "the only means of war that is left to us to fight successfully for somewhat satisfactory terms of peace."[27] In the present and future, "a most ruthless" *Handelskrieg* was Germany's only chance to present an offensive military threat to the British Empire. A campaign against Britain's trade and coastline would also be the only promising course of action in case the British, rather than seek battle, decided to institute a distant blockade of Germany at the Atlantic approaches. In this instance, the German battle fleet or parts thereof would also get directly involved, for Germany would then exercise command of the sea in parts of the North Sea.[28]

US naval strategists, too, believed in the overall value of cruiser-based *Handelskrieg*. The General Board advised it on one of the rare occasions after the turn of the century when it addressed the case of an Anglo-American war. Vigorous cruiser-based commercial warfare against the Royal Navy would be the only option left for the US Navy, with its weaker battle force, the board reckoned in 1906. On that occasion, the agency also stressed the value of a cruiser-based war of commerce and trade against other commercial nations, including Japan, Germany, France, and Italy.[29]

In general, German and US naval strategists were convinced that the benefits of a successful war of trade and economic pressure were enormous, especially if properly conducted according to the tenets of battle-fleet warfare. In their historical works, Mahan and others had demonstrated the importance of commercial maritime warfare as a wartime strategy during the naval wars of the early modern period and the Napoleonic era. More recently, the American Civil War was believed to have taught the same lesson.[30] In fact, the two navies' strategists had little doubt that the economic dimension of naval warfare was gaining more significance than it had ever had precisely because of the tremendous growth of maritime interests and the ever-increasing dependency of industrial economies on maritime trade. Like other military and economic writers across the Western world, US and German naval officers pondered the military ramifications of these developments. Rapid industrialization and the ever-increasing international division of labor within a flourishing world economy were creating unprecedented opportunities for maritime warfare targeting an opponent's seaborne imports.[31]

Viewing a war with Britain as a real possibility in present and future, the Germans took a particularly strong interest in this development. Their country was faced with the prospect of a successful blockade of its coast due to a mixture of geographical circumstance, diplomatic alignments, maritime weakness, and the ever-increasing importance of maritime trade for the German economy. Tirpitz and his collaborators worried a British blockade would interrupt the seaborne supply of raw material and foodstuffs. Their anxieties came into sharp focus during the "war scares" of 1904–1906, which raised the specter of a combined German naval and land war against England and France and perhaps Russia. In such a case, everything depended on whether an enemy blockade would shut down Germany's ability to receive foodstuffs and other imports through neutral Dutch, Belgium, and Scandinavian ports. If Germany could rely on neighboring neutrals for continuous supplies, Tirpitz and others anticipated economic problems of only "more or less local importance," problems that would not pose a serious threat to the sustenance of wartime Germany.[32] But if Germans could not count on trade through neutral countries, they would face great adversity. In 1906–1907, the Imperial Naval Office investigated the issue closely and concluded that if Germany could not use the seaborne trade of neighboring neutrals during a war, feeding its armies and its population would become a major problem within nine months.[33]

Yet the German naval discourse about new economic vulnerabilities stressed not only dangers but also opportunities. Great Britain would be vulnerable, too. Ernst von Halle, one of Tirpitz's close collaborators, concluded that England was "absolutely dependent on an unbroken and undisturbed continuation of its maritime traffic. If this were effectively cut off, England would be forced to conclude peace at any price."[34] Sharing this view, Tirpitz and other strategists explicitly identified the Achilles' heel of England as the "seaborne imports of food stuffs and raw materials" on which hinged continued industrial production and the sustenance of the population.[35] Such views were advanced as the Germans followed the public discussions in England about its ever-increasing economic dependency and the need for military protection of vital import routes in times of war. The findings of the British Royal Commission on Supply of Food and Raw Material in Time of War, published in 1905, captured the German imagination.[36]

Against this backdrop, German naval strategists predicted that even a limited cruiser-based *Handelskrieg* designed as a secondary operation could make a tremendous impact on England. In 1907, Tirpitz calculated that such military action against England's import routes could create economic dislocation, shortages, and moral panic—in his words, "inflation, perhaps famine, layoffs, unrest and similar things." The campaign could inflict enough losses to pose a "considerable" danger, especially to the economic interests of "the City," the community of trading and financial interests in London that would direct English policy.[37] The official planning documents for the use of the handful of existing cruisers overseas struck the same tone. Even if limited in means, cruiser-based commerce destruction would disrupt the opponent's economic life, striking a blow to its war morale and tying down substantial naval forces. In 1911, the commanding officer of the German cruiser squadron envisioned a "considerable disruption" of the English economy and "major interference" with British trade, including a collapse of Australian exports to England, when he discussed the wartime operations of his force. German overseas cruisers could provoke a "panic" that would force the British to send a "large" number of ships to hunt them down, thus relieving "pressure on our home front."[38]

US naval strategists did not study the new economic vulnerabilities and their implications for commercial maritime warfare in the same depth or with the same existentialist urgency as did the Germans. But they nonetheless repeatedly identified the import of food stuffs and raw materials as the key vulnerabilities of the major powers. In 1911, Rear Admiral Bradley Fiske summed up such thinking when he argued that for a "great manufacturing nation" the "stoppage of her over-sea trade by blockade" qualified as the "greatest danger from outside" (besides an invasion, that is); its effect would be "so great that it can hardly be estimated."[39] When, in 1906, the General Board reviewed the US approach to maritime law and commercial warfare, it stressed that the ever-increasing economic dependency of Great Britain, Germany, and Japan on seaborne commerce would open up tremendous opportunities for any opponent.[40] Fittingly, Germany's particular vulnerability to commercial maritime warfare emerged as a central theme in Mahan's thinking after 1904/05. According to him, the British ability to shut down Germany's maritime trade lines was "the strongest hook in the jaws of Germany that the English speaking peoples have."[41]

LAW AND THE LIMITATION OF WAR

While the anticipation of the battle-driven contest of battle fleets, the *Flottenkampf*, took the front seat in military planning and naval construction, US and German naval planners nonetheless conceptualized maritime warfare as a war of economic pressure. In so doing, they moved within a firm regime of military limitation and legal restraint that originated outside the strictures of battle-fleet warfare. Prewar approaches to wartime economic pressures fell short of an active embrace of an all-out war of economic strangulation.

By necessity, the (shared) investment in both commercial warfare and its boundaries showcased itself in the domain of international law. The two navies' policymakers alike opposed any attempt to impose overly severe constraints on commercial warfare by means of maritime law, as they were being considered during the Second Hague Peace conference and the follow-up conference in London exclusively devoted to maritime matters. These conferences set out to codify internationally recognized laws of naval warfare, expanding on the basic framework established by the Declaration of Paris in 1856. The conferences also provided a forum for a far-reaching proposal to confine the maritime war of economic pressure to a bare minimum by providing for the security of all private vessels and cargoes, enemy and neutral, except in cases of contraband and blockade running.[42]

The attempt to radically diminish the possibility of commercial maritime warfare as a viable military strategy through the means of maritime law violated naval reasoning in Germany and the United States. Thus, on both sides of the Atlantic, naval officers opposed providing immunity for private property as it would do away with commerce destruction on the high seas. Preventing the abolition of the *Seebeuterecht*, the right to seize enemy ships and goods and contraband on neutral ships, emerged as a dominant concern of both navies. Taking the issue directly to the emperor and the chancellor, Tirpitz enshrined his view on this matter as official policy, even though he faced considerable opposition from representatives of the Foreign Office and other ministries.[43] In the United States, Mahan and the General Board came out strongly against abolishing a belligerent's right to seize ships and cargoes except in the cases of blockade running and contraband, as proposed by their own government. Accordingly, Rear Admirals Stockton and Sperry, the US naval delegates at the Hague and in London, were most pleased when the official proposal of their own government failed at the Hague Conference and did not surface at the follow-up conference in London.[44] Representatives of both navies reiterated their views on private immunity when they discussed it as a possible item on the agenda for the upcoming Third Hague Peace Conference, which was scheduled for 1915.[45]

Beyond the issue of private immunity, German and US naval elites staked out somewhat different positions concerning the rules governing the conduct of a commercial blockade and commerce destruction on the open sea. The Americans promoted the cause of the blockading power while striking a clear balance between commercial warfare on the open sea and neutral trade.[46] In 1906 the General Board announced that henceforth the United States would resist "any attempt to further limit the right of blockaders."[47] Perhaps most importantly, the representatives of the navy demanded the application of the principle of "continuous voyage" to blockade law. According to this notion, a blockade could affect ships heading toward and cargoes landed in neutral ports whose ultimate destination was the neighboring belligerent power under blockade. During the conference at London, the American naval delegate strongly resisted efforts to radically limit, if not abolish, this notion, even if it were to result in the failure of the entire conference. The United States successfully insisted on the application in principle of this doctrine to the exercise of a blockade, even if only restricted to neutral port–bound cargoes that involved goods of direct military use destined for a neighboring belligerent.[48]

On the issue of how to regulate commercial warfare outside the confines of the blockade, US naval delegates took positions that combined favorable attitudes toward commercial warfare with considerations of neutral trading rights. This approach informed the treatment of the issue of contraband. On the one hand, Sperry, the delegate at the Hague, rejected the abolition of any contraband law, as initially proposed by the British in 1907. Sperry and Stockton, his successor in London, also insisted on the inclusion of the doctrine of "continuous voyage" in contraband law; that is, on the right to seize goods carried in neutral ships heading toward neutral ports as contraband of war if their ultimate destination was believed to be the opposing belligerent power. On the other hand, the Americans argued against any expansive understandings of contraband. They favored specific lists of contraband, defining absolute contraband as goods "exclusively adapted to military use" and its conditional counterpart as articles of dual purpose clearly destined for the enemy's military use.[49] In fact, Sperry had initially favored even the abolition of the latter. The Americans also supported the idea of a "free list" of goods not to be declared contraband under any circumstances, including raw materials for industrial manufacturing and supplies for agricultural production.

Approaching the legal regulation of naval warfare, German naval officers staked out clear positions: the quest to minimize the institution of the blockade combined with the desire to maximize the potential of cruiser-based commercial warfare on the high seas defined their agenda at the two conferences.[50] The imposition of restraints on the exercise of blockades and the "conduct of a legally valid blockade"[51] received top priority as the "truly decisive issue."[52] It was essential to the Germans that a blockade be limited to the enemy coastline and, thus, not extend to neutral neighbors. Moreover, unlike the Americans, the Germans offered restrictive readings of the principle of "effectiveness," which served as the official criterion for the legal validity of any blockade. "Effectiveness" was to require the continuous presence near the blockaded coast of blockading forces capable of preventing, in actuality, both outgoing and incoming maritime traffic. Likewise, the right to seize ships for blockade running was to be restricted to the vicinity of the blockaded coast or, if necessary, the steaming radius of the blockading force.

To facilitate attacks on commercial shipping on the open sea, the Germans sought legal sanction for various practices, among which the right to destroy prizes on the open sea ranked first. Its acceptance was deemed nonnegotiable, for its prohibition would render "illusory" any commercial warfare by a power, like Germany, that lacked a globe-spanning chain of naval stations and depended on the agility and stealth of its commerce destroyers.[53] In contrast to the Americans, the Germans also promoted an expansive reading of the right of belligerent warships to call at neutral ports and receive supplies there and opposed substantive restrictions on the conversion of merchantmen to auxiliary cruisers outside home waters. They felt so strongly about the last issue that they refused to compromise. The issues of conversion remained unsettled at London.

The desire to expand the scale and scope of commerce destruction on the high seas also informed the German approach to contraband. Yet in this case the desire was circumscribed by an interest in protecting Germany's ability to profit from neutral trade in wartime. On the one hand, the Germans opposed the abolition of contraband, as proposed by the British during the Hague Conference. Moreover, they favored a broader definition of contraband goods that could become targets for commercial warfare. On the other hand, the Germans wanted to suspend the doctrine of continuous voyage to protect any goods heading toward neutral ports, a suspension that conveniently did not affect military operations against the seaborne trade of the British Isles.

To ensure such suspensions, the Germans were willing to accept carefully crafted specific lists for both absolute and relative contraband and for free goods. The settlement reached in London resonated with German definitions of interest. In the face of US objections, the Germans consented to applying the notion of "continuous voyage" to goods of absolute contraband. But this concession did not affect their core interests because the Germans managed to place items they considered particularly valuable on the "free list," including key industrial raw materials and agricultural machinery. They also succeeded in extending the key destination criterion for "relative contraband" to include goods destined for the enemy state, not simply its armed forces. The inclusion of foodstuffs resonated with German interests precisely because of the formal exclusion of this kind of contraband from the realm of "continuous voyage." The arrangement thus did not threaten to undermine Germany's ability to receive seaborne imports of foodstuffs through neighboring neutrals.[54]

German-American differences in emphasis and detail reflected varying definitions of national interests. Each navy's positions were based on a careful analysis of military opportunity and geopolitical circumstance. The specter of a hypothetical Anglo-German war shaped the views of Tirpitz and his fellow officers. The belief in the vital importance of continuing trade through the ports of neighboring neutrals in wartime drove the desire to weaken the effectiveness of a blockade by legal means, to protect the seaborne trade of neighboring neutrals, and to suspend the doctrine of "continuous voyage." The prospect of cruiser warfare against England's vital seaborne commerce, its alleged "lifeblood,"[55] underlay the opposition not only to the demand for "private immunity" but to any substantive restriction imposed on commerce destruction by cruisers.

American strategists arrived at their views of commerce destruction on the basis of a careful study of specific scenarios involving the United States as a belligerent, including hypothetical wars against Germany, Japan, and Great Britain. But their particular investment in commercial maritime warfare also evolved from a more general analysis of US interests as a maritime belligerent. As a matter of principle, the Americans wanted to reserve the right to conduct a war of commerce and trade as an open-ended proposition for the future. Far from being a matter of life and death in war scenarios (as with Germany), it offered an attractive military option that bore little risk for the United States. Its navy was bound to be a powerful offensive and defensive weapon. The US merchant marine was small. The riches of the North American continent ruled out the imposition of an effective blockade even by an overwhelmingly superior enemy. The United States, in short, should keep its future military options open rather than behave in an "altruistic" manner and promote neutral rights.[56]

Such a strictly utilitarian reading of the interests of Germany and the United States as belligerent powers resonated well with officers' constructions of their own countries. As aspiring world powers seeking to control their own destiny, their nation-states (allegedly) operated in an antagonistic world of big-power politics. According to naval wisdom, their future depended on military threat and deterrence, not on restrictions on belligerent rights and cooperative security.

At the same time, Germans and Americans accepted the framework of maritime law as a defining feature of military geopolitics. The delineation of the legal boundaries of naval warfare in peacetime was not simply an exercise for public consumption. To be sure, the notion that in wartime belligerent powers would review and, possibly, bend the laws of warfare because of military necessity was widely accepted. But naval officers considered maritime law inviolate, firmly bounding the pursuit of military necessity in wartime. The "weight of neutral power" would always "compel" adherence to the commonly agreed-upon legal rules of warfare, as they were expressed in the Declaration of London, explained Admiral Stockton.[57] Likewise, German naval strategists were not too unsettled by intense public outrage in Britain at the Declaration of London, outrage that culminated in nonratification by the House of Lords. "Either way" the planks of the declaration would become the "foundation for the modern international maritime law" and bound British behavior.[58] It was for the same reasons that, originally, the Germans had fretted over the prospects of the Hague and London conferences. They expected Great Britain, acting for its own advantage, to codify legal rules that would bind the hands of Germans. Given the key German interests, it would be better to prevent any agreement than to accept one that was bound to put Germany at a serious disadvantage in war.[59]

The two navies placed themselves inside the regulatory framework of maritime law. The stipulations of the Declaration of London were incorporated into both navies' legal codes for the conduct of naval warfare.[60] This respect for the law became enshrined in the operations orders with which the German navy went to war in August 1914.[61] It was only fitting that in the spring of 1914, when the head of the German submarine inspection outlined a plan for a future submarine campaign against British trade, this proposal, which was the first of its kind, assumed that the campaign would be waged within the confines of existing maritime law.[62] Likewise, in the first year of the war, the US General Board urged its government to take action against the British because its blockade violated maritime law.[63]

CONCLUSION

After World War I, Carl Schmitt argued that maritime warfare had helped to pioneer "total war," the new mode of war among the great powers in the twentieth century, built on the potentially unlimited use of military means of destruction across the civil-military divide. For the German political theorist, naval warfare had always contained defining "elements" of such a "pure war of extermination" between states. This type of warfare had not been subjected to the same kind of regulation, *Hegung*, as its counterpart on land, while on the other hand not falling outside it as did civil wars and colonial wars, the two constitutive oppositions of regular war between states.[64]

Contrary to such claims, the maritime realm did not function as a (discursive) site of all-out war in the cases of the German and US navies before World War I. What is striking about their prewar approaches to maritime warfare is not the relentless pursuit of the possibilities maritime warfare may have offered for total war. Far from enacting a predilection for the excessive use of military force and an instrumentalization of civilian lives and property for the pursuit of victory, these approaches kept within limits the potentially unrestrained nature of Western maritime warfare as identified by Schmitt. Sharing an outlook, US and German naval planners prepared for a war of economic pressure within clearly defined military and legal confines. Plans for immediate operations against the enemy's seaborne trade remained a sideshow in an overall planning process that prioritized battle fleets and climactic naval combat, in explicit analogy to mainstream practices of land warfare. This orientation shaped military strategy, naval programs, and understandings of military technological means, such as submarines and battle cruisers. Naval operations against an enemy's economy aimed at war supplies, economic dislocation, moral panic, and domestic turmoil, not at mass death and starvation or the destruction of the sustenance, safety, and lives of the larger civilian population.

German and US navies operated within a regime of limitation when they imagined the war at sea in the developing global age. The strictures of maritime law were central to this regime. Emphasizing protection of neutral trade, a restrictive understanding of contraband and blockade law, and due process as far as search, condemnation, and legal recourse were concerned, the law de facto ruled out an all-out war of economic strangulation against an entire enemy nation. Perhaps most importantly, the Declaration of London left little space for a war of economic pressure that targeted foodstuffs for the civilian population: the declaration defined them as conditional contraband liable to seizure only when there was absolute proof that it was destined for enemy armed forces or the enemy state administration, as opposed to civilians.[65]

Before World War I, German and US naval strategists did not anticipate breaking the strictures of maritime law in case of war or preparing for a maritime war of extermination that directly targeted the life and cohesion of the entire enemy nation. Their subsequent embrace of such a war represented a clear departure from previous thinking and practice, which required specific political and military junctures, including the breakdown of the framework of maritime law.[66] Germans and Americans had a common approach to the use of maritime force as they made their own services into the military instruments of belligerent nations in big-power wars at the beginning of the twentieth century. Their firm investments in battle-fleet warfare and the legal delimitation of maritime force lent a distinct shape to the military thought and practice of both navies. It also set German and US maritime-operational approaches apart from those of Britain's Royal Navy, where well before the outbreak of war in 1914, important naval strategists charted different, "extremist" directions (to use Isabel Hull's term) as they looked beyond the confines of battle-fleet warfare, military limitation, and maritime law.[67]

NOTES

1. Geyer and Bright, "Global Violence," and Bright and Geyer, "Regimes of Global Order."
2. Bönker, *Militarism in a Global Age*, offers a comprehensive analysis from which this chapter draws.
3. Mauch and Patel, eds., *Wettlauf um die Moderne*.
4. Eley, "Empire by Land or Sea?," ch. 1 in this volume.
5. Horne and Kramer, *German Atrocities*; Hull, *Absolute Destruction*; Anderson, "A German Way of War?" and "How German Is It?"; Cramer, "A World of Enemies."
6. Geyer, "The Space of the Nation" and "Where Germans Dwell"; H. W. Smith, "When the Sonderweg Debate Left Us" and *The Continuities of German History*.
7. Weigley, *The American Way of War* and "American Strategy."
8. This is an oft-told story. See, for example, Lambi, *The Navy and German Power Politics*, and Spector, *Professors of War*.
9. There is a rich literature on the two navies' operational planning. For a full discussion, see ch. 5 of Bönker, *Militarism in a Global Age*.
10. Hobson, *Maritimer Imperialismus*.
11. Hagan, *This People's Navy*.
12. Olivier, *German Naval Strategy*.
13. Bueb, *Die "Junge Schule" der französischen Marine*, and Røksund, *The Jeune École*.
14. Mahan, *Influence of Sea Power upon History*, and *Influence of Sea Power upon the French Revolution*; Tirpitz, "Erwiderung auf die Schrift von Valois," and his comments on the excerpts from Curt von Maltzahn's *Seelehre*, BA-MA, RMA 3/2.
15. Bönker, "Zwischen Bürgerkrieg und Navalismus," and Sondhaus, *Preparing for Weltpolitik*.
16. On this issue, compare Fiebig-von Hase, *Lateinamerika als Konfliktherd*.
17. Ganz, "Colonial Policy and the Imperial German Navy."

18. A. Lambert, "Wirtschaftliche Macht," and N. Lambert, "Transformation and Technology."

19. Taktische und Strategische Dienstschriften des Oberkommandos der Marine Nr. IX: "Allgemeine Erfahrungen aus den Manövern der Herbstübungsflotte," June 16, 1894, Part II, BA-MA, RM 4/176. Cf. the discussion of "command of the sea" in von Maltzahn, "Das Meer als Operationsfeld."

20. Stockton, *Preparation for War*.

21. Mahan, *Interest of America in Sea Power*, 128, 133.

22. Mahan, *Sea Power in Its Relation*, I, 286.

23. Tirpitz to Bernhard von Bülow, April 29, 1907, *Grosse Politik*, XXIII, 367–372, 370.

24. General Board, "In Case of Strained Relations with Japan," September 1906, NWCA, RG 8, UNOpB; Naval War College, "Strategic Plan of Campaign against Orange," March 15, 1911, and General Board, "Orange War Plan: Strategic Section," March 14, 1914; both in NA, RG 80, General Board, War Portfolio No. 2.

25. Admiral Felix Bendemann, "Entwurf einer Denkschrift," February 2, 1899; Admiralty Staff, "Denkschrift," March 1899; "Denkschrift für einen Operationsplan," December 1899; "Denkschrift zu einem offensiven Vorgehen gegen die Vereinigten Staaten von Nordamerika," January 15, 1902; "Operations–Plan III," March 1903; "Denkschrift zum O–Plan III," March 21, 1903; all in BA-MA, RM 5/5960.

26. Max Grapow, "Denkschrift die Kriegführung Deutschlands gegen England auf der Australischen Station betreffend," November 1901, BA-MA, RM 5/6693. For the following, see the summaries in Lambi, *Navy*, 231–235, 408–410; Overlack, "Function of Commerce Warfare" and "German War Plans in the Pacific."

27. Tirpitz to Bülow, April 20, 1907, *Grosse Politik*, XXIII, 360.

28. Tirpitz to Bülow, February 28, 1907, *Grosse Politik*, XXIII, 350–353.

29. General Board to Secretary of Navy, June 20, 1906, NA, RG 80, General Board, SF 438.

30. For example, Soley, *The Navy in the Civil War*, and von Maltzahn, *Der Seekrieg*, 68–86.

31. The key study is Offer, *The First World War*.

32. Tirpitz to Secretary of War von Einem, March 13, 1906, *Kriegsrüstung*, 205–207, 206.

33. Tirpitz to von Posadowsky-Wehner, January 28, 1907, with enclosure entitled "Untersuchung des Reichsmarineamtes," *Kriegsrüstung*, 218, 219–223. Compare Tirpitz to Bülow, April 20, 1907, enclosure "Über die Bedeutung des Seebeuterechts," *Grosse Politik*, XXIII, 361–367, 365.

34. von Halle, *Handelsmarine*, 57.

35. Tirpitz to Bülow, April 20, 1907, *Grosse Politik*, XXIII, 359; cf. Tirpitz to Bülow, February 28. 1907, *Grosse Politik*, XXIII, 350; Admiral Büchsel, "Denkschrift über die Kriegführung gegen England, 1905," BA-MA, RMA 3/4.

36. von Halle, "Die englische Seemachtpolitik."

37. Tirpitz to Bülow, February 28, 1907, *Grosse Politik*, XXIII, 352. Compare Büchsel to Tirpitz, March 27, 1907, and the enclosure entitled "Gutachten des Admiralstabes der Marine über die Beibehaltung des Seebeuterechtes (vom Standpunkt eine uns aufgezwungenen Krieges gegen E)," BA-MA, RM 5/998.

38. Vice Admiral Krosigk, "Denkschrift," April 1911, BA-MA, RM 5/5925.
39. Fiske, "Naval Power," 683–736, 702, 700, 703.
40. General Board to Secretary of Navy, June 20, 1906, NA, RG 80, SF 438.
41. Mahan to Theodore Roosevelt, ca. July 20, 1906, in Seager and Maguire, eds. *Letters and Papers*, 164–165. For more, see various essays in Mahan, *Some Neglected Aspects of War* and Mahan, *Interest of America in International Conditions*.
42. Coogan, *The End of Neutrality*, and Hobson, *Maritimer Imperialismus*, 63–82.
43. Tirpitz to Bülow, February 28, 1907, April 20, 1907 (twice), May 30, 1907, all in *Grosse Politik*, XXIII, 350–353, 359–372, 378–379; Tirpitz to Müller, April 23, 1907, BA-MA, RM 2/1760; Büchsel to Tirpitz, March 27, 1907, and Tirpitz to Büchsel, April 23, 1907, both in RM 5/998; Imperial Naval Office, "Punktuation, dem Herrn Reichskanzler beim Vortrage am 24. May 1907 überlassen" and "File Note," June 11, 1907, both in RM 5/1000. Tirpitz had already intervened in 1904 during the first round of preparations for the Second Hague Peace Conference. On this issue, cf. Dülffer, "Limitations on Naval Warfare."
44. Mahan to Theodore Roosevelt, December 27, 1904 and ca. July 20, 1906; Mahan to Elihu Root, April 20, 1906, *Letters and Papers*, III, 112–114, 157–159, 164–165; General Board to Secretary of Navy, June 20 and September 28, 1906, NA, RG 80, General Board, SF 438; Sperry to Assistant Secretary of State Robert Bacon, December 15, 1906, Sperry to Wainwright, December 20, 1906, Wainwright to Sperry, December 24, 1906, all in Sperry Papers, Library of Congress, Manuscript Division.
45. "Denkschrift über Seebeuterecht," March 1911, BA-MA, RM 3/4919; Stockton, "International Naval Conference" and "Address on the Codification."
46. The following analysis of the US positions is based upon memoranda and communications in (1) NA, RG 80, General Board, SF 438, (2) Sperry Papers, Subject File "Hague Conference," Library of Congress, and (3) Naval War College Archive, RG 8, SF XLAI.
47. General Board to Secretary of the Navy, June 20, 1906, NA, RG 80, General Board, SF 438.
48. Coogan, *The End of Neutrality*, 113–117, shows how US insistence almost prevented an agreement at the conference after the Germans and British were able to find common ground.
49. Sperry, Report, August 21, 1908, Sperry Papers, Library of Congress.
50. My subsequent analysis draws on a series of memoranda and communications in BA-MA, RM 3/3897, RM 3/4919, RM 5/1001, RM 2/1760, RM 3/4919. In addition, I draw on the correspondence of the naval delegates during the two conferences, in RM 5/999–1000 (Hague); *Grosse Politik*, XXIII, 382–397 (Hague); RM 2/1760, RM 3/4919, and RM 5/1002 (all London).
51. "Instruktion für die Deutsche Delegation zur Londoner Seekriegsrecht-Konferenz," BA-MA, RM 3/4919.
52. Tirpitz to Siegel, June 27, 1907; BA-MA, RM 5/1000.
53. For the term "illusory," see "Aufstellung über Positionen der Marine und anderer Ressorts bezüglich der im Schreiben des englischen Botschafters vom März 1908 aufgeführten seekriegsrechtlichen Fragen, wie sie in den Vorverhandlungen zur II. Haager

Konferenz festgesetzt wurden," BA-MA, RM 3/3897; and Schmidt, "Denkschrift über die Vorverhandlungen zur Londoner Konferenz," June 3, 1908, RM 3/4919.

54. It was for all those reasons that the Germans were most happy with the London Declaration, which, in their view, reflected German military interests. See "Ergebnisse der in London vom 4. Dezember 1908 bis zum 26. February 1909 abgehaltenen Seekriegsrechts-Konferenz," BA-MA, RM 2/1760; Kriege to Bülow, April 20, 1909, BA-MA, RM 3/4919; Tirpitz to Bethmann-Hollweg, March 20, 1909, BA-MA, RM 5/1002.

55. Admiralty Staff, memorandum, July 1906, BA-MA, RM 5/998.

56. Stockton, "Would Immunity from Capture?," 930–943, referred to the official US attachment to private immunity that he did not share as "altruistic."

57. Stockton, "International Naval Conference," 614, and "Address on the Codification," 61, 80.

58. Widenmann to Tirpitz, November 2, 1910, Aiv, "Denkschrift über England und die Londoner Erklärung," December 21, 1910, both in BA-MA, RM 3/3898. Strikingly, Widenmann, a rabid Anglophobe, served as the naval attaché in London at that time.

59. This position was taken in the official instructions for the German delegation at the London Naval Conference; BA-MA, RM 5/999 (enclosed in Imperial Naval Office to Admiralty Staff, July 12, 1907).

60. On the making of the German legal code governing commerce destruction, the *Prisenordnung*, which Wilhelm II approved in September 1909, see the materials in BA-MA, RM 5/1004–1005. For the incorporation of the London Declaration into the US naval war code, see Naval War College to Secretary of the Navy, January 31, 1912, and November 29, 1912; NA, RG 80, General Board, SF 438, and NWCA, RG 8SF XLAI.

61. Operations order, July 30, 1914; in Tirpitz, *Deutsche Ohnmachtspolitik*, 35–36.

62. Spindler, "Der Handelskrieg mit U-Booten," 153–154.

63. General Board to Secretary of Navy, March 24, 1915, NA, RG 80, General Board, SF 438.

64. Schmitt, *Staat, Großraum, Nomos*, 401–430; Schmitt, *Der Nomos der Erde*.

65. My reading of the strictures of maritime law follows Coogan, *The End of Neutrality*, Hobson, *Maritimer Imperialismus*, and Hankel, *Die Leipziger Prozesse*.

66. Bönker, "Ein 'German Way of War'?"

67. Offer, *The First World War*, 215–317; Lambert, "Great Britain and Maritime Law." Lambert, *Planning Armageddon* was published after this essay was written.

FIFTEEN

The Rhineland Controversy and Weimar Postcolonialism

BRETT M. VAN HOESEN

In 1919, as a result of defeat in World War I and ratification of the Treaty of Versailles, Germany relinquished military control over the Rhineland territory.[1] In accordance with the treaty's provisions, Germany's western territory was significantly reduced: Alsace and Lorraine were returned to France, small northern territories were ceded to Belgium, and the Saar Basin was put under international control, its future national affiliation to be determined by plebiscite. The remainder of the Rhineland was to remain under Allied control for fifteen years. Although sections of this considerable region spanning the length of the Rhine had long been under dispute between France and Prussia/Germany, by the start of the 1920s this territory had become a border of great domestic concern and then international scandal authored and perpetuated by the politics of race.[2] In 1920, at the behest of Georges Clemenceau, the French occupational presence along the Rhine was augmented by the addition of colonial troops. This decision, which prompted immediate protests in Germany, inextricably linked the territory with the propagandistic catchphrase "*die schwarze Schmach*" (the black disgrace). Germans retaliated by launching an equally racist propaganda campaign—singling out troops from North Africa, particularly soldiers from Senegal, as violent rapists and sources of moral corruption. While criminal acts did occur on the part of French forces, there were numerous exaggerations and attempts to spur international attention on behalf of German national and local governments as well as a host of private interest groups.

The Rhineland controversy has long served as a ripe arena for examining discourses of nationalism, interwar period diplomacy, Allied postwar military tactics, early-twentieth-century racial theories, and German strategies to revise the Treaty of Versailles. Although significant scholarship on the topic exists, interest in revisiting its historical ramifications has grown since the start of the millennium.[3] This is in large part due to the burgeoning fields of Afro-German studies and black European studies, as well as topics related to German colonialism and imperialism. Recent scholarship has focused upon constructions of gender, race, and nationalism, with additional focus on issues of class. Iris Wigger has argued that the Rhineland controversy should be discussed within the conceptual framework of "interlinked discriminations" associated with racial, sexual, class, and national stereotypes.[4] Other publications have explicitly attended to the fate of children, previously treated as *passive victims*, born of relationships between German women and African soldiers. Scholars, among them Tina M. Campt, have used the children's stories and personal narratives to restore to them a sense of historical agency by arguing that their presence has challenged perceptions of racial difference in twentieth-century Germany.[5] Still newer research continues to push in this direction. The work of Julia Roos focuses on the topic of Rhenish women's rights and so-called *Besatzungskinder*, with particular care for topics involving social welfare, advocacy issues, and paternity suits.[6] Additionally, Lisa Todd has examined the culture of military and civilian interactions with a focus on the perceived escalation of "sexual crises" that occurred in occupied territories during and after the war.[7]

In line with previous scholarship, this essay situates the Rhineland controversy within the larger discourse of German imperialism, with pointed attention to the lingering legacy of colonial issues as they affected postwar attitudes and discourses.[8] International scrutiny of Germany's failures as a colonial power was an important factor in determining the country's postwar standing, including the delay of its entry into the League of Nations until September 10, 1926, and prohibiting Germany from possessing colonial properties. This context shaped German public response to the occupation of the Rhineland and fueled the alarmist rhetoric against the presence of French colonial troops on German soil.

In this chapter I argue that the Rhineland controversy shaped the ambivalently postcolonial character of the Weimar Republic, which had lost its overseas colonies but not the racist and imperialist sensibilities that had emerged alongside them. I consider how we study the Rhineland controversy as a historical event. Most scholarship devoted to the topic has regarded it as relatively short lived (1919–1923), culminating in the Ruhr crisis. While this emphasis is not inaccurate, the narrow time span overlooks the presence of French colonial troops along the Rhine even as late as 1929, and it ignores the fact that the official evacuation of all three Allied zones did not occur until 1930.

Additionally, a limited historical view of the Rhineland controversy underestimates its enduring influence on the popular press and its impact on shaping public opinion beyond 1923. A broader history of the controversy should include the satirical cartoons, illustrations, stories, and poems featured in the Munich-based journal *Simplicissimus*, the Berlin-based publications *Kladderadatsch* and *Berliner Illustrirte Zeitung* (BIZ), and the French periodical *Le Rire*. In 1924, for example, *Kladderadatsch* published a book-format compilation of satirical imagery and text, titled *Rhein und Ruhr*, related to the conflict. These visual tropes of Rhineland propaganda expand our understanding of how visual campaigns targeted other perceived threats, including Bolshevism. While much of the scholarship devoted to the Rhineland controversy rightly identifies two prevailing tropes—the dark-skinned colonial soldier, often morphed into a menacing simian beast, and the passive, victimized, white female—aspects of this recognizable visual language were mirrored in posters and illustrated novella devoted to protesting the reduction of German borderlands to the east.

Lastly, this chapter widens the scope of imagery linked to the Rhineland crisis. Few studies have evaluated stances that counter the racist protest propaganda. At least in a few instances, these crude stereotypes solicited public condemnation and critique. One such case involves the work of the Berlin-based artist Hannah Höch. A member of the avant-garde movement Berlin Dada and a frequent commentator on mass media representations of the New Woman, Höch employed photomontage during the 1920s to critically engage the conservative tenets of political factions and religious leagues involved in framing the Rhineland occupation as a "crisis." Höch's photomontages, particularly their relationship to satirical cartoons from the popular press, embody the lasting impact of the caustic, visual nature of protest propaganda. In a concluding section, I explore how Höch's early criticisms of German racism linked to its colonial legacy have had a lasting effect on avant-garde art in contemporary German society, particularly in the realm of postcolonial visual culture.

WEIMAR POSTCOLONIALISM

France does not stop at the Mediterranean, nor at the Sahara; . . . she extends to the Congo . . . she constitutes an empire vaster than Europe. —CHARLES MANGIN

The bravado of French general Charles Mangin's characterization of France's military might, which at the time included soldiers from Algeria, Morocco,

Tunisia, Senegal, Sudan, Madagascar, Guadeloupe, Martinique, Réunion, and regions of Indochina, spurred the notion that France's occupation of the Rhineland symbolized a *colonial act*. This, coupled with the loss of Germany's former overseas territories, prompted widespread fears of reverse colonization on the part of an aggressive and vengeful French empire. Despite the cultural and racial diversity of the French colonial troops, who numbered roughly 45,000 during the climax of occupation years, German propaganda purposefully denied the geographical breadth of French control and reduced the colonial soldiers to racialized stereotypes, using them as a scapegoat for postwar tensions.[9] As Marcia Klotz has rightly noted, treating the Weimar Republic as a postcolonial state does not correspond with the usual implications of the term. Postcoloniality generally implies a preceding era during which the entity in question was subject to colonial rule. Klotz's solution is to pose a wider definition for the term, to think of the postcolonial as "a historical perspective that sheds light on a given historical topic by orienting it toward its colonial past."[10] Jared Poley speaks instead of "decolonization" in Weimar Germany in order to measure the popular perceptions and deep sense of imperial loss.[11] While this approach is convincing in many respects, it is also problematic, since it means grafting onto the Weimar era a model of decolonization that dates from the 1950s and 1960s. While comparative analyses of other colonial empires is certainly relevant to the study of German colonialism, the specificity of the Weimar postcolonial moment, followed quickly by a resurgence of colonial revisionism and imperial expansion in eastern Europe after 1933, demands special attention. This is particularly the case given that the loss of colonies accompanied Germany's own loss of domestic territory, creating a deeply felt sense of vulnerability and endangerment, a sense that was heightened by the Rhineland occupation and ensuing racial controversy.[12]

The Berlin Conference of 1884–1885, which announced Germany's official presence as a colonial power in Africa, was seen as a major accomplishment of Bismarckian foreign policy. By the beginning of the next century, Germany's success with its colonial territories quickly waned. Throughout the duration of World War I, Germany gradually lost control of its colonies aside from the occupation of German East Africa. Following the war, in conjunction with Paragraph 119 of the Treaty of Versailles and as a component of the League of Nations, the Allies held Germany's former colonial territories as mandates. Great Britain assumed control of German East Africa (Tanganyika), one-sixth of Cameroon, and one-third of Togoland and the South Seas island of Nauru. Australia took control of the Bismarck Archipelago and Kaiser Wilhelmsland. New Zealand became the mandatory of Samoa. The British Union of South

Africa assumed control of German Southwest Africa. France held the mandate for two-thirds of Togoland and five-sixths of Cameroon. Belgium took control of the portion of German East Africa known as Ruanda-Urundi. Japan returned Kiaochow to China and retained the mandate for the Caroline, Mariana, and Marshall Islands.[13] By the end of the war, apathy toward the colonies pervaded contemporary politics, only to be reinforced by a looming economic crisis at home. The Versailles Treaty solidified a correlation between the loss of Germany's colonies and a reduction of its domestic extent. While none of Germany's overseas territories had been economically successful, in March of 1920, just months after ratifying the Versailles Treaty, 414 deputies in the Reichstag voted to renounce the cessation of German colonies. Included in this group of 414 were SPD members who had initially objected to German colonial enterprises. Only the KPD and a majority of the USPD delegates rejected calls to restore the colonies as a means of regaining German economic influence. Despite left-wing dissent, anger over the loss of the colonies among Weimar liberals and conservatives alike sent a clear signal. The Versailles Treaty inadvertently served as a catalyst for renewing German interest in its former colonies. The so-called colonial revisionism of the Weimar era, according to Wolfe Schmokel, indicated "that Germany did not regard the colonial settlement of Versailles as final."[14]

In conjunction with the Reichstag's reevaluation of Paragraph 119, there was a considerable response from former colonial administrators and lobbyists, who became the dominant force in the colonial revisionist campaign. This sentiment manifested itself in a number of venues, including published books, pamphlets, periodicals, calendars, novels, advertisements, theatrical events, school programs, and exhibitions. In 1926 the German Colonial Society still had 250 branches throughout Germany with a total of 30,000 members.[15] Mary E. Townsend, writing in 1928, reported on an active "contemporary colonial movement in Germany" that extended far beyond the framework of colonial associations, "telling the Germans more about their former colonies than they ever knew when those lands were German soil."[16] She noted that magazines such as *Koloniale Rundschau* and *Der Kolonial-Deutsche*, both exclusively devoted to pro-colonial interests, "have a wide circulation although Germany owns no colonies."[17] Townsend also chronicled the appearance of educational venues devoted to colonial studies; they ranged from university programs at Hamburg's Colonial Institute to "colonial weeks" hosted by a number of German cities.

The colonial revisionist movement thus gave a distinctively ambivalent feel to the early years of Weimar postcolonialism. While the colonies may have been lost, the desire for reclaiming them remained strong in many social circles. The movement helped to promote a surprisingly healthy publishing market for books devoted to a range of colonial histories and topics, including topographical and botanical studies set in former colonial locales. Although informative and often scientifically rigorous, these books commemorated a bygone age. Even popular journals such as *Münchner Illustrierte Presse* and BIZ featured photographs and advertisements that played to tropes of colonial fantasies.[18] Collectively, they legitimized, to varying degrees, Germany's quest to regain access to its former colonial territories and kept the spirit of imperial and racial conquest alive.

VISUALIZING THE ENEMY

Given that the Rhineland occupation was perceived by German right-wing revisionists as a threat to future plans for an expanded German *Lebensraum*, it is worth stressing that the same imperial powers that administered its former colonies as League of Nations mandates also controlled regions along the Rhine. The growth of western European imperial power after Versailles heightened German anxieties about its postwar security. The deployment of colonial troops increased fears of German victimization, reinforcing its lack of diplomatic power and restricted sovereignty. Unsurprisingly, this climate fueled a search to define the "enemy" in scandalous fashion, developing a potent propagandistic language to counter the imperial arrogance of the Allied powers—of France, in particular.[19] If Germany's western border was in dispute, its eastern border with Poland was also perceived to be at risk. There the threat was from advancing Bolshevism, a threat that also assumed an equally impressive visual representation. Together, these border conflicts promoted an interrelated visual language of monstrous threats from the east as well as the west; both conflict zones were well represented in the alarmist propaganda posters and other visual materials published in the 1920s.

The mobilizing of race during the Rhineland controversy had its roots in similar propaganda efforts launched during World War I. German anthropologists, according to Andrew D. Evans, were excited by the regional diversity of human specimens generated within the first six months of combat. The presence of thousands of soldiers in prisoner of war camps provided an unprecedented opportunity for scientists to study "non-Europeans on European soil."[20] In the following years, the popular press echoed this fascination by publishing photographs and illustrations of many different nationalities of soldiers made distinguishable by their facial features, body types, military gear, and even their style of marching. Defining national identity was inextricably linked to studying racial difference. While scientific and pseudoscientific philosophies informed popular concepts of race, they were not completely responsible for formulating and perpetuating cultural constructions of *whiteness* and *blackness*. Sander Gilman has convincingly argued that German "models for understanding blackness" were borrowed from other cultural contexts dating as far back as the Middle Ages.[21]

Even before the war, public awareness of and concern over the French use of dark-skinned colonial soldiers in the ranks of their military were pronounced in Germany. Prior to the internment of North African and Senegalese soldiers in Europe, conservative officials demonized French colonial troops as "threatening savages."[22] By 1917 the German Colonial Office had complained that the French use of *la force noire* was endangering European civilization by using the "colored world" against the fatherland.[23] The cover of BIZ from April 8, 1917, reinforced this assessment (see figure 15.1). It depicts a stereotypical interaction between a French colonial soldier and a group of presumably small-town German women and children. The imagery conflates a number of symbols for blackness—including the soldier's caricatured facial features, which referenced the visual vocabulary of minstrel shows—a practice that began well before the US Civil War.[24] The unsettling greeting between the "französischen *Kulturträger*" and the young white child both reinforced prewar stereotypes and prefigured how these soldiers would become potent symbols of German resentment toward French military policies after 1920.

Creating a consistent image of *der Feind* as a black soldier who invaded the gendered and generational zones of women and children did not deter other nuanced versions of this "menace." In a German propaganda poster from the teens reproduced in the March 1919 issue of *Das Plakat* (see figure 15.2), a caricatured French colonial soldier infiltrates the airwaves—purportedly tuning into German communications.[25] The strident message to the military and the masses is that no space is safe from invasion. Images such as these reinforced the idea that while in theory the role of the French colonial troops was the same as that of any other group of Allied soldiers, in reality they functioned as a "subtle kind of psychological warfare" characteristic of the lingering, potent tensions of the postwar years.[26] Despite the fact that the war had ended, the mentality of defensive combat persisted on both sides.[27] If Clemenceau employed the colonial troops in part to punish Germans for crimes inflicted on French civilians during the war, Germans reacted by engineering regional, national, and international protests to the occupation as early as spring 1919, regarding their deployment as a "crisis" and threat to international peace.

FIGURE 15.1 · Cover image, *Berliner Illustrirte Zeitung*, April 8, 1917. Caption reads: "Der erste Gruß aus 'Zivilisation': Ankunft der erstenfranzösischen 'Kulturträger' in den von uns aufgegebenen Ortschaften."

FIGURE 15.2 · German World War I poster, illustrator unknown, featured in the journal *Das Plakat*, March 1919.

The German protest propaganda permeated newspapers, journals, pamphlets, films, and posters, all of which reinforced the stereotype of the colonial soldiers as savages and intentionally raised fears of race mixing. By 1920, the visual language of the propaganda became even more aggressive and grotesque, as the soldiers morphed into menacing gorillas or monsters who carried off innocent female victims with the intention of rape and other violent crimes. The May 1920 cover of *Simplicissimus* (see figure 15.3) illustrates this shift. The heading and subtitle accompanying the illustration read "Black Occupation: A Disgrace for the White Race—but it is happening in Germany." While the sardonic tone may have been intended to poke fun at the tactics of the Rhineland protest propaganda, it simultaneously reinforced the racist language in widespread use. Readers would also have understood how the imagery subtly critiqued French artistic production. The cover illustration was directly based upon a nineteenth-century sculpture titled *Gorilla Kidnapping a Woman*, by the French artist Emmanuel Frémiet, that had won a gold medal at the Third International Art Exhibition held in Munich in 1888. Although considered a laudatory work in the late nineteenth century, Frémiet's depiction of a gorilla abducting a struggling woman was worthy of ridicule by the 1920s. Because Frémiet was French and the fantastical scenario corresponded with German fears over the alleged sexual proclivities of the colonial soldiers, its message would have been immediately discernible to the journal's readership.[28]

The trope of the gorilla as an invading menace was also used by German officials to visualize the threat of Bolshevism, with which the struggles associated with the diminished territories to the east and west were ultimately connected. While the prevailing symbolism of anti-Bolshevik leagues, at least during the teens, often illustrated the fear of communism as a haunting skeleton, it also assumed the guise of a giant hairy beast with claws and fangs by the later teens and twenties.[29] These paradigmatic visual representations were part of a literary phenomenon that originated in the form of illustrated book covers and eventually infiltrated poster designs.[30] As an allegory for death and destruction, Bolshevism signified to some yet another peril of border politics. German posters dating to as early as 1918 (see figure 15.4), replaced the skeleton with a monster bearing a notable resemblance to caricatured renditions of an enraged gorilla. A shared lineage between these two seemingly different representations of Bolshevism is sustained because the simian beast holds a dagger—a weapon consistently brandished by the skeleton. (The dagger was often depicted between the beast's clenched teeth.) Like the overt criticism characteristic of the textual component of the Rhineland protest propaganda, this poster exclaims that "Bolshevism brings war, unemployment, and famine."

FIGURE 15.3 · Cover image, *Simplicissimus*, May 21, 1920. Caption reads: "Black occupation: A disgrace for the white race—but it is happening in Germany."

As the Rhineland controversy continued, alterations to visual and linguistic tactics occurred, including instances conflating anti-Bolshevist and Rhineland imagery. Caricatures from *Simplicissimus* dating to February 1923 (see figure 15.5) captured the continued disdain for the French presence by exaggerating the violent offenses against morality committed by colonial troops. This particular example depicted a menacing gorilla bedecked in military medals, with a sword, gun holster, and dagger in its teeth—coded language for Bolshevism. The alleged damage incurred by the troops is represented by a graveyard littered with crosses. A banner enumerating the atrocities, "78

FIGURE 15.4 · German poster, illustrated by Julius Ussy Engelhard, 1918. "Bolshevism brings war, unemployment, and famine."

Killings from Murder and Manslaughter, 65 Assaults and Invasions, and 170 Moral Offenses," reiterates the extent of the damage. The accompanying title, "To the World's Conscience," implied that although the crimes had been committed by the French, the real onus of blame lay with the world community for allowing the occupation in the first place. The gorilla was a marker of Germany's defensiveness and paranoia about its postwar and postcolonial

FIGURE 15.5 · Caricature from *Simplicissimus*, February 5, 1923. Caption reads: "To the world's conscience: The world was outraged over fairy tales about hacked-off children's hands. But the truth fell on deaf ears."

status. Donna Haraway's analysis of the theoretical and ideological rationales behind the Western fascination with primate culture suggests that "[W]estern primatology has been about the construction of self from the raw material of the other, the appropriation of nature in the production of culture, the ripening of the human from the soil of the animal, the clarity of a white from the obscurity of color, the issue of man from the body of woman, the elaboration of gender from the resource of sex, the emergence of mind by the activation of body."[31]

In 1923 the occupation of the Rhineland reached a climactic point. The Ruhrgebiet, known for its coal and steel production, was targeted by the Allies to recoup unpaid reparations. Starting in early January, Allied forces entered the area. Germany's initial response was passive resistance. Trains full of coal bound for France were surreptitiously rerouted to German cities in unoccupied zones. When the French countered with military force, German workers went on strike.[32] The following months were characterized by extreme inflation that worsened Germany's postwar economic situation. In an attempt to improve the dire economic state of affairs, in summer 1923 the Reichstag proposed negotiated terms for reparations payments; they were summarily declined. German passiveness eventually began to shift to protests, and anti-French demonstrations were launched in many of the occupied cities. At the direction of Prime Minister Raymond Poincaré, the French reacted by ousting German officials from key urban centers and, with permission from the Rhineland Commission, appointed French replacements.[33]

During this period of heightened international diplomatic tension, the African colonial soldier remained a potent scapegoat in the German media. Satirical venues, including the Berlin-based *Kladderadatsch*, provided considerable coverage of the Ruhr occupation. Founded in 1848, the journal was older than *Simplicissimus* and took a slightly different angle. According to Ann Taylor Allen, "*Kladderadatsch* focused on politics in the narrow sense of governmental activity, while *Simplicissimus* explored political attitudes and the social structure which underlay them."[34] As mentioned earlier, in 1924 *Kladderadatsch* published *Rhein und Ruhr*, a collection of satirical caricatures, articles, poems, and songs devoted to the crisis. The compilation spanned several phases of the conflict, chronicling the various ways that the Berlin publication had commented on its associated economic, cultural, political and racial controversies. The cover reinforced the racialized discourses intrinsic to the protest propaganda campaigns. Looming over a cityscape dominated by factory buildings and smokestacks, an exaggerated and monstrous head framed by a halo of bayonets poses a grotesque threat (see figure 15.6). With enlarged pink lips paired with its dark-skin tone and its open mouth showing bared teeth, the figure fused stereotypical representations of the French colonial soldier with the gorilla imagery. The cover strategically employed shock tactics, perhaps as a means to buoy drooping sales of the journal. Since the end of the war, *Kladderadatsch*'s popularity and readership levels were challenged by the dramatic influx of Weimar *illustrierte*. By 1923, Hoffmann Verlag, the original owner, was

FIGURE 15.6 · Cover of the *Kladderadatsch* album *Rhein und Ruhr*. Munich, 1924.

forced to sell it to the Stinnes Company, a move that eventually shifted the journal's political orientation toward more sympathy with the right. Ironically, the marketability of the 1924 *Rhein und Ruhr* verified the discursive dominance of the Rhineland controversy in the public sphere well beyond 1923.

The momentum generated by the Rhineland protest propaganda slowed following the Locarno Treaty in 1925. France agreed to demilitarize the northern territories of the Rhineland and to significantly reduce the number of troops stationed in the south. The number of African soldiers would be significantly reduced. Still, several thousand colonial soldiers were present in parts of the Rhineland for several additional years until their departure in 1930.[35]

CRITIQUING THE PROTEST PROPAGANDA: THE PHOTOMONTAGES OF HANNAH HÖCH

Rhineland controversy scholarship has focused on the politics and ramifications of Germany's aggressive and racist propaganda campaign; the wide range of media included Reichstag speeches, newspaper articles, pamphlets, posters, postcards, and novels. Missing from this body of scholarship, however, is the prospect of counterprotests critiquing the tenets and tactics of the propaganda. Given the political divide in the Reichstag over Germany's neocolonial aspirations, it is not surprising that members of the KPD and USPD denounced aspects of Germany's exaggerated response to the Rhineland occupation. In May 1920 the USPD delegate Luise Zietz addressed the Reichstag. She protested the racist language used against the French colonial population and the disregard for women's issues implied in the conflict. Zietz pointed out that while the government was quick to pinpoint examples of rapes and sexual brutalities on the part of colonial soldiers along the Rhine, it had not directed corresponding outrage at similar acts committed against German women immediately after the war by the Freikorps or against women in the former colonies. Her speech condemned militarism and proclaimed that German colonial politics was a "history of atrocities and oppression of colored peoples by the Germans."[36]

The satirical commentaries on the situation in *Simplicissimus* and *Kladderadatsch* reinforced damaging stereotypes that perpetuated discrimination against the colonial troops and women. A potential arena for counterprotests might have been the realm of the historical avant-garde; given the highly visual nature of the propaganda campaigns, particularly intellectual communities involved with the visual arts. One group poised to critique the situation was Berlin Dada, whose caustic messages in both textual and visual formats left few subjects beyond reproach. The cultural coordinates of what grew to be the Rhineland controversy not only entailed competition between power-hungry European nations but also involved other political factions, religious organizations, and special interest groups. Berlin Dada encompassed scenarios covering a range of political and ideological terrains that were self-consciously declared "cultural crises." In fact, this characterization was a signal to the politically savvy Dadaists that a topic was worth probing, and the Rhineland controversy conformed to a running list of categories consistently devoured by members of the group. These included political conservatism, governmental hypocrisy, militarism, financial catastrophes, religious zealotry, and the scapegoating of the socially disadvantaged by the ruling elite. While photomontages by Raoul Hausmann, Johannes Baader, and John Heartfield, as well as illustrations and published volumes of drawings by George Grosz, vehemently attacked various postwar institutions, their work is bereft of any direct reference to the Rhineland controversy.[37] This void in Dada reaction, especially given the ubiquity of the so-called Black Horror in the press, has one exception, however, in the photomontages of Hannah Höch. Most of these works postdate the official end of Dada in 1923 and the climax of the Ruhr conflict in the same year. Höch commented upon the "crisis" along the Rhine, specifically in regard to constructions of race and gender associated with aspects of Weimar postcolonial politics.

One of Höch's earliest montages (1922) critiquing the visual and linguistic tropes of the Rhineland propaganda is titled *Dada Tanz* (see figure 15.7). While this work has been published in several texts devoted to the history of photomontage, it has rarely been analyzed, presumably due to its seemingly cryptic content in terms of both the imagery and the textual component that runs along the bottom of the collage. The montage plays with recognizable themes of Höch's Weimar vocabulary, including her fascination with dancers and hybrid characters. The scene, set against a backdrop of the French tricolor, stages a dance between two figures. The figure on the far right is a female; her white, mannequin-like face, plumed hat, and *altmodisch* gown ridicule the drama of a society dance, perhaps a waltz. Her partner is a composite: a statuesque female physique with the head, torso, and genitals of a black man. His pronounced blackness overtly contrasts with her artificial whiteness; they are an uncanny pair. The textual component of the work further compounds the elusiveness of this visual message. It reads, "Der Höllenüberschuß fällt in die Kasse des Pfarrers Klatt für unschuldige Berbrecherkinder"; roughly, this translates as "the profit falls into the cashbox of Minister Klatt for the innocent children of criminals." The work is admittedly ambiguous, but the pairing of these two characters and the connotations of exploitation referred to by the text subtly critique the mechanisms of the Rhineland propaganda. These characters sardonically perform the role of two archetypes associated with the conflict: the "good, German woman—a beacon of society" and the "sexualized, black male savage." Their taboo dance plays to the day's inflammatory news stories of willing fraternization between German women and black soldiers. Höch's work appears to critique the hypocrisies inherent in the Rhineland con-

FIGURE 15.7 · Hannah Höch, *Dada Tanz* (Dada Dance), 1922. Photomontage, 12 5/8" × 9 1/16." Collection of Arturo Schwarz, Milan. ©2013 Artists Rights Society (ARS), New York / VG Bild-Kunst, Bonn.

flict and pointedly exploits the ridiculousness of scripting fixed personae for Rhenish women and the occupying forces.

A number of additional montages provided by Höch also engage the visual language of the Rhineland propaganda. In *Die Kokette II* from 1925 (see figure 15.8), Höch diffuses the terror of the enraged gorilla absconding with a white woman (discussed earlier in illustrations from *Simplicissimus*). As the title of the photomontage implies, a flirtatious female figure, represented by a blond-haired *Mädchen*, shares a playful gaze with her simian companion. The two are further unified by attire: she wears the top from a white pantsuit, he dons the bottom. Far from an intimidating scene, the staged playfulness ruptures the hyperbole normally associated with this pairing. Höch's critique of

FIGURE 15.8 · Hannah Höch, *Die Kokette II* (The Coquette II), c. 1925. Photomontage, 13 cm × 13.4 cm. Collection of Marianne Carlberg. ©2013 Artists Rights Society (ARS), New York / VG Bild-Kunst, Bonn.

the role of the New Woman as a pawn of the Rhineland propaganda is implied; rather than a sophisticated, independent female of the twenties, she is just a child. Similarly, if we read the gorilla as a symbol of the colonial soldier, he too is represented as inferior, reduced to a racist stereotype. Other works by Höch from this period, such as *Entführung* (*Abduction*), dated to 1925 (see figure 15.9), also refer to fantastical tales of terrorized German women carried off by hordes of French colonial subjects. To compose this image, Höch clipped a photograph of an African sculpture, probably from the former Congo, from a 1924 issue of *Berliner Illustrirte Zeitung*.[38] The title attributed to the sculpture, *Raub der Jungfrauen* (Abduction of the Virgins), is an obvious product of imposed primitivism (European collectors routinely misinterpreted objects of material culture from other parts of the world). Höch manipulates the reading of this particular sculpture by adding a prototypical head of a Weimar

FIGURE 15.9 · Hannah Höch, *Entführung* (Abduction), from the series *Aus einem ethnographischen Museum*, 1925. Photomontage, 8 3/8" × 8 11/16." Collection Staatliche Museen zu Berlin, Kupferstichkabinett. ©2013 Artists Rights Society (ARS), New York / VG Bild-Kunst, Bonn.

New Woman (marked by her *bubikopf*—her signature bobbed hairstyle) to the torso of one of the two putative virgins. Facing backwards and appearing to vocalize an unsuccessful protest, the New Woman and another female are carried off on horseback by two male warriors. Given the loaded connotation of "abduction," particularly when paired with stereotypes of African men handling German women, Höch's montage mimics yet another trope of the Rhineland propaganda. In this case, she plays to German paranoia concerning African male virility and mocks the propaganda's propensity to characterize the female subject as a helpless victim.

If the three preceding montages employ a playful tone, other works by Höch refer to the seriousness of German concerns about race mixing. In the realm of visual media, there was a long-standing precedent for scornful views of interracial relationships. These convictions strengthened when Germany solidified colonial territories in Africa, the South Seas, and China. In addition to formal administrative policies that frowned upon and in some cases prohibited interracial liaisons, a host of popular media sources, including postcards and cartoons, forewarned the masses against such interactions. As Fatima el-Tayib has shown, German postcards as far back as 1895 illustrated the way in which romantic trysts between German women and black men were openly mocked.[39]

While German propaganda campaigns implored the international community to help oust the French colonial soldiers from the Rhineland, they also spoke to the German populace, to women in particular, to deter consensual fraternization. One strategy involved embellishing reports of soldier maladies. According to German government statistics from the height of the conflict, "100 percent of the native troops were afflicted with syphilis, skin disease, and parasitic worms."[40] They were also allegedly infected with malaria, dysentery, consumption, leprosy, venereal diseases, trachoma, typhus, plague, and cholera. As if this wasn't enough, the colonial troops "were also held responsible for five years of influenza in Europe."[41] Höch appears to reference the long-established societal taboo of interracial amour with her 1925 work *Liebe im Busch* (Love in the Bush; see figure 15.10). This scene depicts two fragmented figures nestled in a stylized wilderness. One dons the visage of a Weimar New Woman, the other the head of a young African boy; their disjointed arms and hands orchestrate a mock embrace. Seen in light of the Rhineland controversy, Höch's imagery immediately disarms the protest propaganda's authorization of the colonial soldiers as menacing, diseased threats. In addition, she again inserts the politicized imagery of the New Woman, a contradictory mass media symbol but one that nonetheless represented women's political and sexual liberation. As with the image of *Die Kokette II*, there is an additional layer of critique imbedded in this work.

While German press coverage of the Rhineland occupation ensured that French colonial troops became synonymous with virulent monsters, another prevailing method of disempowering colonial subjects was to relegate them to the realm of infantilism. Similarly, the New Woman was often parodied in the press. While she purportedly touted a range of newly found freedoms, she was often ridiculed for her confusion about her place with regard to established societal codes ranging from appearance to sexual preferences. In this sense Höch's amorous pair self-consciously functions as a double threat to the political and military establishment. Additionally, her montage, by virtue of its title, also exceeds the discursive boundaries of the Rhineland crisis and per-

FIGURE 15.10 · Hannah Höch, *Liebe im Busch* (Love in the Bush), 1925. Photomontage, 9" × 8 1/2". Modern Art Museum, Fort Worth, Texas. The Benjamin J. Tiller Memorial Trust. ©2013 Artists Rights Society (ARS), New York / VG Bild-Kunst, Bonn.

haps wittingly references sexual relationships between German men and native women at colonial outposts—*im Busch*. As Lora Wildenthal observed, there were specific gendered zones intrinsic to colonial-era discourses concerning interracial relationships and race mixing.[42] Höch's work subtly insinuates the underlying hypocrisy of German colonial policies touted by both male administrators and women's leagues, particularly in relationship to the inflammatory language used to counter the Rhineland occupation.

If sexual relations between black men and white women were a concern integral to the Rhineland controversy, then the potential by-product of these liaisons—offspring—also drew critical attention. Roughly six to eight hundred children were born as a result of consensual and nonconsensual relations between German women and colonial soldiers. While African colonial troops bore the brunt of overt German racism, it was their children who became potent symbols of shame associated with the conflict. As Campt, Grosse, and Lemke-Muniz de Faria have noted, "these black German children were seen to constitute an even greater threat than their fathers."[43] Not only a moral menace in terms of illegitimacy, as German citizens they posed a longer-term threat to national identity.[44] These children were subjected to compulsory sterilization as a result of the National Socialists' *Rassenpolitik* and sterilization law (1933).[45] The eugenic anxieties fueling such medical actions are indirectly referenced in Höch's 1924 montage *Mischling* (Half-Caste; see figure 15.11), which projects the outcome of sexual relationships between white German women and black colonial soldiers. On one level, Höch's photomontage is an acritical experiment with race mixing facilitated by the technology of photomontage. Indeed, in the Weimar popular press there was a healthy pictorial fascination with interchanging facial features; that is, dividing the visage into multiple registers and mixing the eyes, nose, and mouth of people of different racial backgrounds. A publication such as BIZ might seek to aestheticize these fragmented wholes, but this sort of collage practice did not counter the derogatory implications of "othering." Höch's montage certainly embraces an experimental visual sensibility by fusing a photograph of a female from the South Seas with the red lips of a Weimar New Woman. At the same time, her work may also be seen as a critique of the politics of hybridity, a topic directly related to the Rhineland controversy as well as to contemporaneous studies in racial hygiene and eugenics.[46]

CONCLUSION

This chapter has argued that the events associated with the Rhineland controversy were significantly shaped by tactics of visual communication and that the legacy of German colonialism and its impact on the Weimar Republic can be traced through the rich visual culture of the era. Visual images, like other forms of cultural production, can be *reactive* and *proactive*; while they can *reflect* public sentiment, they also can *generate* public discourse. The powerful visual tropes of the Rhineland controversy propaganda inevitably connect with contemporary discussions concerning identity politics, social constructions of race, nationalism, globalization, and the interwoven histories of Europe and Africa. The 2007 exhibition *Global Feminisms*, organized by the Brooklyn Museum of Art, featured the work of the contemporary artist collective Mwangi Hutter. Complicating notions of identity and authenticity, Mwangi Hutter—composed of the married artists Ingrid Mwangi and Robert Hutter—embraces the concept of a *double-bodied artist* in order to explore

FIGURE 15.11 · Hannah Höch, *Mischling* (Half-Caste), 1924. Photomontage, 4 5/16" × 3 1/4". Collection Institut für Auslandsbeziehungen, Stuttgart. ©2013 Artists Rights Society (ARS), New York / VG Bild-Kunst, Bonn.

issues of race and cultural heritage as well as clichés about African and European identities. With a strategically fused biographical narrative, which includes a hybrid place of birth, Nairobi Ludwigshafen, the artists live and work in Germany and Kenya. *Don't call me Neger*, Mwangi Hutter's video installation and performance project from 2000, addresses deep-seated racism and stereotypes with roots in the propaganda of the Rhineland controversy. Showcasing nine different headshots with a single-channel video, Mwangi, whose face is obscured by her flowing dreadlocks, grunts, growls, and shouts, sardonically fulfilling and subversively exploiting presumptions about her "primal" nature as a woman of African heritage.

Other projects, such as *Static Drift* (see figure 15.12), a pair of large-scale

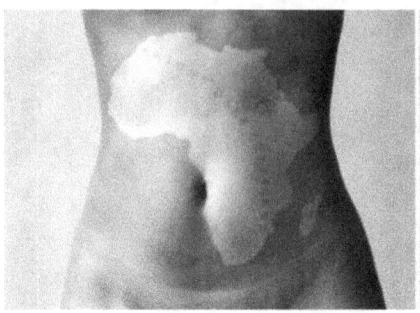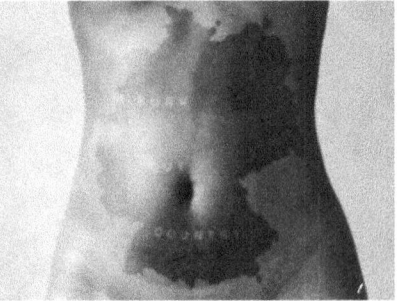

FIGURE 15.12 · Mwangi Hutter, *Static Drift*, 2001. Two chromogenic prints mounted on aluminum. Courtesy of the artist.

digital prints (2001), speak to the duality of Mwangi Hutter's heritage. Again using Mwangi's body to physically inscribe the politics of place, the photographs depict her torso altered by the addition of sun-exposed, stenciled silhouettes of Germany and Africa. With loaded symbolism of light and dark, white and black, the words "Burn Out Country" are read across the darkened map of Germany that symbolically contrasts with Mwangi's lighter skin tone. The reverse colorization is used for the image of Africa; its text is "Bright Dark Continent." This definitive postcolonial stance speaks to Mwangi Hutter's personal narrative, as well as to the sordid heritage of Germany's colonial past. Reversing and confronting the pejorative imagery of conflicts like the Rhineland controversy, Mwangi Hutter and other contemporary artists have the ability to effect social reform; their images become actions for historical intervention and positive change.

One of the most prominent images of German colonial history was referenced in the *Who Knows Tomorrow* exhibition, which ran in Berlin (June 4–September 26, 2010).[47] The sculptural installation *Scramble for Africa* (2003) by British-Nigerian artist Yinka Shonibare, MBE, confronted the legacy of the Berlin West Africa Conference. Installed in the choir loft of Berlin's neo-Gothic Friedrichswerdersche Kirche, Shonibare's jarring presentation of headless male figures wearing Victorian-era suits made from "African cloth" and seated around a table with an outlined map of Africa is the physical embodiment of an unthinkable act. The "story" of Africa, clearly too long and diverse to represent, is solidified into one "picture"—the image of a handful of men seated around a table, dividing a continent, forever changing world history. *Who Knows Tomorrow* is one of the first exhibitions in Germany of contemporary art by artists of African origin to address the history of German colonialism within the larger context of globalization. If museums during the imperial and Weimar period played an integral role in exhibiting the material cultures of colonialism, today many museums are actively involved in fostering transnational discourses that diffuse Eurocentric hegemony and confront controversial histories that continue to have an impact on the cultural and economic dimensions of our globalized world. While such approaches do not negate the wrongs associated with the racist visual rhetoric and human rights atrocities of the Rhineland controversy, they contribute to a world where postcolonial theoretical concerns are put into meaningful personal and political practice.

NOTES

The Charles Mangin epigraph is cited in Nelson, "The 'Black Horror on the Rhine,'" 613.

1. The research for this essay was supported in part by a Junior Faculty Research Grant from the University of Nevada, Reno. An earlier draft of this material, "Critiquing Visual Tropes of the Rhineland Controversy: The Intersection of Popular Press Caricature and Berlin Avant-Garde Photomontage during the Weimar Republic," was presented at the interdisciplinary conference *Transformations in Politics, Culture and Society*, held in Brussels, Belgium, December 6–8, 2002.

2. The purposefully alarmist tenor of the propaganda eventually spurred public outcry in Britain, Italy, Sweden, Norway, the United States, and even France. German-authored protest pamphlets reached as far as Argentina and Peru. The growing international hysteria over the situation eventually prompted the appointment of an investigatory body, the Rhineland High Commission.

3. Nelson, "'Black Horror on the Rhine,'" 606–627; Pommerin, *Sterilisierung der Rheinlandbastarde*; Marks, "Black Watch on the Rhine," 297–334; Lebzelter, "*Die Schwarze Schmach*," 37–58.

4. See Wigger, "*Black Shame*," 33–46. For a lengthier, more complete treatment of this topic, see Wigger, *Die "Schwarze Schmach am Rhein."*

5. See Campt, *Other Germans* and "Afro-German." For additional important sources related to this topic, see El-Tayeb, *Schwarze Deutsche*, and Grosse, *Kolonialismus*.

6. Roos, "Children of the Occupiers," "Women's Rights," and "Nationalism, Racism, and Propaganda." I am grateful to Julia Roos for allowing me to review both her conference paper and early draft of the last article.

7. Todd, "Beware of the Colored Menace" and "Transnational Intimacies?" (conference papers). I am grateful to Lisa Todd for allowing me to review these papers.

8. Campt, Grosse, and Lemke-Muniz de Faria, "Blacks, Germans," 205–229.

9. Nelson, "'Black Horror on the Rhine,'" 610–611. According to Nelson, in 1919, at the peak of the conflict, the French troops totaled 200,000 men. By the winter of 1920, after the treaty was officially in effect, these numbers were reduced to roughly 85,000. In terms of colonial soldiers Nelson notes, "the number of African troops [mainly Algerians, Moroccans and Tunisians] in these totals varied considerably with the season

(in the winters, because of their inability to resist cold, up to half of the 'colonials' were sent into bivouac in southern France), but it seems to have approached 42,000 men in the spring of 1920 and 45,000 in the spring of 1921. . . . Malagasy (Madagascar) regiments arrived on the Rhine at the beginning of April 1919, and the Senegalese came about a month later."

10. Klotz, "Weimar Republic," 135.

11. Poley, *Decolonization in Germany*. For other recent publications that term the post–World War I period the "era of decolonization," see Albrecht, "(Post-)Colonial Amnesia?," 187–196.

12. Baranowski, *Nazi Empire*, 113–115.

13. White, *Mandates*, and Townsend, "Contemporary Colonial Movement," 64–75.

14. Schmokel, *Dream of Empire*, 77.

15. Schmokel, *Dream of Empire*, 2.

16. Townsend, "Contemporary Colonial Movement," 65.

17. Townsend, "Contemporary Colonial Movement."

18. For further information, see my essay "Weimar Revisions," 197–219.

19. Nolan, *The Inverted Mirror*.

20. Evans, "Anthropology at War," 198–199.

21. Gilman, *On Blackness without Blacks*, xii.

22. Koller, "Enemy Images," 141–142. Koller's cross-cultural comparison reinforces the impact of the ongoing debate in France and Germany over use of an *armée noire* from as early as 1909. For an extended discussion, see Koller, "*Von Wilden aller Rassen niedergemetzlt*."

23. Nelson, "'Black Horror on the Rhine,'" 608.

24. Pieterse, *White on Black*.

25. The poster was featured in an essay by Hermine C. Scheutzinger, "Angelsächsischer und deutscher Chauvinismus in der politischen Bildreklame. *Das Plakat* functioned as a venue for poster collectors, designers, illustrators, typographers, and other publishing specialists.

26. Nelson, "'Black Horror on the Rhine,'" 613.

27. Nelson, "'Black Horror on the Rhine,'" 612

28. For a reproduction of Frémiet's sculpture, see Lewis, *Art for All?*, 9.

29. For examples of anti-Bolshevik posters, see Paret, Lewis, and Paret, *Persuasive Images*, 122–124.

30. Simmons, "Grimaces on the Walls," 29–30. Simmons draws a correlation between the imagery of book covers and posters. Although he does not note how representations of Bolshevism assumed simian features, he provides a fascinating, thorough account of other visual representations of Bolshevism—particularly the skeleton as a symbol of death and destruction.

31. Haraway, *Primate Visions*, 11.

32. Trachtenberg, *Reparation in World Politics*, 293.

33. Trachtenberg, *Reparation in World Politics*, 299. US and British positions on France's occupation were considerably unsupportive. The United States, for example,

withdrew its troops from the Rhineland at this time. The British remained diplomatically somewhere in the middle.

34. Allen, *Satire and Society in Wilhelmine Germany*, 13.

35. In 1927 they numbered roughly 2,000; in 1929 nearly 1,000 remained. While such numbers might seem insignificant, they nevertheless allowed the legacy of the occupation to live on in the minds of Germans living along the border territory, as well as those living in urban centers like Berlin and Hamburg that helped to fuel the initial propaganda campaigns.

36. Luise Zietz, Reichstag address, May 1920; cited in Lester, "Blacks in Germany," 115.

37. For instance, George Grosz's *In der Gesicht der Herrschenden Klasse*, 1921, and *Ecce Homo*, 1922, are surprisingly devoid of international political issues.

38. Maud Lavin and Maria Makela note that this photograph appeared in BIZ 33, no. 38 (September 21, 1924), 1095.

39. El-Tayeb, "Africa at Home," 269.

40. Marks, "Black Watch on the Rhine," 301.

41. Marks, "Black Watch on the Rhine."

42. See Wildenthal, *German Women for Empire*, 78–130.

43. Campt, Grosse, and Lemke-Muniz de Faria, "Blacks, Germans," 213.

44. Campt, *Other Germans*, 59–60.

45. Campt, *Other Germans*, 73. For further information about the sterilization policies that impacted Afro-German children, see Pommerin, *"Sterilisierung der Rheinlandbastarde."*

46. Ironically the Rhineland occupation deterred several German geneticists and eugenicists from participating in international meetings devoted to studies in contemporary eugenics. In 1923, German scientists invited to participate on the Permanent Committee on Eugenics claimed that they "would not sit on a committee with French and Belgian eugenicists as long as French and Belgian troops occupied the Ruhr." See Kühl, *The Nazi Connection*, 19.

47. See my essay on the exhibition *"Who Knows Tomorrow*—Berlin and Beyond."

SIXTEEN

Colonialism, Imperialism, National Socialism
How Imperial Was the Third Reich?

BIRTHE KUNDRUS

For many years, German colonialism was perceived as a marginal phenomenon.[1] Germany's rule as a colonial power was judged too late, too superficial, and too short lived to have made a profound impression.[2] But this view has come under pressure, as it ignores the essence of German colonialism in the long global era of imperialism; namely, its transient "real" imperial history and a much longer and more intensive history of imperial intentions. Germany was a latecomer to the race for empires and a country characterized by a dynamic constellation of expectations and frustrations. This is not to deny that there were enormous differences between Germany as a colonial power and countries with a long "real-imperial" past, such as Britain, France, and the Netherlands. Elucidating such dissimilarities (as well as similarities) is no doubt an instructive approach. But we must also be aware that fantasies, plans, and intentions are of importance for the lives and practices of human beings in the past (and present).

While the significance of colonialism for nineteenth- and twentieth-century German history has become increasingly apparent, the precise extent and nature of this impact remains a question for further research. German colonialism is currently the focus of debates about the *Kaiserreich* as well as National Socialism, two case studies of colonialism as a history of violence and brutal foreign rule. One discussion centers on whether the German occupation of eastern Europe in World War II can be described as "colonial";[3] a second asks whether the violent practices that characterized this occupation had their antecedents in formal German colonial rule in the period from 1884 to 1918.[4] A third line connects colonialism, imperialism, and National Socialism by showing that German imperialism set its sights not only on overseas territories—in Africa, Oceania, the Far East, the Near East, and South America—but also on the European continent.[5] In this vein, David Blackbourn recently examined the affective tension associated with eastern Europe as an element of a specific German colonial history.[6] As early as the Wilhelminian period, there were indications that the true parallel to India or Algeria was not Cameroon but central Europe. Blackbourn's conclusion is that, for the German Reich, the colonial caesura was marked not by the country's formal loss of the colonies in 1919 but rather by the end of the German settlements in eastern and central Europe in 1945. This inspired approach raises a new set of questions. How important was classic colonial—that is, overseas—expansion within the context of German history in the first half of the twentieth century when compared with preparations for continental expansion? Did colonialism and the German "drive" to expand in eastern Europe mutually influence one another, and if so, how?[7] In the first two sections of this chapter, I address the intertwined but also competitive history of these two spheres of imperial dreams. A related issue is whether we can categorize Nazi occupation of eastern Europe as a kind of imperial rule or should instead distinguish overseas colonialism, imperialism, and Nazi expansionism from one another on the basis of typological criteria that reflect deviations and analogies. I discuss in a third and final section whether National Socialist rule in eastern Europe can be described as imperial. It is argued here that Nazi expansionist ambitions can indeed be labeled imperialistic but that National Socialism was not imperial nor did it create an empire; instead, the Nazis established a new system of "foreign rule" that broke with core elements of imperial hegemony.

PARALLELS, COMPETITION, REINFORCEMENT

During the Wilhelmine period, there was considerable interest in those regions in central and eastern Europe in which Germans had formerly settled. Since 1900, representatives of the political right, especially those with a *völkisch* orientation, had called for the annexation of these regions, but their demands remained without substantial political results.[8] Whether and how these diverse expansions and political programs were related to (or competed with) one another have not yet been studied in detail. Were the *völkisch* dreams of a "German East" that emerged around 1900 a response to the frustrating political results of German colonial endeavors? Or were they a throwback to the long tradition of yearnings for a "German East"?[9] Philipp Ther's suggestion that the imperial dimension of the *Kaiserreich* must be explored not only in its overseas possessions but also in the sphere of German rule over the Polish population of Prussia's eastern provinces raises further complex issues.[10] Did Germany increasingly perceive Poland as a "substitute colony"[11]—indeed, perhaps even as the only real colony of the German Reich? Heinrich von Treitschke, an influential German historian, has interpreted the history of the Prussian provinces as a "first attempt at German colonialism,"[12] and representatives of the Polish minority in the German parliament, the Reichstag, complained of being treated like the natives of Africa.[13] In fact, many authors who described the situation along Prussia's eastern borders during the Kaiserreich compared it to the settlement of Canada or the "Wild West" rather than to Germany's overseas colonies. Nonetheless, the question remains: is it appropriate to refer to a population as "colonized" that, for the most part, held Prussian/German citizenship and was represented in the German parliament, as was the case with the *Inlandspolen* of eastern Prussia, in contrast to the *Auslandspolen* of Austrian Galicia, for example?[14]

The Polish areas in question were considered part of Prussia/Germany not only according to international law, as in the case of colonies, but also according to the definitions of constitutional law. In his study, "Environmental Chauvinism in the Prussian East," Jeffrey Wilson formulates an unequivocal answer to this question: officials pursued a civilizing mission with respect to both the natural environment and the people who inhabited it, but unlike the colonial natives in German colonies, the inhabitants of the Prussian East were regarded as assimilable. Disciplining the land would also produce a disciplined and *German* populace.[15] This seems to imply that German foreign rule on Prussia's eastern fringes was primarily interpreted as a *national* conflict between Polish nationalism and Germanization;[16] this conflict was settled, at least in certain places and in some periods, by employing colonial concepts. How the Polish minority—as well as the Danish or Alsatian minority—was to be integrated into German society is a question that must still be scrutinized in greater detail, as one aspect of the country's imperial history. In any event, World War I brought new options for territorial expansion.

Between 1914 and 1918, large portions of the Baltic region, Byelorussia, and Ukraine were occupied by German troops, and first steps were taken to prepare these territories for future German settlement. In this respect, the war in the East had a long-range effect for the Germans: for the first time in centuries, parts of eastern Europe extending into Russia were perceived as an area for German expansion. After having been taught in schools and universities that, since the period of "eastern colonialization" by the Teutonic knights, Germans had been destined to raise the East to a higher level of culture, German soldiers were bound to perceive the conquest of these premodern countries as a case of history repeating itself. After the war had been lost, such debates and perceptions nonetheless continued to fuel the notion of a chaotic region that still awaited the ordering and civilizing hand of German rule.[17]

World War I marked the end of the German colonial period as actual history. Yet as Marcia Klotz has pointed out, the Weimar Republic was a postcolonial state in a world that was still colonial.[18] As with the debates on a "German East," the loss of the colonies by no means meant an end to expansionist efforts. On the contrary: domestic political approval for Germany's colonial engagement was greatest at the very moment when the Allies declared the end of the country's colonial mission. When the victors of World War I excluded Germany from the circle of active colonial powers in 1919, the German public reacted with indignation. To make matters worse, the presence of colonialism reached Germany in the shape of real actors—the occupying forces from North Africa, Madagascar, and Indochina.[19] Large parts of the German population concluded that they were now no longer colonizers but instead themselves colonized by both the Allies and the Africans. *Völkisch* German racists reacted vehemently to what they perceived as horrifying. Adolf Hitler wrote that French "Negro hordes" were at the Rhine and conjured up the threat of "an immense, self-contained area from the Rhine to the Congo, filled with a lower race produced gradually from continuous bastardization."[20] This debate, which had its sequel in the discussion about the so-called Rhineland bastards,[21] was symptomatic of the increasing fusion of geopolitical concepts and racist ideas. In this context, the National Socialist movement fueled the belief that Germany would have to assume the role of the guardian of Europe's racial order in a coming "racial war."[22] It was also obvious that this was a colonial twist on a preexisting, fundamentally anti-Semitic worldview of the *völkisch* right. Hitler depicted the deployment of colonial troops as another perfidious act of "world Jewry," designed to secure the Jews' victory in their "racial struggle" with the "Aryans." Moreover, fear of the Reich's occupation by a foreign power was a core element of the revisionist rhetoric of the Weimar Republic.[23] Thus, Hitler was not telling a "story of colonialism"[24] but rather one of anti-Semitism, which now included elements of colonial ideology.

One might ask whether these shock effects of "disappropriation," this sudden shift from power to powerlessness, endured during the Weimar Republic. Did the perceived indignity of losing the colonies and the resulting expansionist vacuum after 1918 intensify the desire to become an imperial power again? How did the lack of a decolonialization phase, the lack of confrontation with the formerly colonized nations, the almost complete lack of migration from the colonies to metropolitan society, affect German society and its politics? Did all of this heighten German "provincialism," as Erich Kästner's ironic parody on Bertolt Brecht's 1930 song "Surabaya Johnny" suggested: *"Du sprachst von Kolonien, / Johnny, sunny Johnny, / und kanntest nur Berlin."* "You spoke of colonies, / Johnny, sunny Johnny, / and only knew Berlin."[25] Or did people come to terms with the situation—indeed, did a part of the German elite even feel "relieved of a burden"? Asked in a survey of two hundred prominent persons from public life whether the German Reich needed colonies, Thomas Mann responded, "The idea of freedom and self-determination has awakened everywhere and will never again be laid to rest. I believe that events have taught us to perceive our freedom from colonial baggage as an advantage."[26] For those interested in the significance of colonialism in a period in which Germany had no colonies of its own, the fact that there has been relatively little research on the critique of colonialism[27] is indeed unfortunate.

At any rate, it is important to keep in mind that while other empires gained in this phase "a more realistic sense of the limitations of their own power,"[28] as Frederick Cooper has noted, in Germany, imperial hubris developed relatively unhampered by political realities. The idea that Germany should ultimately conquer what it was seen as being "entitled to" achieved a new significance with the Nazi rise to power. Moreover, the state established by the Nazis at least *appeared* to merge the goals of pursuing overseas colonialism and expansion to the East.

TURNING EASTWARD

Expansion, the enlargement of living space, or *Lebensraum*, was one of the hallmarks of the Nazi program. But between 1933 and 1945, colonial restitution went hand in hand with the abandonment of classic overseas colonialism, while imperialistic goals were to become most pronounced during the Third Reich. The story of colonialism under National Socialism can be told in two ways. The first version begins by asserting that German colonialism was of great significance in the Third Reich, as evidenced by a surprisingly intense phase of planning and preparation for a new colonial empire. From the end of the 1920s—even more so after the NSDAP, with its international ambitions, seized power—colonial revisionism seemed to experience a renaissance.[29] For many contemporary Germans, the rapid rise of the Nazis led to an almost feverous state of anticipation. For example, entrepreneur Otto Schloifer, who had previously done business in East Africa, noted in 1939, "Now that the

Führer has bestowed upon us military sovereignty, occupation of the Rhineland, and the Greater German Reich, I am confident that he will also restore the colonies."[30] Hopes that the overseas territories would be regained remained alive until the early 1940s. Those who argued in favor of renewing the colonial enterprise referred to Germany's colonial history in the *Kaiserreich* and the colonial revisionism of the Weimar Republic. As in the nineteenth century, colonies were seen as a confirmation of national greatness. Since every nation was entitled to acquire overseas possessions, Germany had to be entitled to an opportunity to annex colonies. For the Nazi leaders, it was difficult to ignore such arguments about national prestige. But the Nazis' rapprochement with the colonial movement was, above all, a tactical move that served two functions. First, by pretending to support the colonial cause without any appreciable efforts, Nazi leaders established ties between parts of the old elite and the Nazi system. However, after the Nazis seized power, most of the colonial organizations were incorporated into the National Socialist system and became part of the *Reichskolonialbund* (Reich Colonial League) and the *Kolonialpolitisches Amt* (KPA, Colonial Policy Office) created in the NSDAP. Franz Ritter von Epp became the head of the NSDAP's colonial office and thus personified continuity in colonial affairs. He had previously served as an army officer in China and German Southwest Africa and as a member of the *Freikorps* in the "*Ruhrkampf*."[31] Like such other old colonialists as Paul Rohrbach and the president of the Reichsbank, Hjalmar Schacht, Epp opposed expansion to the East. He decried it as "*Ostlandreiterei*" ("roaming around in the eastern territories") in 1928.[32]

The second function issuing from colonialism was related to foreign politics. Adolf Hitler, in particular, used the colonial lobby and its goals for strategic games in this sphere. At least until the mid-1930s, Hitler seems to have attached little importance to actually owning overseas colonies; instead, he used German colonial claims to promote improved contacts with England. Once these attempts failed, Hitler began taking colonial rhetoric more seriously. In the excitement of the surprisingly successful blitzkrieg victories of 1939–1940, colonies again seemed to be within reach. In 1941, with the Nazi Reich at the height of its power, demands for the return of the former German possessions were not enough; the German Foreign Office devised plans, styled after those drawn up during World War I, for establishing a German colony in central Africa, with its core territory situated in the Belgian Congo.[33] In the early 1940s plans to reoccupy lost territories were in full swing. Numerous individuals volunteered, ready to depart at short notice for duty in the future African colonies. German experts in colonial affairs and tropical technology made sure they were up to date on the latest developments. The Reich Colonial League had nearly two million members, and considerable sums of money went into colonial research.

On the one hand, these plans revealed close ties to the former German colonial empire. On the other, they illustrate that the old was being combined with the new. What was new was, for example, reference to the idea that the Third Reich was destined to oppose Jewish or Jewish-Bolshevist influence in Africa.[34] Introducing German settlers in large numbers was no longer the order of the day. Individuals with experience in the colonies were hardly available (for age reasons), and plans to create a ten-thousand-man-strong colonial troop force were hampered by the lack of colonial veterans.[35] Moreover, quite a few of the Nazi colonial planners, especially those in the DAF's Institute for Labor Research of the German Labor Front, had moved on, as Karsten Linne has shown in his studies. Pure economic exploitation had become just as obsolete as using extreme violence against the Africans. In the face of impending shortages of labor, the "issue of colonial workers" had to be solved with social policy strategies, and segregation had to be enforced more strictly in order to resolve the *"Mischlingsfrage"* (problem of interracial relations) once and for all. When it came to details, controversies remained. While Hitler opposed the deployment of *"Askari,"* whether in Africa or Europe, the head of the Wehrmacht high command, Wilhelm Keitel, favored their use in the tropics, as did von Epp.[36] In his public appearances, as colonial hero Paul von Lettow-Vorbeck also failed to strike the tones that Joseph Goebbels had expected of him, the Reich propaganda minister labeled him a "reactionary."[37] The Nazi leadership also strove to tap into the colonial experience of other European powers. Branch offices of the KPA in Brussels and Paris were charged with sifting through the French and Belgian colonial documents.[38] The utilization of Italian insights from North Africa seems to have been more intense. Police and SS units traveled to Rome to be trained, and in 1941, German police units were apparently stationed in Libya.[39]

The Nazi leadership also initiated numerous documentary films, including *Mit Dr. Lutz Heck in Kamerun* (1939), and feature films, such as *Carl Peters* (1941), starring Hans Albers, *Ohm Krüger* (1941), and *Germanin* (1943), that took up colonial issues. But Nazi activities to reestablish a German colonial empire did not go beyond the stage of declaration of intent. In terms of actual history, the drive to the east proved stronger.

This brings us to the second version of the history of colonialism in the Third Reich. It begins with the assertion that the *German* colonial past was of very little significance for National Socialism. It was not just the fact that the colonial plans remained just that, namely plans, nor the fact that the true object of desire was eastern Europe; the prioritization of expansion on the European continent was frequently justified by arguing that the old version of colonialism had been a mistake, one the Third Reich abandoned once and for all. Long before seizing power, Hitler had opposed plans to reestablish colonies in Africa.[40] He maintained this position during the war: "One can pursue a colonial policy when one has secured Europe"[41] was the stand the Führer articulated on October 18, 1941, in a meeting at his headquarters. In his so-called political will (February 1945), Hitler even declared all of Spain's, France's and England's colonial undertakings to be failures. Continental peoples should expand only as far as "the geographical connection with the motherland is secured."[42] This belief in being "rooted in the soil" led Hitler to take sides, at least rhetorically, with the colonial peoples; for example, he regretted not having helped the "peoples overseas under French protectorate to gain their independence." Hitler considered the colonial ambitions of the *Kaiserreich* to be a historical "escapade"[43] that had fortunately ended in 1918. Thus, the extensive preparations for the coming colonial empire did not leave the stage of paperwork. Although colonialism of the "old school" saw a new flowering under National Socialism, no serious efforts to seize the former German colonies were initiated. Indeed, with its sights set on eastern Europe, the Nazi leadership positioned itself unequivocally in a state of discontinuity with respect to classic colonialism.

The sharp separation even affected terminology. For example, in February 1938 a national training workshop for *Gau* level administrators of the National Socialist Teachers' Association decided to replace "eastern German colonization" with "eastern German land development" or "reclamation" or "resettlement." The decision was motivated in large part by the members' desire to distance themselves from the "heavy-handed propaganda" of the German colonial enthusiasts.[44] Conversely, one can assume that a simple desire for self-assertion was behind the June 1942 order given by Wenig, von Epp's chief of staff, in which he felt obliged to distance himself from the successful eastern campaign. He ordered that the terms "colonies," "colonial lands," "colonial space," and "colonial" were not to be used "counter to order" for the "occupied eastern territories" but were to be applied only to the overseas territories.[45]

Radical *völkisch* intellectuals in SD and SS circles avoided using the term "empire" not only because they wanted to distinguish the Third Reich from the existing imperial powers. Rather, they argued, this form of rule was hardly congruent with the idea of an "organically developed *Völkergemeinschaft*." Their preferred terms were "*Großraum*" (large space) and its "order" or "administration." Moreover, these concepts were intended as a counterpoint to the ideas of conservative thinkers, such as Carl Schmitt, who expounded theories about the great powers.[46] The concepts were based on a *völkisch* theory of hegemony that universal, binding legal norms—even if defined as vaguely as in the work of Schmitt—were not just obsolete but indeed false. Such concepts held that peoples, not states, were the subjects of large territories. The goal was to structure and administer these territories in a manner that was as efficient, cool, and appropriate to *völkisch* laws as possible. One who took striking exception to this preference for "*Großraum*" and "Reich" was Alfred Rosenberg, Reich minister for the occupied eastern territories. Rosenberg's concept for occupation rule deviated from Hitler's in that he aimed to rely on the Soviet Union's non-Russian peoples in the fight against Moscow's "Jewish Bolshevism." Rosenberg continued to use "imperialism" and referred to his project as "*völkisch* imperialism." In using this term, he highlighted the contrast to French "military imperialism, marked by a mere "spirit of robbery and adventure," and to "economic imperialism," governed by Jewish international financial circles. Moreover, he rejected all German overseas colonial efforts as just miscarried imitations of British endeavors. Central to Rosenberg's vision was living space fit for "Aryan" habitation in eastern Europe.[47]

IMPERIALISTIC BUT NOT AN EMPIRE

How can we interpret this tension between the German colonial movement and the drive to expand to the east? Or to pose the question differently, which version of the story is correct? How significant was the role of German colonialism in the Third Reich? This issue has been at the center of a discussion that has gone on for decades, probably beginning with Hannah Arendt, and the debate has intensified in recent years. As is usual with such debates, controversy centers less on the facts than on their interpretation and evaluation.

Jürgen Zimmerer has reached the conclusion that colonial plans were probably of no great relevance for the political realities of the Third Reich.[48] However, he also maintains that one can trace strands leading from the structures, attitudes, and practices of German colonialism to Nazi imperialism and, in particular, to Nazi modes of warfare and occupation in the East. According to this perspective, the National Socialists' practices of violence followed as cause and effect from formal German colonial rule in the years (1884–1918). Positioning events on a single time scale implies continuity: the racial colonial order as *one* predecessor of the Nazi racial state; the war of annihilation as *one* result of colonial violence; the murder of the Herero as *one* part of the prehistory of the National Socialists' mass crimes. The value of this continuity model lies in how it emphasizes and enhances the significance of colonialism, especially German colonialism, for German history.

The disadvantage of interpretations that frame the Nazi occupation system as "colonial-style" or World War II as the "largest colonial war of conquest in history"[49] is their tendency to exaggerate colonialism's role. Four objections to overestimating the significance of colonialism have been raised. First, in the context of his discussion of Arendt's standpoint, Pascal Grosse has asked why other imperial powers, though having similar colonial-racist attitudes, did not go down the road to totalitarianism. Why did only Germany end in Nazism?[50] Second, scholars have questioned whether it is possible to provide evidence for a process in which a legacy of violence is passed on, especially when the geographical setting, the historical context, and the actors involved have changed.[51] The third objection refers to the actual findings of research.[52] Do the acts of violence perpetrated against the Herero in 1904 and against the populations of eastern Europe indeed resemble one another as closely as is contended? Were the motives, intentions, and practices involved in German violence against Africans the same as those of some forty years later in eastern Europe? Robert Gerwarth and Stephan Malinowski have raised objections to positions that equate colonialism solely with annihilation. They contend that in colonial regimes brutality was just one part of the complex and functional concomitance of annihilation *and* development, of coercive modernization *and* destruction.[53]

A second approach takes up these doubts, concentrates on situational parallels and differences, and asserts that while links do exist between colonialism and National Socialism, these are not so much continuities as analogies that arise from a constellation of foreign rule.[54] Comparing the various forms of colonialism and Nazi occupation rule in the East can uncover similarities in structural features and problems. But the goal of such comparative research is also to determine the unique features of each hegemonic system.[55]

Besides these two approaches, there is a third model, which aims to take up both dimensions and conceptualize the period 1884–1945 under the general heading of imperialism. Here, imperialism is a phenomenon fractured in numerous ways; nonetheless, the concept can be applied to describing the German situation as a single entity. Dirk van Laak takes this track; Wendy Lower's volume on the Ukraine is a further example; Shelley Baranowski argues that Nazi imperialism, though distinct from broader European imperial history, was still imperialism. The challenge facing scholars who apply this method is the pleomorphic phenomenon of nineteenth- and twentieth-century imperialism.

How can these imperialisms be broken down typologically to a point where we might reach the conclusion, after considering all divergent elements and similarities, that National Socialism was similar enough as a form of hegemony to other imperial structures to warrant adding it to the epoch of imperialism? One possible objection to this categorization is the assertion that National Socialism was not a more radical version of imperial rule but, on the contrary, a radical departure from all imperial and colonial antecedents.

The advantage of this approach lies in the fact that it frames the temporal context more precisely, in particular because the importance of World War I is recognized; also, it takes into consideration the European as well as global framework. The effect of these two shifts is to relativize the significance of German colonialism. At this point one might risk arguing that the *German* overseas colonies were completely irrelevant to Hitler's plans but that the goals and interpretative framework in which Nazi expansion occurred were inspired by *European* imperialism—in a very special Nazi reception of imperial pasts and present. I support this argument, which characterizes imperialism as a "sounding board" (Alf Lüdtke) for National Socialism. Rather than emphasize continuities in the stricter sense of cause and effect, this view highlights the more subjective level of how the National Socialists revived, carried on, and developed colonial traditions, how they learned their "lessons of Empire."[56] Thus, Hitler fantasized after a short visit to the newly occupied Ukraine: "The East will be for us what India was for England. If I could only imbue the German people with a sense of what this space will mean for the future! Colonies are a questionable possession; this soil is surely ours."[57] Here, British imperialism remained the frame of reference, but what was at issue was not precise knowledge of British imperial politics, much less the concrete imitation of British policy. When there was talk in the Cultural Department of the Reich Commissariat for the Ukraine in April 1942 about the German occupiers being "really . . . among niggers,"[58] the phrase at first suggests a certain lack of orientation. But this return to colonial *topoi* in fact brought orientation in a foreign, unfamiliar, and uncertain situation, reduced complexity to a compact formula—"imagine it as being like an African colony"—and at the same time legitimated the German presence. Thinking in categories of "natives" and "masters," of "natural" superiority and inferiority and German empowerment, accelerated the development of Nazi rule in eastern Europe and, in this sense, also exacerbated the use of mass violence. To the extent that, for the most part, abstract colonial connotations shaped occupation policies, strategies of separation and forms of dealing with the occupied peoples became more radical. It seems that in most cases these references did not refer to real colonial knowledge, real colonial events, or real colonial structures but can better be described as productive, imaginative transfers. We should recall that historical antecedents are just as frequently revisited because one aims to cut off rather than renew any connection with them. Just as pre–World War I Prussian settlement in the East was considered an instructive example of how things should not be done,[59] the actual imperial efforts of the *Kaiserreich* were also interpreted by the Nazis as misguided. In this sense, it is difficult to decide just how imperial the Third Reich really was. Conceptual distinctions between imperial and nonimperial forms of hegemony should take transitions and shifting boundaries into account.[60] In my assessment, Nazi Germany did act imperialistically but nonetheless must be considered an exception in the lineup of nineteenth- and twentieth-century empires.[61] The Nazi regime is an exception not only because a comparison with these other empires reveals more deviations than analogies but also because the deviations are related to core criteria of imperial rule.

I want to end by explaining this argument against a background of three definitions of empires, chosen from the huge literature on empires and imperialism.[62] Of course, it may be argued that empires and imperialism are marked by ambiguities and that there have been countless ways "to do and undo an empire." Ann Stoler, Carole McGranahan, and Peter C. Perdue follow this path; they prefer the coinage "imperial formations"[63] to capture the dynamic of relationships between parts and the various degrees "of tolerance, of difference, of domination, and of rights" that inhere in empires. I strongly support this concept of empires as variable and highly inconsistent constructs, as these findings correspond well with my own research on the German Empire around 1900.[64] I am aware, too, of the risk of reducing imperialism to a "coherent, monolithic process."[65] But even Stoler and McGranahan know about the risk of overstretching particularities: "If so many of the elements long considered imperial are called into question here, the reader might rightly ask, What are the attributes that still mark something as imperial?"[66] Their answer is, once more, instability, ambiguity, exceptionalism. One can surely agree that the Nazi regime was exceptional. Nevertheless the burning questions for me remain: how can we conceptualize Nazi empire? By thinking it in categories of imperial formations? Or by also reflecting its non- or anti-imperial attributes and approaches?

It seems to me to begin with Jürgen Osterhammel, who defines an empire as "a large scale, hierarchically-ordered association of hegemony, of poly-ethnic and multi-religious character, the coherence of which is maintained by the threat of violence, by administration, indigenous collaboration, and the universalistic programs and symbols of an imperial elite."[67] Aside from the universalistic program, all of these characteristics would seem to apply to National Socialism during World War II. But what if the empire in question declares that its aspirations were based on the goal of eliminating exactly that polyethnic and multireligious character? Indeed, what if this plan to eliminate was the very reason for its existence? *Völkisch* homogeneity was the ultimate National Socialist vision, to be realized in a perpetual campaign. Destruction became a central obsession and "killing became—or at least tended to become—an end in itself."[68] This war of annihilation ended only when its perpetrators were stopped. Empires, however, require foreign populations by definition—or as George Steinmetz has asserted, "Colonialism without the colonized was a contradiction in terms."[69]

That Hitler "tried to form an empire by killing rather than converting"[70] is also one of the arguments made by Mark Mazower.[71] He treats the mythical as well as the destructive dimensions of Hitler's and his collaborators' projects for Nazi rule in occupied eastern Europe. Although Mazower clearly recognizes the imperial aspiration of this project, he nevertheless illuminates the clear cut made by the Nazi leadership. The unrestrained willingness for violent options shocked contemporaries. Here, a state prepared to turn the tables and make Europe itself the object of colonial desires—by the most barbarous means. But the empire failed due to this cruelty. The Nazis lost all chances for cooperation from subject populations. Strong parts of the world's public opinion and especially of the colonized draw from this abandoned mission of conquest the conclusion to delegitimize all imperial desires.

In stressing nationalist skills of empire, Mazower might be read along with Herfried Münkler. The Berlin political scientist did not include the Third Reich in his morphology of empires—with good reason.[72] On a more superficial level, he argues that the existence of the Reich was too short, so that one could not observe it in action. Thus, an important characteristic of empires is lacking; namely, their ability to maintain hegemony. One can declare this deficit to be a lucky coincidence, or give Great Britain, the Soviet Union, and the United States credit for it, or interpret it as further proof of the conclusion that the Third Reich was indeed not an empire. What would seem more significant, however, is a fundamental problem: namely, reconciling the particularism of the National Socialists with Münkler's theory. Internally, the National Socialist state offered its residents who were "Aryan," "hereditarily healthy," "politically trustworthy," and the like a "promise of prosperity." Moreover, there was no lack of *soft skills* in the dealings of the Nazi state with those who were considered to belong to it, as Münkler has emphasized. If there was a mission that had been formulated to legitimate imperial expansion, then one might point to the idea of saving Europe from Jewish Bolshevism.

However, this might be an ambiguous understanding of concepts of "civilizing missions." And in contrast to British or French colonial cultures, the Nazi idea of civilizing "the East" always referred to the nature, not the inhabitants, of those regions. Also, universalism—especially a brand of universalism that "served humanity"—was entirely foreign to National Socialism. In the regime's dealings with the majority of the inhabitants of occupied eastern Europe, the hard facts of power, repression, and mastery were the order of the day. Thus, the center had little appeal for the elites from the periphery, as there was an almost complete lack of the ideological ties offered by an "imperial mission." Presumably, Hitler was only partly interested in being "admired and loved"; his self-understanding was not that of a "global guarantor of order" and a "peacemaker." Moreover, even if one takes into account that the "Greater German Reich" never established a peacetime social order, it cannot be characterized as offering a heightened domestic "level of security" that helped promote prosperity and ensure the progress of civilization and the flowering of culture. Although Münkler perhaps overemphasizes the integrating functions of empires, he nevertheless perceives them as being just as essential as the use of force.[73]

Frederick Cooper perceives empires as permanently facing the challenge of having to integrate countries and peoples and, at the same time, differentiate between them by employing force. The goal of ensuring that colonial subjects were all indeed subjects clashed with the aim of treating different categories of subjects differently. Furthermore, as Cooper reminds us, the most powerful empires frequently were in danger of being taken over by their agents—the settlers who sought alternatives to cooperating with the imperial center.[74] Cooper's argument adds three aspects to the debate. First, he demonstrates that there are significant variations in existing empires and that the dichotomy of subaltern natives and superior colonizers fails to describe realities.[75] Second, he draws attention to where hegemony and its ideologies are limited and fractured.[76] Third, he reminds us of the instability of the processes of racialization.[77] Cooper therefore labels Nazi Germany a "would-be empire"[78]—possibly a very appropriate denotation.

NOTES

1. This chapter uses parts of Kundrus, "*Kolonialismus. Imperialismus, Nationalsozialismus?*"

2. Most recently Wehler, "Transnationale Geschichte?," 165; according to Wehler,

it is hard to explain why "a phenomenon that was, from the perspective of actual history, as secondary as Germany's brief colonial history has been able to attract so much interest."

3. Lower, *Nazi Empire-Building*; Lower and Furber, "Colonialism and Genocide," 372–401.

4. Zimmerer, "Birth of the 'Ostland'"; Zimmerer, "First Genocide of the Twentieth Century."

5. van Laak, *Über alles in der Welt*.

6. Blackbourn, "Das Kaiserreich transnational," 322, and *The Conquest of Nature*, 239–296.

7. The novel *Volk ohne Raum* by Hans Grimm, for example, was extracted from its colonial context and applied to eastern Europe—initially, against the will of the author; Gümbel, *"Volk ohne Raum."*

8. Bley, "Der Traum vom Reich?," 56–70; see also Sweeney, "Pan-German Conceptions of Colonial Empire," ch. 13 in this volume.

9. Thum, ed., *Traumland Osten*.

10. Ther, "Deutsche Geschichte als imperiale Geschichte," 129–148.

11. Conrad, *Globalisierung und Nation*, 124–167.

12. von Treitschke, "Die ersten Versuche deutscher Kolonialpolitik," 339.

13. von Friedeburg, "Konservatismus und Reichskolonialrecht," 371.

14. Wehler, "Polenpolitik im Deutschen Kaiserreich," 184–203; Hagen, *Germans, Poles, and Jews*; Eley, "German Politics and Polish Nationality," 335–364.

15. Wilson, "Environmental Chauvinism in the Prussian East," 30–31.

16. Dickinson, "The German Empire?"

17. Liulevicius, *War Land on the Eastern Front*; Gross, ed., *Die vergessene Front*.

18. Klotz, "The Weimar Republic," 135–147. See also Poley, *Decolonization in Germany*.

19. Cf. Koller, *"Von Wilden aller Rassen."*

20. As quoted in Schmokel, *Dream of Empire*, 18.

21. Cf. Van Hoesen, "Visualizing the Enemy," ch. 15 in this volume.

22. Grosse, "What Does German Colonialism," 115–134.

23. Cf. Koller, *Fremdherrschaft*.

24. Klotz, "The Weimar Republic," 143.

25. Kästner, "Surabaya-Johnny II," 334–335.

26. Mann, "Soll Deutschland Kolonialpolitik treiben?," 624–626.

27. Cf. Stuchtey, *Die europäische Expansion und ihre Feinde*.

28. Cooper, *Colonialism in Question*, 183.

29. Cf. Linne, *Deutschland jenseits des Äquators?*; Schmokel, *Dream of Empire*.

30. As quoted in van Laak, *Imperiale Infrastruktur*, 292.

31. Hildebrand, *Vom Reich zum Weltreich*, 345–390.

32. Schmokel, *Dream of Empire*, 50.

33. Hildebrand, *Vom Reich zum Weltreich*, 449 and passim, 624–629.

34. Cf. Schubert, ed., *Ausschuß für Kolonialrecht*, 467.

35. Dülffer, *Kolonialismus*, 261.

36. Weinberg, "German Colonial Plans and Policies," 485.
37. Mass, *Weiße Helden, schwarze Krieger*, 241.
38. Schmokel, *Dream of Empire*, 140.
39. Weinberg, "German Colonial Plans," 465, 484.
40. Cf. Hitler, *Mein Kampf*, 533.
41. Hitler, *Monologe im Führerhauptquartier*, 94.
42. Similar statements are found in Best, "Grundfragen, 44, 51; cf. Hildebrand, *Vom Reich zum Weltreich*, 716–717.
43. *Hitlers Politisches Testament*, 41–107.
44. Walther, "Imperialismus," 231.
45. Hildebrand, *Vom Reich zum Weltreich*, 728; Fitzpatrick, "Pre-History of the Holocaust?," 1–27.
46. Herbert, *Best*, 279.
47. Rosenberg, *Zukunftsweg*, 9–21; Kamenetzky, *Secret Nazi Plans for Eastern Europe*, 178.
48. Zimmerer, "Birth of the 'Ostland'"; Zimmerer, "Rassenkrieg und Völkermord," 23–48; Zimmerer, "Annihilation in Africa," 51–57.
49. Zimmerer, "Annihilation in Africa," 54.
50. Grosse, "What Does German Colonialism"; also, Hochgeschwender, "Kolonialkriege als Experimentierstätten?," 269–290.
51. Kundrus, "Kontinuitäten, Parallelen, Rezeptionen," 45–62; Gerwarth and Malinowski, "Hannah Arendt's Ghosts," 279–300.
52. Barth, *Genozid*, 128–136; Hull, *Absolute Destruction*; Krüger, "Coming to Terms," 45–49.
53. Gerwarth and Malinowski, "Hannah Arendt's Ghosts."
54. Kundrus, "Kontinuitäten, Parallelen, Rezeptionen."
55. Kundrus, "Von Windhoek nach Nürnberg?," 110–131.
56. Calhoun et al., *Lessons of Empire*. Also, Kakel, *The American West and the Nazi East*.
57. Hitler, *Monologe*, August 8–11, 1941, 55.
58. As quoted in Majer, "Das besetzte Osteuropa," 126. See also Lower, *Nazi Empire-Building*, 109, and Grill, "Robert L. Jenkins," 667–694.
59. Höhn and Seydel, "Der Kampf um die Wiedergewinnung," 61–174.
60. Steinmetz, *The Devil's Handwriting*.
61. Maier, *Among Empires*, 24.
62. Cf. Lieven, *Empire*; ch. 1 explains "A Word and Its Meanings."
63. Stoler, McGranahan, and Perdue, eds., *Imperial Formations*.
64. Kundrus, *Moderne Imperialisten*.
65. Comaroff, "Images of Empire, Contests of Conscience," 165.
66. Stoler, McGranahan, "Refiguring Imperial Terrains," 11.
67. Osterhammel, "Europamodelle und imperiale Kontexte," 172.
68. Reemtsma, "The Concept of the War of Annihilation," 29.
69. Steinmetz, *The Devil's Handwriting*, 44.
70. Snyder, *The Times Literary Supplement*, August 13, 2008.

71. Mazower, *Hitler's Empire*.

72. Münkler, *Imperien*.

73. Even Maier concedes that only "the most predatory empires, such as the Third Reich, have suggested that those conquered have no benefits to gain from being ruled by conquerors." See Maier, "America among Empires?," 27. The absence of any benefit at all for Jews and "Slaves" is also one reason why Stoler and McGranahan's remarks on imperial formations as "states of deferral" (8–9) seem not quite transferable to Nazism.

74. Cooper, *Colonialism in Question*, 24.

75. Cooper, *Colonialism in Question*, 201.

76. Cooper, *Colonialism in Question*, 160.

77. Cooper, *Colonialism in Question*, 29.

78. Cooper, *Colonialism in Question*, 194. Cooper also assigns Japan to this category. Pagden, "Fellow Citizens and Imperial Subjects," 29, refers to the Third Reich as a "short-lived imperial project" and also excludes it from the modern European empires.

Bibliography

ARCHIVES

Archives de l'Institut Pasteur, Paris
Archives Nationales d'Outre Mer
Archives of the Wellcome Trust, Royal Society of Tropical Medicine and Hygiene
Bernhard Nocht Institute Archives, Hamburg
Bundesarchiv, Abteilungen Potsdam (German Federal Archives, Potsdam)
Bundesarchiv Berlin (German Federal Archives)
Bundesarchiv Berlin-Lichterfelde
First Historical Archives, Beijing
Geheimes Staatsarchiv Preußischer Kulturbesitz
Hessisches Staatsarchiv Darmstadt
Humboldt University Archive, Berlin
London School of Hygiene and Tropical Medicine Archives
Militärarchiv, Berlin (German Military Archives)
Politisches Archiv des Auswärtigen Amts Berlin
Sächsisches Staatsarchiv Leipzig
Sperry Papers, Library of Congress
Stadtarchiv Leipzig
Richard Thurnwald papers, Yale University Library
Tanzania National Archives, Dar es Salaam

PERIODICALS

Abdruck aus dem Klinischen Jahrbuch
African World
Akademie der Wissenschaften zu Berlin
Alldeutsche Blätter
Alldeutsche Flugschriften

Allgemeine Zeitung
American Journal of International Law
American Society of International Law Proceedings
Amtsblatt für das Schutzgebiet Kamerun
Annales d'hygiène et de médecine coloniale
Anthropos
Antisemitisches Volksblatt
Archiv für Rassen- und Gesellschafts-Biologie
Archiv für Schiffs- und Tropenhygiene
Augsburger Volkszeitung / Schwäbische Volkszeitung
Bank Börsen-Zeitung
Beihefte z. Archiv für Schiffs- und Tropenhygiene
Beiträge zur Kulturgeschichte von Ostafrika
Berichte über Land- und Forstwirtschaft in Deutsch-Ostafrika
Berliner Illustrirte Zeitung
Berliner Tageblatt
Blätter für Vergleichende Rechtswissenschaft und Volkswirtschaftslehre
Bulletin de la Société de pathologie exotique
Contemporary Review
Dépêche coloniale
Der Fischerbote
Deutsche Arbeit
Deutsche Kolonialzeitung
Deutsche Medizinische Wochenschrift
Deutsche Politik
Deutsche Wacht: Wochenschrift für nationales Deutschtum und sociale Reform
Deutsche Welt: Wochenschrift der Deutschen Zeitung
Deutsche Zeitung
Deutsch-Soziale Blätter
Europäische Gespräche, Hamburger Monatshefte für Auswärtige Politik
Grosse Politik
Hammer: Blätter für deutschen Sinn
Illustrierte Zeitung
Der Islam
Jahrbücher für Nationalökonomie und Statistik
Jahrbuch für Gesetzgebung, Verwaltung und Volkswirtschaft im Deutschen Reich
Jahrbuch über die deutschen Kolonien
Journal of Tropical Medicine
Journal of Tropical Medicine and Hygiene
Klinisches Jahrbuch
Der Kolonialedeutsche
Koloniale Rundschau
Kolonie und Heimat
Die Koralle

Leipziger Illustrierte Zeitung
Leipziger Volkszeitung
Marine-Rundschau
Medizinal Berichte
Mitteilungen der Internationalen Kriminalistischen Vereinigung
Mitteilungen des Seminars für Orientalische Sprachen zu Berlin
Mittheilungen aus dem Verein zur Abwehr des Antisemitismus
Monographien Deutscher Reklamekunstler
Der neue Merkur
Neue Preußische (Kreuz-) Zeitung
Die neue Rundschau
Die Neue Zeit
Pacific Affairs
Der Panther
Die Post
La Presse médicale
Preussische Jahrbücher
Proceedings of the U.S. Naval Institute
La Quinzaine coloniale
Die Reklame
Social Forces
Sonder-Abdruck aus Archiv für Schiffs- und Tropenhygiene
Sonderabdruck aus der Geographischen Zeitschrift
Sonderabdruck aus der Münchener medizinischen Wochenschrift
Sonderabdruck der Illustrierten Auslands- und Kolonialzeitung—"Afrika Nachrichten"
Sozialistische Monatshefte
Staatsbürger-Zeitung
Stenographische Berichte über die Verhandlungen des Abgeordnetenhauses
Stenographische Berichte über die Verhandlungen des Reichstags
Süsserott's Illustrierter Kolonial-Kalender
Le Temps
Times (UK)
Transactions of the Royal Society of Tropical Medicine
Der Tropenpflanzer
Über Land und Meer
Verhandlungen des deutschen Geographentages
Verhandlungen der ersten Hauptversammlung für Vergleichende Rechtswissenschaft und Volkswirtschaftslehre
Volkszeitung
Volk und Rasse
Der Wahre Jacob
Warenzeichenblatt des Kaiserliches Patentamts
Wort und Bild
Zeitschrift für Ethnologie

Zeitschrift für Kolonialrecht
Zeitschrift für Kolonialsprachen
Zeitschrift für Rassenkunde

PRIMARY SOURCES

Aron, Raymond. *La sociologie allemande contemporaine.* Paris: F. Alcan, 1935.
Bartels, Adolf. "Zur Rassenforschung." *Deutsche Welt: Wochenschrift der Deutschen Zeitung,* April 10, 1904.
Barth, William Carl. *Unsere Kolonien im Schulunterricht.* Bielefeld: A. Helmichs Buchhandlung, 1907.
Bartholdy, A. Mendelssohn, ed. "Soll Deutschland Kolonialpolitik treiben? Eine Umfrage aus dem Jahr 1927." *Europäische Gespräche, Hamburger Monatshefte für Auswärtige Politik* 5 (1927): 624–626.
Becker, Carl H. "Der Islam als Problem." *Der Islam* 1 (1910): 1–21.
Becker, Carl H. "Islamisches und modernes Recht in der kolonialen Praxis." *Der Islam* 4 (1913): 169–172.
Bentham, Jeremy. "Anarchical Fallacies." In *The Works of Jeremy Bentham,* vol. 8, edited by John Bowring, 489–534, 521. Edinburgh: William Tait, 1839.
"Bericht über den Verlauf des elften Deutschen Geographentages. Bremen, 17., 18., 19. April 1895." In *Verhandlungen des elften Deutschen Geographentages zu Bremen am 17., 18., und 19. April 1895.* Berlin: Reimer, 1896, x–xi.
Bericht über die Tätigkeit des Agitationskomitees der Sozialdemokratischen Partei Leipzigs für das Jahr 1906–07. Leipzig: Agitationskomitee der Sozialdemokratischen Partei Leipzigs, 1907, 5–6, 7.
Bernstein, Eduard. "Was folgt aus dem Ergebnis der Reichstagswahlen?" *Sozialistische Monatshefte* 13, January–June 1907.
Bernstein, Eduard. "The German Elections and the Social Democrats." *Contemporary Review* 91, April 1907.
Bernstein, Eduard. "Die Kolonialfrage und der Klassenkampf." *Sozialistische Monatshefte* 13 (July–December 1907): 988–996.
Best, Werner. "Grundfragen einer deutschen Großraum-Verwaltung." In *Festgabe für Heinrich Himmler,* 33–60. Darmstadt: Wittich, 1941.
Bromme, Moritz William Theodor. *Lebensgeschichte eines modernen Fabrikarbeiters,* edited by Paul Göhre. Jena: Eugen Diederichs, 1905.
Brose, Maximilian. *Des Deutschen Reiches kolonial-litteratur der letzten zehn Jahre.* Nuremberg: J. P. Raw, 1891.
Brose, Maximilian, ed. *Repertorium der deutsch-Kolonialen Litteratur 1884–1890.* Berlin: Georg Winckelmann, 1891.
Browne, Edward G. *The Reign of Terror in Tabriz: England's Responsibility.* Manchester: Taylor, Garnett, Evans, 1912.
Calwer, Richard. "Der 25. Januar." *Sozialistische Monatshefte* 13 (January–June 1907): 101–107.
Césaire, Aimé. *Discourse on Colonialism,* translated by Joan Pinkham. New York: Monthly Review Press, 1972.

Chronik der königlichen Friedrich-Wilhelms-Universität zu Berlin für das Rechnungsjahr April 1932–März 1935. Berlin: Paul Funk, n.d.

Class, Heinrich. *Denkschrift betreffend die national-, wirtschafts- und sozialpolitischen Ziele des deutschen Volkes im gegenwärtigen Kriege.* 1914. (No additional publishing data available.)

Clifford, Sir Hugh. *German Colonies: A Plea for the Native Races.* London: J. Murray, 1918.

Crusen, Georg. "Die rechtliche Stellung der Chinesen in Kiautschou." *Zeitschrift für Kolonialrecht* 15.2 (1913): 4–17, and 15.3 (1913): 47–57.

Crusen, Georg. "Moderne Gedanken im Chinesenstrafrecht des Kiautschougebietes." *Mitteilungen der Internationalen Kriminalistischen Vereinigung* 21.1 (1914): 134–142.

Degener, Hermann A. L., ed. *Wer ist's?* Leipzig: H. A. Ludwig Degener, 1912.

Dehn, Paul. "Die weltwirtschaftliche Entwickelung." *Alldeutsche Blätter* 1.11 (January 6, 1901): 4–6.

Dehn, Paul. *Weltpolitische Neubildungen.* Berlin: Allgemeiner Verein für Deutsche Literatur, 1905.

Dehn, Paul. *Von deutscher Kolonial- und Weltpolitik.* Berlin: Allgemeiner Verein für Deutsche Literatur, 1907.

Demm, Eberhard, and Hartmut Soell, eds. *Alfred-Weber-Gesamtausgabe*, vol. 10, part 1. Marburg: Metropolis, 2003.

Dernburg, Bernhard. *Zielpunkte des Deutschen Kolonialwesens: Zwei Vorträge.* Berlin: Mittler und Sohn, 1907.

Des Deutschen Reiches kolonial-litteratur der letzten zehn Jahre. Nuremberg: J. P. Raw, 1891.

Deutsche Gesellschaft für Soziologie, *Verhandlungen des Deutschen Soziologentages vom 17. bis 19. September 1928 in Zürich*, 248–288. Tübingen: Mohr, 1929.

Deutsche Kolonialschule. *Der deutsche Kulturpionier. Nachrichten aus der deutschen Kolonialschule Witzenhausen.* Witzenhausen: Werra Verb. Alter Herren V. Wilhelmshof, 1907.

Diercke, Carl, and Eduard Gaebler. *Schul-Atlas für höhere Lehranstalten*, 36th ed. Brunswick: Georg Westermann, 1900.

Dietrich Reimer Verlag. *Verlags-Katalog der geographischen Verlagsbuchhandlung.* Berlin: Reimer, 1895.

Eichler, E. "Im Kampf um die Weltmachtungstellung." *Deutsche Welt*, August 14, 1904.

E. S. *Zur Reorganisation der höheren Schulanstalten vom praktischen Standpunkt aus.* Kassel: Verlag von J. Bacmeister, 1879.

E. S. Mittler und Sohn. *Königliche Hofbuchhandlung und Hofbuchdruckerei.* Berlin: Mittler und Sohn, 1914.

Fabarius, Ernst Albert. "Ausbildung für den Kolonialdienst." *Jahrbuch über die deutschen Kolonien* 2 (1909): 135–148.

Fiske, Bradley A. "Naval Power." *Proceedings of the U.S. Naval Institute* 37 (1911): 683–736.

Förster, Bernhard. *Deutsche Colonien in dem oberen Laplata-Gebiete. Mit besonderer Berücksichtigung von Paraguay. Ergebnisse eingehender Prüfungen, praktischer Arbe-*

iten und Reisen, 1883–1885. Naumburg: Im Selbstverlage des Verfassers, 1886 (self-published).

Freiligrath, Ferdinand. "Löwenritt." In *Deutsches Lesebuch. Für die Bedürfnisse des Volksschul-Unterrichts,* part 4, section 2, 2nd ed., edited by Eduard Bock, 296–298. Breslau: Ferdinand Hirt, 1877.

Frenssen, Gustav. *Peter Moors Fahrt nach Südwest—ein Feldzugsbericht.* Berlin: Grote'sche Verlagsbuchhandlung, 1906.

Frenssen, Gustav. *Peter Moor's Journey to Southwest Africa: A Narrative of the German Campaign,* translated by Margaret May Ward. Boston: Houghton Mifflin, 1908.

Freytag, Gustav. *Soll und Haben.* Leipzig: Hirsel, 1854.

Fryman, Daniel. *Wenn ich der Kaiser wär'—politische Wahrheiten und Notwendigkeiten.* Leipzig: Dieterich'schen Verlagsbuchhandlung, 1912.

Fülleborn, Friedrich. "Reisebericht über einen Besuch der tropenmedizinischen Schulen in England." *Archiv für Schiffs- und Tropenhygiene* 8.7 (1904): 292–299.

Gerstenhauer, Max Robert. "Deutschsüdwestafrika alldeutsch!" *Alldeutsche Blätter* 28, July 9, 1899.

Gerstenhauer, Max Robert. "Der Rassenverderb in Deutsch-Südwestafrika." *Alldeutsche Blätter* 51, December 20, 1900.

Great Britain, Foreign Office, Historical Section. *Treatment of Natives in the German Colonies.* London: HMSO, 1920.

Grimpen, Alb. "Die Negerfrage in Deutschland." *Hammer: Blätter für deutschen Sinn* 7, 1908.

Gründer, Horst. *Geschichte der deutschen Kolonien.* Paderborn: Schöningh, 1912.

Hänsch, Felix. *An der Schwelle des grösseren Reichs. Deutsche Kriegsziele in politisch-geographische Begründung.* Munich: J. F. Lehmann's Verlag, 1917.

Harris, John H. *Dawn in Darkest Africa.* London: Frank Cass, 1968 [1912].

Hartmann, Martin. "Deutschland und der Islam." *Der Islam* 1 (1910): 72–92.

Hasse, Ernst. *Großdeutschland und Mitteleuropa um das Jahr 1950.* Berlin: Thormann und Goetsch, 1895.

Hasse, Ernst. "Europäische oder Weltpolitik?" *Alldeutsche Blätter* 24.9, June 11, 1899, 194.

Hasse, Ernst. *Die Besiedelung des deutschen Volksbodens.* Munich: J. F. Lehmann's Verlag, 1905.

Hasse, Ernst. *Die Zukunft des deutschen Volkstums.* Munich: J. F. Lehmann's Verlag, 1907.

Hasse, Ernst. *Weltpolitik, Imperialismus und Kolonialpolitik.* Munich: J. F. Lehmann's Verlag, 1908.

Henkel, F. "Der Hereroaufstand. Entweder—oder!" *Deutsche Welt,* July 31, 1904.

Herre, P., ed. *Politisches Handwörterbuch.* Leipzig: K. F. Koehler, 1923.

Hilferding, Rudolf. *Das Finanzkapital: Eine Studie über die jüngste Entwicklung des Kapitalismus.* Berlin: Dietz, 1910.

Hitler, Adolf. *Mein Kampf,* translated by James Murphy. London: Hurst and Blackett, 1939.

Hitler, Adolf. *Monologe im Führerhauptquartier,* edited and annotated by Werner Jochmann. Hamburg: Knaus, 1980.

Hitlers Politisches Testament. Die Bormann Diktate vom Februar und April 1945. Hamburg: Knaus, 1981.

Hobson, John A. *The Psychology of Jingoism.* London: Grant Richards, 1901.

Hobson, John A. *Imperialism, a Study.* Ann Arbor: University of Michigan Press, 1965.

Höhn, Reinhard, and Helmut Seydel. "Der Kampf um die Wiedergewinnung des deutschen Ostens. Erfahrungen der preußischen Ostsiedlung 1886 bis 1914." In *Festgabe für Heinrich Himmler*, 61–174. Darmstadt: Wittich, 1941.

Hövermann, Otto. *Kiautschou. Verwaltung und Gerichtsbarkeit.* Tübingen: Mohr, 1914.

H. R. "Zur Kolonial-Frage." *Hammer: Blätter für deutschen Sinn* 6, 1907.

Hugenberg, Alfred. *Innere Colonisation im Nordwesten Deutschlands.* Strasbourg: Verlag von Karl J. Trübner, 1891.

Hugenberg, Alfred. *Streiflichter aus der Vergangenheit und Gegenwart.* Berlin: Scherl, 1926.

Jenetzky, F. W., and E. Hellmuth, eds. *R.u.W. Dietleins Deutsches Lesebuch, Ausgabe D in 4 Teilen für paritätische Mittelschulen.* Part 3: *Der Neubearbeitung*, 1st ed. Leipzig and Berlin: B. G. Teubner, 1909.

J. H. "Innere oder äußere Kolonisation?" *Hammer: Blätter für deutschen Sinn* 5, 1906.

Johst, Hanns. *Ruf des Reiches—Echo des Volkes! Eine Ostfahrt.* Munich: Eher, 1940.

Kamenetzky, Ihor. *Secret Nazi Plans for Eastern Europe. A Study of Lebensraum Policies.* New York: Bookman Associates, 1961.

Karl-Marx-Universität Leipzig, Komittee zur Untersuchung der Verhältnisse an westdeutschen Universitäten. *Eine Dokumentation. Die wissenschaftliche und politische Karriere des Dr. phil. habil Karl Heinz Pfeffer, Professor für Soziologie der Entwicklungsländer an der Universität Münster.* Leipzig, 1996 (no publisher information).

Kautsky, Karl. "Der 25. Januar." *Die Neue Zeit* 25.18, 1906–1907.

Kautsky, Karl. *Sozialismus und Kolonialpolitik: Eine Auseinandersetzung.* Berlin: Vorwärts, 1907.

Kirchhoff, Alfred. *Erdkunde für Schulen nach den für Preußen gültigen Lehrzielen.* Part 2: *Mittel- und Oberstufe*, 127–93. Halle: Waisenhaus, 1893.

Kirchhoff, Alfred. *Die Schutzgebiete des deutschen Reiches zum Gebrauch beim Schulunterricht. Sonderabdruck aus des Verfassers "Erdkunde für Schulen."* Halle: Waisenhaus, 1893.

Kirchhoff, Alfred. "Über die Vorbereitung der Geographielehrer für ihren Beruf." *Verhandlungen des X. Deutschen Geographentages in Stuttgart, 1893.* Berlin: Reimer, 1893.

Kirchhoff, Alfred, ed. *Leitfaden für den Unterricht in der Geographie von Prof. Dr. H. A. Daniel*, 76th ed. Halle: Waisenhaus, 1872.

Kirchhoff, Alfred, ed. *Lehrbuch der Geographie für höhere Lehranstalten von Prof. Dr. H. A. Daniel*, 36th ed. Halle: Waisenhaus, 1873.

K. L. "Thomas Carlyle und die Negerfrage." *Deutsche Welt*, October 31, 1909.

Kleine, Friedrich Karl. "Report of the New Sleeping Sickness Focus and Ikoma." In *Final Report of the League of Nations International Commission on Human Trypanosomiasis.* Geneva: League of Nations Publications, 1928.

Klötzel, C. Z. "Die Erlebnisse deutscher Auswanderer in Persien. Schwere Beschuldigungen gegen Hauptmann Schmude. Der Reichsbeistand der 'Geropers' über die Expedition." *Berliner Tageblatt*, September 23, 1924.

Kohl, Horst, ed. *Die politischen Reden des Fürsten Bismarck 1847–1897*, vol. 11. Stuttgart: Cotta, 1894.
Kolonialpolitisches Aktionskomité, ed. *Kolonialpolitischer Führer*. Berlin: Wedekind, 1907.
Krebs, Emil. "Chinesisches Strafrecht." In *Die Strafgesetzgebung der Gegenwart in rechtsvergleichender Darstellung*, vol. 11, edited by Franz von Liszt and Georg Crusen. Berlin: Liebmann, 1899.
Kriegsrüstung und Kriegswirtschaft. Anlagen zum ersten Band, edited by the Reichsarchiv. Berlin, 1930.
Kronecker, Franz. *Fünfzehn Jahre Kiautschou, Eine kolonialmedizinische Studie*. Berlin, 1913.
Kropatschek, Hermann. *Zur geschichtlichen Entwicklung des geographischen Unterrichts, Separatabdruck aus den Verhandlungen des Zweiten Deutschen Geographentages zu Halle*. Berlin: W. Pormetter, 1882.
Kuhlenbeck, Wilhelm. "Die politischen Ergebnisse der Rassenforschung." *Alldeutsche Blätter*, June 25, 1905.
Külz, Ludwig. "Guinée française und Kamerun." *Amtsblatt für das Schutzgebiet Kamerun* 13–16 (1909): 115–118, 133–144, 144–148, 163–168.
Lange, Friedrich. *Reines Deutschtum: Gründzuge einer nationalen Weltanschauung*. Berlin: Verlag von Alexander Duncker, 1904.
Langenbeck, Rudolf. "Der Erdkundliche Unterricht nach den neuen Lehrpläne." *Sonderabdruck aus der Geographischen Zeitschrift* 1 (1895): 196–207.
Lattmann, Wilhelm. "Küstenklatsch und Kolonialpolitik." *Deutsch-Soziale Blätter*, August 18, 1906.
Laveran, Alphonse. "La section de médecine tropicale au congrès de Londres." *Bulletin de la Société de pathologie exotique* (1913): 546–548.
Laveran, Alphonse, et al. "Instructions données à la mission d'études française qui se rend au Congo en vue d'étudier la maladie du sommeil." *Annales d'hygiène et de médecine coloniale* 10.1 (1907): 95–96.
League of Nations, Health Organisation. *Report of the Second International Conference on Sleeping Sickness, Held in Paris November 5–7, 1928*. Geneva: League of Nations Publications, 1928.
Legrand, Daniel. "La Maladie du sommeil au Cameroun." *La Dépêche coloniale*, June 15, 1929.
Lehmann, Richard. "Der Bildungswert der Erdkunde." *Verhandlungen des elften Deutschen Geographentages zu Bremen am 17., 18., und 19. April 1895*, 191–221. Berlin: Reimer, 1896.
Lenin, Vladimir. *Imperialism, the Highest Stage of Capitalism*. New York: International Publishers, 1939.
Leutemann, Heinrich, ed. *Bilder aus dem Völkerleben von H. Leutemann. Mit erläuterndem Text von Professor Dr. Alfred Kirchhoff*. Fürth: Druck und Verlag von G. Löwensohn, 1888.
Litten, Wilhelm. *Persische Flitterwochen*. Berlin: Georg Stilke, 1925.

Loesch, Karl C., and Wilhelm E. Mühlman. *Die Völker und Rassen Südosteuropas*. Prague: Volk und Reich Verlag, 1943.
Lübbert, H. "Die Fischerei in den deutschen Kolonien." *Der Fischerbote* 5, 1913.
Lugard, Frederick D. *The Rise of Our East African Empire*, vol. 1. London: Frank Cass, 1968 [1893].
Lugard, Frederick. *The Dual Mandate in British Tropical Africa*. London: Blackwood, 1922.
Lugard, Frederick D. *The Dual Mandate in British Tropical Africa*. London: Blackwood, 1926.
Luxemburg, Rosa. "Die Lehren der letzten Reichstagswahl." In *Gesammelte Werke*, vol. 2. Berlin: Dietz, 1972.
Mahan, Alfred Thayer. *The Influence of Sea Power upon History, 1660–1783*. Boston: Little, Brown, 1890.
Mahan, Alfred Thayer. *The Influence of Sea Power upon the French Revolution and Empire, 1793–1812*. 2 vols. Boston: Little, Brown, 1892.
Mahan, Alfred Thayer. *The Interest of America in Sea Power: Present and Future*. Boston: Little, Brown, 1897.
Mahan, Alfred Thayer. *Sea Power in Its Relation to the War of 1812*. Boston: Little, Brown, 1905.
Mahan, Alfred Thayer. *Some Neglected Aspects of War*. Boston: Little, Brown, 1907.
Mahan, Alfred Thayer. *The Interest of America in International Conditions*. Boston: Little, Brown, 1910.
Mann, Thomas. "Soll Deutschland Kolonialpolitik treiben? Eine Umfrage aus dem Jahr 1927." *Europäische Gespräche, Hamburger Monatshefte für Auswärtige Politik* 5 (1927): 624–626.
Martin, Camille. "Publications diverses sur les colonies allemandes." *La Quinzaine coloniale* 13.13, 1909.
Martin, Gustave. *L'existence au Cameroun: Études sociales, études médicales, études d'hygiène et de prophylaxie*. Paris: E. Larose, 1921.
Marx, Karl. *Capital*, vol. 1, translated by Ben Fowkes. New York: Penguin, 1992.
Meineke, Gustave. "Wir sehen in Deutschland eine mächtige Agitation und hören den lauten Ruf nach endlicher Lösung der Colonialfrage!" *Gartenlaube*, 1884.
Meinhof, Carl. "Das Studium der Kolonialsprachen." *Zeitschrift für Kolonialsprachen* 1 (1910–11): 1–4.
Methner, Wilhelm. *Unter drei Gouverneuren: Sechzehn Jahre Dienst in deutschen Tropen*. Breslau: Wilhelm Gottlieb Korn Verlag, 1938.
Mohr, Friedrich Wilhelm. *Handbuch für das Schutzgebiet Kiautschou*. Qingdao: Schmidt, 1911.
Mühlmann, Wilhelm E. "Eckstein und Horn bei Polynesiern und Semiten." *Zeitschrift für Ethnologie* 64 (1932): 173–180.
Mühlmann, Wilhelm E. "Die geheime Gesellschaft der Arioi: Eine Studie über polynesische Geheimbünde, mit besonderer Berücksichtigung der Siebungs- und Auslesevorgänge in Alt-Tahiti." Doctoral diss., Berlin, 1932.

Mühlmann, Wilhelm E. "Die Begriffe 'Ati und Mataeinaa: Ein Beitrag zur politischen Entwicklung und Besiedlungsgeschichte Polynesiens." *Anthropos* 29.5–6 (1934): 739–756.

Mühlmann, Wilhelm E. "Die Frage der arischen Herkunft der Polynesier." *Zeitschrift für Rassenkunde* 1.1 (1935): 3–16.

Mühlmann, Wilhelm E. *Rassen- und Völkerkunde*. Brunswick: Friedrich Vieweg und Sohn, 1935.

Mühlmann, Wilhelm E. "Politisch-katholische Rassenforschung?" *Volk und Rasse* 12 (1937): 35–38.

Mühlmann, Wilhelm E. "Umvolkung und Volkwerdung." *Deutsche Arbeit* 42.1, 1942.

Mühlmann, Wilhelm E. "Echtes und unechtes Slawentum in der deutschen Ostbewegung." *Deutsche Arbeit* 43.3 (1943): 69, 75.

Mühlmann, Wilhelm E. *Assimilation, Umvolkung, Volkwerdung: Ein globaler Überblick und ein Programm*. Stuttgart: Kohlhammer, 1944.

Nadolny, Rudolf. *Mein Beitrag*. Wiesbaden: Limes Verlag, 1955.

Naumann, Edmund. "Geographische Tagesfragen. X. Die Geographie in der Schule." *Allgemeine Zeitung* 29, January 29, 1890.

Neubach, Helmut. *Die Ausweisung von Polen und Juden aus Preußen 1885/86*. Wiesbaden: Harrassowitz, 1967.

Nocht, Bernhard. "Zur Abwehr!" *Sonder-Abdruck aus Archiv für Schiffs- und Tropenhygiene* 23 (1919): 101.

Norem, Ralph A. *Kiaochow Leased Territory*. Berkeley: University of California Press, 1936.

Nowack, F., H. Paust, H. Sieber, and J. G. Steinweller, eds. *Der Unterricht in den Realien. Eine methodische Anweisung mit Lehrproben für die verschiednen Zweige des realistischen Unterrichts in der Volksschule*. Part 1: *Geographie von H. Nowack*, 3rd ed. Breslau: Ferdinand Hirt, 1897.

O.E. "Dernburgs Programm-Rede." *Deutsche Zeitung*, November 30, 1906.

Oehlmann, Ernst., ed. *E. v. Seydlitz'sche Geographie. Ausgabe B. Kleine Schul-Geographie*, 21st ed. Breslau: Ferdinand Hirt, 1897.

Osler, William. *Report of Proceedings on the Occasion of Professor W. Osler, F.R.S., Address "The Nation and the Tropics."* London: Berryman, 1909.

Palyi, Melchior, ed. *Hauptprobleme der Soziologie. Erinnerungsgabe für Max Weber*, 2 vols. Munich and Leipzig: Duncker und Humblot, 1923.

"Papuas." In *Bilder aus dem Völkerleben von H. Leutemann. Mit erläuterndem Text von Professor Dr. Alfred Kirchhoff*, edited by Heinrich Leutemann. Fürth: G. Löwensohn, 1888.

Paquet, A. "Vorwort." In *Chinas Verteidigung gegen europäische Ideen*, edited by Ku Hung-Ming. Jena: Diederichs, 1911: i–xiv.

Paquet, A. *Li, oder Im neuen Osten*. Frankfurt: Rütten und Loening, 1912.

Paquet, A. "Der Kaisergedanke." *Der neue Merkur* 1 (1914): 45–62.

Partsch, Joseph. *Die Schutzgebiete des Deutschen Reiches. Für die Schüler höherer Lehranstalten*. Berlin: Reimer, 1893.

Pischel, Richard, and Karl F. Geldner. *Vedische Studien*, vol. 1. Stuttgart: W. Kohlhammer, 1889.

Pope, William J. "Synthetic Therapeutic Agents." *British Medical Journal*, March 8, 1924.

Präger, Erich. *Die Deutsche Kolonialgesellschaft 1882–1907*. Berlin: Dietrich Reimer / Ernst Vohsen, 1908.

Reismann-Grone, Theodor, and Eduard von Liebert. "Überseepolitik oder Festlandspolitik?" *Alldeutsche Flugschriften* 22. Munich: Lehmann, 1905.

Rohrbach, Paul. *Die Bagdadbahn*, 2nd ed. Berlin: Wiegandt und Grieben, 1902.

Rohrbach, Paul. *Deutschland unter den Weltvölkern: Materialien zur auswärtigen Politik*. Berlin: Fortschritt, 1903.

Rohrbach, Paul. *Deutsche Kolonialwirtschaft*. 2 vols. Berlin-Schöneberg: Buchverlag der Hilfe, 1907, 1909.

Rohrbach, Paul. *Der deutsche Gedanke in der Welt*. Düsseldorf: K. R. Langewiesche, 1912.

Rohrbach, Paul. "Das Kriegsziel im Schützengraben." *Deutsche Politik* 6 (February 4, 1916); quoted by Fischer, *Germany's Aims*, 160.

Rohrbach, Paul. *Weltpolitisches Wanderbuch, 1897–1915*. Königstein im Taunus: K. R. Langewiesche, 1916.

Rohrbach, Paul. *Um die Teufels Handschrift. Zwei Menschenalter erlebter Weltgeschichte*. Hamburg: Dulk, 1953.

Rondet-Saint, Maurice. *Sur les routes du Cameroun et de l'A.E.F.* Paris: Jouve, 1933.

Rosen, Friedrich. *Oriental Memories of a German Diplomatist*. London: Methuen, 1930.

Rosenberg, Alfred. *Der Zukunftsweg einer Deutschen Außenpolitik*. Munich: Eher-Verlag, 1927.

Rössger, Richard. "Die Pflege der Erdkunde in den höheren Schulen." *Deutsche Kolonialzeitung* 44, November 1, 1900.

Rössler, Constantin. *Das deutsche Reich und die kirchliche Frage*. Würzburg: Grunow, 1876.

Sachau, Eduard. *Bericht über die Eröffnung des Seminars für Orientalische Sprachen an der Königlichen Friedrich-Wilhelms-Universität*. Berlin: A. Asher, 1888.

Sachau, Eduard. *Bericht über die Wirksamkeit des Seminars für Orientalische Sprachen*. Berlin: Reichsdruckerei, 1893.

Sachau, Eduard. *Denkschrift über das Seminar für Orientalische Sprachen*. Berlin: Reichsdruckerei, 1912.

Sandwith, F. M. "A Visit to the Tropical School at Hamburg." *Transactions of the Royal Society of Tropical Medicine* 1.1 (1907): 60–67.

Schilling, Claus. "Die Schulen für Tropenmedizin in England." *Klinisches Jahrbuch* (1907): 495–501.

Schilling, Claus. "Bericht über eine Studienreise nach West-Afrika." *Abdruck aus dem Klinischen Jahrbuch* 19 (1908): 1–40.

Schilling, Claus. "Über den ärztlichen Dienst in den deutschen Schutzgebieten." *Beihefte z. Archiv für Schiffs- und Tropenhygiene* 13 (1909): 32–45.

Schilling, Claus. "Welche Bedeutung haben die neuen Fortschritte der Tropenhygiene für unsere Kolonien." *Verhandlungen des deutschen Kolonialkongresses 1910*. Berlin: Verlag Kolonialkriegerdank (1910): 162–185.

Schmitt, Carl. *The Concept of the Political*, translated by George Schwab. 1932. Reprint, Chicago: University of Chicago Press, 2007.

Schmitt, Carl. *Der Nomos der Erde im Völkerrecht des Ius Publicum Europaeum*. Cologne: Greven, 1950.

Schmitt, Carl. *Nomos of the Earth*, translated by G. L. Ulmen. 1950. Reprint, New York: Telos Press, 2003.

Schmitt, Carl. *Staat, Großraum, Nomos. Arbeiten aus den Jahren 1916–1969*, edited by Günter Maschke. Berlin: Duncker und Humblot, 1995.

Schmoller, Gustav. "Die wirtschaftliche Zukunft Deutschlands und die Flottenvorlage." In *Zwanzig Jahre Deutscher Politik (1897–1917): Aufsätze und Vorträge von Gustav Schmoller*, edited by Lucie Schmoeller. Munich and Leipzig: Duncker and Humblot, 1920.

Schmoller, Gustav, Bernhard Dernburg, Walter Delbrück, et al. *Reichstagsauflösung und Kolonialpolitik. Offener stenographische Bericht über die Versammlung in der Berliner Hochschule für Musik am 8. Januar 1907*. Berlin: Wedekind, 1907.

Schrameier, Ludwig Wilhelm. *Aus Kiautschous Verwaltung. Die Land-, Steuer- und Zollpolitik des Kiautschougebietes*. Jena: G. Fischer, 1914.

Schrameier, Ludwig Wilhelm. *Kiautschou. Seine Entwicklung und Bedeutung. Ein Rückblick*. Schriften des Deutsch-Chinesischen Verbandes, 1. Berlin: Curtius, 1915.

Seager, Robert, II, and Doris D. Maguire. *Letters and Papers of Alfred Thayer Mahan*. Annapolis, MD: Naval Institute Press, 1975.

Sembritzki, Emil. *Der Kolonialfreund*. Berlin: Kolonie und Heimat Verlag, 1912.

Severing, Carl. *Mein Lebensweg*, vol. 1: *Vom Schlosser zum Minister*. Cologne: Greven, 1950.

Seÿffert, Rudolf. *Die Reklame des Kaufmanns*. Leipzig: Gloeckner, 1914.

Shahbaz, Yonan. *The Rage of Islam: An Account of the Massacre of Christians by the Turks in Persia*, 3rd. ed. Philadelphia: Judson Press, 1918.

Simon, Hermann, ed. *E. v. Seydlitz'sche Geographie. Ausgabe B. Kleine Schul-Geographie*, 19th ed. Breslau: Ferdinand Hirt, 1881.

Simon, Hermann, and Ernst Oehlmann, eds. *E. v. Seydlitz'sche Geographie. Ausgabe B. Kleine Schul-Geographie*, 20th ed. Breslau: Ferdinand Hirt, 1885.

Soley, James R. *The Navy in the Civil War: The Blockade and the Cruisers*. New York: Scribner's, 1883.

Spellenberg, Friedrich, with Carl Meinhof and Johanna Vöhringer. *Die Sprache der Bo oder Bankon in Kamerun*. Nendeln: Kraus, 1922. Reprint, 1969.

Spindler, Arno. "Der Handelskrieg mit U-Booten." In *Der Krieg zur See 1914–1918*, vol. 1, edited by the Marinearchiv. Berlin: Mittler und Sohn, 1932.

Stein, Adolf. "Die Bastardgefahr." *Deutsch-Soziale Blätter*, July 8, 1908.

Steudel, Emil. "Der Mangel an franzosischen Kolonialärtzen und seine Folgen." *Deutsche Medizinsche Wochenschrift* 10 (1931).

Steudel, Emil. "Die Ärztenot in Afrika." *Sonderabdruck der Illustrierten Auslands- und Kolonialzeitung—"Afrika Nachrichten"* 22 (1930): 1–2.

Stockton, Charles H. *Preparation for War: A Discussion of Some of the Various Elements to Be Considered in the Formation of Plans of Operations and in the Study of Campaigns, Delivered May 31, 1899*. Washington, DC: Government Printing Office, 1899.

Stockton, H. C. "Would Immunity from Capture, during War, of Non-offending Private Property upon the High Seas Be in the Interest of Civilization?" *American Journal of International Law* 1 (October 1907): 930–943.

Stockton, Herbert C. "Address on the Codification of the Laws of Naval Warfare." *American Society of International Law Proceedings* 61 (1909): 61–84.

Stockton, Herbert C. "The International Naval Conference of London, 1908–1909." *American Journal of International Law* 3 (July 1909): 596–618.

Stollwerck, Walter. *Der Kakao und die Schokoladenindustrie. Eine Wirtschafts-Statistische Untersuchung.* Jena: Gustav Fischer, 1907.

Stolze F. and F. C. Andreas. *Die Handelsverhältnisse Persiens, mit besonderer Berücksichtigung der deutschen Interessen.* Gotha: Justus Perthes, 1885.

Stuhlmann, Franz. "Auszüge aus den Berichten der Bezirksämter, Militärstationen und anderer Berichtsstellen über die wirtschaftliche Entwicklung im Berichtsjahr vom 1. Apr. 1901 bis 31. März 1902." *Berichte über Land- und Forstwirtschaft in Deutsch-Ostafrika* 1 (1902–1903): 205–323.

Stuhlmann, Franz. "Übersicht über Land- und Forstwirtschaft in Deutsch-Ostafrika im Berichtsjahre vom 1. Juli 1900 bis 30. Juni 1901." *Berichte über Land- und Forstwirtschaft in Deutsch-Ostafrika* 1 (1902–1903): 1–23.

Stuhlmann, Franz. *Beiträge zur Kulturgeschichte von Ostafrika.* Berlin: Reimer, 1909.

Stuhlmann, Franz. *Handwerk und Industrie in Ostafrika: Kulturgeschichtliche Betrachtungen.* Hamburg: L. Friederichsen, 1910.

Tanon, L., and E. Jamot. "La maladie du sommeil au Cameroun." *Presse médicale* 68, August 23, 1924.

Tappenbeck, Ernst. *Deutsch-Neuguinea.* Berlin: Wilhelm Süsserott, 1901.

Thurnwald, Richard. "Koloniale Eingeborenenpolitik." *Archiv für Rassen- und Gesellschafts-Biologie* 2, 1905.

Thurnwald, Richard. "Die eingeborenen Arbeitskräfte im Südseeschutzgebiet." *Koloniale Rundschau* 10 (1910): 607–632.

Thurnwald, Richard. "Das Rechtsleben der Eingeborenen der deutschen Südseeinseln, seine geistigen und wirtschaftlichen Grundlagen." *Blätter fur Vergleichende Rechtswissenschaft und Volkswirtschaftslehre* 5.5–6, 1910.

Thurnwald, Richard. "Angewandte Ethnologie in der Kolonialpolitik." In *Verhandlungen der ersten Hauptversammlung fur Vergleichende Rechtswissenschaft und Volkswirtschaftslehre*, 59–69. Berlin: Franz Vahlen, 1912.

Thurnwald, Richard. *Forschungen auf den Salomo-Inseln und dem Bismarck-Archipel*, vol. 1. Berlin: Reimer, 1912.

Thurnwald, Richard. "Die Kolonien als Friedensbürgschaft." *Blätter für Vergleichende Rechtswissenschaft und Volkswirtschaftslehre* 14.4–6 (1918): 170–185.

Thurnwald, Richard. "Der Wert von Neu-Guinea als Deutsche Kolonie." *Koloniale Rundschau* 1–2, 1918.

Thurnwald, Richard. *Die menschliche Gesellschaft*, vol. 1. Berlin: Walter de Gruyter, 1931.

Thurnwald, Richard. "Die Neger an der Schreibmachine. Soziale Wandlungen in Afrika. Mit Bildern von der Schomburgh-Afrika-Expedition." *Die Koralle* 8.4 (1932): 154–157.

Thurnwald, Richard. *Black and White in East Africa*. London: Routledge, 1935.
Thurnwald, Richard. "The Crisis of Imperialism in East Africa and Elsewhere." *Social Forces* 15.1, 1936.
Thurnwald, Richard. "The Price of the White Man's Peace." *Pacific Affairs* 9.3, 1936.
Thurnwald, Richard. "Die Kolonialfrage." *Jahrbücher für Nationalökonomie und Statistik* 145 (1937): 66–86.
Thurnwald, Richard. "Kolonialwirtschaftliche Betriebe." *Jahrbücher für Nationalökonomie und Statistik* 148 (1938): 48–62.
Thurnwald, Richard. *Koloniale Gestaltung. Methoden und Probleme überseeischer Ausdehnung*. Hamburg: Hoffmann und Campe Verlag, 1939.
Thurnwald, Richard. "Methoden in der Völkerkunde." In *Kultur und Rasse, Otto Reche zum 60. Geburtstag gewidmet von Schülern und Freunden*. Munich: J. F. Lehmann, 1939.
Thurnwald, Richard. "Die fremden Eingriffe in das Leben der Afrikaner und ihre Folgen." In *Völkerkunde von Afrika*, edited by H. Baumann, R. Thurnwald, and D. Westermann, 455–573. Essen: Essener Verlagsanstalt, 1940.
Thurnwald, Richard. "Aufbau und Sinn der Völkerwissenschaft." *Abhandlungen der Deutschen Akademie der Wissenschaften zu Berlin* 47.3, 1948.
Thurnwald, Richard. "Bericht zu der Sitzung der Arbeitsgemeinschaft Eingeborenenarbeit und -sozialrecht vom 11.7.38 über die Organisierung der Eingeborenenarbeit in Ostafrika und ihre Gestaltungsmöglichkeit auf nationalsozialistischer Grundlage." In *Akademie für Deutsches Recht 1933–1945, Protokolle der Ausschüsse*, vol. 12, edited by W. Schubert, 617–627. Berlin: De Gruyter, 2001.
Tille, Armin. "Alldeutsche Sozialpolitik." *Alldeutsche Blätter* 50, December 16, 1905.
Todd, John L. *Letters*. Senneville, PQ, 1977. Privately published.
Townsend, Mary E. "The Contemporary Colonial Movement in Germany." *Political Science Quarterly* 43.1 (March 1928): 64–75.
Uthemann, Walther, and Otto von Fürth. "Tsingtau. Ein kolonialhygienischer Rückblick auf die Entwicklung des deutschen Kiauschougebietes." Supplement 4, *Beihefte zum Archiv für Schiffs- und Tropenhygiene* 15.4. Leipzig: Barth, 1911.
Vageler, Paul. "Ugogo: Die Vorbedingungen für die wirtschaftliche Erschließung der Landschaft Ugogo in Deutsch-Ostafrika." Supplement to *Tropenpflanzer* 13, 1912.
Verhandlungen des deutschen Kolonialkongresses 1924 zu Berlin am 17. und 18. September 1924. Berlin: Verlag Kolonialkriegerdank, 1924.
Virchow, Rudolf. *Stenographische Berichte über die Verhandlungen des Abgeordnetenhauses*, 64th session, vol. 3, May 8, 1875.
Vohsen, Ernst, and Diedrich Westermann. "Unser Programm." *Koloniale Rundschau* 1 (1909): 1–7.
Volz, B., ed. *Lehrbuch der Geographie für höhere Unterrichtsanstalten von Prof. Dr. H. A. Daniel*, 64th ed. Halle: Waisenhaus, 1885.
Volz, B., ed. *Leitfaden für den Unterricht in der Geographie von Prof. Dr. H. A. Daniel*, 176th ed. Halle: Waisenhaus, 1891.
Volz, B., ed. *Leitfaden für den Unterricht in der Geographie von Prof. Dr. H. A. Daniel*, 210th ed. Halle: Waisenhaus, 1897.

Von Halle, Ernst. "Die englische Seemachtpolitik und die Versorgung Großbritanniens in Kriegszeiten." *Marine-Rundschau* 17 (1906): 911–927 and 19 (1908): 804–815.

Von Halle, Ernst. *Kriegsmarine und Handelsmarine*. Dresden: Zahn und Jaensch, 1907.

Von Hassell, Ulrich. "Die Bilanz der Kolonialpolitik für 1906." *Staatsbürger-Zeitung* (January 4, 1907), morning edition.

Von Liebert, Eduard. *Aus einem bewegten Leben: Erinnerungen*. Munich: J. F. Lehmann Verlag, 1925.

Von Luschan, Felix. "Rassen und Völker." In *Weltgeschichte*, vol. 1, edited by J. von Pflugk-Harttung. Berlin: Ullstein, 1909, 48.

Von Luschan, Felix. *Anthropological View of Race*. New York: Hamburg-Amerika Linie, 1915.

Von Maltzahn, Curt. "Das Meer als Operationsfeld und als Kampffeld." *Marine-Rundschau* (1904): 273–290, 412–426.

Von Maltzahn, Curt. *Der Seekrieg: Seine geschichtliche Entwicklung vom Zeitalter der Entdeckungen bis zur Gegenwart*. Leipzig: Teubner, 1906.

Von Melle, Werner. *Dreißig Jahre Hamburger Wissenschaft, 1891–1921*, vol. 1. Hamburg: Hamburgische Wissenschaftliche Stiftung, 1923.

Von Randow, Albert. "Die Landesverweisungen aus Preußen und die Erhaltung des Deutschtums an der Ostgrenze." *Jahrbuch für Gesetzgebung, Verwaltung und Volkswirtschaft im Deutschen Reich* 10 (1886): 91–125.

Von Schwiessel, Hans Heinrich. "Kolonial-Dummheiten." *Hammer: Blätter für deutschen Sinn* 3, 1904.

Von Seydlitz, Ernest. *Kleine Schul-Geographie. Kleinere Ausgabe des Leitfadens für den geographischen Unterricht*, 13th ed. Breslau: Ferdinand Hirt, 1871.

Von St. Paul-Illaire, Walter, et al. *Taschenbuch für Deutsch-Ostafrika*. Berlin: Wilhelm Weicher, 1911.

Von Tirpitz, Alfred. *Deutsche Ohnmachtspolitik im Weltkriege*. Hamburg: Hanseat Verlagsanst, 1926.

Von Treitschke, Heinrich. "Die ersten Versuche deutscher Kolonialpolitik." In *Deutsche Kämpfe. Schriften zur Tagespolitik*, 334–352. Leipzig: S. Hirzel, 1896.

Von Vietinghoff-Scheel, Leopold. "Grundlinien künftiger innerer Arbeit." *Der Panther* 3.10 (1915): 1198–1221.

Wang, C. D. "Die Staatsidee des Konfuzius und ihre Beziehung zur konstitutionelle Verfassung." *Mitteilungen des Seminars für Orientalische Sprachen zu Berlin* 16.1 (1913): 1–49.

Warburg, Otto. "Zum neuen Jahr." *Der Tropenpflanzer* 12 (1908): 1–22.

Ward, Lester F. *Soziologie von Heute*, translated by Richard Thurnwald. Innsbruck: Wagner, 1904.

Wardein. "Deutsche Kolonialgesellschaft." *Deutsch-Soziale Blätter*, June 12, 1912.

Wawrzinek, Kurt. *Die Entstehung der deutschen Antisemitenparteien 1873–1890*. Berlin: Ebering, 1927.

Weber, Alfred. "Deutschland und der wirtschaftlicher Imperialismus." *Preussische Jahrbücher* 116 (1904): 298–324.

Weber, Alfred. "Das selbstbestimmungsrecht der Völker und der Friede." *Preussische Jahrbücher* 171 (1918): 60–71.

Weber, Alfred. "Deutschland und die europäische Kulturkrise." *Die neue Rundschau* 35 (1924): 308–321.

Weber, Alfred. *Kulturgeschichte als Kultursoziologie*. Leiden: A. W. Sijthoff's Uitgeversmaatschappij, 1935.

Weber, Alfred. "Gibt es wertfreie Soziologie?" In *Einführung in die Soziologie*, 37–43. Munich: Piper, 1955.

Weber, Alfred. *Schriften zur Kultur- und Geschichtssoziologie (1906–1958). Alfred-Weber-Gesamtausgabe*, vol. 8. Marburg: Metropolis, 1997.

Weber, Max. *Die römische Agrargeschichte in ihrer Bedeutung für das Staats- und Privatrecht*. Stuttgart: F. Enke, 1891.

Weber, Max. *Der Nationalstaat und die Volkswirtschaftspolitik*. Freiburg and Leipzig: J. C. B. Mohr, 1895.

Weber, Max. "Hinduismus und Buddhismus." In Max Weber, *Gesammelte Aufsätze zur Religionssoziologie*, vol. 2. Tübingen: Mohr, 1921.

Weber, Max. "Entwicklungstendenz in der Lage der ostelbischen Landarbeiter." In *Gesammelte Aufsätze zur Sozial- und Wirtschaftsgeschichte*, 470–507. Tübingen: Mohr, 1924.

Weber, Max. "The Social Causes of the Decline of Ancient Civilization." *Journal of General Education* 5 (1950–1951): 75–88.

Weber, Max. *The Religion of China: Confucianism and Taoism*. New York: Free Press, 1964.

Weber, Max. *The Agrarian Sociology of Ancient Civilizations*. London: NLB, 1976.

Weber, Max. *Economy and Society*. 2 vols. Berkeley: University of California Press, 1978.

Weber, Max. "The National State and Economic Policy (Freiburg Address)." *Economy and Society* 9 (1980): 428–449.

Weber, Max. *Die Lage der Landarbeiter im ostelbischen Deutschland, 1892*. In *Max-Weber-Gesamtausgabe* 1.3, edited by Martin Riesebrot. Tübingen: Mohr, 1984.

Weber, Max. "The National State and Economic Policy." In *Reading Weber*, edited by Keith Tribe, 188–209. London: Routledge, 1989.

Weber, Max. *Die Wirtschaftsethik der Weltreligionen. Konfuzianismus und Taoismus*. In *Max-Weber-Gesamtausgabe* 1.19, edited by H. Schmidt-Glintzer. Tübingen: Mohr, 1989.

Weber, Max. "Die nationalen Grundlagen der Volkswirtschaft. Vortrag am 12. März 1895 in Frankfurt am Main [Bericht des Frankfurter Journals]." In *Max-Weber-Gesamtausgabe* 4.2. Tübingen: Mohr, 1993.

Werner, Heinrich. *Ein Tropenarzt sah Afrika*. Strasbourg: Heitz, 1953.

White, Freda. *Mandates*. London: Jonathan Cape, 1926.

Wilson, Monica Hunter. *Reaction to Conquest. Effects of Contact with Europeans on the Pondo of South Africa*. London: Oxford University Press, 1936.

Wohltmann, Ferdinand. "Die wirtschaftliche Entwicklung unserer Kolonien." *Der Tropenpflanzer* 7 (1903): 53–66.

Zhengjian, Wang. *Qingdao.* (Qingdao, 1922).
Ziemann, Hans. "Is Sleeping Sickness of the Negroes an Intoxication or an Infection?" *Journal of Tropical Medicine* 5 (October 15, 1902): 309–314.
Ziemann, Hans. "Einige Hauptrichtlinien für die Künftige Sanitäre Koloniale Organisation." Berlin, BArch R1001 5641, Bl. 31–50.
Ziemann, Hans. "Wie erobert man Afrika für die weisse und farbige Rasse? Vortrag gehalten auf den Internationalen Kongress für Hygiene und Demographie zu Berlin, 1907." *Archiv für Schiffs- und Tropenhygiene* 11, 1907.
Zimmermann, Albrecht. "Erster Jahresbericht des Kaiserl. Biologisch-Landwirtschaftlichen Instituts Amani." *Berichte über Land- und Forstwirtschaft in Deutsch-Ostafrika* 1–3, 1902–1911.

SECONDARY SOURCES

Achilles, Robin. *Prügelstrafe und Züchtigungsrecht in den deutschen Kolonien Afrikas: Die Schattenseiten des Kolonialismus—Skandale in den Schutzgebieten.* Munich: GRIN Verlag, 2007.
Adas, Michael. *Machines as the Measure of Men: Science, Technology, and Ideologies of Western Dominance.* Ithaca, NY, and London: Cornell University Press, 1989.
Aitken, Robbie. *Exclusion and Inclusion: Gradations of Whiteness and Socio-economic Engineering in German Southwest Africa, 1884–1914.* New York: Peter Lang, 2007.
Aitken, Robbie. "From Cameroon to Germany and Back via Moscow and Paris: The Political Career of Joseph Bilé (1892–1959), Performer, 'Negerarbeiter,' and Comintern Activist." *Journal of Contemporary History* 43.4 (2007): 597–616.
Albrecht, Monika. "(Post-)Colonial Amnesia? German Debates on Colonialism and Decolonization in the Post-War Era." In *German Colonialism and National Identity*, edited by Michael Perraudin and Jürgen Zimmer, 187–196. London: Routledge, 2010.
Aldrich, Robert. *Greater France: A History of French Overseas Expansion.* Houndmills: Palgrave Macmillan, 1996.
Aldrich, Robert. *Colonialism and Homosexuality.* London: Routledge, 2003.
Allen, Ann Taylor. *Satire and Society in Wilhelmine Germany: Kladderadatsch and Simplicissimus, 1890–1914.* Lexington: University Press of Kentucky, 1984.
Allen, Kieran. *Max Weber: A Critical Introduction.* London: Pluto Press, 2004.
Almaguer, Tomas. *Racial Fault Lines: The Historical Origins of White Supremacy in California.* Berkeley: University of California Press, 1994.
Ames, Eric, Marcia Klotz, and Lora Wildenthal, eds. *Germany's Colonial Pasts.* Lincoln: University of Nebraska Press, 2005.
Amidon, Kevin S. "'Diesmal fehlt die Biologie!' Max Horkheimer, Richard Thurnwald, and the Biological Prehistory of German *Sozialforschung*." *New German Critique* 35.2 (2008): 103–137.
Anderson, Margaret Lavinia. "A German Way of War?" *German History* 22 (2004): 254–258.
Anderson, Margaret Lavinia. "How German Is It?" *German History* 24 (2006): 122–126.

Andriamananjara, Mialy. "Senegal: Africa according to Nicolas Sarkozy." www.global voicesonline.org/2007/08/24/senegal-africa-according-to-nicolas-sarkozy/ (no longer accessible).

Anna, Susanne, Katharina Metz, and Liane Sachs, eds. *Historische Plakate 1890–1914*. Stuttgart: Daco-Verlag Bläse, 1995.

Appadurai, Arjun. *Modernity at Large: Cultural Dimensions of Globalization*. Minneapolis: University of Minnesota Press, 1996.

Arendt, Hannah. *The Origins of Totalitarianism*. New York: Allen and Unwin, 1967.

Arendt, Hannah. *On Violence*. New York: Harvest, 1970.

Ascher, Abraham. "Imperialists within German Social Democracy prior to 1914." *Journal of Central European Affairs* 20 (1961): 397–422.

Aschheim, Steven E. *Brothers and Strangers: The East European Jew in German and German-Jewish Consciousness, 1800–1923*. Madison: University of Wisconsin Press, 1982.

Ash, M. G. "Scientific Changes in Germany 1933, 1945, 1990: Towards a Comparison." *Minerva* 37 (1999): 346.

Austen, Ralph A. *Northwest Tanzania under German and British Rule: Colonial Policy and Tribal Politics, 1889–1939*. New Haven, CT: Yale University Press, 1968.

Aynsley, Jeremy. *Graphic Design in Germany, 1890–1945*. Berkeley: University of California Press, 2000.

Bade, Klaus. *Friedrich Fabri und der Imperialismus in der Bismarckzeit: Revolution—Depression—Expansion*. Freiburg: Atlantis, 1975.

Bade, Klaus. "'Kulturkampf' auf dem Arbeitsmarkt. Bismarcks 'Polenpolitik' 1885–1890." In *Innenpolitische Probleme des Bismarck-Reiches*, edited by Otto Pflanze, 121–142. Munich: Oldenbourg, 1983.

Bade, Klaus. "Imperial Germany and West Africa: Colonial Movement, Business Interests, and Bismarck's 'Colonial Policies.'" In *Bismarck, Europe, and Africa: The Berlin Africa Conference 1884–1885 and the Onset of Partition*, edited by Stig Förster, Wolfgang J. Mommsen, and Ronald Edward Robinson. Oxford: Oxford University Press, 1988.

Badenberg, Nana. "Zwischen Kairo und Alt-Berlin." In *Mit Deutschland um die Welt. Eine Kulturgeschichte des Fremden in der Kolonialzeit*, edited by Alexander Honold and Klaus R. Scherpe, 190–99. Stuttgart: J. B. Metzler, 2004.

Balakrishnan, Gopal, ed. *Debating Empire*. London: Verso, 2003.

Bald, Detlef, and Gerhild Bald. *Das Forschungsinstitut Amani: Wirtschaft und Wissenschaft in der deutschen Kolonialpolitik Ostafrika 1900–1918*. Munich: Institut für Wirtschaftsforschung, 1972.

Balibar, Étienne. "Is There a 'Neo-Racism?'" In *Race, Nation, Class. Ambiguous Identities*, edited by Étienne Balibar and Immanuel Wallerstein, 17–28. London: Verso, 1991.

Ballantyne, Tony, and Antoinette Burton, eds. *Bodies in Contact: Rethinking Colonial Encounters in World History*. Durham, NC: Duke University Press, 2005.

Balzer, Brigitte. *Die preußische Polenpolitik 1894–1908 und die Haltung der deutschen konservativen und liberalen Parteien (unter besonderer Berücksichtigung der Provinz Posen)*. Frankfurt: Peter Lang, 1990.

Baranowski, Shelley. *Nazi Empire: German Imperialism and Colonialism from Bismarck to Hitler.* Cambridge: Cambridge University Press, 2011.

Barkin, Kenneth D. *The Controversy over German Industrialization 1890–1902.* Chicago: University of Chicago Press, 1970.

Barth, Boris. *Genozid: Völkermord im 20. Jahrhundert: Geschichte. Theorien Kontroversen.* Munich: Beck, 2006.

Basler, Werner. *Deutschlands Annexionspolitik in Polen und im Baltikum 1914–1918.* Berlin: Rütten und Loening, 1962.

Bauche, Manuela. "Medizin und Kolonialismus: Schlafkrankheitsbekämpfung in Kamerun, 1900–1914." Master's thesis, Humboldt-Universität, Berlin, 2005.

Bauernfeind, Martina. *Bürgermeister Georg Ritter von Schuh: Stadtentwicklung in Erlangen und Nürnberg im Zeichen der Hochindustrialisierung, 1878–1913.* Nuremberg: Stadtarchiv Nuremberg, 2000.

Bayly, C. A., Sven Beckert, Matthew Connelly, Isabel Hofmeyr, Wendy Kozol, and Patricia Seed. "AHR Conversation: On Transnational History." *American Historical Review* 111.5 (December 2006): 1446, 1459.

Bechhaus-Gerst, Marianne, ed. *Die (Koloniale) Begegnung: AfrikanerInnen in Deutschland 1880–1945, Deutsche in Afrika 1880–1918.* New York: Peter Lang, 2003.

Bechhaus-Gerst, Marianne, and Reinhard Klein-Arendt, eds. *AfrikanerInnen in Deutschland und Schwarze Deutsche: Geschichte und Gegenwart.* Münster: LIT, 2004.

Bechhaus-Gerst, Marianne, and Mechthild Leutner, eds. *Frauen in den deutschen Kolonien.* Berlin: Links, 2009.

Becker, Winfried. "Kulturkampf als Vorwand: Die Kolonialwahlen von 1907 und das Problem der Parlamentarisierung des Reiches." *Historisches Jahrbuch* 106 (1986): 59–84.

Beckert, Sven. "From Tuskegee to Togo: The Problem of Freedom in the Empire of Cotton." *Journal of American History* 92.2 (2005): 498–526.

Belgum, Kirsten. *Popularizing the Nation: Audience, Representation, and the Production of Identity in Die Gartenlaube, 1853–1900.* Lincoln: University of Nebraska Press, 1998.

Benjamin, Walter. "Theses on Philosophy of History." In *Illuminations*, edited by Hannah Arendt and translated by Harry Zohn. New York: Schocken, 1969.

Benninghoff-Lühl, Sibylle. *Deutsche Kolonialromane 1884–1914 in ihrem Entstehungs- und Wirkungszusammenhang.* Bremen: Übersee-Museum, 1983.

Bergen, Doris. "Tenuousness and Tenacity: The *Volksdeutschen* of Eastern Europe, World War Two and the Holocaust." In *The Heimat Abroad: The Boundaries of Germanness*, edited by Krista O'Donnell, Renate Bridenthal, and Nancy Reagin, 267–286. Ann Arbor: University of Michigan Press, 2005.

Berghahn, Volker R. *Germany and the Approach of War in 1914*, 2nd ed. Houndmills: Macmillan, 1993.

Berman, Nina. *Impossible Missions? German Economic, Military, and Humanitarian Efforts in Africa.* Lincoln: University of Nebraska Press, 2004.

Berman, Nina, Klaus Mühlhahn, and Patrice Nganang, eds. *German Colonialism Revisited: African, Asian, and Oceanic Experiences.* Ann Arbor: University of Michigan Press, 2014.

Berman, Russell. *Enlightenment or Empire? Colonial Discourse in German Culture.* Lincoln: University of Nebraska Press, 1998.
Bernardin, Susan, et al. *Trading Gazes: Euro-American Women Photographers and Native North Americans, 1880–1940.* New Brunswick, NJ: Rutgers University Press, 2003.
Bernstein, George. "Anti-Semitism in Imperial Germany 1871–1914: Selected Documents." EdD diss., Teachers College, Columbia University, 1973.
Bhabha, Homi. "Of Mimicry and Man: The Ambivalence of Colonial Discourse." *October* 28 (1984): 125–133.
Bieber, Horst. *Paul Rohrbach, ein konservativer Publizist und Kritiker der Weimarer Republik.* Munich-Pullach: Verlag Dokumentation, 1972.
Biener, Annette S. *Das deutsche Pachtgebiet Tsingtau in Schantung, 1897–1914.* Bonn: Institutioneller Wandel durch Kolonialisierung, 2001.
Blackbourn, David. "Das Kaiserreich transnational. Eine Skizze." In *Das Kaiserreich transnational. Deutschland in der Welt 1871–1914*, edited by Sebastian Conrad and Jürgen Osterhammel, 302–324. Göttingen: Vandenhoeck und Ruprecht, 2004.
Blackbourn, David. *The Conquest of Nature. Water, Landscape and the Making of Modern Germany.* London: Jonathan Cape, 2006.
Blackbourn, David, and Geoff Eley. *The Peculiarities of German History: Bourgeois Society and Politics in Nineteenth-Century Germany.* Oxford: Oxford University Press, 1984.
Blackbourn, David, and Geoff Eley. "Forum: Interview with David Blackbourn and Geoff Eley," *German History* 22.2 (2004): 229–245.
Blanke, Richard. *Prussian Poland and the German Empire 1871–1900.* New York: Columbia University Press, 1981.
Blaut, J. M. *The Colonizer's Model of the World.* New York: Guilford Press, 1993.
Bley, Helmut. *South-West Africa under German Rule 1894–1914.* London: Heinemann, 1971.
Bley, Helmut. *Namibia under German Rule.* Hamburg: LIT Verlag, 1996.
Bley, Helmut. "Der Traum vom Reich? Rechtsradikalismus als Antwort auf gescheiterte Illusionen im Deutschen Kaiserreich 1900–1918." In *Phantasiereiche: Der deutsche Kolonialismus aus kulturgeschichtlicher Perspektive*, edited by Birthe Kundrus, 56–70. Frankfurt: Campus, 2003.
Böhm, Ekkehard. *Überseehandel und Flottenbau: Hanseatische Kaufmannschaft und deutsche Seerüstung 1879–1902.* Düsseldorf: Bertelsmann Universitätsverlag, 1972.
Bolliger, Hans, Guido Magnaguagno, and Raimund Meyer. *Dada in Zürich.* Zürich: Arche, 1985.
Bönker, Dirk. "Zwischen Bürgerkrieg und Navalismus: Marinepolitik und Handelsimperialismus in den USA, 1865–1890." In *Das Militär und der Aufbruch in die Moderne 1860–1890*, edited by Michael Epkenhans and Gerhard P. Groß, 93–115. Munich: Oldenbourg, 2003.
Bönker, Dirk. "Ein 'German Way of War'? Deutscher Militarismus und maritime Kriegführung im Ersten Weltkrieg." In *Das Deutsche Kaiserreich in der Kontroverse. Eine Bilanz*, edited by Sven Oliver Müller and Cornelius Torp, 308–322. Göttingen: Vandenhoeck und Ruprecht, 2008.

Bönker, Dirk. *Militarism in a Global Age: Naval Ambitions in Germany and the United States before World War I*. Ithaca, NY: Cornell University Press, 2012.

Borowsky, Peter. "Paul Rohrbach und die Ukraine." In *Deutschland in der Weltpolitik des 19. und 20. Jahrhunderts*, edited by Imanuel Geiss and Bernd-Jürgen Wendt, 437–453. Düsseldorf: Droste, 1973.

Borscheid, Peter, and Clemens Wischermann, eds. *Bilderwelt des Alltags. Werbung in der Konsumgesellschaft des 19. und 20. Jahrhunderts*. Stuttgart: Steiner, 1995.

Botsch, Gideon. *Politische Wissenschaft im Zweiten Weltkrieg. Die deutschen Auslandswissenschaften im Einsatz 1940–1945*. Schöningh: Paderborn, 2006.

Bourdieu, Pierre. "The Peculiar History of Scientific Reason." *Sociological Forum* 6.1 (1991): 3–26.

Bourdieu, Pierre. "For a Sociology of Sociologists." In *Sociology in Question*, 49–53. London: Sage, 1993.

Bourdieu, Pierre. *The Rules of Art: Genesis and Structure of the Literary Field*. Stanford: Stanford University Press, 1996.

Bourdieu, Pierre. "Rethinking the State: Genesis and Structure of the Bureaucratic Field." in *State/Culture: Historical Studies of the State in the Social Sciences*, edited by George Steinmetz, 53–75. Ithaca, NY: Cornell University Press, 1999.

Bourdieu, Pierre. *Pascalian Meditations*, translated by Richard Nice. Stanford, CA: Stanford University Press, 2000.

Bourdieu, Pierre. "Colonialism and Ethnography: Foreword to Pierre Bourdieu's *Travail et travailleurs en Algérie*," translated by Derek Robbins and Rachel Gomme. *Anthropology Today* 19.2 (April 2003): 13–18.

Bourdieu, Pierre. *Science of Science and Reflexivity*, translated by Richard Nice. Chicago: University of Chicago Press, 2004.

Bourdieu, Pierre. *Sketch for a Self-Analysis*, translated by Richard Nice. Cambridge: Polity, 2007.

Bourdieu, Pierre. *On the State*. Cambridge, UK: Polity, 2014.

Bourke, Eoin. "Two Foxes of Glenarvon." In *Processes of Transposition: German Literature and Film*, edited by Christiane Schönfeld and Hermann Rasche. Amsterdam: Rodopi, 2007.

Bowersox, Jeff. "Raising Germans in the Age of Empire: Education and the Modern Colonial Imagination in Germany, 1871–1914." PhD diss., University of Toronto, 2008.

Bowersox, Jeff. *Raising Germans in the Age of Empire: Youth and Colonial Culture, 1871–1914*. Oxford: Oxford University Press, 2013.

Boyd, John. "Sleeping Sickness: The Castellani-Bruce Controversy." *Notes and Records of the Royal Society of London* 28.1 (1973): 93–110.

Brahm, Felix. "Die Lateinamerika-Beziehungen des Hamburger Tropeninstituts 1900–1945." MA thesis, Universität Hamburg, 2002.

Brehl, Medardus. *Vernichtung der Herero: Diskurse der Gewalt in der deutschen Kolonialliteratur*. Munich: Wilhelm Fink, 2007.

Breuning, E. C. M., and M. E. Chamberlain, eds. *Bedarf Deutschland der Kolonien?* Lewiston, NY: Edwin Mellen, 1998.

Bridenthal, Renate. "Germans from Russia: The Political Network of a Double Diaspora." In *The Heimat Abroad: The Boundaries of Germanness*, edited by Krista O'Donnell, Renate Bridenthal, and Nancy Reagin, 187–218. Ann Arbor: University of Michigan Press, 2005.

Bridgman, Jon M. *The Revolt of the Hereros*. Berkeley: University of California Press, 1981.

Briggs, Laura. *Reproducing Empire: Race, Sex, Science, and U.S. Imperialism in Puerto Rico*. Berkeley: University of California Press, 2002.

Bright, Charles, and Michael Geyer. "Regimes of Global Order: Global Integration and the Production of Difference in Twentieth-Century World History." In *Interactions: Transregional Perspectives on World History*, edited by Jerry H. Bentley, Renate Bridenthal, and Anand A. Yang, 202–238. Honolulu: University of Hawaii Press, 2005.

Broszat, Martin. *Zweihundert Jahre deutsche Polenpolitik*. Frankfurt: Suhrkamp, 1972.

Bublitz, Hannelore. "Zur Konstruktion von 'Kultur' und Geschlecht um 1900: Archäologie 'des Menschen der Moderne.'" In *Der Gesellschaftskörper: Zur Neuordnung von Kultur und Geschlecht um 1900*, edited by Hannelore Bublitz, Andrea Seier, and Christine Hanke, 19–96. Frankfurt: Campus, 2000.

Bublitz, Hannelore, ed. *Das Geschlecht der Moderne: Genealogie und Archäologie der Geschlechterdifferenz*. Frankfurt: Campus, 1998.

Buck-Morss, Susan. *Hegel, Haiti and Universal History*. Pittsburgh: University of Pittsburgh Press, 2009.

Bueb, Volkmar. *Die "Junge Schule" der französischen Marine: Strategie und Politik, 1875–1900*. Boppard: H. Boldt, 1971.

Burke, Timothy. *Lifebuoy Men, Lux Women: Commodification, Consumption, and Cleanliness in Modern Zimbabwe*. Durham, NC: Duke University Press, 1996.

Burleigh, Michael. *The Third Reich: A New History*. London: Macmillan, 2000.

Burton, Antoinette, ed. *After the Imperial Turn: Thinking with and through the Nation*. Durham, NC: Duke University Press, 2003.

Calhoun, Craig, Frederick Cooper, and Kevin W. Moore, eds. *Lessons of Empire: Imperial Histories and American Power*. New York: New Press, 2006.

Campt, Tina Marie. "Afro-German: The Convergence of Race, Sexuality and Gender in the Formation of German Ethnic Identity, 1919–1960." PhD diss., Cornell University, 1996.

Campt, Tina M. *Other Germans: Black Germans and the Politics of Race, Gender, and Memory in the Third Reich*. Ann Arbor: University of Michigan Press, 2004.

Campt, Tina M., Pascal Grosse, and Yara-Colette Lemke-Muniz de Faria. "Blacks, Germans, and the Politics of Imperial Imagination, 1920–60." In *The Imperialist Imagination: German Colonialism and Its Legacy*, edited by Sara Friedrichsmeyer, Sara Lennox, and Susanne Zantop, 205–229. Ann Arbor: University of Michigan Press, 1998.

Canis, Konrad. *Von Bismarck zur Weltpolitik. Deutsche Außenpolitik 1890 bis 1902*. Berlin: Akademieverlag, 1997.

Canning, Kathleen. *Gender History in Practice: Historical Perspectives on Bodies, Class, and Citizenship*. Ithaca, NY: Cornell University Press, 2006.

Césaire, Aimé. *Discourse on Colonialism*, translated by Joan Pinkham. New York: Monthly Review Press, 1972.
Chanock, Martin. *Law, Custom, and Social Order: The Colonial Experience in Malawi and Zambia*. Cambridge: Cambridge University Press, 1985.
Chatterjee, Partha. *The Nation and Its Fragments: Colonial and Postcolonial Histories*. Princeton, NJ: Princeton University Press, 1993.
Chickering, Roger. *We Men Who Feel Most German: A Cultural Study of the Pan-German League, 1886–1914*. Boston: Allen and Unwin, 1984.
Chin, Rita. *The Guest Worker Question in Postwar Germany*. Cambridge: Cambridge University Press, 2007.
Chu, Winson, Jesse Kauffman and Michael Meng. "A Sonderweg through Eastern Europe? The Varieties of German Rule in Poland during the Two World Wars." *German History* 31 (2013): 318–344.
Ciarlo, David M. "Consuming Race, Envisioning Empire: Colonialism and German Mass Culture, 1887–1914." PhD diss., University of Wisconsin–Madison, 2003.
Ciarlo, David. "Globalizing German Colonialism." *German History* 26.2 (2008): 285–298.
Ciarlo, David. *Advertising Empire: Race and Visual Culture in Imperial Germany*. Cambridge, MA: Harvard University Press, 2011.
Ciarlo, David. "Picturing Genocide in German Consumer Culture, 1904–1910." In *German Colonialism and National Identity*, edited by Michael Perraudin and Jürgen Zimmerer. New York: Routledge, 2011.
Clancy-Smith, Julia, and Frances Gouda, eds. *Domesticating the Empire: Race, Gender, and Family Life in French and Dutch Colonialism*. Charlottesville: University Press of Virginia, 1998.
Clifford, James. *The Predicament of Culture*. Cambridge, MA: Harvard University Press, 1988.
Cline, Catherine Ann. "Introduction." In E. D. Morel, *Truth and the War*. New York: Garland, 1972.
Clyde, David. *History of the Medical Services of Tanganyika*. Dar es Salaam: Government Press of Tanzania, 1962.
Cohen, Paul A. *History in Three Keys: The Boxers as Event, Experience and Myth*. New York: Columbia University Press, 1997.
Comaroff, John L. "Images of Empire, Contests of Conscience: Models of Colonial Domination in South Africa." In *Tensions of Empire: Colonial Cultures in A Bourgeois World*, edited by Frederick Cooper and Ann Laura Stoler. Berkeley: University of California Press, 1997.
Connell, R. W. "Why Is Classical Theory Classical?" *American Journal of Sociology* 102.6 (1997): 1511–1557.
Conrad, Sebastian. "Doppelte Marginalisierung: Plädoyer für eine Transnationale Perspektive auf die Deutsche Geschichte." *Geschichte und Gesellschaft* 28 (2002): 145–169.
Conrad, Sebastian. *Globalisierung und Nation im Deutschen Kaiserreich*. Munich: Beck, 2006.

Conrad, Sebastian. *Deutsche Kolonialgeschichte*. Munich: Beck, 2008.
Conrad, Sebastian. *Globalisation and the Nation in Imperial Germany*, translated by Sorcha O'Hanagan. Cambridge: Cambridge University Press, 2010.
Conrad, Sebastian. *German Colonialism: A Short History*, translated by Sorcha O'Hagan. New York: Cambridge University Press, 2012.
Conrad, Sebastian. "Rethinking German Colonialism in a Global Age," *Journal of Imperial and Commonwealth History* 41 (2013): 543–566.
Conrad, Sebastian, and Klaus Mühlhahn. "Global Mobility and Nationalism: Chinese Migration and the Re-territorialization of Belonging, 1880–1910." In *Conceptions of World Order, ca. 1880–1935: Global Moments and Movements*, edited by Sebastian Conrad and Dominic Sachsenmaier, 181–212. New York: Palgrave Macmillan, 2007.
Conrad, Sebastian, and Jürgen Osterhammel, eds. *Das Kaiserreich transnational. Deutschland in der Welt 1871–1914*. Göttingen: Vandenhoeck und Ruprecht, 2006.
Conrad, Sebastian, and Dominic Sachsenmaier, eds. *Competing Visions of World Order: Global Moments and Movements, 1880s–1930s*. New York: Palgrave Macmillan, 2007.
Conte, Christopher A. "Imperial Science, Tropical Ecology, and Indigenous History: Tropical Research Stations in Northeastern German East Africa, 1896 to the Present." In *Colonialism and the Modern World*, edited by Gregory Blue, Martin Bunton, and Ralph Crozier, 246–261. Armonk, NY: Sharpe, 2002.
Conze, Werner. "Nationsbildung durch Trennung. Deutsche und Polen im Deutschen Osten." In *Innenpolitische Probleme des Bismarck-Reiches*, edited by Otto Pflanze, 95–119. Munich: Oldenbourg, 1983.
Coogan, John W. *The End of Neutrality: The United States, Britain, and Maritime Rights 1899–1915*. Ithaca, NY: Cornell University Press, 1981.
Cooper, Frederick. *Colonialism in Question: Theory, Knowledge, History*. Berkeley: University of California Press, 2005.
Cooper, Frederick. "Modernizing Colonialism and the Limits of Empire." In *Lessons of Empire: Imperial Histories and American Power*, edited by Craig Calhoun, Frederick Cooper, and Kevin W. Moore, 63–72. New York: New Press / Norton, 2006.
Cooper, Robert. *The Post-modern State and the World Order*. London: Demos, 2000.
Cooper, Robert. "Grand Strategy." *Prospect* 81 (December 2002): 26–32.
Cooper, Robert. "The New Liberal Imperialism." *The Observer*, April 7, 2002, http://observer.guardian.co.uk/comment/story/0,,680093,00.html (accessed October 10, 2013).
Cooper, Robert. "The Post-modern State." In *Reordering the World: The Long-Term Implications of September 11*, edited by Mark Leonard. London: Foreign Policy Centre, 2002.
Cooper, Robert. *The Breaking of Nations: Order and Chaos in the Twenty-First Century*. New York: Atlantic Press, 2003.
Cramer, Kevin. "A World Of Enemies: New Perspectives on German Military Culture and the Origins of the First World War." *Central European History* 39.2 (2006): 270–298.
Crothers, George Dunlap. *The German Elections of 1907*. New York: Columbia University Press, 1941.

Cunningham, Andrew. "Transforming Plague: The Laboratory and the Identity of Infectious Disease." In *The Laboratory Revolution in Medicine*, edited by Andrew Cunningham and Perry Williams, 209–244. Cambridge: Cambridge University Press, 1992.

Dabringshaus, Sabine. "An Army on Vacation? The German War in China 1900–1901." In *Anticipating Total War: The German and American Experiences*, edited by Manfred F. Boemeke, Roger Chickering, and Stig Förster, 459–476. Cambridge: Cambridge University Press, 1999.

Davis, Christian S. "Colonialism and Antisemitism during the *Kaiserreich*: Bernhard Dernburg and the Antisemites." *Leo Baeck Institute Year Book* 53 (2008): 31–56.

Davis, Christian S. *Colonialism, Antisemitism, and Germans of Jewish Descent in Imperial Germany*. Ann Arbor: University of Michigan Press, 2012.

Deist, Wilhelm. *Flottenpolitik und Flottenpropaganda. Das Nachrichtenbureau des Reichsmarineamts 1897–1914*. Stuttgart: Deutsche Verlags-Anstalt, 1976.

Demm, Eberhard. *Ein Liberaler in Kaiserreich und Republik: Der politische Weg Alfred Webers bis 1920*. Boppard: H. Boldt, 1990.

Demm, Eberhard. "Alfred Weber als Wissenschaftsorganisator." In *Heidelberger Sozial- und Staatswissenschaften: Das Institut für Sozial- und Staatswissenschaften zwischen 1918 und 1958*, edited by Reinhard Blomert, Hans-Ulrich Esslinger, and Norbert Giovannini, 97–116. Marburg: Metropolis, 1997.

Demm, Eberhard. *Geist und Politik im 20. Jahrhundert: Gesammelte Aufsätze zu Alfred Weber*. Frankfurt: Peter Lang, 2000.

Dencker, Berit. "Class and the Construction of the 19th Century German Male Body." *Journal of Historical Sociology* 15.2 (2002): 220–251.

Derks, H. "Social Sciences in Germany, 1933–1945." *German History* 17.2 (1999): 177–219.

Deutsch, Jan-Georg. *Emancipation without Abolition in German East Africa ca. 1884–1914*. Oxford: James Currey, 2006.

Dickinson, Edward Ross. "The German Empire: An Empire?" *History Workshop Journal* 66 (2008): 129–162.

Dirlik, Arif. *Global Modernity: Modernity in the Age of Global Capitalism*. Boulder, CO: Paradigm, 2007.

Doerr, Lambert, ed. *Peramiho 1898–1998: In the Service of the Missionary Church*, vol. 1. Ndanda-Peramiho: Benedictine Publications, 1998.

Drechsler, Horst. *Südwestafrika unter deutscher Kolonialherrschaft*. Berlin: Steiner, 1966.

Drechsler, Horst. *"Let Us Die Fighting": The Struggle of the Herero and Nama against German Imperialism, 1884–1915*. London: Zed, 1980.

Drummond, Elizabeth A. "'Durch Liebe stark, deutsch bis ins Mark': Weiblicher Kulturimperialismus und der Deutsche Frauenverein für die Ostmarken." In *Nation, Politik und Geschlecht. Frauenbewegungen und Nationalismus in der Moderne*, edited by Ute Planert, 147–164. Frankfurt: Campus, 2000.

Duara, Prasenjit. "Imperialism of 'Free Nations': Japan, Manchukuo and the History of the Present." In *Imperial Formations*, edited by Ann Laura Stoler, Carole McGranahan, and Peter C. Perdue, 211–239. Santa Fe: School for Advanced Research, 2007.

Dülffer, Jost. "Limitations on Naval Warfare and Germany's Future as a World Power: A German Debate 1904–1906." *War and Society* 3.2 (September 1985): 23–43.

Dumbuya, Peter A. *Tanganyika under International Mandate, 1919–1946*. Lanham, MD: University Press of America, 1995.

Eckart, Wolfgang U. *Deutsche Ärzte in China 1897–1914. Medizin als Kulturmission im Zweiten Deutschen Kaiserreich*. Stuttgart: Urban und Fischer, 1989.

Eckart, Wolfgang U. "Die Anfänge der deutschen Tropenmedizin—die Gründung des Hamburger Instituts für Schiffs- und Tropenkrankheiten." In *Meilensteine der Medizin*, edited by Heinz Schott, 411–418. Dortmund: Harenberg, 1996.

Eckart, Wolfgang U. *Medizin und Kolonialimperialismus: Deutschland 1884–1945*. Paderborn: Schöningh, 1997.

Eckart, Wolfgang U. "Generalarzt Ernst Rodenwaldt." In *Hitlers militärische Elite*, vol. 1: *Von den Anfängen des Regimes bis Kriegsbeginn*, edited by Gerd R. Ueberschär, 210–222. Darmstadt: Wissenschaftliche Buchgesellschaft, 1998.

Eckart, Wolfgang U. "The Colony as Laboratory: German Sleeping Sickness Campaigns in German East Africa and in Togo, 1900–1914." *History and Philosophy of the Life Sciences* 24.1 (2002): 69–89.

Eckart, Wolfgang U., and Hana Vondra. "Malaria and World War II: German Malaria Experiments 1939–1945." *Parassitologia* 42 (2000): 53–58.

Eckel, Jan. "Herrschaftsstabilisierende Denkmuster in der Geschichtswissenschaft währen des Nationalsozialismus. Eine Skizze der Voraussetzungen, Formen und Entwicklungen." In *Wissenschaft im Einsatz*, edited by Käte Meyer-Drawe and Kristin Platt. Munich: Fink, 2007.

Eckert, Andreas. *Grundbesitz, Landkonflikte und kolonialer Wandel: Douala 1880–1960*. Stuttgart: Steiner, 1999.

Eckert, Andreas, and Albert Wirz. "Wir nicht, die Anderern auch: Deutschland und der Kolonialismus." In *Jenseits des Eurozentrismus: Postkolonial Perspektive in den Geschichts- und Kulturwissenschaften*, edited by Sebastian Conrad and Shalini Randeria, 373–393. New York: Campus, 2002.

Eckert, Andreas, Albert Wirz, and Katrin Brommer, eds. *Alles unter Kontrolle: Disziplinierungsprozesse im kolonialen Tansania 1850–1960*. Cologne: Köppe, 2003.

Eddie, Scott M. "The Prussian Settlement Commission and the Activities in the Land Market, 1886–1918." In *Germans, Poland, and Colonial Expansion to the East: 1850 to the Present*, edited by Robert L. Nelson, 39–63. New York: Palgrave Macmillan, 2009.

Eley, Geoff. "The German Navy League in German Politics, 1898–1914." DPhil diss., University of Sussex, 1974.

Eley, Geoff. "Defining Social Imperialism: Use and Abuse of an Idea." *Social History* 1.3 (1976): 269–90.

Eley, Geoff. "German Politics and Polish Nationality: The Dialectic of Nation-Forming in the East of Prussia." *East European Quarterly* 18 (1984): 335–364.

Eley, Geoff. "Social Imperialism in Germany: Reformist Synthesis or Reactionary Sleight of Hand?" In *From Unification to Nazism: Reinterpreting the German Past*, 154–67. London: Allen and Unwin, 1986.

Eley, Geoff. "Conservatives and Radical Nationalists in Germany: The Production of Fascist Potentials, 1912–1928." In *Fascists and Conservatives: The Radical Right and the Establishment in Twentieth-Century Europe*, edited by Martin Blinkhorn, 64–65. London: Unwin Human, 1990.

Eley, Geoff. *Reshaping the German Right: Radical Nationalism and Political Change after Bismarck.* Ann Arbor: University of Michigan Press, 1991.

Eley, Geoff. *A Crooked Line: From Cultural History to the History of Society.* Ann Arbor: University of Michigan Press, 2005.

Eley, Geoff. "Historicizing the Global, Politicizing Capital: Giving the Present a Name." *History Workshop Journal* 63.1 (Spring 2007): 154–188.

Eley, Geoff. "What Was/Is the Imperial Imaginary? Britain in Europe and the World, 1815–2003." Neale Lecture in British History, University College, London, April 24, 2008. Unpublished MS.

Eley, Geoff. "Imperial Imaginary, Colonial Effect: Writing the Colony and the Metropole Together." In *Race, Nation, and Empire: Making Histories, 1750 to the Present*, edited by Catherine Hall and Keith McClelland, 217–236. Manchester: Manchester University Press, 2010.

Eley, Geoff. "Empire, Ideology, and the East: Thoughts on Nazism's Spatial Imaginary." In *Nazism as Fascism: Violence, Ideology, and the Ground of Consent in Germany, 1930–1945*, edited by Geoff Eley, 131–155. London: Routledge, 2013.

El-Tayeb, Fatima. *Schwarze Deutsche: Der Diskurs um 'Rasse' und nationale Identität, 1890–1933.* Frankfurt: Campus Verlag, 2001.

El-Tayeb, Fatima. "Africa at Home: Europäische Postkarten 1890–1950." In *Der Black Atlantic*, edited by Tina Campt and Paul Gilroy. Berlin: Haus der Kulturen der Welt, 2004.

Enwezor, Okwui. "The Short Century: Independence and Liberation Movements in Africa, 1945–1994—an Introduction." In *The Short Century* (exhibition catalogue). Munich: Prestel, 2001.

Epple, Angelika. "Das Auge Schmeckt Stollwerck." *Werkstatt Geschichte* 45 (2007).

Epstein, James. "Politics of Colonial Sensation: The Trial of Thomas Picton and the Cause of Louisa Calderon." *American Historical Review* 112.3 (2007): 712–741.

Epstein, Klaus. "Erzberger and the German Colonial Scandals, 1905–1910." *English Historical Review* 74.293 (1959): 644–645.

Erichsen, Caspar W. *"The Angel of Death Has Descended Violently among Them": Concentration Camps and Prisoners-of-War in Namibia, 1904–08.* Leiden: Africa Studies Centre, 2005.

Esherick, Joseph W. *The Origins of the Boxer Uprising.* Berkeley: University of California Press, 1987.

Esherick, Joseph W., Hasan Kayali, and Eric van Young. *Empire to Nation: Historical Perspectives on the Making of the Modern World*, 1–13. Lanham, MD: Rowman and Littlefield, 2006.

Evans, Andrew D. "Anthropology at War: Racial Studies of POWs during World War I." In *Worldly Provincialism: German Anthropology in the Age of Empire*, edited by H. Glenn Penny and Matti Bunzl, 198–199. Ann Arbor: University of Michigan Press, 2003.

Evans, Richard J. *Kneipengespräche im Kaiserreich: Die Stimmungsberichte der Hamburger Politischen Polizei, 1892–1914*. Reinbek bei Hamburg: Rowohlt, 1989.

Evans, Richard J. "Proletarian Mentalities: Pub Conversations in Hamburg." In *Proletarians and Politics: Socialism, Protest and the Working Class in Germany before the First World War*. New York: St. Martin's Press, 1990.

Evans-Pritchard, E. E. "Social Anthropology and the Universities in Great Britain." *Higher Education Quarterly* 21 (1967): 167–181.

Fabian, Johannes Fabian. *Time and the Other: How Anthropology Makes Its Object*. New York: Columbia University Press, 1983.

Fall, N. Goné. "Providing a Space of Freedom: Women Artists from Africa." In *Global Feminisms: New Directions in Contemporary Art*, edited by Maura Reilly and Linda Nochlin. London and New York: Merrell / Brooklyn Museum of Art, 2007.

Farley, John. *Bilharzia: A History of Imperial Tropical Medicine*. Cambridge: Cambridge University Press, 1991.

Faught, C. Brad. *Into Africa: The Imperial Life of Margery Perham*. London: I. B. Tauris, 2012.

Fehrenbach, Heide. *Race after Hitler: Black Occupation Children in Postwar Germany and America*. Princeton, NJ: Princeton University Press, 2005.

Feindt, Hendrik, ed. *Studien zur Kulturgeschichte des deutschen Polenbildes 1848–1939*. Wiesbaden: Harrassowitz, 1993.

Fenske, Hans. "Imperialistische Tendenzen in Deutschland vor 1866: Auswanderung, überseeische Bestrebungen, Weltmachtträume." *Historisches Jahrbuch* 97/98 (1978): 336–383.

Fenske, Hans. "Ungeduldige Zuschauer: Die Deutschen und die europäische Expansion 1815–1880." In *Imperialistische Kontinuität und nationale Ungeduld im 19. Jahrhundert*, edited by Wolfgang Reinhardt, 87–123. Frankfurt: Fischer, 1991.

Ferguson, Niall. "America: An Empire in Denial." *Chronicle of Higher Education* (March 28, 2003): B7–B10.

Ferguson, Niall. *Empire: The Rise and Demise of the British World Order and the Lessons for Global Power*. New York: Basic Books, 2003.

Feuerhorst, Ulrich, and Holger Steinle. *Die Bunte Verführung. Zur Geschichte der Bleckreklame*. Berlin: Silberstreif, 1985.

Fiebig-von Hase, Ragnhild. *Lateinamerika als Konfliktherd der deutsch-amerikanischen Beziehungen 1890–1903*. Göttingen: Vandenhoeck und Ruprecht, 1986.

Fischer, Fritz. *Germany's Aims in the First World War*. London: Chatto and Windus, 1967.

Fischer, Fritz. *Krieg der Illusionen. Die deutsche Politik von 1911 bis 1914*. Düsseldorf: Droste Verlag, 1969.

Fischer, Fritz. *War of Illusions: German Policies from 1911 to 1914*. London: Chatto and Windus, 1974.

Fischer, Fritz. *World Power or Decline: The Controversy over Germany's Aims in the First World War*. London: Weidenfeld and Nicolson, 1975.

Fischer, Fritz. *From Kaiserreich to Third Reich: Elements of Continuity in German History 1871–1945*. London: Allen and Unwin, 1986.

Fischer, Hans. *Völkerkunde im Nationalsozialismus. Aspekte der Anpassung, Affinität und Behauptung einer wissenschaftlichen Disziplin*. Berlin: Reimer, 1990.

Fitzpatrick, Matthew P. *Liberal Imperialism in Germany: Expansion and Nationalism 1848–1884*. New York: Berghahn, 2008.

Fitzpatrick, Matthew P. "The Pre-history of the Holocaust? The *Sonderweg* and *Historikerstreit* Debates and the Abject Colonial Past." *Central European History* 41.3 (2008): 1–27.

Fitzpatrick, Matthew P., ed. *Liberal Imperialism in Europe*. New York: Palgrave Macmillan, 2012.

Flachowsky, Sören. *Von der Notgemeinschaft zum Reichsforschungsrat: Wissenschaftspolitik im Kontext von Autarkie, Aufrüstung und Krieg*. Stuttgart: Franz Steiner Verlag, 2008.

Fleischhauer, Ingeborg. *Die Deutschen im Zarenreich. Zwei Jahrhunderte deutsch-russische Kulturgemeinschaft*. Stuttgart: Dva, 1986.

Fletcher, Roger. *Revisionism and Empire: Socialist Imperialism in Germany, 1897–1914*. London: Allen and Unwin, 1984.

Förster, Jürgen. "The Wehrmacht and the War of Extermination against the Soviet Union." http://www1.yadvashem.org/untoldstories/documents/studies/Jurgen_Forster.pdf (accessed May 18, 2009).

Förster, Larissa, Dag Henrichsen, and Michael Bollig, eds. *Namibia-Deutschland, Eine geteilte Geschichte: Widerstand, Gewalt, Erinnerung*. Wolfratshausen: Edition Minerva, 2004.

Förster, Stig, ed. *Bismarck, Europe, and Africa. The Berlin Africa Conference 1884–1885 and the Onset of Partition*. Oxford: Oxford University Press, 1988.

Foucault, Michel. "Society Must Be Defended." Lectures at the Collège de France 1975–1976. New York: Picador, 2003.

Frauendienst, Werner. "Preußisches Staatsbewußtsein und polnischer Nationalismus. Preußisch-deutsche Polenpolitik 1815–1890." In *Das östliche Deutschland*, edited by Göttinger Arbeitskreis, 305–359. Würzburg: Holzner, 1959.

Frech, Stefan. *Wegbereiter Hitlers? Theodor Reismann-Grone: Ein völkischer Nationalist (1863–1949)*. Paderborn: Schöningh, 2009.

Frevert, Ute. *Men of Honor: A Social and Cultural History of the Duel*. New York: Polity, 1995.

Frevert, Ute. "The Taming of the Noble Ruffian: Male Violence and Dueling in Early Modern and Modern Germany." In *Men and Violence: Gender, Honor, and Rituals in Modern Europe and America*, edited by Peter Spierenburg. Columbus: Ohio State University Press, 1998.

Fricke, Dieter. "Der deutsche Imperialismus und die Reichstagswahlen von 1907." *Zeitschrift für Geschichtswissenschaft* 9 (1961): 538–576.

Friedrichsmeyer, Sara, Sara Lennox, and Susanne Zantop, eds. *The Imperialist Imagination: German Colonialism and Its Legacy*. Ann Arbor: University of Michigan Press, 1998.

Fritzsche, Peter. *Reading Berlin 1900*. Cambridge: Cambridge University Press, 1996.

Furber, David B. "Going East: Colonialism and German Life in Nazi-Occupied Poland." PhD diss., State University of New York at Buffalo, 2003.

Furber, David. "Near as Far in the Colonies: The Nazi Occupation of Poland." *International History Review* 26.3 (2004): 541–579.

Furber, David, and Wendy Lower. "Colonialism and Genocide in Nazi-Occupied Poland and Ukraine." In *Empire, Colony, Genocide: Conquest, Occupation, and Subaltern Resistance in World History*, edited by A. Dirk Moses, 372–400. New York: Berghahn, 2008.

Galos, Adam, Felix-Heinrich Gentzen, and Witold Jakóbczyk. *Die Hatakisten. Der Deutsche Ostmarkenverein (1894–1934) — ein Beitrag zur Geschichte der Ostpolitik des deutschen Imperialismus*. Berlin: Deutscher Verlag der Wissenschaften, 1966.

Ganz, A. Harding. "Colonial Policy and the Imperial German Navy." *Militärgeschichtliche Mitteilungen* 21 (1977): 35–52.

Gatrell, Peter. *A Whole Empire Walking: Refugees in Russia During World War I*. Bloomington: Indiana University Press, 2005.

Gehrke, Ulrich. *Persien in der deutschen Orientpolitik während des Ersten Weltkrieges*. Stuttgart: Kohlhammer, 1960.

Geiss, Imanuel. *Der polnische Grenzstreifen 1914–1918. Ein Beitrag zur deutschen Kriegszielpolitik im Ersten Weltkrieg*. Lübeck: Matthiesen, 1960.

Gerlach, Christian. *Kalkulierte Morde. Die deutsche Wirtschafts- und Vernichtungspolitik in Weißrußland 1941 bis 1944*. Hamburg: Hamburger Edition, 1999.

Gerth, Nobuko. "'Between Two Worlds': Hans Gerth. Eine Biographie 1908–1978." *Jahrbuch für Soziologiegeschichte 1999/2000*, 37–38. Opladen: Leske + Budrich, 2002.

Gewald, Jan-Bart. *Herero Heroes: A Socio-political History of the Herero of Namibia 1890–1923*. Oxford: James Curry, 1999.

Gewald, Jan-Bart, and Jeremy Silvester, eds. *Words Cannot Be Found: German Colonial Rule in Namibia: An Annotated Reprint of the 1918 Blue Book*. Leiden: Brill, 2003.

Geyer, Michael. "The Space of the Nation: An Essay on the German Century." In *Strukturmerkmale der deutschen Geschichte des 20. Jahrhunderts*, edited by Anselm Döring-Manteuffel, 21–42. Munich: Oldenbourg Wissenschaftsverlag, 2006.

Geyer, Michael. "Where Germans Dwell: Transnationalism in Theory and Practice." *German Studies Association Newsletter* 31.2 (Winter 2006): 29–37.

Geyer, Michael, and Charles Bright. "Writing World History in a Global Age." *American Historical Review* 100.4 (October 1995): 1034–1060.

Geyer, Michael, and Charles Bright. "Global Violence and Nationalizing Wars in Eurasia and America: The Geopolitics of War in the Mid-nineteenth Century." *Comparative Studies in Society and History* 38.4 (1996): 619–657.

Gilman, Sander L. *On Blackness without Blacks: Essays on the Image of the Black in Germany*. Boston: Hall, 1982.

Glassman, Jonathon. *Feasts and Riot: Revelry, Rebellion, and Popular Consciousness on the Swahili Coast, 1856–1888*. Portsmouth: Heinemann, 1995.

Godoy, Julio. "Recasting Colonialism as a Good Thing." *Global Policy Forum*, July 5, 2005, www.globalpolicy.org/empire/history/2005/0705empgood.htm (accessed October 10, 2013).

Gollwitzer, Heinz. *Die gelbe Gefahr. Geschichte eines Schlagworts. Studien zum imperialistischen Denken*. Göttingen: Vandenhoeck und Ruprecht, 1962.

Gosewinkel, Dieter. *Einbürgern und Ausschließen. Die Nationalisierung der Staatsangehörigkeit vom Deutschen Bund bis zur Bundesrepublik Deutschland.* Göttingen: Vandenhoeck und Ruprecht, 2001.

Gothsch, Manfred. *Die deutsche Völkerkunde und ihr Verhältnis zum Kolonialismus.* Baden-Baden: Nomos, 1983.

Grabowski, Sabine. *Deutscher und polnischer Nationalismus. Der deutsche Ostmarkenverein und die polnische Straz 1894–1914.* Marburg: Herder-Institut, 1998.

Gradmann, Christoph. *Krankheit im Labor: Robert Koch und die medizinische Bakteriologie.* Göttingen: Wallstein Verlag, 2005.

Gradmann, Christoph. *Laboratory Disease: Robert Koch's Medical Bacteriology*, translated by Elborg Forster. Baltimore: Johns Hopkins University Press, 2009.

Grant, Oliver. *Migration and Inequality in Germany 1870–1913.* Oxford: Oxford University Press, 2005.

Grill, Johnpeter Horst. "Robert L. Jenkins, The Nazis and the American South in the 1930s: A Mirror Image?" *Journal of Southern History* 58.4 (1992): 667–694.

Grimmer-Solem, Erik. "Imperialist Socialism of the Chair: Gustav Schmoller and German *Weltpolitik*, 1897–1905." In *Wilhelminism and Its Legacies: German Modernities, Imperialism, and the Meanings of Reform, 1890–1930*, edited by Geoff Eley and James Retallack, 107–122. New York: Berghahn, 2003.

Grimmer-Solem, Erik. *The Rise of Historical Economics and Social Reform in Germany 1864–1894.* Oxford: Oxford University Press, 2003.

Grimmer-Solem, Erik. "The Professors' Africa: Economists, the Elections of 1907, and the Legitimation of German Imperialism." *German History* 25.3 (2007): 313–347.

Gross, Gerhard P., ed. *Die vergessene Front. Der Osten 1914/15. Ereignis, Wirkung, Nachwirkung.* Paderborn: Schöningh, 2006.

Grosse, Pascal. *Kolonialismus, Eugenik und bürgerliche Gesellschaft in Deutschland 1850–1918.* Frankfurt: Campus, 2000.

Grosse, Pascal. "What Does German Colonialism Have to Do with National Socialism?" In *Germany's Colonial Pasts*, edited by Eric Ames, Marcia Klotz, and Lora Wildenthal, 115–134. Lincoln: University of Nebraska Press, 2005.

Grosse, Pascal. "From Colonialism to National Socialism to Postcolonialism: Hannah Arendt's *Origins of Totalitarianism*." *Postcolonial Studies* 9.1 (2006): 35–52.

Gründer, Horst. *Geschichte der deutschen Kolonien.* Stuttgart: Schöningh, 2000.

Gründer, Horst, ed. *"Da und dort ein junges Deutschland gründen": Rassismus, Kolonien, und kolonialer Gedanke vom 16. bis zum 20. Jahrhundert.* Munich: DTV, 1999.

Gümbel, Annette. *'Volk ohne Raum.' Der Schriftsteller Hans Grimm zwischen nationalkonservativem Denken und völkischer Ideologie.* Darmstadt: Selbstverl. der Hessischen Historischen Komm., 2003.

Gungwu, Wang. *China and the Chinese Overseas.* Singapore: Times Academic Press, 1991.

Hachten, Elizabeth. "How to Win Friends and Influence People: Hans Zeiss, Boundary Objects, and the Pursuit of Cross-National Scientific Collaboration in Microbiology." In *Doing Medicine Together: Germany and Russia between the Wars*, edited by Susan Gross Solomon, 159–198. Toronto: University of Toronto Press, 2006.

Hagan, Kenneth J. *This People's Navy: The Making of American Sea Power*. New York: Free Press, 1991.

Hagen, William W. *Germans, Poles, and Jews. The Nationality Conflict in the Prussian East, 1772–1914*. Chicago: Chicago University Press, 1980.

Hake, Sabine. "Mapping the Native Body: on Africa and the Colonial Film in the Third Reich," in *The Imperialist Imagination: German Colonialism and Its Legacy*, edited by Sara Friedrichsmeyer, Sara Lennox, and Susanne Zantop, 163–187. Ann Arbor: University of Michigan Press, 1998.

Hall, Catherine. *White, Male and Middle Class: Explorations in Feminism and History*. New York: Routledge, 1992.

Hall, Catherine. *Civilizing Subjects: Colony and Metropole in the English Imagination 1830–1867*. Chicago: University of Chicago Press, 2002.

Hall, Catherine, ed. *Cultures of Empire: Colonizers in Britain and the Empire in the Nineteenth and Twentieth Centuries: A Reader*. Manchester: Manchester University Press, 2000.

Hall, Catherine, and Keith McClelland, eds. *Race, Nation, and Empire: Making Histories, 1750 to the Present*. Manchester: Manchester University Press, 2010.

Hall, Catherine, Keith McClelland, and Jane Rendall. *Defining the Victorian Nation: Class, Race, Gender, and the Reform Act of 1867*. Cambridge: Cambridge University Press, 2000.

Hall, Catherine, and Sonya O. Rose, eds. *At Home with the Empire: Metropolitan Culture and the Imperial World*. Cambridge: Cambridge University Press, 2006.

Hankel, Gerd. *Die Leipziger Prozesse: Deutsche Kriegsverbrechen und ihre strafrechtliche Verfolgung nach dem Ersten Weltkrieg*. Hamburg: Hamburger Edition, 2003.

Haraway, Donna. *Primate Visions: Gender, Race and Nature in the World of Modern Science*. New York and London: Routledge, 1989.

Harding, Leonhard. "Hamburg's West Africa Trade in the Nineteenth Century." In *Figuring African Trade: Proceedings of the Symposium on the Quantification and Structure of the Import and Export and Long Distance Trade in Africa 1800–1912*, edited by Gerhard Liesegang, H. Pasch, and Adam Jones, 363–391. Berlin: Reimer, 1986.

Hardt, Michael, and Antonio Negri. *Empire*. Cambridge, MA: Harvard University Press, 2000.

Harris, Michael D. *Colored Pictures: Race and Visual Representation*. Chapel Hill: University of North Carolina Press, 2003.

Harrison, Mark. *Public Health in British India: Anglo-Indian Preventive Medicine 1859–1914*. Cambridge: Cambridge University Press, 1994.

Harvey, David. *The Condition of Postmodernity*. Oxford: Blackwell, 1990.

Hastings, Derek. "Fears of a Feminized Church: Catholicism, Clerical Celibacy, and the Crisis of Masculinity in Wilhelmine Germany." *European History Quarterly* 38.1 (2008): 34–65.

Hausen, Karin. *Deutsche Kolonialherrschaft in Afrika. Wirtschaftsinteressen und Kolonialverwaltung in Kamerun vor 1914*. Zurich: Atlantis, 1970.

Hayes, Bascom Barry. *Bismarck and Mitteleuropa*. Cranbury, NJ: Associated University Presses, 1994.

Headrick, Daniel. *The Tools of Empire: Technology and European Imperialism in the Nineteenth Century*. New York: Oxford University Press, 1981.
Headrick, Rita. *Colonialism, Health and Illness in French Equatorial Africa, 1885–1935*. Atlanta: African Studies Association Press, 1994.
Held, Thomas. "Kolonialismus und Werbung." In *Andenken an den Kolonialismus*, edited by Volker Harms. Tübingen: Attempto, 1984.
Henderson, W. O. *The German Colonial Empire, 1884–1919*. London: F. Cass, 1993.
Herbert, Ulrich. *Best: Biographische Studien über Radikalismus, Weltanschauung und Vernunft, 1903–1989*. Bonn: Dietz, 1996.
Herbert, Ulrich. *Geschichte der Ausländerpolitik in Deutschland. Saisonarbeiter, Zwangsarbeiter, Gastarbeiter, Flüchtlinge*. Munich: Beck, 2001.
Herf, Jeffrey. *Reactionary Modernism: Technology, Culture, and Politics in Weimar and the Third Reich*. Cambridge: Cambridge University Press, 1984.
Hering, Rainer. *Konstruierte Nation: Der Alldeutsche Verband 1890 bis 1939*. Hamburg: Christians, 2003.
Herrmann, Ulrich. "Pädagogisches Denken und Anfänge der Reformpädagogik." In *Handbuch der deutschen Bildungsgeschichte*. Vol. 4, *1870–1918. Von der Reichsgründung bis zum Ende des Ersten Weltkriegs*, edited by Christa Berg, 161–171. Munich: Beck, 1991.
Hildebrand, Klaus. *Vom Reich zum Weltreich. Hitler, NSDAP und koloniale Frage 1919–1945*. Munich: Wilhelm Fink, 1969.
Hirschfeld, Yair. *Deutschland und Iran im Spielfeld der Mächte: internationale Beziehungen unter Reza Schah, 1921–1941*. Düsseldorf: Droste, 1980.
Hobsbawm, Eric. "Introduction: Inventing Traditions." In *The Invention of Tradition*, edited by Eric Hobsbawm and Terence Ranger. Cambridge: Cambridge University Press, 1983.
Hobson, Rolf. *Maritimer Imperialismus: Seemachtideologie, seestrategisches Denken und der Tirpitzplan 1875 bis 1914*. Munich: Oldenbourg Wissenschaftsverlag, 2002.
Hochgeschwender, Michael. "Kolonialkriege als Experimentierstätten des Vernichtungskrieges?" In *Formen des Krieges: Von der Antike bis zur Gegenwart*, edited by Michael Hochgeschwender, Dietrich Beyrau, and Dieter Langewiesche, 269–290. Paderborn: Schöningh, 2007.
Höhn, Maria. *GIs and Fräuleins: The German-American Encounter in 1950s Germany*. Chapel Hill: University of North Carolina Press, 2001.
Hollmann, Helga, Lise L. Müller, Heinz Spielmann, Stephan Waetzoldt, Ruth Malhotra, and Alexander Pilipczuk, eds. *Das frühe Plakat in Europa und den USA*. Vol. 3: *Deutschland*. Berlin: Mann, 1980.
Holston, Kenneth. "'A Measure of the Nation': Politics, Colonial Enthusiasm, and Education in Germany, 1896–1933." PhD diss., University of Pennsylvania, 1996.
Homburg, Heidrun. "Werbung—'eine Kunst, die gelernt sein will.'" *Jahrbuch für Wirtschaftsgeschichte* 1 (1997).
Hommen, Tanja. *Sittlichkeitsverbrechen: Sexuelle Gewalt im Kaiserreich*. Frankfurt: Campus, 1999.
Honeck, Mischa, Martin Klimke, and Anne Kuhlmann, eds. *Germany and the Black Diaspora: Points of Contact, 1250–1914*. New York: Berghahn, 2013.

Honold, Alexander, and Klaus R. Sherpe, eds. *Mit Deutschland um die Welt: Eine Kulturgeschichte des Fremden in der Kolonialzeit*. Stuttgart: J. B. Metzler, 2004.

Honour, Hugh, ed. *The Image of the Black in Western Art*. Vol. 4: *From the American Revolution to World War I*. Cambridge, MA: Harvard University Press, 1989.

Hopkins, Anthony G. *An Economic History of West Africa*. New York: Columbia University Press, 1973.

Hoppe, Kirk Arden. *Lords of the Fly: Sleeping Sickness Control in British East Africa 1900–1960*. Westport: Praeger, 2003.

Horne, John, and Alan Kramer. *German Atrocities 1914: A History of Denial*. New Haven, CT: Yale University Press, 2001.

Hotez, Peter J. *Forgotten People, Forgotten Diseases: The Neglected Tropical Diseases and Their Impact on Global Health and Development*. Washington, DC: ASM Press, 2008.

Howe, Stephen. *Empire: A Very Short Introduction*. Oxford: Oxford University Press, 2002.

Hubatsch, Walther. *Grundriß der deutschen Verwaltungsgeschichte 1815–1945*. Series A: *Preußen*. Vol. 22: *Bundes- und Reichsbehörden*. Marburg: Johann Gottfried Herder Institut, 1983.

Hücking, Renate, and Ekkehard Launer. *Aus Menschen Neger machen: Wie sich das Handelshaus Woermann an Afrika entwickelt hat*. Hamburg: Glagenberg, 1986.

Hull, Isabel V. *Absolute Destruction: Military Culture and the Practices of War in Imperial Germany*. Ithaca, NY: Cornell University Press, 2005.

Hunt, Nancy Rose. "Colonial Fairy Tales and the Knife and Fork Doctrine in the Heart of Africa." In *African Encounters with Domesticity*, edited by Karen Tranberg Hansen, 143–171. New Brunswick, NJ: Rutgers University Press, 1992.

Hyam, Ronald. *Empire and Sexuality: The British Experience*. Manchester: Manchester University Press, 1990.

Iliffe, John. "The Effects of the Maji Maji Rebellion of 1905–1906 on German Occupation Policy in East Africa." In *Britain and Germany in Africa: Imperial Rivalry and Colonial Rule*, edited by Prosser Gifford and William Roger Louis. New Haven, CT: Yale University Press, 1967.

Iliffe, John. "The Organization of the Maji Maji Rebellion." *Journal of African History* 8 (1967): 495–512.

Iliffe, John. *Tanganyika under German Rule 1905–1912*. Cambridge: Cambridge University Press, 1969.

Iliffe, John. *A Modern History of Tanganyika*. Cambridge: Cambridge University Press, 1979.

Iliffe, John. *Honour in African History*. Cambridge: Cambridge University Press, 2005.

Isobe, Hiroyuki. *Medizin und Kolonialgesellschaft. Die Bekämpfung der Schlafkrankheit in den deutschen "Schutzgebieten" vor dem Ersten Weltkrieg*. Münster: LIT, 2009.

Issawi, Charles. "The Tabriz-Trabzon Trade, 1830–1900: Rise and Decline of a Route." *International Journal of Middle East Studies* 1.1 (January 1970): 18–27.

Jasanoff, Sheila. "The Idiom of Co-production." In *States of Knowledge: The Co-production of Science and Social Order*. Edited by Sheila Jasanoff, 1–12. New York: Routledge, 2004.

Jeffries, Matthew. *Contesting the German Empire 1871–1918*. Malden, MA: Blackwell, 2008.

Jenkins, Jennifer. "Thinking like an Empire," unpublished MS.
Jenkins, Jennifer. *Weltpolitik on the Persian Frontier: Germany and Iran in the Age of Empire, 1857–1941*. Forthcoming.
Jessop, Bob. *The Capitalist State: Marxist Theories and Methods*. New York: New York University Press, 1982.
Kaczmarczyk, Zdzislaw. "German Colonisation in Medieval Poland in the Light of the Historiography of Both Nations." *Polish Western Affairs* 11 (1970): 3–40.
Kaesler, Dirk. *Die frühe deutsche Soziologie 1900 bis 1934 und ihre Entstehungs-Milieus*. Opladen: Westdeutscher Verlag, 1984.
Kaplan, Amy, and Donald Pease, eds. *Cultures of United States Imperialism*. Durham, NC: Duke University Press, 1993.
Karl, Rebecca E. "Race, Colonialism and History. China at the Turn of the Twentieth Century." In *Philosophies of Race and Ethnicity*, edited by Peter Osborne and Stella Sandford, 97–113. London: Continuum, 2002.
Karl, Rebecca E. *Staging the World. Chinese Nationalism at the Turn of the Twentieth Century*. Durham, NC: Duke University Press, 2002.
Karl, Rebecca. "On Comparability and Continuity: China, circa 1930's and 1990's." *Boundary* 32.2 (2005): 169–200.
Karsten, Rudolph. *Die sächsische Sozialdemokratie vom Kaiserreich zur Republik, 1871–1923*. Weimar: Böhlau, 1995.
Kashani-Sabet, Firoozeh. *Frontier Fictions: Shaping the Iranian Nation, 1804–1946*. Princeton, NJ: Princeton University Press, 1999.
Kästner, Erich. "Surabaya-Johnny II. Frei nach Kipling und Brecht." In *Wir sind so frei. Chansons, Kabarett, Kleine Prosa*, edited by Hermann Kurzke. Munich and Vienna: Carl Hanser Verlag, 1998.
Katouzian, Homa. *State and Society in Iran: The Eclipse of the Qajars and the Emergence of the Pahlavis*. London: I. B. Tauris, 2000.
Kehr, Eckart. *Der Primat der Innenpolitik: Gesammelte Aufsätze zur preußisch-deutschen Sozialgeschichte im 19. und 20. Jahrhundert*, edited by Hans-Ulrich Wehler. Berlin: de Gruyter, 1965. Translated as *Economic Interest, Militarism, and Foreign Policy: Essays on German History*, edited by Gordon A. Craig. Berkeley: University of California Press, 1977.
Kelly, Alfred. *The Descent of Darwin: The Popularization of Darwinism in Germany, 1860–1914*. Chapel Hill: University of North Carolina Press, 1981.
Kershaw, Ian. *The Nazi Dictatorship: Problems and Perspectives of Interpretation*, 4th ed. London: Arnold, 2000.
Ketelsen, Uwe-K. "Der koloniale Diskurs und die Öffnung des europäischen Ostens im deutschen Roman." In *Kolonialismus. Kolonialdiskurs und Genozid*, edited by Mihran Dabag, Horst Gründer, and Uwe-K. Ketelsen, 67–94. Munich: Fink, 2004.
Klein, Thoralf, and Frank Schumacher, eds. *Kolonialkriege: Militärische Gewalt im Zeichen des Imperialismus*. Hamburg: Hamburger Edition, 2006.
Klessmann, Christoph. *Polnische Bergarbeiter im Ruhrgebiet 1870–1945. Soziale Integration und nationale Subkultur einer Minderheit in der deutschen Industriegesellschaft*. Göttingen: Vandenhoeck und Ruprecht, 1978.

Klingemann, Carsten. "Angewandte Soziologie im Nationalsozialismus." *1999. Zeitschrift für Sozialgeschichte des 20. und 21. Jahrhunderts* 4.1 (1989), 21.

Klingemann, Carsten. *Soziologie im Dritten Reich*. Baden-Baden: Nomos Verlagsgesellschaft, 1996.

Klotz, Marcia. "Global Visions: From the Colonial to the National Socialist World." *European Studies Journal* 16 (1999): 37–68.

Klotz, Marcia. "The Weimar Republic: A Postcolonial State in a Still-Colonial World." In *Germany's Colonial Pasts*, edited by Eric Ames, Marcia Klotz, and Lora Wildenthal. Lincoln: University of Nebraska Press, 2005.

Knox, MacGregor. "Conquest, Foreign and Domestic, in Fascist Italy and Nazi Germany." *Journal of Modern History* 56.1 (1984): 1–57.

Knox, MacGregor. "Expansionist Zeal, Fighting Power, and Staying Power in the Italian and German Dictatorships." In *Fascist Italy and Nazi Germany: Comparisons and Contrasts*, edited by Richard Bessel. Cambridge: Cambridge University Press, 1996.

Knox, MacGregor. *Common Destiny: Dictatorship, Foreign Policy, and War in Fascist Italy and Nazi Germany*. Cambridge: Cambridge University Press, 2000.

Koller, Christian. *'Von Wilden aller Rassen niedergemetzeit': Die Diskussion um die Verwendung von Kolonialtruppen in Europa zwischen Rassismus, Kolonial und Militärpolitik, 1914–1930*. Stuttgart: Steiner, 2001.

Koller, Christian. "Enemy Images: Race and Gender Stereotypes in the Discussion on Colonial Troops. A Franco-German Comparison, 1914–1923." In *Home/Front: The Military, War and Gender in Twentieth-Century Germany*, edited by Karen Hagemann and Stefanie Schüler-Springorum, 141–142. Oxford: Berg, 2002.

Koller, Christian. *Fremdherrschaft. Ein politischer Kampfbegriff im Zeitalter des Nationalismus*. New York: Peter Lang, 2005.

Kölling, Bernhard. "Das Öl im Kompass: Zur Geschichte der Zigarre in Deutschland (1850–1920)." *Zeitschrift für Geschichtswissenschaft 1997* 45 (1997).

Kolsky, Elizabeth. "Codification and the Rule of Colonial Difference: Criminal Procedure in British India." *Law and History Review* 23.3 (2005), 631–683.

Kong Xiangji. "Die Jiaozhou-Krise und die Reform-Bewegung von 1898." *Berliner China-Hefte* (December 1997): 42–56.

Konno, Hajime. *Max Weber und die polnische Frage (1892–1920)*. Baden-Baden: Nomos, 2004.

Koponen, Juhani. *Development for Exploitation: German Colonial Policies in Mainland Tanzania, 1884–1914*. Helsinki and Hamburg: Lit Verlag, 1995.

Kopp, Kristin. *Germany's Wild East: Constructing Poland as a Colonial Space*. Ann Arbor: University of Michigan Press, 2012.

Kopp, Kristin. "Constructing Racial Difference in Colonial Poland." In *Germany's Colonial Pasts*, edited by Eric Ames, Marcia Klotz, and Lora Wildenthal, 76–96. Lincoln: University of Nebraska Press, 2005.

Kopp, Kristin. "Gray Zones: On the Inclusion of 'Poland' in the Study of German Colonialism." In *German Colonialism and National Identity*, edited by Michael Perraudin and Jürgen Zimmerer, 33–42. New York: Routledge, 2011.

Kopp, Kristin, and Klaus Müller-Richter, eds. *Die "Großstadt" und das "Primitive." Text—Politik—Repräsentation.* Stuttgart: J. B. Metzler, 2004.

Kouri, E. I. *Der deutsche Protestantismus und die soziale Frage 1870–1919. Zur Sozialpolitik im Bildungsbürgertum.* Berlin: Walter de Gruyter, 1984.

Kramer, Paul A. *The Blood of Government: Race, Empire, the United States, and the Philippines.* Chapel Hill: University of North Carolina Press, 2006.

Kramer, Paul A. "Power and Connection: Imperial Histories of the United States in the World." *American Historical Review* 116.5 (2011): 1348–1391.

Krüger, Gesine. *Kriegsbewältigung und Geschichtsbewusstsein: Realität, Deutung, und Verarbeitung des Deutschen Kolonialkriegs in Namibia 1904 bis 1907.* Göttingen: Vandenhoeck und Ruprecht, 1999.

Krüger, Gesine. "Coming to Terms with the Past." *Bulletin of the German Historical Institute* 37 (2005): 45–49.

Kühl, Stefan. *The Nazi Connection: Eugenics, American Racism, and German National Socialism.* Oxford: Oxford University Press, 1994.

Kundrus, Birthe. *Moderne Imperialisten. Das Kaiserreich im Spiegel seiner Kolonien.* Cologne: Böhlau, 2003.

Kundrus, Birthe. "Von Windhoek nach Nürnberg? Koloniale 'Mischehenverbote' und die nationalsozialistische Rassengesetzgebung." In *Phantasiereiche: Zur Kulturgeschichte des deutschen Kolonialismus*, edited by Birthe Kundrus, 110–131. Frankfurt: Campus, 2003.

Kundrus, Birthe. "Kontinuitäten, Parallelen, Rezeptionen. Überlegungen zur Kolonialisierung des Nationalsozialismus." *Werkstatt Geschichte* 43 (2006): 45–62.

Kundrus, Birthe. "Blind Spots: Empire, Colonies, and Ethnic Identities in Modern German History." In *Gendering Modern German History: Rewriting Historiography*, edited by Karen Hagemann and Jean Quataert, 86–106. New York: Berghahn, 2007.

Kundrus, Birthe, ed. *Phantasiereiche: Zur Kulturgeschichte des deutschen Kolonialismus.* Frankfurt: Campus, 2003.

Kurlander, Eric. *The Price of Exclusion: Ethnicity, National Identity, and the Decline of German Liberalism, 1898–1933.* New York: Berghahn, 2006.

Kuss, Susanne. "Deutsche Soldaten während des Boxeraufstands in China: Elemente und Ursprünge des Vernichtungskrieges." In *Das Deutsche Reich und der Boxeraufstand*, edited by Susanne Kuss and Bernd Martin, 165–182. Munich: Iudicium, 2002.

Lachenal, Guillaume. "Le médecin qui voulut être roi. Médecine coloniale et utopie au Cameroun." *Annales. Histoire, Sciences Sociales* 65.1 (2010): 121–156.

Lahme, Rainer. *Deutsche Außenpolitik, 1890–1894. Von der Gleichgewichtspolitik Bismarcks zur Allianzstrategie Caprivis*, 116–179. Göttingen: Vandenhoeck und Ruprecht, 1990.

Lake, Marilyn, and Henry Reynolds, eds. *Drawing the Global Colour Line: White Man's Countries and the International Challenge of Racial Equality.* Cambridge: Cambridge University Press, 2008.

Lambert, Andrew. "Wirtschaftliche Macht, technologischer Vorsprung und imperiale Stärke: Großbritanniens als einzigartige globale Macht 1860 bis 1890." In *Das Militär* und der Aufbruch in die Moderne 1860–1890, edited by Michael Epkenhans and Gerhard P. Groß, 243–268. Munich: Oldenbourg Wissenschaftsverlag, 2003.

Lambert, Andrew. "Great Britain and Maritime Law from the Declaration of Paris to the Era of Total War." In *Navies in Northern Waters 1721–2000*, edited by Rolf Hobson and Tom Kristiansen, 11–38. London: Frank Cass, 2004.

Lambert, Nicholas. "Transformation and Technology in the Fisher Era: The Impact of the Communications Revolution." *Journal of Strategic Studies* 27 (June 2004): 272–297.

Lambert, Nicholas. *Planning Armageddon: British Economic Warfare and the First World War*. Cambridge, MA: Harvard University Press, 2012.

Lamberty, Christiane. *Reklame in Deutschland 1890–1914: Wahrnehmung, Professionalisierung und Kritik des Wirtschaftswerbung*. Berlin: Duncker und Humblot, 2000.

Lambi, Ivo Nikolai. *The Navy and German Power Politics, 1862–1914*. Boston: Allen and Unwin, 1984.

Langbehn, Victor, ed. *German Colonialism, Visual Culture, and Modern Memory*. London: Routledge, 2010.

Langbehn, Volker, and Mohammad Salama, eds. *German Colonialism: Race, the Holocaust, and Postwar Germany*. New York: Columbia University Press, 2011.

Laukötter, A. "The Time after Adolf Bastian: Felix von Luschan and Berlin's Royal Museum of Ethnology." In *Adolf Bastian and His Universal Archive of Humanity: The Origins of German Anthropology*, edited by M. Fischer, P. Bolz, and S. Kamel. New York: Olms, 2007.

Lebzelter, Gisela. "*Die Schwarze Schmach*: Vorurteile, Propaganda, Mythos." *Geschichte und Gesellschaft* 11 (1985): 37–58.

Lefebvre, Henri. *The Social Production of Space*. Oxford: Blackwell, 1991.

Leitherer, Eugen, and Hans Wichmann, eds. *Reiz und Hülle. Gestaltete Warenverpackungen des 19. und 20. Jahrhunderts*. Stuttgart: Birkhäuser Verlag, 1987.

Lenman, Robin. "Control of the Visual Image in Imperial Germany." In *Zensur und Kultur = Censorship and Culture*, edited John McCarthy and Werner von der Ohe. Tübingen: Max Niemeyer Verlag, 1995.

Lester, Alan. *Imperial Networks: Creating Identities in Nineteenth Century South Africa and Britain*. London: Routledge, 2001.

Lester, Rosemarie K. "Blacks in Germany and German Blacks: A Little-Known Aspect of Black History." In *Blacks and German Culture*, edited by Reinhold Grimm and Jost Hermand. Madison: University of Wisconsin Press, 1986.

Leutner, Mechthild. "Sinologie in Berlin: Die Durchsetzung einer wissenschaftliche Disziplin zur Erschließund und zum Verständnis Chinas." In *Berlin und China*, edited by Heng-yü Kuo, 31–56. Berlin: Colloquium, 1987.

Leutner, Mechthild and Klaus Mühlhahn *"Musterkolonie Kiautschou." Die Expansion des Deutschen Reiches in China. Deutsch-chinesische Beziehungen 1897–1914. Eine Quellensammlung*. Berlin: Oldenbourg Akademieverlag, 1997.

Levy, Richard S. *The Downfall of the Anti-Semitic Political Parties in Imperial Germany*. New Haven, CT: Yale University Press, 1975.

Lewis, Beth Irwin. *Art for All? The Collision of Modern Art and the Public in Late-Nineteenth-Century Germany*. Princeton, NJ: Princeton University Press, 2003.
Lieven, Dominic. *Empire. The Russian Empire and Its Rivals*. London: John Murray, 2000.
Limerick, Patricia Nelson. *The Legacy of Conquest: The Unbroken Past of the American West*. New York: Norton, 1988.
Lindner, Ulrike. "Platz an der Sonne? Die Geschichtsschreibung auf dem Weg in die deutschen Kolonien." *Archiv für Sozialgeschichte* 48 (2008): 487–510.
Lindner, Ulrike. "Colonialism as a European Project in Africa before 1914? British and German Concepts of Colonial Rule in Sub-Saharan Africa." *Comparativ* 19 (2009): 88–106.
Lindner, Ulrike. "Imperialism and Globalization: Entanglements and Interactions between the British and German Colonial Empires in Africa before the First World War." *Bulletin of the German Historical Institute London* 32.1 (May 2010): 4–28.
Linne, Karsten. *Weiße "Arbeitsführer" im "Kolonialen Ergänzungsraum." Afrika als Ziel sozial- und wirtschaftspolitischer Planungen in der ns-Zeit*. Münster: Verlaghaus Monsenstein und Vannerdat, 2002.
Linne, Karsten. *Deutschland jenseits des Äquators? Die ns-Kolonialplanungen für Afrika*. Berlin: Links Verlag, 2008.
Liulevicius, Vejas Gabriel. *War Land on the Eastern Front: Culture, National Identity and German Occupation in World War I*. Cambridge: Cambridge University Press, 2005.
Liulevicius, Vejas Gabriel. *The German Myth of the East: 1800 to the Present*. Oxford: Oxford University Press, 2009.
Longerich, Peter. *Heinrich Himmler: Biographie*. Munich: Siedler Verlag, 2008.
Lonsdale, John. "The Moral Economy of Mau Mau: Wealth, Poverty and Civic Virtue in Kikuyu Political Thought." In Bruce Berman and John Lonsdale, *Unhappy Valley: Conflict in Kenya and Africa. Vol. 2: Violence and Ethnicity*, 315–504. London: James Currey, 1992.
Lonsdale, John. "Moral Ethnicity and Political Tribalism." In *Inventions and Boundaries: Historical and Anthropological Approaches to the Study of Ethnicity and Nationalism*, edited by Preben Kaarsholm and Jan Hultin, 131–150. Roskilde, Denmark: Roskilde University, 1994.
Louis, William Roger. *Ruanda-Urundi, 1884–1919*. Oxford: Oxford University Press, 1963.
Louis, William Roger. "Great Britain and German Expansion in Africa, 1884–1919." In *Britain and Germany in Africa: Imperial Rivalry and Colonial Rule*, edited by Prosser Gifford and William Roger Louis, with Alison Smith, 3–46. New Haven, CT: Yale University Press, 1967.
Lower, Wendy. *Nazi Empire-Building and the Holocaust in Ukraine*. Chapel Hill: University of North Carolina Press, 2005.
Lower, Wendy, and David Bruce Furber II. "Colonialism and Genocide in Nazi-Occupied Poland and Ukraine." In *Empire, Colony, Genocide. Conquest, Occupation, and Subaltern Resistance in World History*, edited by A. Dirk Moses, 372–401. New York: Berghahn, 2008.

Lowry, John S. "African Resistance and Center Party Recalcitrance in the Reichstag Colonial Debates of 1905/06." *Central European History* 39.2 (2006): 244–269.

Lyons, Maryinez. *The Colonial Disease: A Social History of Sleeping Sickness in Northern Zaire, 1900–1940*. Cambridge: Cambridge University Press, 1992.

Maase, Kaspar, and Wolfgang Kaschuba, eds. *Schund und Schönheit. Populäre Kultur um 1900*. Cologne: Böhlau Verlag, 2001.

Macintyre, Ben. *Forgotten Fatherland: The Search for Elisabeth Nietzsche*. New York: Farrar Straus Giroux, 1992.

Madajczyk, Czeslaw, ed. *Vom Generalplan Ost zum Generalsiedlungsplan*. Munich: Saur, 1994.

Madley, Benjamin. "From Africa to Auschwitz: How German South West Africa Incubated Ideas and Methods Adopted and Developed by the Nazis in Eastern Europe." *European History Quarterly* 35.3 (2005): 429–64.

Maier, Charles S. *Among Empires: American Ascendancy and Its Predecessors*. Cambridge, MA: Harvard University Press, 2006.

Maier, Charles S. "America among Empires? Imperial Analogues and Imperial Syndrome." *Bulletin of the German Historical Institute* 41 (2007): 21–31.

Majer, Diemut. "Das besetzte Osteuropa als Deutsche Kolonie (1939–1944): Die Pläne der NS-Führung zur Beherrschung Osteuropas." In *Gesetzliches Unrecht: Rassisches Recht im 20. Jahrhundert*, edited by Micha Brumli, Susanne Meinl, and Werner Renz, 111–134. New York: Campus, 2005.

Mannheim, Karl. "Historicism." In Karl Mannheim, *Essays in the Sociology of Knowledge*, edited by Paul Kecskemeti, 84–133. London: Routledge and Kegan Paul, 1952.

Marashi, Afshin. *Nationalizing Iran: Culture, Power and the State, 1870–1940*. Seattle: University of Washington, 2008.

Marks, Sally. "Black Watch on the Rhine: A Study in Propaganda, Prejudice and Prurience." *European Studies Review* 13.3 (1983): 297–334.

Marks, Sally. *The Illusion of Peace: International Relations in Europe, 1918–1933*, 2nd ed. New York: Palgrave Macmillan, 2003.

Martin, Bradford G. *German Persian Diplomatic Relations 1873–1912*. The Hague: Mouton, 1959.

Martin, Peter. *Schwarze Teufel, edle Mohren. Afrikaner in Geschichte und Bewußtsein der Deutschen*. Hamburg: Junius, 1993.

Mason, Tim. "The Legacy of 1918 for National Socialism." In *German Democracy and the Triumph of Hitler*, edited by Anthony J. Nicholls and Erich Matthias. London: Macmillan, 1971.

Mason, Tim. "Debate: Germany, 'Domestic Crisis,' and War in 1939," with a reply by Richard J. Overy. *Past and Present* 122 (1989): 205–240.

Mason, Tim. "Domestic Crisis and War, 1939." In *Social Policy in the Third Reich: The Working Class and the "National Community,"* edited by Jane Caplan, 294–330. New York: Berg, 1993.

Mason, Tim. "Internal Crisis and War of Aggression, 1938–1939" and "The Domestic Dynamics of Nazi Conquests: A Response to Critics." In *Nazism, Fascism, and the*

Working Class, edited by Jane Caplan, 212–231, 295–322. Cambridge: Cambridge University Press, 1995.

Mass, Sandra. *Weiße Helden, schwarze Krieger. Zur Geschichte kolonialer Männlichkeit in Deutschland 1918–1964*. Cologne: Böhlau, 2006.

Massing, Jean Michel. "From Greek Proverb to Soap Advert: Washing the Ethiopian." *Journal of the Warburg and Courtauld Institutes* 58 (1995): 180–201.

Mauch, Christof, and Kiran Klaus Patel, eds. *Wettlauf um die Moderne: Die USA und Deutschland 1890 bis heute*. Munich: Pantheon Verlag, 2008.

Maurer, Trude. *Ostjuden in Deutschland, 1818–1933*. Hamburg: Christians, 1986.

Mazower, Mark. *Hitler's Empire: How the Nazis Ruled Europe*. New York: Penguin, 2008.

McClintock, Anne. *Imperial Leather: Race, Gender, and Sexuality in the Colonial Conquest*. New York: Routledge, 1995.

McKeown, Adam. "Global Migration, 1846–1940." *Journal of World History* 15.2 (2004): 155–190.

Mead, Geoffrey. "Sense of Structure and Structure of Sense: Pierre Bourdieu's Habitus as a Generative Principle." Ph.D. diss., School of Social and Political Sciences, The University of Melbourne, 2013.

Meissner, Jörg, ed. *Strategien der Werbekunst von 1850–1933*. Berlin: Deutsches Historisches Museum, 2004.

Melk-Koch, M. *Auf der Suche nach der menschlichen Gesellschaft: Richard Thurnwald*. Berlin: Reimer, 1989.

Melk-Koch, M. "Richard Thurnwald." In *Hauptwerke der Ethnologie*, edited by Christian F. Feest and Karl-Heinz Kohl. Stuttgart: A. Kroner, 2001.

Mertens, Myriam. "Chemical Compounds in the Congo: A Belgian Colony's Role in Chemotherapeutic Knowledge Production during the 1920s." Paper presented at the 3rd European Conference on African Studies, Leipzig, June 4–7, 2009.

Mertens, Myriam, and Guillaume Lachenal. "The History of Belgian Tropical Medicine from a Cross-Border Perspective." *Revue belge de philologie et d'histoire*, 90.4 (2012): 1249–1272.

Meyer, Henry Cord. *Mitteleuropa in German Thought and Action, 1815–1945*. The Hague: Martinus Nijhoff, 1955.

Meyer, Henry Cord. *"Drang nach Osten": Fortunes of a Slogan-Concept in German-Slavic Relations, 1849–1990*. Bern: Peter Lang, 1996.

Meyer-Drawe, Käte, and Kristin Platt, eds. *Wissenschaft im Einsatz*. Munich: Fink, 2007.

Michel, Ute. "Wilhelm Emil Mühlmann (1904–1988)—ein deutscher Professor. Amnesie und Amnestie: Zum Verhältnis von Ethnologie und Politik im Nationalsozialismus." *Jahrbuch für Soziologiegeschichte 1991* (1992).

Michel, Ute. "Neue ethnologisches Forschungsansätze im Nationalsozialismus? Aus der Biographie Wilhelm Emil Mühlmann (1904–1988)." In *Lebenslust und Fremdenfurcht*, edited by T. Hauschild. Frankfurt: Suhrkamp, 1995.

Michels, Eckard. "Die WDR-Dokumentation 'Heia Safari' von 1966–67 über Deutschlands Kolonialvergangenheit." *Vierteljahrshefte für Zeitgeschichte* 56 (2008): 467–492.

Miller, Alexei, and Alfred J. Rieber, eds. *Imperial Rule*. Budapest: Central European University Press, 2004.

Mitchell, Philip Euen. *African Afterthoughts*. London: Hutchinson, 1954.

Mitchell, Timothy. "Society, Economy, and the State Effect." In *State/Culture: State-Formation after the Cultural Turn*, edited by George Steinmetz, 76–97. Ithaca, NY: Cornell University Press, 1999.

Moeller, Magdalena M. *Plakate für den blauen Dunst*. Dortmund: Harenberg Kalendar, 1983.

Mogk, Walter. *Rohrbach und das "Größere Deutschland": Ethischer Imperialismus im Wilhelminischen Zeitalter. Ein Beitrag zur Geschichte des Kulturprotestantismus*. Munich: Wilhelm Goldmann, 1972.

Möhle, Heiko, ed. *Branntwein, Bibeln und Bananen: Der deutsche Kolonialismus in Afrika. Eine Spurensuche in Hamburg*. Hamburg: Verlag Libertäre Assoziation, 1999.

Mommsen, Wolfgang J. *Theories of Imperialism*. Chicago: University of Chicago Press, 1982.

Mommsen, Wolfgang J. *Max Weber and German Politics, 1890–1920*. Chicago: University of Chicago Press, 1984. Originally published as *Max Weber und die deutsche Politik 1890–1920*. Tübingen: J. C. B. Mohr, 1959.

Mommsen, Wolfgang J., and Jürgen Osterhammel, eds. *Imperialism and After: Continuities and Discontinuities*. New York: HarperCollins, 1986.

Montoya, Maria E. *Translating Property: The Maxwell Land Grant and the Conflict over Land in the American West, 1840–1900*. Berkeley: University of California Press, 2002.

Mosen, Markus. *Der koloniale Traum. Angewandte Ethnologie im Nationalsozialismus*. Bonn: Holos Verlag, 1991.

Moses, A. Dirk. "Empire, Colony, Genocide: Keywords and the Philosophy of History." In *Empire, Colony, Genocide: Conquest, Occupation, and Subaltern Resistance in World History*, edited by A. Dirk Moses, 3–54. New York: Berghahn, 2008.

Moses, A. Dirk. "Colonialism." In *The Oxford Handbook of Holocaust Studies*, edited by Peter Hayes and John K. Roth, 68–80. New York: Oxford University Press, 2011.

Moses, A. Dirk, ed. *Genocide and Settler Society: Frontier Violence and Stolen Children in Australian History*. New York: Berghahn, 2004.

Moses, A. Dirk, ed. *Empire, Colony, Genocide: Conquest, Occupation, and Subaltern Resistance in World History*. New York: Berghahn, 2008.

Mosse, George. *The Image of Man: The Creation of Modern Masculinity*. New York: Oxford University Press, 1996.

Mühlhahn, Klaus. *Herrschaft und Widerstand in der "Musterkolonie" Kiautschou: Interaktionen zwischen China und Deutschland 1897–1914*. Munich: Oldenbourg, 2000.

Mühlhahn, Klaus. "Staatsgewalt und Disziplin: Die chinesische Auseinandersetzung mit dem Rechtssystem der deutschen Kolonie Kiautschou." In *Kolonialisierung des Rechts. Zur kolonialen Rechts- und Verwaltungsordnung*, edited by Rüdiger Voigt and Peter Sack, 125–156. Baden-Baden: Nomos, 2001.

Müller, Frank Lorenz. "Imperialist Ambitions in *Vormärz* and Revolutionary Germany: The Agitation for German Settlement Colonies Overseas, 1840–1849." *German History* 17.3 (1999): 346–368.

Müller, Fritz-Ferdinand. *Deutschland-Zanzibar-Ostafrika: Geschichte einer deutschen Kolonialeroberung.* Berlin: Rütten and Loening, 1959.

Münkler, Herfried. *Imperien. Die Logik der Weltherrschaft. Vom alten Rom bis zu den Vereinigten Staaten.* Berlin: Rowohlt, 2005.

Nagl, Dominik. *Grenzfälle. Staatsangehörigkeit, Rassismus und nationale Identität unter deutscher Kolonialherrschaft.* Frankfurt: Peter Lang, 2007.

Naranch, Bradley. "'Colonized Body,' 'Oriental Machine': Debating Race, Railroads, and the Politics of Reconstruction in Germany and East Africa, 1906–1910." *Central European History* 33.3 (2000): 299–338.

Naranch, Bradley. "Beyond the Fatherland: Colonial Visions, Overseas Expansion, and German Nationalism, 1848–1885." PhD diss., Johns Hopkins University, 2006.

Naranch, Bradley. "Made in China: Austro-Prussian Rivalry and the Global Unification of the German Nation." *Australian Journal of Politics and History* 56.3 (2010): 367–381.

Nau, H. H. *Der Werturteilsstreit: Die Äußerungen zur Werturteilsdiskussion im Ausschuss des Vereins für Sozialpolitik (1913).* Marburg: Metropolis-Verlag, 1996.

Needham, Joseph. "On Science and Social Change." In *The Grand Titration: Science and Society in East and West,* 123–153. Toronto: University of Toronto Press, 1969.

Neill, Deborah. "Paul Ehrlich's Colonial Connections: Scientific Networks and Sleeping Sickness Drug Therapy Research, 1900–1914." *Social History of Medicine* 22.1 (2009): 61–77.

Neill, Deborah. *Networks in Tropic Medicine: Internationalism, Colonialism, and the Rise of a Medical Specialty, 1890–1930.* Stanford, CA: Stanford University Press, 2012.

Nelson, Keith L. "The 'Black Horror on the Rhine': Race as a Factor in Post–World War I Diplomacy." *Journal of Modern History* 42.4 (December 1970): 606–627.

Nelson, Robert L., ed. *Germans, Poland, and Colonial Expansion to the East: 1850 through the Present.* New York: Palgrave Macmillan, 2009.

Neubach, Helmut. *Die Ausweisung von Polen und Juden aus Preußen 1885/86.* Wiesbaden: Harrassowitz, 1967.

Newman, Louise Michelle. *White Women's Rights: The Racial Origins of Feminism in the United States.* New York: Oxford University Press, 1999.

Nichtweiss, Johannes. *Die ausländischen Saisonarbeiter in der Landwirtschaft der östlichen und mittleren Gebiete des Deutschen Reiches. Ein Beitrag zur Geschichte der preußisch-deutschen Politik von 1890 bis 1914.* Berlin: Rütten und Loening, 1959.

Nipperdey, Thomas. *Deutsche Geschichte 1866–1918,* vol. 1: *Arbeitswelt und Bürgergeist.* Munich: Beck, 1990.

Nipperdey, Thomas. *Deutsche Geschichte 1866–1918,* vol. 2: *Machtstaat vor der Demokratie.* Munich: Beck, 1992.

Noakes, Jeremy, and Geoffrey Pridham, eds. *Nazism 1919–1945,* vol. 3: *Foreign Policy, War, and Racial Extermination. A Documentary Reader.* Exeter: University of Exeter Press, 1988.

Nolan, Mary. *Social Democracy and Society: Working-Class Radicalism in Düsseldorf, 1890–1920.* Cambridge: Cambridge University Press, 1981.

Nolan, Michael E. *The Inverted Mirror: Mythologizing the Enemy in France and Germany, 1898–1914.* New York: Berghahn, 2005.

Northrup, David. *Indentured Labor in the Age of Imperialism, 1834–1922*. Cambridge: Cambridge University Press, 1995.

O'Donnell, Krista, Renate Bridenthal, and Nancy Reagin, eds. *The Heimat Abroad: The Boundaries of Germanness*. Ann Arbor: University of Michigan Press, 2005.

Offer, Avner. *The First World War: An Agrarian Interpretation*. Oxford: Clarendon Press, 1989.

Oldenburg, Jens. *Der deutsche Ostmarkenverein 1894–1934*. Berlin: Logos-Verlag, 2002.

Olivier, David H. *German Naval Strategy 1856–1888: Forerunners to Tirpitz*. London: Frank Cass, 2004.

Orlowski, Hubert. *"Polnische Wirtschaft." Zum deutschen Polendiskurs der Neuzeit*. Wiesbaden: Harrassowitz, 1996.

Orosz, Kenneth J. *Religious Conflict and the Evolution of Language Policy in German and French Cameroon, 1885–1939*. New York: Peter Lang, 2008.

O'Rourke, Kevin H., and Jeffrey G. Williamson. *Globalization and History. The Evolution of a Nineteenth-Century Atlantic Economy*. Cambridge, MA: MIT Press, 1999.

Osterhammel, Jürgen. "Semi-colonialism and Informal Empire in Twentieth-Century China: Towards a Framework of Analysis." In *Imperialism and After: Continuities and Discontinuities*, edited by Wolfgang Mommsen and Jürgen Osterhammel, 290–314. Boston: Allen and Unwin, 1986.

Osterhammel, Jürgen. *Colonialism: A Theoretical Overview*. Princeton, NJ: Markus Wiener, 1997.

Osterhammel, Jürgen. "Transnationale Gesellschaftsgeschichte: Erweiterung oder Alternative?" *Geschichte und Gesellschaft* 27.3, 2001.

Osterhammel, Jürgen. *Kolonialismus: Geschichte, Formen, Folgen*, 4th ed. Munich: Beck, 2003.

Osterhammel, Jürgen. "Lemmata 'Konzessionen und Niederlassungen' and 'Pachtgebiete.'" In *Das große China-Lexikon: Geschichte, Geographie, Gesellschaft, Politik, Wirtschaft, Bildung, Wissenschaft, Kultur*, edited by Brunhild Staiger, 394–397, 551–553. Darmstadt: Wissenschaftliche Buchgesellschaft, 2003.

Osterhammel, Jürgen. "Europamodelle und imperiale Kontexte." *Journal of Modern European History* 2.2 (2004): 157–181.

Osterhammel, Jürgen, and Sebastian Conrad, eds. *Das Kaiserreich transnational. Deutschland in der Welt 1871–1914*. Göttingen: Vandenhoeck und Ruprecht, 2004.

Overlack, Peter. "The Function of Commerce Warfare in an Anglo-German Conflict to 1914." *Journal of Strategic Studies* 20.4 (December 1997): 94–114.

Overlack, Peter. "German War Plans in the Pacific, 1900–1914." *Historian* (Spring 1998): 578–593.

Oyono, Ferdinand. *Une vie de boy*. Paris: Presses Pocket, 1956. Published in English as *The Houseboy*, translated by John French. London: Heineman, 1966.

Pagden, Anthony. "Fellow Citizens and Imperial Subjects: Conquest and Sovereignty in Europe's Overseas Empires." *History and Theory* 44.4 (2005): 28–46.

Paret, Peter, Beth Irwin Lewis, and Paul Paret. *Persuasive Images: Posters of War and Revolution from the Hoover Institution Archives*. Princeton, NJ: Princeton University Press, 1992.

Pascal, Roy. *From Naturalism to Expressionism: German Literature and Society 1880–1918*. London: Weidenfeld and Nicolson, 1973.

Passavant, Paul A., and Jodi Dean, eds. *Empire's New Clothes: Reading Hardt and Negri*. New York: Routledge, 2004.

Peabody, Sue, and Tyler Stovall, eds. *The Color of Liberty: Histories of Race in France*. Durham, NC: Duke University Press, 2003.

Pels, Peter, and Oscar Selemink. "Introduction: Five Theses on Ethnography as Colonial Practice." *History and Anthropology* 8.1 (1994): 1–34.

Penny, H. Glenn. *Objects of Culture: Ethnology and Ethnographic Museums in Imperial Germany*. Chapel Hill: University of North Carolina, 2002.

Penny, H. Glenn, and Matti Bunzl, eds. *Worldly Provincialism: German Anthropology in the Age of Empire*. Ann Arbor: University of Michigan Press, 2003.

Perkins, John A. "The Agricultural Revolution in Germany, 1850–1914." *Journal of European Economic History* 10 (1981): 71–118.

Perras, Arne. *Carl Peters and German Imperialism 1856–1918: A Political Biography*. Oxford: Oxford University Press, 2005.

Perraudin, Michael, and Jürgen Zimmerer, eds. *German Colonialism and National Identity*. New York: Routledge, 2011.

Pesek, Michael. *Koloniale Herrschaft in Deutsch-Ostafrika: Expeditionen, Militär und Verwaltung seit 1880*. Frankfurt: Campus, 2005.

Peterson, Derek. "Morality Plays: Marriage, Church Courts, and Colonial Agency in Central Tanganyika, ca. 1876–1928." *American Historical Review* 111.4 (2006): 983–1010.

Phillips, Richard. *Sex, Politics and Empire: A Postcolonial Geography*. Manchester: Manchester University Press, 2006.

Pierard, Richard Victor. "The German Colonial Society, 1882–1914." PhD diss., Graduate College of the State University of Iowa, 1964.

Pierard, Richard V. "The German Colonial Society." In *Germans in the Tropics: Essays in German Colonial History*, edited by Arthur J. Knoll and Lewis H. Gann. New York: Greenwood Press, 1987.

Pieterse, Jan Nederveen. *White on Black: Images of Africa and Blacks in Western Popular Culture*. New Haven, CT: Yale University Press, 1992.

Platt, Kristin. "'Im ertödtenden Blicke des todten Beschauers.' Krise und tätiges Handeln in Universitätsreden 1933 bis 1934." In *Wissenschaft im Einsatz*, edited by Käte Meyer-Drawe and Kristin Platt. Munich: Fink, 2007.

Poiger, Uta. "Imperialism and Empire in Twentieth-Century Germany." *History and Memory* 17.1–2 (2005): 117–143.

Poley, Jared. *Decolonization in Germany. Weimar Narratives of Colonial Loss and Foreign Occupation*. Oxford: Oxford University Press, 2005.

Pommerin, Reiner. *Sterilisierung der Rheinlandbastarde: Das Schicksal einer farbigen deutschen Minderheit 1918–1937*. Düsseldorf: Droste, 1979.

Porter, Bernard. *The Absent-Minded Imperialists: Empire, Society, and Culture in Britain*. Oxford: Oxford University Press, 2004.

Postone, Moishe. *Time, Labor, and Social Domination: A Reinterpretation of Marx's Critical Theory*. Cambridge: Cambridge University Press, 1993.

Power, Helen J. *Tropical Medicine in the Twentieth Century: A History of the Liverpool School of Tropical Medicine 1898–1990*. London, NY: Kegan Paul International, 1999.

Prakash, Gyan. *Another Reason: Science and the Imagination of Modern India*. Princeton, NJ: Princeton University Press, 1999.

Price, Richard. *An Imperial War and the British Working Class: Working-Class Attitudes and Reactions to the Boer War, 1899–1902*. London: Routledge and Kegan Paul, 1972.

Pugach, Sara. "Afrikanistik and Colonial Knowledge: Carl Meinhof, the Missionary Impulse, and African Language and Culture Studies in German, 1887–1919," 2 vols. PhD diss., University of Chicago, 2001.

Puschner, Uwe. *Die völkische Bewegung im wilhelminischen Kaiserreich: Sprache, Rasse, Religion*. Darmstadt: Wissenschaftliche Buchgesellschaft, 2001.

Pyenson, Lewis. *Cultural Imperialism and Exact Sciences. German Expansion Overseas, 1900–1930*. New York: Peter Lang, 1985.

Ramamurthy, Anandi. *Imperial Persuaders: Images of Africa and Asia in British Advertising*. Manchester: Manchester University Press, 2003.

Reagin, Nancy. "The Imagined Hausfrau: National Identity, Domesticity, and Colonialism in Imperial Germany." *Journal of Modern History* 73 (2001): 54–86.

Reagin, Nancy. "Recent Work on German National Identity: Regional? Imperial? Gendered? Imaginary?" *Central European History* 37 (2004): 273–289.

Reemtsma, Jan Philipp. "The Concept of the War of Annihilation. Clausewitz, Ludendorff, Hitler." In *War of Extermination: The German Military in World War II 1941–1944*, edited by Hannes Heer and Klaus Naumann, 3–35. New York: Berghahn, 2000.

Reichardt, Eike. *Health, "Race," and Empire: Popular-Scientific Spectacles and National Identity in Imperial Germany, 1871–1914*. Lulu.com: 2008.

Reinhard, Wolfgang. "'Sozialimperialismus' oder 'Entkolonisierung der Historie'? Kolonialkrise und 'Hottentottenwahlen' 1904–1907." *Historisches Jahrbuch* 97/98 (1978): 384–417.

Reinhardt, Dirk. *Von der Reklame zum Marketing. Geschichte der Wirtschaftswerbung in Deutschland*. Berlin: Akademie Verlag, 1993.

Renda, Mary A. *Taking Haiti: Military Occupation and the Culture of U.S. Imperialism, 1915–1940*. Chapel Hill: University of North Carolina Press, 2001.

Retallack, James, ed. *Imperial Germany 1871–1918*. Oxford: Oxford University Press, 2008.

Reuveni, Gideon. "Lesen und Konsum: Der Aufstieg der Konsumkultur in Presse und Werbung Deutschlands bis 1933." *Archiv fur Sozialgeschichte* 41 (2001).

Richards, Paul. "Ecological Change and the Politics of African Land Use." *African Studies Review* 26 (1983): 1–72.

Ringer, Fritz K. *The Decline of the German Mandarins: The German Academic Community, 1890–1933*. Hanover, NH: Wesleyan University Press, 1969.

Ringer, Fritz K. *Max Weber—an Intellectual Biography*. Chicago: University of Chicago Press, 2004.

Roberts, Richard. *Litigants and Households: African Disputes and Colonial Courts in the French Soudan, 1895–1912*. Portsmouth: Heinemann, 2005.

Rockel, Stephen J. "'A Nation of Porters': The Nyamwezi and the Labour Market in Nineteenth-Century Tanzania." *Journal of African History* 41 (2000): 173–195.

Røksund, Arne. *The Jeune École: The Strategy of the Weak*. Leiden: Brill, 2007.

Roos, Julia. "Women's Rights, Nationalist Anxiety, and the 'Moral' Agenda in the Early Weimar Republic: Revisiting the 'Black Horror' Campaign against France's African Occupation Troops." *Central European History* 42.3 (September 2009): 473–508.

Roos, Julia. "Children of the Occupiers: The Debate about the Rhenish Besatzungskinder after World War I." Conference paper, German Studies Association, 2010 (unpublished MS).

Roos, Julia. "Nationalism, Racism, and Propaganda in Early Weimar Germany: Contradictions in the Campaign against the *Black Horror on the Rhine*." *German History* 30.1 (March 2012).

Ross, Kristin. *Fast Cars, Clean Bodies: Decolonization and the Reordering of French Culture*. Cambridge, MA: MIT Press, 1995.

Rössler, Mechthild, and Sabine Schleiermacher, eds. *Der 'Generalplan Ost': Hauptlinien der nationalsozialistischen Planungs- und Vernichtungspolitik*. Berlin: Akademie Verlag, 1993.

Rudolph, Karsten. *Die sächsische Sozialdemokratie vom Kaiserreich zur Republik, 1871–1923*. Weimar: Böhlau, 1995.

Rudolph, Karsten. "Das 'rote Königreich': Die sächsische Sozialdemokratie im Wilhelminischen Deutschland." In *Sachsen im Kaiserreich: Politik, Wirtschaft und Gesellschaft im Umbruch*, edited by Simone Lässig and Karl Heinrich Pohl, 77–78. Weimar: Böhlau, 1997.

Ruppenthal, Jens. *Kolonialismus als Wissenschaft und Technik: Das Hamburgische Kolonialinstitut 1908 bis 1919*. Stuttgart: Franz Steiner Verlag, 2010.

Rydell, Robert R. *All the World's a Fair: Visions of Empire at American International Expositions, 1876–1916*. Chicago: University of Chicago Press, 1984.

Said, Edward W. *Representations of the Intellectual—the 1993 Reith Lectures*. New York: Vintage, 1996.

Samuel, Raphael. "Empire Stories: The Imperial and the Domestic." In *Theatres of Memory*. Vol. 2: *Island Stories: Unravelling Britain*. London: Verso, 1998.

Sarkozy, Nicolas. "Speech at University of Dakar." July 28, 2007. www.elysee.fr/elysee/elysee.fr/francais/interventions/2007/juillet/allocution_a_1_universite_de_dakar.79184.html (no longer accessible).

Schaeller, Dominick J. "From Conquest to Genocide: Colonial Rule in Germany Southwest Africa and German East Africa." In *Empire, Colony, Genocide: Conquest, Occupation and Subaltern Resistance in World History*, edited by A. Dirk Moses, 296–324. New York: Berghahn, 2008.

Schlenther, Ursula. "Zur Geschichte der Völkerkunde an der Berliner Universität von 1810 bis 1945." *Wissenschaftliche Zeitschrift der Humboldt-Universität zu Berlin* 9 (1959–1960): 69.

Schlesinger, Walter, ed. *Die deutsche Ostsiedlung des Mittelalters als Problem der europäischen Geschichte*. Sigmaringen: Thorbecke, 1975.

Schmidt, Elizabeth. *Peasants, Traders, and Wives: Shona Women in the History of Zimbabwe, 1870–1939*. Portsmouth: Heinemann, 1992.

Schmidt, Heike. "Colonial Intimacy: The Rechenberg Scandal, Homosexuality and Sexual Crime in German East Africa." *Journal of the History of Sexuality* 17.1 (2008): 25–59.

Schmidt, Heike. "The Maji Maji War and Its Aftermath: Gender, Age, and Power in South-Western Tanzania, c. 1905–1916." *International Journal of African Historical Studies* 43.1 (2010): 27–62.

Schmidt, Oliver R. *"Was Deutschland mit Blut gewann, muss uns wiedergehören und dienen!": Kolonialismus und Jugend in der Weimarer Republik*. Saarbrücken: VDM Verlag, 2008.

Schmidt, Vera. *Die deutsche Eisenbahnpolitik in Shantung, 1897–1914. Ein Beitrag zur Geschichte des deutschen Imperialismus in China*. Wiesbaden: Harrassowitz, 1976.

Schmidt-Glintzer, Helwig. "Einleitung, Editorischer Bericht." In *Max Weber, Die Wirtschaftsethik der Weltreligionen, Konfuzianismus und Taoismus: 1915–1920. Max-Weber-Gesamtausgabe* 1.19, edited by Helwig Schmidt-Glintzer. Tübingen: Mohr, 1989.

Schmidt-Linsenhoff, Viktoria, Kurt Wettengl, and Almut Junker, eds. *Plakate 1880–1914. Inventarkatalog der Plakatsammlung des Historischen Museums Frankfurt. Kleine Schriften des Historischen Museums Frankfurt*, vol. 29. Frankfurt: Dezernat für Kultur und Freizeit, 1986.

Schmokel, Wolfe W. *Dream of Empire: German Colonialism, 1919–1945*. Westport, CT: Greenwood Press, 1980.

Scholz-Hänsel, Michael. *Das exotische Plakat*. Stuttgart: Cantz, 1987.

Schorske, Carl E. *German Social Democracy, 1905–1917: The Development of the Great Schism*. Cambridge, MA: Harvard University Press, 1955.

Schrecker, John E. *Imperialism and Chinese Nationalism: Germany in Shantung*. Cambridge, MA: Harvard University Press, 1971.

Schröder, Hans-Christoph. *Sozialismus und Imperialismus: Die Auseinandersetzung der deutschen Sozialdemokratie mit dem Imperialismusproblem und der 'Weltpolitik' vor 1914*. Hannover: Verlag für Literatur und Zeitgeschehen, 1968.

Schröder, Hans-Christoph. *Gustav Noske und die Kolonialpolitik des Deutschen Kaiserreichs*. Berlin: J. H. W. Dietz, 1979.

Schröder, Martin. *Prügelstrafe und Züchtigungsrecht in den deutschen Schutzgebieten Schwarzafrikas*. Münster: LIT, 1997.

Schubert, Michael. *Der schwarze Fremde: Das Bild des Schwarzafrikaners in der parlamentarischen und publizistischen Kolonialdiskussion in Deutschland von den 1870er bis in die 1930er Jahre*. Stuttgart: Steiner, 2003.

Schubert, Werner, ed. *Ausschuß für Kolonialrecht zusammen mit den Entwürfen des Kolonialpolitischen Amtes (1937–1941)*. Frankfurt: Peter Lang, 2001.

Schultz, Hans-Dietrich. *Die Geographie als Bildungsfach im Kaiserreich. Zugleich ein Beitrag zu ihrem Kampf um die preußische höhere Schule von 1870–1914 nebst dessen Vorgeschichte und teilweiser Berücksichtigung anderer deutscher Staaten*. Osnabrück: Selbstverlag des Fachgebietes Geographie im Fachbereich Kultur- und Geowissenschaften der Universität Osnabrück, 1989.

Schultz, Hans-Dietrich, and Heinz Peter Brogatio. "Die 'Gesellschaft für Erdkunde zu Berlin' und Afrika." In *"... Macht und Anteil an der Weltherrschaft." Berlin und der deutsche Kolonialismus*, edited by Ulrich van der Heyden and Joachim Zeller, 87–93. Münster: Unrast Verlag, 2005.

Schwartz, Frederic J. "Commodity Signs: Peter Behrens, the AEG, and the Trademark." *Journal of Design History* 9.3 (1996): 153–184.

Schwarz, Jürgen. *Bildannoncen aus der Jahrhundertwende: Studien zur künstlerischen Reklamegestaltung in Deutschland zwischen 1896 und 1914*. Frankfurt: Kunstgeschichtliches Institut der Johann Wolfgang Goethe-Universität, 1990.

Seager, Robert, II, and Doris D. Maguire, eds. *Letters and Papers of Alfred Thayer Mahan*. Annapolis: Naval Institute Press, 1975.

Seeberg, Karl-Martin. *Der Maji-Maji-Krieg gegen die deutsche Kolonialherrschaft*. Berlin: Reimer, 1989.

Seelemann, Dirk Alexander. "The Social and Economic Development of the Kiaochou Leasehold (Shantung, China) under German Administration, 1897–1914." PhD diss., University of Toronto, 1982.

Sengupta, Indra. *From Salon to Discipline: State, University and Indology in Germany, 1821–1914*. Heidelberg: Ergon, 2005.

Serrier, Thomas. *Provinz Posen, Ostmark, Wielkopolska. Eine Grenzregion zwischen Deutschen und Polen, 1848–1914*. Marburg: Herder-Institut, 2005.

Shapin, Steven, and Simon Schaffer. *Leviathan and the Air-Pump: Hobbes, Boyle, and the Experimental Life*. Princeton, NJ: Princeton University Press, 1985.

Sheehan, James J. *The Career of Lujo Brentano: A Study of Liberalism and Social Reform in Imperial Germany*. Chicago: University of Chicago Press, 1966.

Short, John Phillip. "Everyman's Colonial Library: Imperialism and Working-Class Readers in Leipzig, 1890–1914." *German History* 21.4 (2003): 445–475.

Short, John Phillip. "Colonialism and Society: Class and Region in the Popularization of Overseas Empire in Germany, 1890–1914." PhD diss., Columbia University, 2004.

Short, John Phillip. *Magic Lantern Empire: Colonialism and Society in Germany*. Ithaca, NY: Cornell University Press, 2012.

Shouzhong, Wang. *Deguo qinlüe Shandongshi* (The German Expansion in Shandong). Beijing, 1987.

Sieg, Katrin. *Ethnic Drag: Performing Race, Nation, Sexuality in West Germany*. Ann Arbor: University of Michigan Press, 2002.

Simmons, Sherwin. "Grimaces on the Walls: Anti-Bolshevist Posters and the Debate about Kitsch." *Design Issues* 14.2 (Summer 1998): 29–30.

Smelser, Ronald, Enrico Syring, and Rainer Zitelmann, eds. *Die braune Elite 2: 21 weitere biographische Skizzen*. Darmstadt: Wissenschaftliche Buchgesellschaft, 1999.

Smith, Helmut Walser. *German Nationalism and Religious Conflict. Culture, Ideology, Politics 1870–1914*. Princeton, NJ: Princeton University Press, 1995.

Smith, Helmut Walser. "The Talk of Genocide, the Rhetoric of Miscegenation: Notes on Debates in the German Reichstag concerning Southwest Africa." In *The Imperialist Imagination: German Colonialism and Its Legacy*. Ann Arbor: University of Michigan Press, 1999, 107–123.

Smith, Helmut Walser. "Eliminationist Racism." In *The Continuities of German History: Nation, Religion, and Race across the Long Nineteenth Century*. Cambridge: Cambridge University Press, 2008.

Smith, Helmut Walser. "Roundtable on 'The Long Nineteenth Century.'" *German History* 26.1 (2008): 72–91.

Smith, Helmut Walser. "When the Sonderweg Debate Left Us." *German Studies Review* 31.2 (2008): 225–240.

Smith, Neil. *American Empire: Roosevelt's Geographer and the Prelude to Globalization*. Berkeley: University of California Press, 2003.

Smith, Woodruff D. *The German Colonial Empire*. Chapel Hill: University of North Carolina Press, 1978.

Smith, Woodruff D. *The Ideological Origins of Nazi Imperialism*. New York: Oxford University Press, 1986.

Smith, Woodruff D. *Consumption and the Makings of Respectability, 1600–1800*. London: Routledge, 2002.

Smith, Woodruff D. "Colonialism and the Culture of Respectability." In *Germany's Colonial Pasts*, edited by Eric Ames, Marcia Klotz, and Lora Wildenthal, 3–40. Lincoln: University of Nebraska Press, 2005.

Snyder, Timothy. "Hitler's Dialectic of Death." Review of Mark Mazower, *Hitler's Empire: Nazi Rule in Occupied Europe*. *Times Literary Supplement*, August 14, 2008.

Sobich, Frank Oliver. *"Schwarze Bestien, rote Gefahr": Rassismus und Antisozialismus im deutschen Kaiserreich*. Frankfurt: Campus, 2006.

Soénius, Ulrich S. *Koloniale Begeisterung im Rheinland während des Kaiserreichs*. Cologne: Rheinisch-Westfälisches Wirtschaftsarchiv, 1992.

Söldenwagner, Philippa. *Spaces of Negotiation: European Settlement and Settlers in German East Africa 1900–1914*. Munich: Martin Meidenbauer, 2006.

Solomon, Susan Gross. "Introduction: Germany, Russia, and Medical Cooperation between the Wars." In *Doing Medicine Together: Germany and Russia between the Wars*, edited by Susan Gross Solomon, 3–34. Toronto: University of Toronto Press, 2006.

Sondhaus, Lawrence. *Preparing for Weltpolitik: German Sea Power before the Tirpitz Era*. Annapolis, MD: Naval Institute Press, 1997.

Sontag, Susan. *Regarding the Pain of Others*. New York: Farrar, Straus and Giroux, 2003.

Sösemann, Bernd. "Die sogenannte Hunnenrede Wilhelms II: Textkritische und Interpretatorische Bemerkungen zur Ansprache des Kaisers vom 27. Juli 1900 in Bremerhaven." In *Historische Zeitschrift*, edited by Theodor Schieder und Lothar Gal, 342–358l. Munich, 1976.

Spector, Ronald. *Professors of War: The Naval War College and the Development of the Naval Profession*. Newport, RI: Naval War College Press, 1977.

Sperber, Jonathan. *The Kaiser's Voters: Electors and Elections in Imperial Germany*. Cambridge: Cambridge University Press, 1997.

Sperling, Walter. "Zur Darstellung der deutschen Kolonien im Erdkundeunterricht (1890–1914) mit besonderer Berücksichtigung der Lehrmittel." *Internationale Schulbuchforschung* 11 (1989).

Spivak, Gayatri Chakravorty. *A Critique of Postcolonial Reason: Toward a History of the Vanishing Present.* Cambridge, MA: Harvard University Press, 1999.

Spohn, Willfried. *Weltmarktkonkurrenz und Industrialisierung Deutschlands 1870–1914. Eine Untersuchung zur nationalen und internationalen Geschichte der kapitalistischen Produktionsweise.* Berlin: Olle and Wolter, 1977.

Stegmann, Dirk. *Die Erben Bismarcks. Parteien und Verbände in der Spätphase des Wilhelminischen Deutschlands: Sammlungspolitik 1897–1918.* Cologne: Kiepenheuer und Witsch, 1970.

Steinmetz, George. "'The Devil's Handwriting': Precolonial Discourse, Ethnographic Acuity, and Cross-Identification in German Colonialism." *Comparative Studies in Society and History* 45.1 (2003): 41–95.

Steinmetz, George. "Return to Empire: The New U.S. Imperialism in Comparative Historical Perspective." *Sociological Theory* 23.4 (2005).

Steinmetz, George. "Imperialism or Colonialism? From Windhoek to Washington, by Way of Basra." In *Lessons of Empire: Imperial Histories and American Power*, edited by Craig J. Calhoun, Frederick Cooper, and Kevin W. Moore, 135–156. New York: Norton, 2006.

Steinmetz, George. *The Devil's Handwriting: Precoloniality and the German Colonial State in Qingdao, Samoa, and Southwest Africa.* Chicago: University of Chicago Press, 2007.

Steinmetz, George. "Transdisciplinarity as a Nonimperial Encounter." *Thesis Eleven* 91.1 (2007): 48–65.

Steinmetz, George. "The Colonial State as a Social Field." *American Sociological Review* 73(4) (August 2008): 589–612.

Steinmetz, George. "The Imperial Entanglements of Sociology in the United States, Britain, and France since the 19th Century." *Ab Imperio* 4 (2009): 1–56.

Steinmetz, George. "Ideas in Exile: Refugees from Nazi Germany and the Failure to Transplant Historical Sociology into the United States." *International Journal of Politics, Culture, and Society* 23:1 (2010): 1–27.

Steinmetz, George, ed. *Sociology and Empire: The Imperial Entanglements of a Discipline.* Durham, NC: Duke University Press, 2013.

Steinmetz, George. "A Child of the Empire: British Sociology and Colonialism, 1940s-1960s." *Journal of the History of the Behavioral Sciences* 49.4 (2013): 353–378.

Steinmetz, George. "État-mort, État-fort, État-empire." *Actes de la recherche en sciences sociales* 201 (2014): 112–119.

Steinmetz, George. "Historicizing and Spatializing Field Theory: A Study of Disciplinary Separation and Interaction between Sociology and History." In *The Sociology of the Social Sciences 1945–2010*, edited by Christian Knudsen, Ole Wæver, and Kristoffer Kropp. Forthcoming.

Steverding, Dietmar. "The Development of Drugs for Treatment of Sleeping Sickness: A Historical Overview." *Parasites and Vectors* 3.15 (2010). www.biomedcentral.com/content/pdf/1756-3305-3-15.pdf (accessed October 10, 2013).

Stichler, Hans Christian. "Das Gouvernement Jiaozhou und die deutsche Kolonialpolitik in Shandong 1897–1909. Ein Beitrag zur Geschichte der deutsch-chinesischen Beziehungen." PhD diss., Humboldt Universität zu Berlin, 1989.

Stöber, Rudolf. *Deutsche Pressegeschichte: Einführung, Systematik, Glossar.* Constance: UVK-Medien, 2000.

Stoecker, Helmuth. *Deutschland und China im 19. Jahrhundert.* Berlin: Rütten and Loening, 1958.

Stoecker, Helmuth, ed. *Kamerun unter deutscher Kolonialherrschaft. Studien,* 2 vols. Berlin: Rütten and Loening, 1960, 1968.

Stoecker, Helmuth, and Peter Sebald. "Enemies of the Colonial Idea." In *Germans in the Tropics: Essays in German Colonial History,* edited by Arthur J. Knoll and Lewis H. Gann. New York: Greenwood Press, 1987.

Stoecker, Holger. "The Advancement of African Studies by the German Research Foundation (GRF), 1920–1945." In *Ordering Africa: Anthropology, European Imperialism, and the Politics of Knowledge,* edited by Helen L. Tilly and Robert J. Gordon. Manchester: Manchester University Press, 2007.

Stoler, Ann Laura. "Making Empire Respectable: The Politics of Race and Sexual Morality in 20th-Century Colonial Cultures." *American Ethnologist* 16.4 (1989): 634–660.

Stoler, Ann Laura. "Rethinking Colonial Categories. European Communities and the Boundaries of Rule." *Comparative Studies in Society and History* 31.1 (1989): 134–161.

Stoler, Ann Laura. "Sexual Affronts and Racial Frontiers: European Identities and the Cultural Politics of Exclusion in Colonial Southeast Asia." In *Becoming National: A Reader,* edited by Geoff Eley and Ronald Grigor Suny. New York: Oxford University Press, 1996, 286–324.

Stoler, Ann Laura. *Carnal Knowledge and Imperial Power: Race and the Intimate in Colonial Rule.* Berkeley: University of California Press, 2002.

Stoler, Ann Laura. "On Degrees of Imperial Sovereignty." *Public Culture* 18.1 (2006): 125–146.

Stoler, Ann Laura, ed. *Haunted by Empire: Geographies of Intimacy in North American History.* Durham, NC: Duke University Press, 2006.

Stoler, Ann Laura, and Frederick Cooper. "Between Metropole and Colony: Rethinking a Research Agenda." In *Tensions of Empire: Colonial Cultures in a Bourgeois World,* edited by Ann Laura Stoler and Frederick Cooper, 1–56. Berkeley: University of California Press, 1997.

Stoler, Ann Laura, and Carole MacGranahan. "Refiguring Imperial Terrains." In *Imperial Formations,* edited by Ann Laura Stoler, Carole McGranahan, and Peter C. Perdue, 3–44. Santa Fe: School for Advanced Research Press, 2007.

Stoler, Ann Laura, Carole McGranahan, and Peter C. Perdue, eds. *Imperial Formations.* Santa Fe: School for Advanced Research Press, 2007.

Struck, Bernhard. *Nicht West—nicht Ost. Frankreich und Polen in der Wahrnehmung deutscher Reisender zwischen 1750 und 1850.* Göttingen: Wallstein, 2006.

Stuchtey, Benedikt. *Die europäische Expansion und ihre Feinde. Kolonialismuskritik vom 18. bis in das 20. Jahrhundert.* Munich: Oldenbourg, 2010.

Sunseri, Thaddeus. *Vilimani: Labor Migration and Rural Change in Early Colonial Tanzania.* Portsmouth: Heinemann, 2002.

Sunseri, Thaddeus. "The Baumwollfrage: Cotton Colonialism in German East Africa." *Central European History* 34.1 (2004): 31–51.
Sutcliffe, Bob, and Roger Owen, eds. *Studies in the Theory of Imperialism*. London: Longman, 1972.
Sweeney, Dennis. "Reconsidering the Modernity Paradigm: Reform Movements, the Social, and the State in Wilhelmine Germany." *Social History* 31.4 (2006): 405–434.
Swett, Pamela E., S. Jonathan Wiesen, and Jonathan R. Zatlin, eds. *Selling Modernity: Advertising in Twentieth-Century Germany*. Durham, NC: Duke University Press, 2007.
Thalmann, Rita. *Protestantisme et nationalisme en Allemagne de 1900 a 1945: D'apres les itineraires spirituels de Gustav Frenssen (1863–1945), Walter Flex (1887–1917), Jochen Klepper (1903–1942), Dietrich Bonhoeffer (1906–1945)*. Paris: Klincksieck, 1976.
Ther, Philipp. "Deutsche Geschichte als imperiale Geschichte. Polen, slawophone Minderheiten und das Kaiserreich als kontinentales Empire." In *Das Kaiserreich transnational. Deutschland in der Welt 1871–1914*, edited by Sebastian Conrad and Jürgen Osterhammel, 129–148. Göttingen: Vandenhoeck und Ruprecht, 2004.
Thomas, Nicholas. "Melanesians and Polynesians: Ethnic Typifications inside and outside Anthropology." In *In Oceania: Visions, Artifacts, Histories*, 133–155. Durham, NC: Duke University Press, 1997.
Thompson, Andrew. *The Empire Strikes Back? The Impact of Imperialism on Britain from the Mid-nineteenth Century*. New York: Pearson Longman, 2005.
Thompson, E. P. "Time, Work-Discipline, and Industrial Capitalism." *Past and Present* 38 (1967): 56–97.
Thum, Gregor, ed. *Traumland Osten. Deutsche Bilder vom östlichen Europa im 20. Jahrhundert*. Göttingen: Vandenhoeck und Ruprecht, 2006.
Timm, K. "Richard Thurnwald: 'Koloniale Gestaltung'—ein 'Apartheids-Projekt' für die koloniale Expansion des deutschen Faschismus in Afrika." *Ethnographisch-Archäologische Zeitschrift* 18 (1977).
Todd, Lisa. "Transnational Intimacies? Sexual Encounters in the Occupied Rhineland, 1919–1923." German Studies Association conference, 2008, unpublished MS.
Todd, Lisa. "Beware of the Colored Menace: Black Men and Sexual Danger in the Occupied Rhineland, 1918–23." German Studies Association conference, 2010, unpublished MS.
Torp, Cornelius. *Die Herausforderung der Globalisierung. Wirtschaft und Politik in Deutschland, 1860–1914*. Göttingen: Vandenhoeck und Ruprecht, 2005.
Trachtenberg, Marc. *Reparation in World Politics: France and European Economic Diplomacy, 1916–1923*. New York: Columbia University Press, 1980.
Tribe, Keith. "Introduction to Weber." *Economy and Society* 9 (1980): 421–427.
Tribe, Keith. "Prussian Agriculture—German Politics: Max Weber 1892–97." *Economy and Society* 12 (1983): 181–226.
Trzeciakowski, Lech. *The Kulturkampf in Prussian Poland*. New York: Columbia University Press, 1990.

Ueberschär, Gerd. "Dokumente zum 'Unternehmen Barbarossa' als Vernichtungskrieg im Osten." In *Der deutsche Überfall auf die Sowjetunion*, edited by Gerd Ueberschär and Wolfram Wette. Frankfurt: Fischer, 1991.

Urena, Lenny. "The Stakes of Empire: Colonial Fantasies, Civilizing Agendas, and Biopolitics in the Prussian-Polish Provinces (1860–1922)." PhD diss., University of Michigan, 2008.

Vagts, Alfred. *Deutschland und die Vereinigten Staaten in der Weltpolitik*, 2 vols. New York: Macmillan, 1935.

Van der Heyden, Ulrich. "Der 'Hottentottenwahlen' von 1907." In *Völkermord in Deutsch-Südwestafrika: Der Kolonialkrieg (1904–1908) in Namibia und seine Folgen*, edited by Joachim Zeller and Jürgen Zimmerer. Berlin: Links, 2003.

Van der Heyden, Ulrich, ed. *Schwarze Biographien: Afrikaner im deutschsprachigem Raum vom 18. Jahrhundert bis zum Ende des Zweiten Weltkrieges*. Berlin: Kai Homilus, 2008.

Van der Heyden, Ulrich, and Joachim Zeller, eds. *Kolonialmetropole Berlin: Eine Spurensuche*. Berlin: Berlin Edition, 2002.

Van der Heyden, Ulrich, and Joachim Zeller, eds. *"... Macht und Anteil an der Weltherrschaft." Berlin und der deutsche Kolonialismus*. Berlin: Unrast, 2005.

Van der Heyden, Ulrich, and Joachim Zeller, eds. *Kolonialismus hierzulande: Eine Spurensuche in Deutschland*. Erfurt: Sutton Verlag, 2008.

Van Hoesen, Brett M. "Weimar Revisions of Germany's Colonial Past: The Photomontages of Hannah Höch and László Moholy-Nagy." In *German Colonialism, Visual Culture, and Modern Memory*, edited by Volker Langbehn, 197–219. London: Routledge, 2010.

Van Hoesen, Brett M. "Postcolonial Cosmopolitanism: Constructing the Weimar New Woman out of a Colonial Imaginary." In *The New Woman International: Representations in Photography and Film from the 1870s through the 1960s*, edited by Elizabeth Otto and Vanessa Rocco, 95–114. Ann Arbor: University of Michigan Press, 2011.

Van Hoesen, Brett M. *"Who Knows Tomorrow*—Berlin and Beyond." *Nka—Journal of Contemporary African Art* 28 (Spring 2011): 78–87.

Van Laak, Dirk. *Imperiale Infrastruktur: Deutsche Planungen für eine Erschließung Afrikas 1880 bis 1960*. Paderborn: Schöningh, 2004.

Van Laak, Dirk. *Über alles in der Welt. Deutscher Imperialismus im 19. und 20. Jahrhundert*. Munich: Beck, 2005.

Väth-Hinz, Henriette. *Odol. Reklame-Kunst um 1900*. Giessen: Anabas, 1985.

Vaughan, Megan. *Curing Their Ills: Colonial Power and African Illness*. Stanford, CA: Stanford University Press, 1991.

Volland, Alexander. "Theodor Fritsch [1852–1933] und die Zeitschrift '*Hammer*.'" PhD diss., Johannes Gutenberg-Universität Mainz, 1993.

Vom Bruch, Rüdiger. *Weltpolitik als Kulturmission: Auswärtige Kulturpolitik und Bildungsbürgertum in Deutschland am Vorabend des Ersten Weltkrieges*. Paderborn: Schöningh, 1982.

Von Friedeburg, Robert. "Konservatismus und Reichskolonialrecht. Konservatives Weltbild und kolonialer Gedanke in England und Deutschland vom späten 19. Jahrhundert bis zum Ersten Weltkrieg." *Historische Zeitschrift* 263 (1996): 345–393.

Von Joeden-Forgey, Elisa. "Race Power, Freedom, and the Democracy of Terror in German Racialist Thought." In *Hannah Arendt and the Uses of History: Imperialism, Nation, Race, and Genocide*, edited by Richard H. King and Dan Stone, 21–39. New York: Berghahn, 2007.

Von Strandmann, Hartmut Pogge. "Consequences of the Foundation of the German Empire: Colonial Expansion and the Process of Political-Economic Rationalization." In *Bismarck, Europe, and Africa: The Berlin Africa Conference 1884–1885 and the Onset of Partition*, edited by Stig Förster, Wolfgang J. Mommsen, and Ronald Edward Robinson, 105–120. Oxford: Oxford University Press, 1988.

Von Strandmann, Hartmut Pogge. "The Kolonialrat, Its Significance and Influence on German Politics from 1890 to 1906." DPhil thesis, University of Oxford, 1970. Published as *Imperialismus vom Grünen Tisch. Deutsche Kolonialpolitik zwischen wirtschaftlicher Ausbeutung und "zivilisatorischen" Bemühungen*. Berlin: Links Verlag, 2009.

Von Strandmann, Hartmut Pogge, ed. *Walther Rathenau: Industrialist, Banker, Intellectual, and Politician. Notes and Diaries 1907–1922*. Oxford: Oxford University Press, 1985.

Von Trotha, Trutz. *Koloniale Herrschaft: Zur soziologischen Theorie des Staatsentstehung am Beispiel des "Schutzgebietes Togo."* Tübingen: J. C. B. Mohr, 1994.

Von Trotha, Trutz. "'The Fellows Can Just Starve': On Wars of Pacification in the African Colonies of Imperial Germany and the Concept of 'Total War.'" In *Anticipating Total War: The American and German Experiences*, edited by Manfred F. Boemeke, Roger Chickering, and Stig Förster, 415–433. New York: Cambridge University Press, 1999.

Von Wolzogen, Christoph. *Zur Geschichte des Dietrich Reimer Verlages 1845–1985*. Berlin: Reimer, 1986.

Wagner, Norbert Berthold. *Die deutschen Schutzgebiete. Erwerb, Organisation und Verlust aus juristischer Sicht*. Baden-Baden: Nomos, 2002.

Walkenhorst, Peter. *Nation-Volk-Rasse. Radikaler Nationalismus im Deutschen Kaiserreich 1890–1914*. Göttingen: Vandenhoeck und Ruprecht, 2007.

Walker, Mack. *Germany and the Emigration 1816–1885*. Cambridge, MA: Harvard University Press, 1964.

Walker, Mark. "National Socialism and German Physics." *Journal of Contemporary History* 24.1 (1999): 63–89.

Walkowitz, Judith R. *Prostitution and Victorian Society: Women, Class and the State*. Cambridge: Cambridge University Press, 1980.

Walther, Daniel Joseph. *Creating Germans Abroad: Cultural Policies and National Identity in Namibia*. Athens: Ohio University Press, 2002.

Walther, Daniel Joseph. "Racializing Sex: Same-Sex Relations, German Colonial Authority, and Deutschtum." *Journal of the History of Sexuality* 17.1 (2008): 11–24.

Walther, Rudolf. "Imperialismus." In *Geschichtliche Grundbegriffe*, 3. Stuttgart: Klett, 1982, 171–236.

Ware, Vron. *Beyond the Pale: White Women, Racism, and History*. London: Verso, 1992.

Warner, Torsten. "Der Aufbau der Kolonialstadt Tsingtau: Landordnung, Stadtplanung und Entwicklung." In *Tsingtau. Ein Kapitel deutscher Kolonialgeschichte in*

China, 1897–1914, edited by Hans-Martin Hinz and Christoph Lind, 84–95. Berlin: Deutsches Historisches Museum, 1998.

Wassink, Jörg. *Auf den Spuren des deutschen Völkermordes in Südwestafrika. Der Herero/ Nama-Aufstand in der deutschen Kolonialliteratur. Eine literaturhistorischen Analyse.* Munich: Meidenbauer, 2004.

Webel, Mari. "Borderlands of Research: Medicine, Empire, and Sleeping Sickness at Lake Victoria and Lake Tanganyika, 1901–1914." PhD diss., Columbia University, 2012.

Wehler, Hans-Ulrich. *Sozialdemokratie und Nationalstaat. Die deutsche Sozialdemokratie und die Nationalitätenfrage in Deutschland von Karl Marx bis zum Ausbruch des Ersten Weltkrieges.* Würzburg: Holzner, 1962.

Wehler, Hans-Ulrich. *Bismarck und der Imperialismus.* Cologne: Kiepenheuer und Witsch, 1969.

Wehler, Hans-Ulrich. "Bismarck's Imperialism 1862–1890." *Past and Present* 48 (1970): 119–155.

Wehler, Hans-Ulrich. "Bismarcks Imperialismus 1862–1890." In *Krisenherde des Kaiserreichs 1871–1918. Studien zur deutschen Sozial- und Verfassungsgeschichte.* Göttingen: Vandenhoeck und Ruprecht, 1970.

Wehler, Hans-Ulrich. "Probleme des Imperialismus." In *Krisenherde des Kaiserreichs 1871–1918. Studien zur deutschen Sozial- und Verfassungsgeschichte.* Göttingen: Vandenhoeck und Ruprecht, 1970.

Wehler, Hans-Ulrich. "Industrial Growth and Early German Imperialism." In *Studies in the Theory of Imperialism*, edited by Robert B. Sutcliffe and Roger Owen, 71–92. London: Longman, 1972.

Wehler, Hans-Ulrich. "Polenpolitik im Deutschen Kaiserreich." In *Krisenherde des Kaiserreichs 1871*, 184–203. Göttingen: Vandenhoeck und Ruprecht, 1979.

Wehler, Hans-Ulrich. *Deutsche Gesellschaftsgeschichte.* Vol. 3: *Von der "Deutschen Doppelrevolution bis zum Beginn des Ersten Weltkrieges, 1849–1914.* Munich: Beck, 1995.

Wehler, Hans-Ulrich. *Politik in der Geschichte: Essays.* Munich: Beck, 1998.

Wehler, Hans-Ulrich. *Umbruch und Kontinuität: Essays zum 20. Jahrhundert.* Munich: Beck, 2000.

Wehler, Hans-Ulrich. *Deutsche Gesellschaftsgeschichte.* Vol. 4: *Vom Beginn des Ersten Weltkrieges bis zur Gründung der beiden deutschen Staaten 1914–1949.* Munich: Beck, 2003.

Wehler, Hans-Ulrich. *Eine lebhafte Kampfsituation. Ein Gespräch mit Manfred Hertling und Cornelius Torp.* Munich: Beck, 2006.

Wehler, Hans-Ulrich. "Transnationale Geschichte—der neue Königsweg historischer Forschung?" In *Transnationale Geschichte. Themen, Tendenzen und Theorien*, edited by Gunilla-Friederike Budde, Sebastian Conrad, and Oliver Janz. Göttingen: Vandenhoeck und Ruprecht, 2006.

Wehler, Hans-Ulrich. *Notizen zur deutschen Geschichte.* Munich: Beck, 2007.

Weigley, Russell F. *The American Way of War: A History of United States Military Strategy and Policy.* New York: Macmillan, 1973.

Weigley, Russell F. "American Strategy from Its Beginnings through the First World War." In *Makers of Modern Strategy from Machiavelli to the Nuclear Age*, edited by Peter Paret, 408–443. Princeton, NJ: Princeton University Press, 1986.

Weinberg, Gerhard L. "German Colonial Plans and Policies 1938–1942." In *Geschichte und Gegenwartsbewusstsein. Historische Betrachtungen und Untersuchungen, Festschrift für Hans Rothfels zum 70. Geburtstag*, edited by Waldemar Besson and Friedrich Freiherr Hiller von Gaertringen, 462–491. Göttingen: Vandenhoeck und Ruprecht, 1963.

Weindling, Paul. *Epidemics and Genocide in Eastern Europe, 1890–1945*. Oxford: Oxford University Press, 2000.

Weisser, Michael. *Cigaretten-Reclame: Über d. Kunst, blauen Dunst zu verkaufen*. Münster: Coppenrath, 1980.

Wernecke, Klaus. *Der Wille zur Weltgeltung: Außenpolitik und Öffentlichkeit im Kaiserreich am Vorabend des Ersten Weltkrieges*. Düsseldorf: Droste, 1970.

Wertheimer, Jack. *Unwelcome Strangers. East European Jews in Imperial Germany*. New York: Oxford University Press, 1987.

Wertheimer, Mildred S. *The Pan-German League, 1890–1914*. New York: Columbia University, 1924.

Wexler, Laura. *Tender Violence: Domestic Visions in an Age of U.S. Imperialism*. Chapel Hill: University of North Carolina Press, 2000.

Wielandt, Ute, and Michael Kascher. "Die Reichstagsdebatten über den deutschen Kriegseinsatz in China: August Bebel und die 'Hunnenbriefe.'" In *Das Deutsche Reich und der Boxeraufstand*, edited by Sussane Kuss and Bernd Martin, 183–201. Munich: Iudicium, 2002.

Wigger, Iris. *Die "Schwarze Schmach am Rhein": Rassistische Diskriminierung, zwischen Geschlecht, Klasse, Nation und Rasse*. Münster: Verlag Westfälisches Dampfboot, 2007.

Wigger, Iris. "*Black Shame*—the Campaign against 'Racial Degeneration' and Female Degradation in Interwar Europe." *Race and Class* 51.3 (January 2010): 33–46.

Wildenthal, Lora. "'She Is the Victor': Bourgeois Women, Nationalist Identities, and the Ideal of the Independent Woman Farmer in German Southwest Africa." In *Society, Culture, and the State in Germany, 1870–1930*, edited by Geoff Eley, 371–396. Ann Arbor: University of Michigan Press, 1996.

Wildenthal, Lora. "Race, Gender and Citizenship in the German Colonial Empire." In *Tensions of Empire: Colonial Cultures in a Bourgeois World*, edited by Frederick Cooper and Ann Laura Stoler, 263–283. Berkeley: University of California Press, 1997.

Wildenthal, Lora. "'When Men Are Weak': The Imperial Feminism of Frieda von Bülow." *Gender and History* 10.1 (1998): 53–77.

Wildenthal, Lora. *German Women for Empire, 1884–1945*. Ann Arbor: University of Michigan Press, 2001.

Wildenthal, Lora. "Notes on a History of 'Imperial Turns' in Modern Germany." In *After the Imperial Turn: Thinking with and through the Nation*, edited by Antoinette Burton, 144–156. Durham, NC: Duke University Press, 2003.

Wilder, Gary. "Unthinking French History: Colonial Studies beyond National Identity." In *After the Imperial Turn: Thinking with and through the Nation*, edited by Antoinette Burton, 125–143. Durham, NC: Duke University Press, 2003.

Wilder, Gary. *The French Imperial Nation-State: Negritude and Colonial Humanism between the Two World Wars*. Chicago: University of Chicago Press, 2005.

Williams, Robert C. *Culture in Exile: Russian Emigrés in Germany 1881–1941*. Ithaca, NY: Cornell University Press, 1972.

Willis, William J., Jr. "Skeletons in the Anthropological Closet." In *Reinventing Anthropology*, edited by Dell Hymes. Ann Arbor: University of Michigan Press, 1999.

Wilson, Jeffrey K. "Environmental Chauvinism in the Prussian East: Forestry as a Civilizing Mission on the Ethnic Frontier, 1871–1914." *Central European History* 41.1 (2008): 27–70.

Wilson, Kathleen. *The Sense of the People: Politics, Culture, and Imperialism in England, 1715–1785*. Cambridge: Cambridge University Press, 1995.

Winkelmann, Ingeburg. "Die bürgerliche Ethnographie im Dienste der Kolonialpolitik des Deutschen Reiches, 1870–1918." PhD diss., Humboldt University, 1966.

Winseck, Dwayne R., and Robert M. Pike. *Communication and Empire: Media, Markets, and Globalization, 1860–1930*. Durham, NC: Duke University Press, 2007.

Wippermann, Wolfgang. *Der 'Deutsche Drang nach Osten.' Ideologie und Wirklichkeit eines politischen Schlagwortes*. Darmstadt: Wissenschaftliche Buchgesellschaft, 1981.

Witt, Peter-Christian. *Die Finanzpolitik des Deutschen Reiches von 1903 bis 1913. Eine Studie zur Innenpolitik des Wilhelminischen Deutschland*. Lübeck: Matthiesen, 1970.

Wolf, Eric R. "Cultural Dissonance in the Italian Alps." *Comparative Studies of Society and History* 5.1 (October 1962): 1–14.

Wolpoff, Milford, and Rachel Caspari. *Race and Human Evolution*. Boulder, CO: Westview Press, 1997.

Wolter, Udo, and Paul Kaller. "Deutsches Kolonialrecht—ein wenig erforschtes Rechtsgebiet, dargestellt anhand des Arbeitsrechts der Eingeborenen." *Zeitschrift für Neuere Rechtsgeschichte* 17 (1995): 201–244.

Worboys, Michael. "The Comparative History of Sleeping Sickness in East and Central Africa, 1900–1914." *History of Science* 32.1 (1994): 89–102.

Worboys, Michael. "Germs, Malaria and the Invention of Mansonian Tropical Medicine: From 'Diseases in the Tropics' to 'Tropical Diseases.'" In *Warm Climates and Western Medicine: The Emergence of Tropical Medicine, 1500–1900*, edited by David Arnold, 181–207. Amsterdam: Rodopi, 1996.

Wright, Marcia. "Local Roots of Policy in German East Africa." *Journal of African History* 9.4 (1968): 621–630.

Wright, Marcia. *German Missions in Tanganyika, 1891–1941: Lutherans and Moravians in the Southern Highlands*. Oxford: Oxford University Press, 1971.

Wright, Marcia. "Maji Maji: Prophecy and Historiography." In *Revealing Prophets: Prophecy in Eastern African History*, edited by David M. Anderson and Douglas H. Johnson. London: James Currey, 1995.

Yufa, Zhang. "Qingdao de shili juan (The Sphere of Influence of Qingdao)." In *Jindai Zhongguo quyushi yantaohui lunwenji* (Essays of the Conference on Regional Modernization in Modern China), edited by Institute of Modern History, 801–838. Academia Sinica. Taipei, 1986.

Zantop, Susanne. *Colonial Fantasies: Conquest, Family, and Nation in Precolonial Germany, 1770–1870*. Durham, NC: Duke University Press, 1997.

Zantop, Susanne. "Colonial Legends, Postcolonial Legacies." In *A User's Guide to German Cultural Studies*, edited by Scott Denham, Irene Kacandes, and Jonathan Petropoulos, 189–205. Ann Arbor: University of Michigan Press, 1997.

Zeller, Joachim. *Weiße Blicke—schwarze Körper. Afrika(ner) im Spiegel westlicher Alltagskultur*. Erfurt: Sutton, 2010.

Zimmerer, Jürgen. "Colonialism and the Holocaust. Towards an Archaeology of Genocide." In *Genocide and Settler Society: Frontier Violence and Stolen Indigenous Children in Australian History*, edited by A. Dirk Moses, 49–76. New York: Berghahn, 2004.

Zimmerer, Jürgen. *Deutsche Herrschaft über Afrikaner: Staatlicher Machtanspruch und Wirklichkeit in kolonialen Namibia*, 3rd ed. Münster: LIT, 2004.

Zimmerer, Jürgen. "Annihilation in Africa: The 'Race War' in German Southwest Africa (1904–1908) and Its Significance for a Global History of Genocide." *Bulletin of the German Historical Institute* 37 (2005): 51–57.

Zimmerer, Jürgen. "The Birth of the 'Ostland' out of the Spirit of Colonialism. A Postcolonial Perspective on Nazi Policy of Conquest and Extermination." *Patterns of Prejudice* 39.2 (June 2005): 197–219.

Zimmerer, Jürgen. "Rassenkrieg und Völkermord. Der Kolonialkrieg in Deutsch-Südwestafrika und die Globalgeschichte des Genozids." In *Genozid und Gedenken. Namibisch-deutsche Geschichte und Gegenwart*, edited by Henning Melber, 23–48. Frankfurt: Brandes und Apsel, 2005.

Zimmerer, Jürgen. "The First Genocide of the Twentieth Century: The German War of Destruction in Southwest Africa (1904–1908)." In *Lessons and Legacies, Volume 8: From Generation to Generation*, edited by Doris L. Bergen, 34–64. Evanston, IL: Northwestern University Press, 2008.

Zimmerer, Jürgen. *Von Windhuk nach Auschwitz? Beiträge zum Verhältnis von Kolonialismus und Holocaust*. Münster: LIT, 2011.

Zimmerer, Jürgen, Birthe Kundrus, Lora Wildenthal, Russell Berman, Jan Rüger, and Bradley Naranch. "Forum: The German Colonial Imagination." *German History* 26.2 (2008): 251–271.

Zimmerer, Jürgen, and Joachim Zeller, eds. *Genocide in German South-West Africa. The Colonial War of 1904–1908 and Its Aftermath*, translated by Edward Neather. London: Merlin, 2008.

Zimmerman, Andrew. *Anthropology and Antihumanism in Imperial Germany*. Chicago: University of Chicago Press, 2001.

Zimmerman, Andrew. "A German Alabama in Africa: The Tuskegee Expedition to German Togo and the Transnational Origins of West African Cotton Growers." *American Historical Review* 110.5 (2005): 1362–1398.

Zimmerman, Andrew. "Decolonizing Weber." *Postcolonial Studies* 9.1 (2006): 53–80.

Zimmerman, Andrew. "'What Do You Really Want in German East Africa Herr Professor?' Counterinsurgency and the Science Effect in Colonial Tanzania." *Comparative Studies in Society and History* 48.2 (2006): 419–461.

Zimmerman, Andrew. "Booker T. Washington, Tuskegee Institute, and the German Empire: Race and Cotton in the Black Atlantic." *Bulletin of the German Historical Institute* 43 (Fall 2008): 12–15.

Zimmerman, Andrew. *Alabama in Africa: Booker T. Washington, the German Empire, and the Globalization of the New South*. Princeton, NJ: Princeton University Press, 2010.

Zimmerman, Andrew. "Race and World Politics: Germany in the Age of Imperialism, 1878–1914." In *The Oxford Handbook of Modern German History*, edited by Helmut Walser Smith. Oxford: Oxford University Press, 2011, 359–377.

Zumbini, Massimo Ferrari. *"Die Wurzeln des Bösen." Gründerjahre des Antisemitismus: Von der Bismarckzeit zu Hitler*. Frankfurt: Klostermann, 2003.

Zurstrassen, Bettina. *Ein Stück deutscher Erde schaffen: Koloniale Beamte in Togo 1884–1914*. Frankfurt: Campus, 2008.

Contributors

DIRK BÖNKER is associate professor of history at Duke University. His research focuses on the history of militarism, warfare, and empire in modern Germany and the United States. He is the author of *Militarism in a Global Age: Naval Ambitions in Germany and the United States before World War I* (2012).

JEFF BOWERSOX is a lecturer in modern German history at University College London. He is the author of *Raising Germans in the Age of Empire: Youth and Colonial Culture, 1871–1914* (2013) as well as articles and essays on German-Polish relations in Upper Silesia, German colonial culture, and Africans in Germany. He is currently working on a history of race and commercial culture in Germany between Kaiserreich and Third Reich.

DAVID CIARLO is associate professor of modern European history at the University of Colorado at Boulder. He received his PhD from the University of Wisconsin–Madison in 2003 and has taught at the Massachusetts Institute of Technology and the University of Cincinnati. His first book, *Advertising Empire: Race and Visual Culture in Imperial Germany* (2011), explores the intersection of colonialism and commerce in the changing imagery of Africans in German visual culture. Essays by Ciarlo are also included in *German Colonialism, Visual Culture and Modern Memory*, edited by Volker Langbehn (2010), and *German Colonialism and National Identity*, edited by Michael Perraudin and Jürgen Zimmerer (2010).

SEBASTIAN CONRAD is professor of modern history at the Free University of Berlin. He is the author of *German Colonialism: A Short History* (2012), *Globalisation and the Nation in Imperial Germany* (2010), and *The Quest for the Lost Nation: Writing History in Germany and Japan in the American Century* (2010).

CHRISTIAN S. DAVIS is associate professor of history at James Madison University. He earned his PhD at Rutgers University in 2005 and is the author of *Colonialism, Antisemitism, and Germans of Jewish Descent in Imperial Germany* (2012). His other publications on German colonialism and anti-Semitism include "'Coddling' Africans Abroad: Colonial Director Paul Kayser and the Education of Africans in Germany, 1891–1896," in the *Journal of Colonialism and Colonial History*, and "Colonialism and Antisemitism during the *Kaiserreich*: Bernhard Dernburg and the Antisemites," in the *Leo Baeck Institute Year Book*.

GEOFF ELEY is the Karl Pohrt Distinguished University Professor of Contemporary History at the University of Michigan. He has published widely in German history of the nineteenth and twentieth centuries, including his first book, *Reshaping the German Right: Radical Nationalism and Political Change after Bismarck* (1980; new ed., 1991), and a general reinterpretation of German history, jointly authored with David Blackbourn, called *The Peculiarities of German History* (German ed., 1980; English ed., 1984). His essays in the German field range widely, from the later nineteenth century to the present. He is currently finishing a book to be called "Genealogies of Nazism: Conservatives, Radical Nationalists, Fascists in Germany 1860–1930," while a companion volume, *Nazism as Fascism: Violence, Ideology, and the Ground of Consent in Germany, 1930–1945*, is currently in press. His edited volumes include *Society, Culture, and the State in Germany 1870–1930* (1996); *The "Goldhagen Effect"* (1997); and (with Jan Palmowski) *Citizenship and National Identity in Twentieth-Century Germany* (2007). With Ron Suny, he edited a reader on nationalism, *Becoming National* (1996), and with Nicholas Dirks and Sherry Ortner, a reader on social theory, *Culture/Power/History* (1993). His general history of the left in Europe, *Forging Democracy*, appeared in 2002, and a study of the shifting popularity of social history and cultural history during the past four decades, *A Crooked Line*, was published in 2005. A jointly authored book with Keith Nield, *The Future of Class in History: What's Left of the Social?*, appeared in February 2007.

JENNIFER JENKINS is associate professor of German and European history at the University of Toronto, where she holds a Canada Research Chair in modern German history. She is the author of *Provincial Modernity: Local Culture and Liberal Politics in Fin-de-Siècle Hamburg* (2003) and numerous articles. She is currently at work on two books: "Weltpolitik on the Persian Frontier: Germany and Iran in the Age of Empire," an exploration of Germany's global interactions in the Middle East and Central Asia from the Crimean War to Operation Barbarossa, and "Germany among the Global Empires, 1850 to the Present," for the Wiley-Blackwell series A New History of Modern Europe.

BIRTHE KUNDRUS is professor of social and economic history at the University of Hamburg. She earned her PhD at the University of Bielefeld and is the author of *Kriegerfrauen: Familienpolitik und Geschlechterverhältnisse im Ersten und Zweiten Weltkrieg* (1995) and *Moderne Imperialisten. Das Kaiserreich im Spiegel seiner Kolonien* (2003). She is also the editor of *Phantasiereiche: Zur Kulturgeschichte des deutschen Kolonialismus* (2003) and is the German regional editor of *A Historical Companion to Postcolonial Literatures—Continental Europe and Its Empires*, edited by Prem Poddar, Rajeev S.

Patke, and Lars Jensen (2008). In 2012 she coedited with Dierk Walter a volume, *Transkulturelles Lernen in Imperialkriegen*. She has published on German history, especially National Socialism and the German Empire, and also on the history of violence and genocide. A jointly edited volume with Sybille Steinbacher on *Kontinuitäten und Diskontinuitäten. Der Nationalsozialismus in der Geschichte des 20. Jahrhunderts*, appeared in 2013.

KLAUS MÜHLHAHN is a professor of Chinese history at the Freie Universität Berlin. His work examines China's cultural and social development in an international and global context. He has written on a wide range of subjects, including China's relations with Europe, in particular Germany; the evolution of modern Chinese law; and the history of human rights in China. His book *Criminal Justice in China—A History* (2009) won the John King Fairbank Prize of the American Historical Association. In 2014 he published the coedited volume (with Nina Berman and Patrice Nganang), *German Colonialism Revisited: African, Asian, and Oceanic Experiences*.

BRADLEY NARANCH is visiting assistant professor of history at the University of Montana. His recent publications include "Between Cosmopolitanism and German Colonialism: Nineteenth-Century Hanseatic Networks in Emerging Tropical Markets," in *Cosmopolitan Networks in Commerce and Society 1660–1914*, edited by Margrit Schulte-Beerbühl and Andreas Gestrich (2011); and "Made in China: Austro-Prussian Overseas Rivalry and the Global Unification of the German Nation," *Australian Journal of Politics and History* (September 2010). He is completing a book manuscript for Oxford University Press on German statecraft, globality, and empire in the nineteenth century.

DEBORAH J. NEILL is associate professor of history at York University in Toronto, Canada. Her research explores the intersection of European colonialism, internationalism, humanitarianism, and health in the nineteenth and twentieth centuries. She is the author of *Networks in Tropical Medicine: Internationalism, Colonialism, and the Rise of a Medical Specialty, 1890–1930* (2012).

HEIKE I. SCHMIDT is Lecturer in Modern History, Department of History, University of Reading. She works on nineteenth and twentieth century Zimbabwe and Tanzania. Her research encompasses "new" colonial history, gender history, historical anthropology, and social history, with a focus on violence, gender, memory, power, and identity. Dr. Schmidt's publications include *Colonialism and Violence in Zimbabwe: A History of Suffering* (2013) and *African Modernities: Entangled Meanings in Current Debate*, edited with Jan-Georg Deutsch and Peter Probst (2002).

JOHN PHILLIP SHORT is associate professor of modern European history at the University of Georgia. He is the author of articles on the social, cultural, and visual history of German imperialism and of *Magic Lantern Empire: Colonialism and Society in Germany* (2012).

GEORGE STEINMETZ is the Charles Tilly Collegiate Professor of Sociology and German Studies at the University of Michigan. Before coming to Michigan in 1997 he taught at the University of Chicago as a tenured professor of sociology and history, and he was a senior research associate at Chicago until 2002. Steinmetz is the author of *The Devil's Handwriting: Precoloniality and the German Colonial State in Qingdao, Samoa, and Southwest Africa* (2007), and *Regulating the Social: The Welfare State and Local Politics in Imperial Germany* (1993), and editor of *Sociology and Empire: The Imperial Entanglements of a Discipline* (2013). He is currently completing "Imperial Intellectuals: Sociologists and the French and British Colonial Empires, 1930s–1960s." He has edited two other books, written one hundred articles, and codirected the historical documentary film *Detroit: Ruin of a City*.

DENNIS SWEENEY is associate professor of history at the University of Alberta in Edmonton, Alberta, Canada. He is the author of *Work, Race, and the Emergence of Radical Right Corporatism in Imperial Germany* (2009) and numerous essays on German labor, heavy industry, liberalism, socialism, and modernity. He is finishing a book on radical nationalism, empire, and the colonial genealogy of the racial state in Germany from 1890 to 1924.

BRETT M. VAN HOESEN is assistant professor of art history and a faculty associate in the Gender, Race, and Identity Program at the University of Nevada, Reno. Recent publications include "Re-Visioning Germany's Colonial Past: Tactics of Weimar Photomontage and Documentary Photography," in *German Colonialism, Visual Culture, and Modern Memory*, edited by Volker Langbehn (2010); "Postcolonial Cosmopolitanism: Constructing the Weimar New Woman out of a Colonial Imaginary," in *The New Woman International: Photographic Representations from the 1870s through 1960s*, edited by Elizabeth Otto and Vanessa Rocco (2011); "Carl Einstein and the Lessons of László Moholy-Nagy" in *Carl Einstein and the European Avant-Garde*, edited by Nicola Creighton and Andreas Kramer, (2012); and "The Culture of Critique?: Avant-Garde and Popular Press Photomontage in the Age of Weimar Postcolonialism" in *Weimar Colonialism*, edited by Florian Krobb and Elaine Martin (2014). She is completing a book manuscript on the legacy of Germany's colonial history in the arts and visual culture of the Weimar Republic.

ANDREW ZIMMERMAN is professor of history at George Washington University. He is the author of *Anthropology and Antihumanism in Imperial Germany* (2001) and *Alabama in Africa: Booker T. Washington, the German Empire, and the Globalization of the New South* (2010). He is currently working on a global history of the American Civil War.

Index

advertising, 13, 20, 187–206; as colonialist fantasy, 189; colonial motifs in, 195–202, 205; for consumer products, 191–192; for German colonies, 191; imperialist ideology in, 187, 188; increasing visuality of, 195, 203

Africa: in colonial geography, 171; European medicine in, 80; European sovereignty over, 93, 95; proposed Nazi colonizing of, 64–65; as static nature, 96

Africans: in advertisements, 187, 195–196, 198, 200, 202, 203–206; in colonialist discourse, 7, 13, 101, 211; compared to German workers, 216; contemporary postcolonial artists, 324–327; in geographic instruction, 178; German fears of miscegenation with, 273–274, 275, 311, 321–322, 323–324; in Höch's photomontages, 318–322; interactions with settlers, 119, 120–121, 124; Pan-German views of, 273–274; peasantization of, 100; as post–World War I occupation soldiers, 302, 303–304, 305, 307, 315, 316–317, 322, 333; in Rhineland propaganda, 304, 308–311, 315–316; in Thurnwald's work, 59; transformation into labor force, 96–99, 100, 236, 257. *See also* Naturvölker

African sleeping sickness, 79–81, 97, 99; success of German program, 81; transnational research partnerships, 79–80

agriculture (Africa), 97–98; German programs for, 97–98, 103, 258

Amani Institute (German East Africa), 98–99, 104, 106; under British control, 105

anticolonialism. *See* anti-imperialism

anti-imperialism: among German intelligentsia, 54–55; among German working class, 210–211; and Thurnwald, 63

anti-Semites: 13; concerns for cultural degeneracy, 237; divisions among, 229, 232–233, 234, 235–238, 239, 242; fusion with anti-Slavism, 256–257; and Herero War, 233–234, 236–237; racial arguments of, 232, 235, 237, 333; views on colonialism, 228–242; "yellow peril" discourse among, 260

Anti-Semites Petition (1880), 235

Arendt, Hannah, 254, 338, 339

Augsburger Volkszeitung (journal), 216

Bartels, Ludwig, 218, 232
Baster peoples, 274
Bayer (pharmaceutical company), 79, 85
Bayer 205 (medicine), 83, 85, 87
Bebel, August, 241
Becker, Carl, 103
Belgium: Pan-German aims for, 276, 277
Bentham, Jeremy, 94–95
Bergmann and Company, 187, 188–189, 205

Berlin Colonial Congress (1905), 216
Berlin Conference (1884–85), 34, 93, 94, 95, 99, 105, 246, 305; General Act of, 93, 94, 246
Berlin Dada, 304, 317–318
Berlin Ethnological Museum, 56, 59, 61
Berliner Illustrirte Zeitung (BIZ, newspaper), 304, 307, 308, 320, 324
Berliner Lokal-Anzeiger (newspaper), 198
Bernstein, Eduard, 212, 215–216, 217
Bethmann Hollweg, Theobald von, 28, 278
Bieberstein, Adolf Marshall von, 150
Bismarck, Otto von, 150, 228, 246, 252
Blohm, Emil, 118
Blücher, Wipert von, 160
Boer War, 216
Boers (South Africa), 273, 274
Bourdieu, Pierre, 60, 61, 64
Boxer Rebellion (China), 7–8, 51, 138–139, 213, 216
Bülow, Bernhard von, 213, 214, 234
Burundi. *See* German East Africa
Bushmen (San people), 274

Cameroon, 76, 228, 305; African sleeping sickness in, 80, 83, 84, 85; cocoa production, 198
Caprivi treaties (1892–4), 27
Catholic Center Party (Germany), 13, 101, 234, 246, 253; and Hottentot elections, 211, 213, 214
Catholicism (German): in *Kulturkampf*, 251
China, 7, 12, 51, 129–143, 171, 179, 216; "coolie" trade, 259–260; German colonies as semi-colonial, 131, 132–133, 142–143; resistance to colonization, 130; M. Weber's studies of, 51–52, 53–55. *See also* Kiaochow
Chinese: interactions with German settlers, 130; legal treatment of, 135–136; settler communities, 134–135
Christian Social Party (Germany), 228, 231, 234
Class, Heinrich, 253, 275, 276–277, 278
Clausewitz, Karl von, 286
Clemenceau, Georges, 302, 308
Clifford, Hugh, 81–82
cocoa, 198–199, 200, 201
colonialism (German): anti–Semites' views on, 228–242; connections with Holocaust, 2; different forms of, 129–130, 131, 134, 139, 142, 255; discursive approaches toward, 2, 4, 10, 37, 223; domestic attitudes toward, 210–211, 212–213, 218, 219, 220–221, 222, 224n8, 333; of East Prussia, 246; and education, 12, 102–103; as form of modernization, 5, 26; and gender, 2; in German social science, 58–59, 94, 103; within German studies, 3–4, 5–6; historiography of, 1–3, 19–20, 22–23, 330; as imperial (expansionist) program, 4, 6, 9, 23–24, 26–28, 132, 150, 164, 176, 229, 230, 234, 268–269, 335; Nazi appropriation of, 15–16; and postcolonial studies, 2; and race, 4, 6–7, 32, 38, 223; and science, 11, 78, 94, 96, 98–99, 101, 103; SPD criticisms of, 216–217, 218–219; and transnational history, 2, 6, 20, 21, 24, 25, 29–31. *See also* continuity with Nazi Germany, 15–16, 35–36, 38, 266, 330–331, 334–335, 338–339; discontinuity with Nazi Germany, 336–338, 339; internal colonialism
colonies (German): administration of, 94, 95–96, 112–113, 117–118, 131; advertisements for, 191; agricultural cultivation of, 97–98; economies of, 198; in German school curriculum, 182–183; households in, 114; as military bases, 130–131; post–World War I loss of, 81–82, 94, 104; as sites for exploitation, 175–176, 269; as sites for German settlers, 230–231, 235, 238, 268–269, 273; as sites for missionary work, 231; tropical medicine research in, 10–11, 74–88
Colony and Home in Words and Pictures (magazine), 203, 205
Confucianism, 51, 52; as anticolonial ideology, 138
Congo (Belgian) 83, 85, 100, 104; African sleeping sickness in, 79; Nazi colonial plans for, 335
Cooper, Frederick, 110, 143, 334, 343
cotton: German West African economy, 100
Crusen, George, 136
Culture Station Kwai (German East Africa), 98, 99, 106

Dabaodao (China). *See* Kiaochow
Dada, 15

412 · Index

Damara people, 274
Dar es Salaam (German East Africa): German settlers in, 113–114
Das Plakat (journal), 308
Declaration of London, 296, 297
De Groot, J. J., 52, 54
Dehn, Paul, 150, 271
Delbrück, Clemens von, 28
Der Islam (journal), 103
Der Kolonial-Deutsch (journal), 306
Dernburg, Bernhard, 100, 101, 102, 103, 214, 218, 229, 238, 242, 257; anti–Semites' views of, 240–241
Deutschebund, 231
Deutsche-Soziale Blätter (journal), 230–231, 236, 237, 241
Deutsche Tabakbau-Gesellschaft Kamerun, 199–200
Deutsche Tageszeitung (journal), 240
Deutsche Wacht (journal), 230, 239
Deutsche Welt (journal), 232, 236
Deutsche Zeitung (journal), 232, 236, 237, 240
Die Gartenlaube (newspaper), 198, 200
Die Reichsbote (journal), 239
Die Woche (newspaper), 195

Eastern Europe: compared to Africa, 340; as a form of German colonialism, 9, 14, 331, 332–333; under Nazi rule, 343; and *Umvolkung* (trans-folking), 49
Eastern Marches Society (*Ostmarkenverein*), 252–253, 255
education, 12; colonial geography, 171; colonialism in Imperial German schools, 171; pedagogical critiques of, 173; reforms of [*Reformpädagogik*], 173; training colonial settlers, 102–103. *See also* geography
Ehrlich, Paul, 78, 83; and African sleeping sickness, 79
Emile cigars, 196–197
empire: challenges to, 343; characteristics of, 341–342; compared to imperialism, 19–20; as German national self-definition, 170; in geography instruction, 171, 172, 179; and globalization, 25
Epp, Franz Ritter von, 335, 336
Erzberger, Mathias, 129
ethnology (German), 60, 63, 65, 72n102, 178, 181

Europeans: as carriers of civilization, 178–179
Evangelical Workers Associations, 217, 219

Fabri, Friedrich, 189
Feldmann, Oskar, 79
Ferguson, Niall, 25
Fischer, Eugen, 64
Fischer, Fritz, 21, 23, 27
Fischer Controversy. *See* Fischer, Fritz
Flottenkampf. *See* navy (Germany)
Flottwell, Eduard, 247–248
Fontaine, Theodor, 111
Förster, Bernhard, 235
Förster-Nietzsche, Elisabeth, 235
France: investment in Iran, 153; postwar attitude toward German scientists, 82, 84; postwar German fears of, 305; postwar military strength of, 304–305; transnational relations with German scientists, 77, 79, 80, 81; use of colonial soldiers, 308
Frank, Hans, 47
Franke, Adolf, 147, 148, 155, 156, 157, 158, 159
Franke, Otto, 54
Free Conservative Party, 266
Freiligrath, Ferdinand, 171
Frémiet, Emmanuel, 311
Frenssen, Gustav, 21, 219
Freytag, Gustav, 250, 255
Fritsch, Theodor, 229, 237
Fülleborn, Friedrich, 77

Gaomi (China), 138, 139
Gare War (German East Africa, 1908), 120, 121–122
General German League. *See* Pan-German League
geographers: instructional objectives, 171–172, 173, 182–183; proposed use of colonial imagery in instruction, 174; reforms proposed by, 173–174; use of German colonies in instruction, 182–183
geography: and German colonies, 182–183; an imperial instruction, 171; instructional history of, 172–175; land-and-people [*Land-und-Leute*] approach, 174–176, 177; practical applications of, 175–176; schools' adoption of, 176–177; textbooks, 177–179, 181, 182.
German Colonial Bulletin, The, 203

German Colonial Calendar, The, 191, 193
German Colonial News, The: advertisements in, 190, 191, 192, 193–195, 196–198, 203
German Colonial Office, 56, 205, 229, 239, 257, 308
German Colonial Society, 13, 20, 56, 80, 190–191, 192, 198; advertisements by, 191; aims, 190; in Hottentot elections, 211, 214, 217; influence on print culture, 190 membership, 190, 202, 306
German Colonial Union, 189
German Communist Party (KPD), 306, 317
German Conservative Party, 217, 266
German East Africa, 76, 94–96, 109–124, 198, 305, 306; administration of, 95–96, 112–113, 117–118; African sleeping sickness in, 79, 80; agriculture, 96; British control of, 305; criminal cases in, 110, 113, 115–116, 118–120, 121–123, 124; economy, 95–96; German settlers in, 11, 98, 109, 113, 114, 117–118; military stations in, 112; missionaries in, 117
German Empire (1871–1918): acquisition of colonies, 246; "civilizationist" discourse in, 38–39; colonialist/imperial discourse in, 8, 10, 20, 23–24, 26, 171, 253, 270–271; discourse in, 28–29, 278; economy, 27, 28, 111, 258; education, 171; loss of colonies, 81–82, 94, 104, 305, 333; militarism in, 284; *Mitteleuropa* and masculinity, 111; modernization of, 111, 114, 170; nationalist agitation within, 31, 265; racial attitudes in, 13; support for colonial development, 233, 258; unification, 31, 111, 170, 248
German Foreign Office, 151, 152, 154, 155, 156, 157, 158, 190, 229, 292, 335
German Independent Social Democratic Party (USPD), 306, 307
German New Guinea, 56, 60, 62, 198
German Reform Party, 228, 230, 231, 234, 235, 239
German Social Party, 228, 230, 231, 233, 234, 235, 237, 241
German Southwest Africa, 2, 76, 210–211, 228, 237, 252, 256, 257; Pan–German racial discourses about, 267, 273–276, 280; South African control over, 305–306
German Tropical Medicine Society, 82
German West Africa, 253; economy, 95, 99–100

Germanin (film), 87–88
Germany, Federal Republic of (West Germany): colonial memory in, 21–22
Gerstenhauer, Max Robert, 273–274
Gliess, Franz, 120, 121
Goebbels, Joseph, 336
Gossler, Gustav von, 173
Götzen, Graf von, 113, 120
Great Britain: acquisition of German colonies, 104–105, 109; colonial science of, 76–79, 80–81, 105; economic vulnerability of, 291; German naval strategy against, 289, 290–291; postwar attitude toward German scientists, 81–82, 83, 85; seizure of Iran, 152; transnational relations with Germans, 76, 77, 79, 80–81, 151

Halle, Ernst von, 290
Halle Colonial Academy (Halle University), 62
Hamburg Colonial Institute, 102, 103, 306
Hamburg Colonial Society, 54
Hamburg group (tropical medicine): loss of transnational relationships in Africa, 81–82, 87; racial views of, 78; transnational relationships, 77, 87. *See also* Institut für Schiffs- und Tropenkrankheiten
Hammer (magazine), 229, 237, 238, 241
Hänsch, Felix, 279
Harris, John H., 104
Hartmann, Georg, 153
Hartmann, Martin, 103
Hasse, Ernst, 33, 265, 267, 269–270, 271–272, 275
Hegel, Georg Wilhelm Friedrich: attitude toward China, 52
Heia Safari (television program), 21
Heine, Theodore Thomas, 7, 8
Henrici, Ernst, 228
Hentze, Adolf, 257
Herero people, 2, 7, 217, 257, 274, 338. *See also* Herero Wars
Herero Wars (1904–08), 7, 21, 104, 202, 232, 236, 237, 257, 274; German attitudes toward, 210–211, 213; SPD criticisms of, 217
Hindenburg, Paul von, 156
Hitler, Adolf, 16, 333, 335, 336, 340, 342; anti-colonial views of, 337
Hobson, J. A., 211, 212

Höch, Hannah, 15, 304, 318; *Dada Tanz*, 318–319; *Die Kokette II*, 319–320; *Entführung*, 320–321; *Liebe im Busch*, 322, 323; *Mischling*, 324, 325
Holocaust (World War II): connections with colonialism, 2
Hönig and Bauhardt Cocoa, 199
honor. *See* propriety
"Hottentot" elections (1906–07), 13, 20–21, 100–101, 202, 210–223, 229, 240, 241; electoral outcome of, 220–221; nationalist rhetoric in, 213–214
Hottentots. *See* Nama people
Hugenberg, Alfred, 253, 268, 277, 278
Hunneman, Albert, 154
Hutter, Mwangi, 324–327

Illustrated Colonial Calendar, 203, 205
Illustrated German Colonial Calendar, 205
imperialism (German): as colonial program, 4, 6, 9, 23–24, 26–28, 132, 150, 164, 176, 229, 230, 234, 269–270; compared to empire, 19–20; competing ideologies of, 230; and concept of "humanitarianism," 93–94, 179; concept of "imperial formations," 341; conceptions of space, 267, 270–271, 272–273, 275, 278, 279; everyday life/attitudes towards, 19–20; ideology in advertisements, 187, 188; in Nazi Germany, 338, 339–340; Pan-German agitation for, 265–280; "social imperialism," 23–24, 36–37; as sounding board for Nazi Germany, 340
India: 55, 179
Institut für Schiffs- und Tropenkrankheiten (Hamburg), 74, 76, 77. *See also* Hamburg group
"internal colonialism," 246, 268
Iran, 147–164; German economy in, 149, 150, 152, 153; German investment in, 150, 152–154, 162; German missions in, 150–151; German refugees in, 12, 150–152, 153–154, 162–164; modernization of, 152–154; relations with Germany, 149–150, 152; Russian German [*Russlanddeutsche*] refugees in 147, 148, 155–162; seizure by Britain, 152; state policies on refugees, 155. *See also* Tabriz *and* Tehran
Islam: colonial study of, 103–104

Jaeschke, Paul, 137–138, 139
Jeune École, 286
Jews: in colonial movement, 229, 239; compared with Chinese, 260; German attitudes toward, 256; and German colonial policy 240; immigration to Prussia, 256, 275; proposed resettlement of, 278–279. *See also* Dernburg, Bernhard
Johnston, Harry, 81
Jomini, Antoine-Henri, 286

Kaiser. *See* Wilhelm II
Kaiserreich. *See* German Empire
Kaiser-Wilhelms-Land (New Guinea), 181
Kamerun. *See* Cameroon
Kautsky, Karl, 101, 220, 222
Keitel, Wilhelm, 336
Kiaochow (China), 7, 12, 51, 129–130, 132–143, 216, 255, 289, 306; Chinese boycott in, 140–141; Chinese communities, 134–135, 137, 140; civilian administration of, 135; conflicts in, 137–138, 140; economy, 133–134, 137, 142; ; German-Chinese college in, 141; German community in, 12, 134, 136–137; German investment in, 140; legal system in, 135–136; Naval administration of, 130, 132, 133–134; prostitution in, 137; punishments in, 136; racial spaces in, 134, 137; as semi-colonial, 131, 132–133, 142–143. *See also* China
Kipungu, 121
Kirchhoff, Alfred, 181, 182
Kladderadatsch (journal), 304, 315
Kleine, Friedrich Karl, 77, 83, 87
Knapp, Georg Friedrich, 258
Koch, Robert, 75, 76, 78; research into African sleeping sickness, 79, 80, 99
Koloniale Rundschau (journal), 306
Kolonialrat, 96–97
Ku Hung-Ming, 52
Kuhlenbeck, Ludwig, 274
Kuhn, Philalethes, 80
Kuhnle, Friedrich, 115–116
Kulturkampf, 250–251
Külz, Ludwig, 77

Lange, Friedrich, 231–232, 234
Langenbeck, Rudolf, 174
Lattmann, Wilhelm, 231, 233, 235, 241

Laveran, Alphonse, 75, 79
League of Nations, 11, 104–105, 303
Lebensraum, 14, 64, 230, 231, 234, 253, 334; Pan-German agitation for, 266
Lehmann, Richard, 176
Lehrer–Zeitung (journal), 249
Leipziger Illustriete Zeitung (magazine), 205
Leipziger Volkszeitung (journal), 216, 217, 221, 222
Lenin, V. I., 212
Lettow-Vorbeck, Paul von, 336
Leutwein, Theodor, 237
Liebert, Eduard von, 33, 271
Litten, Wilhelm, 151, 152
Lugard, Frederick, 95, 101
Luschan, Felix von, 56, 59, 61
Luxemburg, Rosa, 220

Mahan, Alfred Thayer, 286, 288, 291, 292
Maji–Maji War (German East Africa, 1905–1907), 117, 213
Mann, Thomas, 334
Mannheim, Karl, 48, 61
Manson, Patrick, 75
Martin, Gustave, 84
masculinity: colonial notions of, 109–110, 117–120, 122, 124
Mass Observation (Great Britain), 65
Matzat, Heinrich, 174
Mauss, Marcel, 47
Mehring, Franz, 217
Meinecke, Gustav, 190
Methner, Wilhelm, 113
Mitteleuropa: in German discourse, 28–29; versus colonialism, 34
Mitteleuropäischer Wirtschaftsverein, 27
Morel, E. D., 100, 104
Moroccan Crisis (1905), 27, 213
Moroccan Crisis (1911), 27, 34, 221
Mühlmann, Wilhelm, 47, 48–50, 63; affinity with Nazism, 48, 65, 66; *Unvolkung* theory, 49–50
Münchner Illustrierte Presse (journal), 307
Münkler, Herfried, 342–343

Nama people, 2, 211, 257, 274
nation: definitions of, 114
National Liberal Party (Germany), 217, 220, 266

nationalists (German), 14, 21, 30; and colonial discourse of, 30–31, 222; demands for Eastern European colonization, 331; relations with Polish nationalists, 248; role in Hottentot elections, 213–214, 215, 217; support of Polish independence, 247. See also *völkisch* nationalism
Naturvölker (native peoples), 32, 78, 251; in geographic instruction 179, 181–182. See also Africans
Naumann, Friedrich, 21, 278
Naval Law (1900), 28
naval strategists (Germany), 283, 284; antiblockade policy, 294, 297; commercial warfare policy of, 294–295, 297; and maritime law, 296; support of cruiser warfare, 286, 289, 291, 294
naval strategists (United States), 283, 287–288, 291; commercial warfare policy, 293, 295; and maritime law, 296; strategy, 285–286, 287–288, 289
naval warfare: defined as commercial war, 286, 288, 289–290, 292, 293, 297; as total war, 296–297
navalism: definition, 283–284
navy (Germany), 283–298: annexation of Qingdao, 51; battle-fleet [*Flottenkampf*] strategy, 285–286, 287, 288, 292; connection with German colonialism, 35–36; expansion of, 27; jurisdiction of Kiaochow, 132; naval buildup, 283; similarities to US navy, 285; strategy against Great Britain, 289, 290; support for colonialism, 15, 132; vulnerabilities of, 290
Navy League (Germany), 20–21, 202, 214
Nazi Germany (1933–1945): colonial cinema in, 336; colonial institutions in, 335; colonial policy of, 47, 336; colonial workers, 336; continuity with colonialism, 15–16, 35–36, 38, 266, 330–331, 334–335, 338–339, 341; discontinuity with colonialism, 336–338, 339, 341, 342, 343; eliminationist policy, 342; and German social science, 47, 48, 63–66; *Lebensraum*, 334; and *Russlanddeutsche*, 161–162; *Rassenpolitik* in, 324; and tropical medicine, 87–88
Nazi Party: colonial views in, 334; in Iran, 161–162; influence of Pan-German ideas on, 266; political mission of, 342–343

Needham, Joseph, 95
Neue Deutsche Volkszeitung (journal), 260
Nocht, Bernhard, 82
NSDAP. *See* Nazi Party
Nueva Germania (Paraguay), 235
Nyamwezi people, 98, 99

Odol mouthwash, 195–196, 197, 205
Ogburn, W. F., 58
Ostmarkenroman, 250, 256. *See also* Poland (German)
Ottoman Empire, 163

Pahlavi, Reza Shah, 152–153, 154
Pan-German League, 27, 212, 214, 228–229, 253, 265–280; colonial policy, 268–269, 273–274; composition, 266; customs union plan, 269–270, 278; imperialist discourse within, 265–265–268, 271–272, 274–276; mission, 268. *See also* Pan-German movements; racial discourse of, 267, 273–276, 278–279
Pan-German movements: 265–280; biopolitical racial ideology of, 267–268, 273–279, 280; debate over World War I, 276–279; "Greater Germany" discourse in, 34, 265–266, 267, 268–270, 276–277, 278, 280; imperial discourse within, 14, 33–34, 35, 36, 265–268, 271–272, 279. *See also* Pan-German League
Papua peoples: in geography instruction, 181
Paquet, Alfons, 55
Pasha, Emin (Karl Oscar Theodor Schnitzer), 229, 239, 242; anti-Semites' views of, 239
Pasteur, Louis, 75
Pasteur Institute, 79, 80, 84
Perserflüchtlinge. *See Russlanddeutsche*
Persia. *See* Iran
Pfeffer, Karl-Heinz, 50
Poland, 2, 8, 35, 48, 51, 247, 250, 307; German notions of, 249; as German colony, 332
Polanyi, Karl, 47
Poles: forced expulsions of, 252; German civilizing mission toward, 249, 250, 252, 254, 260–261, 269, 332; legal status, 248; nationalist aspirations of, 248; Pan-German opinions of, 250, 253, 254, 255, 260–261, 269, 274–275, 332; in Prussia, 247–261, 275, 332
polnische Wirtschaft, 250. *See also* Poles
propaganda, 14, 15, 190. *See also* advertising
propriety: colonial notions of, 109–110, 112, 114, 116–117, 123
Prussia, East: agricultural economy, 32; in German imaginary, 14, 250, 255; internal colonization of, 35, 36, 100, 246, 249, 252, 253, 332, 341; Jewish immigration into, 256; Poles in, 247, 248; Polish policy in, 248–249; *Kulturkampf* in, 250–251; politics of settlement of, 253, 254; Weber's thesis on, 53

Qajar Dynasty (Iran), 149
Qing Dynasty (China), 12
Qingdao (China). *See* Kiaochow

race: in advertisements, 187, 195–196, 198, 200, 202, 203–206; in agricultural labor, 258–259; anthropological studies of, 307–308; and anti-Semitism, 231–232, 235; biopolitical notions of, 267, 273–276; as a category, 32–33; in colonialist discourse, 4, 6–7, 32, 38, 223, 307–308; colonial policies toward, 134; in geography instruction, 171, 175, 178; in German sociology, 59–60; German views of, 13, 114–115, 122; and humanitarianism, 104; Pan-German notions of, 267, 273–279, 280; racialization of Poles, 249, 250, 254, 256; *Rassenpolitik* in Nazi Germany, 324; in Rhineland propaganda, 304, 308–311, 315–316; and *Russlanddeutsche*, 161–162; and tropical medicine, 78, 87
Randow, Albert von, 256
rape: in German law, 116
Rathenau, Walter, 28
Rathgen, Karl, 103
Reformpädagogik. *See* education
Reismann-Grone, Theodor, 33, 44n62, 271
Rhein und Rhur, 304, 315–316
Rhineland (Germany), 302–326: Allied occupation of, 302, 307; anti-Bolshevism in, 304, 307, 311–313; anti-French sentiment in, 313–315; controversy over African colonial troops in, 302, 303–304, 307; Ruhr Crisis, 315

Rhineland Controversy. *See* Rhineland
Richthofen, Ferdinand von, 52, 54
Riquet (cocoa manufacturer), 201
Rodenwaldt, Ernst, 87
Rohrbach, Paul, 27, 29, 42n42, 335
Roloff, Gustav, 28
Rosen, Friedrich, 151
Rosenberg, Alfred, 50, 338
Royal Prussian Colonization Commission (*Königlich Preußische Ansiedlungskommission*), 252
Rückwanderer. See *Russlanddeutsche*
Russlanddeutsche, 147–148, 155–162; emigration to Germany, 156–157; ethnic identity of, 159–162; German documentation of, 158–159, 160, 161–162; and German Foreign Office, 157–158, 159, 161; Iranian government views of, 157–158, 159, 160; and Nazi Germany, 161–162; philanthropy for, 160
Rwanda. *See* German East Africa

Sachau, Eduard, 102
Sahm, Berta, 115–116
Salm-Horstmar, Otto zu, 278
Schacht, Hjalmar, 335
Scheer, Dora, 160
Scheer, Eduard, 160
Schilling, Claus, 77, 78, 80, 87
Schmidt, Wilhelm, 50
Schmitt, Carl, 93–94, 296–297, 338
Schmoller, Gustav, 28, 100, 101
Schnitzer, Carl. *See* Pasha, Emin
Schulenburg, Friedrich Werner von, 147–148, 152, 154, 155–157, 158–159, 161
Schulgeographen. *See* geographers
Schünemann, Max, 151
science: and German colonialism, 11, 78, 94, 96, 98–99, 101, 103, 105–106; as form of sovereignty, 94–95. *See also* tropical medicine
semicolonialism. *See* China and Kiaochow
Seminar for Oriental Languages (Humboldt University), 102, 112
Severing, Carl, 214
Shandong province (China), 130; German annexation of, 131–132
Shonibare, Yinka, 326
Simplicissimus (periodical), 6, 8–9, 304, 311, 312, 314, 315

Six, Franz, 50
Slavs: compared with Africans, 7, 8
Social Democratic Party (SPD)(Germany), 13, 27, 101; and Hottentot elections, 214–215, 220–221; mobilization of working class, 215–216, 218, 219, 222; opposition to anti–Semitism, 241; opposition to colonialism, 216–217, 218, 219, 221, 222–223, 253; pro-colonialist attitudes within, 211, 212, 213, 215, 217, 219, 234
social imperialism. *See* imperialism
Social Reich Party (Germany), 228
sociology (German), 10, 46–68, 68n2; as applied discipline, 58; division between historicists and positivists, 53; and scientific autonomy, 46
Sociologus (journal), 58
Solf, Wilhelm, 60
Sonderweg thesis, 2, 284
Songea (German East Africa), 117–123
Sonnenburg, Liebermann von, 236
Sorokin, P. A., 58
Soviet Union (USSR): German refugees [*Russlanddeutsche*] from, 147–148, 155–156; state policies of, 148
Sperry, Charles Stillman, 292, 293
Staatsbürger-Zeitung (journal), 228, 236, 239, 240
Stiegler, Joseph, 120–122
Steudel, Emil, 85
Stockton, Charles, 292, 293
Stoecker, Adolf, 231, 235–236, 242
Stoler, Ann Laura, 129, 250, 257, 341
Stollwerck (cocoa manufacturer), 201–202
Studt, Konrad von, 248, 249
Stuhlmann, Franz, 97, 98
Sun Yat-Sen, 141

Tabriz (Iran): German economy in, 150; German settlers in, 148, 151–152, 161; Russian troops in, 151–152. *See also* Iran
Taidongzhen (China). *See* Kiaochow
Taixizhen (Chian). *See* Kiaochow
Tanzania. *See* German East Africa
Tehran (Iran): German school of, 150; German settlers in, 149, 154, 160, 161; Nazi Party in, 161–162. *See also* Iran
Thilenius, Georg, 103
Third Reich. *See* Nazi Germany

Thurnwald, Richard, 10, 47–48, 55–66, 67–68; academic career, 55–56, 57–58; affinity with Nazism, 47, 63–66; anticolonialism and cultural hybridity, 63; anti-Semitic views of, 63, 64, 65; founds *Sociologus*, 58; and German ethnology, 61, 65; and German sociology, 57–58; research in New Guinea, 56; views on colonialism, 47, 58–59, 61, 62, 64; views on native policy, 60, 61–62; views on race, 59–60, 65
Tiedemann, Christoph von, 246
Tille, Armin, 275–276
Tirpitz, Alfred von, 132–133, 286, 288, 289, 290, 291, 292, 295, 296
Togo, 31, 76, 87, 100, 104, 106, 228, 259, 305
Todd, John, 76
tropical medicine (German), 10–11, 74–88, 97; British/French attitudes toward, 81–82, 83–84, 85, 86; German predominance in, 76; as imperial project, 75, 78, 84–85, 86, 87; loss of German predominance in, 81–85, 86; transnational cooperation in, 74–75, 76–78, 79–80, 86
Tropical Medicine Society (Germany), 77
Trotha, Lothar von, 213, 218
Truppel, Oskar von, 140
Tuskegee expedition (Togo), 31–32, 33, 259
Tuskegee Institute (US), 100, 259

Über Land und Meer (newspaper), 200
Uganda: African sleeping sickness in, 79–80, 83
Umvolkung (trans-folking), 49
Union of Defense against Anti-Semitism, 239, 241
United States: agricultural economy, 32; involvement in colonial science, 105; military strategy in, 284–285 naval buildup, 283

Versailles, Treaty of (1919), 93, 94, 302, 303, 305, 306
Virchow, Rudolf, 251
visuality: history of, 188
Vohsen, Ernst, 96, 190
völkisch nationalism, 231, 232, 237, 266, 331; hegemony theory of, 338
Volkskörper, 275–276, 278–279, 280. *See also* race: Pan-German notions of

Waldersee, Alfred von, 138–139
Wang Ching Dao, 54
Warner, Lloyd, 65
Washington, Booker T., 31–32, 259; and M. Weber, 32;
Weber, Alfred: academic career, 48; opposition to German imperialism, 48, 66; scientific objectivity, 48, 66
Weber, Max, 10, 29, 31, 50–55, 57, 66–67, 258–259, 260; academic career, of 47, 53, 54; and B. T. Washington, 32; and German imperialism, 48; racial attitudes, 48; scientific theories of, 46, 47–48, 53; work on China, 51–52, 53–55; work on India, 55;
Wehler, Hans-Ulrich, 21, 23, 26, 36–37
Weimar Germany (1918–1933): anti-Bolshevism in 304, 307, 311–313; colonial movement in, 306–307; loss of Rhineland territory, 302; postcolonial attitudes in, 15, 303, 306, 317, 333–334; as postcolonial state, 305
Weltpolitik, 14, 26, 27, 230, 231, 234, 272; and M. Weber, 48, 51; and China, 51
Werner, Ludwig, 230, 231, 235, 241
Wilhelm Köhler (firm), 203–205
Wilhelm, Richard, 52, 54
Wilhelm Süsserott (firm), 203, 205
Wilhelmine Germany. *See* German Empire
William II, 8, 27, 94, 132, 270
Windhorst, Ludwig, 246
Witzenhausen Colonial School, 102
women (German): in advertisements, 189, 198; in colonies, 109, 114, 115; in Höch's photomontages, 318–322, 324; press parodies of, 322; in Rhineland propaganda, 304, 311–312
women (Polish), 256

Yuan Shikai, 139

Zeimann, Hans, 77, 78, 87
Zeiss, Hans, 87
Zeitschrift für Völkerpsychologie und Soziologie. *See Sociologus*
Zhou Fu, 140
Zietz, Luise, 317
Zimmerman, Albrecht, 99
Zimmeran, Oswald, 230

www.ingramcontent.com/pod-product-compliance
Lightning Source LLC
Chambersburg PA
CBHW061341300426
44116CB00011B/1944